A Guide to Developing Client/Server SQL Applications

The Morgan Kaufmann series in Data Management Systems

Series Editor, Jim Gray

A Guide to Developing Client/Server SQL Applications
Setrag Khoshafian (Portfolio Technologies, Inc.)
Arvola Chan (Versant Object Technology)
Anna Wong (CLaM Associates)
Harry K.T. Wong (Nomadic Systems)

The Benchmark Handbook for Database and Transaction Processing Systems
Edited by Jim Gray (Digital Equipment Corporation)

Camelot and Avalon: A Distributed Transaction Facility
Edited by Jeffery L. Eppinger (Transarc Corporation)
Lily B. Mummert (Carnegie Mellon University)
Alfred Z. Spector (Transarc Corporation)

Database Modeling and Design: The Entity-Relationship Approach
Toby J. Teorey (University of Michigan)

Readings in Object-Oriented Database Systems
Edited by Stanley B. Zdonik (Brown University)
David Maier (Oregon Graduate Center)

Readings in Database Systems
Edited by Michael Stonebraker (University of California at Berkeley)

Deductive Databases and Logic Programming
Jack Minker (University of Maryland)

A Guide to Developing Client/Server SQL Applications

Setrag Khoshafian

Arvola Chan

Anna Wong

Harry K.T. Wong

Morgan Kaufmann Publishers
San Francisco, California

The authors dedicate this book to the freedom of Nagorno-Karabagh.

Publishers' Acknowledgement: A special thanks is owed to Setrag Khoshafian and Arvola Chan for the diligence, creativity, and extra effort they invested in bringing this book to publication.

Sponsoring Editor: Bruce M. Spatz
Production Manager: Yonie Overton
Copyeditor: Susan Festa
Composition/Text Design:
S.M. Sheldrake Graphic Design & Production
Proofreaders:
Lynn Meinhardt, Sharilyn Hovind, Gary Morris
Cover Design: Sandra Popovich

Morgan Kaufmann Publishers, Inc.
Editorial Office:
340 Pine Street, Sixth Floor
San Francisco, CA 94104

96 95 94 6 5 4 3 2

Library of Congress Cataloging-in-Publication Data

A Guide to developing client/server SQL applications / Setrag Khoshafian ... [et al.].
p. cm. -- (The Morgan Kaufmann series in data management systems)
Includes bibliographical references and index.
ISBN 1-55860-147-3
1. Data base management. 2. SQL (Computer program language) 3. Application software. I. Khoshafian, Setrag. II. Series.
QA76.9.D3G835 1992
005.75'65--dc20 92-8628
CIP

Contents

Preface

We believe that an understanding of client-server architecture is key to understanding computing in the 1990s. In the history of computing, this decade will certainly be recognized as the era that launched LAN-based client-server computing. Replacing and augmenting mainframe applications with "downsized" client-server applications is promoting a quiet revolution in information management processes within large corporations. Although local area networks have been around for more than a decade, it is only recently that LAN-based applications for cooperative corporate computing are starting to appear en force. The client-server architecture is the foundation of such distributed cooperative computing applications, and database servers are the repositories that store the shared information in client-server architectures.

Client Servers and LANs

In a client-server architecture, workstations or personal computers request services from various servers on a local area network. The "local" processing enabled by personal computers has been one of the most important components that has helped to reshape the information age and encourage the proliferation of client-server computing.

In the 1960s, users interacted with mainframes through punched card readers and "dumb" terminals; these "users" were sophisticated, trained professionals. This mode of interaction with both mainframes and minicomputers continued throughout the 1970s. Then, in the early 1980s, the personal computer was introduced, and within a decade, the PC business exploded into a multibillion dollar industry. It is ironic that machines designed for isolated "personalized" computation became the backbone (or shall we say the "front" bone) of distributed client-server computing, threatening the very mainframes and minicomputers whose adherents initially shrugged PCs off as "toys."

The need to share resources (files, printers) gave rise in the mid 1980s to the practice of interconnecting PCs through local area networks, with an underlying network operating system. Typically, data sharing was accomplished through a file-server client-server architecture. With file servers, all data filtering, computations, and manipulation took place on the client side; the concurrently shared files were stored on the server.

Client Servers and the Relational Data Model

Relational database servers were introduced in the late 1980s and have become increasingly popular in the early 1990s. They provide relational database management system support on servers in client-server architectures. The relational data model was originally conceived by Dr. E.F. Codd in the early 1970s as a means to provide more flexibility in organizing large data bases and to alleviate some of the problems of the earlier navigational (network and heirarchical) models.

Relational databases and relational database servers are prevailing largely because of several inherent advantages. For example, relational query languages, such as Structured Query Language (SQL), are much more declarative than the navigational languages of the earlier models. This allows the user to specify what is wanted from the database in a high-level declarative style of programming, stating "what" is to be accessed from the databases rather than "how" to access it. Furthermore, the relational model is simple and elegant. The underlying theory is based on the mathematically well founded and well understood concepts of relational algebra and first-order predicate calculus. Relational algebra consists of only a few operations: set operations (union, intersection, difference, and Cartesian product) and relational operations (selection, projection, and join). And last, relational database servers provide much more functionality, or "intelligence" than file servers. The database server maintains integrity, provides security of database objects, supports transactions, and optimizes queries against the database.

Purpose of This Book

Which brings us to the purpose and scope of this book. We believe SQL database servers will play a crucial role in downsizing mainframe applications to client-server LAN-based systems. We also believe professionals involved either in downsizing, upgrading, or the development of new client-server applications (e.g., MIS managers, database administrators, database application developers, etc.) will need to have a vigorous and comprehensive understanding of the issues involved in the development of robust client-server database applications. We attempt to meet these needs and target our book primarily to the database application developer. The book could also be used in advanced database courses as it provides a comprehensive understanding of SQL relational databases and the emerging client-server technologies.

In this book, we concentrate primarily on *SQL database application development*. In fact, many of the discussions are relevant to database application development on minicomputers and mainframes. However, we also provide a very comprehensive presentation of all the SQL data definition, SQL data manipulation, transaction management, system administration, performance tuning, benchmarking, application programming interface, and distributed computing issues in client-server application development.

We purposefully concentrate on topics related to the development of SQL client-server applications through programming interfaces. This book does not cover PC database application development tools such as form generators, report generators, graphical user interface development environments, and the like. We do intend to follow this book with a second volume that concentrates on the front-end client development tools for client-server application development. Typically, these tools are supported by tool vendors whose products interface with one or more back-end server products. The tools vary greatly in functionality and scope. One recent survey identified about 150 front-end tool products for database servers! Even as this book is going to press, this number is expected to rise. We believe a comprehensive analysis of all the features of front-end products and tools requires a volume by itself. However, in order to assist our readers in their overall understanding of the criteria for evaluating front-end application products, we have included in the Appendix 12 "rules" that pertain to client application environments accessing server data.

Organization and Contents

In this book, we analyze the relevant standards and examine four database server products. The standards are ANSI/ISO SQL, SAA SQL, and the SAG SQL, which represent the main proposed standards for SQL. The database server products we survey are the IBM OS/2 Extended Edition Database Manager, the ORACLE Server for OS/2, the Microsoft SQL Server, and DEC's VAX Rdb/VMS. Although many other database servers are currently being sold by leading vendors, we feel these four products provide a good cross section of database servers. Our selection includes major computer vendors, database vendors, and feature list of all existing servers (that is, SQL constructs, application programming interface alternatives, performance tuning constructs, database administration tools, transaction management alternatives, and so on).

In Chapter 1, we provide a brief introduction to client-database–server architectures. We also describe some of the attributes found in several database servers currently available.

In Chapter 2, we discuss the various aspects of relational database design. We illustrate the steps involved in the top-down design of relational database client-server applications, and we explain the different types of integrity constraints. In addition, we review the 12 rules of relational databases developed by Dr. E.F. Codd and point out how these rules can be useful in evaluating relational database server products.

In Chapters 3 and 4, we present the data definition and data manipulation constructs of Structured Query Language, respectively. Besides illustrating the DDL and DML SQL constructs in the standards, we compare the various SQL dialects of the aforementioned four database servers. In addition to data definition constructs, which are used to create tables and views, we cover system catalogs of the various SQL database servers and illustrate how each server handles privileges. In Chapter 4, we compare the features of the SELECT, INSERT, DELETE, and UPDATE data manipulation constructs both in the standards and in the four servers.

Database servers are used to implement transactions that run concurrently against shared databases. In Chapter 5, we provide a comprehensive comparative analysis of the concurrency control and recovery features of four database servers.

Implementing adaptable and resilient client-server applications requires database administration utilities and features such as backup, automatic system recovery, auditing, and data import and export. We discuss these operations and how they are handled in four servers in Chapter 6.

The performance of client-server database applications are affected by many often tunable factors, including indexing, background writing, optimization, and clustering. This is the focus of Chapter 7 in which we analyze and compare the performance-related factors of four database servers.

Performance is one of the criteria often used when selecting a server. Benchmarking, a method for measuring the performance of a system in a controlled environment using a standardized methodology, is the topic of Chapter 8. Here, we discuss five industry-standard database/transaction benchmarks used to compare database-server performance.

Application programming interfaces are the system tools that allow client-server applications to access server data. Dynamic SQL, embedded SQL, and module language are a few of the tools used by clients to retrieve and update databases. In Chapter 9, we discuss the different types of application program interfaces supported by the standards and the database server products.

We realize that considerable confusion and hype exists in the commercial database world over the definition of a distributed database. We tackle this discussion in Chapter 10. While many years of research have gone into the development of technical solutions for distributed database problems, the first commercial distributed database systems have emerged only recently with a very rudimentary set of capabilities. In Chapter 10, we examine the rules for distributed databases outlined by Dr. Chris Date. These rules are the most often quoted yardsticks for assessing the capability of a distributed database system. Our discussion divides these rules into three groups, along the dimensions of autonomy, distribution transparency, and heterogeneity.

In addition to client-server architectures, the most significant technologies changing the software industry today are *object orientation, multimedia,* and *artificial intelligence.* In Chapter 11, we discuss how these technologies can be integrated in SQL. We illustrate the meaning of intelligent databases in the context of the Intelligent SQL prototype. We also illustrate how object-oriented and other advanced features are proposed in the upcoming SQL2 and SQL3 standards.

Finally, in Chapter 12 we provide a summary and conclusion.

Acknowledgments

We would like to thank those who helped us in the preparation and production of this book. First and foremost, we thank our spouses and children for their patience and support. This book took longer than anticipated and our publishing editor, Mr. Bruce Spatz, was extremely patient, understanding, and supportive throughout the entire process. For this we are grateful. We also would like to express our gratitude to the editor of the series, Dr. Jim Gray, who enthusiastically supported this project. Very helpful comments were provided by Joe Celko, Robert Orfali, Rick Cattell, Donald Slutz, and Richard Finkelstein, who participated as reviewers. The book has benefitted from their criticism and encouragement. We also thank Rick Trutna and Patti Pasley, who contributed to the editing of the book. Finally, last but not least, we would like to thank our Morgan Kaufmann production team: production manager, Yonie Overton; copyeditor, Susan Festa; and graphic artist, Jay Nitschke, for the fine and professional job that is clearly reflected in this book.

Chapter 1

An Introduction to Client-Server Technology

Client-server computing is the latest trend in the development of database systems and local area network (LAN) technology. As LANs have found broader acceptance in business enterprises, users have been busy discovering new and different ways to use and share data. Driven by the need for more efficient ways to share and access information, client-server computing, which allows applications to store and access data from a LAN-based database server, is "an idea whose time has come."

The client-server model applied to database applications provides a number of distinct advantages over early technology. Foremost, client-server technology allows you to optimize the use of hardware and software resources at both the *front-end* application (the client computer) and the *back-end* database server (a centralized "repository" of shared database information). The move toward client-server architecture is primarily important for database applications because it improves the performance of accessing shared data in a LAN environment and allows more users to access the same data, often using their existing PC software.

In this chapter, we provide an overview of several important aspects of client-server database applications and technology. We begin our discussion in Section 1.1 with a look at the trends and forces at work in today's data processing market, most notably, the widespread acceptance of LAN technology, application *downsizing* trends, and the natural evolution of database products toward client-server architecture. In Section 1.2, we present a historical perspective of database systems from host-based terminal access programs and file-server–based systems to the client-server application programs and database servers of today.

An introduction to client-server architecture is provided in

Section 1.3. Here, we discuss the advantages of client-server database systems over host and file-server–based database systems. This is followed, in Section 1.4, by a discussion of Structured Query Language (SQL), the standard interface for data access to relational databases.

We address the opportunities and challenges facing client-server technology in Section 1.5. Then, in Sections 1.6 and 1.7, we examine database servers and present criteria we feel are important when selecting one.

We conclude the chapter in Section 1.8 with an introduction to four popular database servers currently available and a comparison of their features.

1.1 Trends and Forces at Work in the Database Market

The market for database system software is presently one of the fastest growing segments of the computer industry. While database systems have always been a major focus of larger minicomputer and mainframe applications, their numbers in the PC marketplace are steadily growing. Additionally, developers of other PC software applications such as spreadsheets and word processors continue to add features that allow access to server data.

A look at today's database market reveals a number of different trends at work. First, the "year of the LAN" has finally arrived. While the LAN started out as a way to share expensive resources such as hard disks and printers, LANs are increasingly being used to access expensive and vital business data. Thus, the LAN is beginning to live up to its long-awaited promise.

The success story of the LAN has not unfolded without the introduction of new problems. For example, the LAN has brought about a proliferation of data, stored in a number of different formats, so that data used by one application often is not directly accessible by another. But, client-server computing provides a way out of this dilemma and offers a solution for standardizing and streamlining the way in which applications operating on a LAN can access data.

Another significant trend in the database market is the availability of less expensive, but more powerful, PCs and workstations that can be considered for downsizing applications, which, until a few years ago, were the exclusive domain of larger, more expensive minicomputers and mainframes. This trend is evidenced by sales and market surveys indicating that corporations and other business enterprises are purchasing more PCs and workstations as compared to mainframes and minicomputers. Moreover, an increasing number of these computers are being linked together on a LAN.

As PC and LAN technology become more sophisticated, new opportunities will arise for system developers and designers, both in converting applications to the newer, smaller, more powerful, and less expensive platforms, and in providing solutions to totally new business problems such as integrating notebook- and pen-based computers into database management systems.

The maturing of database management systems (DBMS) and application software themselves is a final force affecting the database market. Since its introduction in the early 1980s, the PC has proved to be a fertile breeding ground for new ideas and the design of new application programs. Database software being no exception, the 1990s have provided us with a powerful new paradigm for accessing data and for providing a cooperative computing solution—applications developed using the client-database–server model.

Taking advantage of a client-server architecture, you can combine the features of *user-friendly* graphical interfaces and the flexibility typical of applications running on a PC, with access to relational database technology provided by a database server. Also, the development of standards for accessing SQL database servers makes it possible to develop more portable applications and to access data from more diverse or *distributed* sources.

1.2 A Historical Perspective

As perhaps other texts describing the evolution of database technology point out, early database applications were run on large centralized computers, which were first accessed by *dumb* terminals and then by *smart* terminals or workstations. Since computing power and computer resources generally were expensive, they were concentrated on a larger computer or mainframe. As such, interaction with the computer was limited and was concerned for the most part with sending *batch* data requests to the centralized host computer for simple data retrieval and display. This is illustrated in Figure 1.1.

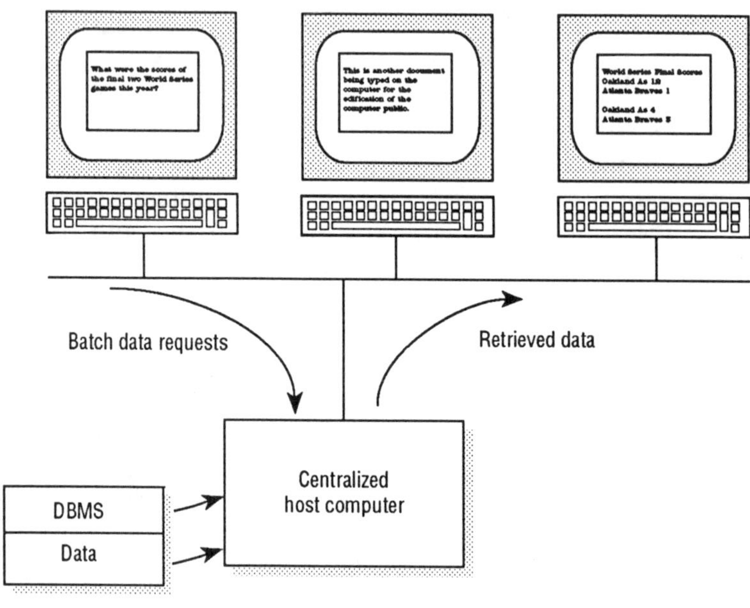

Figure 1.1: Terminal-based computing.

While this configuration is still widely used, it evolved in some situations so that applications running on a central computer included a more elaborate user interface, still displayed on either dumb or smart terminals, but with all user interaction processed by the central computer. This is shown in Figure 1.2. This type of system required a great deal more computing power and resources, however, since the mainframe or minicomputer now needed to handle each user's individual interaction with the application in addition to any data processing requests.

Host computer is managing display of application, user interaction, and data processing for both terminals and PCs.

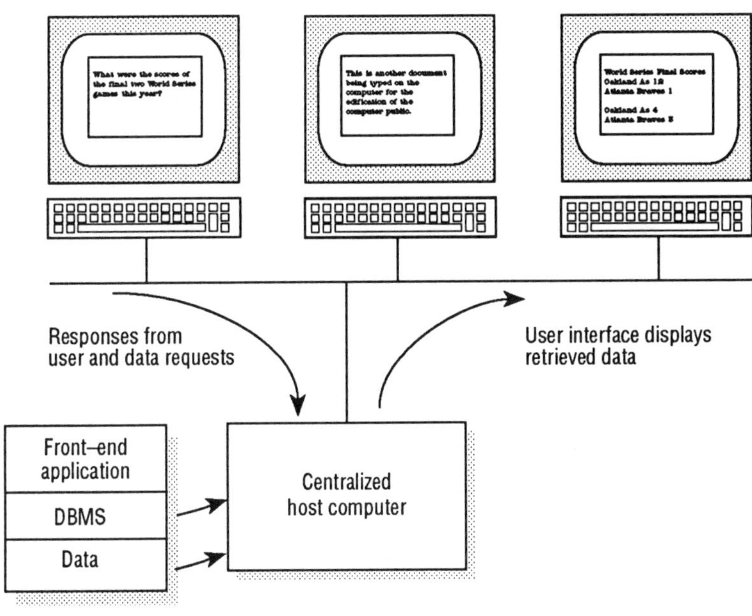

Figure 1.2: User interface management on a host.

When PCs with sufficient local processing and storage capabilities were introduced, programs such as Lotus 1-2-3 and dBASE II came into wide use. Users could now define and manipulate their own local data separate from data previously stored in an organization's larger computer. Figure 1.3 illustrates stand-alone PC applications. PCs also provided applications with more graphical user interfaces (GUIs) that were easier to use and more interactive. However, each new PC application stored and maintained data in its own way, and soon data proliferated in a number of different formats and file locations.

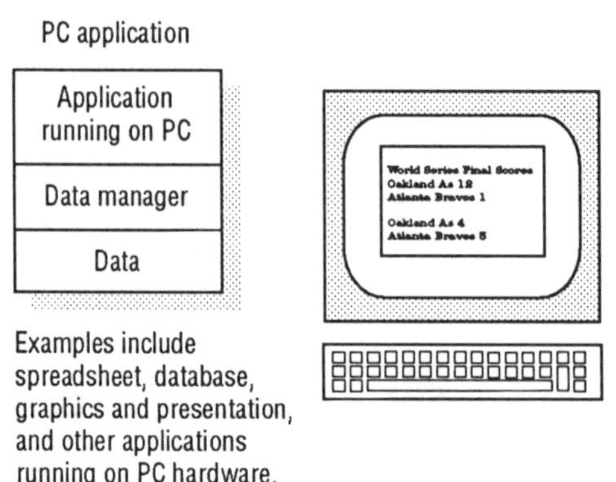

Figure 1.3: Stand-alone applications running on PCs.

The introduction of the LAN and increasingly powerful PCs marked the next stage in the evolution of the PC. Users could now link their PCs together, establishing a hub or file-server computer to store common shared data, as illustrated in Figure 1.4. The file-server computer took on the role of maintaining data and shipping entire files to each PC or workstation as requested, so the PC could perform more processing of data locally.

This arrangement worked fine as long as the number of users and the amount of data being accessed on the file-server computer was small. However, the file server could quickly become a bottleneck when processing larger amounts of data or when more users began accessing it, thereby increasing network traffic. Also, the file server generally was not well equipped to deal with larger issues such as maintaining the security or integrity of data, handling concurrent updates by different users, or providing services such as backup and recovery of data.

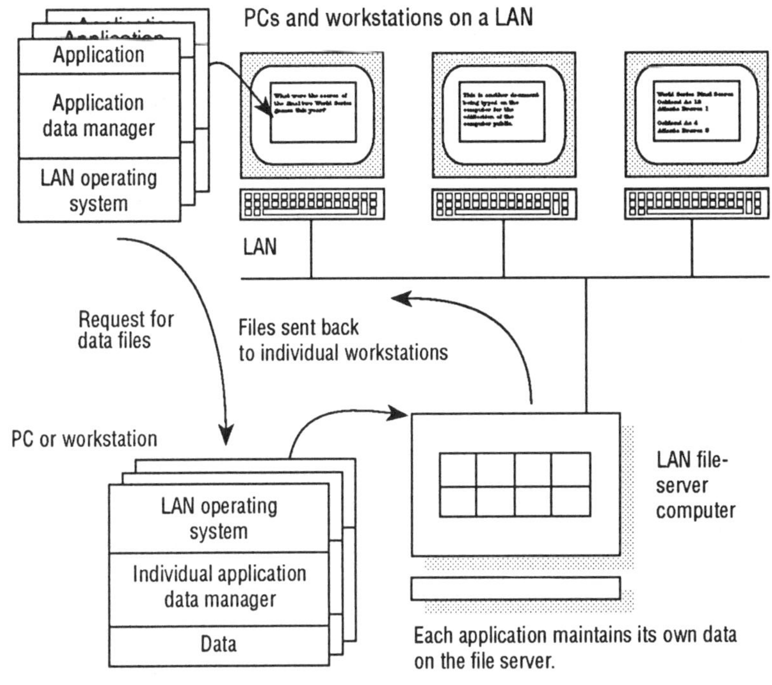

Figure 1.4: File-server architecture.

1.3 Client-Database–Server Architecture

The deficiencies of file-server technology have led to the development of products that use client-database–server architecture. Client-server configurations attempt to make the best use of both hardware and software resources by separating functions into two parts: the front-end portion of applications running on client computers or workstations, and the back-end database server, which stores and manages data requests. Figure 1.5 illustrates a client-server architecture with a database server. Data on the database server is stored only once and may be accessed concurrently by many different applications, including databases, spreadsheets, and business graphic packages.

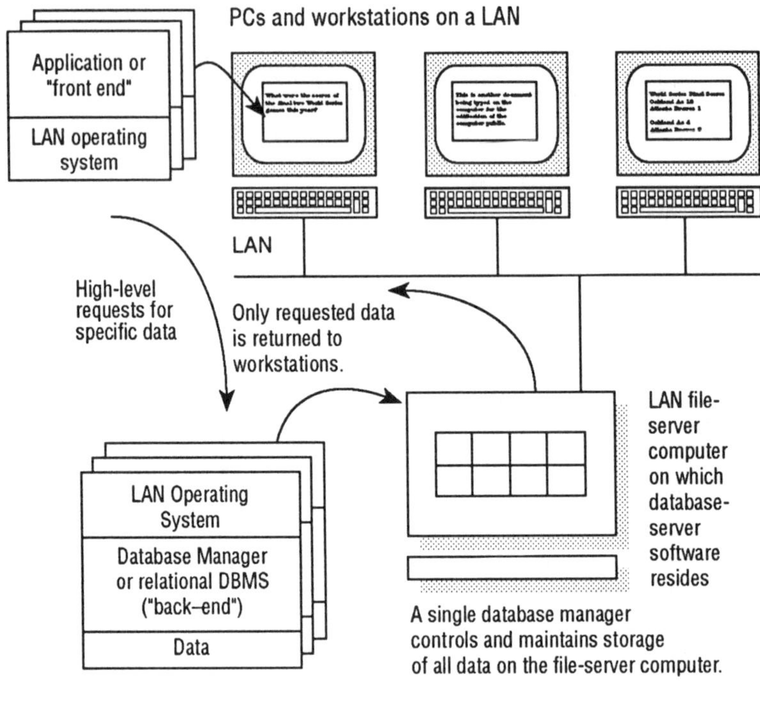

Figure 1.5: Client-server architecture with database server.

In contrast to traditional file-server configurations, the database server processes requests for data and ships only the requested data back to applications running on client PCs. The PC, then, is only responsible for running the user's application, handling user interaction, and generating requests for data. Instead of processing data, the client PC can focus on the user's application and take advantage of increasingly sophisticated GUIs available on PC or workstation hardware. In performing only database management tasks, the database server provides maintenance of data integrity, error recovery and security controls, and generally improves the user's ability to concurrently access and update data.

Client-server database computing generally offers a number of advantages over other types of systems:

- *Client-server applications provide a more efficient division of labor.* Both the client and database server can be dedicated to the tasks for which they are best suited. The client server can be used for presentation of a graphical user interface and handling user interaction with the application, whereas the database server is reserved for high-performance, large volume data processing with security, integrity, and concurrency control.

- *Client-server architecture provides an opportunity for both horizontal and vertical scaling of resources to do the job.* For example, you can distribute the work of processing data requests, such as queries or updates, to multiple processors on the same network (horizontal scaling), or you can move the relational database management system (RDBMS) to a larger, more powerful computer (vertical scaling).
- *Applications using client-server architecture generally can be run on smaller client computer configurations with better performance.* Since most of the work of database processing has been *offloaded* to the server, inexpensive PCs can serve as effective workstations running applications that access server data. Additionally, network traffic is reduced since applications send only specific data requests to the database server, and, in turn, only that requested data is sent back to the client PC or workstation.
- *Users can stay with the same familiar and favorite tools they've grown accustomed to using on the PC.* A majority of the most common types of applications have already been modified to access server data, and new applications are being written specifically to take advantage of client-server configurations. As better and simpler tools make application development easier and, in some cases, allow end-users to design their own applications, the application backlog at many companies can be reduced.
- *Clients can access more data.* SQL is typically used as the common data access language for database servers. This standard improves access of data from both heterogeneous and homogeneous sources and improves application portability on different platforms.
- *Increasingly valuable data can be properly safeguarded against loss or improper access.* As data processing is returned to centralized database management systems equipped for the job, important aspects of database applications such as security, data integrity, concurrency, and backup and recovery are returned to management information system (MIS) and information system (IS) personnel.

- *Less expensive and more powerful PC hardware and software are providing business problem solutions that are cheaper to implement than the database applications they replace.* In fact, it's not uncommon for firms downsizing existing database applications to use client-server architecture to build comparable systems at costs ranging from one-tenth to one-half that of the previous systems. Companies are now looking at converting both mission-critical and online transaction processing applications to those that use client-server technology and a broader mix of PC, minicomputer, and mainframe resources.

1.4 SQL and the Relational DBMS

In the client-server model, the database server processes data requests from various front-end applications running on PCs. With most servers on the market today, these requests are made using SQL commands accessing data stored in a relational database. SQL is well suited for this purpose since it provides a concise nonprocedural method of requesting data. A client PC's application sends a single SQL statement to the server, and the server returns only the requested data back to the client.

There are several benefits of using SQL as the data access method for client-database–server applications. First, application programming for specifying data requests is simplified, and for the most part is portable for applications running on different platforms. Consequently, network traffic is reduced since only the data request and the requested data are sent out over the network. Second, standardizing on SQL allows different applications to access data stored in the same format. It also makes the task of accessing distributed database servers possible since data residing on homogeneous (or even heterogeneous) sources use the same database access language. However, while complete standardization is the goal, it is still a long way off. On the positive side, though, a number of PC users' most familiar and favorite tools and applications already incorporate SQL and can access server data.

1.5 Opportunities and Obstacles for Client-Server Technology

While it's easy to see the opportunities for client-server applications, ranging from the continued downsizing of existing applications to the development of applications that address new target markets, there is a need for caution and careful consideration of options when choosing both client- and database-server hardware and software. And, until more success stories exist to counterbalance the horror stories that will always abound, there will be skepticism and doubt from those with a vested interest in the existing technology and those concerned with the bottom line.

For the present, both program designers and application developers still need to overcome significant obstacles in the conversion and downsizing of user applications to run on PC, workstation, and server-based systems. For instance, program designers must continue to satisfy user demands by developing and modifying their software to work with both new and existing hardware and software configurations. They must also adapt to a changing database-server environment, particularly as standards evolve. Additionally, applications developers must keep up with the new technology and apply it in the production of working systems, which must be solid, reliable, delivered on schedule, and within budget.

Support is also a major concern as companies put new systems in place, especially mission-critical ones. Companies must make sure they get the necessary support to bring the system up, to provide training for users, and to change or fix the system over time. Changeover to systems that use more PC-based resources will inevitably alter the way companies purchase both hardware and software, which, in turn, brings up the support issue again. Whereas in the past companies may have looked to a single vendor for both the hardware and software used in a database application, now they might consider multiple source vendors, each providing key components of their system.

With these requirements in mind we now take a closer look at the features provided by the database server itself, identifying specific criteria you can use to evaluate individual servers.

1.6 The Database Server

The database server is a LAN-based database management system that stores client data and provides other services such as data update and retrieval, concurrency control (for multiple users accessing the same data), transaction processing, backup and recovery, and database security.

Relational database servers based on SQL provide database engines that process SQL statements submitted by various clients.

Database servers then perform the relational operations necessary to retrieve the requested data and pass it back it over the network to each client. Figure 1.6 shows the interaction between client and server for data retrieval.

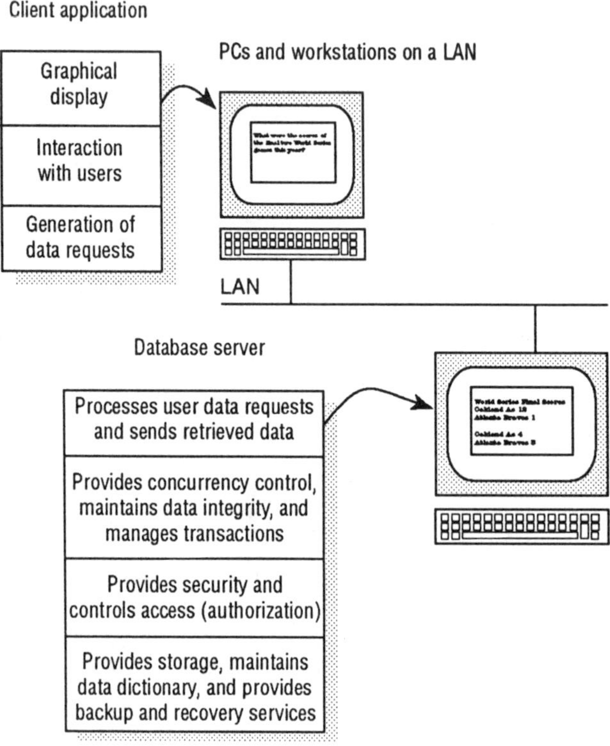

Figure 1.6: *Delegation of services using the client-database–server model.*

Database servers that use SQL remove the burden of specifying how to access server data. Instead, users or applications simply specify "what" data they want, not "how" to get it. This idea, referred to as *data independence*, is extremely important in the design of relational database management systems for the many benefits and the simplification in database applications it provides. For example, by not requiring programs to specify how to retrieve data from a database, data independence frees developers from having to perform complex query processing or having to spend countless hours tuning application codes to run in particular configurations. Plus, applications are easier to maintain since less programming changes are required if the application's requirements change or if the structure or content of accessed data is changed.

SQL provides a key role in database systems that implement client-server architecture. Data processing requests are relegated to the back-end database server, while the front-end application running on a user's PC or workstation generates SQL data requests and handles user interaction. In addition to making more efficient use of computing resources, this separation of roles provides better overall system performance.

1.7 Evaluating Features of Individual Database Servers

While their basic operation is the same, individual database servers generally differ in their implementation of particular features. For this reason, it is important to carefully look at the features and specific operations each product provides when you are evaluating database servers. Several of the key features to consider are highlighted below. Each of these functional areas is covered at greater length in the sections that follow.

SQL and connectivity options (for remote database access): The database server should implement SQL commands that conform, when possible, to existing SQL standards. Also, the server should support common network communication protocols and application interface standards for establishing client application connections.

Database server objects and data dictionary: Although most database servers provide the same objects, their exact implementation and support of various data operations may differ. Similarly, the data dictionary, which is used in relational databases to access information about stored data, may vary widely among database servers.

Optimization and performance: The database server may incorporate sophisticated optimization algorithms and techniques to determine the best methods to access specified data. For distributed databases, this optimization may be expanded to include data access from remote sites. In general, the overall performance of database servers is affected by other factors such as the number of currently connected users and the number of concurrent queries and updates being performed.

Data integrity control: Data integrity control ranges from enforcement of *entity integrity* for column values of individual rows in a single table to *referential integrity* for column values of rows in different tables.

Transaction processing: This feature processes a series of updates as a single transaction. All operations within the transaction must be completed before changes are committed in a database; otherwise, partial updates will be rolled back—restoring the database to its pretransaction state. This situation is complicated by the fact that different transactions may be performed simultaneously by different users accessing the same database.

Concurrency, deadlock avoidance, and multiuser access control: The database server attempts to balance user accessibility with updatability. To avoid conflicts between users reading or updating data and to maintain consistent data, the database server uses *locking* (on the individual row, page, or table) and *multiversioning* to maintain consistency of data stored and retrieved from the database.

Security and authorization checking: Most database servers provide security and authorization checking to prevent unauthorized access or tampering. The specific implementation of security features on a particular server dictates how database administrators add users and assign access and privileges necessary to perform various database operations.

Backup, recovery, and other database administration facilities: Database servers generally include facilities and/or utilities for backup and recovery of data. They are also capable of other database administration operations such as performance monitoring, user and access privilege assignment, and data schema and rule definition. While often overlooked, these features can be the Achilles' heel of an otherwise well designed database management system.

1.7.1 Implementation of Standard SQL

When accessing a database server, you specify a SQL statement that is passed to the server where it is executed, and data is returned. The key to this operation is that the particular SQL statement you send to a database server depends on the particular SQL implementation that server uses. Therefore, when evaluating SQL database servers, conformance to existing SQL standards is an important criterion.

While IBM originally defined SQL and incorporated it into products such as SQL/DS and DB2, other vendors have now created their own versions and have added their own SQL extensions. Currently, both the American National Standards Institute (ANSI) and International Standards Organization (ISO) have formed committees to define SQL standards that would make it easier for users to access data from diverse sources and would simplify system integration tasks. The ANSI/ISO SQL standard includes (1) the basic standard X3.135-1986 document ratified in 1986 and (2) addendum 1, which specifies the syntax and semantics of referential integrity constraints.

In 1989, these two documents were integrated as a new edition titled "ANSI Database Language SQL with Integrity Enhancement," which is ANSI X3.135.1-1989. The ANSI SQL standard specifies the syntax and semantics of Data Definition Language (DDL) commands, Data Manipulation Language (DML) commands, and embedded SQL commands within a host language.[1]

In addition to the ANSI/ISO SQL standard, several other important standards have been developed. (These will be described in greater detail in Chapter 11.) For example, X/Open, which provides a definition based loosely on the ANSI standard, takes into account the capabilities of leading relational database management systems available in the UNIX market and System V environments. IBM's Systems Application Architecture (SAA) specification is the IBM perspective or blueprint for providing portable and consistent applications across its major computing systems. And, Remote Database Access (RDA) is a proposed ISO Open Systems Interconnection (OSI) standard designed to facilitate access to server databases from client workstations and from other database servers. Finally, the SQL Access Group, a consortium of hardware and software vendors, has developed a SQL Access specification that addresses the issues of interoperability and portability of SQL-based applications.

---

1 This document describes two levels of conformance to the SQL standard. Level 2 is the complete language (SQL) minus integrity enhancements that specify various semantic integrity constraints, including default values, CHECK constraints, UNIQUE constraints, and referential integrity constraints. Level 1 is a subset of Level 2, which is primarily intended to be the intersection of existing SQL implementations. In the future, whenever we refer to the ANSI SQL standard we mean the Level 2 adherence specified within this particular document.

1.7.2 Connectivity and Remote Database Access

Using the client-database–server architecture, client application software and database server software reside on different computers. SQL statements and other commands are sent from the client application to the database server, which then passes back data and messages. This communication takes place over a LAN linking one or more client computers with one or more database servers. When evaluating products, it is important to consider several aspects of this client-database–server communication.

The first thing to note is the particular operating system, hardware, and network platforms that a database server runs on. Not only will these platforms dictate available connectivity options, but they can also affect horizontal and vertical scaling options (respectively, the ability to add multiple servers on the same network, or to access data from database-server software running on larger computers). This, in turn, may affect opportunities for accessing data from distributed databases through internetwork communications achieved using database links, gateways, or bridges.

Software running on a client workstation sends data requests and receives data back using several different components. First, the application programming interface (API) to the database server dictates the type of communication that may take place between client and server. Handling communication via the API is built into the client application software. Or, if you are designing your own client software, you must specify the type of operations available to the application by defining API calls.

Data communication between client and server takes place over the specific network protocols supported by a particular database server and the LAN that is established. For example, client-server software primarily runs on LANs that connect PCs, and therefore the major protocols to consider are

(1) NetBIOS (standard provided for most PC LANs),
(2) Extended NetBIOS or NETBEUI (used for Microsoft Lan Manager and compatibles),
(3) SPX/IPX (used in Novell NetWare), and
(4) VINES (used in Banyan networks).

You should look carefully at the type and variety of protocol options supported by a particular database server since available options will ultimately affect your ability to connect different hardware and application software to your database server.

1.7.3 Database Objects and Data Dictionary

SQL database servers are somewhat consistent in the types of primary database objects they use to store and maintain data—these being tables, views, and indexes. Within these basic types of objects, however, there are typically differences among various servers. Such differences relate to the data types supported, the types of indexes supported, and the level of null value support the database engine provides. Beyond the basic support for objects that store actual data, different database servers provide support for other objects such as synonyms, triggers, rules, and so on. When evaluating a database server, you will want to look closely at the database objects it supports. The existence of particular database object types or features will greatly enhance and facilitate application development. For example, triggers and rules are very useful for enforcing integrity constraints in mission-critical applications.

According to the inventor of the relational model, Dr. E.F. Codd, in a relational database all data stored in the database should be available and accessible using the same methods; that is, the data should be stored and retrieved from columns and rows within one or more tables or views. In addition to tables or views that store actual user data, a special set of tables, usually referred to as the *data dictionary,* stores all other *system* information. For example, the data dictionary typically contains the names of all user-defined tables and views in a database, information on the definition of indexes on particular tables, and statistical information describing the contents of tables. Users or application developers can query the data dictionary just as they would ordinary tables and views. The data dictionary is also helpful to the query optimizer in determining the best way to access data.

1.7.4 Optimization and Performance

Performance is a critical factor in the selection of a database server, yet it is one of the most elusive and difficult-to-quantify attributes of database server operation. In general, performance of a database server has two components: the first measure is the performance or response time for execution of standard operations using a prescribed database-server workload and configuration; the second measure is the database server's *throughput,* or the total amount of work a particular server can perform as its workload changes. Generally, the overall performance of a database server, as noticed by any one user accessing it, will degrade as the workload and/or the number of users accessing it increases.

There are two ways to monitor or measure performance. First, you can perform the actual tasks you need, using the exact configuration and workload you expect to use in a real application. This, perhaps, is the best test of performance since once you're done, you can be assured of a fairly accurate measure of how you can expect the database server to perform under actual situations or "real life." The second method of measuring performance is with standard benchmark tests. While benchmarks may be quicker and cheaper, their results may be less accurate or less indicative of the performance you might get using actual data in a real work environment. Like automobile measurements, "your mileage may vary." Also, the latitude provided in implementing various benchmark tests makes the claimed results provided by manufacturers suspect and open to controversy (see Chapter 8).

When evaluating database servers, be sure also to check for any built-in features or tools for monitoring and/or providing better performance. The speed with which a particular database server can perform database operations depends in large part on the internal methods used to execute them. For example, query execution speed is dependent on both the access methods chosen and any query optimization or statistical analysis used in the selection of a particular method. Thus, the performance of different database servers may vary widely and is related to the flexibility and degree with which a server's built-in query optimizer can choose the best access method.

In addition to out-of-the-box performance of a database server, which relies on built-in optimization, some database servers provide other means for performance tuning. For instance, users can specify options that control the way the database server performs particular operations such as specifying the type of locks used, controlling the location of database objects, defining clustered indexes, or adjusting options for other memory, processor, and disk usages.

1.7.5 Data Integrity and Transaction Management

A major advantage of a database server is the level of control and maintenance of data integrity it can provide over other types of database management systems. By consolidating data processing and transaction management in a single place, the database server engine, the database server can keep track of specified integrity constraints, ranging from single entity—single or multiple column values in specified rows—to referential integrity—involving comparison of values entered in multiple tables or other complex conditions or business rules (see Chapter 5).

An adjunct to the maintenance of data integrity through integrity constraints is transaction processing management, which is also incorporated into the operation of the database server engine. Every database server must manage updates and ensure the integrity of data against failed transactions or lost updates. For example, the database server must provide recovery when a transaction violates data constraints or when all the resources necessary to complete a transaction are not available.

For the most common type of transaction failures, simple database update logging allows *rollback* (restoring the database to its pretransaction state) and *rollforward* (reapplying transaction changes) capabilities. Most database servers available today include standard transaction commands such as COMMIT and ROLLBACK, but many do not support ROLLFORWARD. There are, however, still many differences among servers. For example, the way in which you define transactions, how and where transactions are logged, and how transactions can be applied, committed, rolled back, or rolled forward all vary somewhat on different servers.

The ability of a database server to maintain data integrity and manage transaction processing is an important area that warrants considerable attention when evaluating database servers.

1.7.6 Concurrency Control

Managing the concurrent access of data by a number of users who are running the same or different client application software is an important job of all database servers. Unlike many other traditional database management systems, SQL-based database servers handle the concurrent access of data automatically, freeing end-users and developers alike from managing this difficult and complex task at the application level. In addition to maintaining data integrity and handling transactions, the database server must also try to maximize the accessibility of data while minimizing the disruption one user may cause to another. This process is generally referred to as *concurrency control*.

To prevent users from disrupting each other or from overwriting each other's updates, database servers must provide a level of *isolation* and *read consistency* such that each workstation client querying data sees a consistent view of the data, which remains constant for the duration of the query. On the other hand, it is also important that when users wish to update data, the latest data is available to them, and thus they are not updating old data that has already been modified. If the data cannot be updated, an appropriate message or error is returned.

Chapters 5 and 7 contain more information on data accessibility and read consistency or isolation, particularly as they relate to transaction processing and the concurrency control options generally implemented in current database servers. For now, we can generalize and say that database servers typically provide some sort of *locking*—shared or exclusive, and row-, page-, or table-level locks—and/or *multiversioning* of data. Both of these features function to provide read consistency (or a "snapshot") of data stored or retrieved from a database, as well as a mechanism to detect and resolve deadlocks automatically. Locking generally provides the most assurance of being able to complete updates but provides the least amount of concurrency, with concurrency being reduced as locks escalate from shared to exclusive, or as locks progress from table- to page- to row-level. Multiversioning provides higher levels of read consistency and concurrency, however, with increased overhead from the different versions of data that must be maintained for separate users.

1.7.7 Security and Authorization Checking

Earlier we touched on the general capability of database servers to provide centralized security and authorization checking aimed at preventing unauthorized database access or data tampering. Typically, a database server provides a database administrator with a facility to add users and to assign access privileges to various database objects defined in a database. Then, each user's authorization is automatically checked prior to performing a requested online operation.

Most database servers have implemented the standard SQL commands GRANT and REVOKE; however, there are many differences among servers in the actual privileges that may be specified using these two commands. Depending on the security mechanism of a server, privileges can range from single GRANT and

REVOKE on database tables to very elaborate privileges for various data definition commands (e.g., CREATE TABLE, DROP INDEX, CREATE RULE).

1.7.8 Database Administration Facilities

Database administrators (DBAs) must perform many tasks in the installation, setup, and maintenance of a database management system. For example, when installing a new database server, the DBA must set up new equipment and networks and install various hardware, as well as operating system and network software. Then, in setting up databases, the DBA must define the data *schema* for database objects that users may access, first defining the structures and then populating the structures with data. The DBA is also responsible for defining security access to new databases and specifying access privileges for new database objects. Finally, the administrator, along with users and developers, must build, install, and debug client application software.

Through time, the DBA must continue to monitor and tune the database server's performance, modifying the system as needed, adding to or altering the database, or adding new hardware, software, and network options. The DBA is also responsible for correcting problems that arise and for performing routine and emergency backup and recovery procedures.

What are we getting at here? Well, there are numerous tasks that a database administrator is expected to perform—from the most important or critical tasks to the most mundane and time consuming. Therefore, to help make database administration and maintenance easier, most servers provide their own facilities. When looking for a database server, be sure to consider the tasks that its particular facilities enable you to perform, how easy or automated they are, and how thorough they are in completing all of the operations your database administrator will be doing—not just once, but many times over the life of the system.

Typically, database servers include facilities for operations such as backup and recovery of data, and for other database administration operations such as performance monitoring, user and access privilege assignment, data schema and rule definition, and so on. As we mentioned earlier, these features, while often overlooked, can be a vulnerable point in an otherwise well designed database management system.

1.8 Survey of Currently Available Database Servers

In this section, we review and compare four SQL-based database servers currently available: the IBM OS/2 Extended Edition Database Manager, the ORACLE Server for OS/2, the DEC Rdb/VMS, and the Microsoft SQL Server.

Certainly, there are a number of other leading servers and server vendors who offer very powerful database-server functionalities. Among these vendors, we can list Informix, Gupta, and Hewlett-Packard. While it would be ideal to compare all the features of the many servers available on the market today, this is neither the intent nor the scope of this book. Rather, we attempt in this book to discuss the major issues and trends in SQL-based database servers.

We have chosen these four servers in order to include the major computer vendors as well as the major database vendors. In addition, our selections address the PC-based (OS/2) and the minicomputer (VMS) platforms. And, finally, we feel the features and approaches of these four servers provide a very good, if not comprehensive, coverage of the major functionalities and approaches offered by relational database servers.

Before beginning our discussion of individual servers, we offer the following list of questions to consider when evaluating any database server.

- *What are the overall features of the database server, that is, what hardware, operating systems, and network platforms does it run on?*
- *What type of application support is provided with the server—both end-user and application development?*
- *How complete is the database server in its SQL implementation?*
- *Does the database server adhere to SQL and other database, connectivity, and application development standards?*
- *What database objects, such as user-defined tables, views, indexes, triggers, and rules, are defined by the database server?*
- *What system database objects are defined in the server's data dictionary?*
- *How does the database server handle data integrity, security and access control, and backup and recovery operations?*
- *What are the database server's capabilities in the areas of*

transaction processing, concurrency, row-, page-, table-level locking and multiversioning support, and optimization and performance?

1.8.1 IBM OS/2 Extended Edition Database Manager

The IBM Extended Edition (EE) Database Manager is an OS/2-based SQL database server accessible to either DOS or OS/2-based clients over protocols supported by the OS/2 Communications Manager and LAN Requestor software as part of the IBM System Application Architecture (SAA) blueprint. As such, the OS/2-based database server is intended to participate in distributed database access ranging from PC and OS/2 platforms to databases residing on AS/400 machines and DB2 residing on IBM mainframes. The SAA architecture is intended to provide application portability across various IBM computer platforms, so database applications can be developed and distributed by IBM as well as a host of other third-party horizontal and vertical application developers.

The OS/2 Extended Edition Database Manager provides a Level 1 ANSI, SAA-compliant implementation of SQL that is mostly consistent with DB2. In addition, it provides SQL cursors, both static and dynamic embedded SQL commands, and a full range of SQL data types and objects. The Extended Edition Database Manager also includes an embedded SQL programming interface for host languages that currently include C and Fortran. It supports definition of both entity and referential integrity constraints plus declarations (in the CREATE TABLE command) for both primary and foreign keys.

The transaction processing capabilities of the Extended Edition Database Manager include COMMIT and ROLLBACK commands and row-level locking. In addition, this server employs cost-based optimization of query and transaction processing and allows performance monitoring and tuning via memory and disk space allocation and configuration.

The Extended Edition Database Manager features a Query Manager facility for executing interactive SQL queries and performing all other database administration tasks such as security and authorization setup, backup and recovery, and import and export.

1.8.2 ORACLE Server

Advertisements for the ORACLE Server indicate that this SQL database server runs on more hardware, software, and network platforms than any other relational database. In the PC and workstation environments, Oracle Corporation's Server runs on UNIX, OS/2-based computers, and the Macintosh. Applications may access the ORACLE Server from DOS, OS/2, UNIX, or Macintosh client computers using a number of different protocols, including NetBIOS, NetBEUI, TCP/IP, and Novell's IPX/SPX.

An assortment of tools such as SQL*Forms, SQL*Reports, SQL*Menus, and CASE are available with the ORACLE Server. It also features an embedded SQL programming interface for a number of host languages such as C, Fortran, and Cobol, and another API called the ORACLE Call Interface (OCI) for application program development. In addition, the ORACLE Server is a major platform for numerous third-party and other horizontal and vertical applications.

The ORACLE Server is a Level 1 ANSI, SAA-compliant implementation of SQL, which is patterned after IBM's DB2 product. Like the IBM DB2, it provides SQL cursors, both static and dynamic embedded SQL commands, and a full range of SQL data types and objects. Oracle's PL/SQL provides procedural extensions to SQL and allows entire blocks of statements to be sent to the server in one block.

Data integrity constraints for null, unique, and qualified (with CHECK) column value entries, plus declarations for primary and foreign keys are available with the ORACLE database. In addition, this product boasts an automatic sequence number generator for generating unique integers used as primary key values, and a large collection of expression operators and functions. The ORACLE Server supports GRANT and REVOKE commands for both adding new users and specifying connection privileges in addition to standard SQL access privileges.

The full transaction processing support of the ORACLE database includes COMMIT, ROLLBACK, and ROLLFORWARD capabilities and complete backup and recovery facilities, which allow full or incremental automated and online backups if desired. Both row- and table-level locking are supported and multiversioning is available for maintaining read consistency. The ORACLE Server employs syntax-based optimization—such that the actual construction of SQL statements and queries may affect performance—and it allows performance tuning via memory and disk space allocation and configuration.

For database administration, the ORACLE Server offers a SQL*DBA facility. Additionally, SQL statements may be executed using the SQL*Plus facility. In the OS/2 environment, ORACLE provides a Presentation Manager-style interface that utilizes menu-driven operations for database administration functions.

1.8.3 DEC Rdb/VMS

Digital Equipment Corporation's Rdb/VMS product is a relational DBMS that runs solely under the VAX/VMS operating system. The Rdb/VMS supports two different interfaces: VAX SQL, which can execute interactive and embedded static and dynamic SQL commands; and RDO, a proprietary Digital language that is gradually being phased out as the SQL interface gains in popularity. In addition, Digital has licensed tools from ASK Corporation (formerly INGRES) and modified them to access the Rdb/VMS. Client computer access is available by VAX SQL Services, a SQL-based API that uses the DECnet networking protocol to provide client application access to Rdb from VMS and Ultrix workstations, as well as from DOS-based and Macintosh computers.

DEC's Rdb/VMS provides a superset of the Level 1 ANSI implementation of SQL. In addition to a full set of interactive and embedded static and dynamic SQL commands that can be used with Ada, C, Cobol, Fortran, Pascal, or PL/1 programming languages, and a full range of SQL data types and objects, the Rdb/VMS offers a number of other SQL extensions designed to facilitate enforcement of data integrity and triggers for definition of business rules. DEC's Rdb/VMS also supports GRANT and REVOKE commands for adding new users and specifying connection privileges beyond standard SQL access privileges.

This product features full transaction processing support, including COMMIT and ROLLBACK commands, and full backup and recovery facilities that allow full or incremental automated and online backups. Row-level locking is supported, as is multiversioning, which improves concurrency and maintains read consistency. The Rdb/VMS utilizes a cost-based optimizer, but it also allows performance tuning via memory and disk space allocation and configuration.

1.8.4 Microsoft SQL Server

The Microsoft SQL Server is a SQL database server running under OS/2 and is based on RDBMS technology developed by Sybase.

Sybase itself sells database servers that run on various other UNIX systems and on VAX/VMS computers. In the OS/2 environment, the SQL Server requires *named-pipe* network support, which is currently provided by Microsoft LAN Manager (or compatible products such as those provided by IBM and 3Com) or Novell's NetWare Requestor for OS/2 software. Applications may access the OS/2 SQL Server from DOS and OS/2 client computers.

For application development operations, the SQL Server utilizes a DB-LIBRARY C language API. The Server is also a major platform for third-party and other horizontal and vertical applications.

While the SQL Server provides a Level 1 implementation of SQL called TRANSACT-SQL, it lacks certain standard SQL commands that provide cursor support and standard forms of static and dynamic SQL statements. This product does provide a full range of SQL data types and other database objects.

The SQL Server contains extensions called *triggers* that allow specification of entity and referential integrity constraints used to enforce business and application data rules. Users may write TRANSACT-SQL programs (which, in addition to SQL, contain procedural commands), which are stored and executed from the SQL Server's data dictionary.

Standard data integrity constraints for null and unique column value entries and a large collection of expression operators and functions are part of the SQL Server's package. This product also supports GRANT and REVOKE commands for specifying SQL access privileges. (TRANSACT-SQL provides a large collection of system procedures for other operations such as adding users, defining database connections, and so on.)

Users of the SQL Server have access to full transaction processing support including COMMIT TRANSACTION and ROLLBACK TRANSACTION commands. Additionally, the SQL Server introduces a *savepoint* and a SAVE TRANSACTION command to provide more flexibility in processing transactions. And, the Server offers full backup and recovery capability for both database files and transaction logs using TRANSACT-SQL commands or the System Administrator Facility (SAF) program.

While the SQL Server provides only page-level locking, it does support different types of locks (shared or exclusive) to increase concurrency. The SQL Server also incorporates a cost-based query optimizer and allows performance tuning via database and transaction log disk space allocation and clustered indexes.

For performing database administration operations and executing interactive TRANSACT-SQL statements, the SQL Server employs two facilities—isql and SAF. While isql provides a command line interface, SAF utilizes a Presentation Manager-style menu interface system.

1.9 Summary

In this chapter, you were given a brief introduction to client-database server architecture, some tools with which to evaluate database servers, and a synopsis of the attributes of several database servers available today. The succeeding chapters will focus on specific aspects of client-server architecture, database servers, and relational database management systems. Each chapter will first present conceptual information and then survey the specific features or operations of individual products.

Chapter 2
Relational Database Design

In Chapter 2, we present an overview of the various concepts and issues involved in the design of relational databases. The goal of relational database design is to specify a database structure that best captures the real world semantics of the problem domain by representing the entities and relationships of the problem domain as directly as possible. Additionally, the design seeks to provide the best integrity and performance of the application programs that access the database.

Alternative designs have different characteristics, and tradeoffs often exist. For instance, a more *normalized* schema (i.e., a schema that involves more tables) might provide better integrity but might result in poorer performance for some frequently occurring database queries and updates. Therefore, it is impossible to list the "rules" for designing databases that have the best performance and best capture the semantics of the problem domain. However, certain guidelines can be used to develop "well-formed" databases. The following sections on normalization and entity-relationship modeling provide a number of useful guidelines for designing well-behaved, well-modeled, and high-performance relational databases.

Database design is the first and perhaps the most fundamental step in developing efficient client-server applications. Besides the *conceptual* design it also entails the *physical* and performance-critical design of the database. This chapter concentrates primarily on the issues involved in the conceptual design of databases for client-server applications. Chapter 3 will focus on the SQL data definition constructs to define the structure of relational databases in client-server applications, and Chapter 7 will detail the performance-enhancing features and tuning options for database servers, concentrating on the physical database design options.

In the sections that follow, Section 2.1 provides the "top-down" algorithms for relational database design, whereas the remaining sections take a "bottom-up" approach in discussing the main issues explicitly involved in the design of semantically consistent and high-performance relational databases. Section 2.2 focuses on the integrity constraint specification in relational databases, and Section 2.3 covers normalization alternatives for relational databases. These integrity constraint and normalization concepts are used to map semantic or entity-relationship (ER) diagrams onto relational schemata. A general discussion of semantic data modeling, with special emphasis on the entity-relationship data model, is provided in Section 2.4. Section 2.5 presents a partial answer to the controversial and unresolved question, When is a DBMS relational? This is accomplished through a discussion of the rules for relational databases devised by Ted Codd, the originator of the relational model. The contents of the chapter are then summarized in Section 2.6.

2.1 Introduction

Relational database design deals with disciplines and guidelines that are used in the construction of high-performance and semantically consistent relational databases. A relational database has three main components: structure, integrity constraints, and instances or rows of records in each relation.

In the relational world, a database structure is a collection of *relations* or *tables*. Each table is organized into rows and columns. The persistent objects of an application are captured in these tables, as illustrated in Figure 2.1. The database consists of a collection of tables or relations R_1, ..., R_n. Each table R_i has columns C_{i1}, ..., C_{im}. Each column C_{ij} has a *type,* which represents a set of permissible values called its *domain.* This type indicates that column values will be elements of its domain. Tables can be *base tables* or *view tables.* Base tables are the actual data stored in the database. View tables, also called *views,* are tables produced from relational commands operating on the base tables. These *virtual tables* don't actually exist in the database. Rather, they are produced upon request by a user and defined in terms of one or more base tables. The specification of the tables (base or views), their columns, and the types of the columns are part of the *schema* of the database. A database management system uses a *Data Definition Language (DDL)* to *define* the schemata of persistent databases. Throughout this book, the terms *table* and *relation* are interchangeable. Similarly, in some cases, the words *column* and *attribute* are also interchangeable.

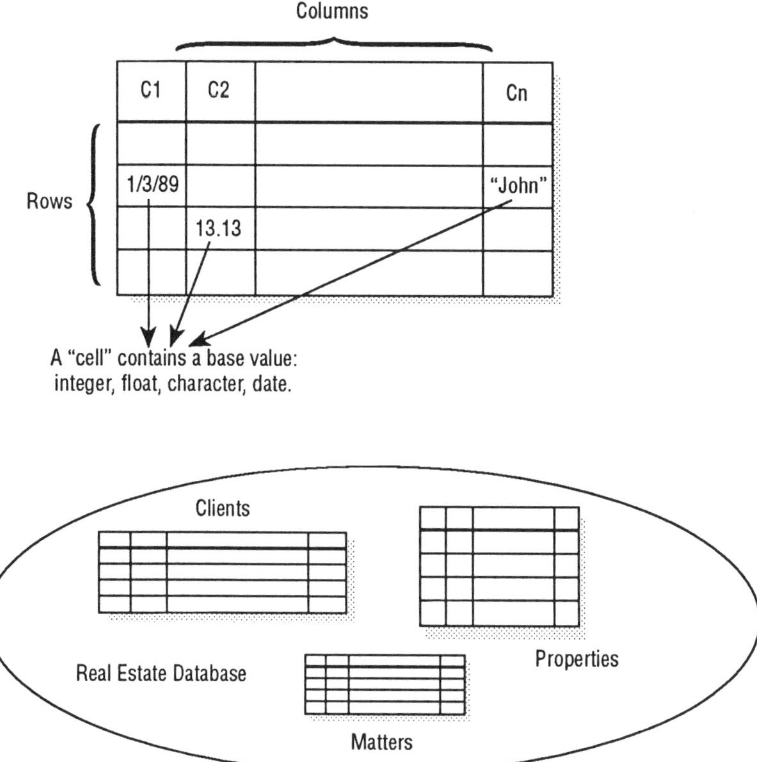

Figure 2.1: Relational databases containing tables.

The *integrity constraints* on individual relations, column values, and row values of an individual table are also defined in the schema through the DDL as are *constraints on relationships* between values in multiple tables.

Each relation in a populated database contains zero or more rows. The values and structure of these rows are determined through the schema of the database. If r is a row in relation R_i, then it will have values (some of which could be NULL) for columns C_{i1} through C_{in} of R_i. We shall use the dot "." notation r.C_{ij} to indicate the C_{ij} column value of r. Also, as mentioned earlier, we shall also use the term *attribute* for C_{ij}; thus, r has attributes C_{i1}, ..., C_{in}, and its C_{ij} attribute value is r.C_{ij}. The actual querying, inserting, deleting, and updating of rows of relations is done through a *Data Manipulation Language (DML)*.

Relational, or more specifically SQL, DDL constructs will be discussed in Chapter 3 where we will discuss the definition of tables, views, and integrity constraints. In addition, most commercial relational database management systems allow different users *privileges* for accessing or updating persistent relational database objects for security control. Security will be discussed in Chapter 6.

In a relational database, the same information can be structured in many different ways. For instance, we can have a database D1 with three tables and another database D2 with 10 tables both containing exactly the same information. In fact, the number of tables containing the same persistent database information can range from one to almost the total number of columns in the database. Figure 2.2 illustrates this point. The specification of the number and structure of the database tables is part of the database design and is typically the responsibility of database professionals.

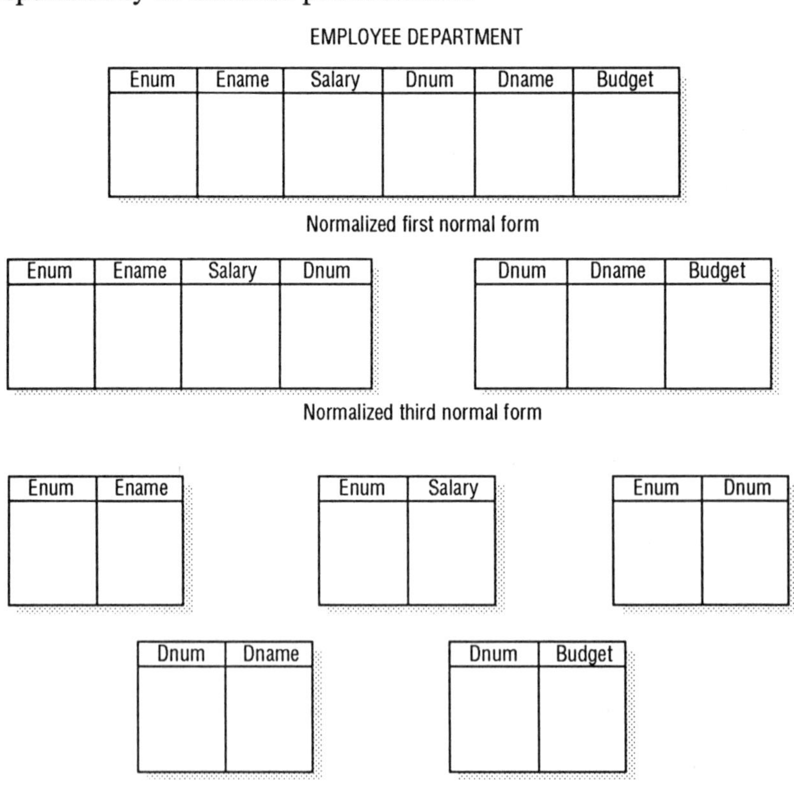

Figure 2.2: *Different "levels" of normalization.*

The database professional—most often the *database administrator*—is responsible for tailoring the conceptual structure, the physical auxiliary structures, the integrity rules, and the security control for particular applications and problem domains. Therefore, this individual must be concerned with the conceptual design as well as the physical design of the database. The conceptual design is primarily concerned with the specification of the *enterprise* model, which is shared by all users of a corporation. The physical design is concerned with the placement of the database onto physical storage and the subsequent efficient access and manipulation of the database. The ANSI/SPARC Study Group for database management systems has proposed an ANSI/SPARC architecture standard, which is shown in Figure 2.3.

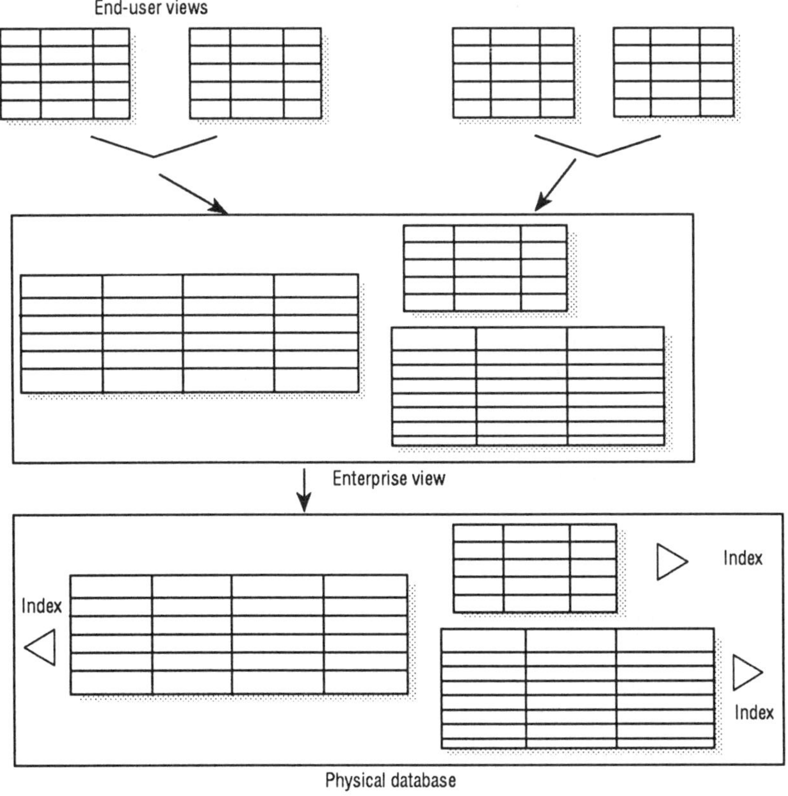

Figure 2.3: *The ANSI/SPARC architecture standard.*

The ANSI/SPARC standard recognizes three different user classes or levels: *end-users, the enterprise,* and *database professionals. End-users* are nontechnical users running programs that access specific components of a corporate database. These individuals access the *external level* of the architecture, which is also called the database's *logical view.*

The global conceptual corporate database is shared by all end-user applications throughout the *enterprise.* This corresponds to the *conceptual level* of the architecture. In some cases, the conceptual level is obtained by integrating several individual views or external schemata. Corresponding to this level, the *conceptual schema* models the persistent objects in a business. As far as relational databases are concerned, both views and base tables could be used to construct the conceptual schemata. In a particular application, the end-user external schemata are built on top of a common conceptual design.

In addition to designing the conceptual schema, the database administrator (DBA) designs and specifies different aspects of the *physical databases,* which are actually stored in persistent storage media. This corresponds to the *internal level* or *storage level* in the ANSI/SPARC architecture. In most relational database management systems, the physical storage objects are themselves relations or tables. Mapping a conceptual schema onto an internal physical schema involves

(1) Further normalizations,
(2) Additional integrity constraints,
(3) Specification of auxiliary structures such as indexes,
(4) Specification of data placement alternatives,
(5) Possible replication of data, and
(6) Fragmentation of data.

Each of the issues introduced here will be discussed in greater detail throughout this book.

2.1.1 Top-down Design

This section presents an overview of each of the four major steps for designing a consistent and efficient relational database for a business. Each step includes many intricacies and subtasks that are beyond the scope of this book. Here, we concentrate instead on the *relational, aspects* of the database design.

A number of algorithms and strategies for designing relational databases have been developed. The paragraphs that follow present the main steps for a top-down design of a relational database. The relational database can be managed by any one of the database management systems discussed in this book or by any other relational DBMS that provides the necessary data definition constructs for expressing the relations and integrity constraints presented in this chapter.

Roughly, the top-down design of relational databases involves four steps:

STEP 1: Identify entities and relationships (ER) of the problem domain.

STEP 2: Merge the external end-user views and generate conceptual model.

STEP 3: Map ER diagram of conceptual model onto relational schema.

STEP 4: Implement the physical design.

Step 1: Identify Entities and Relationships of the Problem Domain

This step involves understanding the problem domain for particular users and user views and, subsequently, specifying the *nodes* and *links* in terms of entities and relationships. Through this step, the database designer models the problem domain of the individual user views or business functions and determines its correspondence to the external level of the three-layered architecture. In this process, the *entities*, that is, the people, places, environment, objects, events, and roles, can be specified, along with the *relationships* between these entities.

Identifying entities involves the specification of the *attributes* of the entities. The attributes of an entity or relationship describe various characteristics and features about the entity; for example, the Name of an entity, Person, or the Budget of an entity, Department. Note that here the term "attribute" is used somewhat differently than column values for rows, although, as we shall see, in most instances these entity attributes will actually be mapped onto columns of relations.

The entities and relationships are translated into *entity-relationship* (ER) diagrams, which depict all the attributes of the entities and relationships. Again, there are a number of alternative strategies for representing ER diagrams, or, more generally, representing semantic data models. Sometimes these ER diagrams can be used to specify various integrity constraints on the persistent database objects. Entity-relationship diagrams are discussed at greater length in Section 2.4.

Step 2: Merge Views

The integration of the different user views into one global and consistent business ER model involves *merging* the different entities and relationships into one consistent model. The resulting model incorporates all the individual user views. This step constructs the logic of the business, and hence corresponds to the second logical level of the three-layered architecture described in the previous section.

Step 3: Map ER Diagram Onto a Relational Schema

Depending upon the particular ER or semantic modeling constructs, a number of well-known algorithms can be used to generate *normalized* databases which have desirable integrity and performance characteristics.

Step 4: Implement the Physical Design

Based on the specifications of the problem domain and the different applications of the enterprise being modeled, the database professional must specify a number of performance tuning constructs and auxiliary structures. These include storage clusters, indexes, data replication, and so on. The resulting relational schema is the actual physical schema, corresponding to the third logical level of the three-layered architecture.

Figure 2.4a illustrates a simple example involving Clients, Properties, and Client Appointments for managing the Properties. As we have assumed a single view in this example, step 2 is not necessary.

In Figure 2.4a, the ER diagram depicts a many-to-many (n-by-m) relationship between Clients and Properties. In a n-by-m relationship, for each entity instance on the "n" side of the relationship there could possibly be many entity instances on the "m" side of the relationship, and vice versa. For example, a client might own many properties, and the same property can be co-owned by multiple clients. Figure 2.4a also shows a one-to-many relationship between a client and his/her appointments. By a one-to-many (1-by-n) relationship, we mean for each entity instance on the "1" side of the relationship there could be many entity instances on the many or "n" side of the relationship. However, each entity instance on the "n" side of the relationship can be related to only one entity instance on the "1" side of the relationship. Figure 2.4b illustrates how the ER diagram is mapped onto a SQL schema. We have incorporated the appropriate primary and foreign key constraints as well as some indexes for accelerated access on certain attributes.

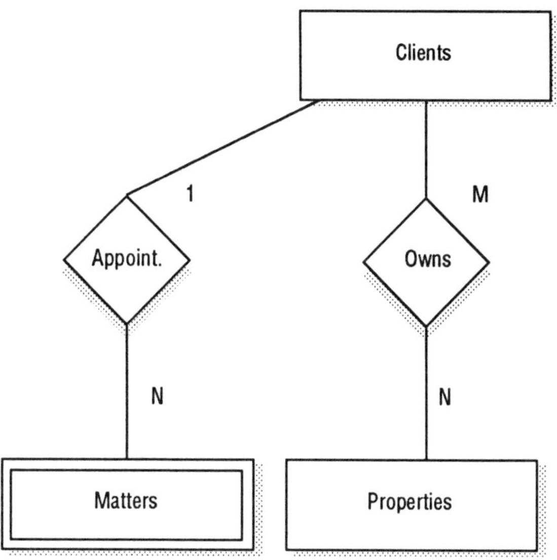

Figure 2.4a: A simple ER diagram.

Clients

ID	Name	Address	Phone	—
1101	John	13 Main St.	(612) 523-4313	—
1131	Mark	14 Dayton		—

Clients–Properties

CID	PID
1101	3121
1101	3341
1131	3121

CID, PID — Primary key
CID — Foreign key of clients
PID — Foreign key of properties

Properties

ID	Address	Price	—
3121	13 Main St.	$100,000	—
3341	14 Dayton	$200,000	—

Matters

CID	Date	Note	—
1101	10/22/91	Price inquiry	—
1131	02/01/92	Accept offer	—

CID, Date — Primary key
CID — Foreign key of clients

Figure 2.4b: An ER diagram mapped onto a SQL schema.

In addition to these four main steps for designing a relational database, the database professional must specify integrity constraints that capture the semantics and consistency of the database. Moreover, in order to avoid anomalies and further enhance the overall efficiency of the database access, alternative normalization strategies should be taken into account. These issues are the focus of the succeeding sections.

2.2 Integrity Constraints

Through transactions, database management systems map one *consistent* (correct) database state onto another. (Transactions will be discussed in greater detail in Chapter 5.) The consistency of the database is typically expressible through *predicates* or conditions on the current state of the database. The predicates that capture the consistency of a database are called *integrity constraints*. Generally, a number of integrity constraints must be enforced on a database state to guarantee its consistency. Examples of some simple integrity constraints are

- The age of a person cannot be a negative number.
- An account balance must be less or equal to the sum of the deposits.
- If an employee works for a department, a record for that department must exist in the database.
- The social security number of each employee must be unique in the set of all employees.
- A person must have a Name; the Name attribute cannot be empty or null.

As these examples suggest, many types of integrity constraints must be imposed on a database to maintain its consistency. These integrity constraint types are organized into several categories: unique/primary key constraints, referential or foreign key constraints, NOT NULL constraints, domain constraints, integrity rules, and triggers.

2.2.1 Key Constraints

A *key* or a *candidate key* is simply one or more columns (attributes) of a relation that uniquely identifies a row. If a key consists of more than one attribute, it is called a *composite key*.

The Social Security Number of a person, the Unique Vehicle Identification Number of a car, or the Project Number in a department are typical examples of keys. A *unique key* constraint specifies that the values of an attribute in a relation (set of rows) must not have any duplicates. Therefore, unique key constraints identify keys or candidate keys. For instance, the Persons table in Figure 2.5 illustrates two candidate keys: the columns Last Name and First Name taken together represent one key, and the column Social Security Number by itself is the other key.

A *primary key* is a designated key with values that serve as identifiers for the relation. A relation might have many keys; the primary key is one of the keys that serve as the identifier of the rows of the relation. An attribute that is not involved in the primary key is called a *nonkey* attribute. Primary keys are used in referential integrity constraints, which are discussed in the next section. In Figure 2.5, Social Security Number is designated as the primary key.

Persons

Last Name	First Name	Soc. Sec. Num.	Date of Birth	—
Smith	John	111-22-3333	10/01/45	—
Wong	Paul	444-55-6666	02/01/52	—
Williams	John	777-88-9999		

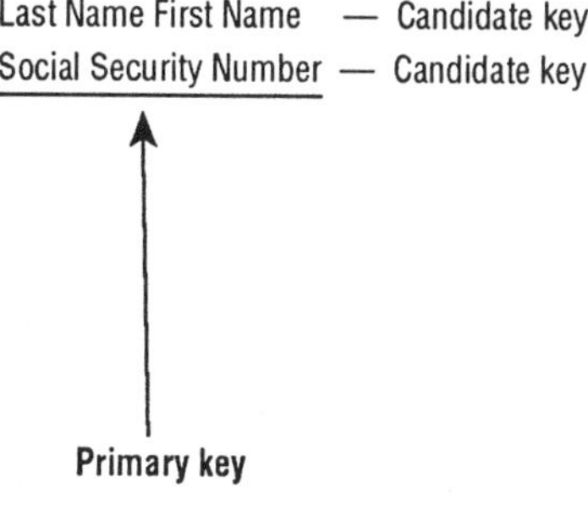

Figure 2.5: Persons table containing two keys.

When a primary key of a table T1 (the *referenced table*) appears as column values in another table T2 (the *referencing table*), it is called a *foreign key* in the referencing table. Therefore, a foreign key is one or more attributes of a table (called the referencing table) whose values correspond to primary key values of another table (called the referenced table).

The actual syntax used to specify unique constraints, primary constraints, and foreign key constraints in different SQL-based database management systems will be presented in Chapter 3.

2.2.2 Referential/Foreign Key Constraints

In a relational model, databases or schemata describe a collection of *flat* (*first normal form*) tables. (Normalization is discussed in Section 2.3.) The most frequently used mechanism for establishing the relationships among the tables and columns of a relation are the referential or foreign key constraints. A referential constraint indicates that attribute values in one relation are actually primary key values in another relation. For example,

- The ManagerID (e.g., Social Security Number) of a department's manager is a foreign key of an employee record (row) in the Employees table.
- Similarly, the DepartmentID in the Employees relation is a foreign key of a record (row) in the Departments table. These are depicted in Figure 2.6.
- In the Clients-Properties many-to-many relationship, the ClientID (CID) and PropertyID (PID) are each foreign keys of a client and a property in the relations Clients and Properties, respectively.

Each of the foreign key values is actually a "surrogate" of a foreign object. By a surrogate, we mean a logical pointer or an identifier of the object. Therefore, the referential integrity constraint specifications attempt to guarantee that "dangling" references to objects do not exist. In our examples, this means

- For each ManagerID in Departments, there must exist an Employee row whose primary key value (Social Security Number) is that ID appearing in Departments.
- Similarly, for each DepartmentID appearing in the Employees table, there must exist a Departments row with that ID as key.
- Also, for each ClientID-PropertyID pair, there must exist a client in the Clients table with that ID and a property in the Properties table with a key the PropertyID.

If a database management system supports referential integrity constraints, it will disallow the insertion or modification of a foreign key value with no corresponding object in the foreign table. We will discuss referential integrity constraints at greater length in Chapter 3.

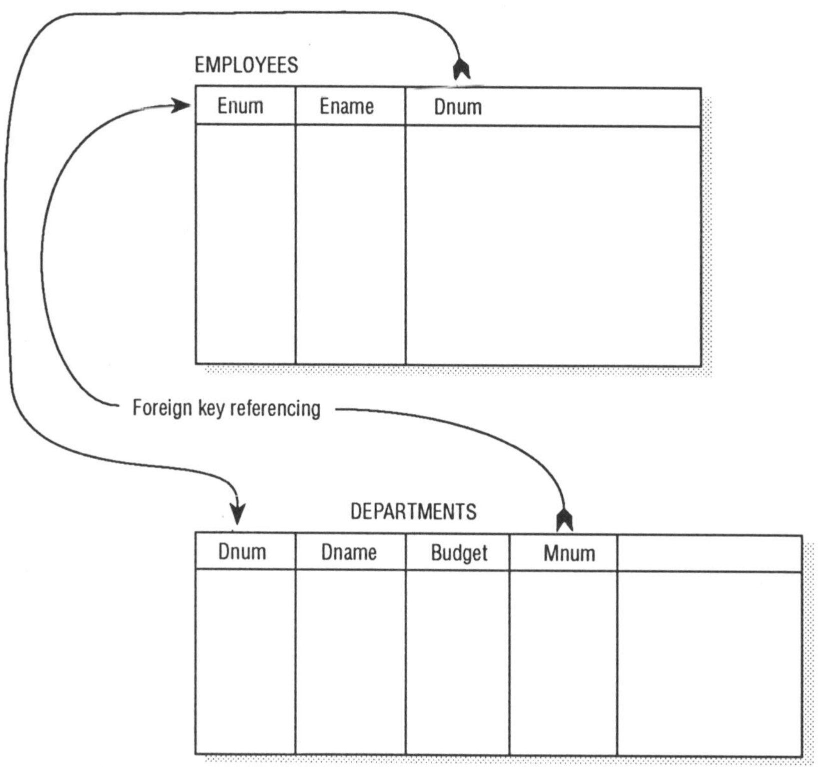

Figure 2.6: Employees and Departments tables foreign key references.

2.2.3 NOT NULL Constraints

Relational databases must support three-valued logic through NULL values. A NULL value represents a "missing" column value. NULL values are essential to support referential integrity (e.g., the requirements that primary keys must be NOT NULL) and various kinds of statistical analysis (such as a survey questionnaire where the respondent does not answer a question). Suppose you wish to obtain the average test scores of all students in a class. If some of those scores are null—either missing or unavailable for privacy reasons—should you treat the null values as zeros, or should you ignore the records?

The underlying relational system must support NULL values and three-valued logic. However, in many cases, values of some columns must not be empty or NULL. For instance, each employee must have a salary, every person must have a name, and each department must have a budget. NOT NULL constraints are automatic for unique or primary key attributes, but in some cases, they are also useful for columns that are not primary keys (e.g., neither the salary nor the balance of an account can be NULL). In general, when an attribute or a column is declared to be of type T, then the attribute values in the table can be T-values or NULL. For instance, if Age is of type Integer, then the Age of a person can be an integer value greater than or equal to zero or NULL. Remember that the null value represents missing or unknown information. Thus, if the Age of John is NULL, it indicates that we do not know John's age. Therefore, when we declare

> Column C is of type T
> (e.g., Column Age is of type INTEGER),

then

> permissible values of C = all T values in the system plus NULL
> (e.g., Permissible values of Age =all INTEGER values (0, +/-1, +/-2, ...) plus NULL).

When a NOT NULL constraint is specified for a column, the range of values for that column are the values included in the type of the column only (i.e., the NULL value is not valid).

As we'll see in Chapters 3 and 4, SQL supports the null-value concept using the keyword NULL and a number of predicates such as IS NULL or NOT NULL. The NOT NULL constraint is used in table definitions to indicate that the column values cannot be null. A number of other predicates (such as IS NULL) are used in the data manipulation part of SQL to check for NULL values of columns.

2.2.4 Domain Constraints

Typically, relational databases come with a collection of built-in data types. The values of columns in the populated relations are drawn from these built-in data type *domains* (i.e., the permissible values of the type). The minimum data types generally provided are CHARACTER strings and NUMERIC (INTEGER and FLOATING POINT). For instance, if Age is declared to be of type INTEGER (a numeric type), then the Age attribute or column value in each row of the table must be an integer (or NULL if it is allowed).

Other built-in data types include long bit-string (for multimedia data) and logical (TRUE, FALSE) data types. In Chapter 3, we will describe the built-in data types found in the four database servers surveyed in this book.

In some cases, just specifying a built-in type is not enough. For instance, although each Age is an integer (which can be either a positive or a negative number), the age of a person cannot be negative. Also, the salary of a person must be within a prescribed range. Therefore, we must impose an integrity constraint on the domain of columns as well. The general form of a domain constraint consists of the built-in or derived domain type and the restriction predicate. For example, the Age domain constraints should be defined as follows:

Domain type: INTEGER
Restriction predicate: >= 0

In a certain sense, domain constraints are a form of *subtyping* [Khoshafian and Abnous, 1990], as supported in some object-oriented systems. These systems provide a number of built-in types and allow users to construct their own subtypes, specializing the system-defined types. However, domain constraints in relational systems are a highly restricted form of subtyping in that they restrict only the permissible values for a column. They cannot introduce new operators that either extend or override the operators of their supertype. Later, in Chapter 11, we will see that it is possible to have more general object-oriented features in SQL and to allow the construction of abstract data type hierarchies. A subtype can specialize both structure (values) and behavior (operations).

2.2.5 Integrity Rules

Thus far we have discussed only special types of integrity constraints—those that apply to column values. Specifically, these have been: unique or primary key constraints used to indicate that the values of particular columns must be unique within the relation; non-null constraints used to indicate that column values cannot be NULL; and domain constraints used to restrict the values of columns.

These common constraints are quite useful. While it is conceivable to have many more special types of constraints, there are a number of situations not covered by a set of special constraint types. Therefore, it is useful to have a more general mechanism for defining types of (arbitrary) constraints. For example, assume we have two tables, Employees and Departments, where employees have salaries and departments have budgets. A constraint on the database is

- The sum of the employees' salaries must not exceed 50% of their department's budget.

Assume we have two tables, Clients and Properties. Two nontrivial constraints on the database are

- If the client is not a U.S. citizen, he/she cannot own 50% of California beaches!
- If a property is co-owned by many clients, then the total assets of all the co-owners must exceed the property value.

It is unreasonable to have a special integrity constraint category for each of these constraints. Rather, we need a general mechanism by which users can express integrity rules. This general mechanism must provide the constructs for (1) defining the integrity and (2) specifying the actions to be taken when an integrity rule is violated.

The integrity rule will be declared as a predicate that must not be violated. Typically, the sublanguage used to define integrity constraint is the Data Manipulation Language of the underlying database management system plus a number of constructs for defining the integrity rule itself (e.g., CHECK or ASSERT). When an integrity constraint is violated, the system will generally raise an exception that will probably end up aborting the transaction that caused the violation. In Chapter 3, we will cover the specific syntax and semantics used to define integrity constraints for the different servers.

The general integrity constraint mechanism subsumes the special integrity constraints discussed in the previous sections. For instance, if we have a general integrity constraint definition mechanism, we will be able to define the unique, primary, non-null, referential or domain constraints. The difference between the constraints is that the special integrity constraints are *supported by the system*, whereas the general integrity constraint mechanism is *user defined.*

It could be argued that one does not need the *system-defined* "special" integrity constraints at all. While there is some merit to this argument, there are also advantages to supporting some integrity constraints explicitly by a database management server. One such advantage is that it provides the users with a clear and useful list of the most frequent integrity constraint categories. In most cases, the users do not need to worry about defining the integrity constraint explicitly each time they need it for an application. In a sense, it is similar to *code sharing*. The system supports these special integrity constraints, and all applications can use them without needing to recode from scratch each time. In addition, since the integrity constraints are *system defined,* there is the potential for better performance in supporting or checking the constraints by the underlying system.

Because of these advantages and the need for expressing more general integrity constraints, future systems most likely will support both mechanisms. They will provide a number of integrity constraint categories, but will also allow the user to define special integrity constraints through an integrity constraint definition sublanguage.

2.2.6 Triggers

The integrity constraints discussed so far have been primarily predicates or assertions that should not be violated in order to maintain a correct or consistent database. If a database operation such as an *update* violates an integrity constraint, the system will probably raise an *exception* or error condition. The most reasonable response to this exception is the abortion of the transaction that violated the integrity constraint.

Triggers are somewhat different from the integrity constraints previously discussed. They are activated upon the execution of certain database operations or when certain conditions are satisfied. Therefore, conceptually, a trigger consists of a *condition* component and an *action* component. The condition can be either a particular state of the persistent database or the execution of a database operation. The action is a database program that attempts to ensure the integrity of the database state when the condition (either a predicate or a database operation) is satisfied.

Database management systems that support triggers often use the execution of database operations as the condition for activating the trigger. Some common database operations that can activate triggers are

- Retrieval or SELECT operations, which read from the persistent database;
- Update operations, which modify the values of attributes of existing rows;
- Inserts of one or more rows in a table; and
- Deletes of existing rows from a table.

Given a consistent and correct state of a database, the only way integrity constraints could be violated is through the operations that modify the state of the database, such as updates, inserts, and deletes. If the condition is one of these operations, the trigger mechanism could be used to enforce integrity of the database through programs that ensure that integrity constraints are maintained. Unlike the previous declarative schemes that allowed the system to enforce integrity constraints (and raise exceptions when constraints are violated), the trigger mechanism allows the database application developer to ensure that integrity constraints are maintained through the action that is activated upon the condition.

Let us examine the "dangling reference" problem of referential integrity constraint through triggers. In Figure 2.7, Column 2 in Table 2 is a foreign key that references Column 1 in Table 1, its primary key. The Action is either an UPDATE of Column 1 in Table 1 or a DELETE of a row of Table 1. In either case, we might have a value of Column 2 in a row of Table 2 without a corresponding Column 1 value in a row of Table 1. To guarantee the integrity constraint and avoid the dangling reference problem, the Action part of a DELETE of a row of Table 1 would be either to: (1) set the corresponding Column 2 values of rows in Table 2 to NULL or (2) delete the Table 2 rows that have invalid Column 2 values. This is a *cascaded* delete, which could cause other rows of other tables to be deleted.

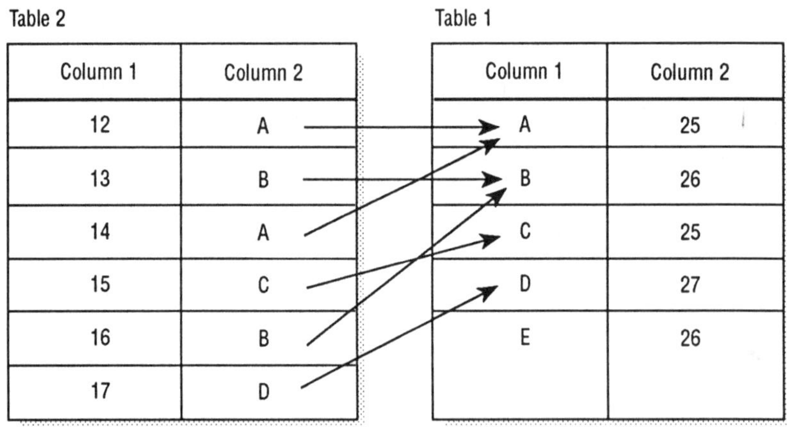

Figure 2.7: *Foreign key references from Table 2 to Table 1.*

Triggers can also support other types of integrity constraints (such as domain constraints and non-NULL constraints). In fact, the trigger mechanism could allow the user to support *all* the integrity constraints on the database. Triggers are complementary to other integrity constraint mechanisms because they allow users (database designers and application developers) to explicitly program the enforcement of the integrity constraint. For instance, the user could declare a foreign key/referential constraint by either a special referential integrity constraint supported by the system, or a declarative assertion or integrity rule expressed by the designer.

As far as enforcement of the referential constraint, integrity constraints raise exceptions only when the constraint is violated. It is the responsibility of the programmer or application developer to realize that foreign keys must exist as primary key values in the referenced table before they are inserted in the referencing table. Triggers facilitate such enforcement of the integrity constraints. With UPDATE and DELETE triggers on the referenced table, the application developer can make sure the referencing table entries are consistent.

2.3 Normalization

Integrity constraints capture the *conditions* for correct and consistent database states. In relational databases, the persistent database states are contained in a collection of tables. Normalization deals with the *structure* of the persistent database tables. By structure, we mean the number of tables, the type (columns and their domains) of each table, and the relationships among the table columns.

Relational database design is primarily the result of two functions: (1) the specification of relational table structures and (2) the normalization plus the specification of integrity constraints. Of course, other data definition components are also required to design a relational database. These components include external views, security, and performance enhancer and auxiliary structures.

Relational databases allow users to design and represent the same information through different schemata or structures. Each of these alternative schemata possesses different modeling and performance characteristics. Normalization in relational database design provides guidelines for designing "well-formed" and high-performance database schemata based on the underlying theoretical relational model. In practical terms, the normal forms are helpful in designing relational databases that prevent unnecessary data duplication, inconsistencies in the database, update, insert, and delete anomalies, and information loss problems. In addition, normal forms function in a positive manner to enhance the maintainability, extensibility, and performance of database applications.

Several types or forms of normalization differ in the extent to which the information in a database is partitioned within tables. Generally, the more normalized a database, the more tables it contains. However, this does not mean that the database state size (i.e., the sum of the sizes of the tables contained in the database) will be *larger.* Because normalization attempts to avoid unnecessary data replication, the overall size of a database state for a more normalized database actually could be *smaller.*

In relational database theory, about five normal forms exist. Fifth normal form is the most restrictive, whereas first normal form is the least constrained. In this section, we concentrate primarily on the first three normal forms. We believe relational databases in third normal form possess most of the primary advantages over unnormalized databases. Additional normalizations could result in more complex databases and application. This could adversely affect the performance and maintainability of the database and the applications.

An extensive discussion of normalization is beyond the scope of this book. For more information on this topic, see Armstrong [1974]; Beeri et al. [1977]; and Maier [1983].

2.3.1 Dependency Relationships

One of the most fundamental concepts used in normalization is the notion of *dependency.* Dependency relationships specify how the values of one or more columns (attributes) of a relation are dependent on the values of other columns of the relation. The simplest form of dependency is *functional dependency,* and in the class of functional dependencies, the most obvious are the dependencies of the nonkey attributes on the values of the key attributes of the relation. Consider the following functional dependencies:

- The first and last name of a person determines his/her salary: the composite <First Name, Last Name> is a composite key of the Person relation.
- The DeptID of a department determines the budget of the department: DeptID is the primary key of the relation Department.
- The number of years and experience of an employee determines his/her rank.
- The residency of a person (which state) and his/her taxable income determines his/her state tax rate.

The first two examples are clearly dependencies of columns on the (primary) key attributes. The dependencies in the latter two examples are less obvious. As we will see in the sections that follow, depending upon the normalization of the tables involved in the relational schema, these examples could be rendered to "cleaner" dependencies, which avoid the pitfalls of unnormalized schemata (e.g., update anomalies).

Here is a more formal definition of dependencies.

> Columns <C_{d1}, ..., C_{dn}> are functionally dependent of columns <C_{f1}, ..., C_{fm}> if for each value of <C_{f1}, ..., C_{fm}>, there is only one functionally determined value of <C_{d1}, ..., C_{dn}>.

This is indicated through:

$$C_{f1}, ..., C_{fm} \longrightarrow C_{d1}, ..., C_{dn}.$$

Assume C_{p1}, ... C_{pk} is the primary key of relation R. Then if C_{d1}, ..., C_{dn} functionally depend on a proper subset of the primary key, we say C_{d1}, ..., C_{dn} are partially dependent on the primary key. Otherwise C_{d1}, ..., C_{dn} are fully dependent on the primary key.

Note that *each key functionally determines all the other attribute values*. However, *other* functional dependencies could involve either nonkey attributes or attributes that are part of a primary key. Most of the normalization schemes discussed in the following sections attempt to avoid these types of functional dependencies.

2.3.2 First Normal Form

The predecessors of the relational model were the *network* and *hierarchical* models. In both models, it was possible for an attribute to reference a *set* or collection of objects, capturing the one-to-many (in the case of hierarchical) or many-to-many (in the case of network) relationships between "child" and "parent" entities.

The *first normal form constraint* of the relational model differs from the network and hierarchical models: it requires the attribute (column) values in a relation to be only *atomic*. More specifically, if R is a relation with columns C_1, ..., C_n, then the domain of each C_{ij} must be the domain of an atomic type (such as an INTEGER, CHARACTER string, or DATE). In particular, the C_{ij} values cannot contain *repeating groups* (i.e., sets of atomic values or sets of tuples).

As a simple example, assume each Parent has a Name, Social Security Number, Job Title, and Children attributes. Each child has a Name and Date of Birth attribute. Figure 2.8a presents a hierarchical representation of the data in which the relationship between Parent and Children is one-to-many. (Section 2.4 covers one-to-many relationships in greater detail). For a relational representation in first normal form, Figure 2.8b represents the same data in two tables: Parent and Children. Note that ParentID is a foreign key in the

Children relation. But, as the example illustrates, each column value in both relations is atomic—unlike Figure 2.8a where the Children attributes are sets of tuples.

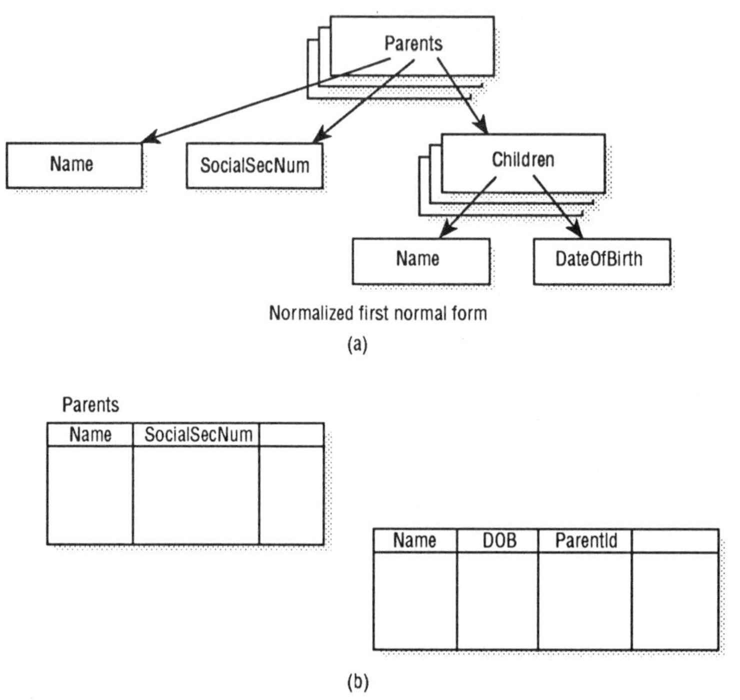

Figure 2.8: Hierarchical model (a) and relational representation (b) in first normal form.

The first normal form constraint is a fundamental requirement for relational models. In fact, it is the *only* requirement that can be—and in most cases is—enforced by the underlying database management system. The system requires that column values be instances of their domains. And in most cases, the domains of the column values are the domains of system-defined types (Integer, Character String, Date, etc.). Any attempt to set the value of a column to anything but a value in the domain of its type will result in an error. More specifically, it will be impossible to set the value of a column to a set of atomic values or tuples.

In summary, a relational database in first normal form satisfies the following constraints: (1) each entry in a table represents one data item (i.e., no repeating groups); (2) all instances within each column are the same, that is, they are instances of the domain of the column's type; (3) each column has a unique name; (4) all rows are unique (i.e., no duplicates); and (5) the order of viewing the rows and columns does not affect the semantics of any function using the table.

2.3.3 Second Normal Form

The second normal form further restricts the first normal form and requires that there be no nonkey attributes that partially depend on the primary key. As discussed earlier, the first normal form is the only normal form that is enforced by the system. In most implementations of relational systems, the other normal forms are enforced by the designer. These normal forms give the "obvious" guidelines for separating attributes that pertain to different abstract entities in different relations, and grouping the attributes that pertain to the same abstract entity together in one relation.

In Section 2.4, we discuss a number of simple algorithms for transferring entity-relationship models onto normalized relational models so that the relations are in third normal form. In this way, the pitfalls of unnormalized models are avoided.

To illustrate the advantages of the second normal form constraint, assume we have one large table Clients-Properties-ALL containing *all* the information on clients and properties. See Figure 2.9. The primary key of the relation is the composite CID, PID.

Clients–Properties–All

CID	PID	CName	CAddress	CPhone	•••	PAddress	Price	•••

Figure 2.9: Clients-Properties-ALL table.

The relation is in the first normal form, but there are several problems. Namely,

(1) The information about a client is replicated for each property of the client, which causes an overhead in data replication.

(2) Whenever we update information about a client or property (such as credit status, address, or income), we should update all tuples that contain information about the client or the property.

(3) Since primary key attributes cannot be NULL, we cannot enter client information (e.g., CID, Name, Address) if a client does not have any properties. Similarly we cannot enter or update information about a property if it is not currently owned by a client.

(4) By the same token, deletions are also problematic. For instance, if we delete all the properties of a client, we lose the information about the client (e.g., CID, Name, Address).

These problems occur because some of the attributes are determined *partially* on the primary key. That is, the client attributes are determined by the CID. We can avoid such pitfalls by using the second normal form.

Second normal form is violated when an attribute that is not part of the primary key is partially determined by the primary key. This means each nonkey attribute must depend on all the attributes in the primary key.

More formally, if $C_{k1}, ..., C_{kn}$ is the primary key of a relation, then the relation is in second normal form if it *does not* have any nonkey attribute Cp such that

$$C_{ki1}, ..., C_{kij} \longrightarrow C_p,$$

where $C_{ki1}, ..., C_{kij}$ is a *proper* subset of $C_{k1}, ..., C_{kn}$.
According to the previous example we had

CID —> CName
CID —> CAddress,

and so on. Similarly,

PID —> Price
PID —> PAddress,

and so on.

These functional dependencies all violate the second normal form constraint. Figure 2.4b shows how the same information could be represented in three tables, Clients, Properties, and Clients-Properties, which are all in second normal form. All the pitfalls of first normal form relations are avoided and this second normalized model is clearer, cleaner, and more maintainable.

2.3.4 Third Normal Form

The third normal form further restricts the second normal form by requiring that nonkey attributes depend *only* and *fully* on the primary key. The second normal form guarantees that a nonkey attribute does not depend *partially* on the primary key. However, the second normal form does not restrict other types of dependencies. For instance, we can have a relation in second normal form and yet have a dependency:

> Ni —> Nj
> (from a nonkey attribute Ni to another nonkey attribute Nj).

Let us slightly modify the Properties relation example and assume each Property has a manager—PropertyManager—and the manager's phone number—ManagerPhoneNumber. A property manager can manage multiple properties. The only key of Properties is PropertyID. The relation is in the second normal form, but we have the following functional dependency:

> PropertyManager —> ManagerPhoneNumber.

The dependency of an attribute on another nonkey attribute can create certain problems. Specifically,

- A property manager's phone number is replicated for every property that he/she manages.
- If we change the phone number of a manager, we must consistently change the phone numbers of all Properties tuples that have the same manager.
- If we drop all properties managed by a particular property manager, we would lose his/her phone number.

These problems are similar to the consistency problems of relations that are not in second normal form. Note that the ManagerPhoneNumber is functionally dependent on the PropertyID primary key in two ways: directly through the functional dependency PropertyID —> ManagerPhoneNumber and transitively through PropertyID —> PropertyManager —> ManagerPhoneNumber.

A relation is in third normal form if it is in second normal form and no nonkey attributes are transitively dependent on the primary key. The third normal form constraints avoid the problems and anomalies of the previously mentioned examples.

The property manager example can be normalized to third normal form if we remove the ManagerPhoneNumber attribute from the relation Properties and instead introduce a relation ManagerPhones with the attributes Manager (primary key) and Phone Number. Thus, the PropertyManager attribute in Properties becomes a foreign key corresponding to Manager in the ManagerPhones referenced relation.

2.4 Entity-relationship Data Modeling

We have discussed the integrity constraints and normalization strategies that are essential for well-designed relational databases. However, as stated in Section 2.1, to begin designing relational databases, we usually first design an *entity-relationship (ER) data model.* This data model is subsequently mapped onto a relational schema.

In its most abstract form, an entity-relationship data model is a node and link representation of the object space structure in a problem domain. The motivation for designing the data models is to model the real world as closely as possible. More specifically, entity nodes in an entity-relationship model represent real world entity types, which could be related to other entity types either through relationship nodes or links. Similar to types in programming languages, an entity type represents a set of objects (entities), all having the same *attributes*. An attribute is a function that can apply to an entity in the entity type. The name of an entity type also identifies the *extension* (set of all instances) of the entity type. Relationships are represented as nodes "connecting" one or more entity types.

Researchers have developed a number of graphical representations of entity-relationship models. The forerunner of these models is the famous ER model, introduced by Chen [1976]. The ER model schema consists of (1) rectangles representing entity types, (2) ovals representing ranges of attributes, and (3) diamonds representing relationships (i.e., aggregation).

Relationships can be one-to-one (each person has a one spouse), many-to-one (a person has many children), or many-to-many (employees can work in different departments and many employees work in the same department). The cardinality of these relationships are usually labeled on the arcs of the relationship. One-to-one relationships are represented with the labels "1" on the other side. One-to-many are represented as the label "1" on the side that involves one entity and the label "N" on the side that involves many entities. Many-to-many relationships are labeled with "N" and "M" on each side, respectively. Figure 2.10 illustrates the way in which relationships are labeled.

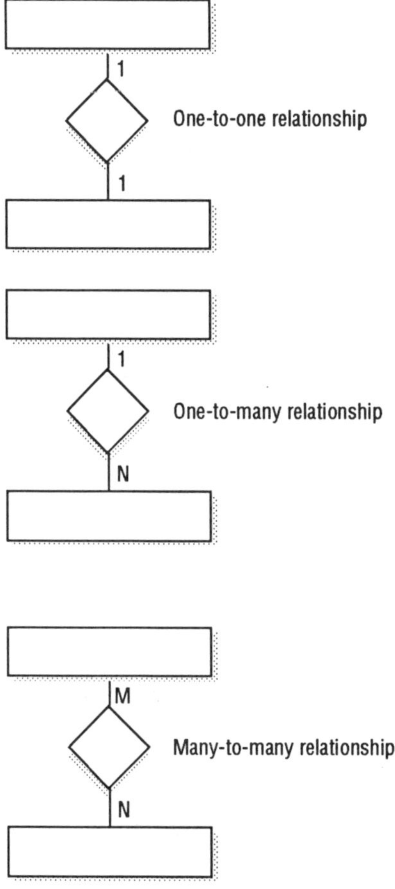

Figure 2.10: Labeling of relationships.

As a more concrete example, Figure 2.11 depicts the attributes of the entity type Person. Each person has a Name, Date of Birth, Social Security Number, and so on. Figure 2.11 also illustrates the Address entity type and the relationship "Resides" between Person and Address. This is a one-to-many relationship as each person can reside at one address, and many people can reside at the same address.

An entity type can be related to itself. Figure 2.12 is a slightly more generalized model of the Clients-Properties example where each client has a spouse. In this model, "Owns" is a many-to-many relationship between Clients and Properties.

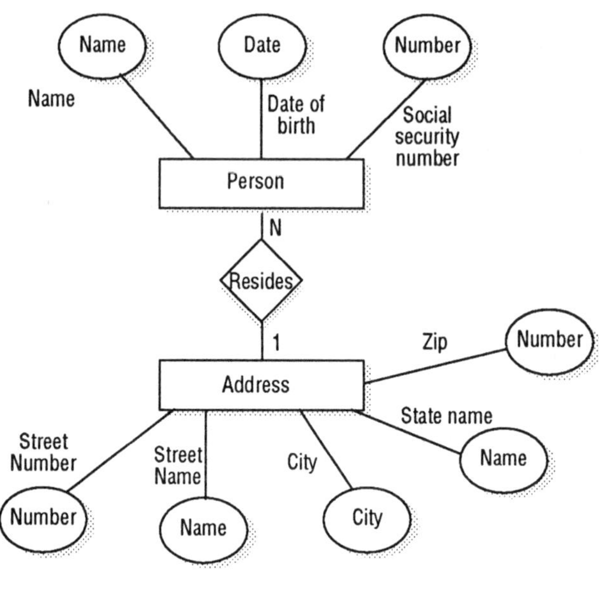

Figure 2.11: Attributes of the entity type Person.

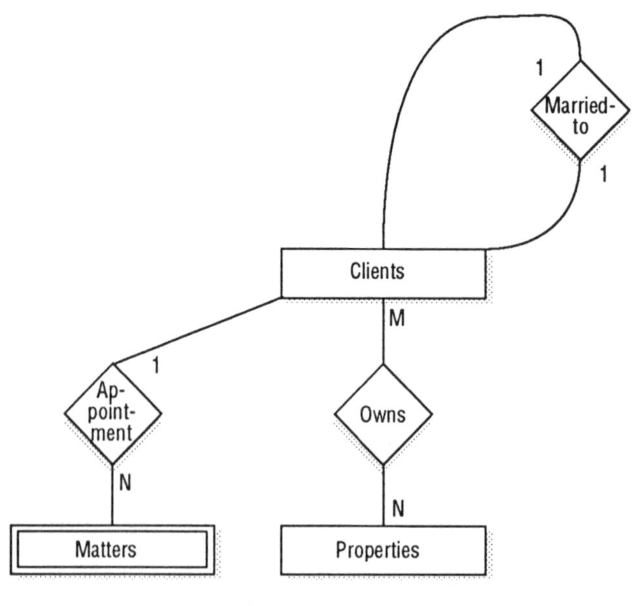

Figure 2.12: Clients-Properties example.

2.4.1 Alternative Constructs and Extensions

In this section, we discuss additional constructs and extensions to the basic ER modeling previously described. Specifically, we explain how *keys, weak entities,* and *inheritance* could be represented in entity-relationship diagrams. Some of these constructs were illustrated in previous examples.

For instance, in Figure 2.11, the Social Security Number attribute of Person is a *key*. Similarly, the composite <StreetNumber, StreetName> is a *key* of Address.

Sometimes an entity is entirely dependent on the existence of another entity. The dependent entity is called the *weak entity.* In our RealEstate example, each client makes a number of appointments to deal with matters of concern. The entries in Matters are dependent on the clients. Figure 2.4a illustrated this using a double rectangle.

In some cases, it is useful to have an entity type "inherit" attributes from one or more existing entity types. For instance, both Real Estate Agents and Clients are Persons. A simple diagram with "is-a" *inheritance* is shown in Figure 2.12. With inheritance hierarchies we would replicate all the common attributes of agents and clients such as name, date of birth, address, and so on. Inheritance of entity types provides a natural and powerful mechanism for organizing the structure of the entities. The original entity ER model did not incorporate inheritance hierarchies. However, several extensions of ER and semantic data models did introduce inheritance relationships. For instance, the attributes Name, Social Security Number, Date of Birth, and Address of Persons will be inherited by Clients and Agents. The attributes of Clients will be the combination of the attributes of Persons and the attributes of Clients defined specifically for the Client entity type. In Chapter 11, we will discuss inheritance at greater length.

Keys, weak entities, and inheritance represent only a sample of those constructs that have been introduced and defined for ER modeling. Researchers have developed many other variations and extensions to the original ER model introduced by Chen in 1976. However, the most significant extension continues to be the inheritance relationship.

Researchers have also developed a number of graphical representation alternatives for ER models. For example, *Database Modeling and Design* by Toby J. Teorey (from the series in *Data Management Systems* by Jim Gray) follows a representation developed by Reiner et al. [1985]. Figure 2.13 uses this alternative representation to illustrate some entity types and their relationships. Note that the cardinality of the relationship is indicated by the color of the diamond. A one-to-one relationship is white, a one-to-many relationship is white on the one side and black on the many side, and a many-to-many relationship is black.

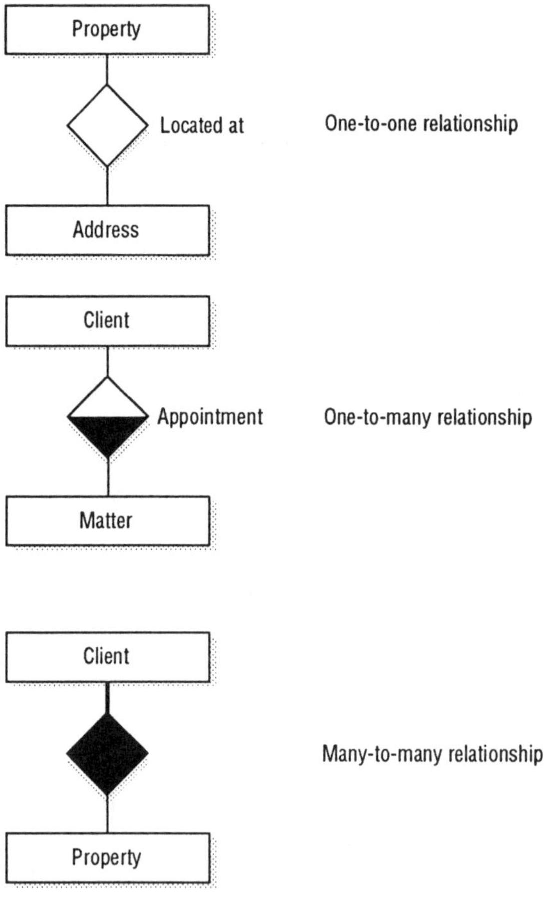

Figure 2.13: *An alternative representation of the ER model (per Reiner).*

A third alternative uses a "crow's foot" representation for the many side of the relationship [Everest, 1986]. In this model, diamonds are not used to represent relationships. Rather, the relationship name is a label on the link between two entities. Oracle's CASE.METHOD product uses this method [Barker, 1989]. In Figure 2.14, a portion of the real estate database schema is shown using this alternative representation.

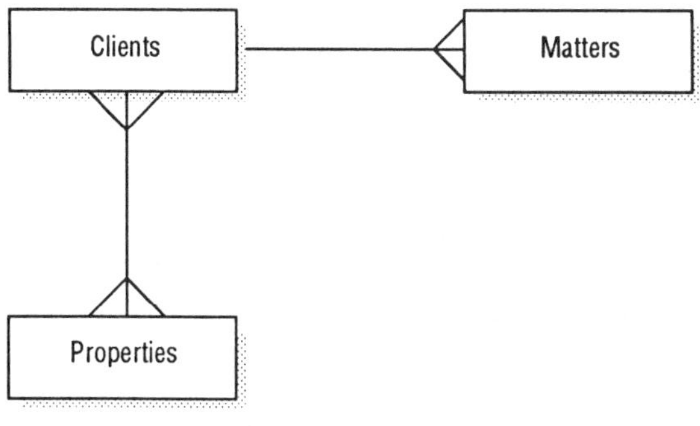

Figure 2.14: A "crows foot" representation of the ER model.

The alternative representations are equivalent. Entity types and relationships can be represented using any of these (and other) alternative schemes. Standards do not exist, and different CASE and database data modeling products will choose one or the other of these strategies.

2.4.2 Mapping ER Diagrams Onto Relational Schemata

As mentioned earlier, it is much simpler to first design the schema of a database using an ER model and then map the ER schema onto a relational schema using the SQL Data Definition Language. This mapping can be performed either automatically by the system or by the database professional.

For instance, IBM's Repository Manager provides an entity-relationship abstraction to its clients. The entities and relationships are mapped onto DB2 schemata automatically by the Repository Manager. Alternatively, the database administrator can map the ER diagram that is generated for the database application onto a SQL schema. In either case, the steps in mapping ER diagrams onto relational schemata are well known and well understood. We outline the basic mappings and algorithm below.

To develop the mapping algorithm we need to generate relation schemata for the entity types, relation schemata for the relationships, and various integrity constraints to capture the semantics of the various constraints and annotations of the ER diagrams.

Starting with an ER diagram, it is possible to apply a simple algorithm to generate a normalized relational schema. The relations will, in fact, be in the third normal form. The basic algorithm follows.

- For each entity type, create a table whose columns correspond to the attributes of the entity.
- For each one-to-one relationship, include the key of onc of the entities as a foreign key in the other entity's table definition.
- For each one-to-many relationship, include the primary key of the parent entity as a foreign key in the many children's relation.
- For each many-to-many relationship, create three tables: one table for each entity and a relationship table whose columns are the primary keys of the relationship entities.

Note that for the relationships we use foreign keys. This means we need to introduce either foreign key constraints or triggers to maintain the integrity. As illustrated earlier, Figure 2.4a shows the ER diagram of the RealEstate database, and Figure 2.4b shows the SQL schema generated for the ER diagram.

If additional constraints and annotations exist in the ER diagram, these too must be mapped onto triggers or integrity constraints. For instance, a weak entity must be mapped onto an existential integrity constraint. Using triggers or more elaborate referential integrity constraint mechanisms requires the following actions:

- If a parent entity is deleted, then all corresponding weak entities must be deleted.
- If the key of a parent entity is modified, then all the foreign key values of the corresponding weak entities must be modified.

In Chapter 3, we'll illustrate how the CASCADE construct can be used in conjunction with referential integrity constraints to cascade the deletes of referenced (parent) rows to referencing (child) rows, especially when the children are weak entities.

This brief discussion illustrates the fact that you can simply map basic ER diagrams onto relational schemata. To capture the semantics of relationships, we need to include referential integrity constraints. In some cases the referential integrity constraint must support the CASCADE construct. If the database management system (DBMS) does not support referential integrity constraints, the integrity must be preserved through triggers implemented by a database administrator. This is the case with the SQL Server. For a more detailed discussion on mapping ER diagrams onto relational schemata refer to Teorey [1990].

2.5 When Is a DBMS Relational?

So far, we have discussed some fundamental aspects of relational database design. For example, in order for the database professional to design and implement correct, semantically consistent, high-performance database applications, the underlying DBMS must possess certain features. Specifically, the system must enable the specification of different integrity constraints; it must support different normalization constructs; and, finally, it must allow the specification of primary keys, indexes, clustering hints, and so on. In other words, for a DBMS to be *relational,* it must support those features that enable the database application programmer to design correct, consistent, and efficient relational databases.

What is the specific list of criteria used to determine if a commercial DBMS is relational? This is a controversial question. The relational model has gained widespread user acceptance, which has led to a rush among vendors to claim that their product is in some way relational. In fact, most novel database applications are being developed in relational systems. Therefore, to survive in the database world, vendors must provide relational features or features that, at least, claim to be relational.

Concerned that the full power and implications of the relational approach were being watered down, Dr. E.F. Codd, the inventor of the relational model, has suggested a number of definitions or specifications for determining whether a system is relational. Codd has identified a Relational Model Version 1 and a Relational Model Version 2. The Relational Model Version 1 (RM/V1) consists of 50 or so features published by Codd between 1968 and 1988. In his recent book on the Relational Model Version 2, he describes some 333 features of the Relational Model Version 2 (RM/V2). In this work, Codd points out

> *A DBMS product is fully relational in the 1990s if it fully supports each and every one of the features of RM/V2 defined in this book.*
> *[Codd, 1990]*

A description or even an abbreviation of the 333 features identified by Codd is beyond the scope of this book. (Codd's book on the RM/V2, as well as some of his other papers, is included in the references.) In fact, we tend to doubt that *any* product will ever satisfy Dr. E.F. Codd's definition of being relational (according either to RM/V1 or RM/V2). However, some of the characterizations and features clarified by Dr. Codd throughout the years are very useful in understanding the different features of relational products. In particular, we believe *Codd's Twelve Rules* [Codd, 1985], which defines a set of rules for what really constitutes a relational DBMS, is very useful. These rules forms a yardstick against which the "real" relational DBMS products can stand up and be counted.

If a DBMS does not implement a significant fraction of these rules, it is probably not worth further examination. If it scores poorly in implementing the rules, complete revision of applications is generally necessary because of the shaky foundation of the underlying data model.

In the remainder of this section, we first discuss the 12 rules themselves, reorganized into functional classifications of foundational rules, structural rules, integrity rules, data manipulation rules, and data independence rules. We then present the advantages offered by systems that observe the rules. The taxonomy here follows Parsaye et al. [1989].

2.5.1 Foundational Rules: Rule 0 and Rule 12

Foundational rules include Codd's Rule 0 and Rule 12, which help determine whether a DBMS is relational.

> **Rule 0:** For any system that is advertised as, or claimed to be, a relational database management system, that system must be able to manage databases entirely through its relational capabilities.
>
> **Rule 12:** If a relational system has a low-level (single-record-at-a-time) language, that low level cannot be used to subvert or bypass the integrity rules and constraints expressed in the higher level relational language.

To qualify for Rule 0, all management capabilities of the system must be subsumed by its relational interface. (The "relational interface" in this context means a set-at-a-time operational language—SQL, for example.) Rule 0 disqualifies those systems that use nonrelational facilities to achieve data management capabilities, including data definition, data manipulation, query, integrity, security, and performance enhancement.

Rule 12 precludes those products that claim to have a relational interface but actually provide the user with a pre-existing, low-level, record-at-a-time interface "for performance reasons." These claims usually convince the user that such an interface will maintain the same integrity constraints imposed by the set-at-a-time relational interface. However, a record-at-a-time interface often compromises the integrity of the database without the knowledge of the user or the database administrator.

If a DBMS cannot satisfy the foundational rules, Codd says it is not truly relational. Many network-based or hierarchical-based DBMSs offering a relational front end typically fail to satisfy these rules.

2.5.2 Structural Rules: Rule 1 and Rule 6

In Codd's view, a relational database must support several structural features. Codd's Rule 1 and Rule 6 are included in our structural rules category.

> **Rule 1:** All information in a relational database is represented explicitly at the logical level and defined in exactly one way—by values in tables.
>
> **Rule 6:** All views that are theoretically updatable are also updatable by the system.

Rule 1, subtitled the *Information Rule,* asserts that for a DBMS to be relational, all information (even system catalog information) regarding table names, column names, domain names, view definitions, security, and integrity constraints must be stored in the system catalog as tables themselves.

Rule 6 explicitly addresses views. It is commonly known that updating views can produce inconsistent results (because they are associated with multiple base tables). This rule states that if a view is theoretically updatable, then the DBMS should be able to perform the update. No system truly supports this feature, however, because all theoretically updatable views cannot yet be identified. DB2 currently supports a subset of theoretically updatable views, but even though certain views are clearly updatable, DB2 has no algorithms for recognizing such views.

2.5.3 Integrity Rules: Rule 3 and Rule 10

Data integrity is one of the most important elements of database management and was discussed in some detail in Section 2.2. Two of Codd's rules deal with data integrity.

> **Rule 3:** NULL values (distinct from the empty character string or a string of blank characters) are supported in fully relational DBMSs for representing missing information and inapplicable information in a systematic way, independent of data type.

Rule 10: Integrity constraints specific to a particular relational database must be definable in the relational data sublanguage and storable in the catalog, not in the application programs.

In Rule 10, Codd specifies that integrity constraints must be stored in the DBMS data catalog rather than in application programs or user interfaces. This convention supports centralized control and integrity constraint enforcement. If a constraint is changed (e.g., the price ceiling of a property in a particular zone), the change and enforcement will be performed within the catalog. Thus, you will not have to rewrite the application programs. Also, because constraints are stored only once in a catalog, you will never have multiple versions of constraints, each enforced by different application programs. Isolating application programs from changes in integrity constraints is referred to as *integrity independence.*

Consider a system not based upon a relational model that includes user-defined integrity constraints built into the database schema definition. If any constraints within the system are changed, the associated database may have to be completely reloaded and each associated application may have to be rewritten. Thus, such systems cannot usually guarantee good data quality.

2.5.4 Data Manipulation Rules: Rules 2, 4, 5, and 7

Besides data definition (schemata) specifications, a relational DBMS should support a Data Manipulation Language. Four of Codd's rules apply to various features of the DML.

Rule 2: Each and every datum (atomic value) in a relational database is guaranteed to be logically accessible by resorting to a combination of table name, primary key value, and column name.

Rule 4: The database description is presented at the logical level in the same way as ordinary data, so that authorized users can apply the same relational language to its interrogation as they apply to the regular data.

Rule 5: A relational system may support several languages and various modes of terminal use (e.g., the fill-in-the-blanks mode). However, there must be at least one language whose statements are expressible as character strings and that is comprehensive in supporting all of the following items: data definition, view definition, data manipulation (interactively and by program), integrity constraints, authorization, and transaction boundaries (begin, commit, and rollback).

Rule 7: The capability of handling a base relation or a derived relation applies not only to the retrieval of data but also to the insertion, update, and deletion of data.

Rule 2 guarantees that the query language allows the user to access all the data in the database (to which the user has access privileges). In a relational DBMS, you cannot restrict access to some area of the database by the query language. Rule 4 specifies that relational databases do not have different languages for manipulating metadata and regular data. Additionally, only one logical structure (relation or table) is used to store system information for manipulation. Rule 5 requires that the query language used by the system use set-at-a-time statements (as opposed to a single-record navigational language). In addition, Rule 7 stipulates that operations that change the contents of the database should be set-at-a-time statements.

2.5.5 Physical Data Independence: Rule 8

Physical data independence deals with the separation of physical storage and performance aspects from the logical structures of data that an application sees. Codd's Rule 8 addresses this concept.

Rule 8: Application programs and terminal activities remain logically unimpaired whenever any changes are made in either storage representations or access methods.

Rule 8 allows the database administrator to tune the performance and to rearrange the physical organization of the relational DBMS without affecting running applications. SQL, for example, achieves full physical database independence by specifically excluding access to low-level database structures.

Suppose a database administrator drops an index on a column in a table. All programs that access that table should continue to run without recompilation or modification. However, in many nonrelational systems, a change in physical database structure brings a halt to the programs that operate on the data. Thus, database modifications on nonrelational systems consequently could require considerable modifications to associated applications.

2.5.6 Logical Data Independence: Rule 9

Logical data independence also separates application programs from data restructuring, as designated by Codd's Rule 9.

> **Rule 9:** Application programs and terminal activities remain logically unimpaired when information-preserving changes of any kind that theoretically permit unimpairment are made to the base tables.

According to this rule, you can also alter the logical structure of the database if all the information is preserved without affecting the running of applications. View structures that hide the logical structure alteration are a key aid to this operation. For example, if two tables are combined without information loss, you can define a view that is a projection of the combined table. Thus, it will appear to the user (or application program) that nothing was changed.

2.5.7 Distribution Independence: Rule 11

Distribution independence indicates that an application program that accesses a DBMS should perform without modification if the data is moved from computer to computer in a network environment. This is noted in Codd's Rule 11.

> **Rule 11:** A relational DBMS has distribution independence.

In other words, the data should appear to be centralized on a single machine, and the responsibility of locating and recomposing the data should always reside with the system.

2.5.8 Advantages of Conforming to Strict Relational Criteria

Relational database management systems that adhere to the rules discussed above offer numerous advantages. First, they employ a complete high-level query language that insulates the user and application programs from the physical and logical mechanisms that implement the data management capabilities. Such systems also utilize the same language for data and metadata with all the benefits of the high-level query language, as well as greater flexibility in database restructuring. In addition, the mechanisms supplied for data independence ensure longevity of applications. Thus, both users and developers are guarded against modifying programs in the event of low-level reorganizations of the database. And, the mechanisms that implement integrity constraints guarantee additional correctness of data. Finally, database systems that adhere to relational rules offer ease of distribution as neither the users nor the application programs are required to know where the data is physically located.

2.6 Summary

In this chapter, we discussed the various aspects of relational database design. First, we presented the four major steps in the top-down design of relational databases.

In addition, we discussed the importance of specifying integrity constraints in the design of relational databases. We saw that some of these integrity constraints can be specified when mapping the ER model onto a relational database. For instance, referential integrity constraints are identified in the ER-to-relational mapping phase. However, there are additional constraints that must be specified, including domain or range constraints on table columns, NULL constraints, UNIQUE constraints, and other general integrity constraints.

To prevent various insert, update, and delete anomalies, a relational database must be normalized. This chapter presented the definition of the first three normal forms as well as the algorithm for mapping an ER model onto a third normal form relational database. Finally, the last part of the chapter focused on the 12 rules for relational databases devised by E.F. Codd and outlined the advantages offered by systems that adhere to these rules.

Chapter 3

Data Definition

In Chapter 2, we provided an overview of relational databases, covering relational database design, integrity constraints for relational databases, and desirable features for relational database management systems. In this chapter, we concentrate on the SQL database language for defining relational databases.

Structured Query Language (SQL) consists of three categories:

(1) *Data Definition Language (DDL).* The DDL constructs are used to create and destroy tables, indexes, views, integrity constraints, and so on.

(2) *Data Control Language (DCL).* The DCL constructs are used primarily by a database administrator to enroll and drop users, to grant and revoke privileges to users, and so on.

(3) *Data Manipulation Language (DML).* The DML allows users to SELECT, INSERT, UPDATE, and DELETE from persistent database tables.

Our focus in this chapter is primarily on the data definition, or DDL, constructs. In order to illustrate how various privileges could be granted to or revoked from database objects, we also discuss the GRANT and REVOKE DCL constructs of the SQL servers. Chapter 6 will present a more comprehensive discussion of the security features of the various servers.

Relational database management systems typically store the descriptive data about the database, or *metadata,* in relational tables. In other words, information about the structure of the tables, such as the number of the columns, the name and type of each column, and so on, are also stored in relational tables. One important advantage of this strategy is that SQL statements can be used to query and possibly even update these *meta* tables. Depending upon the product or context, the tables containing various types of information about the content and structure of the database are called *system catalogs, metadata,* and *data dictionaries.* In this chapter, we also discuss the tables that constitute the system catalogs of the various servers.

We begin our discussion in Section 3.1 with an introductory overview of various data definition constructs in SQL. The data types supported in the different standards are then presented in Section 3.2, followed by a discussion on the construction of databases and schemata in Section 3.3.

In Sections 3.4 through 3.7, we focus on the SQL constructs for defining and dropping tables and views, for granting and revoking privileges, and for implementing various integrity constraints. We then proceed with a discussion on system catalogs and the SAG catalog tables in Section 3.8.

In Section 3.9, we examine the data definition constructs of four popular SQL servers. This includes a survey of the data types, schema definition, table and view creation, integrity constraint and privilege definition, and system catalogs of each product. A chapter summary is provided in Section 3.10.

3.1 An Overview of Data Definition in SQL

The SQL Data Definition Language (DDL) provides constructs for defining databases, tables, views, authorization privileges (actually DCL as discussed in Chapter 6), and integrity constraints.

Varying SQL "standards" and dialects provide different levels of support for each of these DDL constructs. These standards include the ANSI SQL89 standard, the SQL Access Group (SAG) SQL, and the database language of IBM System Application Architecture (SAA). Each of these is described in this chapter.

In most systems, the data dictionaries contain the table definitions, the views, the integrity constraints, authorization, and other primitives stored in various system tables. The collection of these system tables is called the *system catalog*. In fact, as mentioned above, the terms *data dictionary, metadata, system tables,* and *system catalog* are often used interchangeably. In this chapter, however, we primarily use the term *system catalog* to indicate the tables that contain the definitions (structure) of the databases.

At the outset, it should be emphasized that what we present here is an overview and summary of the data definition (metadata) constructs in the servers. We have attempted to capture the most important aspects of the data definition constructs that the different servers provide. However, this chapter must not be considered a comprehensive reference on specific database servers or standard definition constructs. Rather, you should refer to the documentation provided with individual servers, which are listed in the bibliography [ANSI, 1986, 1989; DEC, 1990a-1990d; IBM, 1988, 1989a-1989d; Microsoft, 1990a-1990d; Oracle, 1989a-1989g; SAG, 1990; and X/Open SQL, 1989]. Our aim here is to present only an overview of all the data definition constructs of the SQL database servers and some of the differences in servers with regard to data definition. We emphasize the conceptual design constructs of the servers, placing less emphasis on the physical data definition constructs, such as clusters, indexes, and the like, which will be covered in Chapter 6. In addition, we compare the data definition constructs of the SAA and the SAG standards with those of the ANSI SQL89 standard. We also demonstrate additional or more specific distinguishing data definition features of the servers.

As a word of caution, we are analyzing and surveying only particular versions of the standards and products. It is very likely that these standards and products will evolve to include more advanced features. Hence, in the foreseeable future, some of our characterizations might be obsolete. However, as far as standards are concerned, these typically take much longer to evolve. In fact, the functionality of most of the products discussed in this book will probably continue to incrementally improve. Subsequent revisions of this book will incorporate any changes to and enhancements of these standards and products.

3.2 Data Types

SQL databases are constructed on top of a collection of system-supported built-in data types. Each data type specifies a set of values. Values of individual columns within SQL tables are elements of these sets. In some SQL dialects, it is possible to further restrict these data types and create user-specified *domains*. However, all these domains are actually subsets of the system-supported data types. For instance, INTEGER is a built-in data type; however, five-digit client IDs are a subset of the set of all possible integers. The client ID values must be elements of the pool of five-digit positive integer values presenting valid client identifiers.

In some cases, a column value can be missing or NULL. As we discussed in Chapter 2, NULL is distinct from all domain values of individual data types. Most SQL systems support the notion of a NULL value. However, sometimes certain columns are not allowed to have NULL values. For example, if the Social Security Number of the Persons table is a primary key and as such each person must have a social security number, then a NULL value would not be allowed.

The ANSI SQL89 standard supports two fundamental data types: number and character string. A value that is not NULL can be either a character string or a number. A character string and a number cannot be compared with each other. Specific servers typically extend the alphanumeric data types with other types, such as date, time, money, logical, long binary, and so on.

3.2.1 Character Data Type

The character data types contain characters of the implementation-defined character set. A character string is a sequence of one or more characters usually indicated through CHARACTER (n). Its length, n, is the maximum number of characters in the character sequence. Character strings are comparable. String comparison is performed in accordance with the implementation-defined character collating sequence. When the character strings being compared are not equal, the shorter string is right padded with blanks before the comparison. The standard uses CHAR and CHARACTER as synonyms.

Character string literals or *constants* are usually delimited by single or double quotes, depending upon the particular dialect of SQL. The following are valid character string literals:

- "John Smith"
- 'This is a description of the department record'
- "Note: The client is interested in a property in the greater L.A. area with a value not to exceed $100,000"

Of course, these character string values are specified as character column values in SQL tables. As we will see in Chapter 4, users can search the content of character string-valued attributes (columns) using exact matches or *wildcards*. Ordering predicates (< , > , <= , >=, and so on) are all applicable to character string-valued attributes.

The semantics of a character string-valued attribute is basically lexicographic ordering comparing the corresponding characters left-to-right. For instance, "John" > "Joan" because "h" comes after "a" (and the first two characters are the same).

3.2.2 ANSI SQL89 Number Data Type

A number is either an *exact numeric value* or an *approximate numeric value*. All numbers are comparable. An exact numeric value has a precision (p) and a scale (q) component. Precision is a positive integer greater than zero that represents the number of significant decimal digits in the number. Scale is a non-negative integer. For a scale of q (and an integer value of the p significant digits equals n), the numeric value is equal to $n*10^{-q}$. For example, if the scale is two, and we have five significant digits 15237, then the numeric value is

$$15237*10^{-2} = 152.37$$

The standard uses DEC and DECIMAL as synonyms and INT and INTEGER as synonyms. DECIMAL, NUMERIC, INTEGER, and SMALLINT are exact numeric literals. These literals are either integers, signed integers, decimals (with a decimal point), or signed decimals. The following numbers are valid exact numeric literals:

235, -540, 12.34, -0.47

FLOAT, REAL, and DOUBLE PRECISION column data types are approximate numeric values. These numbers span a larger interval of values than the fixed-point numbers. They have a range determined by an exponent, and a precision determined by a mantissa, or fraction, component. All approximate numeric values of a certain type (single or double) are converted internally to a common format. If the system allows, say, a three-digit exponent value and a five-digit mantissa, then positive approximate numeric values will range from

$$0.10000 * 10^{-999} \text{ to } 0.99999 * 10^{999}$$

Literals for floating or approximate numeric values use "E" to indicate the exponent. Some examples of valid approximate numbers are

0.345E12, -12.44E2, -0.235E-3

The actual range of values allowed for exact and approximate numeric values is *not* specified in the ANSI SQL89 standard. Instead, it is left to the implementation.

3.2.3 SAG Data Types

The SQL Access Group (SAG) standard *does* specify ranges for character strings and numbers. Table 3.1 compares the ANSI SQL89 standard data types and the SAG data types and presents the ranges of SAG data types.

ANSI SQL89	SAG Standard	Range in SAG
CHARACTER(n)	CHARACTER(n)	1 <= n <= 254
———	CHARACTER VARYING(n)	1 <= n <= 254
SMALLINT	SMALLINT	Absolute values less than 32,768
INTEGER	INTEGER	Absolute values less than 2,147,483,648
DECIMAL(P, S)	DECIMAL(P,S)	1 <= P <= 15 with 0 <= S <= P
NUMERIC(P, S)	NUMERIC(P,S)	1 <= P <= 15 with 0 <= S <= P
REAL	REAL	Approximate numeric with absolute values between 1.0E-38 and 1.0E+38
FLOAT	FLOAT	Approximate numeric with absolute values between 1.0E-38 and 1.0E+38
DOUBLE PRECISION	DOUBLE PRECISION	Approximate numeric with absolute values between 1.0E-38 and 1.0E+38

Table 3.1: Comparison of ANSI SQ89 and SAG data types.

As shown, SAG supports the CHARACTER VARYING data type. The CHARACTER VARYING(n) type represents variable length character strings with a maximum string length of "n."

As mentioned earlier, the SAG standard specifies the ranges of the numeric and character values. In the SQL standard, these are defined by the implementation. Also, the ranges indicated in Table 3.1 are the *minimum* values. In other words, some implementations could support larger range values for the numeric and character types.

3.2.4 SAA Data Types

The IBM System Application Architecture (SAA) standard also specifies ranges for character strings and numbers. Like the SAG range values, the ranges in SAA are *minimum* range values for compliance; actual implementations could provide larger ranges for the SAA types.

In addition to the numeric and character data types, SAA also supports GRAPHIC (and VARGRAPHIC), DATE, TIME, and TIMESTAMP data types. Table 3.2 presents a comparison of the ANSI SQL89 standard data types and the SAA data types. The ranges of the SAA data types are also included.

GRAPHIC and VARGRAPHIC are used to store double-byte characters. In most cases, these double-byte character strings are used for more complex international character strings such as Kanji.

The DATE data type is used to represent a day under the Gregorian calendar. A date is a triple expressed as year, month, day. Examples of valid dates are 534-12-30, 1915-4-24, and 1990-8-2.

The TIME data type is also a triple representing a point in time, up to minutes, in a 24-hour day. Thus, 12.10.05 and 23.45.15 are valid times.

The TIMESTAMP data type is a seven-part value representing a specific point in time down to the granule of a microsecond. A TIMESTAMP consists of a date, time, and microsecond formatted accordingly; for example, 1990-5-1312.25.33.000234.

Like most SQL systems that support DATE, TIME, and TIMESTAMPS, the SAA standard does not include explicit constants to represent values of these data types. Instead, date, time, and timestamp values can be represented as character strings. In embedded applications (i.e., when SQL is embedded in a host language such as C), we must assign a date, time, or timestamp column value to a character string-valued variable in order to retrieve its value. However, the exact format of the date, time, or timestamp depends upon the product or country where the values are manipulated. For instance, the USA format for July 28, 1955 is 7/28/1955, whereas the European format is 28.7.1955, and the Japanese is 1955-7-28.

3.3 Databases and Schemata

In most SQL dialects and implementations, the tables, indexes, and other persistent objects are stored in databases. In typical systems, a database has a unique database name and contains tables, views, privileges, integrity constraints, and all other information pertaining to a particular domain or application.

ANSI SQL89	SAA Standard	Range in SAA
CHARACTER(n)	CHARACTER(n)	1 <= n <= 254
———	VARCHAR(n)	1 <= n <= 4000
———	GRAPHIC(n)	1 <= n <= 127
———	VARGRAPHIC(n)	1 <= n <= 2000
SMALLINT	SMALLINT	Absolute values less than 32,768
INTEGER	INTEGER	Absolute values less than 2,147,483,648
DECIMAL(P, S)	DECIMAL(P,S)	1 <= P <= 15 with 0 <= S <= P
FLOAT	FLOAT	Approximate numeric with absolute values between 5.4E-79 and 7.2E+75
———	DATE	Range of dates between 0001-01-01 and 9999-12-31
———	TIME	A three-part time value: hour, minute, second ranging between 00.00.00 and 24.00.00
———	TIMESTAMP	A seven-part date and time value: date (three parts), time (three parts) microsecond (one part)

Table 3.2: Comparison of ANSI SQ89 and SAA data types.

The ANSI SQL89 standard uses the CREATE SCHEMA statement for creating databases. A schema is created by a specified authorization identifier in an environment. In the ANSI Standard SQL, the concept of an environment is implementor defined. Among other things, a schema consists of: (1) a schema authorization clause, (2) any number of the table definition statements, (3) view definition statements, and (4) privilege definition statements.

The schema authorization clause specifies the creator of a schema. Each table definition statement defines and specifies a table, while each view definition statement defines a view. The privilege definition statement grants certain privileges for accessing particular tables to particular users. Each of these concepts is defined in more detail in subsequent sections of this chapter. As a simple example, we illustrate how some of the real estate database tables are created. The real estate database in this example is a simplified version of the real estate database illustrated in Figure 2.4. In particular, each client can own multiple properties, but a property is owned by one client. Also, the name of the client, not his/her id, is the primary key in the client table. The following construct creates the schema and some of the tables for the RealEstate database.

```
CREATE SCHEMA RealEstate
AUTHORIZATION John

CREATE TABLE Clients
(Name          CHAR(36),
WPhone      CHAR(12),
HPhone      CHAR(12),
Address     CHAR(100),
SS#         CHAR(11), ...)
CL_Type     CHAR(1)

CREATE TABLE Properties
(APN        CHAR(22),
State-Code  CHAR(2),
Owner       CHAR(36),
SalePrice   INTEGER,
NumUnits    INTEGER
...)
```

Both the SAG and SAA SQLs include the notion of databases

containing table definitions, views, privileges, and the like. However, these two standards do not support the CREATE SCHEMA language construct explicitly. Instead, in SAG, the user is allowed to open and connect to a database through a session environment statement. For instance, the following statement allows John to connect to the university database:

```
CONNECT TO University
USER John
```

Needless to say, John must have the access right to connect to the database. In addition to the CONNECT statement, SAG supports the corresponding DISCONNECT statement, which terminates the connection between the user (or application program) and the database environment of the last database to which the user was connected.

3.4 Tables

As stated earlier, each database in SQL is a collection of tables. A table is a two-dimensional structure that consists of a row of column headings and zero or more rows of data values. Figure 3.1 is an example of a simple table for Clients.

Name	WPhone	HPhone	Address	SS#	CL_Type
John Smith	555-1212	555-3636	13 Main St	111-22-3333	B
Mark Black	555-5656	555-7878	2 Dayton St.	444-55-6666	B

Figure 3.1: A Clients table.

A column of a table has a description and a position within the table. The description of a column includes its data type and whether the column can contain null values. The column value is the smallest selectable or updatable unit of data in a table. Each data row contains exactly one value for each column specified in the column heading. This corresponds to the first normal form constraint described in Section 2.3.2. All the values in a given column have the same type as the data type specified in the column.

For example, Name in Clients is a fixed-length character string with length less than or equal to 36 characters. If it is not acceptable to have NULL values for names of clients (after all, we should know the names of those we are selling to), this will be indicated in a NOT NULL constraint in the following manner:

Name CHAR(36) NOT NULL.

A row is the smallest unit of data that can be inserted into or deleted from a table. The rows of a table are unordered, while the columns of a table are ordered. The number of columns in a table represents the degree of that table. For example, the Clients table in Figure 3.1 has a degree greater than four.

A *base table* is a table that exists physically. It is defined by the table definition of the SQL Data Definition Language. In addition to base tables, SQL also allows the definition of *virtual tables* or *views,* which are described in the next section. In the schema example described earlier, all tables are base tables.

Sometimes, after a table is created through a CREATE TABLE statement, the user might wish to drop the table entirely from the database or modify the definition of the table by either dropping or adding columns. In the ANSI SQL89 standard, it is possible only to create tables in the context of a schema. The notion of dropping a table or altering its definition is not supported. However, both the SAG and SAA standards do support the following statements:

DROP TABLE: Removes an existing table from the database.

ALTER TABLE: Adds a column to a table.

For instance, the following statement will drop the Matters table from the RealEstate database:

DROP TABLE Matters.

In addition, the following specifications will add the column BusinessAddress to the Clients table:

ALTER TABLE Clients

ADD (BusinessAddress CHAR(50))

3.5 Views

A *view* is a *virtual table,* that is, a table that does not exist in physical storage. The CREATE TABLE statement in SQL creates a base table. A view is defined in terms of one or more base tables using a VIEW definition, which consists of a view name, and a query containing the column names, plus view-defining conditions.

A view is not usually stored; rather, it is recomputed when it is referenced. A view can be used for security purposes to limit the availability of data to the user. For example, to create a view that contains the name, address, and social security number of all clients who are buyers, we use the following format:

```
CREATE VIEW Buyers (BName, BAddress, BSS#)
AS SELECT Name, Address, SS#
    FROM Clients
    WHERE Cl_Type = "B"
```

In this example, the view Buyers has three columns: BName, BAddress, and BSS#. Each column type is the same as Name, Address, and SS# of Clients. The view Buyers can now be accessed by a SELECT statement, just like any other base table.

Sometimes views can be updatable. That is, in some cases it is possible to apply the INSERT, DELETE, or UPDATE data manipulation statements of SQL (to be discussed in Chapter 4) to a view. Defining updatable views involves only one base table; therefore, updatable views are typically subtables of existing base tables. In the following example, the view ClientState, which contains the client name and the state where he/she owns property, is not updatable:

```
CREATE VIEW ClientState (CName, State)
AS SELECT C.Name, P.State_Code
    FROM Clients C, Properties P
    WHERE C.Name = P.Owner_Name
```

The ANSI SQL89 does allow the definition of views, but it does not support the notion of dropping a view. However, both SAG and SAA SQL allow users to drop views by using the construct DROP VIEW Buyers.

3.6 Privileges

In the ANSI SQL89 standard, an *authorization identifier* is specified for each schema. The authorization identifier specifies the owner of the schema and permits certain privileges for the tables and views of that schema. Privileges include INSERT, DELETE, SELECT, and UPDATE for both tables and views.

To perform an action on a table or a view, the associated authorization identifier must grant the necessary privileges. This is performed through the Data Control Language (DCL) constructs of SQL, which will be discussed further in Chapter 6. The owner of a table has all the privileges for that table, and the owner of a view has all the applicable privileges for that view. For instance, the view owner always holds SELECT privileges for that view. In the case of an updatable view, if the owner of the underlying base table holds INSERT, UPDATE, and/or DELETE privileges, then the view owner holds those same privileges for the view.

The owner of an object can grant privileges for that object to other authorization identifiers by using the GRANT operation. By specifying WITH GRANT OPTION in the GRANT operation, the owner can allow the recipient of the privilege to grant that same privilege to other authorization identifiers.

For instance, if John created the RealEstate schema and would like to give SELECT privilege for the Clients table to Jim and ALL privileges (SELECT, INSERT, UPDATE, and DELETE) to Mary, he would use the following statements:

```
GRANT SELECT ON Clients TO Jim

GRANT ALL ON Clients TO Mary WITH GRANT OPTION
```

In the second statement, Mary, who is the recipient of the privilege, can, in turn, grant privileges for Clients to other users.

Besides granting privileges, both the SAG SQL and the SAA SQL dialects support the notion of revoking privileges through a REVOKE command. For example, John can revoke the SELECT privilege from Jim by implementing the statement

```
REVOKE SELECT ON Clients FROM Jim
```

3.7 Integrity Constraints

In Chapter 2, we discussed several forms of integrity constraints including null, primary key, foreign key, and other more general constraints. Here, we discuss the SQL syntax and semantics for these integrity constraint constructs.

3.7.1 NULL Constraints

The ANSI SQL89, the SAG SQL, and the SAA SQL all support the notion of a NULL value and NOT NULL constraints. As we saw from earlier examples, to indicate that the social security number must not be NULL, we would use the construct

SS# CHAR(11) NOT NULL

3.7.2 Unique and Primary Key Constraints

All standards also support unique and primary keys. For example, to indicate that the id of a client is unique in the Clients table, we use the UNIQUE(ID) clause. In addition, to indicate that a social security number is unique, the UNIQUE(SS_Number) construct can be used. On the other hand, to indicate that the name of a client is the primary key, we use the PRIMARY KEY (Name) clause.

3.7.3 Foreign Keys and Referential Integrity Constraints

The SQL standard supports FOREIGN KEY and REFERENCES constructs to help maintain the referential integrity within the database. To indicate that the Owner_Name in the Properties table is a foreign key referencing the primary key Name in the Clients table, the following construct is used:

FOREIGN KEY (Owner) REFERENCES Clients

A foreign key always corresponds to the primary key in the referenced table—in this case, the column Name in the Clients table.

3.7.4 CHECK Constraint

The SQL standard also supports the CHECK constraint construct, which can be used to introduce more general and ad hoc integrity rules and constraints. For instance, the following construct can be used to indicate that the type of a client is either B for Buyer, S for Seller, or N for neither:

CHECK(CL_Type IN ("B", "S", "N"))

If an integrity constraint is violated, an exception indicates that a violation of the integrity constraint occurred while executing a statement. Of course, given a database with a consistent state (i.e., one in which all integrity constraints are satisfied), the only way integrity constraints could be violated is through an INSERT, DELETE, or UPDATE data manipulation statement.

3.8 System Catalogs

Most relational database management systems provide a number of system tables or system catalogs that contain all the information on the structure of the database. In other words, the system tables or catalogs contain everything that is defined through the Data Definition Language.

Since the system catalogs in most servers are stored in tables, SQL can be used to query the system tables in order to obtain various facts about the structure or contents of the database. For instance, the user can query various tables in the system catalog to answer the following questions:

- *What are the names of the tables contained in this database?*
- *What are all the integrity constraints defined for a particular table T?*
- *Which view uses a particular table T?*
- *Who has authorization to update tables T1 and T2?*

This elegant and uniform approach to data access, uses the same language for data definition and data manipulation and thus requires that the user learn only a single language or mechanism for accessing the database content and structure.

The ANSI SQL89 standard and the *Common Programming Interface Database Reference Manual* of SAA [IBM, 1988] do not specify particular schemata for defining system catalogs. However, system catalog definition is supported by the SAG SQL. The catalog tables are "read only" tables that store information regarding the authorization and structure of the database tables.

Each of the catalog tables in SAG SQL is called a view. Do not to confuse the SAG system *views,* which are tables describing the metadata, with user-defined *views* on base tables or other views. The important thing to remember is that users can only access and select data from the SAG views; they cannot update these views.

The system view tables in SAG include:

TABLES view: Among other things, this system table contains information about the owner of the table, the name of the table, and the type of the table (i.e., whether it is a base table, view, or system table).

COLUMNS view: This system table first identifies the table to which a column belongs. It then specifies the names and types of columns.

SQL_LANGUAGES view: All the SQL dialects and languages that are supported by the system are stored in this table. Its columns contain information about the organization of a particular SQL dialect, the year a particular standard was adopted, the level of conformance (ANSI SQL89 has Level 1 and Level 2 conformance), whether integrity enhancements (referential integrity constraints) are supported, and the name of the vendor of the SQL system.

SERVER_INFO view: This table holds information on the various attributes of the server. Among other things, server attributes contain server-specific information, such as whether the server is case sensitive, the maximum length of an identifier, the maximum length of a column, or the maximum length of a row of a table in the SQL system supported by the server. Each server attribute has a name, which is associated with an attribute value. Therefore, the server information is stored in the following pairs format: (SERVER_ATTRIBUTE, ATTRIBUTE_VALUE).

As an example, to obtain the data type of the SalePrice column in the Properties table, we use the following construct:

```
SELECT DATA_TYPE
FROM COLUMNS
WHERE TABLE_NAME ="Properties"
AND COLUMN_NAME="SalePrice"
```

Here, the DATA_TYPE column contains the name of the data type for a particular column of a given table.

As another example, to determine the maximum permitted length of a row in a table in the system, the following query can be used:

```
SELECT ATTRIBUTE_VALUE
FROM SERVER_INFO
WHERE SERVER_ATTRIBUTE = “TABLE_LENGTH”
```

3.9 Case Studies

In this section, we present the data definition constructs in each of the four SQL servers surveyed in this book. When applicable, we compare the capabilities to those servers with the ANSI89 SQL standard.

3.9.1 IBM OS/2 Extended Edition Database Manager

We now examine the data types, database creation, tables, views, privileges, and system catalogs supported by the IBM OS/2 Extended Edition Database Manager.

Data Types

The SQL dialect of the IBM OS/2 Extended Edition Database Manager supports character strings, numeric data types, and date and time data types. The IBM Extended Edition data types are very similar to the SAA SQL data types, which were summarized in Table 3.2.

Character strings. There are three options for specifying character string types in the IBM Extended Edition:

> **CHAR(n):** Used for fixed-length character strings. The maximum length of a CHAR is 254 bytes.
>
> **VARCHAR(n):** Used for varying-length character strings. The maximum length in the IBM Extended Edition is 4,000 bytes. A maximum length must be specified when declaring columns of type VARCHAR.
>
> **LONG VARCHAR:** Used for long varying-length fields. The maximum length is 32,700 bytes. The length does not need to be specified when declaring columns of type LONG VARCHAR.

Numeric data types. The IBM Extended Edition supports four numeric data types:

> **SMALLINT:** Used to declare two-byte integers.
>
> **INTEGER (or INT):** Used to declare four-byte integers.
>
> **DECIMAL(p,s) (or DEC(p,s)):** Used to declare fixed-point decimal numbers. p is the precision (i.e., the total number of digits), and s is the scale (i.e., the number of digits to the right of the decimal point). The scale is always less than or equal to the precision. The precision can vary from 1 to 31.
>
> **FLOAT:** Used for precision floating point numbers. Each floating point number consumes eight bytes and can have 15 significant digits. The absolute values of floating point numbers range from 2.2*10E-307 to 1.8*10E308.

Date. A date is a three-part (year/month/day) valued data type that designates a day in a Gregorian calendar. The year is between 0001 and 9999, the month is between 1 and 12, and the day is between 1 and 28, 29, 30, or 31, depending on the month. A date consumes four bytes.

Time. A time is also a three-part valued data type consisting of an hour (between 0 and 24), a minute (between 0 and 59), and a second (between 0 and 59). A time consumes three bytes.

Timestamp. A timestamp incorporates a date, a time in that date, and a fractional part. The seven specific parts of a timestamp are year, month, day, hour, minute, second, and microsecond.

Schemata and Databases

IBM Extended Edition databases are created through a procedural call that can be invoked from C, COBOL, FORTRAN, or Pascal. The name of the procedure is *SQLCRED* and the general format of the call is

```
SQLCRED(cmt_length, spare1, db_length, drive,
    cmt_codepage, comment, sqlca, spare2, database)
```

The name of the database is given in the *database* argument. Additionally, *drive* specifies the OS/2 drive (c:, d:, etc.) that should contain the database being created, and *sqlca* points to a SQL Communications Area (SQLCA) data structure. This structure contains information on the statement or call that has been executed. It returns various codes and diagnostic data.

To use a created (and populated) database to access data, update data, or create new metadata (e.g., tables), the user must execute a START USING DATABASE call:

```
SQLGSTRD(spare1, db_length, use. sqlca, spare2, database)
```

In this statement, *database* is the name of the database to be started (opened). The user can also drop a database using the *SQLDRPD* call, which deletes all the files associated with the database.

Tables

Like most table creation statements, the CREATE TABLE statement of the IBM Extended Edition specifies the name of a table, column definitions, and integrity constraints. After defining a table, the user can add additional columns to the table through the ALTER TABLE statement. Consider the following example, which adds column BusinessAddress to Clients table:

```
ADD BusinessAddress        CHAR(30)
```

The ALTER TABLE statement can also be used to ADD referential integrity constraints, to ADD or DROP a primary key, or to DROP a foreign (referential) key. Additionally, the entire table can be dropped through the DROP TABLE statement. For example, to drop the table of the queries of all the clients, we have

```
DROP TABLE PropertyQueries
```

Views

The CREATE VIEW statement in the IBM Extended Edition specifies the view name, optional renaming of the columns of the view, the SELECT statement defining the view, and the WITH CHECK OPTION.

A view can be either read only or updatable. The WITH CHECK OPTION applies only to updatable views. With this constraint, if an insert or update does not satisfy the constraints of the view (as specified in the WHERE clause of the SELECT statement defining the view), then the update or insert will be rejected.

For instance, assume we have an Employees table defined via the following statement:

```
CREATE TABLE Employees(
    Name    CHAR(20),
    SS#     DECIMAL(11),
    Salary  DECIMAL(10,3))
```

Now, consider the following example of CREATE VIEW:

```
CREATE VIEW RichEmployees(RName, RSS#, RSalary)
    AS
    SELECT *
    FROM Employees
    WHERE Salary >= 100000
    WITH CHECK OPTION
```

The following insert will be rejected:

```
INSERT INTO RichEmployees
    VALUES("John Smith", 111223333, 25000)
```

The insert is rejected, since it violated the constraint of the view—salary must be greater than or equal to $100,000.

Privileges

The IBM OS/2 Extended Edition system has an elaborate authorization control mechanism based on an authorization hierarchy. The System Administrator (SYSADM) is at the top of the hierarchy. Below the SYSADM is the Database Administrator (DBADM) who, among other things, can create databases and provide a user with access to a database. All DBADM authorizations are also SYSADM authorizations (i.e., SYSDADM authorizations are a superset of DBADM authorizations). In addition to the DBADM authorizations, the SYSADM can also introduce remote databases to the system, restore a database, and drop a database.

The only users who can perform actions on the database as a whole are those with SYSADM or DBADM authority. Other "ordinary" users have *table* privileges, which they can GRANT to other users or REVOKE from other users.

In IBM OS/2 Extended Edition, the GRANT and REVOKE commands are used to grant and/or revoke the following privileges:

Database: Privilege used to connect to a database or create a table in a database.

Table: Privilege used to SELECT, INSERT, DELETE, UPDATE, etc. a table.

Program: Privilege used to execute a program accessing a database.

Index: Privilege used to create or drop an index on a table.

Consider the following example that grants the connect to a database privilege to Ted:

```
GRANT CONNECT ON DATABASE TO Ted
```

The table privilege is the most common and is actually supported in the SQL standard. The program privileges address programs (access plans) that access and/or update objects in a database (e.g., tables).

Integrity Constraints

When creating a table, the user can specify the following constraints with the IBM Extended Edition:

Not NULL constraint: Indicates that the column cannot take NULL values.

Not NULL primary key: Indicates the column is a primary key (and cannot take NULL values).

Referential integrity constraint: Specifies the foreign keys that are references (keys) of another table.

The referential integrity constraint in the IBM Extended Edition allows the user to specify what should happen when a row of a referenced (parent) table is deleted and key values of that row (foreign keys) are in referencing tables (children). For example, the column Owner in the Properties table is also a foreign key of the Clients table. What should happen when, say, we delete John Smith's entry from the Clients table and John has some properties (i.e., there are some rows in Properties whose Owner_Name column value is "John Smith")?

The IBM Extended Edition provides mechanisms for specifying the "rules" for what should happen when a referenced column is deleted or updated or when a row of a referencing table is inserted. The most interesting of these are the delete rules, which are summarized as follows:

(1) The user can specify that the DELETE of the parent row must propagate (or cascade) to all the children rows that reference the parent. Therefore, in our example, if we delete John Smith, all the properties of John in the Properties table must also be deleted. This is accomplished through the ON DELETE CASCADE option.

(2) The user can prohibit the deletion of a parent row if there are children rows that reference the parent. Thus, the system can prohibit the deletion of John Smith's row from the Clients table if John has some properties in the Properties table. This is accomplished through the ON DELETE RESTRICT option.

(3) Finally, the user can specify that if a parent row is deleted, then foreign key values of the children rows must be set to NULL. In our example, this option can be used to delete John Smith's row. However, all foreign key values in the Properties table that formally had John Smith as owner will be set to NULL. This is accomplished through ON DELETE SET NULL option.

Below is the definition of that part of the Properties table with the referential integrity constraint. It specifies that ON DELETE of a client's row, the delete of the parent (i.e., the client) must cascade to deletes of his/her properties.

```
CREATE TABLE Properties
                (APN            CHAR(22),
                 State-Code     CHAR(2),
                 Owner          CHAR(36),
                 SalePrice      INTEGER,
    PRIMARY KEY (APN)
    FOREIGN KEY (Owner)
    REFERENCES Clients
    ON DELETE CASCADE
```

System Catalogs

The IBM Extended Edition has many system catalog tables, which are created by executing a CREATE DATABASE command. These system catalog tables can be taxonomized into three categories. The first category includes catalog tables that contain the definition of tables, columns, indexes, views, and integrity constraints. Table 3.3 lists some of the tables in this category.

SYSTABLES	Contains the definition of each table in the database
SYSCOLUMNS	Contains the definition of each column in a table of the database
SYSINDEXES	Contains the definition of each index for each table in the database
SYSVIEW	Contains the definition of each view in the database
SYSRELS	Contains the definition of the referential integrity constraint dependencies in between the referenced/referencing tables of the database

Table 3.3: *The system catalog tables in IBM Extended Edition—table definitions.*

The second category consists of catalog tables containing information on access plans. An access plan contains all the facts necessary for executing an application program against the Extended Edition database engine. An application program with embedded SQL statements is bound to a specific database; this binding produces an access plan object. Information on the access plan, the users of the access plan, the SQL statements that are executed through the access plan, and so on are all stored in system catalog tables. Table 3.4 lists some of the access plan catalog tables found in the IBM Extended Edition. Access plans and the resulting optimization through the use of access plans will be discussed in more detail in Chapter 7.

SYSPLAN	Contains information on each access plan
SYSPLANDEP	Contains information on the dependencies between access plans
SYSSTMT	Contains information on the SQL statement processed through the access plan

Table 3.4: *The system catalog tables in IBM Extended Edition—access plans.*

Catalog tables containing information about the different users and their privileges (i.e., authorization) represent the third category of tables. Some of the catalog tables in this category are included in Table 3.5.

SYSDBAUTH	Includes all the users that can access different objects in the database
SYSPLANAUTH	Contains information on users who can access specific access plans
SYSTABLAUTH	Contains information on authorization of users for specific views and base tables
SYSINDEXAUTH	Contains information on user privileges for accessing indexes

Table 3.5: *The system catalog tables in IBM Extended Edition—authorization.*

3.9.2 ORACLE Server

Data Types

The ORACLE Server supports character string, numeric, date, and raw binary data types, as well as ROWID for row ids.

Character strings. The ORACLE Server supports three options for specifying character string types:

> **CHAR(n) (or CHARACTER(n)):** Used for fixed-length character strings. The maximum length of a CHAR is 255 letters, numbers, or symbols.
>
> **VARCHAR(n):** Used for varying-length character strings. The maximum length is also 255 characters. A maximum length must be specified when declaring columns of type VARCHAR.
>
> **LONG or LONG VARCHAR:** Used for varying-length character strings of up to 65,535 bytes.

Numeric data types. The numeric data types supported by the ORACLE Server include

> **NUMBER (or NUMBER (*), NUMBER(*, scale), NUMBER(precision), NUMBER(precision, scale)):** Used to store fixed and floating point numbers. The ranges are numbers from plus or minus 10^{-129} to plus or minus 10^{124}. As usual, precision indicates the total number of digits, and If scale indicates the number of digits to the right of the decimal point.
>
> **FLOAT (or REAL, FLOAT(*), FLOAT(precision)):** Used to store floating point numbers. A minimum precision can be specified with FLOAT(p).
>
> **DECIMAL (or DECIMAL (*), DECIMAL(*, scale), DECIMAL(precision), DECIMAL(precision, scale)):** Same as NUMBER.
>
> **INTEGER:** Used to represent integers with a precision of 38.

In the ORACLE Server, all numbers are stored in the same internal format. For all numeric types, the decimal precision of a number ranges from 1 to 38, and the scale ranges from -84 to 127.

Date. The DATE data type can store date and time precision. Each date value can be composed of the century, year, month, day, hour, minute, and second. The default format of a date is dd-mm-yy. Dates can range from January 1, 4712 BC to December 31, 4712 AD.

Binary data types. Two commands are used to store binary data in the ORACLE Server:

RAW(s): Used to store raw bits of binary data of size s bytes. The maximum size of s is 255.

LONG RAW: Used to store raw binary data with a size of up to 65,535 bytes.

ROW identifiers. The ORACLE Server also has a ROWID type that stores the internal row identifier of a row. The row identifier is actually the physical address of the row. ROWIDs *are not* surrogates or object identities (as explained in Khoshafian and Copeland, [1986]). The ROWID of a table's row can change if the row moves, and it is possible to retrieve a row using its ROWID. However, ROWIDs cannot be updated.

Schemata and Databases

In the ORACLE Server, a CREATE DATABASE command is used to create databases, to specify different parameters for the name and size of the database, and to designate the maximum number of users who can have concurrent access to the database. The CREATE DATABASE command also specifies the log files for storing the redo logs and the data files that are used to store the content of the database. Redo logs are used to reconstruct the database after media failure (e.g., a disk crash).

Consider the following example. If the RealEstate database redo logs should be stored in RE.LOG, the data (content of the tables) should be stored in RE.DAT, and we would like to allow at most 20 people to mount and open the database simultaneously, we have

```
CREATE DATABASE RealEstate
                    LOGFILE RE.LOG
                    DATAFILE RE.DAT
                    MAXINSTANCES 20'
```

To use the information in a database, a user must *connect* to the database. In embedded SQL (i.e., SQL embedded in a host programming language such as C), this is achieved through the CONNECT statement. Embedded SQL will be discussed in greater detail in Chapter 9.

Tables

In addition to column and integrity constraint specifications, the CREATE TABLE statement in the ORACLE Server allows the user to specify different storage allocation parameters, different active transactions parameters, and if desired, the loading of a table from a query.

Tablespaces. In the ORACLE Server, the objects of a database are stored in one or more tablespaces. Each tablespace is a logical partition of the database containing one or more tables or indexes. Tablespaces are created through a CREATE TABLESPACE command, which specifies the operating system files that are to store and contain the tablespace. There is always at least one tablespace called SYSTEM, which contains all the system tables. The user can utilize this default tablespace or create additional tablespaces. If a user has a number of tablespaces to choose from, he/she must specify the one to use for a table in the CREATE TABLE statement.

Fill factors. A tablespace consists of a number of physical data blocks, which are the smallest units of storage. Another often used term for a block is *data page*. In the CREATE TABLE statement, a user can specify the percentage of a block that should remain free when allocating a new block for the table through the PCTFREE parameter. Additionally, through the PCTUSED parameter, users can specify the minimum percentage of utilized space in a block. These parameters should be set according to the access and update patterns and frequencies of a table.

Transaction parameters. Another category of parameters are those dealing with transactions. Through the MAXTRANS parameter, the user can specify the maximum number of transactions that can access and update a block (smallest I/O unit) that stores rows of the table. Via the INTRANS parameter, the user can specify the number of transactions entries that are initially allocated within a block. This will incur a space overhead.

Initializing the table. Besides these and other storage and performance-related parameters, the user can also specify a SQL SELECT statement that can obtain rows to initialize a table.

Consider the following example. Assume we want to create a table ClientStateProp that contains the Name, SS#, Business, State, and County of all the clients who hold a property in the County of the State. Assume also that we like to allow at most 10 transactions to concurrently update a block of the table. Finally, assume the Tablespace is SYSTEM and we would like each block to be 75% utilized. Then the CREATE TABLE is

```
CREATE TABLE ClientStateProp
                    (Name                CHAR(20),
                    SS#    CHAR(11),
                    Business        CHAR(3),
                    State           CHAR(2),
                    County          CHAR(3))
                    PRIMARY KEY (SS#, State, County)
                    TABLESPACE SYSTEM
                    PCTUSED 75
                    MAXTRANS 10
                    AS
                            SELECT      C.Name, C.SS#,
                                        C.Business, P.State,
                                                P.County
                            FROM Clients C, Properties P
                            WHERE C.Name = P.Owner
```

Views

In the ORACLE Server, views are created and dropped through the CREATE VIEW and DROP VIEW statements. CREATE VIEW also supports the WITH CHECK OPTION, which prohibits updates or inserts that violate the view constraint.

The following example creates the view JohnsProps, which contains John Smith's properties:

```
CREATE VIEW JohnsProps
                    AS
                    SELECT *
                    FROM Properties
                    WHERE Owner = "John Smith"
                    WITH CHECK OPTION OWN
```

Here the names and types of the columns of JohnsProps will be the same as the names and types of the columns of Properties. As illustrated, ORACLE allows the user to specify a name for the WITH CHECK OPTION constraint. In this example the name is OWN.

Privileges

There are basically three categories of user and/or access privileges in ORACLE. These categories correspond to the privileges granted to the database administrator (DBA), individual users, and all valid users or the PUBLIC.

Using the GRANT statement, certain users can grant privileges for (1) accessing the database, (2) creating objects in tablespaces, and (3) operating on objects.

Accessing the database. The specific database access privileges supported by the ORACLE Server are CONNECT and RESOURCE. The CONNECT statement is used to allow users access to a database. Similarly, the RESOURCE statement is used to grant the privilege of creating tables, views, and other database objects. Both privileges are granted exclusively by the DBA. Consider the following examples of the CONNECT and RESOURCE statements:

```
GRANT CONNECT TO Bob, Mary

GRANT CONNECT, RESOURCE TO Jim, Terry
```

Creating tablespace objects. The RESOURCE privilege allows users to create objects in specific tablespaces. The following example grants Ted the privilege of creating up to five megabytes of database objects in the EmpDept tablespace:

```
GRANT RESOURCE(5M) ONE EmpDept TO Ted
```

In addition, the DBA can grant to users the privilege of creating tables, views, and other database objects, through the RESOURCE privilege. For example, the DBA can allow Jim and Terry to create database objects and connect to the database through:

```
GRANT CONNECT, RESOURCE TO Jim, Terry
```

Operation on objects. The specific privileges in this category include ALTER, DELETE, INSERT, INDEX, and SELECT privileges on tables or views. These privileges could also be granted using WITH GRANT OPTION, which allows the person being granted the privilege to grant the privilege to other users.

For example, assume Terry has ALL PRIVILEGES on the Clients table. Then she could grant INDEX privilcges on the Clients table to Mark:

```
GRANT INDEX ON Clients
                    TO Mark
                    WITH GRANT OPTION
```

With this privilege, Mark can create indexes on Clients and also allow other users to create indexes by granting them the same privilege.

Privileges in all of these three categories can be taken away through the REVOKE construct. The following example revokes connect privilege from Bob and Mary:

```
REVOKE CONNECT FROM Bob, Mary
```

Integrity Constraints

Integrity constraints can be *table constraints,* which apply to the table or multiple columns of the table, or *column constraints,* which apply to an individual column. ORACLE provides a number of table and column integrity constraints:

Unique and primary key constraints: The following statements define the primary key and unique constraints for the Clients table:

```
PRIMARY KEY (Name) and UNIQUE (SS#).
```

Not NULL constraints

Checks for constraints on column values: This constraint could involve multiple columns. For instance, if each property has a number of units, we must have the constraint

```
CHECK(NUM_UNITS >= 1).
```

Referential integrity constraints: In the RealEstate database example, a Matters table is used to store the appointments entered, reviewed, or canceled by a client. The Matters table creation is as follows:

```
CREATE TABLE Matters
        (CName      CHAR(36),
        CDate       DATE,
        NOTES       VARCHAR(255),
        Type        CHAR(15),
        Topic       CHAR(20),
        PRIMARY KEY(CName, CDate)
        FOREIGN KEY (CName)
        REFERENCES Clients
        CONSTRAINT ClientAppt)
```

In the above example, the name of the integrity constraint is ClientAppt. Whenever an attempt is made to INSERT or UPDATE a Matters row where a corresponding client (as indicated through the CName foreign key) does not exist in the Clients table, the operation will be rejected. Similarly, the system will reject DELETES of clients who have appointments stored in the Matters table.

System Catalogs

The ORACLE Server provides comprehensive system catalogs called *data dictionary views*. The system catalog information is contained in three types of views:

(1) The DBA view permits access to all the available information in the system catalogs.
(2) The PUBLIC view allows users to access information available to any user in general, but not specific protected information that is accessible only to the DBA.
(3) The individual view allows access to particular users for those system table views that are pertinent to them.

ORACLE has four main categories of system tables. The first group is composed of the data dictionary views, which contain the data definitions for various tables, views, columns, and so on. Table 3.6 lists and describes specific data dictionary views.

CATALOG	Various tables, views, synonyms, and sequences
IND-COLUMNS	COLUMNS comprising INDEXES on the TABLES
SEQUENCES	Definition of sequences
SYNONYMS	Definition of synonyms
TABLES	Definition of tables
TAB-COLUMNS	Definition of the columns, tables, and views
VIEWS	Statement defining the views

Table 3.6: *Data dictionary views in the ORACLE Server.*

The second group includes those system tables that store privilege information on tables, columns, and the like. Table 3.7 summarizes these tables.

COL_GRANTS	Definition of the grants on columns
TAB_GRANTS	Definition of all the grants on objects
TABLE_PRIVILEGES	Grants on objects for which the user is the grantor, grantee, or owner

Table 3.7: Authorization system tables in the ORACLE Server.

The third group of system tables stores auditing information describing the various accesses and access patterns to the tables and other objects in the databases. The primary view in this group is TAB_AUDITS_OPTS, which contains the auditing information.

Finally, the fourth group includes those tables that store information on the different tablespaces and physical clusters that store the database. These tables are listed in Table 3.8.

FREE_SPACE	Information on free extents in tablespaces
SEGMENTS	Storage allocated for all database segments
TABLESPACES	Information on all accessible tablespaces
TS_QUOTAS	Tablespace quotas

Table 3.8: Storage management system tables in the ORACLE Server.

3.9.3 DEC Rdb/VMS

Data Types

DEC's Rdb/VMS supports character strings, numeric data types, byte strings, and date data types.

Character strings. This product supports three types of character strings:

CHAR (or CHAR(n)): Used to indicate fixed-length strings of characters up to 16,383 bytes.

VARCHAR(n): Used to indicate varying-length character strings up to 16,383 bytes.

LONG VARCHAR: Equivalent to VARCHAR.

Numbers. The Rdb/VMS supports the following numeric data types:

SMALLINT: Used to declare two-byte integers with sizes ranging from -2^{15} to 2^{15}.

INT: Used to declare four-byte integers with sizes ranging from -2^{31} to 2^{31}.

TINYINT: Used to declare one-byte integers with values ranging from -127 to 127.

QUADWORD: Used to designate signed 64-bit quadwords ranging in value from -2**63 to 2**63.

For DECIMAL and NUMERIC data types, there is no direct support in the underlying DIGITAL Standard Relational Interface (DSRI) database engine. Instead, these data types are converted as follows:

DECIMAL(1) (NUMERIC(1)) to DECIMAL(4) (NUMERIC(4)) are converted to SMALLINT.

DECIMAL(5) (NUMERIC (5)) to DECIMAL(9) (NUMERIC (9)) are converted to INTEGER.

DECIMAL(10) (NUMERIC (10)) to DECIMAL(18) (NUMERIC (18)) are converted to QUADWORD.

DECIMAL(19) (NUMERIC(19)) and larger are converted to DOUBLE PRECISION.

The Rdb/VMS supports the following floating point numbers:

FLOAT(n): If n is less than 25, FLOAT indicates a 32-bit floating point number; if n is greater than 25, it indicates a 64-bit floating point number.

REAL: For 32-bit floating point numbers.

DOUBLE PRECISION: For 64-bit floating point numbers.

Long byte strings. This data type is used for fields up to 6,513 bytes long. It is specified accordingly. For example, **LIST OF BYTE VARYING(n).**

Date. The format of the DATE data type in the Rdb/VMS is dd-mmm-yyyy (indicating day, month, year). Sixty-four bits are used for storing a date; this corresponds to the VAX absolute date data type.

Schemata and Databases

In the Rdb/VMS, the CREATE SCHEMA statement is used to create databases. Of course, CREATE SCHEMA also includes the capability to create *schema elements,* which are tables, views, indexes, grant and revoke statements, and so on. In addition to these basic schema elements, the Rdb/VMS provides a rich set of parameters used to store and access the schemata. A comprehensive treatment of all the elements in a schema definition in Rdb/VMS is beyond the scope of this book. Some of the elements of the CREATE SCHEMA statement in DEC's Rdb follow:

Authorization: The authorization identifier in the Rdb/VMS is an attachment or database handle, which, in many statements, is used to attach and make requests from a particular database. The RDB$DBHANDLE contains the value of the authorization identifier.

File paths: File path specifications indicate where the schema should be created, where (in which file) the snapshot should be created, and so on.

Dbkey scoping: Each record in the Rdb/VMS comes with a unique database key. The dbkey scoping parameter indicates whether a dbkey of a deleted row can be reused immediately after the transaction that performed the delete or after the attachment session of the user with the database is terminated.

COLLATING sequencing: VMS provides a number of national character sets, such as French and German. The CREATE COLLATING SEQUENCE statement in the CREATE SCHEMA statement of the Rdb/VMS allows the user to give a name to a collating sequence and to bind it to a national character set.

Control over maximum number of users: The Rdb/VMS supports limiting the number of users accessing the schema simultaneously. More specifically, this element indicates the maximum number of users who can be attached to the database identified by the schema at one time.

Number of VAXcluster nodes from which users can access the schema: Currently, VMS allows a maximum of 64 VAXcluster nodes, which is also the maximum number of VAXcluster nodes from which a user can access a particular schema.

Buffer parameters: Buffer parameters indicate the size of the buffer in blocks, the number of buffers allocated for each process, and the number of buffers allocated for recovery purposes.

Snapshot settings: The Rdb/VMS utilizes snapshot settings to indicate whether and/or how the snapshot file should be updated by a transaction that modifies a record.

Protection parameters: The protection parameters of the Rdb/VMS specify whether the protection is ANSI or Access Control List (ACL). Briefly, the difference between these two approaches deals with the way access privileges are granted. ANSI allocates all privileges to the user, and ACL allocates the first element matching a user's ID in an ordered set of authorization IDs.

Storage settings: Storage settings indicate the number of data pages allocated to a schema, the size of pages in blocks, the fill factor (percentage of used space) in a page, and so on.

The definition of the schema elements: In the Rdb/VMS, users can define elements such as tables, views, indexes, domains, and triggers.

Consider the following example of schema parameters for the RealEstate database. (These statements should be followed by the more basic schema element definiteness, such as CREATE TABLE, CREATE VIEW, and so on.)

```
CREATE SCHEMA RealEstate
        AUTHORIZATION Bob
                    DBKEY SCOPE IS TRANSACTION
                    COLLATING SEQUENCE GREEK GREEK
                    NUMBER OF USERS 100
                    NUMBER OF VAXCLUSTER NODES IS 35
                    NUMBER OF RECOVERY BUFFERS IS 25
                    PROTECTION IS ANSI
                    ALLOCATION IS 500
                    PAGE SIZE IS 4
                    PAGE FORMAT IS UNIFORM
                    ...

                    CREATE TABLE ...
```

Tables

The CREATE TABLE statement in the Rdb/VMS incorporates column definitions, table constraints, or, if desired, a table definition derived from an existing table definition.

Column definitions. As usual, the basic column definition includes a column name and a data type. For data types, the Rdb/VMS allows the specification of either a domain name or a basic data type such as INTEGER, CHAR, or any of the types previously discussed. Domains specify restrictions on base type values and are discussed at greater length later in this chapter.

Column definitions can also include the following elements:

Default values: The user can specify a default value for columns. For instance, the user might insert a row in the table without specifying a value for a particular column. As an example, if the column definition includes the DEFAULT clause, then the default value will be assigned to the column. In this way, if Bob Donavan is the default manager of all employees when they get hired, then the Manager column will be defined as

```
Manager    CHAR(30) DEFAULT "Bob Donavan"
```

Column constraints: Columns could be assigned constraints such as the primary key constraint, unique constraint, not NULL constraint, referential integrity constraint, and other ad hoc check constraints.

Computed columns: The column can be derived from values of existing columns. For instance, if a table called Finances contains a column Revenue and a column Expenses, then we can define a new column called Profit, which is computed as the difference between Revenue and Expenses. This operation is completed using the COMPUTED BY clause.

Output formatting clauses: For both table definitions and view definitions, the Rdb/VMS supports the notion of formatting the output or display of the column values for interactive SQL users. For instance, the user can specify a query header to display the name that should be used for a column when values are returned and displayed to the user. The following example specifies the header "Born" for the Dob column:

```
Dob    DATE
QUERY HEADER IS 'B'/'o'/'r'/'n'
```

Integrity constraints for tables: In addition to specifying integrity constraints for columns, the CREATE TABLE statement in the Rdb/VMS can also specify integrity constraints involving several columns of a table. For instance, if we incorporate two columns, FirstName and LastName, then only the combination of FirstName and LastName column values are Unique (assuming we do not have two people with the same name in the database). Integrity constraints in the Rdb/VMS are discussed in more detail later in this chapter.

Table definitions. It is possible to define the structure of a table from an existing data definition though a FROM clause. This clause allows many tables and applications to share the same table definition and structure:

```
FROM path-name
```

ALTER TABLE statement. Besides the CREATE TABLE statement, the Rdb allows users to use the ALTER TABLE statement to add a column, drop a column definition, add or drop an integrity constraint, and alter the definition of a column through, for instance, changing the data type of a column.

DROP TABLE statement. A table T could be dropped from a database essentially via the statement DROP TABLE T.

Additionally, if other tables and views are dependent on the table definition, the user can also drop those tables and views using DROP TABLE T CASCADE. If this option is not specified (or if the user specifies DROP TABLE T RESTRICT), the drop will fail if any other view or table definitions depend on the dropped table.

Views

The CREATE VIEW statement in the Rdb/VMS can incorporate the SELECT expression, the WITH CHECK option, and formatting and display options.

The JohnsProps view definition example used in our discussion of the ORACLE Server is a valid view definition example for the Rdb/VMS—and for many other relational database management systems.

As with table definitions, a view might also be dropped with the CASCADE or RESTRICT options. The CASCADE option will also drop any view that uses the view being dropped. For example, if view V2 uses view V1 as in

```
CREATE VIEW V2
AS
        SELECT *
        FROM V1
```

Then, when we say DROP VIEW V1 CASCADE, both V1 and V2 will be dropped.

Privileges

When creating a schema in Rdb/VMS, the user can specify whether privilege protection is ANSI or ACL. With ACL type privilege protection, the search for a user's access rights or privileges is *order dependent*. The ACL scheme follows VAX/VMS's Access Control List Entries protection mechanism. On the other hand, the ANSI privilege scheme *does not* depend on an ordered list. Rather, it gathers the access privilege list and checks if a user is assigned the specific privilege for the operation being performed.

Corresponding to the different protection modes, the GRANT and REVOKE statements vary somewhat in their syntax and semantics. Both ANSI and ACL GRANT statements support the more "conventional" granting of SELECT, INSERT, DELETE, ALTER, and UPDATE privileges. These privileges could be given to schemata, tables, or columns. For instance,

```
GRANT SELECT ON SCHEMA AUTHORIZATION Bob
TO Jim
```

allows Jim to perform SELECTs on tables in the schema.

One additional difference between ANSI and ACL is that ACL incorporates a POSITION n clause, which specifies the position to be entered in the ACL list for the user who is being granted the privilege. For instance,

```
GRANT SELECT ON Clients
TO [Group2, Norman]
POSITION 5
```

indicates that the fifth entry in the ACL list of privileges is SELECT privilege on clients for Norman in Group 2. In this example, this privilege will supersede all other privileges subsequently granted to Norman.

Privileges could also be granted to every member of a group using the construct [Group2, *]. Then, if the privileges granted to [Group2, *] are positioned before, say, [Group2, Norman], then [Group2, Norman] will match the former. This will offer Norman only the privileges offered to the group and not additional privileges (if any) granted to Norman specifically.

The ANSI and ACL GRANT statements differ further in that the

ANSI GRANT incorporates a WITH GRANT OPTION clause, which allows the user to GRANT the privilege to other users. It also allows the person being granted the privilege to, in turn, grant the privilege to other users.

Integrity Constraints

Rdb SQL has a rich collection of column and table integrity constraints. In the CREATE TABLE statement, column constraints are specified immediately after the column name and column type specification. They can refer only to the column being defined. Table constraints are specified after all column specifications, and they can refer to any of the columns in the table defined in the CREATE TABLE statement. Rdb's available integrity constraints include:

- Not NULL constraint
- Primary and unique key constraints
- Default values (including NULL)
- Foreign keys—imposed through a trigger
- CHECK constraints for specifying more ad hoc integrity constraints

In the previous sections, we presented examples of these integrity constraints. As usual, the referential integrity constraint is one of the most important integrity constraints. To guarantee integrity of the database, the Rdb/VMS allows the user to specify triggers, which are activated on INSERT, DELETE or UPDATE of a table. It is up to the user to specify what should happen in a trigger. For example, assume the user wants to delete the rows of properties for which the owner's record is deleted. To do this, the user can create a trigger to delete the property rows after the delete of the client's row:

```
CREATE TRIGGER ZapOwner
                    AFTER DELETE ON Clients
                    ON Properties
                    (DELETE FROM Properties P
                    WHERE P.Owner = Clients.Name)
```

The Rdb/VMS also incorporates the notion of a DOMAIN (which is actually a ratified SQL2 ANSI standard proposal). Among other uses, Rdb domains provide (1) collating sequence specifications, (2) default clauses, and (3) editing or formatting specifications.

For instance, we can specify that the collating sequence of a particular domain is GERMAN through

```
CREATE COLLATING SEQUENCE GERMAN GERMAN
    CREATE DOMAIN GERMAN_NAME CHAR(30)
        COLLATING SEQUENCE IS GERMAN
```

Then, in a CREATE TABLE statement, we can specify the German name of a person with the German National Character Set) through the following statement:

```
GName     GERMAN_NAME
```

System Catalogs

In the Rdb/VMS, a number of system tables or catalogs store database structure, content, and user access information. All system catalogs in Rdb are pre-pended with "RDB$" or "RDBVMS$". They can be categorized into four groups.

The first group consists of system relations that contain the data definitions of tables, views, columns (fields in Rdb), and so on. Table 3.9 lists several data definition system catalogs in the Rdb/VMS.

RDB$FIELDS	The definition of each field (column) in the database
RDB$RELATION _FIELDS	The columns (fields) defined for each relation
RDB$RELATIONS	The relations defined in the database

Table 3.9: Data definition system tables in the DEC Rdb/VMS.

System relations that store the privileges for the different database objects make up the second group of Rdb system catalogs. The information stored in these systems is primarily defined in RDBVMS$PRIVILEGES.

The third group of system catalogs is made up of various system relations that contain information on storage parameters. Table 3.10 lists some of these system relations.

And finally, the fourth category includes those system relations that store information on the integrity constraints. Table 3.11 summarizes the most important of these tables.

RDB$DATABASE	Information on the file that stores the database
RDB$INDICES	Definition of the indexes in the database
RDBVMS$STORAGE _MAP_AREAS	Stores the various properties of storage areas containing database objects

Table 3.10: Storage management system tables in the DEC Rdb/VMS.

RDBVMS$TRIGGERS	Contains definitions of the triggers
RDB$CONSTRAINTS	Stores the name and definition of each integrity constraint
RDBVMS$INTER RELATIONS	Stores information on the referential dependencies of tables

Table 3.11: Integrity constraint system tables in the DEC Rdb/VMS.

3.9.4 Microsoft SQL Server

Data Types

The Microsoft SQL Server supports character string, numeric, date and timestamp, binary, and multimedia (text and image) data types.

Character strings: There are two options for specifying character string types in the Microsoft SQL server:

CHAR(n): Used for fixed-length character strings. The maximum length of a CHAR is 255 letters, numbers, or symbols.

VARCHAR(n): Used for varying-length character strings up to 255 characters. A maximum length must be specified when declaring columns of type VARCHAR.

Numeric data types: There are four numeric data types in the Microsoft SQL Server:

SMALLINT: Used to declare two-byte integers whose sizes range from -2**15 to 2**15.

INT: Used to declare four-byte integers whose sizes range from -2**31 to 2**31.

TINYINT: Used to declare one-byte integers whose values range from 0 to 255 inclusive.

MONEY: This data type is quite unique for SQL Server. All money types must be preceded by a "$" sign. Money values range from -922,337,203,685,447.5807 to +922,337,203,685,447.5807. All SQL aggregate functions can apply to columns of type MONEY.

FLOAT: Used for double-precision floating point numbers. Each floating point number consumes eight bytes.

Datetime and timestamp. In addition to character strings and numeric data types, the SQL Server also supports DATETIME, and TIMESTAMP data types:

DATETIME: Internally, a DATETIME is stored in eight bytes. The first four bytes store the number of days from January 1, 1990, and the other four bytes store the number of milliseconds after midnight on that day with accuracy up to 0.003 seconds. The earliest possible date is January 1, 1753. DATETIME has a default representation, and DATETIME values should be entered using single or double quotes.

TIMESTAMP: A timestamp is an eight-byte binary value that is updated every time a row is inserted or updated. To have a TIMESTAMP column, both the column and its data type must be called TIMESTAMP.

Binary data types. The following binary data types are supported in the Microsoft SQL server:

BINARY(n): Represents fixed-length binary data up to 255 bytes.

VARBINARY(n): Represents varying-length binary data up to 255 bytes.

BIT: Columns of this type hold either zero or one value.

Multimedia data types. The SQL Server has two multimedia data types, TEXT and IMAGE, which are used to store (almost arbitrarily large) text and image data values.

TEXT: Used to store text data; values can be as large as two gigabytes.

IMAGE: Primarily intended for storing image data; can store up to two gigabytes of hexadecimal binary data.

Stored Procedures

The data definition constructs of the Microsoft SQL Server use a rather unique feature called *stored procedures*. These stored procedures are actually SQL program-incorporated control structures. These stored procedures are compiled (and optimized) once, and they can be invoked repeatedly by different users and applications. Invoking a stored procedure is usually more efficient than recompiling and executing frequently used SQL statements from scratch. Chapter 7 will discuss stored procedures in more detail.

In addition to user-defined stored procedures, the SQL Server supports a number of system procedures. These procedures are supplied by the SQL Server and are used to provide different functionalities and specifications of data definition constructs. In fact, in many cases the SQL Server utilizes stored system procedures to achieve functionalities that are usually provided through the SQL data definition constructs directly in other servers.

Schemata and Databases

The SQL Server's TRANSACT-SQL incorporates a CREATE DATABASE statement. With this statement, the user can specify the name of the database, the size (or amount of space) allocated to the database (in megabytes), and the devices that contain the database.

For example, to indicate that the RealEstate database must be stored in files RE1 and RE2, where for each, the system allocates 10 megabytes is

```
CREATE DATABASE RealEstate
ON RE1 = 10, RE2 = 10
```

The size of a database can range from 2 to 2**15 megabytes.

Other constructs associated with databases are executed through stored procedures. For instance, the stored procedure *sp_diskdefault* is used to change the default device drive of the database. Similarly, *sp_logdevice* is used to indicate the database device in which the system log should be stored. Information about databases on the SQL Server is obtained through *sp_helpdb*.

Tables

The CREATE TABLE definition of the Microsoft SQL Server is rather simple, specifying the column definitions with NULL (i.e., default value of a column whose value is not provided) and NOT NULL (for the not Null constraint). Consider the following example:

```
CREATE TABLE Person(
                Name        CHAR(20) NOT NULL,
                DATE        DATE  NULL,
                SS#         INTEGER NOT NULL,
                Salary              MONEY NULL)
```

Other specifications such as default values for columns, triggers, indexes, foreign keys, rules, and so on, are done with separate CREATE statements and stored procedures.

For instance, the primary key of a table is defined through the stored procedure *sp_primarykey*. Similarly, foreign key references are defined through *sp_foreignkey*.

Views

The CREATE VIEW statement in TRANSACT-SQL specifies the name of the view, the optional renamed column names, and the select statement that defines the view. The following example defines a view RichPeople where the column names are the same as those of People:

```
CREATE VIEW RichPeople
                AS
                        SELECT *
                        FROM People
                        WHERE Salary > $50,000
```

The user can rename the view through the stored procedure *sp_rename*. Additionally, the user can get information on which views or tables depend through invoking the stored system procedure *sp_depends*.

Privileges

Like most SQL database management systems, privileges in the Microsoft SQL Server are achieved through GRANT/REVOKE statements. The SQL Server supports GRANT permission for objects, and GRANT permission for statements.

The objects for which different types of permission could be granted with the SQL Server include tables, views, and stored procedures.

The SQL Server provides a number of statements for which different types of permission could be granted. These include:

CREATE DATABASE

CREATE DEFAULT

CREATE PROCEDURE

CREATE RULE

CREATE TABLE

CREATE VIEW

DUMP DATABASE

DUMP TRANSACTION

In addition to the system administrator and individual users, the Microsoft SQL Server supports groups of users, PUBLIC (which includes all users that are not in a group), and ALL (which includes all users). Thus, to grant SELECT permission on Clients to PUBLIC, we have the statement

```
GRANT SELECT ON Clients TO PUBLIC
```

And, to grant INSERT permission on Clients to group 1 and Mark we have

```
GRANT INSERT ON Clients TO Group1, Mark
```

Groups are created through the stored procedure *sp_addgroup*. Users are added to groups through the stored procedure *sp_adduser.* The user can obtain information on groups and permissions in the databases through the stored procedures *sp_helpgroup* and *sp_helprotect,* respectively.

Integrity Constraints

The SQL Server supports a number of integrity constraint constructs, including the following:

NULL and not NULL constraints: Used for column declarations in CREATE TABLE statement.

Primary keys and foreign keys: Specified through sp_primarykey and sp_foreignkey stored procedures, respectively.

Triggers: The CREATE TRIGGER statement allows users to specify triggers for INSERT, DELETE, or UPDATE operations on rows of tables. Since TRANSACT-SQL supports control structures, the SQL statement that is executed in a trigger could contain control structures. The following example creates a trigger to indicate large numbers of properties owned by clients:

```
CREATE TRIGGER PropertyAlert
            ON Properties
            FOR INSERT
            IF (SELECT COUNT(*)
                FROM Properties P, Clients C
                WHERE
                            C.Name = P.Owner_Name) > 1000
      THEN
      PRINT
      "There are now more than 1000 properties owned by clients"
```

System Catalogs

Like most database management systems, the system tables in the SQL Server store and maintain information about the database content, structure, and users.

SYSCOLUMNS	Contains the definition of columns in views and tables
SYSDEPENDS	Stores dependencies between stored procedures, tables, and views
SYSINDEXES	Includes definition of indexes for the tables
SYSKEYS	Stores definitions of primary and foreign keys
SYSLOGS	Contains the transaction log
SYSOBJECTS	Contains the definitions of tables, views, triggers, stored procedures, and other objects in the database
SYSPROTECTS	Stores information about the different privileges and permissions
SYSSEGMENTS	Stores disk space information
SYSUSERS	Stores information on the users of the database

Table 3.12: System tables in the Microsoft SQL Server.

The SQL Server has user databases and a number of special system databases. These include the master database, the model database, the temporary database, and a sample pubs (publications) database.

Table 3.12 lists several of the system tables contained in all the databases of the SQL Server. The master database contains additional system tables, some of which are listed in Table 3.13.

SYSCONFIGURES	Stores user-specified configurations
SYSDEVICES	Stores various information on dump devices, database storage devices, disk partitions, and so on
SYSLOCKS	Stores the active locks
SYSLOGINS	Stores SQL Server user accounts
SYSMESSAGES	Stores error and/or warning messages

Table 3.13: Other system tables in the Microsoft SQL Server.

3.10 Summary

In this chapter, we concentrated on the data definition constructs and system catalogs of the various the Microsoft SQL database servers. We also illustrated how the various servers handled privileges, which is actually a data control construct.

We saw that the various standards and servers support different data types. Table 3.14 summarizes the various data types supported by the different servers and compares them to ANSI the SQL 89 standard.

All the servers, except the IBM Extended Edition, incorporate a CREATE SCHEMA or DATABASE statement. This statement is used to create tables, views, integrity constraints, indexes, privileges, and so on. In the IBM Extended Edition, the schema creation is achieved through a call interface.

In regard to integrity constraints, all the servers we discussed support NOT NULL, UNIQUE, and PRIMARY KEY constraints. In the Microsoft SQL Server, primary keys are indicated through calling a stored procedure. The integrity constraints supported by the four servers in our discussion are summarized in Table 3.15.

ANSI SQL89	IBM EE	ORACLE Server	DEC Rdb/VMS	Microsoft SQL Server
CHARACTER	CHARACTER	CHARACTER	CHARACTER	CHARACTER
———	VARCHAR	VARCHAR	VARCHAR	VARCHAR
———	LONG VARCHAR	LONG VARCHAR	LONG VARCHAR	LONG VARCHAR
			TINYINT	TINYINT
INTEGER	INTEGER	INTEGER	INTEGER	INTEGER
FLOAT REAL	FLOAT	FLOAT REAL	FLOAT REAL	FLOAT
DECIMAL	DECIMAL	DECIMAL	DECIMAL	DECIMAL
DOUBLE PRECISION	———	———	DOUBLE PRECISION	———
———	———	———	———	MONEY
———	DATE	DATE	DATE	DATETIME
———	TIME	———	———	DATETIME
———	TIMESTAMP	———	———	TIMESTAMP
———	———	RAW LONG RAW	LONG BYTE STRING	BINARY VARBINARY
———	TIMESTAMP	ROWID	DBKEY	TIMESTAMP
———	———	———	———	BIT
———	———	———	———	IMAGE
———	———	———	———	TEXT

Table 3.14: The data types in various servers.

IBM EE	ORACLE Server	DEC Rdb/VMS	Microsoft SQL Server
FOREIGN KEY With CASCADE	FOREIGN KEY	———	sp-foreignkey
———	CHECK	———	———
———	———	TRIGGER	TRIGGER
———	———	DOMAIN	———

Table 3.15: Integrity constraints in various SQL servers.

Chapter 4
Data Manipulation

As we stated earlier, Structured Query Language (SQL) can be categorized into three groups: the Data Definition Language (DDL), the Data Manipulation Language (DML), and the Data Control language (DCL). In Chapter 3, we saw how the Data Definition and Control languages are used to define the structure and security of a database. In this chapter, we focus on the Data Manipulation Language which functions to retrieve or modify data in a database.

We begin our discussion in Section 4.1 with a brief overview of the different data manipulation operations in SQL. Then, in Section 4.2, we turn our attention to the SQL noncursor operations INSERT, SELECT, DELETE, and UPDATE. We describe the manner in which null values are treated in SQL in Section 4.3. This is followed, in Section 4.4, by a lengthy examination of the noncursor operation statements supported by the four SQL servers we have selected to study in this book. Finally, we include several tables in Section 4.5 summarizing the noncursor operations supported by each of the four SQL servers.

4.1 An Overview of Data Manipulation in SQL

The SQL Data Manipulation Language defines statements that manipulate data in a database by retrieving, inserting, deleting, and updating data. The DML can be divided into three categories, which are based on the nature of the operation: (1) cursor operations, (2) noncursor operations, and (3) transaction termination operations.

4.1.1 Cursor Operations

A *cursor* is a SQL object associated with a specific SELECT operation. Cursors provide a mechanism for sequentially accessing a set of selected records and processing the records one at a time. DECLARE CURSOR, OPEN, FETCH, DELETE:positioned, UPDATE:positioned, and CLOSE are cursor-related SQL statements.

The DECLARE CURSOR statement is used to define a cursor. A cursor definition consists of a cursor name and a cursor specification. The specified SELECT statement in a cursor specification is executed when the cursor is opened by the OPEN statement. After the execution of an OPEN statement, the cursor is positioned before the first row of the selected set. To advance a cursor to the next record and to retrieve the values of that record the FETCH statement is used. The current record can be deleted by the DELETE:positioned statement and updated by the UPDATE:positioned statement. When a cursor is closed by the CLOSE statement, the association between the cursor and the selected set of records is destroyed.

4.1.2 Noncursor Operations

SQL has four noncursor operation statements: INSERT, SELECT, DELETE, and UPDATE.

After defining a database, the INSERT statement is used to load the actual data values into a table. Retrieving data from a database is accomplished with the SELECT statement. The DELETE statement removes rows of data from a table, and the UPDATE statement is used to update columns in rows of a table.

4.1.3 Transaction Termination Operations

A *transaction* is a sequence of operations that is atomic with respect to recovery and concurrency. COMMIT and ROLLBACK are the two transaction termination statements in SQL.

The COMMIT statement terminates the current transaction, closes any opened cursors in the current transaction, and causes all the updates made by the current transaction to be permanent. The syntax of a COMMIT statement is as follows:

<commit statement> ::= COMMIT WORK

The ROLLBACK statement terminates the current transaction, closes any opened cursors in the current transaction, and cancels all the updates made by the current transaction. The syntax of a ROLLBACK statement is

<rollback statement> ::= ROLLBACK WORK

4.2 Noncursor Operation Statements

In this chapter, we concentrate our discussion on the noncursor operation statements—INSERT, SELECT, DELETE, and UPDATE. In addition to the tables in the RealEstate database introduced in Chapter 3, we use the employee (Emp), department (Dept), and standard salary (StdSalary) tables in this chapter. Table 4.1 lists all the employees in the Emp table, Table 4.2 includes all the departments in the Dept table, and Table 4.3 contains the standard salaries for each department.

EmpNo	EName	DeptNo	Mgr	Salary	HiredDate
1001	Smith	10	2001	1700	2/2/89
1002	Jones	10	2001	1200	1/1/90
1003	Brown	20	2002	2000	3/15/87
1004	Green	20	2002	1500	9/13/89
1005	White	30	2003	2000	1/1/90
1006	Bays	30	2004	2200	8/1/88
1007	Taylor	30	2004	3000	6/15/90
2001	Kramer	10	2002	3000	12/1/87
2002	Lowe	20	3001	3500	5/1/89
2003	Morton	30	3001	2800	11/15/88
2004	Tracy	30	3001	3100	7/1/89
3001	Peterson	99		6000	12/1/85

Table 4.1: Employees in Emp table.

DeptNo	DName	MinSalary	MaxSalary
10	Human Resource	1200	4000
20	Sales	1500	4300
30	Accounting	2000	4500
40	Security	1000	3500
99	President	5000	

Table 4.2: Departments in Dept table.

DeptName	StdMinSal	StdMaxSal
Human Resource	1000	3000
Sales	1500	3500
Accounting	1800	3600
Customer Support	1700	3700
Technician	2000	4500
President	5000	
Janitor	2500	5000

Table 4.3: Departments in StdSalary table.

4.2.1 INSERT Statement

The INSERT statement inserts a row or a set of rows into a specified table. The syntax of an INSERT statement is stated as follows:

```
<insert statement> ::=
    INSERT INTO <table name> [ ( <insert column list> ) ]
    {
                    VALUES (<insert value list>)
            |       <query specification>
    }
```

The INSERT statement that includes a VALUES clause is used to add a single row of data to a table. For example, to add a security department with a department number of 40, a minimum salary of $1,000, and a maximum salary of $3,500 to the Dept table, we execute the following SQL statement:

```
INSERT INTO Dept VALUES (40, "Security", 1000, 3500)
```

And, to add a real estate property, we have the following SQL statement:

```
INSERT INTO Property
        VALUES ("13788", "CA", "John Smith", 250000)
```

The INSERT statement with query specification is used to insert multiple rows of data into a table. (See Section 4.2.2 for a description of a query specification.) In the following example, the HighIncome table has the same data definition as the Emp table. To add all the employees who earn more than $3,000 to the High Income table, HighIncome, we execute the SQL statement that follows:

```
INSERT  INTO HighIncome
            SELECT      *
            FROM        Emp
            WHERE       Salary > 3000
```

As a result, three rows are inserted.

In all INSERT statements, the table specified in the INTO clause of the statement must be updatable. Moreover, that table must not be identified in a FROM clause of the query specification or any subquery contained in the query specification. If the table specified is a view with the WITH CHECK OPTION specification, then the inserting rows must satisfy the view-defining condition.

The number of columns specified in the optional insert column list should match the number of columns specified in the inserting rows. Each specified column must be unique and must be contained within the specified table. Moreover, the data type of the column and the corresponding values in the inserting rows must be compatible. For columns not specified in the insert column list, null values are inserted. In the example that follows, a new department is added to the Dept table even though the salary information is unavailable. The value of the MinSalary and MaxSalary columns will be set to NULL:

```
INSERT  INTO Dept (DeptNo, DName)
VALUES          (50, "Customer Support")
```

To add a personal record for John Smith, we execute the following SQL statement:

```
INSERT  INTO Person (Name, Dob, SS#, Salary)
VALUES          ("John Smith", "02/03/58", 553981908, 3000)
```

4.2.2 SELECT Statement

The SELECT statement is used to retrieve values from the tables that satisfy specified conditions. A SELECT statement can be used to retrieve a single row of results and store them in the specified select target list. This type of SELECT statement is called a singleton SELECT statement. Its syntax is as follows:

```
<select statement> ::=
        SELECT [ ALL | DISTINCT ] <select list>
        INTO <select target list>
        <table expression>
```

A SELECT statement can also be used in a cursor specification to retrieve a set of rows to be manipulated using a cursor. The syntax of the cursor specification is

```
<cursor specification> ::=   <query expression>
                             [ <order by clause> ]
<query expression> ::= <query term>
                       | <query expression> UNION [ALL] <query term>
<query term> ::= <query specification> | ( <query expression> )
<query specification> ::=
        SELECT [ ALL | DISTINCT ] <select list> <table expression>
```

In the pages that follow, we examine the syntax and semantics of several important elements of the SELECT statement.

Select List

The syntax of the select list is

```
<select list> ::=
                  <value expression> [{, <value expression>}...]
        |         *
```

Each element in the select list generates a column in the resulting table. Therefore, every column of the resulting table has the same data type, length, and precision as the value expression from which the column was derived. If the value expression in the select list consists of a single column, then the resulting column has the same name as the column specified. Otherwise, the resulting column is unnamed. For example, to select the state code and sale price of John Smith's property, we specify the State-Code and SalePrice columns in the select list of a SELECT statement as follows:

```
SELECT   State-Code, SalePrice
FROM     Property
WHERE    Owner = "John Smith"
```

The result is

State-Code	SalePrice
CA	250000

To select the employee number and salary of Smith, we execute the following SQL statement:

```
SELECT   EmpNo, Salary
FROM     Emp
WHERE    EName = "Smith"
```

The retrieved result is

EmpNo	Salary
1001	1700

The number of columns selected equals the number of elements in the select list. If an asterisk (*) is specified in the select list, then every column of the table specified in the FROM clause of the table expression is selected. To list all the employees in Department 30, we specify an asterisk in the select list and execute the SQL statement

```
SELECT    *
FROM      Dept
WHERE     DeptNo = 30
```

As a result, every column in the Dept table is retrieved as follows:

EmpNo	EName	DeptNo	Mgr	Salary	HiredDate
1005	White	30	2003	2000	1/1/90
1006	Bays	30	2004	2200	8/1/88
1007	Taylor	30	2004	3000	6/15/90
2003	Morton	30	3001	2800	11/15/88
2004	Tracy	30	3001	3100	7/1/89

If DISTINCT is specified in a SELECT statement, then duplicate rows in the result table are eliminated. For example, to display the managers of Department 30, the DISTINCT keyword is specified in the select list as follows:

```
SELECT    DISTINCT Mgr
FROM      Dept
WHERE     DeptNo = 30
```

The retrieved results are

Mgr
2003
2004
3001

Value Expression

A value expression is used to specify a value. It can be a value specification, a column specification, a set function specification, or an arithmetic operation of two value expressions. The arithmetic operators supported are plus (+), minus (-), multiply (*), and divide (/). The unary plus (+) and unary minus (-) operators are also supported. SQL does not allow arithmetic operations on operands of character data type. In the following example, the expression -123*2 and the salary range (which is the result of MaxSalary minus MinSalary) for the Sales department are retrieved:

```
SELECT    -123*2, MaxSalary - MinSalary,
FROM      StdSalary
WHERE     DeptName = 'Sales'
```

The result is

	MaxSalary - MinSalary
-246	2000

Value specification. A value specification designates a value that is not selected from a table. The value can be represented as a parameter, a variable, a literal, or the special keyword USER of the character data type. The value specified by USER is listed in the module authorization identifier clause of the module that contains the SQL statement.

A parameter specification consists of a parameter name and an optional indicator parameter. Similarly, a variable specification consists of a variable name and an optional indicator variable. If the value of an indicator parameter or an indicator variable is negative, then the value specified by the parameter name or the variable name is null. Otherwise, the value of the parameter or variable is the value specified by the parameter name or the variable name. For example, to select the literal "The user is", the current user name, an arithmetic expression, and a variable Var, we execute the following SQL statement:

```
SELECT   "The user is", USER,
         Var INDICATOR Var_indicator * 2 - 3,
         Var INDICATOR Var_indicator
FROM     Dept
WHERE    DeptNo = 40
```

The result is

The user is	USER		
The user is	Smith	243	123

The value of Var is 123, because the value of the indicator variable, Var_indicator, equals 0.

Column specification. Column specification designates a column, which can be qualified by a table name or a correlation name. In the following example, the EName column is qualified with the correlation name Employee:

```
SELECT Employee.EName
  FROM Emp Employee
 WHERE Employee.DeptNo = 10
```

The retrieved results are

Employee.EName
Smith
Jones

In the following query, the correlation names Mgr and Employee are used to represent the two different invocations of the Emp table:

```
SELECT    Mgr.EName, Mgr.EmpNo, Mgr.DeptNo
FROM      Emp Employee, Emp Mgr
WHERE     Employee.Mgr = Mgr.EmpNo
```

The retrieved results are

Mgr.EName	Mgr.EmpNo	Mgr.DeptNo
Kramer	2001	10
Lowe	2002	20
Morton	2003	30
Tracy	2004	30
Peterson	3001	99

Set function specification. Set function specification designates a value that is the result of some function. The ANSI SQL89 functions are described in Table 4.4.

All the ANSI SQL89 standard functions, with the exception of COUNT(*), operate on the collection of scalar values in one column of a table and produce a single scalar value. The SUM and AVG functions work only on numeric arguments. The DISTINCT keyword eliminates any duplicate values from the column before applying the function. If DISTINCT is specified in the function, then the argument must be a column reference. Otherwise, the argument can be a value expression.

Set functions are nonrecursive; therefore, the argument cannot reference any set functions. Except for the COUNT(*) function, any null values in the argument are eliminated before the function is applied. Applying AVG, MIN, MAX, or SUM functions to an empty argument will result in a null value. For example, to select the number of total employees, and the maximum, minimum, and average salary of the employees, we execute the following SQL statement:

```
SELECT    COUNT(*), MAX(Salary),
          MIN(Salary), AVG(Salary)
FROM      Emp
```

SQL Function	Description
COUNT (*)	Returns the number of rows in a table, including duplicate rows and rows with NULL values
COUNT (DISTINCT <column>)	Returns the number of the known values in a column, eliminating any duplicate values
AVG (DISTINCT <column>)	Returns the average of the known values in a column, eliminating any duplicate values
AVG ([ALL] <value expression>)	Returns the average of the known values in a column
MAX (DISTINCT <column>)	Returns the largest known value in a column
MAX ([ALL] <value expression>)	Returns the largest known value in a column
MIN (DISTINCT <column>)	Returns the smallest known value in a column
MIN ([ALL] <value expression>)	Returns the smallest known value in a column
SUM (DISTINCT <column>)	Returns the total of all known values in a column, eliminating any duplicate values
SUM ([ALL] <value expression>)	Returns the total of all known values in a column

Table 4.4: *ANSI SQL89 functions.*

The result is

COUNT(*)	MAX(Salary)	MIN(Salary)	AVG(Salary)
12	6000	1200	2666

Table Expression

A table expression specifies a table or a grouped table. A table expression is composed of a FROM clause, an optional WHERE clause, an optional GROUP BY clause, and an optional HAVING clause.

FROM clause. A FROM clause specifies the list of tables from which the resulting table will be derived. Table names (as well as correlation names) in the FROM clause must be unique. If the FROM clause contains only one table, then the result of the FROM clause is the table identified by that one table name. Otherwise, the result of a FROM clause is the extended Cartesian product of the specified tables. In the following example, only one table is specified in the FROM clause to list all the departments in the Dept table:

```
SELECT    *
FROM      Dept
```

The result of the query will retrieve all rows and columns from the Dept table:

DeptNo	DName	MinSalary	MaxSalary
10	Human Resource	1200	4000
20	Sales	1500	4300
30	Accounting	2000	4500
99	President	5000	

To query multiple tables, we specify both the Dept and StdSalary tables in the FROM clause as follows:

```
SELECT    *
FROM      Dept, StdSalary
WHERE     DeptNo = 10
```

The retrieved results are

DeptNo	DName	MinSalary	MaxSalary	DeptName	StdMinSal	StdMaxSal
10	Human Resource	1200	4000	Human Resource	1000	3000
10	Human Resource	1200	4000	Sales	1500	3500
10	Human Resource	1200	4000	Accounting	1800	3600
10	Human Resource	1200	4000	Customer Support	1700	3700

10	Human Resource	1200	4000	Technician	2000	4500
10	Human Resource	1200	4000	President	5000	
10	Human Resource	1200	4000	Janitor	2500	5000

If the table specified in the FROM clause is a grouped view, then the FROM clause can contain only that table. Furthermore, the table expression cannot contain a WHERE clause, a GROUP BY clause, or a HAVING clause.

WHERE clause. A WHERE clause specifies a table by applying a search condition to each row of the result from a preceding FROM clause. The table resulting from the WHERE clause contains data that satisfied the search condition. Each column specification directly contained in the search condition must be a column of the table specified in the preceding FROM clause or an outer reference. An *outer reference* is a column specification that does not reference any of the columns in tables specified in the FROM clause of a subquery. Instead, the column specification references a column of a table specified in the FROM clause of the query containing the subquery. In the following example, Dept.DeptNo is the outer reference. That is, Dept.DeptNo is not a column of the Emp table; rather, it is a column of the Dept table, which is a table specified in the FROM clause of the main SELECT statement.

```
SELECT    *
FROM      Dept
WHERE     DeptNo IN
          (SELECT DeptNo FROM Emp
          WHERE Emp.DeptNo = Dept.DeptNo)
```

The results are

DeptNo	DName	MinSalary	MaxSalary
10	Human Resource	1200	4000
20	Sales	1500	4300
30	Accounting	2000	4500
99	President	5000	

GROUP BY clause. A GROUP BY clause specifies a grouped table derived from the result of the previously specified clause. Each column specification in the GROUP BY clause (the "grouping" column) must be a column in the result of the previously specified clause. The GROUP BY clause partitions the result into a minimum number of groups such that all values of each grouping column are identical. In the example that follows, a GROUP BY clause is used to list all employees by department number:

```
SELECT      *
FROM        Emp
GROUP BY    DeptNo
```

The retrieved results are

EmpNo	EName	DeptNo	Mgr	Salary	HiredDate
1001	Smith	10	2001	1700	2/2/89
1002	Jones	10	2001	1200	1/1/90
2001	Kramer	10	2002	3000	12/1/87
1003	Brown	20	2002	2000	3/15/87
1004	Green	20	2002	1500	9/13/89
2002	Lowe	20	3001	3500	5/1/89
1005	White	30	2003	2000	1/1/90
1006	Bays	30	2004	2200	8/1/88
1007	Taylor	30	2004	3000	6/15/90
2003	Morton	30	3001	2800	11/15/88
2004	Tracy	30	3001	3100	7/1/89
3001	Peterson	99		6000	12/1/85

HAVING clause. A HAVING clause specifies a restriction on a grouped table by eliminating groups that do not satisfy a search condition. For example, to list all employees according to department number with department number less than or equal to 20, a GROUP BY and a HAVING clause are specified as follows:

```
SELECT      *
FROM        Emp
GROUP BY    DeptNo
HAVING      DeptNo <= 20
```

The results are

EmpNo	EName	DeptNo	Mgr	Salary	HiredDate
1001	Smith	10	2001	1700	2/2/89

1002	Jones	10	2001	1200	1/1/90
2001	Kramer	10	2002	3000	12/1/87
1003	Brown	20	2002	2000	3/15/87
1004	Green	20	2002	1500	9/13/89
2002	Lowe	20	3001	3500	5/1/89

Search Condition

A search condition specifies the value of a condition to be TRUE, FALSE, or UNKNOWN. The result of a search condition is derived by applying the specified Boolean operators to the conditions that result from the application of each specified predicate to a given row of a table or a given group of a grouped table. In descending order, the order of precedence for the Boolean operators is expression within parentheses, NOT, AND, and OR.

Operators at the same precedence level are applied from left to right. For example, to select the name, employee number, and salary of all the employees whose salary is less than $2,000 and who were hired after 9/1/89, we execute the following SQL statement:

```
SELECT   EName, EmpNo, Salary
FROM     Emp
WHERE    Salary < 2000
AND      HiredDate > '9/1/1989'
```

The results are

EName	EmpNo	Salary
Jones	1002	1200
Green	1004	1500

Predicate. A predicate specifies a condition that returns a value of TRUE, FALSE, or UNKNOWN. The result of a predicate is derived by applying a predicate to a given row of a table or a given group of a grouped table. The ANSI SQL89 standard lists seven types of predicates: COMPARISON, BETWEEN, IN, LIKE, NULL, QUANTIFIED, and EXISTS.

The COMPARISON predicate specifies a comparison of two values. The following are comparison operators:

= (equal)

<> (not equal)

< (less than)

> (greater than)

<= (less than or equal to)

>= (greater than or equal to)

If either one of the operands in a comparison is the null value, then the result of the comparison is unknown. In the example below, no rows are retrieved because one of the operands in the comparison is NULL and the result of the comparison is unknown:

```
SELECT   EName, DeptNo
FROM     Emp
WHERE    EName > NULL
OR       DeptNo >= NULL
OR       NULL = NULL
```

The comparison of two character strings is performed by the comparison of each individual character with the same ordinal position. When two character strings are compared for equality and the strings do not have the same length, a working copy of the shorter string is made and padded on the right with space so that it is the same length as the other string. Consider the following strings equality comparison, even though 'abc' is not the same as 'abc ', the comparison returns TRUE because the shorter string 'abc' is padded with space for the comparison:

```
SELECT   EName, DeptNo
FROM     Emp
WHERE    'abc' = 'abc '
AND      EmpNo < 1003
```

The results are

EName	DeptNo
Smith	10
Jones	10
Lowe	3500
Tracy	3100

To select the name and salary of all the employees having a salary greater than or equal to $3,000 and who are not in Department 99, the comparison operator >= is used:

```
SELECT   EName, Salary
```

```
FROM     Emp
WHERE    Salary >= 3000
AND      DeptNo <> 99
```

The results are

EName	Salary
Taylor	3000
Kramer	3000
Lowe	3500
Tracy	3100

The BETWEEN predicate compares a value to a specified range of values. The data type of the value expressions in a BETWEEN predicate must be comparable. The expression "A BETWEEN B AND C" is equivalent to the expression "A>=B AND A<=C." For example, to select the name and salary of all the employees having a salary ranging from $1,500 to $2,000, we use the BETWEEN predicate:

```
SELECT   EName, Salary
FROM     Emp
WHERE    Salary BETWEEN 1500 AND 2000
```

This results in

EName	Salary
Smith	1700
Brown	2000
Green	1500
White	2000

The IN predicate specifies a quantified comparison. The value expression is compared with a list of values returned from a subquery or from a list of values specified in the IN value list. The expression "A IN B" is equivalent to "A = ANY B" where B denotes the list of values with which to be compared. In the following example, the IN predicate is used to select the name and salary of all the employees who are in Department 10, 20, or 99:

```
SELECT   EName, Salary
FROM     Emp
WHERE    DeptNo IN (10, 20, 99)
```

The results are

EName	Salary
Smith	1700
Jones	1200
Brown	2000
Green	1500
Kramer	3000
Lowe	3500
Peterson	6000

In the next example, to select the department number and department name of employees who earn more than $3,000, a subquery and the IN predicate are used. The subquery returns all the department numbers with employees earning more than $3,000 and the IN predicate is used to compare the Dept.DeptNo with the retrieved Emp.DeptNo as follows:

```
SELECT   DeptNo, DName
FROM     Dept
WHERE    DeptNo IN (   SELECT   DeptNo
                       FROM     Emp
                       WHERE    Salary > 3000)
```

The results are

DeptNo	DName
20	Sales
30	Accounting
99	President

The LIKE predicate specifies a pattern-matching comparison. Only character data can be compared with a LIKE predicate, and wildcard characters can be used in the pattern matching. In the pattern, if an escape character is not specified, then an underscore character represents an arbitrary character specifier, while a percent sign represents an arbitrary string specifier. If an escape character is specified, any character that follows the escape character must be another escape character, an underscore, or a percent sign. Both the escape character and the character that follows it represent a single occurrence of the second character. The expression "A LIKE B" is unknown if either A or B is NULL. In the following example, to select names that are five characters long and that begin with 'Smit', or to select names that end with a character 'n' from the employee table, the LIKE 'Smit_' and LIKE '%n' clauses are used:

```
SELECT   EName
FROM     Emp
WHERE    EName LIKE 'Smit_'
OR       EName LIKE '%n'
```

The selected results are

EName
Smith
Green
Brown
Morton
Peterson

As another example, to list all the names that start with 'Smit_', the ESCAPE character '^', together with the '_' character, is used to represent the literal '_'. In this case, the '_' does not function as a wildcard character:

```
SELECT   name
FROM     clients
WHERE    name LIKE 'Smit^_%' ESCAPE '^'
```

No row is retrieved because there are no names like 'Smit_'.

The LIKE predicate does not pad strings with blanks as does the = predicate. Thus two strings compared equal to each other might not return TRUE when compared using the LIKE predicate. This is illustrated in the following example:

```
SELECT   EName, DeptNo
FROM     Emp
WHERE    'abc' LIKE 'abc '
```

No row is retrieved because the comparison of 'abc' LIKE 'abc ' returns FALSE.

The NULL predicate tests for a null value. The result of a NULL predicate is either TRUE or FALSE. Thus, if the value specified A is NULL, then the expression "A is NULL" is TRUE. For instance, to select the name and employee number of all the employees without a manager, we use the NULL predicate as follows:

```
SELECT    EName, EmpNo
FROM      Emp
WHERE     Mgr IS NULL
```

This results in

EName	EmpNo
Peterson	3001

The QUANTIFIED predicate specifies a quantified comparison. For instance, let A denote the result of a value expression, and let B denote the result of a subquery. The result of the expression "A <comp op> <quantifier> B" is derived by applying the implied comparison predicate "A <comp op> B" to every value in B. If B is empty or the implied comparison predicate is TRUE for every value of B, then "A <comp op> ALL B" is TRUE. If B is empty or if the implied comparison predicate is FALSE for every value of B, then "A <comp op> [SOME | ANY] B" is FALSE. As an example, to list the department name for any department that has employees, we use the following SQL statement:

```
SELECT    DISTINCT DName
FROM      Dept
WHERE     DeptNo = SOME (SELECT DeptNo FROM Emp)
```

The results are

DName
Human Resource
Sales
Accounting
President

And, to list the department name for any department with a department number different from all the employees' department numbers, we execute this SQL statement:

```
SELECT    DISTINCT DName
FROM      Dept
WHERE     DeptNo <> ALL (SELECT DeptNo FROM Emp),
```

which results in

DName
Security

The EXISTS predicate tests for an empty set. The expression "EXISTS B" is TRUE if and only if the set B is not empty. For example, to list the name and number of all employees whose salary is at least 10% higher than the minimum salary in their department, we execute

```
SELECT   EName, EmpNo
FROM     Emp
WHERE    EXISTS ( SELECT   *
                  FROM     Dept
                  WHERE    Emp.DeptNo = Dept.DeptNo
                  AND      Emp.Salary > MinSalary * 1.1)
```

The results are

EName	EmpNo
Smith	1001
Brown	1003
Taylor	1007
Kramer	2001
Lowe	2002
Morton	2003
Tracy	2004
Peterson	2005

Subquery. A subquery specifies a multiset of values derived from a table expression. A subquery must produce a single column of data as its query result. Therefore, the degree of the table expression must be one if a wildcard (*) is specified in the result specification of a subquery of any predicate other than an EXISTS predicate. For an EXISTS predicate, the degree of the table expression is not important because it checks for existence of rows and returns TRUE if any row is returned from the subquery. The table expression cannot contain a GROUP BY clause or a HAVING clause or cannot reference a grouped view if a subquery is specified in a COMPARISON predicate. In addition, the keyword DISTINCT can be specified only once in a subquery, excluding any subquery contained in that subquery.

In the following example, two subqueries are used to list the name, employee number, salary, and department number of the employees having the highest salary in their department:

```
SELECT    EName, EmpNo, Salary, DeptNo
FROM      Emp Outer
WHERE     DeptNo IN (
              SELECT    DeptNo
              FROM      Dept
              WHERE     Emp.DeptNo = Dept.DeptNo)
              AND       Salary = (
                      SELECT    MAX(Salary)
                      FROM      Emp Inner
                      WHERE     Outer.DeptNo = Inner.DeptNo )
```

The results are

EName	EmpNo	Salary	DeptNo
Kramer	2001	3000	10
Lowe	2002	3500	20
Tracy	2004	3100	30
Peterson	3001	6000	99

To list the name of a person who owns a property and earns $3,000, we execute the statement

```
SELECT    Name
FROM      Person
WHERE     Name IN(SELECT Owner FROM Property)
AND       Salary = 3000,
```

which results in

Name
John Smith

Select Target List

The syntax of the select target list is

```
<select target list> ::=
        <target specification>
        [{, <target specification>}...]
```

```
<target specification> ::=
                    <parameter specification>
         |          <variable specification>
```

If a select target list is specified, the table expression cannot include a GROUP BY or a HAVING clause and cannot identify a grouped view. The number of elements in the select list and the select target list must be the same, and the data type of the *i*-th element in the select list must be compatible with the data type of the *i*-th element in the select target list. In addition, the table expression can retrieve at most one row of data. If no data is retrieved, the SQLCODE parameter is set to +100. Otherwise, the retrieved data is assigned to the select target list. If the assignment succeeds, SQLCODE is set to zero. Otherwise, SQLCODE is set to a negative number. For example, the following SQL statement stores the Social Security Number of John Smith into the variable ClientID:

```
SELECT    Social Security #
INTO      ClientID INDICATOR :CIndicator
FROM      Clients
WHERE     Name = 'John Smith'
```

As a result, the variable ClientID is set to 10, and the variable indicator CIndicator is set to zero. SQLCODE is also set to zero.

UNION Clause

The UNION clause is used to derive a result table by combining rows from two tables. The number of returned columns should be the same in both tables. Moreover, the data type of each corresponding columns in the two tables must be compatible. If the ALL keyword is specified, then all rows that are in either of the two tables are included in the result. Otherwise, any duplicate rows are eliminated from the result. All columns in the resultant table are unnamed. In the example that follows, the UNION ALL clause is used to retrieve all the department names in both the Dept and the StdSalary table:

```
SELECT    DeptName
FROM      Dept
UNION ALL
SELECT    DeptName
FROM      StdSalary
```

The results are

DeptName
Human Resource
Human Resource
Sales
Sales
Accounting
Accounting
Security
Customer Support
Technician
President
President
Janitor

In the next example, the UNION clause is used to retrieve all the department names in both the Dept and the StdSalary table. Since the ALL keyword is not specified, any duplicates are eliminated.

```
SELECT    DeptName
FROM      Dept
UNION
SELECT    DeptName
FROM      StdSalary
```

This produces the following list:

DeptName
Human Resource
Sales
Accounting
Security
Customer Support
Technician
President
Janitor

ORDER BY Clause

The ORDER BY clause is used to specify the ordering of rows in the retrieved result. The syntax of an ORDER BY clause is

```
<order by> ::=        ORDER BY <sort specification list>

<sort specification> ::=

        { <unsigned integer> | <column specification> } [ ASC | DESC ]
```

A <sort specification> specifies a sort column and a direction. If the DESC keyword is specified, then the direction of the sort column is descending; otherwise, it is ascending. The order of the <sort specification> in the <sort specification list> determines the relative significance of the sort columns. The first specified sort column is the most significant, with each successively specified sort column being less significant.

If a column is specified in the <sort specification>, then that column must be a column in the specified FROM table list. If an unsigned integer is specified in the <sort specification>, then that integer must be greater than zero and not greater than the number of columns returned from the resultant set. The sort column is the column in the retrieved column list with the ordinal position specified by the <unsigned integer>. For example, to list department numbers in descending order, we execute the following SQL statement:

```
SELECT      *
FROM        Dept
ORDER BY    1 DESC
```

The resultant list is

DeptNo	DName	MinSalary	MaxSalary
99	President	5000	
40	Security	1000	3500
30	Accounting	2000	4500
20	Sales	1500	4300
10	Human Resource	1200	4000

Outer Join

An outer join is used to join two or more tables together. This convention returns all rows from one table that satisfy a specified condition, regardless of whether other tables contain matching rows. As a result, the outer join extends the result of a normal join by returning all the rows returned by the simple join as well as the rows from one table that do not match any row from the other tables. As outer join is not addressed in the ANSI SQL89 standard, its syntax and implementation vary from product to product. Basically, three types of outer join exist: (1) full outer join, (2) left outer join, and (3) right outer join.

Full outer join. A full outer join of two tables is performed by executing a normal join using the provided matching condition. For each row in the first table that satisfies the condition but does not match a row in the second table, a row containing the values of the columns in the first table and null values for columns in the second table is added to the query results. Then, for each row of the second table that satisfies the condition but does not match a row in the first table, a row containing the values of the columns in the second table and null values for columns in the first table is added to the query results.

For example, to select the department number and name of all the departments and the corresponding standard minimum and maximum salaries, we use a full outer join as follows:

```
SELECT    DeptNo, DName, StdMinSal, StdMaxSal
FROM      Dept, StdSalary
WHERE     Dept.DName *=* StdSalary.DeptName
```

This results in

DeptNo	DName	StdMinSal	StdMaxSal
10	Human Resource	1000	3000
20	Sales	1500	3500
30	Accounting	1800	3800
40	Security	Null	Null
99	President	5000	Null
Null	Customer Support	1700	3700
Null	Technician	2000	4500
Null	Janitor	2500	5000

Left outer join. A left outer join is performed by executing a normal join on two tables. Then for each row in the first table that satisfies the condition but does not match a row in the second table, a row containing the values of the columns in the first table and null values for columns in the second table is added to the query results.

For instance, to select the department number and name of all the departments and the corresponding standard minimum and maximum salaries, we use the following left outer join:

```
SELECT    DeptNo, DName, StdMinSal, StdMaxSal
FROM      Dept, StdSalary
WHERE     Dept.DName *= StdSalary.DeptName,
```

which produces

DeptNo	DName	StdMinSal	StdMaxSal
10	Human Resource	1000	3000
20	Sales	1500	3500
30	Accounting	1800	3800
40	Security	Null	Null
99	President	5000	Null

Right outer join. A right outer join of two tables is performed by executing a normal join on two tables. Then for each row in the second table that satisfies the condition but does not match a row in the first table, a row containing the values of the columns in the second table and null values for columns in the first table is added to the query results. In the example that follows, a right outer join is used to select the department number and name of all the departments and the corresponding standard minimum and maximum salaries.

```
SELECT    DeptNo, DName, StdMinSal, StdMaxSal
FROM      Dept, StdSalary
WHERE     Dept.DName =* StdSalary.DeptName
```

The results are

DeptNo	DName	StdMinSal	StdMaxSal
10	Human Resource	1000	3000
20	Sales	1500	3500
30	Accounting	1800	3800
99	President	5000	Null
Null	Customer Support	1700	3700
Null	Technician	2000	4500
Null	Janitor	2500	5000

Nested SELECT Statements

A search condition may be specified in the WHERE clause of a table expression and may reference a subquery in its predicate. A subquery is a special form of a SELECT statement, consisting of a result specification and a table expression. Therefore, a table expression that specifies a search condition with a subquery may contain another table expression, which in turn may contain another table expression. In other words, a SELECT statement may be nested with multiple subqueries one inside the other. This type of statement is referred to as a *nested SELECT* statement.

Because of the recursive nature of the SELECT statement, SQL is capable of constructing complex queries. For instance, to select the name and department number of all employees in departments having a minimum salary less than or equal to the standard minimum salary, we have the following nested SELECT statement:

```
SELECT DISTINCT   EName, DeptNo
FROM              Emp
WHERE             DeptNo IN (
            SELECT    DeptNo
            FROM      Dept
            WHERE     MinSalary <= (
                  SELECT    StdMinSal
                  FROM      StdSalary
                  WHERE     DName = DeptName))
```

The results are

EName	DeptNo
Brown	20
Green	20
Lowe	20
Peterson	99

4.2.3 DELETE Statement

The DELETE statement deletes all those rows in the specified table that satisfy the specified search condition. The syntax of the DELETE statement is as follows:

```
<delete statement: searched> ::=
        DELETE FROM <table name>
        [ WHERE <search condition> ]
```

The table specified in the DELETE statement must be updatable. Moreover, it must not be a table identified in the FROM clause of any subquery contained in the search condition. An optional WHERE clause can be used to determine the rows to be deleted. If a WHERE clause is not specified in a DELETE statement, then all rows in the specified table are removed. For example, to delete the Customer Support department, a WHERE clause is specified:

```
DELETE FROM     Dept
WHERE           DName = "Customer Support"
```

As a result, only those rows with DName equal to Customer Support are removed.

On the other hand, all the employees in the employee table are deleted in the next example because no WHERE clause is specified:

```
DELETE FROM     Dept
```

4.2.4 UPDATE Statement

The UPDATE statement updates rows in the specified table that satisfy the specified search condition. The syntax of the UPDATE statement is

```
<update statement: searched> ::=
        UPDATE <table name>
        SET <set clause:searched>
            [ {, <set clause:searched> } ... ]
        [WHERE <search condition> ]

<set clause:searched> ::=
        <column name> =
            { <value expression> | NULL }
```

The table specified in the UPDATE statement must be updatable. Moreover, that table must not be a table identified in the FROM clause of any subquery contained in the search condition. If the specified table is a view with the WITH CHECK OPTION specification, then the update must conform to the view-defining condition.

Each column name specified in the <set clause:searched> clause must be unique and must be a column of the specified table. The column data type and the corresponding value must be compatible. Moreover, the value expression of a SET clause cannot contain a set function specification. The SET clauses are executed in parallel. Thus, in the following example, the MinSalary and MaxSalary values are swapped:

```
UPDATE    Dept
SET       MinSalary = MaxSalary,
          MaxSalary = MinSalary
```

An optional WHERE clause can be specified to select the rows to be updated. If no WHERE clause is specified in an UPDATE statement, then every row in the specified table is updated. For instance, to change the department name and department number for the Customer Support department, a WHERE clause is specified:

```
UPDATE    Dept
SET       DName = "Customer Service",
          DeptNo = 70
WHERE     DName = "Customer Support"
```

Alternatively, the WHERE clause is not specified in the UPDATE statement that follows. Therefore, the UPDATE applies to every row in the specified table. As a result, the sale price of every property is increased by 20%.

```
UPDATE    Properties
SET       SalePrice= SalePrice*1.2
```

4.3 The Treatment of Nulls

In SQL, a value has no logical subdivision and is either a null or a non-null value. A non-null value can be a character string or a number. A null value is distinct from all non-null values; it represents an “unknown” or a “not applicable” value.

There is no logical representation of a null value. If a null value is specified in a SQL statement, the keyword NULL is used.

If a null value is to be assigned to a table column, the column must be allowed to contain null values. If a null value is assigned to a host variable, the associated indicator variable is set to -1. For a non-null value in a host variable, the indicator variable, if present, is set to zero.

4.3.1 Three-valued Logic

The null value creates a three-valued logic for SQL search conditions. For any given row, the result of a search condition may be TRUE, FALSE, or NULL. Whenever one of the columns used in evaluating the search condition contains a null value, the result of the search condition is NULL.

The truth tables for AND, OR, and NOT in three-valued logic are presented in Figure 4.1, where T = TRUE, F = FALSE, and U = UNKNOWN or NULL.

AND	T	F	U
T	T	F	U
F	F	F	F
U	U	F	U

OR	T	F	U
T	T	T	T
F	T	F	U
U	T	U	U

NOT	T	F	U
	F	T	U

Figure 4.1: *Truth tables for AND, OR, and NOT with NULL(U) values.*

SQL provides a special null value test to determine whether the result of a search condition is NULL. The syntax for the NULL predicate is

<column name> IS [NOT] NULL

If NOT is not specified, the result of the predicate is TRUE if the value referenced in the column is NULL. Otherwise, the result of the predicate is FALSE.

Apart from the NULL predicate, comparing a null value with any value, even with another null value, always returns the unknown value. Therefore, we cannot test for a NULL value using a simple comparison search condition such as COL1 = NULL.

Even if the comparison test is syntactically correct, the rules for handling NULL values in comparison conditions cause the test to behave differently than the user might expect. For instance, if SQL encountered a row where the COL1 column was NULL, the search condition would result in NULL = NULL.

Because the values on both sides of the equal sign are unknown, the rules of SQL logic evaluate the result as NULL. Since the search condition does not produce a TRUE value, the row is excluded from the query results. This result is different from the equality comparison for non-null values. Thus, to test for NULL values, we use the NULL predicate COL1 is NULL.

4.3.2 SQL Access Implicit (System) Comparisons

Null values and non-null values are handled differently in system-generated comparisons. For example,

- If a unique index is specified on a column that can contain null values, all null values are considered equal and more than one null value is allowed in that column.
- In the GROUP BY clause, null grouping column values are considered equal.
- In the ORDER BY clause, null values are equal and are either greater than or less than all non-null values.
- In the SELECT DISTINCT context, all null values are considered equal.
- In the set functions evaluation, null values are eliminated regardless of whether the DISTINCT option is specified (except that COUNT(*) counts all the rows in a table including all null values).

4.4 Case Studies

The remainder of this chapter is devoted to an examination of the syntax and semantics of the noncursor operation SQL statements in the IBM OS/2 Extended Edition, ORACLE Server, DEC Rdb/VMS, and Microsoft SQL Server.

4.4.1 IBM OS/2 Extended Edition Database Manager

With the IBM OS/2 Extended Edition, for each table referenced in a SELECT statement, the user must have at least one of the following access privileges: SYSADM authority, DBADM authority, CONTROL privilege, or SELECT privilege.

Additionally, to execute the INSERT, DELETE, or UPDATE statement, the user must have at least one of the following privileges for the target table: SYSADM authority, DBADM authority, CONTROL privilege, or INSERT, DELETE, or UPDATE privilege in accordance with the type of SQL statement.

INSERT Statement

The IBM Extended Edition INSERT statement is syntactically and semantically the same as the ANSI SQL89 standard.

With the enforcement of referential integrity, for each constraint defined on a table, each non-null insert value of the foreign key must match a primary key value of the parent table.

SELECT Statement

In the IBM Extended Edition, a SELECT statement is composed of a fullselect and an optional ORDER BY clause, an optional UPDATE clause, or an optional FETCH clause. A *fullselect* consists of a subselect and an optional set operator followed by a subselect or a fullselect. In addition to supporting the ANSI SQL89 standard UNION operator, the EXCEPT and INTERSECT operators are supported by this server. The set operators UNION, EXCEPT, and INTERSECT correspond to the relational operators union, difference, and intersection. The syntax of the IBM Extended Edition SELECT statement is

```
<select statement> ::=
        <fullselect>
            [     <order by clause> [ <fetch clause> ]
```

```
                |       <update clause>
                |       <fetch clause> ]
    <fullselect> ::=
            { <subselect> | ( <fullselect> ) }
            [ { { INTERSECT | EXCEPT | UNION }
                [ ALL ]
                { <subselect> | ( <fullselect> ) }
            } ...]
```

The set operators are used to derive a result table by combining two result tables. A UNION operation results in all rows that are in either of the two tables; an EXCEPT operation results in all rows that are in the first table but not in the second; and an INTERSECT operation results in all rows that are in both tables. Duplicate rows are removed from the result table unless the ALL option is specified. Operations within parentheses are performed first. If no parentheses are specified in the query, the operations are performed from left to right with the exception of INTERSECT operations, which are performed before the UNION or EXCEPT operations.

For example, to select the name of all the departments in either the Dept or the StdSalary table, we use a UNION operator as follows:

```
SELECT    DName
FROM      Dept
UNION
SELECT    DeptName
FROM      StdSalary
```

The results are

DName
Human Resource
Sales
Accounting
Security
President
Customer Support
Technician
Janitor

In the next example, an EXCEPT operator is used to select the name of all the departments that are in the Dept table but not in the StdSalary table:

```
SELECT   DName
FROM     Dept
EXCEPT
SELECT   DeptName
FROM     StdSalary
```

The result is

DName

Security

And, to select the name of all the departments in both the Dept and the StdSalary tables, we use the INTERSECT operator and execute the following SQL statement:

```
SELECT   DName
FROM     Dept
INTERSECT
SELECT   DeptName
FROM     StdSalary
```

The results are

DName

Human Resource

Sales

Accounting

President

Customer Support

Technician

Janitor

FETCH Clause

The syntax of an IBM Extended Edition FETCH clause is as follows:

```
<fetch clause> ::=
        FOR FETCH ONLY
```

The FETCH clause designates that the cursor is for fetch only. Therefore, no UPDATE or DELETE statements should reference the specified cursor. The FETCH clause is not supported in the ANSI SQL.

As an example, to list the name and employee number of all the employees in Department 30 in descending order of employee number, we execute the SQL statement below. It should be noted that the FETCH clause is specified to signal that the cursor associated with this SELECT statement is not updatable.

```
SELECT     EName, EmpNo
FROM       Emp
WHERE      DeptNo = 30
ORDER BY   EmpNo DESC
FOR FETCH ONLY
```

The results are

EName	EmpNo
Tracy	2004
Morton	2003
Taylor	1007
Bays	1006
White	1005

UPDATE Clause

The syntax of an IBM Extended Edition UPDATE clause is

```
<update clause> ::=
        FOR UPDATE OF <column name> [ {, <column name> }... ]
```

The UPDATE clause allows a cursor UPDATE statement to refer to a list of specified columns. Only those columns specified can be updated by the cursor UPDATE statement. Moreover, the columns specified must be columns of the table or view identified in the FROM clause of the fullselect.

The UPDATE clause cannot be used if the result table is read only or if the FROM clause of the SELECT statement identifies a system table. The UPDATE clause is not supported in the ANSI SQL.

For example, to select the names and employee numbers of all the employees, an IBM Extended Edition UPDATE clause is used. Note that the UPDATE clause is specified to signal that the cursor associated with this SELECT statement is updatable, that is, the salary and manager can be updated by the cursor.

```
SELECT              EName, EmpNo
FROM                Emp
WHERE               DeptNo = 30
FOR UPDATE OF       Salary, Mgr
```

The results are

EName	EmpNo
White	1005
Bays	1006
Taylor	1007
Morton	2003
Tracy	2004

Search Condition

The syntax for the COMPARISON predicate, the IN predicate, and the EXISTS predicate are similar to the ANSI SQL89 standard. However, in ANSI SQL89, the predicate specifies the subquery rather than the fullselect.

In the IBM Extended Edition, a fullselect referenced in the predicate must return only one column; this is the case with the ANSI SQL89 standard as well. However, a fullselect in the IBM Extended Edition may be composed of two or more subselects related by set operators; a subquery in the ANSI SQL89 standard cannot contain a set operator.

In the example that follows, a subquery containing an INTERSECT operator is used with an IBM Extended Edition IN predicate to select the name and department number for all departments that are in both the Dept and the Emp tables:

```
SELECT    DName, DeptNo
FROM      Dept
WHERE     DeptNo IN (   SELECT      DeptNo
                        FROM        Emp
                        INTERSECT
                        SELECT      DeptNo
                        FROM        Dept)
```

The results are

DName	DeptNo
Human Resource	10
Sales	20
Accounting	30
President	99

The IBM Extended Edition does not support the ANSI SQL89 standard ESCAPE clause in the LIKE predicate.

Value Expression

In the IBM Extended Edition, scalar functions are supported in addition to the set functions. Scalar functions are specific to the IBM Extended Edition and are not specified in the ANSI SQL89 standard. A scalar function can be used whenever an expression can be used.

The special registers CURRENT DATE, CURRENT TIME, and CURRENT TIMESTAMP are not supported in the ANSI SQL89 standard. In the example that follows, an IBM Extended Edition CURRENT DATE keyword is used to select today's date:

```
SELECT    EName, HiredDate, CURRENT DATE,
FROM      Emp
WHERE     LENGTH(EName) < 5
```

The results are

EName	HiredDate	CURRENT DATE
Bays	8/1/88	1/1/99
Lowe	5/1/89	1/1/99

SELECT INTO Statement

The SELECT INTO statement selects at most one row of data and assigns the retrieved values to host variables. This statement can only be embedded in an application program.

The data type of the host variable must be compatible with the retrieved value. If an error occurs as a result of an arithmetic expression or a numeric conversion in the SELECT INTO list, no value is assigned to the host variable or to later variables, although any values that have already been assigned to variables remain assigned. For example, to select Smith and his employee number into the program variables emp_name and emp_number, we use an IBM Extended Edition SELECT INTO statement as follows:

```
SELECT   EName, EmpNo
INTO     :emp_name, :emp_number
FROM     Emp
WHERE    EName = 'Smith'
```

As a result, the program variable emp_name contains the value 'Smith' and emp_number contains the value 1001.

DELETE Statement

The IBM Extended Edition DELETE statement may specify a correlation name, which can be used within the search condition to designate the table. In the following example, a correlation name is used in the DELETE statement to remove all the departments from the Dept table that are also in the StdSalary table:

```
DELETE   FROM Peterson.Dept Department
WHERE    DName IN
         (SELECT DeptName FROM StdSalary
         WHERE Department.DName = DeptName)
```

If the specified table is a parent, the rows selected for deletion must not have any dependents in a relationship with a delete rule of RESTRICT. The delete operation also must not cascade to descendent rows that are parent rows in a relationship with a delete rule of RESTRICT.

UPDATE Statement

The IBM Extended Edition UPDATE statement may also specify a correlation name, which may be used within the search condition to designate the table. Consider the following example of an IBM Extended Edition UPDATE statement:

```
UPDATE   Emp
SET      Salary = Salary *1.1
WHERE    DeptNo IN
         (SELECT DeptNo FROM StdSalary
         WHERE DeptName = "Sales"
AND      Emp.DeptNo = StdSalary.DeptNo
```

The UPDATE statement must not change the primary key value. If a column to be updated is part of a primary key, then only one row should be selected for update. Also a non-null update value of a foreign key must be equal to a value of the primary key of the parent table.

4.4.2 ORACLE Server

In the ORACLE Server, a subquery can return more than one column. Therefore, a multicolumn nested SELECT and a multicolumn UPDATE statement are supported.

INSERT Statement

The INSERT statement in the ORACLE Server is similar to the ANSI SQL89 INSERT statement except that the target table may be referenced in a subquery. Consider the following example of an ORACLE INSERT statement, which adds minimum and maximum salary to departments if the minimum and maximum salary information is missing:

```
INSERT INTO     Dept (MinSalary, MaxSalary)
        SELECT  StdMinSal, StdMaxSal
        FROM    StdSalary
        WHERE   DeptName IN (
                SELECT  DName
                FROM    Dept
                WHERE   MinSalary IS NULL
                AND     MaxSalary IS NULL)
```

SELECT Statement

In the ORACLE Server, a SELECT statement can retrieve any number of records. SELECT in the ORACLE Server is similar to the DECLARE CURSOR statement in the ANSI SQL89 standard, except that SELECT works interactively. The syntax of an ORACLE SELECT statement is as follows:

```
<fullselect statement> ::=
        <select statement>
        [{ <select operator> <select statement> }...]
        [ORDER BY <order by list>]
        [FOR UPDATE OF <column name list> [NOWAIT] ]
```

The UPDATE clause in the SELECT statement locks the selected rows of the tables. Once the rows are locked, other users cannot update them until the locks arc released by a COMMIT or ROLLBACK statement. The UPDATE clause is not supported in the ANSI SQL89 standard.

With the NOWAIT clause specified in a SELECT statement, if the rows selected by the UPDATE clause cannot be locked because they are in use, the SELECT statement will terminate instead of waiting until the lock request succeeds. NOWAIT is not supported in the ANSI SQL89 standard.

The following is the list of ORACLE select operators:

```
<select operator> ::=
        {UNION | INTERSECT | MINUS}
```

In the ORACLE Server, the keyword ALL is not supported in the UNION operation. Rather, the INTERSECT and MINUS operators are used to combine the results of two SELECT commands into a single result. INTERSECT returns the results existing in both the SELECT commands, and MINUS returns the results retrieved in the first but not the second SELECT. Neither the INTERSECT nor the MINUS operators is supported in the ANSI SQL89 standard.

Select List

The select list in the ORACLE Server and the ANSI SQL89 standard consists of either a wildcard (*) or a list of expressions. However, in ORACLE a table name can be used to qualify the wildcard (*) and an optional alias can be used to specify an expression. If an expression has an alias, that alias will be displayed as the column heading of the expression.

For example, to select all columns in the Dept table and the employee name such that the department number in the Dept table is the same as the department number of an employee whose employee number is 1001, we execute the following SQL statement:

```
SELECT    Dept.*, EName EmployeeName
FROM      Dept, Emp
WHERE     Dept.DeptNo = Emp.DeptNo
AND       EmpNo = 1001
```

In the result, EmployeeName is displayed as the column heading for EName:

DeptNo	DName	MinSalary	MaxSalary	EmployeeName
10	Human Resource	1200	4000	Smith

In the ORACLE Server, the optional CONNECT BY clause following the WHERE clause can be specified in a SELECT statement with the following syntax:

```
<connect clause> ::=
        CONNECT BY
        {  PRIOR {<expression> <operator> <expression> |
           <expression> <operator> PRIOR <expression> }
        [START WITH <search condition>]
```

The CONNECT BY clause specifies that rows are retrieved in a tree-structured hierarchical order. The condition supplied to the CONNECT BY clause is used to define the relationship used to connect table rows into a tree [Oracle, 1989b, p. B-80]. The optional START WITH clause specifies a condition that identifies the row(s) used as the root(s) of the tree. If there is no START WITH clause, SELECT returns a series of trees starting with each selected row.

The PRIOR operator is used to define the parent-child relationship in the tree-structured query. The parent is represented by the expression after the PRIOR keyword, and the child is represented by the expression before the keyword. The CONNECT BY clause and the concept of a tree-structured query is not supported in the ANSI SQL89 standard.

In our next example, an ORACLE CONNECT BY clause is used to select the hierarchical structure of the Peterson's company:

```
SELECT              EName Employee, EmpNo Number,
                    Mgr Manager, DeptNo
FROM                Emp
CONNECT BY PRIOR    EmpNo = Mgr
START WITH          DeptNo = 99
```

The results are

Employee	Number	Manager	DeptNo
Peterson	3001		99
Lowe	2002	3001	20
Brown	1003	2002	20
Green	1004	2002	20

Kramer	2001	2002	10
Smith	1001	2001	10
Jones	1002	2001	10
Morton	2003	3001	30
White	1005	2003	30
Tracy	2004	3001	30
Bays	1006	2004	30
Taylor	1007	2004	30

Subquery

In the ORACLE Server, a subquery is similar to a SELECT command except that the retrieved rows are not displayed, but rather, they are fed back into the surrounding SQL command. The ORDER BY and FOR UPDATE OF clauses cannot be used in a subquery in ORACLE. This limitation is also true of the ANSI SQL89 standard. However, the CONNECT BY clause is acceptable in the ORACLE subquery, but not in the ANSI SQL89 standard. Moreover, a subquery in the ORACLE Server can return more than one column of values. The select list of a subquery and the select list of a SELECT statement are syntactically the same.

Value Expression

In the ANSI SQL89 standard set functions, if the keyword DISTINCT is specified, only a column name can be used as an argument. In the ORACLE Server, the argument of a set function can be an expression even if the keyword DISTINCT is specified. Furthermore, in ORACLE, the COUNT(<expression>) function accepts an optional ALL keyword, but in the ANSI SQL89 standard, the ALL keyword is not acceptable in a COUNT function. Besides supporting the set functions, the ORACLE Server supports a set of built-in arithmetic, string, group, date, and special functions.

For example, to select the number of distinct department numbers in the Employee table, we execute the SQL statement below. (Note: In ORACLE, the argument of a set function can be an expression even if the keyword DISTINCT is specified.)

```
SELECT   COUNT(DISTINCT DeptNo+10)
         "Total Number of Departments"
FROM     Emp
```

The result is

Total Number of Departments
4

In the ANSI SQL89 standard, a value specification includes a parameter, variable, literal, and USER. In the ORACLE Server, an expression cannot contain substitution variables. However, besides USER, the pseudocolumns ROWID, ROWNUM, SYSDATE, LEVEL, and UID are valid entries of the SELECT clause. For example, to select the SYSDATE, the last day of this month, and the name and department number of Smith, we have the following SQL statement:

```
SELECT    SYSDATE Today,
          LAST_DAY(SYSDATE) "Last Day of this Month",
          EName Name, DeptNo Department,
FROM      Emp
WHERE     EName = 'Smith'
```

The result is

Today	Last Day of this Month	Name	Department
01-JAN-99	31	Smith	10

Search Condition

In the ORACLE Server, the NOT EQUAL operator can be represented as !=, ^=, or <>. In the ANSI SQL89 standard, only the <> representation is valid. The BETWEEN, IN, NULL, and EXISTS predicates are used in the same manner in both the ANSI SQL89 standard and ORACLE. However, in ORACLE, the LIKE predicate does not support an optional ESCAPE clause, and the quantified predicate does not support the keyword SOME.

Consider the following example of a search condition in ORACLE. To select the department number of the employees with department number not equal to 10, we execute

```
SELECT    DISTINCT      DeptNo "Department Number"
FROM      Emp
WHERE     DeptNo ^= 10
```

The results are

Department Number
20
30
99

Outer Join

In the ORACLE Server, the outer join operator (+) must follow a column reference within a join condition. In addition, an outer join must contain a WHERE clause with a condition in the following format:

<table1.column> (+) = <table2.column>   (Right Outer Join)

OR

<table1.column> = <table2.column> (+)   (Left Outer Join)

Extra "null" column values are created temporarily for the table with the outer join operator. These values are joined against all rows from the other table so that all rows in the other table are returned. For example, to select the department number and name of all the departments in the Dept table, and to select the corresponding standard minimum and maximum salaries, we use the following ORACLE outer join statement:

```
SELECT    DeptNo, DName, StdMinSal, StdMaxSal
FROM      Dept, StdSalary
WHERE     Dept.DName = StdSalary.DeptName (+)
```

The results are

DeptNo	DName	StdMinSal	StdMaxSal
10	Human Resource	1000	3000
20	Sales	1500	3500
30	Accounting	1800	3800
40	Security	Null	Null
99	President	5000	Null

To select the department number and name of all the departments, and to select the corresponding standard minimum and maximum salaries, we execute the following SQL statement:

```
SELECT    DeptNo, DName, StdMinSal, StdMaxSal
FROM      Dept, StdSalary
WHERE     Dept.DName (+) = StdSalary.DeptName
```

The results are

DeptNo	DName	StdMinSal	StdMaxSal
10	Human Resource	1000	3000
20	Sales	1500	3500
30	Accounting	1800	3800
99	President	5000	Null
Null	Customer Support	1700	3700
Null	Technician	2000	4500
Null	Janitor	2500	5000

Multicolumn Nested SELECT

In the ORACLE Server, a condition may be a comparison with any or all members in a list or a query. A query in the ORACLE Server is the same as a SELECT statement. Therefore, multiple columns can be specified in the select list of a query, and multicolumn nested SELECT statements are supported. For example, to select all the departments with both the minimum and maximum salary higher than the standard, we execute the following multicolumn nested SELECT statement:

```
SELECT   DName
FROM     Dept
WHERE    (MinSalary, MaxSalary) > (
         SELECT   StdMinSal, StdMaxSal
         FROM     StdSalary
         WHERE    DeptName = DName)
```

The results are

DName
Human Resource
Accounting

DELETE Statement

The DELETE statement in the ORACLE Server is similar to the ANSI SQL89 standard except that the search condition may reference the target table. Moreover, an alias for the target table may be specified, as shown in the following example:

```
DELETE FROM    Emp Outer
WHERE          EmpNo IN (
               SELECT  Mgr
               FROM    Emp Inner, Dept
               WHERE   Inner.Salary = Dept.MinSalary)
```

As a result, any manager with workers earning minimum salary are removed.

UPDATE Statement

The ORACLE Server has two forms of UPDATE statement. One form is compatible with the ANSI SQL89 UPDATE statement, except that an optional alias can be specified for the target table. The other form of UPDATE statement, which is not supported in ANSI SQL89, has the following syntax:

```
<update statement: searched> ::=
        UPDATE <table name> <alias>
        SET ( <set clause: subquery> [ {, <set clause: subquery> } ... ]
        [ WHERE <search condition> ]
<set clause: subquery> ::=
        ( <column> [ {, <column> } ...] )
            = ( <query> )
```

In the above statement, a subquery may be used to update the values of the specified columns. If the SET clause contains a subquery, then the subquery must return exactly one row for each row being updated. If no rows are returned, then the value will be set to NULL. The SET clause may intermix assignments of expressions and subqueries. Both the subquery and the search condition may reference the target table.

The following example uses a subquery to perform a multicolumn update:

```
UPDATE    Dept
SET       (MinSalary, MaxSalary) = (
                    SELECT  StdMinSal, StdMaxSal
                    FROM    StdSalary
                    WHERE   DeptName = DName),
```

```
                DeptNo = DeptNo - 5
        WHERE   DeptNo = (
                        SELECT  MIN(DeptNo)
                        FROM    Dept)
```

As a result, the minimum salary, maximum salary, and department number of the lowest department number in the department table are modified.

4.4.3 DEC Rdb/VMS

The SQL extension supported in DEC's Rdb/VMS is similar to the ANSI SQL89 standard. All the features supported in ANSI are supported in the Rdb/VMS. In addition, the Rdb/VMS supports some scalar functions, arithmetic operations, special registers, and predicates that are not supported in the ANSI SQL89 standard.

INSERT Statement

The syntax of the Rdb/VMS INSERT statement is

```
<insert statement> ::=
        INSERT INTO <table name>
            [ ( <insert column list> ) ]
        { VALUES ( <insert value list> )
            [ RETURNING DBKEY [INTO <parameter>] ]
        | <query specification> }
  |
        INSERT INTO CURSOR <cursor name>
        VALUES ( <insert value list> )
```

In the above statement, the RETURNING DBKEY clause is used to return the database key (DBKEY) value of a newly inserted record. This clause is used with the insertion of a single row of data. When the DBKEY value is valid, subsequent queries can use the DBKEY to access the record directly. The RETURNING DBKEY clause is specific to Rdb and not supported in the ANSI SQL89 standard.

In this example, to add a department to the StdSalary table, a Rdb INSERT statement is used:

```
INSERT INTO              StdSalary
VALUES                   ("Quality Control", 800, 2500)
RETURNING DBKEY INTO     :dbkey
```

As a result, one row is inserted, and the DBKEY of the newly inserted row is stored in the dbkey program variable.

An INSERT statement with a cursor can be used to assign values to a column of the LIST OF BYTE VARYING data type. In this case, the column name list and the RETURNING DBKEY clause must be omitted, and no <query specification> should be specified in the INSERT statement. This form of INSERT statement is not supported in the ANSI SQL89 standard.

As an example, let us assume that the Dept table has an additional column, JobDescription, of LIST OF BYTE VARYING data type. First, we declare a TabCursor cursor for inserting the department name and job description into the Dept table. Next, we declare a ListCursor cursor for inserting JobDescription into the department table based on the current position of the TabCursor. We then open the TabCursor. We use the Rdb INSERT CURSOR statement to add an advertising department to the TabCursor, and then open the ListCursor. Finally, we use the Rdb INSERT CURSOR statement to add a job description to the JobDescription column of the Dept table using the ListCursor. The inserted value describes the advertising department. The sequence of Rdb/VMS SQL statements are as follows:

```
DECLARE   TabCursor INSERT ONLY TABLE CURSOR
FOR       SELECT       DName, JobDescription
          FROM         Dept;
DECLARE   ListCursor INSERT ONLY LIST CURSOR
FOR       SELECT       JobDescription
          WHERE        CURRENT OF TabCursor;
OPEN TabCursor;
INSERT INTO CURSOR     TabCursor (DName)
VALUES                 ("Advertising");
OPEN ListCursor;
INSERT INTO CURSOR     ListCursor
VALUES                 ("Promote the new line of products");
```

As a result, a row containing data of LIST OF BYTE VARYING data type is inserted.

SELECT Statement

The syntax of the Rdb/VMS SELECT statement is

```
<select statement> ::=
        <select expression>
        [ ORDER BY <order by column list> ]
    [ LIMIT TO <row limit> ROWS ]
```

In the above statement, the LIMIT TO clause specifies the number of rows in the result table. If the row limits specified by the LIMIT TO clause is greater than the number of resulting rows, all the retrieved rows are returned and no error message is generated. The LIMIT TO clause is not supported in the ANSI SQL89 standard.

Consider the following example of a Rdb/VMS SELECT statement with the LIMIT TO clause:

```
SELECT          Emp.EName
FROM            Emp
WHERE           DeptNo = 10
LIMIT TO 1 ROW
```

As a result, one employee in department 10 is displayed:

```
Emp.EName
Smith
```

Search Condition

Predicates in Rdb/VMS search conditions are similar to those of ANSI SQL89. However, Rdb/VMS supports several additional search predicates: CONTAINING, LIKE, STARTING WITH, and UNIQUE.

The syntax of the Rdb/VMS CONTAINING predicate is as follows:

```
<containing predicate> ::=
        <value expression> [NOT] CONTAINING
                <value expression>
```

The CONTAINING predicate tests whether a second string expression is found within the first string expression. The CONTAINING predicate is case insensitive. In the following example, a CONTAINING clause is used to select the name of all property owners whose name contains the 'MITH' string:

```
SELECT   Owner
FROM     Property
WHERE    Name CONTAINING 'MITH'
```

The result is

Owner

John Smith

In Rdb/VMS the LIKE predicate accepts the IGNORE CASE clause to perform case insensitive comparisons. The ESCAPE clause and the IGNORE CASE clause cannot be specified in the same Boolean expression. For instance, to select the name of all employees whose name contains the 'MITH' string, we execute the following SQL statement:

```
SELECT   EName
FROM     Emp
WHERE    EName LIKE '%MITH%' IGNORE CASE
```

The result is

EName

Smith

The syntax of the STARTING WITH predicate is

```
<starting with predicate> ::=
        <value expression> [NOT] STARTING WITH
                <value expression>
```

The STARTING WITH predicate tests whether the first characters of the first value expression match those specified in the second value expression. The STARTING WITH predicate is case sensitive. In the example that follows, the STARTING WITH clause is used to select the name of all property owners whose name begins with the 'Jo' string:

```
SELECT   Owner
FROM     Property
WHERE    Owner STARTING WITH 'Jo'
```

The result is

```
Owner
John Smith
```

The syntax of the Rdb/VMS UNIQUE predicate is as follows:

```
<unique predicate> ::=
        UNIQUE ( <column select expression>)
```

The UNIQUE predicate tests whether the result table specified in the column select expression has exactly one row. An asterisk wildcard in the column select expression that refers to a multicolumn table is acceptable to a UNIQUE predicate because it only checks for the existence of rows. In this example, a UNIQUE predicate is used to select the managers who manage only one employee:

```
SELECT   Mgr
FROM     Emp Outer
WHERE    UNIQUE (SELECT EmpNo
                 FROM Emp Inner
                 WHERE Inner.Mgr = Outer.EmpNo)
```

The result is

```
Mgr
2003
```

Value Expression

A Rdb/VMS value expression is similar to that of the ANSI SQL89 standard. There are, however, several notable differences. First, the DBKEY keyword, which represents the value of an internal pointer to a table row, is supported in Rdb. In addition, Rdb supports the SUBSTRING function. And lastly, a string concatenation operator || is supported in Rdb. This operator is used to link two value expressions of data type CHAR, VARCHAR, or LONG VARCHAR.

In the following example, the SUBSTRING function and the string concatenation operator are used in the Rdb/VMS value expressions:

```
SELECT   EName, 'is of department: ' || DeptNo
FROM     Emp
WHERE    SUBSTRING(EName FROM 1 FOR 3) LIKE 'Smi%'
```

The result is

ENname	is of department: DeptNo
Smith	is of department: 10

DELETE and UPDATE Statements

The DELETE and UPDATE statements in Rdb/VMS are similar to the ANSI SQL89 standard DELETE and UPDATE statements except that a correlation name for the target table may be specified in Rdb.

4.4.4 Microsoft SQL Server

The version of SQL supported in the Microsoft SQL Server is called TRANSACT-SQL. TRANSACT-SQL can be executed interactively using the utility program isql. In isql, each batch of TRANSACT-SQL commands must be terminated by an end-of-batch signal, which is the go command on a line by itself. Consider this example of an interactive isql section:

```
SELECT EName FROM Emp
SELECT DName FROM Dept
go
```

As a result, the names of all the employees are displayed; then, the names of all the departments are displayed.

TRANSACT-SQL can be embedded in a program. It does not require a statement terminator. The dbcmd( ) routine is used to add text to the command buffer. The user can call dbcmd( ) repeatedly to store a batch of commands in the command buffer. Since the dbcmd( ) routine concatenates text to the existing buffer, a blank must appear between the end of one line and the beginning of the next to prevent the two lines from running together. The dbsqlexec( ) routine is used to send a batch of commands to the SQL Server. The dbcmd( ) and dbsqlexec( ) routine calls are illustrated in this example:

```
dbcmd(dbProc, "SELECT EName FROM Emp");
dbcmd(dbProc, "SELECT DName FROM Dept");
dbsqlexec(dbProc);
```

This results in the sequential execution of both of the SELECT statements.

In TRANSACT-SQL, an optional database name and owner name can be specified to fully qualify a table. In the next example, the table name and column name are fully qualified with the database name and owner name:

```
SELECT   Confidential.Peterson.Emp.EmpNo
FROM     Confidential.Peterson.Emp
WHERE    Confidential.Peterson.Emp.EName = 'Smith'
```

The result is

EmpNo
1001

Trigger

In TRANSACT-SQL, a trigger is a stored procedure associated with a particular table. It is used to enforce the referential integrity on tables. Three kinds of triggers are supported by TRANSACT-SQL: an INSERT trigger, which is executed when a row is inserted; an UPDATE trigger, which is executed when data is modified; and a DELETE trigger, which is executed when a row is deleted.

A table can be associated with at most three triggers. Moreover, only one of each (INSERT, UPDATE, or DELETE) can be associated with a table. A trigger action is record oriented (instead of set oriented) and is executed after the update, delete, or insert action.

Two logical tables, *inserted* and *deleted,* can be referenced in a trigger for data manipulation. Structurally, the inserted and deleted tables are similar to the table on which the trigger is defined. During an INSERT or UPDATE action, the inserted table contains the newly inserted or updated data. During a DELETE action, the deleted table contains the current deleted data. A trigger can reference data in the inserted or deleted table to determine whether these data are valid and to perform the appropriate action. A trigger is not recursive; thus the result of one trigger cannot induce the execution of another trigger.

For example, the SQL statement that follows creates an INSERT and UPDATE trigger that enforces the referential integrity on the DeptNo column in the Emp and Dept tables. Whenever a DeptNo is inserted or updated in the Emp table, that DeptNo must be a valid department number in the Dept table.

```
CREATE ValidDeptNo TRIGGER ON EMP
FOR INSERT, UPDATE AS
IF NOT EXISTS
```

```
                (SELECT DeptNo FROM inserted
                WHERE DeptNo =
                (SELECT DeptNo FROM Dept))
        BEGIN
                Print("Invalid Department Number.")
        END
```

The next SQL statement is used to create a DELETE trigger that enforces the referential integrity on the DeptNo column in the Emp and Dept tables. Here, whenever a DeptNo is removed from the Dept table, that DeptNo must not be a DeptNo of any employee in the Emp table.

```
        CREATE EnforceDeptNo TRIGGER ON DEPT
        FOR DELETE AS
        IF EXISTS
                (SELECT DeptNo FROM deleted
                WHERE DeptNo IN
                (SELECT DeptNo FROM EMP) )
        BEGIN
                Print("Department number in use, cannot be deleted.")
        END
```

Due to the record-oriented nature of a trigger, it is difficult to maintain a unique sequence of numbers in a table using a trigger. In the following example, a trigger is created to maintain a unique sequence of EmpNo in the NewEmp table. (Note: The NewEmp table is similar to the Emp table, except that the NewEmp table has a timestamp column. A timestamp is unique and can be used to uniquely identify a record.)

```
    CREATE UniqueEmpNo TRIGGER ON NewEmp
    FOR INSERT AS
    DECLARE @curMaxNum int, @lastInsMinTS timestamp,
                    @insMinTS timestamp, @insRecNum int
    /*
    ** curMaxNum is the current maximum EmpNo in NewEmp.
    ** lastInsMinTS is the timestamp of the last modified record.
```

```
** insMinTS is the timestamp of the first inserted record.
** insRecNum is the total number of inserted records.
** In order to speed up the trigger action, the maximum integer value,
    ** 2147483647 is used as the inserted value of the EmpNo.
*/
        SELECT @lastInsMinTS=0x0
        SELECT @insRecNum = COUNT(*) FROM inserted
                    WHERE EmpNo = 2147483647
IF @insRecNum != 0
BEGIN
        /* Get the current maximum valid EmpNo from Emp. */
        SELECT @curMaxNum = ISNULL(MAX(EmpNo),0)
        FROM NewEmp
        WHERE EmpNo < 2147483647
        /* Update each newly inserted records. */
        WHILE @insRecNum > 0
                    BEGIN
                    /* Advance insMinTS to the next record to be update. */
                    SELECT @insMinTS = MIN(inserted.timestamp),
                            FROM inserted
                            WHERE inserted.timestamp > @lastInsMinTS
                    /* Get the EmpNo of the to be updated record. */
                    SELECT @curRecNum = inserted.EmpNo
                            FROM inserted
                            WHERE inserted.internal_timestamp =
                            @insMinTS
                    IF (@curRecNum = 2147483647)
                    BEGIN
                    /* Update the newly inserted record. */
                            UPDATE NewEmp
                            SET EmpNo = @curMaxNum+1
                            WHERE timestamp = @insMinTS
                            /* Advance the curMaxNum value. */
```

```
                    SELECT @curMax = @curMaxNum+1
                END
                SELECT @lastInsMinTS = @insMinTS
                SELECT @insRecNum = @insRecNum-1
        END     /* while loop */
    END
```

Whenever a record is inserted to the NewEmp table, the UniqueEmpNo trigger is executed. For instance, to insert records into the NewEmp table, we execute the following SQL statement:

```
    INSERT INTO     NewEmp
                    SELECT      2147483647, EName, DeptNo, Mgr,
                                Salary, HiredDate, null
                    FROM        Emp
```

In the above example, after the records have been inserted into the NewEmp table, the UniqueEmpNo trigger is executed for each record inserted. This maintains a unique sequence for the EmpNo column.

INSERT Statement

Minor syntactic differences exist between the TRANSACT-SQL and the ANSI SQL89 INSERT statement. In TRANSACT-SQL, the INTO keyword is optional, and the search condition in an INSERT statement may reference the target table. The following example shows a TRANSACT-SQL INSERT statement that does not have the INTO keyword and whose search condition references the target table Confidential Peterson Emp:

```
    INSERT  Confidential.Peterson.Emp (EName, DeptNo)
            SELECT      "ToBeHired", DeptNo
            FROM        Dept
            WHERE       DeptNo IN (
                SELECT  DeptNo
                FROM    Confidential.Peterson.Emp
                WHERE   Confidential.Peterson.Emp.Salary
                        <= Dept.MinSalary
                AND     Confidential.Peterson.Emp. DeptNo
                        = Dept.DeptNo)
```

As a result, for every employee whose salary is less than or equal to the minimum salary of the department, a new employee will be hired in the department.

TRANSACT-SQL also supports an insert trigger for a table. The trigger takes a specified action when an INSERT command is issued on that table. In addition, TRANSACT-SQL allows users to create and bind a rule to a column to restrict the domain of legal values in that column. A TRANSACT-SQL INSERT statement fails if it violates domain or integrity rules or if there are data type mismatches in the insert columns.

SELECT Statement

The syntax of a TRANSACT-SQL full SELECT statement is

```
<full select statement> ::=
        <select statement>
        [ORDER BY <order by list>]
        [COMPUTE <compute column list>
            [BY <column name list> ] ]
        [FOR BROWSE]
```

TRANSACT-SQL supports the COMPUTE clause in a SELECT statement. A COMPUTE clause is used with aggregate functions to generate control break summary values. COMPUTE is not supported in the ANSI SQL89 standard.

If the COMPUTE BY clause is used, the ORDER BY clause must also be used. The columns listed after COMPUTE BY must be identical to, or a subset of, the ORDER BY column list, and they must be in the same left-to-right order. The COMPUTE keyword can be used without BY to generate grand totals and grand counts.

In the example that follows, a TRANSACT-SQL COMPUTE BY clause is used to generate a summary of the average minimum and maximum salaries for each department:

```
SELECT        DName, MinSalary, MaxSalary
FROM          Dept
ORDER BY      MinSalary, MaxSalary
COMPUTE       AVG(MinSalary), AVG(MaxSalary)
BY            MinSalary, MaxSalary
```

The results are

DName	MinSalary	MaxSalary
Security	1000	3500
	Avg	
	1000	
		Avg
		3500

DName	MinSalary	MaxSalary
Human Resource	1200	4000
	Avg	
	1200	
		Avg
		4000

DName	MinSalary	MaxSalary
Sales	1500	4300
	Avg	
	1500	
		Avg
		4300

DName	MinSalary	MaxSalary
Accounting	2000	4500
	Avg	
	2000	
		Avg
		4500

DName	MinSalary	MaxSalary
President	5000	Null
	Avg	
	5000	
		Avg
		Null

To display the name and the minimum and maximum salary of a department in ascending order of minimum and maximum salary plus a grant summary of the average minimum and maximum salary, we have the SQL statement that follows. (Note: The COMPUTE clause is not followed by a BY clause; therefore, the grand total of the minimum salaries and the grand total of the maximum salaries in all the departments are displayed.)

```
SELECT        DName, MinSalary, MaxSalary
FROM          Dept
ORDER BY      MinSalary, MaxSalary
COMPUTE       AVG(MinSalary), AVG(MaxSalary)
```

The results are

DName	MinSalary	MaxSalary
Security	1000	3500
Human Resource	1200	4000
Sales	1500	4300
Accounting	2000	4500
President	5000	Null
	Avg	
	2140	
		Avg
		4075

In a TRANSACT-SQL SELECT statement, the FOR BROWSE clause allows users to perform an update while viewing. For example, to select information on all properties and prepare to update the results, we execute the statement

```
dbcmd(dbProc, "SELECT * FROM Property FOR BROWSE");
```

The set operator UNION is not supported in a TRANSACT-SQL SELECT statement.

In TRANSACT-SQL, the column name can be qualified by a database name, an owner name, and a table name, whereas in the ANSI SQL89 standard, the column name can be qualified only by a table name. Moreover, expressions are accepted in the TRANSACT-SQL ORDER BY clause but not in the ANSI SQL89 standard.

Consider the following example of a SELECT statement referencing a fully qualified column name and using an expression in the ORDER BY clause:

```
SELECT     Confidential.Peterson.Dept.DName
FROM       Confidential.Peterson.Dept
ORDER BY   (Confidential.Peterson.Dept.MaxSalary -
           Confidential.Peterson.Dept.MinSalary) DESC
```

The results are

DName

Human Resource

Sales

Accounting

President

The syntax of a TRANSACT-SQL SELECT ... INTO statement is as follows:

```
<select statement> ::=
        SELECT [ ALL | DISTINCT ] <select list>
        [INTO <table name>]
        <table expression>
```

The SELECT...INTO statement in TRANSACT-SQL is used to create a table. The INTO clause in TRANSACT-SQL accepts a table name as an argument and creates a table using the result of the select statement. In the ANSI SQL89 standard, the SELECT...INTO statement is used to retrieve data and store it into host variables. Thus, the TRANSACT-SQL INTO clause is syntactically and semantically different from the ANSI SQL89 standard INTO clause.

In the example that follows, a TRANSACT-SQL SELECT ... INTO statement is used to create a new table, HighIncome, that is identical to the employee table. HighIncome contains information on employees who earn more than $3,000.

```
SELECT   *
INTO     HighIncome
FROM     Emp
WHERE    Salary > 3000
```

With the TRANSACT-SQL select list it is possible to use a column heading to replace the default column name or expression. Moreover, in TRANSACT-SQL, the user can specify built-in functions in the select list of a TRANSACT-SQL SELECT statement. For example,

```
SELECT   "Average Price" = AVG(Salary), "Of",
         Today = GETDATE( )
FROM     Emp
```

As a result, the average salary of the employees as of today is displayed:

Average Price	Of	Today
2666	Of	01-01-99

The arithmetic operator % (modulo) and the string concatenation operator + are supported in TRANSACT-SQL but not in the ANSI SQL89 standard. Moreover, in the TRANSACT-SQL, the bitwise operators & (and), | (or), ^ (exclusive or), and ~ (not) are supported. In the statement that follows, the TRANSACT-SQL string concatenation operator is used:

```
SELECT    EmpNo, "Employee Name : "+EName
FROM      Emp
WHERE     DeptNo = 99
```

The results are

EmpNo	Employee Name : EName
3001	Employee Name : Peterson

TRANSACT-SQL supports its own built-in functions as well as aggregate functions, whereas the ANSI SQL89 standard supports only aggregate functions. In TRANSACT-SQL, the keyword ALL is not supported in an aggregate function, and the optional keyword DISTINCT is not supported in the MAX and MIN functions. In the ANSI SQL89 standard, if the DISTINCT keyword is specified, only a column name can be used. When the DISTINCT keyword is specified in TRANSACT-SQL, an expression, in addition to column names, can be used.

Consider the following example of a TRANSACT-SQL aggregate function:

```
SELECT    "Average salary of department 20"=AVG(
          DISTINCT Salary+300)
FROM      Emp
WHERE     DeptNo = 20
```

As a result, the average salary of employees in Department 20 is retrieved:

Average salary of department 20
2633

Parameters, variables, and USER are valid entries in an expression in the ANSI SQL89 standard; they are not supported in TRANSACT-SQL.

FROM Clause

The syntax of a TRANSACT-SQL FROM clause is

<from clause> ::=

FROM <table reference> [{, <table reference>}...]

<table reference> ::=

<table name> | <view name> **[HOLDLOCK]**

The optional keyword HOLDLOCK in the above statement restricts a shared lock on the table or view by holding it until the transaction has been completed. The HOLDLOCK construct is not supported in ANSI.

The table name specified in the TRANSACT-SQL FROM clause can be qualified with a database name and an owner name; thus, tables in different databases can be used in the query. This feature is not supported in the ANSI SQL89 standard.

In the following example, the table name in a TRANSACT-SQL FROM clause is fully qualified:

```
SELECT    Confidential.Peterson.Emp.EName
FROM      Confidential.Peterson.Emp.Emp,
          Public.Smith.Clients
WHERE     Confidential.Peterson.Emp.EName =
          Public.Smith.Clients.Name
```

The results are

Ename
Smith
Taylor
Peterson

GROUP BY Clause

The syntax of a TRANSACT-SQL GROUP BY clause is

<group by clause> ::=

GROUP BY **[ALL]** <aggregate free expression>

[{, < aggregate free expression >}...]

In TRANSACT-SQL, the keyword ALL ensures that all groups in the results are used, including those rows that failed the search condition. For instance, to select all departments with minimum salary greater than $1,500 and to group results according to department name, we execute the SQL statement

```
SELECT      *
FROM        Dept
WHERE       MinSalary > 1500
GROUP BY    DName
```

The results are

DeptNo	DName	MinSalary	MaxSalary
30	Accounting	2000	4500
99	President	5000	

The next example is similar to the previous one except that the keyword ALL is specified in the GROUP BY clause to ensure that all groups in the results are used, including those rows that failed the search condition:

```
SELECT      *
FROM        Dept
WHERE       MinSalary > 1500
GROUP BY    ALL DName
```

Because the ALL keyword is specified in the GROUP BY clause, all departments are selected:

DeptNo	DName	MinSalary	MaxSalary
10	Human Resource	1200	4000
20	Sales	1500	4300
30	Accounting	2000	4500
40	Security	1000	3500
99	President	5000	

The comparison operators !> and !< are supported in TRANSACT-SQL but not in the ANSI SQL89 standard. The ANSI SQL89 standard operator <> is represented as != in TRANSACT-SQL, as shown here:

```
SELECT      EName, Salary
FROM        Emp
WHERE       Salary !> 2000
AND         DeptNo != 30
```

As a result, the name and salary of employees whose salary is not greater than $2,000, and who are not in Department 30 are retrieved:

EName	Salary
Smith	1700
Jones	1200
Brown	2000
Green	1500

The quantifier keyword SOME and the " = ALL <subquery> " predicate is supported in the ANSI SQL89 standard but not in TRANSACT-SQL.

In TRANSACT-SQL, only literals are supported in the <in value list>, whereas in the ANSI SQL89 standard, parameters, variables, and USER are supported. In the following example, the literals 10, 20, and 30 are specified in the <in value list> :

```
SELECT    DName
FROM      Dept
WHERE     DeptNo IN (10, 20, 30)
```

The results are

DName
Human Resource
Sales
Accounting

In TRANSACT-SQL, the LIKE comparison works on datetime columns as well as on character columns. When datetime columns are used, TRANSACT-SQL automatically converts them to characters and then performs the comparison. The datetime data type is not supported in the ANSI SQL89 standard.

In addition to supporting the % and _ string-matching wildcards as in the ANSI SQL89 standard, TRANSACT-SQL supports [] and [^]. [] represents any single character within a specified range (e.g., [abcde] means matching a single character of a, b, c, d, or e). [^] represents any single character not within a specified range. The ANSI SQL89 standard ESCAPE clause is not supported in TRANSACT-SQL.

For example, to display the name and salary of employees whose name starts with a character 'B' or 'T' and does not have 'a' or 'o' as the third character, we execute the following SQL statement:

```
SELECT    EName, Salary
FROM      Emp
```

```
WHERE    EName like '[BT]_[^ao]%'
```

The results are

EName	Salary
Bays	2200
Taylor	3000

Outer Join

The outer join operators =* and *= are supported in TRANSACT-SQL. Join operators are not supported in the ANSI SQL89 standard. Left outer join (*=) includes all rows from the first table that meet the restrictions specified in the statement. The second table generates values if there is a match on the condition. Otherwise, the second table generates null values.

For example, to select the department number and name of all departments in the Dept table, and to select the corresponding standard minimum and maximum salaries, we use the TRANSACT-SQL left outer join:

```
SELECT   DeptNo, DName, StdMinSal, StdMaxSal
FROM     Dept, StdSalary
WHERE    Dept.DName *= StdSalary.DeptName
```

The results are

DeptNo	DName	StdMinSal	StdMaxSal
10	Human Resource	1000	3000
20	Sales	1500	3500
30	Accounting	1800	3800
40	Security	Null	Null
99	President	5000	Null

Right outer join (=*) includes all rows from the second table that meet the restrictions specified in the statement. The first table generates values if there is a match on the condition. Otherwise, the first table generates null values. Consider the following example:

```
SELECT   DeptNo, DName, StdMinSal, StdMaxSal
FROM     Dept, StdSalary
WHERE    Dept.DName =* StdSalary.DeptName
```

The results are

DeptNo	DName	StdMinSal	StdMaxSal
10	Human Resource	1000	3000
20	Sales	1500	3500
30	Accounting	1800	3800
99	President	5000	Null
Null	Customer Suppor	t1700	3700
Null	Technician	2000	4500
Null	Janitor	2500	5000

DELETE Statement

TRANSACT-SQL supports two types of DELETE statements. The first type is similar to the ANSI SQL DELETE statement except that the FROM keyword is optional and the target table may be referenced in the search condition. For example, to delete all employees with salaries greater than or equal to that of their managers, we execute the following SQL statement:

```
DELETE     Emp Outer
WHERE      Salary >= (
                  SELECT     Salary
                  FROM       Emp Inner
                  WHERE      Outer.Mgr = Inner.EmpNo)
```

Since no employees in the Emp table earn more than their manager, no row is deleted.

The second type of TRANSACT-SQL DELETE statement is not supported in the ANSI SQL89 standard. In this statement, an optional FROM clause follows the DELETE table name. The additional FROM clause allows the user to delete rows from one table based on data stored in other tables, giving the user the power of an embedded SELECT statement. The syntax of this DELETE statement is

```
<delete statement: searched> ::=
        DELETE [ [<database>.] <owner>. ]
                  <table name> | <view name>
        [ FROM [ [<database>.] <owner>. ]
                  <table name> | <view name>
                  [ { , [ [<database>.]<owner>.]
                            <table name> | <view name> } ... ]
```

```
        ]
        [ WHERE <search condition> ]
```

The following example achieves the same goal as the previous example: to delete all employees whose salary is greater than or equal to their manager. However, the TRANSACT-SQL DELETE ... FROM statement is used in this example. With the FROM clause supported in the TRANSACT-SQL DELETE statement, the SQL statement is simplified:

```
DELETE   Emp
FROM     Emp Outer, Emp Inner
WHERE    Outer.Salary >= Inner.Salary
AND      Outer.Mgr = Inner.EmpNo
```

The user can define a delete trigger that takes a specified action when a DELETE command is issued on a specified table.

UPDATE Statement

TRANSACT-SQL also supports two types of UPDATE statements. The first type is similar to the ANSI SQL89 standard UPDATE statement except that the search condition in the TRANSACT-SQL UPDATE statement may reference the target table, and the table name can be fully qualified with the database name and owner name. The second type of TRANSACT-SQL UPDATE statement is not supported in the ANSI SQL89 standard. In this statement, an optional FROM clause follows the SET clause. The additional FROM clause allows the user to update rows from one table based on data stored in other tables, giving the user the power of an embedded SELECT statement. The syntax of this UPDATE statement is as follows:

```
<update statement: searched> ::=
        UPDATE <table name>
        SET <column> = { <expression> | NULL }
            [ {, <column> = { <expression> | NULL } }...]
        [ FROM <table name> [ {, <table name> } ... ]
        [ WHERE <search condition> ]
```

In our final example, a TRANSACT-SQL UPDATE ... FROM statement is used to set the minimum and maximum salary of all departments to be 10% higher than the standard:

```
UPDATE   Dept
SET      MinSalary = StdMinSal * 1.1,
         MaxSalary = StdMaxSal * 1.1
FROM     Dept, StdSalary
WHERE    (Dept.DName = StdSalary.DeptName)
```

The user can define an update trigger that takes a specified action when an UPDATE command is issued on a specified table or on a specified column of a table.

4.5 Summary

In this chapter, we focused on the syntax and semantics of the noncursor operation SQL statements in the ANSI SQL89 standard, the IBM OS/2 Extended Edition, the ORACLE Server, DEC's Rdb/VMS, and the Microsoft SQL Server. Tables 4.5 through 4.8 summarize the syntactic differences among the different systems.

INSERT Statement	ANSI SQL89	IBM EE	ORACLE Server	DEC Rdb/VMS	Microsoft SQL Server
Referential integrity	No	Yes	No	No	Yes
References the target table in a subquery	No	No	Yes	No	Yes
INSERT INTO CURSOR statement	No	No	No	Yes	No

Table 4.5: Comparison of INSERT statement in SQL servers.

SELECT Statement	ANSI SQL89	IBM EE	ORACLE Server	DEC Rdb/VMS	Microsoft SQL Server
ESCAPE clause in the LIKE predicate	Yes	No	No	No	No
Outer join	No	No	Yes	No	Yes
Built-in scalar functions	No	Yes	Yes	Yes	Yes
Multicolumn selected in a subquery	No	No	Yes	No	No
Nonstandard clauses*	No	Yes	Yes	Yes	Yes
Set operator(s)†	Yes	Yes	Yes	Yes	No
Special predicates‡	No	No	No	Yes	No
UNION ALL	Yes	Yes	No	Yes	No
= ALL (<subquery>)	Yes	Yes	Yes	Yes	No
The SOME keyword	Yes	Yes	No	Yes	No
Special arithmetic operators§	No	No	Yes	No	Yes

Table 4.6: *Comparison of SELECT statement in statement in SQL servers.*

* *Nonstandard clauses*

IBM EE:	FOR UPDATE OF clause and FOR FETCH ONLY clause
ORACLE Server:	FOR UPDATE OF clause and CONNECT BY clause
Rdb/VMS:	LIMIT TO clause
SQL Server:	FOR BROWSE clause and COMPUTE clause

† *Set operators*

ANSI:	UNION
IBM EE:	EXCEPT, INTERSECT, UNION
ORACLE Server:	INTERSECT, MINUS, UNION
Rdb/VMS:	UNION

‡ *Special predicates*

Rdb/VMS:	CONTAINING, STARTING WITH, and UNIQUE

§ *Special operators*

ORACLE Server:	PRIOR operator
SQL Server :	% (modulo), & (bitwise and), | (bitwise or), ^ (bitwise exclusive or), ~ (bitwise not), and + (string concatenation)

DELETE Statement	ANSI SQL89	IBM EE	ORACLE Server	DEC Rdb/VMS	Microsoft SQL Server
Alias for the target table	No	Yes	Yes	Yes	No
References the target table in a subquery	No	Yes	Yes	No	Yes
References a list of tables in the FROM clause of a DELETE statement	No	No	No	No	Yes

Table 4.7: Comparison of DELETE statement in SQL servers.

UPDATE Statement	ANSI SQL89	IBM EE	ORACLE Server	DEC Rdb/VMS	Microsoft SQL Server
Alias for the target table	No	Yes	Yes	Yes	No
References the target table in a subquery	No	Yes	Yes	No	Yes
Multicolumn UPDATE	No	No	Yes	No	No
Supports an optional FROM clause in an UPDATE statement	No	No	No	No	Yes

Table 4.8: *Comparison of UPDATE statement in SQL servers.*

Chapter 5
Transaction Processing

Improved multiuser support and data integrity are important motivations for migrating client-based file-server database applications to a client-server architecture. In this chapter, we discuss the notion of transaction processing in a multiuser database system. Our objectives are to define the correct behavior for synchronizing accesses to the database system by concurrent users and to discuss the recovery management required to preserve the integrity of the database in the event of failure. And, as in previous chapters, we examine case studies of transaction processing in four popular database servers.

5.1 Transaction Definition and Example

Loosely speaking, a transaction is a sequence of operations (including database definition operations and database manipulation operations) that is atomic with respect to recovery. That is, either the entire sequence of operations or nothing at all is applied to the database. More stringent definitions for transactions require each transaction to possess a number of properties commonly referred to as the ACID properties: atomicity, consistency, isolation, and durability.

To illustrate the semantics of transaction processing, we make use of the banking environment hypothesized in the TP1 transaction performance benchmark [Anon. et al., 1985]. (This benchmark will be described further in Chapter 8.) This hypothetical bank has one or more branches and a number of accounts. Each branch of the bank has a number of tellers. The database models the cash positions associated with the branches, tellers, and accounts under this application environment. This is illustrated in Figure 5.1. A TP1 transaction represents the work performed when a customer makes a deposit or a withdrawal to or from an account. Each transaction is carried out by a teller at a particular branch on an account that was opened either at that branch or some other branch. The transaction debits or credits a bank account, performs the standard double-entry bookkeeping, and then returns a reply to the teller's terminal.

Each deposit and withdrawal transaction involves the following sequence of database operations or steps:

(1) The balance of the affected account record is modified to reflect the deposit or withdrawal.
(2) The balance of the affected branch record is modified to reflect the deposit or withdrawal.
(3) The balance of the affected teller record is modified to reflect the deposit or withdrawal.
(4) A new record is inserted into the history table, identifying the account, branch, teller, amount of deposit or withdrawal, and time of the transaction.

In the sections that follow, we describe what is meant by the atomicity, consistency, isolation, and durability properties required of each transaction.

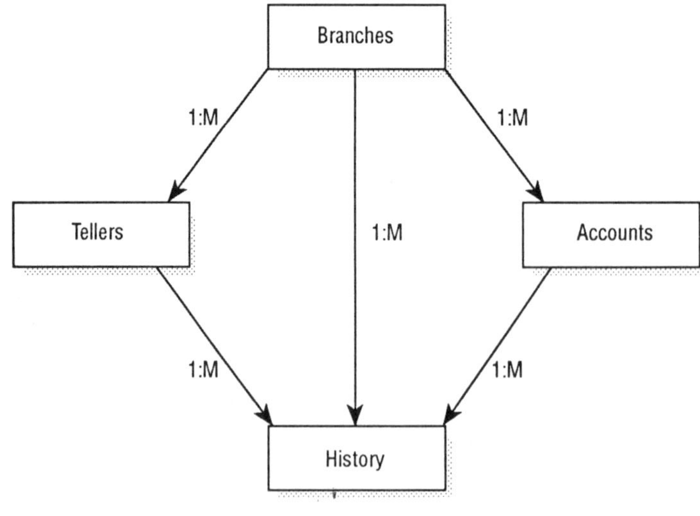

Figure 5.1: TP1 database schema.

5.1.1 Atomicity

The database system must ensure that all operations performed by a successfully committed transaction are reflected in the database and that the effects of a failed transaction are completely undone from the database. In other words, the transaction must be atomic. Thus, a successful TP1 transaction must update an account record, a teller record, and a branch record, and must insert a history record. On the other hand, if a TP1 transaction fails because of concurrency control or another reason, its effects, if any, on the accounts table, the tellers table, the branches table, and the history table must be completely reversed.

5.1.2 Consistency

A database state is said to be *consistent* if all associated semantic integrity constraints (e.g., domain constraints, entity constraints, referential integrity constraints) are satisfied. The execution of a transaction, in the absence of interference from other concurrent transactions, is assumed to take the database from one consistent state to another consistent state. For example, in the TP1 database, the following consistency constraints should be preserved by each transaction:

(1) The sums of the balance columns in the accounts table, the tellers table, and the branches table should all be equal.
(2) For a given branch, the sum of the balances for those tellers assigned to that branch must be equal to the branch's own balance.
(3) The history table should contain one record for each committed transaction and no records for any failed transactions.

In the course of executing a transaction, the consistency constraint may be momentarily violated. For example, the first constraint above will not be satisfied immediately after step 1 of the TP1 transaction (described earlier). Rather, consistency will be restored only after steps 2 and 3 have been executed. In general, the collective logic of all steps within a transaction must be designed to take the database from one consistent state to another. Thus, if transactions were performed on a database in a strictly serial fashion, consistency would be guaranteed. The challenge in implementing an efficient concurrency control scheme is to permit the interleaving of operations from multiple transactions, while preserving the consistency of the database.

5.1.3 Isolation

In a multiuser environment where concurrent applications may access the same data, it is important that the interleaving of database operations originating from different transactions does not give rise to anomalies. The database system provides a safeguard against mutual interference between concurrent transactions; this is referred to as *isolation*. A system may provide different levels of isolation among concurrently executed transactions. The level of isolation required for a given application environment usually has a direct impact on synchronization overhead and, consequently, on the transaction throughput that can be achieved. The different levels of isolation provided are described in the sections that follow.

Serializability

The 1989 ANSI SQL standard stipulates that the execution of concurrent transactions be *serializable*. That is, the interleaved execution of operations from concurrent transactions must produce the same effects on the database as though the transactions were executed in some serial order. However, many SQL-based database systems don't support serializability as the default isolation level because of the limited concurrency afforded to transactions when serializability is enforced. The proposed SQL2 standard addresses this issue by enabling different adjustable levels of isolation among concurrent transactions, thus allowing for different performance tuning options.

Lost Updates

Minimally, the database system must guarantee that if two concurrent applications attempt to update the same database object at the same time, neither update will be lost. For example, consider an account with a balance of $10,000. Two co-owners of this account simultaneously go to different tellers and attempt to withdraw $1,000 each. At the end of these two transactions, the account should be left with a balance of $8,000. Now suppose we have the following sequence of interleaved operations from the two transactions:

(1) Teller 1 reads an account balance of $10,000.
(2) Teller 2 also reads an account balance of $10,000.
(3) Teller 1 decrements the read account balance with the amount of the withdrawal, setting the new balance to $9,000.
(4) Teller 2 also decrements the read account balance with the

amount of the withdrawal, again setting the new balance to $9,000.

Thus, if two concurrent transactions are not properly synchronized and the above interleaved execution sequence is allowed to occur, the transaction (withdrawal) performed by the first user (teller) is effectively lost. In Section 5.2.1, we examine techniques that can guard against such lost update situations.

Dirty Read

Dirty read refers to the following anomaly: transaction T_1 modifies a row of a table; transaction T_2 then reads this modified row before T_1 commits. If T_1 aborts and its updates get rolled back at this point, T_2 would have read a row that has never been committed and that should not be considered as ever having existed.

Even though dirty read may not be desirable for many applications, it is sometimes tolerated as it affords improved concurrency. For instance, consider a statistical query that computes an aggregate value over all rows in a huge table. It may not be desirable to stop all other transactions from modifying the table while the time-consuming query is being processed. At the same time, the query result may hardly be affected by the additional synchronization because of the sheer number of rows in the table. Under such circumstances, it may be appropriate to allow dirty read for the long query and thereby not impose synchronization overhead on other transactions.

Cursor Stability

Even though the ANSI SQL standard stipulates that transactions must be serializable, many database system vendors find that this requirement is not conducive to good performance. For many applications, a guarantee of *cursor stability* is often sufficient. That is, if an application performs retrievals and updates via a SQL cursor, it is sufficient to guarantee that a row fetched through a cursor does not yield uncommitted data. Moreover, cursor stability leads to less synchronization conflicts than serializability. As soon as a transaction's cursor has moved off a particular row, other transactions are free to access (read or modify) that row. With serializability, a transaction is not permitted to modify a row that has previously been read or modified by another in-progress transaction; thus, the transaction may be forced to wait for the previous transaction to commit or abort before it is allowed to proceed.

Repeatable Read

Repeatable read refers to the following phenomenon that can occur under cursor stability. Transaction T_1 reads a row from a table via a SQL cursor and then moves off that row. Transaction T_2 now modifies or deletes the same row that T_1 has read, and then T_2 commits. If T_1 tries to reread the previously read row, it will discover that either the row's fields have changed or the row is no longer available for reading. To guarantee that reads are repeatable, a database system must ensure that database objects read by a transaction are not modified or deleted by other transactions prior to the termination (commit or rollback) of the former transaction. Again, this implies more blocking on concurrent transactions that need to access database objects already accessed by other transactions. It should be noted that repeatable read is a stronger consistency requirement than cursor stability (i.e., repeatable read implies cursor stability).

Phantom

Consider an audit transaction T_1 designed to verify that the consistency constraints associated with the TP_1 database are not violated. The transaction computes the sum of the balances of all tellers assigned to the San Francisco branch (i.e., it performs an aggregate computation on tellers as step 1) and then tries to verify that this sum is equal to the balance of the San Francisco branch (i.e., it performs a primary-key–based retrieval on branches as step 2). Now suppose a second transaction T_2 adds a new teller to San Francisco, and a third transaction T_3 performs an account deposit by this new teller. If both T_2 and T_3 are executed in between steps 1 and 2 of T_1, then by the time T_1 performs step 2, the branch balance for San Francisco will not match the sum of the teller balances computed in step 1. This anomaly arises because T_2 is allowed to create a *phantom* teller record that satisfies the selection criterion of T1, but that T_1, did not see. In Section 5.2.1, we will examine index-locking techniques that can guard against phantoms. Suffice to say, concurrency control schemes that guarantee serializability also prevent phantoms.

SQL2 Isolation Levels

In the proposed SQL2 standard, the level of isolation for read operations within a transaction is determined by an isolation level, which is designated via a SET TRANSACTION statement. Level 3, the default isolation level, guarantees that all transactions are serializable. Isolation level 2 prevents dirty reads and nonrepeatable reads from occurring, but it does not preclude the phantom phenomenon. And, while isolation level 1 guarantees that dirty reads do not occur, it does not guard against nonrepeatable reads or the phantom phenomenon. Level 0 provides the least protection, as it allows dirty reads, nonrepeatable reads, and phantoms. Table 5.1 summarizes the isolation levels supported in the proposed SQL2 standard.

Anomalies	Level 0	Level 1	Level 2	Level 3
Dirty Read	x	–	–	–
Nonrepeatable Read	x	x	–	–
Phantom	x	x	x	–

Table 5.1: Permissible anomalies with SQL2 isolation levels.

5.1.4 Durability

The database system must be able to preserve the effects of all committed transactions as well as database consistency in the presence of system and media failures. That is, if the database system fails while transactions are running, only the work done by the in-progress transactions should be lost, and all updates performed by committed transactions should persist in the database. Similarly, if a disk crash affects tables in the database, it must be possible to reconstruct the most recent consistent state of the database, which should include all committed transactions and should not include the effects of updates performed during incomplete transactions.

To guarantee transaction durability, the updates performed by a transaction must be recorded in some durable medium at commit time. A durable storage medium is traditionally a stable storage medium that is inherently nonvolatile, such as a magnetic disk, an optical disk, or a magnetic tape.[1] Durability of transactions implies that sufficient

1 Nowadays, a durable medium can also be constructed from a volatile medium, such as semiconductor memory, through coupling with an uninterruptible power supply (UPS). The latter allows the contents of the volatile memory to be transferred to another inherently nonvolatile storage medium before any data is lost in the event of an external power failure.

redundancy is built into the transaction processing mechanism to guarantee recoverability from any single point of failure. The two most common single points of failure are the failure of an individual durable medium containing the database and a system crash or hang.

Recovery from a failure of the durable database storage medium is achieved by mirroring the medium. Alternatively, you can keep an archival snapshot of the database along with a redo log of updates performed to the database since the time the snapshot was taken. Failure of the durable medium containing the redo log is also considered a single point of failure. Here, recovery can be achieved by saving another archival snapshot of the database using the current database contents from the durable database storage medium, thereby truncating and restarting the redo log.

Recovery from a system crash or hang requires undoing the effects of in-progress transactions that might have been applied to the stable database prior to the system failure. Typically, an undo log is maintained for this purpose. The undo log contains *before* images of objects modified by in-progress transactions. On recovery from a system failure, the undo log can be used to undo the updates of incomplete transactions.

5.1.5 Scope of a Transaction

A transaction is a delimited sequence of database operations that is treated as the unit for consistency and recovery. Most database systems impose restrictions on what type of operations can be bracketed as recoverable units. Some systems support the predeclaration of the nature of a transaction (e.g., READ ONLY vs. READ WRITE), so as to select the kind of isolation from other transactions. Most systems will start a transaction implicitly when a user submits the first SQL statement. Additionally, some systems will commit the implicitly started transaction as soon as the SQL statement is executed. In most implementations, data definition operations cannot be included as part of a general transaction; in fact, each such operation is often treated as an implicit transaction.

Implicit Transaction Start

Neither SQL nor SQL2 provides explicit language constructs to start transactions. Thus, a transaction is implicitly started when an application performs the first database definition or database manipulation operation after commitment of the last transaction.

Automatic Transaction Commit

Some systems support the notion of automatic commit whereby each SQL statement is treated as a separate implicit transaction. In other words, each SQL statement implicitly starts a transaction, and, if successfully executed, is implicitly committed as a transaction. To allow more general transactions that span multiple SQL statements, it must be possible to enable and disable the auto commit mechanism.

Schema Updates

Schema update refers to the modification of the database schema as a result of addition, deletion, or modification of schema objects such as tables, views, and indexes. In general, processing a SQL DML statement requires the generation of an access plan based on access paths existing in the database. The validity of such access plans may be adversely affected by schema updates. For example, an access plan that depends on a particular index will be invalidated if that index is dropped. Thus, schema updates must be carefully synchronized against regular DML operations.

The proposed SQL2 standard does not allow intermixing database definition and database manipulation operations within the same transaction. The existing SQL standard, on the other hand, leaves such restrictions to the implementation. Additionally, many database-server implementations do not permit multiple database definition operations within the same transaction. Thus, each database definition operation often is treated as an implicit transaction. In fact, when a DDL statement is processed, previously executed DML statements are often implicitly committed, and a special type of transaction that allows the execution of a single DDL statement is implicitly started.

5.2 Concurrency Control

Concurrency control is the process of synchronizing the actions of concurrent transactions, thereby guarding against mutual interference. Most known concurrency control algorithms make use of some form of locking, timestamp ordering, or commit time certification [Bernstein et al., 1987]. Since locking-based algorithms are widely used in commercial database implementations, we concentrate our discussions in this section on locking.

5.2.1 Locking

Locking is the most commonly used mechanism for synchronizing concurrent transactions. The simplest form of locking is based on obtaining exclusive control on a resource. For example, each database object that may be accessed by a transaction has a lock associated with it. Before accessing a database object, a transaction must first acquire the corresponding lock; this gives temporary control of the object to the transaction and allows it to make different kinds of access to the object.

A generalization of exclusive locking involves the existence of multiple lock modes associated with the same database object; for example, a shared read mode and an exclusive write mode. This allows a transaction to declare its intention on the kind of operation it will perform on a database object when the lock is acquired. Intention locking also allows concurrent transactions with compatible intentions (e.g., reading) to simultaneously hold compatible locks against the same database object.

The locks acquired by a transaction must be released with a certain discipline in order to guarantee serializability. *Two-phase* locking refers to the clear demarcation of a transaction into a growing phase and a shrinking phase. During the growing phase, all locks must be acquired, possibly incrementally. During the shrinking phase, all locks are released, again, possibly incrementally. The growing phase must be completed before the shrinking phase can commence.

Theoretically, a transaction does not need to complete its database updates before releasing some of its acquired locks. Serializability can still be assured if transactions follow the two-phase locking discipline and if transactions adhere to the protocol of locking a database object before accessing it. In practice, most database systems do not start releasing locks until a transaction has completely finished its execution. This guards against the need for cascaded rollbacks. That is, if transaction T_2 acquires a lock on an object that transaction T_1 has modified prior to T_1's commit, it is possible that T_2 may have to be rolled back if T_1 subsequently rolls back. Likewise, the commitment of T_2 would have to be conditional on the commitment of T_1.

Lock Modes

If two transactions need to read the same database object, they can both proceed as long as they guard against other transactions updating that database object. In general, multiple read locks may be held by different transactions on the same database object. However, only a single write lock can be outstanding on a database object at one time. The granting of multiple locks, possibly of different modes, against the same database object is left to the lock manager or scheduling component of a database system. This activity is governed by a *compatibility matrix* as shown in Table 5.2.

	Shared	**Exclusive**
Shared	Y	N
Exclusive	N	N

Table 5.2: A simple lock mode compatibility matrix.

Each column in the compatibility matrix represents an outstanding lock mode held by one transaction on an object, and each row represents a newly requested lock mode on the same object by another transaction. The matrix essentially indicates whether the new request is compatible with a request that has already been granted.

Multigranularity Locking

The locking granularity supported by a database system can affect the bookkeeping overhead for locks as well as the level of concurrency. Very often, a database system will support locking at different granules (e.g., at the row, table, storage area, or database level) to suit the needs of different transactions. In general, the larger the granule, the lower the bookkeeping overhead. On the other hand, the use of large-granule locks limits the level of concurrency available to concurrent transactions. Multigranularity locking allows different transactions to set locks at different levels. Thus, long transactions that access large portions of the database can use coarser granules than short transactions that involve only small portions of the database.

The implementation of multigranularity locking requires that conflicting locks on two overlapping granules cannot be set. For example, a transaction T_2 should not be allowed to lock a table if another transaction T_1 has already locked a row within that table. It would be inefficient to require that all outstanding row locks be tested for overlap against an incoming table lock request before the table lock can be granted. However, such conflict testing can be streamlined through the use of intention locks.

Intention Locks

With multigranularity locking, objects in a database can be organized hierarchically in the form of a tree (such that each object has a single parent) or as a directed acyclic graph (such that each object may have multiple parents). Figure 5.2 illustrates a hierarchy of lock types. Each database contains multiple storage areas; each storage area contains multiple tables; and each table contains multiple rows. A lock on an object also implicitly locks all descendants of that object. Thus, a read lock on a storage area implicitly locks all tables contained in that area for reading.

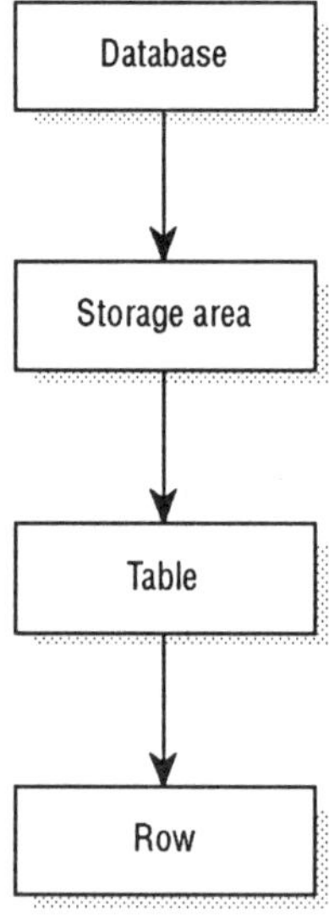

Figure 5.2: A hierarchy of lock granularity.

To lock a fine-granule object, a transaction must first lock one or more of its ancestors in some less restrictive lock mode. The objective is to propagate the effect of fine-granule locking activities to a containing coarser granule, using an appropriate *intention lock.*[2] Thus, a transaction must set an *intention read (IR)* lock on a table

[2] Holding an appropriate intention lock on a coarse-granule object entitles a transaction to acquire a more restrictive, but compatible, lock on a descendant object.

before setting read locks on rows contained in that table. Similarly, a transaction must set an *intention write (IW)* lock on a table before setting write locks on rows contained in that table. Sometimes, a transaction might want to read many rows within a table and modify only a small number of rows. This can be accomplished by setting a *read intention write (RIW)* lock on the table, and then setting write locks on rows that need to be modified. The RIW lock on the table implicitly locks all rows within the table for reading. Thus, it is not necessary to lock individual rows for reading. The compatibility matrix for different lock types in the multigranularity locking scheme is summarized in Table 5.3.

	R	**W**	**IR**	**IW**	**RIW**
R	Y	N	Y	N	N
W	N	N	N	N	N
IR	Y	N	Y	Y	Y
IW	N	N	Y	Y	N
RIW	N	N	Y	N	N

Table 5.3: *Compatibility matrix for multigranularity locking.*

A lock mode LM_1 is said to be stronger than another lock mode LM_2 if the set of lock modes with which LM_1 is compatible is a subset of those lock modes with which LM_2 is compatible. Thus, R (read) is stronger than IR (intention read), and W (write) is stronger than IW (intention write). In general, when a lock request is submitted on behalf of one transaction, the lock manager must determine if incompatible locks are held by other transactions. If the requesting transaction already holds a stronger lock on the affected object, the request is automatically granted. On the other hand, if the request is for a stronger lock than the one already held by the transaction or if the transaction does not currently hold any lock on the affected object, the request must be tested for compatibility with locks held by other transactions.

According to Table 5.3, neither R (read) nor IW (intention write) is stronger than the other. This is because R is compatible with {R, IR}, whereas IW is compatible with {IR, IW}, and neither {R, IR} nor {IR, IW} is a subset of the other. On the other hand, RIW (read intention write) is stronger than both R (read) and IW (intention write). Thus, if a transaction holding a read lock on an object wants to acquire an intention write lock on the same object, the lock manager will try to upgrade the transaction's lock on the object to read intention write.

The protocol for multigranularity locking on an object x within a tree-structured database object space can be summarized as follows:

(1) If x is not the root of the object space, then a transaction can set a read lock or an intention read lock on x if the transaction has already set an intention read lock, an intention write lock, or a read intention write lock on x's parent.

(2) If x is not the root of the object space, then a transaction can set a write lock or an intention write lock on x if the transaction has already set an intention write lock on x's parent.

(3) To read x, a transaction must hold a read lock on x, a write lock on x, a read lock on an ancestor of x, a write lock on an ancestor of x, or a read intention write lock on an ancestor of x.

(4) To write x, a transaction must hold either a write lock on x or a write lock on an ancestor of x.

(5) A transaction must not release an intention lock on x as long as it is holding a lock on any child of x.

When the object space is a directed acyclic graph (DAG) rather than a tree, the multigranularity locking protocol is slightly more complicated:

(1) If x is not the root of the object space, then a transaction can set a read lock or an intention read lock on x if the transaction has already set an intention read lock or an intention write lock on some parent of x.

(2) If x is not the root of the object space, then a transaction can set a write lock or an intention write lock on x if the transaction has already set an intention write lock on some parent of x.

(3) To read x, a transaction must hold a read lock on x, a write lock on x, a read lock on an ancestor of x, or a read intention write lock on an ancestor of x.

(4) To write x, a transaction must hold either an explicit write lock on x or an implicit write lock on x by virtue of a write lock on some ancestor of x. In addition, the transaction must hold a write lock or an intention write lock along every path that leads from the root of the object space to x.

(5) A transaction must not release an intention lock on x as long as it is holding a lock on any child of x.

Figure 5.3 depicts a DAG-structured object space.

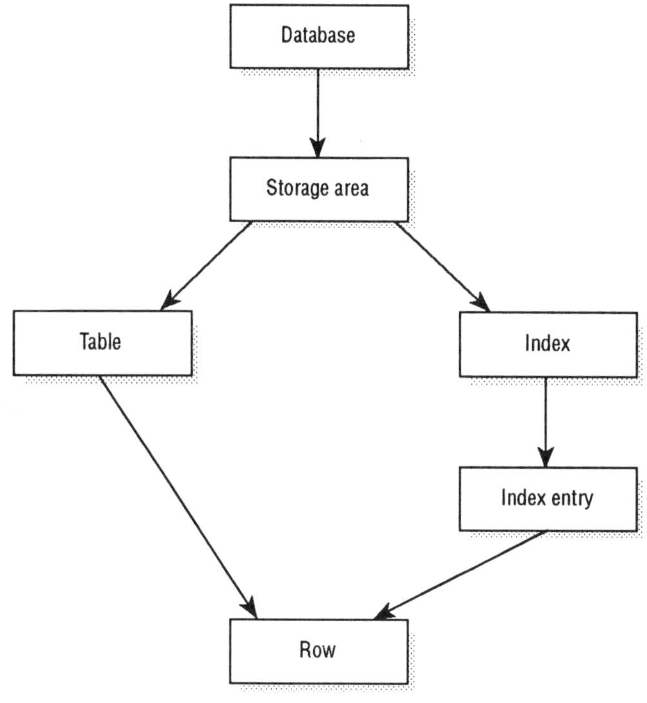

Figure 5.3: A graph-structured object space.

In order to read lock a row, a transaction can set an intention read lock on either the containing table or on the index entry that points to the row. To write lock a row, a transaction must set not only an intention write lock on the containing table, but also an intention write lock on every index entry that points to that row.

Lock Mode Conversion

Concurrency can be improved through the support of multiple lock modes. A transaction must acquire a more restrictive lock on a database object if its intended action on that database object warrants the more restrictive lock. However, this implies that a transaction holding a read lock on a database object must convert that lock into a write lock prior to modifying that database object. Since other read locks on the same database object may be outstanding, it is not always possible to satisfy the conversion request immediately.

A transaction can hold only one lock on a database object at any time, although it may request a lock many times on the same object. Normally, a conversion is performed to obtain a lock mode that is more restrictive than the one currently held. For a row-level lock, the only meaningful conversion is from read (share) to write (exclusive). In the case of multigranularity locking, the intention write lock mode and the read lock mode are not directly comparable (neither one is more restrictive than the other). Thus, when a transaction holding an intention write lock requests a read lock, or vice versa, the originally held lock is upgraded to a read intention write lock, subject to compatibility with locks held by other concurrent transactions.

For example, the rows associated with a SQL cursor can be individually read locked as an application fetches rows through the cursor. It is necessary to convert the read lock into a write lock only when the application decides to delete the current record in the cursor. When a SQL cursor is declared, it is also possible to attach a FOR UPDATE OF clause. Typically, when a row is fetched through such a cursor, the database system immediately acquires a write lock on the row in question, avoiding the need for any subsequent lock conversion operations.

Lock Escalation

Since there is a performance tradeoff between the low bookkeeping overhead for coarse-granule locking and the higher concurrency afforded by fine-granule locking, most database systems support multigranularity locking. Concurrency is maximized through the use of fine-granule locks. However, if a transaction acquires many fine-granule locks, it becomes advantageous to replace a number of these fine-granule locks with a coarser-granule lock in order to reduce the bookkeeping overhead.[3] This action is called *lock escalation*. Typically, lock escalation is performed by the database system on an as needed basis and is completely transparent to the application. If two or more transactions need to escalate their row-level locks into a table-level lock at the same time, deadlocks can occur.

---

3 This is particularly true for those systems that allocate a fixed amount of internal lock tablespace for keeping track of locking information.

Deadlocks

When transactions acquire locks incrementally on an as needed basis, it becomes possible for each of two transactions to be waiting for a lock that the other is holding; therefore, forward progress is stalled. This situation is called a *deadlock*. Deadlocks can also arise because of lock conversion and/or escalation operations. For example, if both T_1 and T_2 are holding read locks on the same row, and if both desire to upgrade their read locks to write locks, then neither can proceed because the other is holding a lock that blocks the lock conversion operation.

Deadlocks can be identified through the construction of a waits-for graph (WFG), which shows the relationships of transactions waiting for other transactions. A deadlock occurs if there is a cycle in the WFG. WFGs can be constructed on a periodic basis, or they can be maintained continuously. In the latter case, a deadlock can be identified immediately when a transaction is blocked because it is waiting for a lock.

Deadlocks can be resolved by picking one of the transactions involved in a cycle in the WFG as a victim, and then rolling it back. The victim selection process can be optimized on the basis of the amount of lost work that would result from rolling back each of the involved transactions. When continuous deadlock detection is used, it is often simplest to victimize the last transaction that closes a loop in the WFG.

Deadlocks can be prevented through the use of *timeouts* or by never allowing one transaction to wait for another. In this way, a transaction that cannot obtain a desired lock can be aborted and automatically restarted (after some delay) in the hope that by the time it once again needs to acquire the previously unavailable lock, the conflicting transaction(s) has terminated.

Another possible deadlock avoidance scheme is to require transactions to explicitly lock all the needed tables up front. Alternately, if tables in a database are totally ordered, and if all transactions acquire table locks in the same order, deadlocks can also be avoided.

Livelocks

A transaction can be repeatedly deadlocked; each time, it may be picked as the victim, aborted, and then restarted. This phenomenon is called *cyclic restart* or *livelock*. In order to avoid livelocks, the victim selection algorithm for deadlock resolution must take into consideration the number of times a given transaction was previously aborted due to deadlocks.

A lock scheduler that favors read locks over write locks can also lead to livelocks. Since two read locks on the same object are compatible, a transaction that requests a write lock on an object may have to wait indefinitely because of transactions that continually request read locks on the same object. This situation occurs when lock requests are granted solely on the basis of their compatible with outstanding locks.

Explicit Table Locking

It is not easy for the database system to infer an application's intent to access a large percentage of the rows within a table. Thus, the system may have to begin using row-level locking and escalate to table-level locking once it sees that the application is acquiring a large number of row locks. To save the overhead of escalation and to avoid the risk of deadlocking during escalation, many database systems allow the application to explicitly lock tables. In some cases, it is possible for a transaction to reserve or preclaim all required tables in the desired lock modes. Here, the database system will not start the transaction until all the needed locks have been granted. Once started, a transaction that makes use of such a locking option is guaranteed that it can run to completion without concurrency conflicts with other transactions.

Index Locking

One way to avoid the phantom problem described earlier is with *index locking.* When a transaction makes use of an index to locate rows with a particular index key value, it is required to set a read lock on the corresponding index key. Likewise, when a transaction inserts a new row, it is required to set a write lock on all the affected index keys. Thus, a read lock on the index key Location='SF' not only will lock existing rows with location equal to SF, but it will also prevent other transactions from inserting rows with location equal to SF into the table and from changing an existing row's location to SF.

When queries are processed by sequential scanning, index locking is not applicable. Instead, it is necessary to set a table lock that conflicts with all write locks on index keys.

5.2.2 Multiversion Concurrency Control

A multiversion concurrency control algorithm creates a new version, or copy, of a database object for each update transaction. Typically, a multiversion concurrency control algorithm is used to improve concurrency between readers and writers. Readers can be guaranteed to see a consistent snapshot of the database, while writers, who do not conflict with other writers, can run without any hindrance or delays caused by concurrent readers. Thus, the nonrepeatable read and phantom problems can be solved for read-only transactions without locking out other transactions.

A multiversion concurrency control algorithm must be able to determine the appropriate version of a database object that a given transaction should read. It must also incorporate some kind of *garbage collection* mechanism to get rid of old versions that are no longer of interest to in-progress and future transactions.

We now describe several multiversion concurrency control schemes. The schemes differ in terms of the maximum number of versions that can be kept for a given object and in the way versions are labeled.

Supporting up to Two Versions

Multiversion concurrency control can be used in conjunction with two-phase locking. Bayer et al. [1980] present a multiversion, two-phase locking scheme that supports up to two versions of each database object. Under this scheme, if an object has two versions, only one can be written by a committed transaction; the other must be written by a transaction that is still in progress. Readers are allowed to read the old committed version. When an update transaction commits, it goes through a certification process, converting its write locks into certify locks. In this process, the current transaction waits for other transactions that have set read locks on database objects for which it has created new versions. When it successfully acquires certify locks for all objects it has written, old versions of those objects are garbage-collected.

For instance, when an update transaction T_1 modifies a database object x under a multiversion concurrency control scheme, it sets a write lock on x and creates a new version x_{new} for it. If another transaction T_2 needs to read x, it acquires a read lock that does not conflict with the outstanding write lock on x. T_2 is then allowed to read the old version of x, x_{old}. When T_1 has finished processing and is ready to commit, it acquires a certify lock for all objects it has written. In this case, however, the certify lock on x will not be granted until T_2 commits or aborts. Thus, keeping only two versions of each database object, readers are allowed to read the old version while updaters are creating new versions; updaters, however, must still wait for readers to finish before they can acquire the appropriate certify locks.

Additionally, allowing an arbitrary number of versions of a database object may further reduce conflicts between readers and writers.

Supporting an Arbitrary Number of Versions

The most common implementation of multiversion concurrency control combines the use of locking and timestamp ordering. Read and write transactions set read and write locks as they do in two-phase locking. When updating a database object, an out-of-place update is performed (such that old versions are not overwritten), and the versions are chained in reverse chronological order. When an update transaction commits, object versions it has created are assigned a transaction timestamp corresponding to the time of the transaction's commitment. Read-only transactions, on the other hand, don't set locks. They obtain a timestamp at the beginning of the transaction and use that timestamp to define the consistent snapshot of the database it should see. Essentially, for each database object, the read-only transaction sees the latest version with a timestamp that is smaller than the read-only transaction's own initiation timestamp. As long as update transactions set read locks on the objects they read (thereby reading the latest versions of those objects), this scheme can provide serializability of all transactions.

Avoiding the Use of Commit Timestamps

A further refinement of the above scheme is to use a commit list instead of timestamp. In this case, each object version is labeled with a transaction number (assigned at the beginning of transaction) instead of a commit timestamp, which cannot be assigned until the transaction is ready to commit. This change eliminates any need to reread each modified object and to rewrite the assigned timestamp if there is insufficient buffer space to cache updates until the transaction ends. When a read-only transaction begins, it saves a snapshot of the current commit list, which defines what set of transactions have committed as of that point. When traversing the version chain of a particular object, a read-only transaction simply reads the first encountered version created by a transaction that is on the read-only transaction's saved commit list. However, even though the commit list can be represented quite compactly, it still takes more space to represent as compared to a single timestamp.

By maintaining an arbitrary number of versions of an object, garbage collection becomes an important issue. Essentially, an old version must be saved for as long as those read-only transactions require it for a consistent snapshot. As those transactions terminate, old versions can safely be garbage-collected. An integrated multiversion concurrency control and recovery scheme that makes use of an on-disk ring buffer for storing old versions is described by Chan et al. [1983].

5.2.3 Optimistic Concurrency Control

Rather than requiring each transaction to hold an appropriate lock before allowing it to perform any operation on a database object, it is possible to perform the operation and to check from time to time whether the operations performed so far are safe. Essentially, when a transaction is ready to commit, its set of actions can be reviewed to determine if it might have done something to cause it not to be serializable with respect to other transactions. The process of determining whether a transaction's commit can be safely processed is called *certification.* Concurrency control algorithms that make use of certification are sometimes referred to as being *optimistic*. This is because an optimistic assumption is made that the read-set of a transaction remains unchanged by other transactions over the course of the former transaction, and that it is not necessary to lock the read-set to prevent it from changing.

To facilitate the certification process, the read-set and write-set[4] of each transaction must be kept track of. When a transaction T_i is to be certified, read-set (T_i) must be tested for overlap against write-set (T_j), for all other active transactions T_j in the system. Furthermore, write-set (T_i) must be tested for overlap against read-set (T_j) and write-set (T_j), for all other active transactions T_j in the system. T_i is certified (and therefore committed) only if none of the above comparisons shows any overlap. If overlaps are found between write-set (T_i) and read-set (T_j) or write-set (T_j), T_j must also be aborted because the read-set and write-set information does not identify the order/timing of conflicting read/write operations. Thus, if T_i's write-set overlaps with T_j's read-set, it is possible that T_j might have already read T_i's output, thereby necessitating a cascaded rollback. When a transaction is certified, it is removed from the list of active transactions, so information about its read-set and write-set can be forgotten.

Because of the potential space requirements for tracking the set of rows read or written by transactions, optimistic concurrency control is seldom used in commercial database implementations. There is,

4 These are the sets of database objects read and written by the transaction.

however, a restricted class of transactions that read and write individual rows identified through the use of primary keys. In this case, rather than testing for read-set and write-set overlap among transactions, it is possible, through the use of a timestamp mechanism, to certify that the row read by a transaction has not changed since the time it was read. When an update operation is submitted, the transaction specifies the timestamp of the object version that was read. If the timestamp for the object in the database matches the timestamp read by the transaction, then the update operation is safely performed. This type of transaction control uses less space than optimistic concurrency control, which was discussed previously.

5.3 Recovery Management

To implement the atomicity and durability properties of transactions, a database system must be prepared to undo the effects of failed transactions. In addition, it must be prepared to redo the effects of committed transactions in the event of a media failure.

To speed up database access, portions of the stable database may be cached in volatile memory. In general, the cache buffers may be shared by different concurrent transactions, or each transaction may manage its own portion of the cached database. To guarantee that the updates performed by a transaction persist, the updates must be written from the cache to the stable storage medium prior to the commitment of the transaction. This may be in the form of either entries to the recovery log or as direct modifications to the stable database, as shown in Figure 5.4.

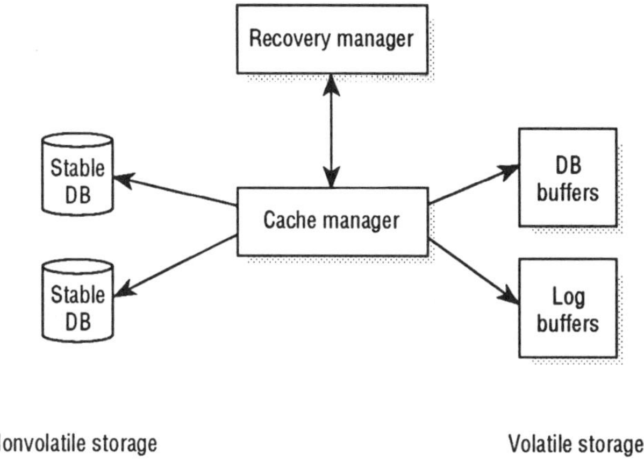

Figure 5.4: Recovery management.

Upon recovery from a system failure, it may be necessary to undo the effects of all incomplete transactions that were active at the time of the system failure. Additionally, it may be necessary to redo all transactions that were committed but whose updates have not yet been recorded in the stable database. *Before images* are used for undoing transactions, while *after images* are used for redoing transactions.

Before Images and After Images

The *before images* of a transaction consist of the previous values of objects modified by that transaction. Before images are used to recover from system failures and to undo the effects of failed transactions. In addition, before images are sometimes used in multiversion concurrency control algorithms to improve concurrency, by allowing a transaction to read a somewhat out-of-date, but consistent, snapshot of the database without setting read locks. As in the case of locking, before images can be kept at the record level or at the block level.

The *after images* of a transaction consist of the new values of objects modified by that transaction. After images are used to recover from system and media failures by redoing the effects of committed transactions. After image logging can be performed at a physical level or at a logical level. For example, when a record is inserted, logical logging would only record insertion of the record itself, whereas physical logging would also record corresponding insertions and updates to the associated indexes.

The write ahead log (WAL) protocol is typically used to govern the sequencing of write operations to before and after image logs, as well as to write operations to the stable database. By force writing the recovery logs and updates to the database itself at the end of the transaction, recovery from system failures can be simplified. This is sometimes referred to as a *transaction-oriented checkpointing* policy. However, to improve performance, it is often desirable to buffer the modified database pages in main memory and to write modified database pages back to stable storage as part of the page replacement process (i.e., the process of replacing database pages in the buffer pool that have not been used recently with pages that need to be accessed by transactions) and at periodic checkpoints (when all modified pages in the buffer pool are written). Fuzzy checkpoints are sometimes used to further minimize the amount of synchronized writing required at a checkpoint. (Additional checkpointing strategies are described later in this section.)

Transaction Failures

A transaction failure is usually related to concurrency control or consistency. For example, a transaction may be involved in a deadlock and become the victim transaction that is rolled back. A transaction may also abort in order to avoid potential deadlock situations; that is, a transaction may timeout and wait for a lock, or it may abort and restart when a lock request cannot be granted. Such transaction failures are related to concurrency control. On the other hand, a consistency-related transaction failure might occur when incorrect input data violates certain integrity constraints that are automatically enforced by the database system. Even though SQL-based database systems are supposed to automatically undo the effects of a failed SQL statement, the logic of the transaction may be such that the entire transaction is aborted whenever any statement fails.

To undo the effects of a transaction that is rolled back, its before images must be reapplied to the database. For multiversion concurrency control algorithms, this can be as simple as flipping a bit to indicate that the transaction is unsuccessful and that object versions created by this failed transaction should be ignored.

System Failures

A system failure may be due to either hardware or software problems. The general assumption is that the contents of volatile memory are lost after a system failure. As a result, all database cache buffers are also lost.

The actions required for recovering from system failure depend on the checkpointing policy in force.[5] For transaction-oriented checkpointing, only incomplete transactions that were in progress at the time of the system failure need to be undone. For other less restrictive forms of checkpointing, it may be necessary to redo transactions that have committed, but whose updates were buffered and were not yet written to the stable database.

Media Failures

To recover from media failure, it is important to perform logging on a device with a failure mode that is independent of the stable database. That is, it should be highly unlikely that the logging device and the stable database can fail at the same time. Furthermore, a complete snapshot of the database must have previously been saved so that log entries beyond the time the snapshot was taken can be reapplied to reconstruct the latest state of the database. Backup of an entire database may be completed online while transactions are executing, or offline such that transactions are prevented from executing while the backup procedure is in progress.

An alternative to logging is *disk mirroring*—maintaining multiple copies of identical disk blocks on different disk drives. As soon as media failure is detected in one drive, processing can be switched to the other drives. Under normal operations, different readers can be directed to different copies of the same logical disk block; this improves performance by providing parallel reads.

Recovery Strategies

The kind of information that must be recorded in the course of a transaction to provide for system failure recovery depends on how updates to the stable database are performed. Two possible update strategies are *in-place updating* and *out-of-place updating*. In-place updating physically changes the value of a database object in the stable database; thus, the old value is lost. Out-of-place updating does not directly overwrite the old value of the database object. Instead, it creates a new version for it. Periodically, these new versions are integrated into the stable database. For example, consider the shadow page strategy. Instead of updating the original copy of a database

---

5 That is, if updates made by a transaction are required to be written back to the stable database before the transaction can be considered committed or if writing to the recovery logs is sufficient to guarantee durability. See further discussions on checkpointing later in this section

page, the updated copy is written as a shadow page. Eventually, the shadow page must replace the original page. The shadow page can either be copied to the original page slot at some later time, or the page table can be adjusted accordingly to reflect this replacement.

Because in-place updating directly modifies the stable database, it is necessary to keep enough information to undo the updates of a transaction in the event of a transaction or system failure. This information is typically kept in an *undo log*. Because volatile memory is considered lost during a system crash, and because the undo log is needed for undoing incomplete updates of failed transactions prior to the system crash, the undo log must be kept in stable storage. To minimize input/output (I/O), an undo log may be cached in volatile memory. However, flushing the undo log cache must be carefully synchronized with flushing the database cache to ensure that the undo log entry is written to stable storage before a database object is updated in the stable database.

The caching strategy also has a big impact on recovery from transaction and system failures. When transactions are short, it is possible to buffer all updates performed by a transaction up to the transaction's commit point and to minimize the need to rollback the effects of the transaction.[6] This is referred to as the *no steal* buffer strategy [Harder and Reuter, 1983]. Except for special-purpose systems where all transactions are predefined and uniformly short, the no steal strategy is not a generally viable solution. Thus, most general-purpose database systems employ a *steal* buffer strategy in which uncommitted updates may be written to the stable database because cache buffers in volatile memory are needed to satisfy other database operations.

Another dimension of recovery management is the strategy for *commit processing*. To guard against media failures, a transaction typically writes to both the stable database and the redo log (which is used to store the after images of transactions). Provided the redo log is written to stable storage at commit time, there is no immediate need to write updates back to the stable database from the cache. Such updates could be written back asynchronously as part of the cache replacement process. Thus, database objects that are frequently accessed may be read from and written back into the cache many times before being written back once to the stable database. This is referred to as the *no flush* strategy [Ozsu and Valduriez, 1991].

---

6 In this case, caching is done on per transaction basis and buffers are not shared among transactions.

Should a system failure occur, the stable database may not reflect all updates made by committed transactions. As a result, the redo log is used to redo appropriate transactions. Alternatively, a transaction can always make sure that its updates are written back to the stable database at commit time, thereby making it unnecessary to redo transactions on recovery from system failure. This is referred to as the *flush* strategy [Ozsu and Valduriez, 1991].

The four strategies that follow combine the steal/no steal and flush/no flush options:

Steal/No Flush: This strategy is referred to as an *undo/redo* algorithm [Bernstein et al., 1987]. It requires the least amount of synchronized disk writes and is most commonly used in commercial implementations. Steal/no flush imposes no restrictions on the amount of updates performed by a transaction as it does not require buffering of all updates until transaction end. The salient features of this strategy are described later in this chapter.

Steal/Flush: This strategy is referred to as an *undo/no redo* algorithm by Bernstein et al. [1987]. Force writing updated pages at the end of a transaction eliminates the need to redo committed transactions on system recovery. This leads to a simpler recovery algorithm but more force writing of updates at transaction end. As with steal/no flush, there is no restriction on the amount of updates performed by a transaction.

No Steal/Flush: Bernstein et al. [1987] refer to this strategy as a *no undo/no redo* algorithm. Modified data pages are completely buffered and are not written back to the stable database prior to the transaction's commit point. Consequently, no undo is necessary should the transaction abort. Redo is also rendered unnecessary by flush writing updated pages at commit time along with the use of an out-of-place update strategy.

No Steal/No Flush: This is referred to as a *no undo/redo* algorithm by Bernstein et al. [1987]. As in no steal/flush, undo is unnecessary because updates are buffered until transaction end. Because modified data pages are not flush written at the commit point, redo may be necessary on recovery from system failure.

Logging Granularity

Just as locking can be applied at the table, page, or row level, logging can also be applied at different granularities. Because pages are the actual units of transfer between the stable database in nonvolatile storage and the database buffers in volatile storage, undo and redo operations are simplest if applied at the page level. On the other hand, logging at the page level unnecessarily increases the size of the log entries and, consequently, the amount of input/output (I/O) overhead. Therefore, the most commonly used logging granule is a row within a page. To accommodate multiple records of varied length within the same page, it is common practice to include on the page a *line table* that identifies the offset and length of each *line* (i.e., a row or a portion of a row that spans multiple pages) within the page, and to map a row into one or more lines. (It is necessary to map a row into multiple lines on different pages only if the row is too long.) In this way, rows can be identified by a page number plus a line number; moreover, a row can be expanded and contracted within a database page and the index entries that point to the row need not be updated. Thus, a typical log entry might contain the following information:

- The transaction ID—a unique means of identifying the transaction in question.
- The operation, such as insert, delete, or update, performed on a line within a database page.
- The before image of the row for update and delete.
- The after image of the row for insert and update.

Physical logging describes the update operation in terms of physical changes made to specific data pages. *Logical logging* describes the update in terms of the logical database operations performed. Thus, a logical log record for an insertion operation would only identify the table, the columns, and the corresponding values that are inserted into the database. Insertion of information about the row in auxiliary access structures like indexes is implicit. Physical logging records the physical addresses and changes to all pages modified by the insertion of a new row, including the page receiving the row as well as index structures that point to the row. Physical logging records a larger amount of information but requires simpler recovery procedures; it is more commonly used in commercial database systems.

Bidirectional log records include both undo and redo information. Separate redo and undo logs lead to more I/O, but a more compact redo log is more convenient for media failure recovery. The undo log for a transaction can be garbage-collected as soon as the transaction is committed. Keeping both the undo and redo logs in the same sequential file makes it more difficult to garbage-collect the undo portions of the recovery log.

Checkpointing

Checkpointing is the activity of writing information to stable storage during normal operations in order to reduce the amount of work required at recovery time. Suppose some database pages are frequently updated. If we rely on only the least recently used page replacement algorithm for writing modified pages back to the stable database, then hot spots within the database may not be written back for a long time. As a result, recovery processing will essentially require the redoing of *all* committed transactions from the beginning of the log. Checkpointing flush writes pages from the database buffers in volatile storage back to the stable database, thereby creating a fire wall before which operations of committed transactions do not have to be redone, and operations of aborted transactions[7] do not have to be undone.

Bernstein et al. [1987] identified several different checkpointing strategies: the commit-consistent checkpoint, the cache-consistent checkpoint, and the fuzzy checkpoint.

Commit-consistent checkpoint. This kind of checkpoint can be taken by forcing a quiescent point within the database system, essentially stopping new transactions from entering the system and waiting for all in-progress transactions to be completed. All dirty database buffers are then written back to the stable database, and a checkpoint record is written. The advantage of taking commit-consistent checkpoints is that on recovery, it is never necessary to go before the latest checkpoint in the log to locate entries for undoing a transaction that aborts after the checkpoint. However, forcing a quiescent point within the database system may not be acceptable for many application environments.

Cache-consistent checkpoint. This commonly used checkpointing strategy is achieved by temporarily suspending database operations and by writing all dirty database buffer pages back to the stable database. This strategy guarantees that all transactions committed before the checkpoint do not have to be redone. On the other hand, transactions aborted after the checkpoint may have entries in the log before the checkpoint that are required for the undo operation.

Fuzzy checkpoint. A further optimization of the cache-consistent

---

7 This refers to only transactions that have been aborted as of the time of the checkpoint. Transactions that abort after the checkpoint still must be undone and they may have before images that are positioned before the checkpoint record in the log.

checkpoint notion is that of a fuzzy checkpoint. This concept minimizes the number of database buffers that have to be flush written at the time of each checkpoint. Instead of flushing all dirty database buffers, taking a fuzzy checkpoint entails writing only those dirty buffers that have not been written since the penultimate checkpoint (i.e., the previous checkpoint). In this case, the checkpoint record would also keep track of those buffers that have become dirty since the previous checkpoint. This information is then used in a subsequent checkpoint to determine what pages need to be flush written.

Restart Idempotence

After a system failure, the database system must go through a restart or system recovery procedure. It is possible for the system to encounter another failure even before the restart is completed. This leads to an important requirement: *restart idempotence*. That is, if the restart procedure is interrupted at any point and is reapplied from the very beginning, it must produce the same result in the stable database as if the first execution successfully ran to completion. In fact, any number of incomplete executions of restart, followed by a successful execution, must still produce the same correct result.

Since a restart assumes that cache buffers in volatile storage are lost, it completely relies on information from the stable database and from the recovery log to carry out its actions. In other words, a restart must ensure that the stable database is always in such a state that a new execution of restart can be correctly carried out. This requires that writes to the stable database during restart be carefully ordered.

Log Sequence Numbers

Log sequence numbers (LSNs) assigned to each log entry help to ensure that restart is idempotent and that undo and redo log entries are not applied unnecessarily. Whenever a page is modified, it is also assigned a LSN, corresponding to the LSN of the entry describing the modification to the page in question. Each log entry keeps track of the LSN of the previous page modification (old LSN) and the LSN of the following page modification (new LSN). During recovery processing, the LSN of a log entry is used to determine if an undo action or a redo action must be reapplied.

Consider an example where transaction T_1 is known to have committed and the following log entry is encountered:

Log record: insert row (with line number 1) into page 10

old LSN for page 10 = 100

new LSN for page 10 = 110

Suppose the LSN for page 10 in the stable database is 100. This indicates that the stable database still has the before image of T_1. Therefore, the insert row operation should be reapplied.

Consider another log entry for this same transaction:

Log record: modify row (with line number 2) in page 20

old LSN for page 20 = 200

new LSN for page 20 = 220

Suppose the LSN for page 20 in the stable database is 230. This indicates that page 20 in the stable database was already overwritten by a transaction more recent than T_1. Therefore, the modify row operation does not have to be reapplied.

Now consider another transaction T_2, which is known to have aborted. Suppose the following log record for T_2 is encountered:

Log record: insert row (with line number 1) into page 30

old LSN for page 30 = 300

new LSN for page 30 = 330

Suppose the LSN for page 30 in the stable database is 300. This indicates that T_2's update on page 30 was not yet written to the stable database or was previously undone; hence, there is no further need for undo.

Consider yet another log record for T_2:

Log record: delete row (with row number 2) from page 40

old LSN for page 40 = 301

new LSN for page 40 = 332

Suppose the LSN for page 40 in the stable database is 332. This indicates that the stable database still has the update of the aborted transaction T_2. Therefore, the operation must be undone using the before image of the deleted row from the log entry.

Undo/Redo

Based on the previous discussions on cache-consistent checkpointing, restart idempotence, and the use of log sequence numbers to avoid unnecessary undo/redo operations, we now outline an undo/redo algorithm for recovering from system failures. (This discussion assumes the use of page-level locking and the holding of transaction locks until they are committed or aborted.)

During normal operation, the following types of records are entered into the recovery log:

Insert/Delete/Update: This type of record identifies the transaction issuing the operation, the LSN of the previous log record for the same transaction, the address of the database record being operated on (i.e., its page number, offset, and size), the latter's before image and after image, and the old and new LSNs associated with the page containing the record.[8]

Commit: This type of record identifies the transaction being committed.

Abort: This type of record identifies the transaction being aborted.

Checkpoint: This type of record identifies a list of transactions active at the time of the checkpoint.

When a transaction is committed, a commit record is added to the log. This record and all preceding log records are flush written to stable storage. Database pages modified by a transaction are not required to be flush written at commit time. However, the write ahead log (WAL) protocol must be observed such that the log entry describing a page update operation must be written to stable storage before the modified page is written back to the stable database.

When a transaction is aborted, the before images in its log records are used to undo the actions of the transaction. Since these log records are linked in reverse chronological order, the before images are also reapplied in reverse chronological order. After the transaction's updates have been undone, an abort record is flush written to the log.

The checkpoint procedure is invoked periodically to flush dirty pages from the cache. This limits the amount of undo and redo necessary for system recovery. While the checkpoint procedure is in progress, all read, write, commit, and abort operations are suspended. The checkpoint record is appended to the log as the last step of the checkpoint procedure.

The restart procedure scans the recovery log in two passes. First, a backward scan from the end of the log is used to undo uncommitted transactions. Then, a forward scan from the last checkpoint in the log is used to redo updates of committed transactions.

---

[8] The new LSN associated with the page containing the record is simply the LSN for the log record itself.

The backward scan builds a list of committed transactions, a list of aborted transactions, and a list of incomplete transactions. When a commit or abort record is encountered, the corresponding transaction is added to the appropriate list. When an update record is encountered, the corresponding transaction is checked for inclusion in the committed list or in the aborted list. If not found, the transaction is added to the incomplete list. If the update record belongs to an aborted or incomplete transaction, the before image portion of the log record is applied to undo the effects of the update operation. Effectively, the actions of an aborted or incomplete transaction are undone in reverse chronological order. For transactions that were active at the last checkpoint but that were never committed, it is necessary to go beyond the last checkpoint in the backward scan to undo their updates.

When the last checkpoint record is reached, a list of committed transactions is collected in reverse chronological order. These transactions are reapplied in chronological order. In other words, the actions of each committed transaction should be reapplied in chronological order. Redo is complete when the end of the log is reached. The restart procedure is completed by adding abort records for all incomplete transactions (so as to leave the log in a consistent state), and by taking a new checkpoint (so that subsequent restarts will not have to go through the same undo and redo operations already taken in the current restart).

5.4 Case Studies

In this section, we examine and contrast the concurrency control and recovery management strategies in each of the servers covered in this book: the IBM OS/2 Extended Edition Database Manager, ORACLE Server, DEC Rdb/VMS, and Microsoft SQL Server.

5.4.1 IBM OS/2 Extended Edition Database Manager

The IBM OS/2 Extended Edition Database Manager uses locking to implement concurrency control. In addition, it supports three levels of isolation: cursor stability (CS), repeatable read (RR), and uncommitted read (UR). Its default isolation level is cursor stability.

The granularity for specifying isolation levels is an individual application program. The desired isolation level can be specified either at the time an embedded SQL application is precompiled, or if a bind file is generated by the precompilation, when the bind utility is used to bind the application to a particular database (see Chapter 7).

Cursor stability (CS) means that a row lock is held only while the cursor is positioned over that row. When the cursor is advanced, the lock on the previous row is released. Cursor stability applies only to data that is read. All modified rows remain locked until the transaction commits or aborts.

Repeatable read (RR) requires that row locks be held until the end of a transaction. If the transaction rereads a row multiple times, repeatable read guarantees that identical values are returned, with the exception that updates performed by the transaction are visible to the transaction itself. Since repeatable read keeps read locks for a longer duration, it offers less concurrency, but more data integrity, than cursor stability.

Uncommitted read (UR) allows the user to not set any read locks to perform a fetch or *select into host-variable* operation. It offers the highest degree of concurrency but at the expense of data integrity. Logically, nonexistent data could be read if transactions whose uncommitted updates were read are ultimately rolled back. In general, schema changes made by other concurrent applications are usually not visible to an application that is run at the uncommitted read isolation level.

The IBM Extended Edition implements multigranularity locking as discussed in Section 5.2.1. It supports the following lock modes on database objects. The compatibility of these lock modes is summarized in Table 5.4.

Intent None (IN): The lock owner can read any data within the object, including uncommitted data, without further locking at a lower level.

Intent Share (IS): This is identical to the intention read lock mode described earlier.

Share (S): This mode is identical to the read lock mode described earlier.

Intent Exclusive (IX): This is identical to the intention write lock mode described earlier.

Share With Intent Exclusive (SIX): This lock mode is identical to the read intention write lock mode described earlier.

Exclusive (X): This is identical to the exclusive lock mode described earlier.

Super Exclusive (Z): This is essentially an exclusive lock on the schema of the locked object. This lock mode is acquired prior to the dropping or schema alteration of the associated object. Schema alteration includes adding or dropping indexes and/or columns.

Mode A / Mode B	IN	IS	S	IX	SIX	X	Z
IN	Y	Y	Y	Y	Y	Y	N
IS	Y	Y	Y	Y	Y	N	N
S	Y	Y	Y	N	N	N	N
IX	Y	Y	N	Y	N	N	N
SIX	Y	Y	N	N	N	N	N
X	Y	N	N	N	N	N	N
Z	N	N	N	N	N	N	N

Table 5.4: Compatibility matrix for IBM Extended Edition table locks.

Version 1.2 of the IBM Extended Edition supports only before image journaling. It does not provide for recovery from media failure.

Dynamically Prepared Statements

In the IBM Extended Edition, cursors can be declared using the WITH HOLD option. By default, dynamically prepared statements within a transaction are released at the end of the transaction. Prepared statements referenced by cursors declared with the WITH HOLD option are retained at transaction commitment. When a transaction is rolled back, dynamic statements prepared within the transaction are also rolled back.

Record-level Locking

Record-level locking provides a high degree of concurrency. Record locks are implicitly set, that is, they are not under application control. Intention locks at the table level are automatically used to achieve multigranularity locking.

Table Locking

The LOCK TABLE statement is used to lock an entire table, exclusively or nonexclusively, under application control. Table locking is typically done in anticipation of batch-oriented operations on the table to minimize the bookkeeping overhead.

Lock Escalation

Lock escalation occurs when too many locks are issued on the database. To achieve lock escalation, the IBM Extended Edition requires that the next application process that requests a lock convert its row locks on a table into a table lock to reduce the overall number of outstanding locks. This process is repeated until sufficient locks are freed by one or more processes.

The maximum number of locks that an OS/2 process running Extended Edition Database Manager can hold is a configurable parameter. Sometimes a process may receive the escalation request even though it holds few or no locks on the target table. The reason is that one process may be holding many locks (although the number is less than the configuration parameter of locks per process) on rows of the target table. That process may not necessarily request another lock or access the database except to end the transaction. In the meantime, another process may come along and request a lock that triggers the escalation request. Like lock conversion, lock escalation in the IBM Extended Edition is subject to deadlocks.

Repeatable Read

In the IBM Extended Edition, repeatable read is implemented by locking all rows that are retrieved and by holding on to those locks until the end of a transaction. Since no other transactions are allowed to modify the rows read by a transaction until the latter commits, the retrieving transaction is guaranteed that its read operations are repeatable.

Cursor Stability

Cursor stability is implemented in the IBM Extended Edition by locking each row touched by a transaction for the duration that the cursor is positioned over that row. No other transaction is allowed to update or delete that row as long as the cursor is positioned over it. Cursor stability is strictly a weaker requirement than repeatable read (i.e., repeatable read implies cursor stability, but not vice versa).

Uncommitted Read

Uncommitted read is applicable only to read-only cursors. An intent none lock is set at the table level to prevent schema changes; no further lock is set at the row level for reading. For updatable cursors, the uncommitted read synchronization level behaves the same way as the cursor stability synchronization level; that is, locks will still be held on rows that are updated.

Deadlock Detection

In the IBM Extended Edition, periodic deadlock detection is performed by an asynchronous thread in a system background process called the deadlock detector. The deadlock detector looks for a cycle in the waits-for graph and selects a deadlocked transaction to roll back. The process that hosts the transaction is awakened, and it takes care of rolling back the effects of the victim transaction and releasing its locks. The deadlock detection interval may impact on overall performance. It is a configurable parameter.

5.4.2 ORACLE Server

The ORACLE Server also uses locking to synchronize concurrent read-write transactions. Two types of locks are of interest to users: data locks and dictionary locks. Data locks protect data and support two levels of granularity: table locks, which lock entire tables, and row locks, which lock selected rows only. Dictionary locks protect the schema or structure of database objects. They can be further classified as parse locks versus DDL locks. A dictionary lock held in share mode is called a *parse lock*. It is acquired at the beginning of a query on tables referenced in the query to guard against schema changes on those tables by other transactions. A dictionary lock held in exclusive mode is called a *DDL lock*. It is acquired for SQL statements performing DDL operations that are potentially incompatible with other outstanding SQL statements.

The default locking employed for queries guarantees a read-consistent result for every query. This is implemented using a multiversion concurrency control algorithm that effectively makes use of information recorded in the undo log (rollback segments in the ORACLE Server terminology) to reconstruct a consistent database snapshot for the reader.

The ORACLE Server supports a form of multigranularity locking that varies slightly from the scheme discussed in Section 5.2.1. The granules supported are tables and rows. The following table lock modes are supported by ORACLE:

Row Share/Share Update (RS): This mode is equivalent to the combination of the intention read and intention write modes discussed earlier. Recall that a transaction holding an intention read (intention write) lock on a table is expected to further set read (write) locks on desired rows. In the ORACLE Server, these two modes are collapsed into one because the only lock mode that can be set at the row level is exclusive. As we shall see, this is partially a consequence of the ORACLE Server's multiversion concurrency control mechanism, which obviates the need for share locks at the row level. The ORACLE Server automatically acquires a RS lock when it comes across a SELECT ... FOR UPDATE statement.

Row Exclusive (RX): This mode is analogous to the intention write mode discussed earlier. The transaction is expected to further set exclusive (write) locks at the row level. The ORACLE Server automatically acquires a RX lock when it comes across an INSERT, DELETE, or UPDATE statement.

Share (S): This is analogous to the read mode discussed earlier and is only used to implement user-controlled LOCK TABLE statements. It is not explicitly used by the ORACLE Server.

Share Row Exclusive (SRX): This mode is analogous to the read intention write mode described earlier. It is used to look at an entire table and to perform selective updates. SRX allows other transactions to lock rows in the table but not to lock the entire table in share mode. This lock mode is not implicitly used by the ORACLE Server.

Exclusive (X): This mode is analogous to the write mode presented earlier. It is used only in user-controlled LOCK TABLE statements.

The compatibility matrix for these lock modes is shown in Table 5.5.

Explicit Locking

ORACLE supports explicit locking, both at the row and table levels. A SQL SELECT ... FOR UPDATE statement may be used to explicitly lock rows within a table. The LOCK TABLE statement, on the other hand, can be used to lock an entire table in row share, row exclusive, share update, share, share row exclusive, or exclusive mode. Furthermore, a NO WAIT option may be specified to indicate that if the desired table lock cannot be granted because of resource conflicts, the transaction should be notified immediately.

	RS	RX	S	SRX	X
RS	Y	Y	Y	Y	N
RX	Y	Y	N	N	N
S	Y	N	Y	N	N
SRX	Y	N	N	N	N
X	N	N	N	N	N

Table 5.5: Compatibility matrix for the ORACLE Server table locks.

Lock Conversion and Escalation

In ORACLE, lock conversion typically occurs at the request of a transaction. If a transaction holding an explicit table lock requests another lock mode on the same table, conversion will be attempted. The resulting lock mode on the table may not be exactly the lock mode requested. Instead, a more restrictive lock mode (compared to the previously owned lock mode and the currently requested lock mode) may result. This happens when the requested lock mode and the previously owned lock mode are not directly comparable; that is, neither one is strictly more restrictive than the other.

ORACLE does not escalate locks automatically. Lock escalation only happens when a transaction that is holding row locks requests an explicit table lock.

Deadlock Detection

When the ORACLE Server detects a deadlock, it rolls back the current statement of one of the transactions involved in the deadlock. It is up to the transaction's logic to decide whether to retry the statement or to roll back the entire transaction.

Read Consistency

ORACLE implements a multiversion concurrency control algorithm that allows queries to see a consistent snapshot of the database without setting locks, thereby not impeding other transactions from updating the same data. When a read-consistent view is needed, ORACLE utilizes information in the rollback segments (undo log) to reconstruct older data blocks where necessary. This happens if a data block is changed between the time a query is started and the time the data block is accessed. Only blocks that have changed since the query began need to be reconstructed; others can be read directly from the cache or from the stable database. ORACLE's multiversion mechanism allows readers to access true multiple logical versions of the same table. It does not impose the two-version restriction discussed in Section 5.2.2. By default, the consistent database snapshot afforded to each SQL SELECT statement is as of the time the associated cursor is opened. The query sees all updates that were committed as of the query's start, plus any updates made by the transaction that encapsulates the query in question.

Occasionally, if a query is long or if update-intensive applications are running concurrently, the ORACLE Server may not be able to return a read-consistent snapshot of the database because blocks from the rollback segments might have been recycled. In such cases, an error message, "Snapshot too old," will be returned. The user's available options are

(1) restart the query in the hope that fewer updates will be running concurrently,
(2) explicitly lock tables so that it will not be necessary to reconstruct old data blocks, or
(3) increase the individual size of and/or the total number of rollback segments.

Overriding ORACLE's Default Concurrency Control

By default, each query within a transaction sees a consistent snapshot of the database as of the query's initiation time. Thus, if the same query is issued within a transaction twice, it is liable to see somewhat different results if concurrent update transactions modify some of the rows retrieved by the query. Likewise, a transaction that makes use of multiple queries to test consistency constraints spanning multiple tables may find that the information retrieved in different queries is somewhat inconsistent. To guard against such inconsistencies, ORACLE offers the SET TRANSACTION READ-ONLY statement. The statement instructs ORACLE to evaluate all subsequent queries in the context of the current transaction using a snapshot of the database as of the time the transaction was initiated. There are several restrictions imposed on a read-only transaction:

- The SET TRANSACTION statement must be the first statement in the transaction.
- Only queries are allowed in the transaction.
- A COMMIT, ROLLBACK, or a DDL statement will terminate the transaction.
- All queries within the transaction see a consistent snapshot of the database.
- Other users may continue to query or update the same data.
- The read-only transaction will see only updates that have been committed as of its own initiation time.
- Long running read-only transactions may receive the "Snapshot too old" error message.

If the above restrictions are too stringent for a transaction, one option is to use explicit TABLE LOCKING statements. Alternatively, the parameter SERIALIZABLE in the configuration file init.ora can be set to true. By default, this parameter is set to false in ORACLE Version 6 implementations.

ORACLE's default locking scheme does not guarantee serializability. By default, ORACLE's read consistency mechanism makes use of a snapshot that is effective as of the start of each explicit or implicit query. (An explicit query is a SELECT statement; an implicit query is any SELECT statement nested within an INSERT, or an implicit SELECT operation induced by the WHERE clause within an UPDATE or DELETE statement.) The only way to turn off these defaults and to ensure that multiple queries within a transaction see the same consistent database snapshot is to declare a transaction to be read only. Thus, if a transaction T_1 needs to insert into two different tables using the results of the same query by executing the query twice, it is possible that the first query does not see the updates of another transaction T_2, while the second query does see the updates of T_2. Therefore, the result of this interleaved execution of the two transactions is neither equivalent to the serialization order of T_1 followed by T_2, nor to the serialization order of T_2 followed by T_1. Under this scenario, serializability can be achieved only by overriding ORACLE's locking scheme either by using the LOCK TABLE statement, or setting locks on rows that are read using the FOR UPDATE clause in conjunction with a SELECT statement.

Sequence Generation

In the ORACLE Server, the sequence generator is used to generate sequence numbers (as unique identifiers) for rows within a table. Two concurrent transactions may create rows that are assigned different sequence numbers. Rolling back one of these transactions will not affect the other's ability to commit. However, the sequence numbers generated on behalf of a failed transaction will be lost forever.

Table Locking

The following is an example for table locking in the ORACLE Server:

```
LOCK TABLE <table name>
IN SHARE ROW EXCLUSIVE MODE
NO WAIT
```

A row share (same as share update) table lock allows concurrent access to the table; it conflicts with an exclusive lock on the same table. A row exclusive lock is similar to a row share lock, with the exception that it also conflicts with a share lock on the same table. A share row exclusive lock is used to lock an entire table to do selective updates; it is also used to allow other users to look at rows in the table but not to lock the table in share mode or to update rows.

The NO WAIT option in the table locking statement specifies that if a resource is not available, control should be returned immediately to the application. By default, a transaction may have to wait indefinitely for a requested lock.

SELECT FOR UPDATE

ORACLE's FOR UPDATE option in a select statement causes locks to be set on the selected rows. This can be considered a form of explicit locking at the row level. It is used for locking a row without actually modifying it. For example, if an application desires to perform an update based on the existing values of a row, it is necessary to ensure that the values of the dependent row are not changed by someone else before the application's updates are performed.

SELECT ... FOR UPDATE statements first execute the query to identify the rows that qualify for selection, and then set locks on them.

Savepoints

The ORACLE Server supports the use of savepoints in order to subdivide a transaction into smaller portions. At any point within a transaction (after the completion of a particular SQL statement), a transaction may create a savepoint with the following syntax:

SAVEPOINT savepoint_ID

where savepoint_ID is a SQL identifier or a host variable. Subsequently, the transaction can be rolled back to that savepoint using the syntax

ROLLBACK [WORK] TO [SAVEPOINT] savepoint_ID

If the same savepoint_id is used in two different SAVEPOINT statements within the same transaction, then the subsequent savepoint effectively overwrites the previous one. When a transaction is rolled back to a previous savepoint, all locks acquired after the savepoint are released.

Redo Logging

Redo log files are used to recover from system and media failures. They should be stored on disk drives that are separate from database files. The redo log under the ORACLE Server can be used in either an *archivelog* mode or a *noarchivelog* mode. The log mode is selected either when the database is initially created or with the ALTER DATABASE statement when the database is closed and there are no active transactions against it.

In *archivelog* mode, all changes made to the database are logged, and the log entries are managed in such a way that they can be used to reconstruct the stable database in the event of a media failure. To facilitate media failure recovery, an offline redo log must be used in conjunction with the online redo log. In addition, the database must be physically backed up periodically.

The online redo log files are needed under both the archivelog mode and the noarchivelog mode. The archivelog mode facilitates both system failure recovery and media failure recovery. On the other hand, the noarchivelog mode performs garbage collection to the log in such a way that only system failure recovery can be guaranteed. When an online log is full, its contents must be saved or garbage-collected before it can be reused. Under the archivelog mode, the contents of an online log file must be archived before the file can be reused. The online redo log contains two or more operating system files.

An offline log is needed only under the archivelog mode. It consists of all redo log files that have been archived. Typically, the offline log is kept in a removable stable storage medium that may require some manual action to bring it online.

When a database is accessed under the noarchivelog mode, online backups cannot be performed. Instead, the database can be backed up only while it is shut down. The checkpoint interval is the number of redo log blocks used as a threshold to trigger a checkpoint.

Rollback segments are used to save the before images of transactions. Each rollback segment can accommodate only a limited number of transactions. Long running queries can increase the demand for rollback segments. If the data needed to generate a read-consistent block from a rollback segment is overwritten, the query will get the "Snapshot too old" error.

If noarchivelog is used, media failure can be recovered only by using a snapshot of the database taken while it was offline. All transactions committed beyond the point the snapshot was taken are lost.

Backups

An *image backup* is a block-by-block copy of the database. It is a physical copy that records the location of all data in order to restore the data to the same form.

An *export* is a logical backup. It moves database data to an operating system file. Export uses a read-consistent view of an individual table. If an export for the entire database is taken, it is recommended that all tables be locked in share mode. Treating this operation as a read-only transaction may not work because of the possibility of a "Snapshot too old" error. The export saves the data and database definitions in a format that only ORACLE understands. The restore can be targeted for a different device or different ORACLE database.

5.4.3 DEC Rdb/VMS

DEC's Rdb/VMS uses table-level, page-level, and row-level locking for concurrency control to guarantee transaction serializability. It supports both preclaim and timeout strategies to avoid deadlocks, and it uses separate recovery unit journal (RUJ) and after image journal (AIJ) files to support transaction, system, and media recovery. Rdb/VMS also implements a special snapshot (SNP) file mechanism to improve concurrency of read-only transactions.

Concurrency Control

With Rdb, the characteristics of a transaction can be explicitly specified using a SET TRANSACTION statement. The characteristics of all subsequent transactions can also be specified using a DECLARE TRANSACTION statement. Furthermore, tables can be explicitly reserved in a SET TRANSACTION statement.

Rdb supports three types of transactions: *read-only* transactions, *read-write* transactions, and *batch-update* transactions. Read-write is the default.

Read-only transactions are supported via a SNP file, while read-write transactions use both the RUJ file and the AIJ file. Batch-update transactions do not update the RUJ file or the SNP file and therefore cannot coexist with read-only transactions.

Tables can be reserved by specifying a share mode and a lock type:

SET TRANSACTION <transaction mode>

RESERVING <table name>

FOR <mode of sharing> <lock type>

The mode of a transaction can be either read only, read write, or batch. Read-only transactions are supported using a snapshot file multiversion mechanism discussed later in this section. Read-write transactions are synchronized using locking. In general, row-level locks are used, except when tables are reserved in the protected read (PR), protected write (PW), or exclusive (EX) modes discussed below.

Rdb/VMS supports the following modes of sharing:

Shared: With this mode, other users can work with the same table. Depending on the options those users choose, they can have read-only or read-write access to the table.

Protected: This mode allows other users to read rows from the same table, but it does not allow those other users write access.

Exclusive: With this mode, other users cannot have access to the same table.

The lock type indicates the intended access to the table:

Read: Rows can be retrieved but not updated.

Write: Rows can be both retrieved and updated.

Table 5.6 shows the compatibility matrix of DEC's Rdb/VMS table locks.

	SR	SW	PR	PW	EX
SR	Y	Y	Y	Y	N
SW	Y	Y	N	N	N
PR	Y	N	Y	N	N
PW	Y	N	N	N	N
EX	N	N	N	N	N

Table 5.6: Rdb/VMS lock compatibility matrix.

A transaction that specifies a reserving clause is not started until all the specified tables are available in at least share mode. Actual processing will not commence until all the specified tables are available in the specified modes. Lock modes more restrictive than originally reserved may also be necessary in the course of performing the transaction.

The shared read and shared write options set row-level locks. They permit high concurrency but are subject to deadlocks. The protected read option disallows write access to the same table by other read-write transactions. The protected write option disallows both read and write access by other read-write transactions.

Row-level locking is always used if a read-write transaction is processed using a table scan, and if the table in question was reserved in a prior SET TRANSACTION statement with the EXCLUSIVE option.

A WAIT or NOWAIT specification can also be attached to a SET TRANSACTION statement. If NOWAIT is specified, an error will immediately be returned as soon as the transaction encounters an object that it cannot lock successfully. If WAIT is specified, the maximum amount of time allowable for waiting for a lock can also be indicated.

The default characteristics of a transaction include (1) read and write access to all declared databases, (2) indefinite wait for locks that are required, and (3) repeatable reads and the absence of phantoms.

Rdb allows schema updates to be bracketed by transactions. In other words, there is no need to treat each SQL DDL statement as a separate transaction. However, schema updates that conflict with access plans generated for compiled queries must wait for the termination of applications that have compiled those queries.

Adjustable Lock Granularity

As we will see in Chapter 7, Rdb uses a process-oriented model for transaction processing. Transactions originating from distinct applications are processed by distinct operating system (OS) processes. Internally, Rdb makes use of the VMS Distributed Lock Manager to maintain locks on a database resource at table, page, and row levels to synchronize with Rdb processes running other applications. This form of multigranularity locking is quite different from the multigranularity locking implemented in other systems. The objective is to maintain as few locks as possible.

When a query needs access to a specific table, Rdb first determines if other OS processes are accessing the same table. If not, it locks the entire table. At the same time, Rdb sets up an asynchronous notification routine (called an *asynchronous system trap*), which the VMS Distributed Lock Manager uses to notify Rdb of other processes' attempts to lock the same table. Subsequently, if other transactions try to access rows from the same table and the former transaction's copy of Rdb is notified, Rdb may decide to keep the table lock. Alternatively, Rdb may decide to acquire the appropriate row-level locks and then demote its own table lock to a less restrictive level. By default, the adjustable lock granularity capability is enabled. It is disabled using the ADJUSTIBLE LOCK GRANULARITY IS DISABLED option of the ALTER SCHEMA statement.

Read-only Transaction Support

Rdb makes use of a snapshot file to allow read-only transactions to see consistent snapshots of the database without setting locks, thereby not conflicting with update transactions. When the snapshot file option is enabled, update transactions write before images of each updated row to the snapshot file. Read-only transactions use the snapshot file to access those rows that have been updated since the time of its initiation, thereby seeing a consistent database snapshot that is effective as of that time. If snapshot files are not enabled when an attempt is made to start a database in read-only mode, only read transactions will be allowed, and they will be synchronized through record-level locking by default.

It should be noted that unlike rollback segments in the ORACLE Server, snapshot files in Rdb are not used in regular transaction and system recovery. Rather, they are maintained expressly for eliminating conflicts between read-only and update transactions. With snapshot files enabled, additional I/O overhead is incurred by update transactions.

Snapshot files are enabled by default in Rdb. They can be deferred or reset using the ALTER SCHEMA statement

```
ALTER SCHEMA FILENAME <file_name>
SNAPSHOT IS ENABLED <IMMEDIATE / DEFERRED> ;
```

When deferred snapshot files are used, read-only transactions wait for all update transactions to begin writing to the snapshot files before starting. Once snapshot-file writing has started, subsequent read-only transactions do not have to wait. When all read-only transactions complete, subsequent updates do not write to the snapshot files. Snapshot files can also be disabled altogether using the SNAPSHOT IS DISABLED option.

It is important to note that batch-update transactions and transactions that reserve tables in exclusive mode do not write to snapshot files. Hence, such transactions are not able to start while read-only transactions are in progress, and vice versa.

The snapshot file is automatically expanded as necessary. The initial allocation for a snapshot file is 100 pages. The SNAPSHOT EXTENT IS option is used to specify the number of pages added to the SNP file when the initial allocation is exceeded. Alternatively, the.SNP file can be automatically expanded by a specified percentage of its current size as follows:

```
ALTER SCHEMA FILENAME <file_name>
SNAPSHOT EXTENT IS
(MINIMUM OF <m> pages, MAXIMUM OF <n> pages,
PERCENT GROWTH IS <p>) ;
```

Before Image Journaling

Each user process maintains a separate recovery unit journal (RUJ) file to keep track of before images of transactions it processes. On system recovery, all RUJ files for processes that were active prior to the system failure must be available. The before images of a transaction in a RUJ file are cleaned up once the transaction terminates. The RUJ file is not written by batch-update transactions. If the transaction fails, the operation cannot be rolled back. The corrupted database can only be recovered from the most recent backup.

Snapshots

As discussed, the snapshot (SNP) file is used to store before images of read-write transactions to permit read-only transactions to see a consistent state of the database. A single SNP file can be shared by multiple concurrent users. The SNP file is not updated by batch-update transactions or by transactions that reserve tables in exclusive write mode.

After Image Journaling

After image journaling is optional in Rdb/VMS. If enabled, a single after image journal (AIJ) file is created for the entire database for logging after images of updates performed for each transaction. The initial size of the allocated AIJ file is adjusted using the JOURNAL ALLOCATION IS option for the ALTER SCHEMA statement. The size of incremental allocations is specified using the JOURNAL EXTENT IS option. The after images of a transaction, along with the database pages modified by the transaction, are flush written to stable storage at transaction end. Thus, no redo is necessary to recover from a system failure. Unlike the SQL Server and ORACLE, the AIJ file in Rdb is not preallocated a fixed amount of space. Instead, it grows incrementally and indefinitely.

After Image Journal Archival

In Rdb, the RMU/BACKUP/AFTER_JOURNAL command copies the contents of the database's AIJ file to a backup AIJ file (typically on magnetic tape). On completion, the online AIJ file is truncated to a size of zero.

The procedure operates in two modes:

Catchup mode: Transactions can continue to write to the online AIJ file while the latter's contents are being copied to the backup AIJ file.

Quiet-point mode: A quiet-point lock suspends all transaction activities. The remainder of the online AIJ file is copied to the backup AIJ file before the quiet-point lock is released.

Normally, the contents of the online AIJ file that exist at the beginning of the backup operation are copied to the backup AIJ file using the catchup mode. In the meantime, other transactions can continue to append to the online AIJ file. When the backup procedure is finished copying the original portion of the AIJ file, it goes into the quiet-point mode to copy the newly appended portion of the AIJ file and to truncate the online AIJ file. When the online AIJ file grows beyond the size specified in the /THRESHOLD option, the backup procedure immediately goes into the quiet-point mode and prevents transactions from appending to the AIJ file until its contents are backed up.

In addition to manual initiation, the AIJ file backup procedure can be set up to run on a periodic basis.

Online Backup

Backing up a database is carried out as a read-only transaction and therefore is done in parallel with other read-write transactions. Batch-update transactions and transactions that reserve tables for exclusive write, however, cannot be present because they do not post updates to the SNP file.

The RMU/BACKUP/ONLINE command starts a read-only transaction and makes use of the SNP file where necessary. Therefore, SNP files must be enabled. During online backup, batch transactions that attempt to reserve tables in exclusive mode are disallowed because they do not write before images to the SNP files.

5.4.4 Microsoft SQL Server

The SQL Server uses page-level locking for concurrency control and periodic checkpointing to flush write modified database pages back to stable storage. It uses the write ahead log (WAL) protocol to ensure transaction recoverability. It also employs a physical logging strategy, thereby logging insert, delete, and update operations on data records and to indexes. In general, the SQL Server does not allow DDL statements inside user-defined transactions.

Implicit Transactions

Transactions in the SQL Server can be bracketed with explicit BEGIN TRANSACTION and COMMIT TRANSACTION calls. When a SQL statement is not explicitly bracketed, it is implicitly treated as an individual transaction.

Cursor Stability

By default, read locks are not held until the end of a transaction in the SQL Server. They are used only to guard against reading uncommitted updates and are released as soon as possible. The HOLD LOCK option is used on a SELECT statement immediately after the WHERE clause to flush the retention of read locks until transaction end.

Timestamp

The SQL Server supports a timestamp data type. Every time a row is modified, a column of type timestamp is automatically assigned a unique eight-byte timestamp that is monotonically increasing. This timestamp is guaranteed to be unique within the database. Even if multiple rows are inserted or modified by the same SQL statement, each row is assigned a unique timestamp. Thus, the timestamp column can be treated as a unique system-generated primary key. It is similar to system-generated sequence numbers in the ORACLE Server, with the exception that the key space is nonsequential.

Browse Mode Support

The timestamp column values in the SQL Server are used to implement a simple form of optimistic concurrency control. This mechanism is particularly suited for allowing multiple users to concurrently browse rows of a table and to selectively perform updates. Essentially, no locks are held on the rows that have been read. If a user U_1 desires to update a particular row, the timestamp for the row last read by this user is compared against the timestamp of the row currently stored in the database. If there is a mismatch, then between the time U_1 reads the row and the time he/she decided to perform the update, another user U_2 had already performed an update on the same row. In this case, U_1 has no choice but to refresh his/her copy of the row before reapplying the update.

Page-level Locking

The SQL Server uses page-level locking on data rows and indexes. Write locks are held until the end of the transaction. Read locks, by default, are released as soon as the transaction finishes reading the page. However, when the HOLDLOCK option is specified, read locks are held until the end of the transaction.

Savepoints

The SQL Server allows users to specify savepoints within a transaction and to selectively roll back to a previously established savepoint.

Multidatabase Transactions

A transaction that updates tables in multiple databases will automatically open a transaction in each of the databases referenced. The transaction in the original database is considered the master transaction.

Backup

The SQL Server allows databases to be backed up even while users are actively accessing those databases. The DUMP DATABASE command makes an exact snapshot of the database. Changes made after the start of the backup are not included in the backup. As soon as the SQL Server receives the DUMP database command, it checks the transaction log for recently committed transactions and makes sure that the updates for those transactions have been reflected in the stable database. The SQL Server keeps track of which sections of the database have been backed up. If an ongoing transaction requests a change to data that has already been backed up, there is not a problem. However, if a transaction attempts to modify a portion of the database that has not yet been backed up, the system immediately rearranges the backup sequence so it can back up that particular section of the database next. After backing up that section, the SQL Server executes the change requested by the transaction.

The SQL Server also has the ability to backup the transaction log. The DUMP TRANsaction command makes a backup of all entries in the log that deal with committed transactions. Backing up the transaction log is less complicated than a full database backup because transactions being run during the log backup simply append to the log. They do not write over existing entries. Thus, backing up the transaction log only involves copying log entries to the backup device and then deleting the entries from the online transaction log.

5.5 Summary

In this chapter, we defined a transaction as a sequence of database operations that is atomic with respect to recovery. That is, either the entire sequence of operations or nothing at all is applied to the database. A more formal definition of transaction processing requires each transaction to satisfy the atomicity, consistency, isolation, and durability properties.

We also discussed the ways in which database systems implement concurrency control to synchronize the activities of concurrent transactions and to guard against mutual interference. Concurrency control algorithms in the literature fall into three main categories:

locking, timestamp ordering, and optimistic. Current commercial implementations are mostly based on locking. The lockable database granules may include database, table, page, and row. Generally speaking, the finer the locking granule, the higher the bookkeeping overhead and the higher the degree of concurrency.

We saw that concurrency can also be improved through the use of multiple lock modes. A transaction can declare its intention on the kind of operation it will perform to a database object, thereby allowing other transactions with compatible intentions to hold compatible locks on the same database object. The locks acquired by a transaction must be released with a certain discipline to guarantee serializability. Two-phase locking refers to the protocol that no locks are released by a transaction until it has acquired all locks needed for its processing. Even though it is permissible to start releasing locks before the end of a transaction, most implementations release locks at transaction end to avoid the complication of cascaded rollbacks.

We discussed recovery management and its importance in guaranteeing the atomicity and durability of transactions. Most commercial implementations use the write ahead log (WAL) protocol to support recovery from transaction failures, system failures, and media failures. Here, before images are written to the recovery log prior to any in-place update in the database, and after images are written to the recovery log before a transaction is committed. Before images are used to undo the updates of transactions that are rolled back; they are needed for both transaction recovery and system recovery. Some systems exploit before images to implement multiversion concurrency control, thereby ensuring that read-only transactions do not conflict with read-write transactions. After images are used to redo the updates of transactions that must be rolled forward; they are needed for both system recovery and media recovery. To minimize the amount of synchronized writes to the database, most high-performance systems implement periodic checkpointing to write modified database pages back to the database, rather than forcing writes to happen before a transaction is considered committed.

Finally, we examined the concurrency control and recovery management strategies in four database servers: the IBM Extended Edition, ORACLE Server, DEC Rdb/VMS, and Microsoft SQL Server. Table 5.7 presents a comparison of these concurrency control features and Table 5.8 compares the recovery management features of these systems.

Concurrency Control Features	IBM EE	Oracle Server	DEC Rdb/VMS	Microsoft SQL Server
Cursor Stability	Y	Y	Y	Y
Deadlock Detection	Y	Y	Y	Y
Deadlock Detection Interval Specification	Y	N	Y	N
Dirty Read	Y	N	N	N
Explicit Table Lock	Y	Y	Y	N
Implicit Page Lock	N	N	Y	Y
Implicit Row Lock	Y	Y	Y	N
Implicit Table Lock	Y	Y	Y	Y
Implicit Transaction Start	Y	Y	Y	Y
Intention Lock	Y	Y	N	Y
Livelock Detection	N	N	N	Y
Lock Conversion	Y	Y	Y	Y
Lock Escalation	Y	N	N	Y
Multiversion Concurrency Control	N	Y	N	N
No WAIT Option	N	Y	Y	N
Optimistic Concurrency Control	N	N	N	Y
Phantom	N	N	N	N
Repeatable Read	Y	Y	Y	Y
Serializability	Y	Y	Y	Y
Serializability as Default	Y	N	Y	N

Concurrency Control Features	IBM EE	Oracle Server	DEC Rdb/VMS	Microsoft SQL Server
Snapshot Read	N	Y	Y	N
Timeout	N	Y	Y	N

Table 5.7: Comparison of concurrency control features in four servers.

Recovery Management Features	IBM EE	ORACLE Server	DEC Rdb/VMS	Microsoft SQL Server
After Image Logging	Y	Y	Y	Y
Before Image Logging	Y	Y	Y	Y
Bidirectional Logging	Y	N	N	Y
Checkpoints	Y	Y	N	Y
Logical Logging	N	N	N	N
Media Recovery	N	Y	Y	Y
No Steal/Flush	N	N	N	N
No Steal/No Flush	N	N	N	N
Online Backup	N	Y	Y	Y
Physical Logging	Y	Y	Y	Y
Steal/Flush	N	N	Y	N
Steal/No Flush	Y	Y	N	Y

Table 5.8: Comparison of recovery management features in four servers.

Chapter 6
Database Administration and Maintenance

Database administration is concerned with establishing and maintaining the environment in which data is manipulated and stored. The activities involved in the efficient administration of a database are numerous and include tasks such as installing a database system, enrolling and dropping users, backing up and restoring a database, and importing and exporting a database or a database table. In addition, the database administrator is responsible for overseeing recoveries from media and system failures and for controlling and auditing database access and authorization.

In this chapter, we first provide an overview of these database administration tasks. We then proceed to describe the types of facilities provided by four database products for performing these tasks.

6.1 Installation

Database installation is the process of establishing the directory structure for the database management system, copying the software to the appropriate directory, setting up the database administrator account, and initializing the database system. In a client-server architecture, the installation process involves the installation of both the client workstation and the server machine. If the required operating system and the network support have been installed and configured appropriately, installation is a straightforward process. For the IBM Extended Edition Database Manager, ORACLE Server, and Microsoft SQL Server, OS/2 and the appropriate network software must be installed before the server is installed. Similarly, the VMS operating system and DECnet must be installed before Rdb is installed.

6.2 Database Startup and Shutdown

In order to access information in a database, that database must be started. When a database is shut down, users of a database cannot access information in the database. With the ORACLE Server and the SQL Server, a default database is started when you connect to the server. However, after connecting to a server with the IBM Extended Edition and DEC's Rdb, you must explicitly start a database to access data.

6.3 Enrolling and Dropping Users

To prevent unauthorized persons from accessing a database system, the security mechanism of the system must control user access. The access control in a database system creates user accounts and passwords to control the log-in process.

In this way, a user must have a user account in order to access a database system. A database administrator is a user account that is created during the initial database installation. Because the database administrator has a broad range of permissions and is responsible for enrolling and dropping users, this individual is considered a superuser. Enrolling a user in a database involves creating a new user account and password for that user; this allows a user to access information in that database. Dropping a user from a database is the process of removing a user account, thus disabling a user from accessing information in that database.

A user must log in to the database system by entering a user name and password. The database system makes sure that the user name and password are valid before allowing a user to use a database system and access data in a database.

6.4 Checkpointing

The database administrator must provide efficient recovery of databases for the users. One mechanism that enhances the recovery speed is checkpointing. The checkpointing process, which was discussed in Chapter 5, consists of the following steps:

(1) Freeze all the transactions that are modifying the database.

(2) Save the location of the next entry to be written in the transaction log file.
(3) Write all pages that have been modified since the last checkpoint to the database device.
(4) Write a checkpoint record to the saved location in the transaction log file.
(5) Unfreeze all frozen transactions.

After checkpointing, all completed transactions are written to disk. Thus, the recovery process is shortened because it can start at the checkpoint location.

6.5 Backup

Backup is the process of saving the database contents, usually by saving all the associated database files to a storage medium, so that data can be retrieved in case of recovery. However, even with database backup, transactions executed since the last backup may be lost. To prevent losing all the effects of the executed transactions since the last backup, the transaction log should be backed up periodically. The transaction log contains every change to the database and is usually substantially smaller than the database; thus it can be backed up more frequently. All committed transactions recorded in a transaction log that has been backed up can be recovered on database reconstruction. To recover from a disk failure, a database is first recreated on disk from its latest backup copy, then the effects of all the committed transactions that were stored in the backup transaction log are reconstructed.

In addition to the backup utilities supported by a particular operating system to backup database files, each database server also provides its own backup utilities for database backup. To restore a system to a reasonably current status when a database becomes corrupt, frequent backup is recommended.

6.6 Recovery

Recovery refers to the process of restoring the database to a consistent state after a system or media failure. Because a transaction is a logical unit of work that is atomic with respect to recovery, it is considered the basic unit of recovery.

Recovery guarantees that all incomplete transactions are undone completely from the database; it also guarantees that successfully completed transactions exist in the database. In some systems, recovery from system failure is automatic. However, recovery from media failure often requires the database administrator to restore the database from the backup files. Thus, to facilitate recovery from media failure, the database and the transaction log file should be backed up periodically to some other medium. In the case of media failure, the database is first restored from the most current database backup. The successive incremental transaction log backups are then applied to restore the database to a consistent state.

6.7 Data Import and Export

Import involves loading data from a foreign format operating system file to a database system. Export is the unloading of data from a database system to an operating system file, which can then be loaded to other database systems and file systems.

The importing and exporting of data can be useful in a number of situations. For example, import and export can facilitate backup by saving snapshots of table definitions or data offline. In addition, these processes enable data to be moved from a database on one computer to a database on another computer. And finally, import and export functions can provide protection against database corruption. For instance, because export copies only the logical contents of the database and does not make an exact copy of the database files, it can help recover from structural damage of a database.

6.8 Authorization Administration

Authorization administration governs the enrolling or dropping of users from a database. As we mentioned earlier, a user must be enrolled in a database in order to access data in that database.

Authorization administration also governs a user's access to certain database objects based on granting and revoking of privileges. In order to access a database object, a user must have the appropriate privileges. There are two different categories or levels for assigning privileges to the database system: the account level and the relation level.

The account level: The database administrator specifies the particular privileges that each account holds independent of the relations in the database. These privileges can include

CREATE	To create a base table
CREATE VIEW	To create a view
ALTER	To add or remove columns from tables
DROP	To delete tables or views
MODIFY	To insert, delete, or update records
SELECT	To retrieve information from the database using a SELECT query

The relation level: The database administrator controls the privileges to access each individual relation or view in the database. These privileges include

SELECT	To retrieve records from a table
UPDATE	To update records in a table
DELETE	To delete records from a table
INSERT	To insert records into a table
ALTER	To add or remove columns from tables

The owner of a table is given all privileges on that table and can pass on these privileges to other users by granting privileges to them. The user who grants privileges to other users is called a *grantor;* the user who receives privileges from a grantor is called a *grantee.* In some RDBMSs, the owner of a table has the choice of granting a privilege to another user with or without the *GRANT OPTION.* If the GRANT OPTION is given, the grantee can also grant that privilege to other users with or without GRANT OPTION. In this way, privileges on a table can propagate to other users without the knowledge of the table owner.

Revoking a privilege involves canceling a privilege that has been given to a certain user. When a grantor revokes certain privileges from a grantee, the grantee loses the granted privileges. Moreover, if the grantee was given the GRANT OPTION and granted the privileges to other users, those users also lose their privileges. Therefore, a database system that allows propagation of privileges must keep track of how the privileges were granted so that privileges can be revoked correctly.

6.9 Auditing

Auditing is a security feature that allows the database administrator and users to track database use. All accesses and operations applied to the database are recorded in a database log file. Auditing occurs at the database level and at the database object level:

Auditing access to the database: The database administrator monitors the result of attempts to connect and disconnect from the database. The DBA can also monitor the granting and revoking of privileges.

Auditing access to database objects: The owners of database objects monitor the access to their objects. Moreover, they can selectively audit different types of SQL statements executed against their database objects.

6.10 Case Studies

In this section, we examine how each of the four servers we have been discussing handles database administration and maintenance functions.

6.10.1 IBM OS/2 Extended Edition Database Manager

The IBM Extended Edition Database Manager is a database management system that runs under OS/2. It consists of the Database Services, Remote Data Services, and Query Manager components. Database Services provides users with an application programming interface for writing programs to access Database Manager databases. Remote Data Services provides users with data management functions for remote databases on a network connection. To access remote databases, the Communication Manager must be installed. Communication Manager provides the communications support code governing the information exchange between computers. Query Manager provides menus, panels, and associated contextual help to prompt the user through the process of retrieving and manipulating database data.

A workstation can be identified as a database server, a database requestor, or both a database server and a database requestor. A database server has one or more databases that can be shared with a database requestor. A database requestor has no local database, and thus depends on sharing access to a database that resides on a database server. A database requestor uses Advanced Program-to-Program Communication (APPC) to communicate with a database server. APPC is an application programming interface that provides system network architecture for application programs that process distributed transactions.

Installation

The IBM Extended Edition supports three methods of installing Database Manager: custom installation, basic configuration installation, and advanced installation.

Custom installation creates a customized diskette that contains specific instructions for installing each OS/2 component. The administrator prepares the custom install diskette. The custom install diskette contains a user configuration file that provides the system with the user's hardware and software configuration and information to configure the workstation for communications and Remote Data Services functions.

The basic configuration method installs the necessary OS/2 components and creates the required Communication Manager configuration file for a workstation. The configuration file contains the APPC profiles needed for Remote Data Services. The basic configuration installation establishes the necessary APPC profiles for each Database Requestor workstation to communicate with one Database Server workstation. When a Database Requestor workstation needs to communicate with more than one Database Server workstation, additional APPC profiles must be created.

With the advanced method, the necessary OS/2 components are installed. In addition, this method enables the user to build the configuration file that contains the necessary profiles for APPC. However, advanced installation does not build any APPC profiles. A configuration file must be created after installation is completed and the Communication Manager must be reinstalled with the newly created configuration file.

Database Manager Startup and Shutdown

The Database Manager is started automatically by the Query Manager. Therefore, the easiest way to start Database Manager is to enter the Query Manager. An alternative is to enter the STARTDBM command at the OS/2 command prompt. To start the Database Manager via a program, the user must execute a program that contains the sqlestar( ) routine call.

To shut down Database Manager, the user enters the STOPDBM command at the OS/2 command prompt. The Database Manager can also be shut down via a program by executing the sqlestop( ) routine call.

Database Startup and Shutdown

In Query Manager, the environment routine START USING DATABASE connects an application program to a database. Conversely, the environment routine STOP USING DATABASE disconnects an application program from a database.

Enrolling and Dropping Users

Controlling database access involves both access to and within Database Manager. Access to Database Manager is validated by the *User Profile Management* utility outside Database Manager.

Each request to access Database Manager is associated with an ID. This ID is the user ID or group ID within User Profile Management and Query Manager. It is also the authorization ID within Database Services. User Profile Management verifies that the user ID is valid before passing the user information on to Database Manager. Database Services then determines if the user is authorized for the requested action.

User Profile Management provides user ID validation and user and group management facilities. Additionally, User Profile Management provides three levels of authority: user, administrator, and local administrator.

All users can log in, view their own privileges, change their own passwords, add comments to their own profiles, and log off.

Administrators are authorized to add or delete users. They can create, change, and delete groups of users. They can also specify other user types, password options, and the access status of a user.

A local administrator is authorized to grant and revoke user privileges within Database Manager on the local workstation but has no administrator capabilities outside of Database Manager. There is only one local administrator on each workstation. If a second user is given the local administrator user type on a workstation, the user type of the first local administrator is changed to user.

Adding or dropping a user involves logging on to the User Profile Management utility as an administrator and perform the appropriate action.

Access Privileges

The IBM Extended Edition controls database access through the use of privileges granted to users and groups. Administrative authorities are privileges covering a set of objects. The IBM Extended Edition defines two administrative authorities: system administrator (SYSADM) and database administrator (DBADM). These authorities can grant or revoke the privileges of other users on existing database objects.

SYSADM authority has control over all Database Manager resources except the directories and system catalogs that are created and maintained by Database Manager. SYSADM authority includes all the privileges of DBADM authority for any database on the system. Additionally, SYSADM authority is local to a workstation and does not extend to remote databases.

DBADM authority includes all database, index, plan, and table privileges, as well as the ability to grant and revoke these privileges to and from other users. When DBADM authority is granted, BINDADD, CONNECT, and CREATETAB privileges are directly granted by Database Manager. Only a user with SYSADM authority can grant or revoke DBADM authority. Table 6.1 describes the database, index, plan, and table privileges in the IBM Extended Edition Database Manager, and Table 6.2 summarizes the privileges and authorities hierarchy in this server.

Privileges	Description
Database Privileges	Database privileges involve actions on a database. Only users with SYSADM or DBADM authority can grant and revoke database privileges. ▸ BINDADD enables a user to create new access plans in the database. The access plan creator automatically has CONTROL privilege for that plan. ▸ CONNECT enables a user to access the database. ▸ CREATETAB enables a user to create tables in the database. The table creator automatically has CONTROL privilege on the table.
Index Privileges	Index privileges involve the ability to create and drop indexes using the CONTROL privilege for indexes.
Plan Privileges	Plan privileges involve the ability to create and execute database access plans. ▸ CONTROL provides a user with control over an access plan in a database. A user with CONTROL privilege also has the BIND and EXECUTE privileges. ▸ BIND enables a user to rebind an access plan. ▸ EXECUTE enables a user to execute an existing access plan.

Privileges	Description
Table Privileges	Table privileges involve action on tables or views. ▸ CONTROL privilege on a table allows users to access a specific database object and to grant and revoke privileges to and from other users on that object. A user with CONTROL privilege is directly granted all the table privileges. The creator of a database object automatically has CONTROL privilege on that object. ▸ ALL gives the user INDEX, ALTER, SELECT, INSERT, DELETE, UPDATE, and REFERENCES privileges on a table. ALL gives the user SELECT, INSERT, DELETE, and UPDATE privileges on a view. ▸ ALTER enables a user to modify a table. ▸ DELETE enables a user to delete rows from a table or view. ▸ INDEX enables a user to create an index on a table. ▸ INSERT enables a user to insert an entry into a table or view. ▸ REFERENCES enables a user to create a referential constraint on a table. ▸ SELECT enables a user to retrieve rows from a table or view. This privilege also allows a user to run the EXPORT utility or to create a view on a table. ▸ UPDATE enables a user to change an entry in a table or view.

Table 6.1: *Description of the database, index, plan, and table privileges in the IBM Extended Edition Database Manager.*

SYSADM					
DBADM					
CREATETAB (Databases)	BINDADD (Databases)	CONNECT (Databases)	CONTROL (Indexes)	CONTROL (Access, Plans)	CONTROL (Tables, Views)
				BIND	ALL
				EXECUTE	ALTER
					DELETE
					INDEX
					INSERT
					REFERENCES
					SELECT
					UPDATE

Table 6.2: *Privileges and authorities hierarchy in the IBM Extended Edition Database Manager.*

Grant Privileges

The user must have SYSADM, DBADM, or CONTROL privilege on a database object to grant privileges on that object. The SQL GRANT command enables the specified privileges on a database object. The syntax of the GRANT command is as follows:

```
<GRANT statement> ::=
            GRANT <db_privilege_list> ON DATABASE TO <id_list>
    |       GRANT <table_privilege_list> ON TABLE <name> TO
                    <id_list>
    |       GRANT <plan_privilege_list> ON PROGRAM <name> TO
```

```
                <id_list>
|       GRANT CONTROL ON INDEX <name> TO <id_list>

<db_privilege_list> ::= <db_privilege> [ {, <db_privilege> }... ]
<db_privilege> ::=      DBADM     |
                        BINDADD |
                        CONNECT |
                        CREATETAB

<table_privilege_list> ::=  ALL [PRIVILEGES]    |
                            <table_privilege>[ {, <table_privilege> }... ]

<table_privilege> ::=       CONTROL             |
                        ALTER           |
                        DELETE          |
                        INDEX       |
                        INSERT          |
                        REFERENCES |
                        SELECT          |
                        UPDATE
<plan_privilege_list> ::= <plan_privilege> [ {, <plan_privilege> }... ]
<plan_privilege> ::=        CONTROL     |
                        BIND  |
                        EXECUTE
```

The grant privileges to database statement does not specify a database name; therefore, the action applies to the currently connected database.

Revoke Privileges

The user must have SYSADM, DBADM, or CONTROL privilege on a database object to revoke privileges on that object. Additionally, the user must have SYSADM or DBADM authority to revoke CONTROL privilege from another user. The SQL REVOKE command disables the specified privileges on a database object. The syntax of the REVOKE command is as follows:

```
<REVOKE statement> ::=
        REVOKE <db_privilege_list> ON DATABASE FROM <id_list>
  |     REVOKE <table_privilege_list> ON TABLE <name> FROM
              <id_list>
  |     REVOKE <plan_privilege_list> ON PROGRAM <name> FROM
              <id_list>
  |     REVOKE CONTROL ON INDEX <name> FROM <id_list>
```

The revoke statement does not specify a database name; therefore, the action applies to the currently connected database.

Backup

The IBM Extended Edition supports two ways of backing up and restoring a database: the user can use either the Database Services application programming interface or the Query Manager to back up or restore a database.

Database Services backup. Database Services provides an application programming interface routine SQLGBACK for backing up a database. The user must have SYSADM or DBADM privilege in order to execute the SQLGBACK routine.

Only local databases can be backed up using the SQLGBACK routine. Moreover, the user should execute the environment command START DATABASE MANAGER before calling this routine. To establish a starting point that contains all the database information, the user should back up the entire database first. After the starting point is created, the user can back up only those files that have changed since the last backup. Or, the user can create a new base and starting point by backing up the entire database again. Since the SQLGBACK routine uses the OS/2 backup utility, the restrictions for the OS/2 backup utility also apply. Before calling the back up routine, the diskette must be in the specified drive or an error returns.

The SQLGBACK routine connects to the database in an exclusive mode and locks out other applications until the backup is completed. Therefore, if other applications are connected to the database, the SQLGBACK routine fails.

IBM Extended Edition's Database Services SQLGDRES routine restores a database to a prior backed-up state. The database must have been backed up previously with the SQLGBACK routine to use the SQLGDRES routine for restoration. The user must have SYSADM privilege to execute the SQLGDRES routine.

The SQLGDRES routine restores only local databases. Similar to the SQLGBACK routine, the SQLGDRES routine connects to the database in an exclusive mode.

The SQLGDRES routine should be executed only if the database was damaged or destroyed. The routine first drops the database and then restores it.

Query Manager backup. The BACKUP DATABASE and RESTORE DATABASE utilities in Query Manager enable a user to back up and restore a database.

The BACKUP DATABASE utility provides the user with two methods to back up an IBM Extended Edition database: the user can back up an entire database or only those files that are new or that have changed since the last backup. Only users with SYSADM or DBADM authority can back up the database. The BACKUP DATABASE utility uses the OS/2 backup utility; therefore, the restrictions of the OS/2 backup utility also apply. For the changes-only backup, the user must insert the diskettes that were used on the previous backup in order to keep the file assignments correct.

Query Manager's RESTORE DATABASE utility restores a database to its previously backed-up state. Therefore, the database must have been previously backed up with the BACKUP DATABASE utility. The user must have SYSADM authority to execute this utility.

The RESTORE DATABASE utility requires that the database exist on the workstation before it can be restored. The authorized user can also create an empty database and then restore the data in the database. None of the databases on the workstation can be in use while the database is being restored.

Recovery

Database Services uses a circular logging method to store changes to the database. When a table is modified by an application program, the changes are recorded in the recovery log file. The changes are committed to the database if the application program is completed successfully. Otherwise, the changes are rolled back so that the table remains unchanged.

The IBM Extended Edition provides several functions for system recovery: BACKUP, RESTORE, IMPORT, and EXPORT. If a database is corrupted or accidentally deleted, and the database has been backed up, an authorized user may be able to restore it by using the RESTORE utility. If a table has been exported and is accidentally deleted, an authorized user may be able to restore it by using the IMPORT utility.

Data Import and Export

The IMPORT and EXPORT utilities enable a user to move data between an IBM Extended Edition database and other database systems and file systems. The OS/2 file formats supported by the IBM Extended Edition Database Manager are described in Table 6.3:

File Format	Description
DEL	Delimited ASCII for exchange with dBASE II, III, or III Plus, BASIC program, the IBM Personal Decision Series, DB2, and SQL/DS. DB2 and SQL/DS files can be imported only
ASC	Nondelimited ASCII for importing data from other applications
WSF	Worksheet formats
IXF	The preferred method for exporting data from a table, so that the data can be imported later into the same table or into another IBM EE Database Manager table

Table 6.3: The OS/2 file formats supported by the IBM Extended Edition Database Manager.

IMPORT utility. The IMPORT utility inserts data from an OS/2 file into an IBM Extended Edition Database Manager table. If the table or view receiving the imported data already contains data, the user can replace or append the data in the existing table or view with the data in the OS/2 file.

To import data into a new table, the user must have SYSADM, DBADM or CREATETAB privilege for the database. To import data into an existing table or view, the user must have either one of SYSADM, DBADM, or CONTROL privilege for the table/view, or SELECT, INSERT, and DELETE privilege for the table/view. To append data to an existing table or view, the user must have SELECT and INSERT privileges for the table or view.

EXPORT utility. The EXPORT utility exports data to an OS/2 file from an IBM Extended Edition Database Manager database. The user must have SYSADM, DBADM, CONTROL, or SELECT privilege for each table involved in the export.

6.10.2 ORACLE Server

The ORACLE Server is based on a client-server architecture in which a database application is divided into two parts: a client front end and a database-server back end. At the client front end, data is entered and retrieved from the database by executing end-user application programs. The server back end executes the relational database management system and enforces integrity. The back end database-server machine must service multiple clients simultaneously, thereby requiring a multitasking operating system such as OS/2.

Installation

The installation of the ORACLE Server involves two steps: setting up the server and setting up the client workstations.

Server installation. The ORACLE Server for OS/2 installation creates the directory structure for all the ORACLE products. The ORACLE_HOME directory is the main directory that holds ORACLE Server for OS/2 subdirectories and files. The default directory for ORACLE_HOME is \ORACLE6. Table 6.4 summarizes the subdirectories of ORACLE_HOME.

Subdirectory	Description
\BIN	Holds executable programs and batch files for ORACLE Server, Server Manager, SQL*Net drivers, and ORACLE tools
\DBS	Holds the files that contain the ORACLE database
\LIB	Holds the dynamic link libraries used by the server and other ORACLE products
\LOADER	Holds the SQL*Loader files
\PRO	Holds files used by PRO*C

Table 6.4: Description of the ORACLE_HOME subdirectories.

Table 6.5 describes the ORACLE programs that can be installed during server installation.

Program	Description
RDBMS	The Version 6.0 multiuser ORACLE RDBMS
SQL*DBA	A command line database tool that performs database administration functions
Server Manager	A menu-driven database administration utility that runs under OS/2 Presentation Manager
SQL*Loader	A utility for loading data from ASCII, dBASE III PLUS, and Lotus 1-2-3 files
EXP	A utility for writing data from an ORACLE Version 6.0 RDBMS database to an operating system file
IMP	A utility for reading data from export files into an ORACLE Version 6.0 RDBMS

Table 6.5: ORACLE programs installed during server installation.

All ORACLE programs can be installed by running the ORAINST utility. This involves inserting the diskette labeled "OS/2 install" in drive A and typing

```
[C:\] A:ORAINST
```

The user then follows the installation procedures, selecting all the ORACLE programs for install.

Client installation. The installation of an ORACLE client workstation is similar to the installation of ORACLE Server. The only difference is in the selection of products to be installed.

To establish a client workstation to run ORACLE tools, the following software from the ORACLE Server for OS/2 diskettes is required:

- Utilities (includes SQL*DBA)
- SQL*Loader
- SQL*Net

If the database is to be administered in Presentation Manager, the Server Manager diskette is also required. And, to develop C-interface programs, the additional software Pro*C must be installed.

ORACLE Server Database Startup and Shutdown

The database administrator is responsible for starting up and shutting down a server database. Starting an ORACLE Server database involves (1) starting an "instance" to allocate the database processes, (2) mounting a database so that the database is associated with the previously started instance, and (3) opening a database to enable normal database operations on the mounted database. An ORACLE database is often referred to as an instance because an instance contains all of the software codes and information necessary for a database to function.

The SQL*DBA STARTUP command is used to start, mount, and open a database:

```
SQLDBA> STARTUP;
```

Shutting down an ORACLE database involves (1) closing the database so that it is unavailable for general database operations by normal users, (2) dismounting the database to disassociate it from the current instance of ORACLE, and (3) shutting down an instance so that the database processes are removed from ORACLE's memory.

Before any shut down commands can be issued, the DBA must be disconnected from the database via the DISCONNECT command at the SQL*DBA prompt:

```
SQLDBA> DISCONNECT;
```

The SQL*DBA SHUTDOWN command is used to close and dismount a database and shut down an instance after all users have disconnected:

```
SQLDBA> SHUTDOWN;
```

To close and dismount a database and shut down an instance without waiting for all users to disconnect, the following statement is entered from the SQL*DBA prompt:

```
SQLDBA> SHUTDOWN IMMEDIATE;
```

Enrolling and Dropping Users

ORACLE has two levels of security—database access security and database object security. Database access security refers to the rights to access a database as a whole, while database object security refers to the rights to access specific database objects within a database.

A user must have the CONNECT privilege to connect to an ORACLE database. To create database objects in a database, a user must have the RESOURCE privilege on the tablespace of the database. A user with DBA privilege has all power of the CONNECT and RESOURCE privileges. Moreover, this user can perform any type of database operation with the ORACLE Server.

When a user is created, regardless of the privileges the user has been granted, his/her default tablespace (for creating database objects and temporary segments) is set to SYSTEM. To reduce contention for disk space and possibly improve ORACLE's performance, each user's default tablespace can be changed to a tablespace other than SYSTEM. This is done by using the ALTER USER command. The following example changes the tablespace of john from the default, which is SYSTEM, to the tablespace called usertablespace:

```
ALTER USER john DEFAULT TABLESPACE usertablespace
```

Creating New Users

The DBA can use the following forms of the GRANT statement to create new users. The first statement grants either a CONNECT or DBA privilege to a user with an optional password:

```
GRANT [ CONNECT | DBA ] TO <username>
                                   [ {, <username>}... ]
          IDENTIFIED BY <password>
                                   [ {, <password>}... ]
```

The next statement grants the CONNECT privilege and, optionally, the RESOURCE privilege to a user with an optional password:

```
GRANT CONNECT [, RESOURCE ] TO <username>
                              [ {, <username>}... ]
          IDENTIFIED BY <password>
                              [ {, <password>}... ]
```

Grant Privileges to Users

Existing users can be granted the RESOURCE or DBA privileges using a simpler form of the GRANT command:

```
GRANT [RESOURCE | DBA] TO <username>
```

Revoke Privileges From Users

Privileges can be revoked from users using the REVOKE command:

```
REVOKE [ CONNECT ] [, RESOURCE ] [, DBA] FROM <username>
```

A user must have the CONNECT privilege to connect to an

ORACLE database. Revoking the CONNECT privilege from a user is equivalent to dropping the user from the database since the user cannot connect to the database.

When a user is dropped, the database objects created by this user are affected as follows:

(1) Database objects created by the dropped user continue to exist.
(2) All users granted privileges to use those objects can continue to use them.
(3) If the username is recreated, the username will own all database objects previously created by that username.
(4) To drop database links created by the user, the DBA will temporary need to recreate the username, connect as that user, drop the database links, and then drop the username again.
(5) All other database objects owned by a dropped user may be dropped by the DBA using the DROP command that specifies the creator of the object.

Checkpoints

Checkpoints automatically occur when the redo log files become full. During checkpointing, the Database Writer (DBWR) process writes all modified database buffers in the System Global Area (SGA) to the database files. The completion of a checkpoint insures that all the log entries prior to the checkpoint in the online redo log are written to disk and are no longer needed for database instance recovery. When recovery is necessary at some time after the checkpoint is taken, it can start at the checkpoint location.

The checkpointing process consists of storing the location of the next entry to be written in the redo log file, writing the modified database buffers to disk, and then writing the stored location to the control file and database files. The database system does not halt activity, and current transactions are not affected when the checkpoint is in progress.

By periodically saving the changes to the database, checkpoints allow an online redo log file to be archived or reused. Moreover, it reduces the time required by database instance recovery.

Backup

Operating system backups of ORACLE's database files, redo log files, and control files are necessary.

Offline database backup. To perform a full offline database backup, the database must be shut down. Operating system commands or a backup utility is then used to make backups of all the database files, redo log files, and database control files. After the backup process is completed, the database is restarted.

Online database backup. To perform an online database backup, the database must be running in ARCHIVELOG mode. The first step is to archive any filled redo log files. Next, the SQL*DBA ALTER DATABASE BEGIN BACKUP command must be executed from a DBA account. Then, the SQL*DBA utility is exited to return to the operating system prompt, and the operating system commands or a backup utility are used to make backups of all the database files, redo log files, and database control files. When the backup process is completed, the SQL*DBA ALTER DATABASE END BACKUP command is executed from a DBA account.

Recovery

To recover from disk failure using the EXPORT and IMPORT utilities, the database structure, including all tablespaces and users, must be recreated. Then the appropriate export files must be imported to restore the database to the most current state.

System failure recovery. ORACLE automatically performs database instance recovery when necessary upon the startup of a database. The following steps are carried out:

(1) All the changes recorded in the online redo log files are reapplied. This restores the committed changes not applied to the database, uncommitted transactions recorded in the log, and rollback segments.
(2) Any changes that were not committed are undone using the rollback segments. This removes the uncommitted changes that were applied by the redo log.

Media failure recovery. To recover from disk failure with no loss of work, it is necessary to make frequent online backups of the database and to archive the redo log files by

(1) Restoring the database with the most current backup files.
(2) Reapplying to the database all the changes recorded in the redo log files dating from the time of the database backup.
(3) Undoing any changes that were not committed by using the rollback segments.

If the online redo log files are not archived, the database should be backed up frequently. The steps for recovery from media failure in this situation are

(1) Restore the database using the most recent backup files.
(2) Re-enter any work done since the backup was performed.

Data Import and Export

ORACLE's EXPORT utility allows all data to be backed up while the database is open and available for use. Three modes of export are supported:

User mode: Exports all objects owned by a user.

Table mode: Exports all or a specific table owned by a user.

Full database mode: Exports all objects of the database.

The DBA can perform any of the following types of exports:

Incremental export: Involves only the export of data modified since the last incremental export.

Cumulative export: Involves only the export of data modified since the last complete export.

Complete export: Involves the export of all database data.

ORACLE's IMPORT utility allows users to restore database information held in previously created export files. It is the complement utility to EXPORT.

Authorization Administration: GRANT Statement

The GRANT statement provides specified privileges on a database or a database object to a user. ORACLE supports three forms of the GRANT statement: (1) grant access to a database, (2) grant access to a tablespace, and (3) grant various types of access to database objects. Each of these forms is described below.

Grant access to a database. The syntax of this type of GRANT statement is as follows

```
<grant> ::=
        GRANT <database privilege>
                [ {, <database privilege> }...]
        TO <user> [ {, <user>}...]
        [ IDENTIFIED BY <password> {, <password> }... ]
```

```
<database privilege> ::=
        { DBA | RESOURCE | CONNECT }
```

Only users with DBA privilege can use this form of the GRANT statement to grant database access to other users. However, all users can use this form of GRANT statement to change their passwords.

The DBA privilege allows a user to bypass many standard privileges that are normally required to use database objects. This privilege also allows a user to perform certain database administration tasks such as CREATE TABLESPACE and CREATE ROLLBACK SEGMENT.

The RESOURCE privilege permits a user to create such database objects as tables, indexes, clusters, and sequences.

The CONNECT privilege enrolls a new username to the database. With CONNECT privilege, a user may connect to the database and access any objects for which he/she has been given the appropriate privilege.

Grant access to a tablespace. The syntax of this GRANT statement is

```
<grant> ::=
        GRANT RESOURCE [ ( <quota> [K | M ] ) ]
        ON <tablespace>
        TO { PUBLIC | <user> [ {, <user> }...] }
```

Only users with DBA privilege can execute the grant access to database space statement. This form of the GRANT statement provides additional flexibility and control compared to the previous form of the GRANT <database privilege> statement.

Grant various types of access to database objects. The syntax of this GRANT statement is as follows:

```
<grant> ::=
        GRANT
        { <object privilege> [ {, <object privilege>}...]
                | ALL [PRIVILEGES ]
        }
        ON [<user>.] <object>
        TO { <user> | PUBLIC } [ {, <user>}...]
        [ WITH GRANT OPTION ]
```

```
<object privilege> ::=
        { ALTER | DELETE | INDEX | INSERT | REFERENCES |
        SELECT | UPDATE }
```

This statement grants the specified privilege on a database object to the specified user. If the privilege was granted with the WITH GRANT OPTION privilege, a user may pass this sequence of privileges to another user.

Authorization Administration: REVOKE Statement

The REVOKE statement removes specified privileges on a database or a database object from a user. ORACLE supports three forms of the REVOKE statement.

The first form of the REVOKE statement is used to remove user privileges:

```
REVOKE { [ CONNECT ] [, RESOURCE ] [, DBA] }
        FROM <user> [ {, <user>}...]
```

Revoking the CONNECT privilege from a user is equivalent to dropping a user because a user must have CONNECT privilege to connect to an ORACLE Server database.

The second form of the REVOKE statement is used to revoke tablespace access from the specified users:

```
REVOKE RESOURCE on <tablespace>
        FROM <user> [ {, <user>}...]
```

The third form of the REVOKE statement is used to revoke the specified privileges on a database object from the specified users:

```
REVOKE { {<object privilege> [{,<object privilege>}...]}
            | ALL   }
        ON [<user>.] <object>
        FROM { <user> | PUBLIC } [ {, <user>}...]
```

Auditing

Auditing is a security feature used to monitor the user activity within a database system. In ORACLE, all auditing records are stored in a table in the database dictionary called the AUDIT_TRAIL. ORACLE provides two levels of auditing: auditing database access, and auditing access to database objects.

The DBA has control over auditing database access, whereas the owners of database objects have control over auditing access to their objects.

Auditing database access. By default, auditing database access is disabled. To enable system auditing, the DBA must set the AUDIT_TRAIL parameter of the INIT.ORA file to TRUE and restart the database after the INIT.ORA file is edited. Then the DBA must set the systemwide auditing option by issuing an AUDIT command:

```
<option>:: = {CONNECT | DBA | NOT EXISTS | RESOURCE}
AUDIT { { <option> [ {, <option> } ... ]} | ALL
        [ WHENEVER [NOT] SUCCESSFUL ]
```

Table 6.6 describes the options included in the AUDIT command.

Option	Description
CONNECT	Audits all actions requiring the CONNECT privilege
DBA	Audits all actions requiring the DBA privilege, including all uses of GRANT, REVOKE, AUDIT, NOAUDIT, CREATE (or DROP) PUBLIC SYNONYM, and CREATE (or DROP) DBLINK statements
NOT EXISTS	Audits all references to objects that result in the "... does not exist" error
RESOURCE	Audits all actions requiring the RESOURCE privilege including all uses of the CREATE, ALTER, and DROP commands on database objects
ALL	Audits all actions of database activity. Equivalent to specifying the CONNECT, DBA, NOT EXISTS, and RESOURCE options of the AUDIT command
WHENEVER	Records one audit record in the AUDIT_TRAIL access, either for successful attempts, unsuccessful attempts, or both (if neither is specified)

Table 6.6: *The options supported in the AUDIT command of ORACLE.*

Systemwide auditing options are disabled by the DBA using the following form of the NOAUDIT command:

```
NOAUDIT { { <option> [ {, <option> } ... ] } | ALL}
        [ WHENEVER [NOT] SUCCESSFUL ]
```

Auditing access to database objects. Owners of a table, view, or sequence can audit their database object usage if the DBA has enabled systemwide auditing. The available auditing options for tables, views, and sequences are presented in Table 6.7.

Option	Table	View	Sequence
ALTER	Yes	No	Yes
AUDIT	Yes	Yes	Yes
COMMENT	Yes	Yes	No
DELETE	Yes	Yes	No
GRANT	Yes	Yes	Yes
INDEX	Yes	No	No
INSERT	Yes	Yes	No
LOCK	Yes	Yes	No
RENAME	Yes	Yes	No
SELECT	Yes	Yes	Yes
UPDATE	Yes	Yes	No

Table 6.7: Description of the available auditing options in ORACLE.

The default auditing options for a table, view, or sequence are the same as the auditing options specified for a table referred to as DEFAULT. Only the DBA can set the auditing options of the DEFAULT table by using the following form of the AUDIT command:

```
AUDIT { { <option> [ {, <option> } ... ] } | ALL} ON DEFAULT
        [ BY { SESSION | ACCESS } ]
```

[WHENEVER [NOT] SUCCESSFUL]

BY SESSION specifies the insertion of only one record in the AUDIT_TRAIL, per user, for each session that includes an audited action. BY ACCESS specifies the insertion of one record in the AUDIT_TRAIL each time an audited action is performed.

The DBA can disable the default database object auditing options by using the following NOAUDIT command:

NOAUDIT { { <option> [{, <option> } ...] } | ALL} ON DEFAULT

[WHENEVER [NOT] SUCCESSFUL]

Owners of a table, view, or sequence can explicitly set the auditing option of their object using the following form of the AUDIT command:

AUDIT { { <option> [{, <option> } ...] } | ALL} ON <object name>

[BY { SESSION | ACCESS }]

[WHENEVER [NOT] SUCCESSFUL]

where <object name> is the name of a table, view, or sequence. All auditing options specified by the owner of a database object override the default auditing options set in the table DEFAULT.

Auditing options on a table, view, or sequence can be disabled by the owner of the database object using the following form of the NOAUDIT command:

NOAUDIT { { <option> [{, <option> } ...] } | ALL} ON <object name>

[WHENEVER [NOT] SUCCESSFUL]

6.10.3 DEC Rdb/VMS

As we have seen earlier, Rdb is the relational database management system produced by Digital Equipment Corporation that runs under VAX/VMS. Rdb provides language interfaces to VAX SQL and RDO. VAX SQL supports embedded SQL and interactive SQL access, whereas RDO supports a proprietary Digital database language.

Server Installation

The Rdb installation process consists of a series of questions and informational messages.

The system disk should be backed up before performing the installation. Moreover, DECnet should be up and running. To start the installation, the DBA invokes the VMSINSTAL command procedure from a privileged account with adequate quotas, such as the SYSTEM account. The VMSINSTAL procedure is in the SYS$UPDATE directory, which is a restricted directory. Thus, a user must have SETPRV privilege to run VMSINSTAL. The VMSINSTAL procedure is invoked as follows:

```
@SYS$UPDATE:VMSINSTAL <product-name> <device-name>
    OPTIONS N
```

The <product name> for Rdb is RDBVMStypnnn, where **typ** represents the type of kit (DEV for the full development kit, RTO for the run-time kit, and INT for the interactive kit), and **nnn** represents the version number prefixed with zero. The <device name> is the name of the device on which you plan to mount the media. Finally, OPTIONS N is an optional parameter that indicates you want to see the release notes question.

To install the full development kit for DEC's Rdb Version 4.0, the following command is entered from disk drive MTA1:

```
@SYS$UPDATE:VMSINSTAL RDBVMSDEV040 MTA1
```

All the installation questions that appear must then be answered. When the entire installation procedure is completed, the LOGOUT command is executed to log out of the privileged account.

Opening and Closing Rdb Databases

In Rdb, opening and closing a database describes the process of mapping and unmapping database root (RDB) file global sections. The RDB file contains all the database-specific information loaded into memory that is essential to operating the database. Maintenance operations that modify the RDB file characteristics require exclusive access to the database and cannot take place when the RDB file is mapped.

Database opening. To open a database in Rdb, a user must follow these steps:

(1) Check to make sure the database root file has not been moved.
(2) Allocate page pool space for the database root file.
(3) Create and map the database root file into the global section.
(4) Start the recovery processes, if necessary.
(5) Initialize the after image journal (AIJ) file, if any.

A Rdb database can be opened in one of two ways:

(1) With the RMU/OPEN command: only users with sufficient Rdb privilege (ADMINISTRATOR) for the database or with VMS BYPASS or SYSPRV privileges can execute an RMU/OPEN command to open the database. By default, Rdb allows automatic opening and closing of the database. However, if the OPEN IS MANUAL option is specified in the schema, a privileged user must issue a RMU/OPEN command before any user can access the database.

(2) With the SQL DECLARE statement: in interactive SQL, a user attaches to a database using the following DECLARE statement:

```
<declare scheme> ::=
            DECLARE SCHEMA FILENAME <database name>
```

Exiting from SQL closes the specified database because the SQL user was the only active user. If a database is created with automatic opening, a SQL DECLARE statement from a user will open the database as if the RMU/OPEN command was issued.

Database closing. Closing a database involves terminating user processes and unmapping database root file global sections.

A database is closed by executing the RMU/CLOSE command; this command controls the process of eliminating active users in a specific database and unmaps global sections. By default, an RMU/CLOSE command terminates all user processes currently accessing the specified database. If the user does not want to terminate active user processes immediately, the /NOABORT option is specified in the RMU/CLOSE command. With the /NOABORT option, active transactions are allowed to finish rather than being forced off the database immediately.

Enrolling and Dropping Users

User accounts must have certain privileges and quotas to work with Rdb. That is, each account must have at least the TMPMBX and NETMBX privileges and must have sufficient quotas to be able to use Rdb. User account quotas are stored in the file SYSUAF.DAT. The AUTHORIZE utility is used to verify and change the user account quotas.

Revoking either the TMPMBX or NETMBX privileges from the user, or lowering the user's account quota will drop the user from a database.

Backup

Rdb's RMU commands are used to backup a database, to check the integrity of the backup file, and to restore the database. Database backups can be performed online on an open database or on a closed database. A database backup can be done in full or incrementally.

The RMU/BACKUP command performs a full or an incremental backup of an entire database, excluding all read-only storage areas, unless these are explicitly included. During an online backup, other users may be attached to the database and can execute any type of transaction that does not conflict with the read-only online backup transactions.

A full RMU/BACKUP command backs up the RDB file and all RDA files in all the storage areas into a single database backup file (RBF). An incremental backup backs up the RDB file and all database pages that were changed since the most recent full backup into a single RBF file. A user must always create a full database backup file for a database before creating any incremental database backup files for that database.

The RMU/DUMP/BACKUP_FILE command is used to verify the integrity of the backup file created by the RMU/BACKUP command and to detect media errors.

The RMU/RESTORE command restores a database to the condition it was in at the time of the last full or incremental backup.

The RMU/BACKUP/ONLINE command performs a backup of the database online, without closing the database or denying access to users. When the RMU/BACKUP/ONLINE command is entered, it takes out a quiet-point lock and waits for all active read-write exclusive or batch-update transactions to complete; processing proceeds when the database reaches a quiet point. One of the benefits of online backup is that it permits concurrency with all other types of transactions (with the exception of read-write exclusive or batch-update transactions).

The RMU/BACKUP/INCREMENTAL <file name> command performs an incremental backup operation.

Recovery

Rdb handles system failure recovery automatically. To recover from a media failure, the database administrator must first restore the database from backup files.

System failure recovery. Rdb automatically detects abnormal termination of a user's transactions. If abnormal termination is detected, rollback and recovery are initiated without causing any data inconsistency.

Media failure recovery. Restoring a database from a backup file produces a database that is current up to the point of the most recent backup. If a database has after image journaling, a user can use the .AIJ file to complete the recovery by rolling forward all transactions up to the most recent COMMIT statement.

The following steps will recover the database to a known, consistent state:

(1) Restore the database from the last full backup operation using the RMU/RESTORE command. The RMU/RESTORE command performs a full restore operation of an entire database from one or more RBF files created by the RMU/BACKUP command.

(2) Update the restored database from the last incremental backup operation using the RMU/RESTORE/INCREMENTAL command. This command performs an incremental database restore operation.

(3) Use the RMU/RECOVER command to apply the transactions in the .AIJ files to the fully restored copy of the database. Thus, all transactions that were committed before a disk failure are reapplied to the database. The .AIJ files should be restored in the order of their relative age, with the oldest one first and the latest one last.

(4) Verify the integrity of the database with the RMU/VERIFY command.

(5) Use the RMU/BACKUP command to perform a full online database backup to a new disk or tape that specifies a database name that is different from the previous backup copy.

Data Import and Export

Rdb supports three methods of loading or importing dáta from existing data files into a database. The first method involves the use of a high-level language program that reads rows or records and then uses the STORE statement to store them in the database. As an alternative, the IMPORT statement in interactive Rdb/VMS SQL can be used to create a database from a previously exported file. The third option is to use the RMU/LOAD command, which reads sequential RMS files created by an application program or the RMU/UNLOAD command, and automatically stores them into the database.

To use the RMU/LOAD command, the sequential RMS file must

be in a fixed record length format. In addition, each record must be completely filled; blank fields must be filled with spaces. The number and data types of the columns specified in the database table must agree with the number and data types of the fields in the input file.

The load operation depends on the existence of two files: the RMS record definition (RRD) file, which contains the metadata or points to the data dictionary where the metadata can be found, and the sequential RMS data file (UNL), which contains data to be loaded.

To unload or export data from a database to data files Rdb supports the RMU/UNLOAD command, which unloads data from database tables to RMS files, and the EXPORT statement in interactive Rdb/VMS SQL, which copies the entire database to a file.

Authorization Administration

At the time the database is created, the user must specify whether the database protection mechanism is ANSI style or access control list (ACL) style.

In ACL style databases, the access privilege set is order-dependent. Each entry in an ACL consists of an identifier and a list of privileges assigned to the identifier. When a user tries to perform an operation on a schema, the system reads the access control list from top to bottom, comparing the identifier of the user with each entry. When it finds a matching entry, it grants the privilege and stops the search. Any identifier that does not match an entry in the access control list is treated as the entry [*,*], which is equivalent to the PUBLIC user in SQL. If no entry has the identifier [*,*], then users with unmatched identifiers are denied all access to the database.

In ANSI style databases, the access privilege set is order-independent. The system first matches the user to an entry in the access privilege set. The system then gets the associated privileges, and then the privileges defined for PUBLIC. PUBLIC always has an access privilege entry even if it has no access to the database. ANSI style databases grant access to the creator when an object is created.

Since there are two styles of privilege access in Rdb, the GRANT and REVOKE statements support these two different styles.

GRANT Statement: ACL Style

The ACL style GRANT statement creates or adds privileges to an entry in the Rdb access privilege set, called the access control list, for a schema, table, view, or column. The syntax of the ACL style GRANT statement is as follows:

```
<grant> ::=
    GRANT
    { <schema privs> ON SCHEMA AUTHORIZATION <auth id list>
    | <table privs> ON [TABLE] <table or view name list>
    | <column privs> ON COLUMN <column name list>
    }
    TO <user list>
<schema privs> ::=
    {       ALL PRIVILEGES | <privilege list> }
<privilege list> ::=
    <privilege> [ {, <privilege> }... ]
<privilege> ::=
    {       SELECT | INSERT | OPERATOR | DELETE | CREATETAB |
            ALTER | DROP | DBCTRL | DBADM | SHOW |
            REFERENCES | UPDATE | SECURITY | DISTRIBTRAN
    }
<table privs> ::=
    {       ALL PRIVILEGES |
            < table privilege> [ {, <table privilege>}...]
    }
<table privilege> ::=
    {       SELECT | INSERT | OPERATOR | DELETE | CREATETAB |
            ALTER | DROP | DBCTRL | SHOW |
            REFERENCES [ ( <column name list> ) ]
            UPDATE [ ( <column name list> ) ]
    }
<column name list> ::=
    <column name> [ {, <column name>}...]
<column privs> ::=
    { ALL PRIVILEGES |
            <column privileges [ {, <column privilege>}...]
    }
```

<column privilege> ::=

{ UPDATE | REFERENCES }

<user list> ::=

<user specification> [{, <user specification>}...]

<user specification> ::=

{ PUBLIC | <identifier>

[AFTER { PUBLIC | <identifier> }

| POSITION <n>

]

}

<identifier> ::=

<id> [{ + <id> }...]

<id> ::=

{ <uic identifier> | <general identifier> |

<system identifier>

}

GRANT Statement: ANSI Style

The syntax of the ANSI style GRANT statement is similar to the ACL style GRANT statement except that the WITH GRANT OPTION clause is supported. Moreover, only PUBLIC or the <uic identifier> is supported in the <user specification>.

<user specification> ::=

{ PUBLIC | <uic identifier> }

REVOKE Statement: ACL Style

The REVOKE statement removes the granted privilege from a user. The syntax of the ACL style REVOKE statement is

<revoke> ::=

REVOKE

{ { <schema privs> | ENTRY } ON SCHEMA AUTHORIZATION <auth id list>

| { <table privs> | ENTRY } ON [TABLE] <table or view name list>

| { <column privs> | ENTRY } ON COLUMN <column name list>

```
}
FROM <user list>
```

If the ENTRY privilege is specified in the REVOKE statement, the entire entry in the ACL, including the identifier, is deleted.

REVOKE Statement: ANSI Style

The syntax of the ANSI style REVOKE statement is similar to the ACL style REVOKE statement except that the ENTRY privilege is not supported and in the <user specification> clause only PUBLIC or the <uic identifier> is supported.

Auditing

The Rdb monitoring process collects and maintains information about database users and other overall activities. Rdb monitor runs under the SYSTEM account in a detached process called RDMS_MONITOR. The monitoring process controls database access, initiates the automatic recovery procedure, and maintains a log of database activity.

Specifically, the monitoring process keeps track of current database users. In addition, it records certain database activity, including the nature of each attach request, in the monitor log file.

The RMU/MONITOR command is used to start or stop the monitoring process. The RMU/MONITOR/STOP command stops the process, while the RMU/MONITOR/START command starts the process.

The Rdb Management Utility (RMU) SET AUDIT and SHOW AUDIT commands are used to modify and display information about users of a specific database, users of all databases, or database statistics.

6.10.4 Microsoft SQL Server

The Microsoft SQL Server provides both the SQL Server Administration Facility (SAF) and the isql utility program for users to administer a SQL Server database. The SAF provides menus that help users to perform many system administration tasks without entering TRANSACT-SQL statements directly. Additionally, SAF's SQL Query window allows users to execute TRANSACT-SQL statements and system procedures. The isql utility allows users to enter TRANSACT-SQL commands and system procedures interactively or in batch files.

Installation

The SQL Server is based on a client-server architecture. The server software of the SQL Server requires an OS/2 system to run. The SQL Server workstation can run under either MS-DOS or OS/2.

Server installation. If the user intends to install the server machine as a network server, both network server software and network workstation software must be installed in the machine before the SQL Server is installed.

The **Setup** program is used to install SQL Server software on the server machine. The Setup program is a menu-driven utility that provides step-by-step instructions. When installing the SQL Server, the Setup program first makes sure that the named-pipe interprocess communication (IPC) exists on the server. Then Setup loads the server software and utility programs from the setup disks and modifies the config.sys file to include the appropriate library path. Setup also creates the *master* database to the user's specification.

To start the installation process, the user inserts the **"SQL Server setup"** disk in Drive A and types

```
a:setup [ /remote ]
```

If the user wants to install or delete software on a remote computer system the /remote switch must be specified. The Setup program prompts the user for any information required to carry out the installation. One piece of the information required is the case sensitivity of character data and object names. If the user chooses case-sensitive data, character data retrieved from a database must contain the same uppercase and lowercase letters it contained when it was entered into the database. Object names must also contain the same uppercase and lowercase letters used when the object was created. With non-case-sensitive data, the character data and object name are insensitive to uppercase and lowercase letters. When the installation is completed, the user must reboot the computer to effect the change to config.sys.

Workstation installation. The installation of workstations is similar to the server installation. The Setup program is used to install the workstation. If the user chooses to install a workstation, the Setup program copies the utility programs and programming tools to the workstation. Setup also modifies the config.sys and the autoexec.bat files to contain the appropriate information.

SQL Server Startup

SQL Server can be started up in multiuser or single-user mode. To start SQL Server in multiuser mode, the user issues the following net command at the operating system prompt:

```
net start sqlserver
```

To start SQL Server in single-user mode, the sqlservr program is executed at the operating system prompt as follows:

```
sqlservr /d <master phys name> [/m] [ /e <error log phys name> ]
```

The /d <master phys name> option specifies the full path name of the master database device. The optional /m option specifies that SQL Server is started in single-user mode. And, the optional /e <error log phys name> option specifies the full path name of the error log file for SQL Server system-level error messages.

The sqlservr utility can be executed from the server or from a workstation. For example, to start SQL Server in a single-user mode, with the master database located in the c:\sql\data directory, execute the sqlservr utility is executed at the server operating system prompt as follows:

```
sqlservr /d c:\sql\data\master.dat /m
```

SQL Server Shutdown

To shut down the SQL Server, the following net command is issued at the operating system prompt:

```
net stop sqlserver
```

The SQL Server can also be shut down by using the SHUTDOWN command in TRANSACT-SQL:

```
SHUTDOWN [ WITH NOWAIT ]
```

Without specifying the WITH NOWAIT option, the SHUTDOWN command waits for all currently executing SQL statements or stored procedures to finish and then performs a checkpoint on every database before shutting down the SQL Server. With the NOWAIT option specified, the SQL Server is shut down immediately.

Database Startup and Shutdown

The USE command in TRANSACT-SQL starts a specified database:

```
use <dbname>
```

To shutdown the current database, the USE statement is issued on another database.

Special Users

In the SQL Server, three types of special users administer and control the system: the system administrator (sa), the database owners (dbo), and the database object owners. Table 6.8 describes these three types of SQL Server users.

System Administrator (sa)	The sa is responsible for administrative tasks unrelated to specific applications. These tasks include installing the SQL Server, managing storage, creating user databases, setting up user accounts, granting permissions to SQL Server users, and fine-tuning the SQL Server. When the SQL Server is installed, the sa is the database owner of the master database. The sa is also treated as the database owner of any databases he or she uses. Moreover, the sa has permission to use all TRANSACT-SQL statements and system procedures.
Database Owner (dbo)	The dbo creates a database and is responsible for administrative tasks related to that database. These tasks include adding users to the database, granting permissions within the database, backing up and restoring the database, and creating tables, procedures, rules, defaults, triggers, and views.
Database Object Owner	A database object owner is the creator of a particular database object. The database object owner must grant permissions on their database object to other users in order for these users to access the object.

Table 6.8: Special users in the Microsoft SQL Server.

Enrolling and Dropping Users

All users must have a log-in name, a password, and a default database before they can work on the SQL Server. The sa is responsible for adding new users to the SQL Server. In addition, each user must have a user name to access a SQL Server database. A user name is different from a log-in ID, which allows a user to access the SQL Server but not any user database. The system procedures related to adding and dropping new users are as described in Table 6.9.

System Procedure	Description
sp_addlogin	Used by the sa to add a log-in name for a new user
sp_password	Used to change a user's password; users can change their own password. The sa can change any user's password
sp_defaultdb	Used to change a user's default database
sp_droplogin	Used by the sa to drop a user from the SQL Server
sp_adduser	Used by the sa or dbo to assign a user name in the current database
sp_helpuser	Used to display user information in a database
sp_dropuser	Used by the sa or dbo to drop a user from a database

Table 6.9: *System procedures for adding and dropping new users in the Microsoft SQL Server.*

A database group is made up of several users with the same permissions. The sa or database owner can add or drop a group to the current database using the system procedures described in Table 6.10.

System Procedure	Description
sp_addgroup	Used to add a group to the current database
sp_changegroup	Used to change a user's group within the current database
sp_helpgroup	Used to display information on groups within the current database
sp_dropgroup	Used to delete a group from the current database

Table 6.10: *System procedures for adding and dropping groups in the Microsoft SQL Server.*

Checkpoints

The SQL Server supports both automatic checkpoints and the TRANSACT-SQL CHECKPOINT statement. The schedule of automatic checkpoints depends on the recovery interval configuration option and the system activity. The maximum acceptable recovery time is specified in the recovery interval configuration option. Alternatively, the database owner can force a checkpoint by issuing the TRANSACT-SQL CHECKPOINT statement.

Backup

The DUMP DATABASE and DUMP TRANSACTION TRANSACT-SQL statements are used to backup a database in the SQL Server:

```
DUMP DATABASE <database name> TO <dump device>
```

Dumping a database backs up an entire database. The transaction log cannot be backed up separately from the database itself if it is stored in the same database device as the database. When the transaction log is stored on a database device other than the one containing the remainder of the database, the database owner should back up the transaction log more frequently than the database. This is accomplished using the following statement:

```
DUMP TRANSACTION <database name> [ TO <dump device>]
        [ WITH TRUNCATE_ONLY | WITH NO_LOG ]
```

In this statement, the <dump device> specifies the logical name of the dump device to which the specified database or transaction log is dumped. A dump device is the hard disk files or diskette files to which the database is dumped.

The WITH TRUNCATE_ONLY option removes the inactive part of the log by not backing it up. The WITH NO_LOG option is similar to the WITH TRUNCATE_ONLY option as it also removes the inactive log portion. In addition, the WITH NO_LOG option saves space by not recording the dump transaction procedure in the transaction log.

If a user executes DUMP DATABASE and never executes DUMP TRANSACTION, the transaction log will never be cleared out and eventually will become very large. Therefore, each time a user executes DUMP DATABASE, he/she should also execute DUMP TRANSACTION WITH TRUNCATE_ONLY to clear out the log.

Recovery

In the SQL Server, system recovery is handled automatically by the server. However, the user must back up the database files in order to recover from media failure. Every time the SQL Server is restarted, it automatically recovers from system failure. To recover from media failure, the database owner must dump the database and transaction log at regular intervals, and then load the dumped database when necessary.

Data Import and Export

The TRANSACT-SQL LOAD DATABASE and DUMP DATABASE statements are used to import and export an entire database.

The DUMP DATABASE command exports the entire database to a dump device:

```
DUMP DATABASE <database name> TO <dump device>
```

The LOAD DATABASE command loads a backup copy of a user database from the dump device:

```
LOAD DATABASE <database name>
        FROM <dump device>
```

SQL Server's bulk copy utility program (bcp) moves data between the SQL Server and an operating system file. To use bcp, a user must have a SQL Server account and the appropriate permissions on the database tables and operating system files. To copy data out of a table, a user must have SELECT permission on that table. To copy data into a table, a user must have INSERT permission on the table. When the transfer is complete, the program reports the number of rows successfully copied together with some performance information.

Authorization Administration

The SQL Server recognizes four types of users in its permissions system: the system administrator database owners, database object owners, and other users of the database.

The system administrator (sa) is the special user who handles tasks not specific to an application. There are no restrictions on what the sa can do within SQL Server. Moreover, only the sa can grant CREATE DATABASE permission.

Database owners have full permission to do anything inside their assigned database and are responsible for granting permissions to other users. Database owners can grant permissions on the following commands to other users: CREATE DEFAULT, CREATE PROCEDURE, CREATE RULE, CREATE TABLE, CREATE VIEW, DUMP DATABASE, DUMP TRANSACTION, and GRANT and REVOKE of object permissions.

Database object owners create database objects and are automatically granted all object permissions on those database objects. Users other than the object owner are automatically denied all permissions on the object unless they are granted by the owner. By default, the following command permissions are granted to the owner of a table and cannot be transferred to other users: ALTER TABLE, CREATE INDEX, CREATE TRIGGER, DROP TABLE, TRUNCATE TABLE, and UPDATE STATISTICS.

The permission to use the GRANT and REVOKE commands cannot be transferred. However, the object owner can grant and revoke SELECT, INSERT, DELETE, UPDATE, and EXECUTE permission to other users.

The SQL Server has two categories of permissions: object and command. The SELECT, UPDATE, INSERT, DELETE, and EXECUTE commands are called object permissions because they always apply to database objects.

Command permissions are not object specific and can be granted only by the sa or a database owner. Command permissions apply to the following commands: CREATE DATABASE, CREATE DEFAULT, CREATE PROCEDURE, CREATE RULE, CREATE TABLE, CREATE VIEW, DUMP DATABASE, and DUMP TRANSACTION.

Command and object permissions are granted or revoked with the GRANT and REVOKE commands.

The syntaxes for GRANT and REVOKE on command permissions are as follows:

```
GRANT { ALL | <command list> }
        TO { public | <name list> }
REVOKE { ALL | <command list> }
        FROM { public | <name list> }
```

In these statements, ALL specifies all the command permissions. Only the sa can use ALL to assign command permissions because only the sa can grant or revoke CREATE DATABASE permission.

The <command list> option specifies a list of command permissions. The keyword public specifies all users in the current database. The <name list> option specifies a list of database users' names separated by commas.

The syntaxes for GRANT and REVOKE on object permissions are as follows:

```
GRANT { ALL | <permission list> }
        ON { <table name> [(<column list>)] |
                <view name> [(<column list>)] |
                <stored procedure name> }
        TO { public | <name list> }
REVOKE { ALL | <permission list> }
        ON { <table name> [(<column list>)] |
                <view name> [(<column list>)] |
        FROM { public | <name list> }
```

In these statements, ALL specifies that all permissions applicable to the specified object are granted or revoked. Additionally, <permission list> specifies a list of permissions granted or revoked. When permissions are granted or revoked on a table or a view, the permission list can include SELECT, INSERT, DELETE, and UPDATE. When permissions are granted or revoked on columns, the permission list can include SELECT and UPDATE. And, when permissions are granted or revoked on stored procedures, the only permission possible is EXECUTE.

6.11 Summary

In this chapter, we examined the database administration features in the IBM Extended Edition, ORACLE Server, DEC Rdb/VMS, and Microsoft SQL Server. Table 6.11 presents a summary of the administration tasks supported by each of these products.

Database Administration	IBM EE	ORACLE Server	DEC Rdb/VMS	Microsoft SQL Server
Checkpoint	No	Yes	No	Yes
Database Backup Utility	Yes	Yes	Yes	Yes
Incremental Backup	Yes	No	Yes	No
Automatic System Failure Recovery	Yes	Yes	Yes	Yes
Auditing	No	Yes	Yes	No
Data Import and Export	Yes	Yes	Yes	Yes
Grant With Grant Option	Yes	No	Yes	No
Incremental Backup	Yes	No	Yes	No

Table 6.11: *Summary of the database administration tasks in four servers.*

Chapter 7

Performance Tuning and Optimization

Many factors affect the performance of client-server database applications. These include

Computation architecture—the manner in which the server schedules processing on behalf of clients.

Database organization—how the server structures the database in stable storage to provide locality of reference and associative access.

Access path selection—the server's ability to optimize the selection of an access plan for a given database query.

Client-server communication discipline—the mechanism by which requests and responses are transmitted between clients and the server.

Concurrency control—the ability of the server to synchronize concurrent operations from multiple clients in order to provide the desired level of transaction isolation.

Buffering strategy—how the server caches database pages in random access memory and flushes modified pages back to the database.

In this chapter, we first discuss each of these performance-related factors. We then go on to examine the performance-enhancing features and tuning options supported by four popular database servers.

7.1 Computational Architecture

The simplest way to organize multiuser database access is to have one operating system process work on behalf of each of the concurrent users, with these processes sharing some common RAM-resident data structures such as lock tables and cache buffers. The major advantage of this organization is the strong correspondence between entities of user interaction and entities of the operating system. As a result, taking advantage of the scheduling and multiuser isolation facilities of the operating system is straightforward. This organization is often referred to as the *Process Model.*

The Process Model does have a limitation: every time a user issues an input/output (I/O) request that cannot be satisfied by data present in the cache buffers, a process switch is required to allow requests from other users to be serviced while the first user waits for the I/O operation to complete. In most operating systems, this switch is expensive in terms of CPU time. Moreover, process creation (which also can be expensive in many operating systems) is required for each user session, and the processes required in a system with high concurrency can be so numerous that main memory can become a bottleneck.

To minimize these drawbacks, many database and transaction processing systems perform their own scheduling. In other words, they are small monitors that run above the underlying host operating systems. These monitors are specialized to deal with database transactions instead of general-purpose processes. They implement more optimized scheduling strategies for database management that reduce process-switching overhead. Essentially, these monitors eliminate the overhead of process creation and the memory required to support a large number of processes. For implementation simplicity, many such monitors just single-thread the execution of transactions. That is, they complete the execution of a request from one user before scheduling a request on behalf of another user. As a result, computation-intensive transactions (e.g., ones that perform aggregate computations over large volumes of data) can monopolize the server, causing poor response for other transactions.

The *Server Model* is an alternative organization for providing multiuser support. In this mode, server processes exist independent of users and transactions. Users obtain services from the server processes through request messages. A server process is assigned to work on behalf of a user dynamically, given the user's transaction identifier. A server may interleave its service for transactions from multiple users. When a server executes a recoverable action for a particular transaction, the log records are tagged with the corresponding transaction identifier. This allows the actions performed on behalf of a user transaction to be committed atomically or rolled back in their entirety. The Server Model reduces overhead for process creation and process switching. The number of processes is no longer dependent on the number of existing user sessions or in-progress transactions because when a server is finished with its actions on behalf of one transaction, it can begin servicing another one.

The IBM OS/2 Extended Edition Database Manager utilizes a pure Process Model and allocates a separate operating system process to support each client session, whereas the Microsoft SQL Server uses a pure Server Model, employing a single operating system process that multithreads and schedules activities on behalf of multiple users. Like the IBM OS/2 Extended Edition, the ORACLE Server allocates an additional operating system process to anchor the activities on behalf of each user. However, ORACLE also makes use of several dedicated operating system processes for logging and writing modified database pages back to stable storage, thus allowing such operations to be batched together in a more efficient manner. DEC's Rdb/VMS uses a Process Model primarily for local data access. When Rdb databases are accessed remotely through the SQL Services interface, a process pool mechanism (akin to the Server Model) is employed to minimize the process creation and switching overhead.

7.2 Physical Database Design

Physical database design refers to the selection of various options for organizing data on disk and the maintenance of auxiliary access paths to facilitate associative database access. The database designer typically makes decisions regarding the choice of fields (or combination of fields) to index and the type of organization for these indexes, the choice of clustering criteria for rows within tables, and the selective placement of tables and indexes on disk volumes.

7.2.1 Indexing

Indexes are optional auxiliary data structures associated with tables. Given an index key value, the rows that contain that value can be directly located through an index. Generally, indexes are created to provide keyed access to rows within a table and to enforce uniqueness of rows within a table.

Because of the physical data independence afforded to SQL data manipulation statements, indexes can be added or dropped any time without affecting the logical correctness of existing SQL applications. The logic will continue to work, although performance can be affected.

Indexes can be created on one or more columns. For example, an index can be created on the combination of the last name and first name columns. The ordering of columns in multicolumn indexes is significant. Typically, only selection predicates involving either all or a prefix of the ordered columns within a multicolumn index can be resolved using the index. Once created, an index is automatically maintained by the database system. Because of the overhead of index maintenance during insertions, deletions, and updates, indexes should be chosen judiciously.

B^+-tree Index

An index organized as a B^+-tree can be used to search for rows with a specific index key value or to search for rows satisfying a range predicate. It can also be used for retrieving rows in index key order without physically sorting the table.

Figure 7.1 illustrates the structure of a B^+-tree index. The upper (nonleaf) blocks of a B^+-tree contain index data that point to lower level index blocks. For a large table, it may take three or more page accesses to look up an entry in a B^+-tree. The leaf blocks together contain all the index key values, along with pointers to the rows that contain each of the index key values. The leaf blocks of a B^+-tree index are chained. Just by traversing the leaf blocks and following the row pointers, it is possible to retrieve all rows in index key order.

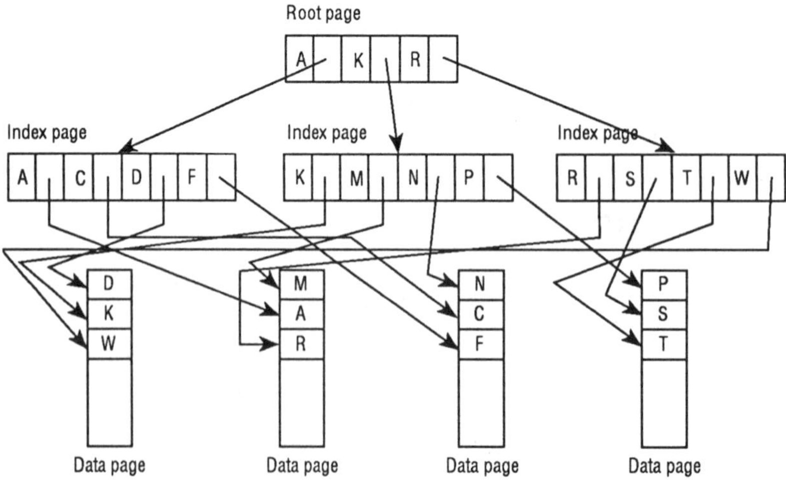

Figure 7.1: B^+-tree index.

Hashed Index

A hashed index provides more efficient access to rows with a specific index key value but it cannot be used for range retrieval. If properly organized, a direct key access to a hashed index can, on the average, be accomplished in slightly greater than one, but much less than two, page accesses.

Index Compression

Index compression provides several benefits. A compressed index requires less storage and fewer I/O operations to retrieve data. In addition, more efficient query processing is possible when the index is used in place of the corresponding table.

In a compressed index, information within index nodes is compressed so that it takes up less space. As a result, the total number of nodes in the index is reduced. Typically, index compression on an alphanumeric field is achieved by storing a fixed-length prefix of the field in the index. However, the resulting precision loss implies that any uniqueness constraint on the field can no longer be enforced using the compressed index. Also, selection predicates involving such an index may have to be retested against rows identified by the index.

7.2.2 Clustering

Clustering is a means of structuring the data in one or more tables so that rows likely to be used together are placed physically close together. As in the case of indexing, the introduction of clustering is logically transparent to SQL applications.

Clustering Index

With a clustering index, rows are sorted on an ongoing basis so that their physical order is the same as their logical (indexed) order. The bottom, or leaf level, of a clustering index contains the actual data pages of the table. When the placement of rows are to be controlled through the use of a clustering index, the physical location of a row may be changed as rows are inserted, deleted, or modified in the key field. Consequently, the presence of a clustering index can affect the maintenance cost of nonclustered indexes. Any time a row is relocated to maintain physical sorted order, all nonclustering index entries that point to the same row must be modified to reflect the new location of that row.

Multitable Clustering

In addition to clustering rows within a table, it is often advantageous to cluster rows from multiple tables that are logically related (i.e., that share common columns) and are therefore likely to be accessed together. Multitable clustering is particularly useful for facilitating join operations between tables based on one-to-one and one-to-many relationships. The disadvantage of multitable clustering is in the higher cost for sequentially scanning rows from a single table within a cluster; the rows will be spread out over a larger number of blocks, compared with the same table stored separately from other tables.

7.2.3 Distributing Input/Output

Allocating database components to different physical files and placing of these files on specific devices can significantly impact database performance. To reduce the activity on an overloaded disk, it is useful to move one or more of its heavily accessed files to a less active disk. The purpose of distributing input/output is to roughly equalize the amount of I/O to and from each disk. Techniques for distributing I/O include

(1) Storing database files and log files on different disks,
(2) Striping or partitioning table data on different disks
(3) Storing tables and their associated indexes on different disks

Some database servers permit the designation of specific files for certain database components. Separating the database from the log for uncommitted transactions reduces the time to find a particular data item or storage segment. Locating these files on different disk drives reduces disk access times even further because a single disk read head does not have to jump between files.

ORACLE can split a database into physical tablespaces. Each table can be assigned to a different tablespace, if desired. It is also possible to store a table and its indexes in separate tablespaces. SQL Server's support for multiple databases also allows for the physical separation of tables, but a table may not be separated from its indexes. ORACLE and the SQL Server explicitly allocate files of a fixed size for use by a database. When the predefined space has been exhausted, new files must be created. ORACLE's CREATE DATABASE, CREATE TABLESPACE, and ALTER TABLESPACE commands create files and allocate the appropriate tablespaces.

Like ORACLE, Rdb uses the notion of storage areas to control the placement of tables and indexes. However, Rdb does not require disk storage space to be completely pre-allocated. The SQL Server uses DISKINIT to create a file of desired size; CREATE DATABASE and ALTER DATABASE simply allocate existing files to databases. The IBM OS/2 Extended Edition automatically creates and allocates files when databases are created, expanding and adding files as needed. In fact, the IBM Extended Edition uses its own directory naming scheme, and it adds files as the database grows rather than expanding a single file. These file management schemes are much simpler than those of ORACLE, the SQL Server, and Rdb, but an Extended Edition database is limited to a single disk partition.[1] Databases in ORACLE, Rdb, and the SQL Server, on the other hand, can span multiple disk volumes/partitions.

7.3 Query Optimization

A hallmark of the relational data model and the SQL language is the notion of data independence, or the separation of storage and access details from the application's logic and code. Data independence comes along with the use of a nonprocedural query language like SQL, which allows users to specify the characteristics of the data they want rather than the access paths that should be traversed to locate the desired data. With data independence, database designers are free to tune the physical organization of the database to optimize for a prevailing access pattern, without incurring the prohibitive cost of rewriting existing applications. The database server is expected to optimize queries based on its knowledge of data characteristics and available access paths in order to provide a high level of performance. The end-user orientation of relational database technology and the relegation of optimization responsibilities to the database system are particularly important in reducing application backlogs in large MIS departments.

Given a SQL query and an existing database organization, a database server should find an efficient way to process that query among the many access paths that are available. To understand the complexity of the access path selection process, it is helpful to examine the basic strategies used for selecting rows of interest from a given table. An appreciation of the processing freedom available to the query optimizer for ordering multitable operations can also assist in understanding this process.

Table scan: All data pages that contain rows from a table can be sequentially scanned to locate all rows that meet a given search

---

1 The recovery log optionally can be placed on a separate disk drive.

criterion. Each page that contains rows from the table in question is accessed exactly once.

Index order scan: The rows in a table can also be scanned in index key order. This option can be useful for locating all rows that fall within a range of index key values. Sometimes, this access method is used to produce output rows in the index key order, even when the search criterion has nothing to do with the index key column(s). The purpose is to cluster together rows with the same index key value to facilitate processing of subsequent join operations or to avoid the cost of an explicit sort operation producing the desired output order for the query.

Indexed access: When only a subset of the rows in a table are to be selected based on values for the key column(s) in an index, those rows can be located by using an index without searching the entire table.

The server can select the access plan for a given query based on heuristics, or it can systematically estimate the costs of different possible access plans and choose the best one. These approaches are described further in the sections that follow.

7.3.1 Heuristics-based Optimization

An example of a heuristics-based optimizer is found in the implementation of the Version 6 kernel of the ORACLE Server [Oracle, 1989b]. The ORACLE optimizer chooses an execution plan based on the following criteria:

- The syntax of the SQL statement
- The predicates, or conditions, of the WHERE clause of the SQL statement
- The structures and definitions of the database objects named in the SQL statement
- Any indexes that exist on these database objects

ORACLE's query optimizer does not make use of statistical information about the database to select a particular access path. After parsing and performing semantics checks on a query, the optimizer makes use of access path information obtained from the system catalog to determine what indexes are available for accessing tables referenced in the query. Some applicable rules follow

- Single-column indexes can be used for resolving equality and range predicates.

- Multicolumn indexes are only usable if a prefix subset of the index columns is referenced.
- Indexes cannot be uscd to resolve IS NULL and IS NOT NULL predicates.
- Indexes cannot be used to resolve predicates that involve column expressions.
- Indexes can be used to evaluate aggregates like MIN and MAX (and expressions involving these aggregates) when the table is not restricted by selection predicates.
- Indexes are not used to process DISTINCT and GROUP BY constructs in SQL statements. Instead, an explicit sort operation is always performed.
- Multiple indexes on the same table are used to resolve a conjunction of multiple predicates if the indexes are nonunique column indexes and if the predicates are equalities. However, only a maximum of five indexes can be merged. If both a unique and a nonunique index are available, only the unique index will be used.
- Multiple indexes on the same table are used to resolve a disjunction of multiple predicates only if all of the predicates are resolvable using indexes. IN predicates (e.g., emp# in (x, y, z)) are treated like disjunctions.

The ORACLE optimizer uses multiple indexes to resolve a query, which is accomplished by merging the ROWIDs obtained from two or more index searches. However, other available indexes are not used if a unique or concatenated index is usable because these access paths are considered near-optimal. Once the optimizer has identified all of the available access paths for a given table, it ranks them in the following order:[2]

1. ROWID = constant
2. Unique index = constant
3. Entire unique concatenated index = constant
4. Entire cluster key = corresponding cluster key from the same cluster
5. Entire cluster key = constant
6. Entire nonunique concatenated index = constant
7. Nonunique single-column index = constant
8. Entire noncompressed concatenated index >= constant
9. Entire compressed concatenated index >= constant

---

2 The lower the rank order, the faster the access path.

10. Most leading noncompressed concatenated index specified
11. Most leading compressed concatenated index specified
12. Unique indexed column BETWEEN two constants or LIKE 'F%'
13. Nonunique indexed column BETWEEN two constants or LIKE 'F%'
14. Unique indexed column < or > constant (unbounded range)
15. Nonunique indexed column < or > constant (unbounded range)
16. Sort/merge (joins only)
17. MAX or MIN of a single indexed column
18. ORDER BY an entire index
19. Full table scan

Every predicate connected by AND is assigned a rank. If the query involves only a single table, the lowest rank (fastest access path) predicate is used to drive the selection processing. Joins are ranked on the number of tables that are joined without an index; they have priority over Cartesian products. If ranks for two tables being joined are equal (e.g., when there is no index available for the join), tables in the FROM clause are selected from right to left. ORACLE uses a sort merge join only if indexes are not available.

With knowledge of ORACLE's access path selection rules, it is possible to coerce the ORACLE optimizer to avoid certain access paths. Consider the following query:

```
SELECT    EName
FROM      Emps
WHERE     EName LIKE 'Sm%'
AND       DeptNo = 50;
```

If indexes are available on both name and deptno, only one of them will be chosen by the optimizer. If there are more rows that satisfy the name predicate than those that satisfy the deptno predicate, the optimizer can be coerced into choosing the NAME index by modifying the query as follows:

```
SELECT    EName
FROM      Emps
WHERE     ENameLIKE 'Sm%'
AND       DeptNo = 50 + 0;
```

Consider the following nested SQL query:

```
SELECT    DName, DeptNo
FROM      Depts
WHERE     DeptNo NOT IN (SELECT DeptNo
                         FROM   Emps)
```

The index on emps is not used because the subquery that searches the emps table does not have a WHERE clause.

Now consider the following equivalent nested SQL query:

```
SELECT    DName, DeptNo
FROM      Depts
WHERE     NOT EXISTS ( SELECT DeptNo
                       FROM   Emps
                       WHERE  Depts.DeptNo=
                              Emps.DeptNo)
```

The WHERE clause in the subquery names the DeptNo column of the Emps table, so the index DeptNo_index is used.

7.3.2 Cost-based Optimization

Cost-based optimization uses statistics known about the database to estimate the cost of different access strategies for processing a query and for selecting an efficient processing strategy. Costs are usually measured in terms of a weighted sum of CPU and I/O costs. The relevant statistics include: the number of rows in a table, and the width of each row; the number of distinct values in an index key column; and a histogram of the distribution of key values within an index key column.

Except in those systems where histograms are maintained, it is typical to assume that index key values are uniformly distributed among rows. The *selectivity* of an index is the fraction of total number of rows that can be expected to have a specific index key value. When a histogram is not maintained, it is often estimated as the reciprocal of the number of distinct values in the index key column (or combination of key columns).

When a retrieval predicate involves two or more index key columns, it is possible to combine together the row ID lists obtained from multiple indexes to pinpoint the set of rows that qualify for the selection. For conjunctions, row ID lists can be intersected; for disjunctions, row ID lists can be unioned. To estimate the fraction of rows that satisfy a conjunction or a disjunction of predicates, it is customary to simply assume that the predicates are uncorrelated and that selectivities for the indexes involved can effectively be multiplied. For example, consider two uncorrelated predicates P_1 and P_2 with selectivities S_1 and S_2, respectively. The selectivity of P_1 and P_2 is estimated as S_1*S_2, and the selectivity of P_1 or P_2 is estimated as $S_1 + S_2 - S_1*S_2$.

An access plan defines how a query should be processed. It determines whether a table should be retrieved using a table scan or an index scan. It also determines how and when a row from one table is joined with a row from another table. The decision to choose one access plan for a query over other access plans is primarily based on the estimated cost, which depends on three factors:

(1) The scans used for each involved table
(2) The join implementations used in the access plan
(3) The order in which tables involved in the query are joined

The type of scan used to obtain rows from a table has a direct effect on the cost of an access plan. There are two forms of scans:

Table scan: Retrieves all the rows from a table by examining all nonempty ages that potentially store rows for that table.

Index scan: Uses an index to retrieve rows from a table.

A table scan examines all the data pages that contain rows from the table. However, each page is examined only once. On the other hand, an index scan accesses each index page once and then follows pointers from the index pages to access the associated rows. Data pages that are not pointed to by index entries are not touched. In an index scan, each data page that is pointed to by multiple index entries may have to be accessed multiple times. The cost of using a table scan is, in general, different from that of using an index scan. It cannot be assumed that one is always more costly than the other.

When a B^+-tree index is used to perform an index scan, rows are delivered in index key order. This ordering can sometimes be used to speed up processing of a join. A join implementation that requires its inputs to be ordered by the join column values will benefit from a scan that produces rows in that order. Otherwise, it is necessary to incur the cost of an explicit sort operation before the join can be performed.

To determine whether an index scan or a table scan is less costly, we need to look at the number of page accesses required for each scan. We must also determine whether the scan provides a useful ordering to facilitate a subsequent operation. An output order is said to be *interesting* if it can be used by some join implementation or if it is the desired output order for the query.

The second factor that affects the cost of an access plan is the actual join implementations used. It is obvious that different join implementations incur different costs. A merge-scan join has a cost formula that is quite different from that of a nested loop join. In general, the cost of a join implementation depends on the cardinality of the two tables involved and whether the input rows are correctly ordered. A merge-scan join on a table whose rows are already ordered by the join column avoids a costly sort operation prior to the merge-scan join. Similarly, the cost of a nested loop join is particularly affected by the cardinalities of the inner and outer tables.

The third factor influencing the cost of an access plan is the order in which the tables are joined. The selection of outer versus inner table is also very important. The join implementation often performs better if the outer table is the smaller of the two tables. Furthermore, the output order of the rows from a join often depends on the order of the outer table. As stated previously, an output order of a join that is used to facilitate a subsequent join in a sequence of join operations can reduce the overall cost of the access plan.

One naive way to select an optimal access plan is to exhaustively enumerate all possible access plans and estimate the associated cost of each. However, the number of possible access plans can be astronomical for complex queries. In fact, the number of possible access plans grows exponentially with the number of types of scans, the number of tables involved in the query, and the number of feasible join implementations.

Consider a system that makes use of m possible strategies for processing a join operation. Given a query with n join operations, there are $n!$ possible orders for processing the join operations, since these operations are commutative and associative. Thus, there are $(m^{**}n)\ n!$ possible processing strategies. A brute force enumeration of all processing strategies can be computationally prohibitive.

The technique of dynamic programming is often used for pruning the strategy space and for keeping track of undominated partial strategies to ultimately support the construction of a globally optimal strategy for processing the entire query. The idea is to prune suboptimal partial strategies and to avoid computing the cost associated with an optimal partial strategy more than once, by identifying equivalent classes of partial strategies that produce the same intermediate results. For each equivalent class, only the lowest cost strategy that produces the associated intermediate result needs to be tracked.

First, all the possible scans along with their estimated costs are enumerated for each table involved in the query. Pruning techniques are then used to determine if a partial access plan that uses one of the enumerated scans can ever be part of an optimal access plan. If it is not possible, then the partial access plan is pruned. (One scan can be shown to be dominated by another and therefore will never be part of an optimal access plan.)

The next level of enumeration expands the undominated partial access plans for individual tables to produce intermediate results—each containing two tables involved in the query. Pruning techniques are again used to prune away those expanded partial access plans that will never be part of an optimal access plan.

At the third level, intermediate results that involve two tables can be joined with intermediate results that contain a single table to obtain another intermediate result that contains three tables, and so on.[3] When the enumeration is complete, an optimal access plan emerges. The effectiveness of this dynamic programming approach lies in its ability to prune entire classes of access plans. When a partial access plan is pruned, all access plans that can be generated from the expansion of this pruned partial access plan are also eliminated from further consideration.

Pruning Scans That Produce an Uninteresting Order

A scan that produces an uninteresting output order can be pruned if it is not the least expensive scan. If the least expensive scan produces an interesting output order, it is retained for the remainder of the enumeration process. If the least expensive scan does not produce an interesting order, it still should be retained because it may be more efficient than all the scans with an interesting order. This can happen when the uninteresting order scan is so inexpensive that adding to it the cost of an explicit sort operation would still be less expensive than following an index to obtain rows in the index key order. Morever, when the next join implementation does not require its inputs to be sorted on the join column, like the nested loop join implementation using a table scan access path, the least expensive uninteresting order scan will be more efficient. Note that this pruning method does not prune away any scan that gives an interesting order, unless its cost is higher than the cost associated with some other scan plus the cost of an explicit sort operation.

---

3 In general, an intermediate result that contains n tables can be obtained from joining intermediate results that contain p and q tables, respectively, such that $p + q = n$.

Delaying Cartesian Products

One of the most expensive operations in query processing is the Cartesian product. The cardinality of its output is the product of the cardinalities of its inputs. Not only does the Cartesian product take a long time to evaluate, but its output requires a large amount of temporary storage. Therefore, every effort should be made to avoid processing a Cartesian product or to delay its processing as long as possible.

The way to avoid a Cartesian product is by recognizing that if there is no join predicate between two tables A and B, then the join between these two tables is a Cartesian product. However, performing a Cartesian product cannot be totally avoided in some queries. In these cases, it is usually a good heuristic to delay forming a Cartesian product for as long as possible. Consider the following example:

```
SELECT    T1.A, T2.B, T3.C
FROM      T1, T2, T3
WHERE     T1.X = T2.Y
AND       T2.R = T3.S
```

The following join sequences delay forming Cartesian products:

((T1, T2), T3)[4]

((T2, T1), T3)

((T2, T3), T1)

((T3, T2), T1)

The sequences cause a delay because join conditions exist between T1 and T2 and between T2 and T3. On the other hand, these join sequences do not make use of the heuristics:

((T1, T3), T2)

((T3, T1), T2)

Pruning Strategies Within an Equivalence Class

Before discussing pruning within an equivalence class, a little background knowledge on dynamic programming is useful. As stated in Selinger et al. [1979], the cost of joining the $(k+1)^{th}$ table is independent of the way in which the first *k* tables have been joined, for a particular output order of the first *k* tables with the same access

4 This notation indicates that T1 is joined with T2, and then that result is joined with T3.

structures. The output order is the order in which the output tables are produced when performing a join.

Consider two join sequences ((T1, T2), T3) and ((T2, T1), T3). In both cases, T3 is the inner table. There are only three ways the composite tables (T1, T2) and (T2, T1) can affect the cost of joining with table T3, given a particular join algorithm:

- The cardinality of the composite tables (T1, T2) and (T2, T1)
- The ordering of rows in the composite tables (T1, T2) and (T2, T1)
- The access structures that are available to the composite tables (T1, T2) and (T2, T1)

The cardinality of the outer table has a direct effect on the number of times the inner table will be accessed. The ordering of rows in (T1, T2) and in (T2, T1) may reduce the cost of some subsequent join if the ordering is an interesting one.

Finally, the absence of an access structure that is required by the chosen join algorithm would mean an additional cost in building the access structure. Now suppose that (T1, T2) and (T2, T1) have the same output order and access structures. The only remaining factor that can influence the joining cost is the cardinality of (T1, T2) versus (T2, T1). However, the cardinalities of (T1, T2) and (T2, T1) should be the same since the number of qualifying rows for a join between two tables T1 and T2 is independent of which table is used as the outer table and of the join algorithm actually used. Therefore, if the output orders of (T1, T2) and (T2, T1) are the same, and if the access structures available to (T1, T2) and (T2, T1) are the same, then (T1, T2) and (T2, T1) should incur the same cost in joining with T3. Furthermore, the intermediate results produced by joining T1 with T2, or by joining T2 with T1, are equivalent.

We define an *equivalence class* as a set of join sequences that have the same tables involved and the same output order. Thus, in the above example, the join sequences (T1, T2) and (T2, T1) belong to the same equivalence class {T1, T2} since they both produce unordered results. Pruning within an equivalence class takes into consideration the fact that join sequences within an equivalence class affect the cost of subsequent joins in the same manner. Therefore, only the least expensive join sequence that produces a particular intermediate result needs to be considered; all others can be discarded. Thus, if (T1, T2) and (T2, T1) are in the same equivalence class, and if the cost of performing (T1, T2) is lower than that of performing (T2, T1), then (T2, T1) cannot be part of an optimal processing strategy for the overall query.

Pruning Similar Equivalence Classes

We say that two equivalence classes are similar if the tables involved in both equivalence classes are the same. For example, the equivalence class of strategies that produce the join of {T1, T2, T3} in T1.a order and the equivalence class of strategies that produce the join of {T1, T2, T3} in T2.b order are similar.

At a given stage of the join sequence, an output order is said to be *locally interesting* if the order can be used to reduce the cost of some subsequent join or to avoid a final sorting operation on the query output. Suppose also that we want to join five tables R, S, T, U, and V. Suppose also that a join with table R as the inner table will be cheaper if the outer table is ordered by R1.a. Similarly, the preferred outer table orders are S.b, T.c, U.d, and V.e, respectively. Thus, to tables U and V, any output order of {R, S, T} that is ordered by R1.a, R2.b, or R3.c can be considered uninteresting since the two remaining joins with U and V cannot take advantage of these orders to reduce their processing costs. Likewise, after joining {R, S, T, U}, an output order of U.d is also considered uninteresting for the remaining join with V.

Using the concept of locally interesting order, we can group similar equivalence classes having output orders that are locally uninteresting into one equivalence class. This is possible because equivalence classes with locally uninteresting orders do not allow subsequent joins to take advantage of their output orders.

Access Path Enumeration Example

Consider the following query:

```
SELECT    accounts.a#, branches.bname, owners.oname
FROM      accounts, branches, owners
WHERE     accounts.b# = branches.b#
AND       accounts.o# = owners.o#
AND       branches.location = "Northern California"
AND       owners.name > "Smith"
```

In this example, the access paths for all the individual tables with their local predicates are enumerated. This enumeration is shown in Figure 7.2.

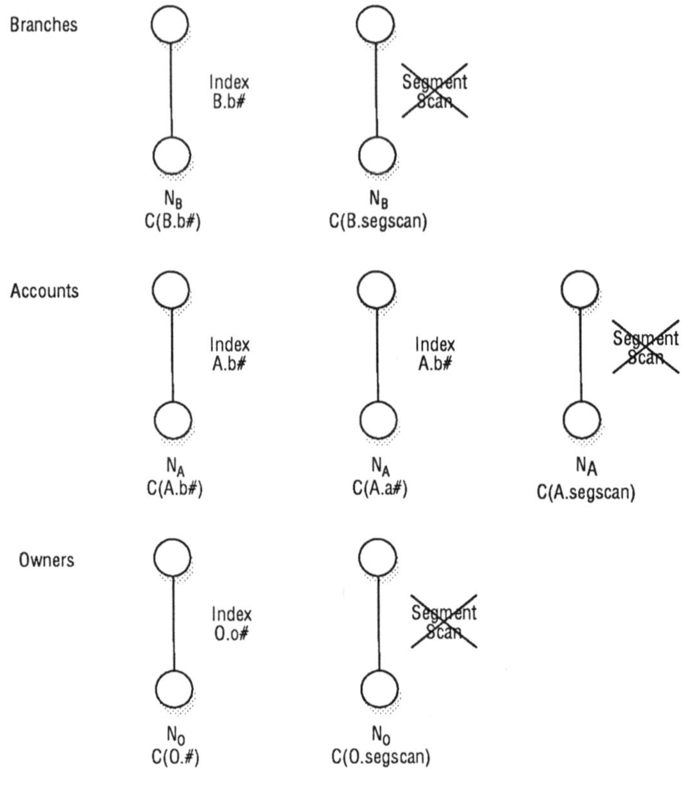

Figure 7.2: Access paths for individual tables.

There are three access paths for accounts: a nonclustering index on b#, a clustering index on o#, and a table scan. The first two access paths are retained because they both deliver rows in interesting orders. Furthermore, let's assume that using the clustering index access path is less expensive than the table scan. The table scan access path can therefore be pruned because it is dominated by the clustering index access path.

There are two access paths for branches: a clustering index on b# and a table scan. The table scan is pruned because it is dominated by the clustering index access path.

Owners also has two access paths: a clustering index on o# and a table scan. Again, the table scan is pruned because it is dominated by the clustering index access path.

The pruned search tree that is retained at the end of single table enumeration is shown in Figure 7.3. The notation C(B.b#) represents the cost of scanning the branches table via the index on b# and applying all other local predicates on branches from the query (in this case branches.location = "Northern California"). The notation N_B means the number of rows from branches that satisfy the local predicates.

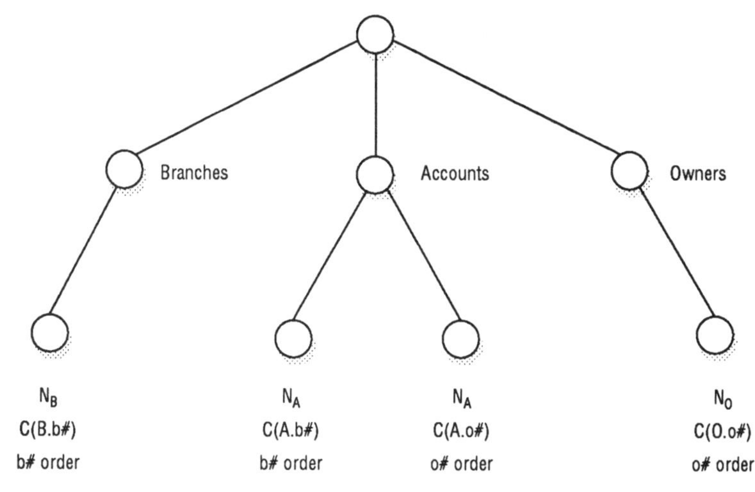

Figure 7.3: Search tree for single tables.

The search tree is expanded to cover intermediate results that contain pairs of tables. This is achieved by joining a second table to any of the individual tables in Figure 7.3 using nested loop index joins. This enumeration is shown in Figure 7.4. This notation (Accounts, Branches) represents an intermediate result obtained by joining Accounts with Branches, regardless of which table is used as the outer table. The notation N_{AB} represents the cardinality of the resulting table. The corresponding costs of forming two-table intermediate results using nested loop index joins, as well as merge joins, are shown in Figure 7.5. The notation C_B(A.b#) represents the cost of using the b# index on Accounts to find the matching rows for a given row from branches.

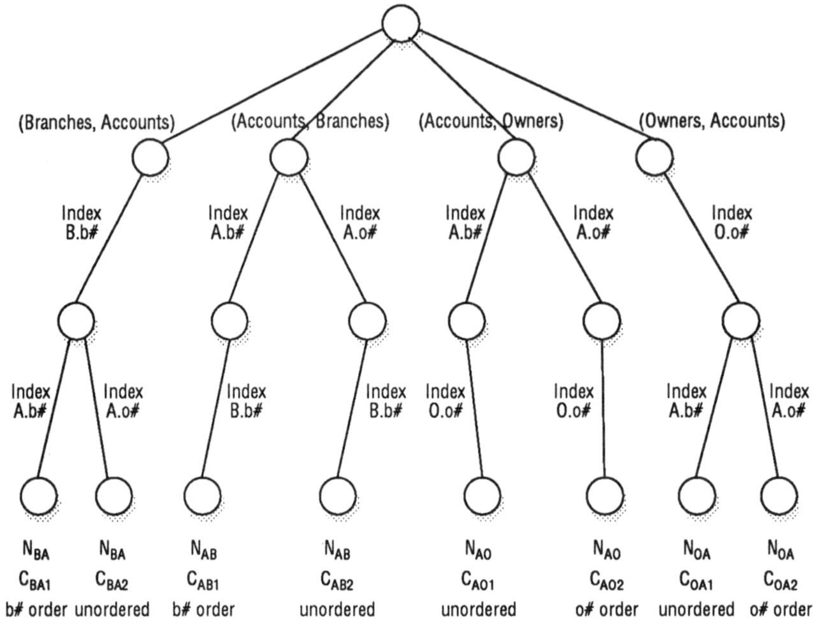

Figure 7.4: *Search tree for two tables (nested loop join).*

$C_{BA1} = C(B.b\#) + N_B * C_B(A.b\#)$

$C_{BA1} = C(B.b\#) + N_B * CB(A.o\#)$

$C_{BA1} = C(A.b\#) + N_A * C_A(A.b\#)$

$C_{BA1} = C(A.o\#) + N_A * C_A(B.b\#)$

$C_{BA1} = C(A.b\#) + N_A * C_A(O.o\#)$

$C_{BA1} = C(A.o\#) + N_A * C_A(O.o\#)$

$C_{BA1} = C(O.o\#) + N_O * C_O(A.b\#)$

$C_{BA1} = C(O.o\#) + N_O * C_O(A.o\#)$

$C_{BA1} = C_{merge}(B{,}b\#, A.b\#)$

$C_{BA4} = C_{sort}(A.o\#) + C_{merge}(B.b\#, Temp1)$

$C_{BA3} = C_{merge}(A.b\#{,}B.a\#)$

$C_{AB4} = C_{sort}(A.o\#) + C_{merge}(Temp2, B.b\#)$

$C_{AO3} = C_{sort}(A.b\#) + C_{merge}(Temp3{,}O.o\#)$

$C_{AO4} = C_{merge}(A.o\#{,}O.o\#)$

$C_{OA3} = C_{sort}(A.b\#) + C_{merge}(O.o\#, Temp4)$

$C_{OA4} = C_{merge}(O.o\#, A.o\#)$

$C_{AB} = \min(C_{AB1}, C_{AB2}, C_{AB3}, C_{AB4}, C_{BA1}, C_{BA1}, C_{BA3}, C_{BA4})$

$C_{AO} = \min(C_{AO1}, C_{AO2}, C_{AO3}, C_{AO4}, C_{OA1}, C_{OA1}, C_{OA3}, C_{OA4})$

Figure 7.5: *Costs for two table joins.*

Let us next consider the use of merge joins. Figure 7.6 shows the enumeration. Since the b# index on Branches and the b# index on Accounts both deliver rows in b# order, no extra merge steps are required and the resulting table is in b# order. On the other hand, when the o# index is used as the access path for Accounts, it is necessary to sort the resulting rows on b# into a temporary table Temp1 before the merge join can be performed.

Notice that in Figures 7.4 and 7.6, none of the intermediate results is in an interesting order (i.e., usable for the remaining join). Therefore, the search tree can be pruned to retain only the most economical way to produce each of (Accounts, Branches) and (Accounts, Owners) with the corresponding costs of C_{AB} and C_{AO}, respectively.

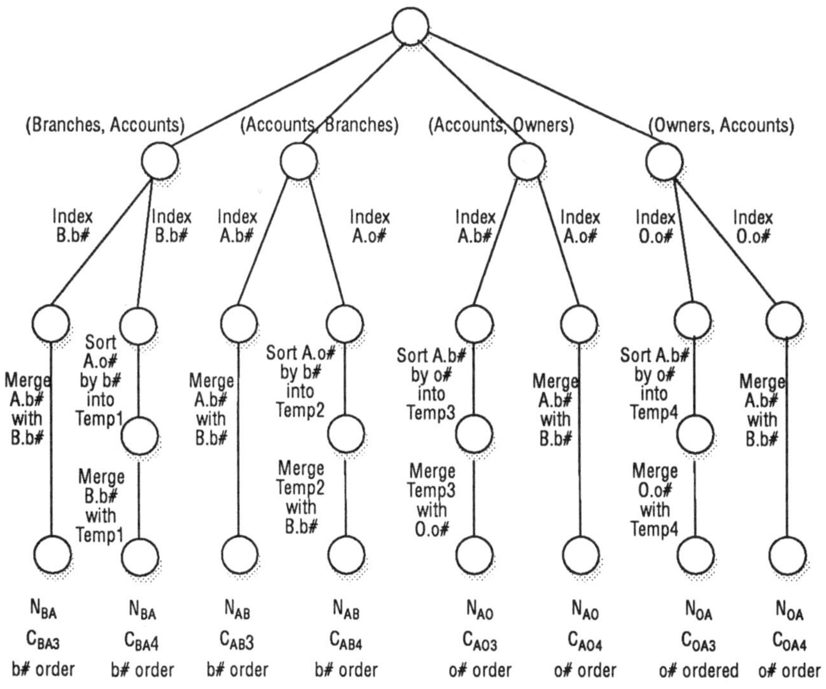

Figure 7.6: Search tree for two tables (merge join).

Finally, let's consider expanding the search tree to produce intermediate results that contain three tables. In general, we can use either a two-table intermediate result as the outer table and a single table as the inner table, or the roles of the two operands can be reversed. For the nested loop method, it is generally preferable to use the two-table intermediate result as the outer table. This is because rows from the two-table intermediate result can be pipelined, avoiding the need to save the intermediate result in a temporary table. Figure 7.7 shows the search tree for forming three-table intermediate results—in this case, the final result of the query.

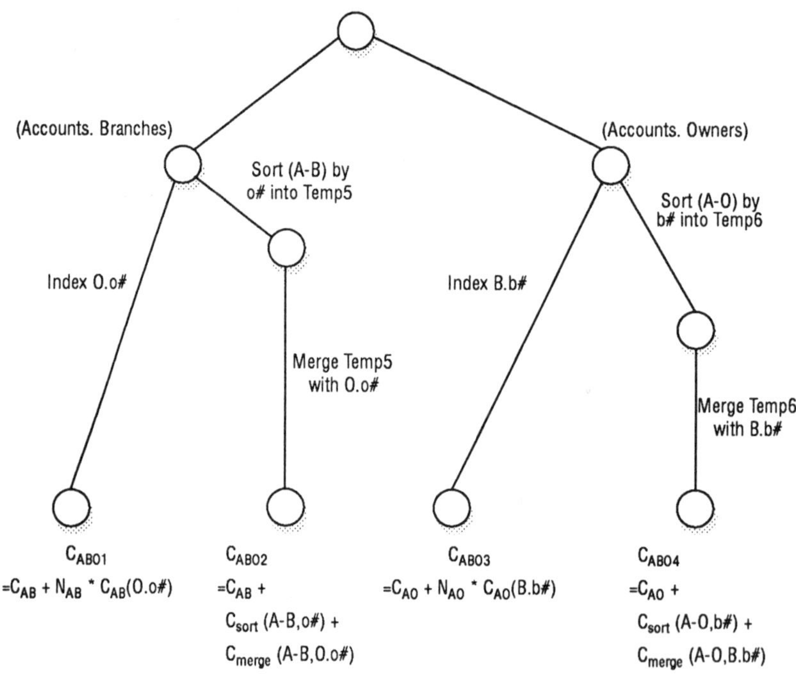

Figure 7.7: Search tree for three tables (nested loop join and merge join).

7.3.3 Flattening of Nested SQL

The semantics of nested SQL queries are defined via nested iteration. Standard implementation approaches all use nested iteration. As a result, the same sub-query may be evaluated multiple times. The flattening of a nested SQL query into a canonical, non-nested query allows set-at-a-time processing, eliminates redundant operations, and generally opens up more opportunities for optimization. A taxonomy of nested SQL queries, along with approaches for their flattening and optimization, have been proposed in Kim [1982].

Type-A Nesting

A nested predicate is type-A if the inner query block Q does not contain a join predicate that references a table in the outer query block and if the SELECT clause of Q consists of an aggregate function over a column in an inner table [Kim, 1982]. An example of a type-A nested query follows:

```
SELECT  a#
FROM    accounts
WHERE   b# = (   SELECT  max(b#)
                 FROM    branches )
```

This query can be transformed into two sequential subqueries:

Subquery 1:

```
SELECT  max (b#)
FROM    branches
INTO    :bno
```

Subquery 2:

```
SELECT  a#
FROM    accounts
WHERE   b# = :bno
```

Type-N Nesting

A nested predicate is type-N if the inner query block Q does not contain a join predicate that references a table in the outer block and if the SELECT clause of Q does not contain an aggregate function [Kim, 1982]. An example of a type-N nested query follows:

```
SELECT  a#
FROM    accounts
WHERE   b# IN (  SELECT  b#
                 FROM    branches
                 WHERE   location = "Northern California" )
```

This query can be transformed into two sequential subqueries:

Subquery 1:

```
temp1 =
        SELECT    b#
        FROM      branches
        WHERE     location = "Northern California"
```

Subquery 2:

```
        SELECT    a#
        FROM      accounts, temp1
        WHERE     accounts.b# = temp1.b#
```

As we shall see later in this section, the above transformation is only valid when each row in the accounts table joins with a single row in the branches table. Otherwise, subquery 1 must be modified to select the distinct set of b# in order to produce the same result set as the original query.

Type-J Nesting

A type-J nested predicate results if the WHERE clause of the inner query block contains a join predicate that references the table of an outer query block and if the table is not included in the FROM clause of the inner query block. Additionally, the SELECT clause of the inner query block should not contain an aggregate function [Kim, 1982]. The following is an example of type-J nesting:

```
        SELECT    a#
        FROM      accounts
        WHERE     o# IN (   SELECT    o#
                            FROM      owners
                            WHERE     balance = - overdraft_limit )
```

This query can be transformed into an equivalent non-nested query:

```
        SELECT    a#
        FROM      accounts, owners
        WHERE     accounts.o# = owners.o#
        AND       accounts.balance = - owners.overdraft_limit
```

Again, the above transformation is appropriate only if each row in the accounts table joins with a single row in the owners table.

Type-JA Nesting

Type-JA nesting is present if the WHERE clause of the inner query block contains a join predicate that references the table of an outer query block and if the inner SELECT clause consists of an aggregate function over an inner table [Kim, 1982]. For example,

```
SELECT    oname
FROM      owners
WHERE     o# = (    SELECT  max(o#)
                    FROM    accounts
                    WHERE   balance = - overdraft_limit )
```

This query can be transformed into two sequential subqueries:

Subquery 1:

```
temp =
SELECT    max(o#), balance
FROM      accounts
GROUP BY  balance
```

Subquery 2:

```
SELECT    oname
FROM      owners, temp
WHERE     - owners.overdraft_limit = temp.balance
```

Pitfalls of Flattening

Consider the following two queries on the parts and orders tables below:

Q1:

```
SELECT    part#, description
FROM      parts
WHERE     part# IN (      SELECT   part#
                    FROM    orders)
```

Q2:

```
SELECT    parts.part#, parts.description
FROM      parts, orders
WHERE     parts.part# = orders.part#
```

Parts			Orders		
part#	description quantity	qoh	order#	part#	
101	bolt	10	10001	101	1
102	nut	5	10002	101	1
103	hammer	1	10003	102	1
		10004	102	NULL	

The semantics of Q1 is to iterate over all rows in the parts table and to test if each row satisfies the IN predicate. Since the nested subquery does not contain any correlated variables, it would suffice to evaluate this subquery only once and to save the corresponding result for testing against each row in the parts table. Q1 yields

part#	description
101	bolt
102	nut

whereas Q2 yields

part#	description
101	bolt
101	bolt
102	nut
102	nut

Q1 and Q2 would produce the same results had the relationship between parts and orders been one-to-one or many-to-one. The two queries are not equivalent in the above scenario because one row from parts can join with multiple rows in orders. Some systems attempt to provide syntax-independent optimization by converting nested SQL queries into equivalent non-nested ones in order to improve performance. However, such normalization must be done carefully, or unnecessary duplicates may result in the output, and the semantics of the original nested query will not be preserved.

It should be noted that Q1 is equivalent to the semijoin of parts by orders based on the part# columns. (That is, the selection of those rows from parts that join with one or more rows from orders.) If the database system internally supports the semijoin operation, Q1 can be processed quite efficiently.

Consider the following queries:

Q3:

```
SELECT   part#
FROM     parts
WHERE    qoh > ALL (   SELECT  quantity
                       FROM    orders
                       WHERE   orders.part# = parts.part#)
```

Q4:

```
SELECT   part#
FROM     parts
WHERE    qoh > MAX (   SELECT  quantity
                       FROM    orders
                       WHERE   orders.part# = parts.part#)
```

Q4 is not a valid transformation of Q3 for the parts and orders tables shown earlier. This is because the MAX function is computed over non-null values, whereas the ALL comparison preserves NULL values. Thus Q3 returns parts 101 and 103, while Q4 returns parts 101 and 102, and implementations that perform the above transformation are erroneous.

7.3.4 Timing of Optimization

Optimization can be performed at compile time or run time. Systems that do not support compile time optimization typically allow queries to be optimized once at the beginning of a user session, into an in-memory execution tree which can then be invoked an unlimited number of times during that session.

Some systems allow the generation of the access plan for a query to be deferred, while at the same time they allow use of the generated access plan across multiple sessions. Such delayed binding enables a more flexible development approach. An application can be developed against a development database and can then be adapted for execution against a production database. This arrangement provides the advantages of compile time optimization without its restrictions.

To allow for reuse of an access plan across sessions, the database system must track the dependency of access plans on schema objects. When schema objects are deleted or modified, the affected access plans must be identified and flagged so that the generation of a new access plan will be forced prior to the next execution.

7.4 Minimizing Communication Overhead

SQL is ideally suited for use in a client-server environment because of its set-orientation. A client can submit a nonprocedurally specified SQL query to the server and the latter can optimize its processing by selecting from existing access paths as well as considering the dynamic generation of additional access paths (e.g., creating a sorted temporary or an index on the fly). Once a query has been submitted to the server, a pipeline effectively has been set up between the client and the server, and the client can start fetching rows from the server.

Very often, the client-interface package provided by the database software vendor will buffer a sliding window of the result set. Thus, each fetch operation submitted by the application will not have to be mapped into a separate invocation of the server. As a result, the message overhead between the client and the server incurred in the processing of a SELECT statement can easily be kept to a minimum. For statements that are more record-oriented (e.g., the INSERT statement), other batching mechanisms are required to hold down the communication overhead. Several possible approaches are

- Using an array interface
- Batching multiple SQL statements as a single request
- Adding control structures to the request specification to permit the server to execute selected batched statements conditionally
- Using a stored procedure/module implementation to permit code sharing among multiple users

Array Interface

An array interface can be used in an embedded SQL environment. (See Chapter 9 for discussions on the embedded SQL approach for interfacing with a server.) Instead of fetching a row into host variables that represent individual column values, host variables that represent arrays can be specified. In this case, multiple rows can be fetched in a single call. Likewise, instead of inserting a single row using host variables that represent individual column values, host variables that represent arrays can be used. Thus, multiple rows can be inserted into the database in one batched request to the server. Similarly, array host variables can be used to direct the server to execute delete and update statements multiple times, each time using as parameters an element from each of the specified arrays. Much of ORACLE's efficiency in dealing with insert- and update-intensive applications is derived from its support of an array interface.

Batching

When a callable interface is used between the client and the server (as in the Microsoft SQL Server and DEC Rdb/VMS), the client interface can be directed to batch multiple SQL statements as one request to the server. The SQL Server allows a user to place multiple SQL statements (possibly of different types) in a command buffer, to be sent as one request to the server. The execution of the batch is terminated as soon as any of the statements within the batch fails.

Whereas the SQL Server parses each of the batched statements on the fly, SQL Services (Rdb's client interface), which supports a callable interface patterned after dynamic SQL, requires that statements be prepared before their batched execution can be effected. (A discussion of dynamic SQL interface will be presented in Chapter 9.) Furthermore, in the case of retrievals, batching in SQL Services is limited to the fetching of multiple rows from a cursor associated with a prepared statement. In the case of updates, multiple INSERT/DELETE/UPDATE statements may be batched using an execution flag. As long as the flag is not turned on, commands are accumulated and processing is deferred. Like Rdb, ORACLE supports a transaction execution mechanism whereby multiple prepared SQL statements can be executed as one batch.

Control Structures

Both the SQL Server and the ORACLE Server support the use of control-of-flow constructs in the specification of a batch of SQL statements to be executed as a unit by the server. These extensions provide for the declaration of variables, and the conditional/unconditional execution of SQL statements. The SQL Server's extended SQL dialect is called TRANSACT-SQL, while ORACLE's dialect is called PL/SQL. TRANSACT-SQL can be used at execution time to specify a batch of source SQL statements to be executed at the server. It can also be used as the language for defining stored procedures that can be invoked multiple times. PL/SQL, on the other hand, is used in a manner akin to the embedding of SQL in a host programming language. Instead of directing the server to execute a standard SQL statement, the application can invoke the server to execute an entire PL/SQL block, thereby minimizing the communication overhead between the client and the server.

Stored Procedures

A limitation of the PL/SQL approach to batching of SQL statements is that each PL/SQL block is specified inline within an application. There is no support for the encapsulation of a PL/SQL block as a procedure that can be invoked from other PL/SQL blocks. In fact, the implementation of PL/SQL does not provide for code sharing between multiple (possibly concurrent) incarnations of the same application. Each application must incur the cost of having a PL/SQL block parsed and optimized once, before it can be executed one or more times within the application. The stored procedure implementation in the SQL Server, on the other hand, provides for the invocation of a stored procedure from other stored procedures. Once a stored procedure has been optimized, its execution plan is saved as a persistent object in the database and it can be used any number of times in the future. In fact, the SQL Server maintains a cache of stored procedures that have recently been invoked. Thus, in an online transaction processing environment, the same optimized access plan for a stored procedure can be shared among multiple client applications.

7.5 Concurrency Control Tuning

As we discussed in Chapter 5, most database systems use locking to implement concurrency control. Thus, locks that are held on database objects are a major source of contention. Some systems support concurrency control tuning options that can reduce such contention. Both ORACLE and Rdb support a multiversion concurrency control mechanism that eliminates conflicts between read-only transactions and update transactions. With ORACLE, it is necessary to adjust the number of rollback segments to make sure that there is sufficient room for before images needed by read-only transactions. Likewise, Rdb allows snapshots to be immediate or deferred. If snapshots are deferred, then no performance penalty is imposed on update transactions that start at a time when there are no active read-only transactions. However, read-only transactions will be forced to wait for update transactions that do not write to the snapshot file to complete, before they themselves can begin. The SQL Server defaults to non-two-phase locking (releasing read locks as quickly as possible) to minimize conflicts. The IBM OS/2 Extended Edition Database Manager uses lock escalation to limit the number of outstanding locks in order to minimize the amount of bookkeeping.

7.6 Buffering Strategy

The strategy employed by a server for buffering database pages in random access memory has a significant impact on performance. In Chapter 5, we examined the checkpointing strategies used in different servers. In servers that make use of periodic checkpointing, such as the IBM Extended Edition Database Manager, the ORACLE Server, and the Microsoft SQL Server, the overhead for committing a transaction is much reduced because only the recovery log entries may have to be force written. Database pages that have been modified by the committing transaction can stay in the database cache. They can be displaced and written back to the stable database as part of a least-recently-used page replacement process, or they can be written at the time of a checkpoint. Conversly, for systems like Rdb that make use of a transaction-oriented checkpointing strategy, more synchronized updates to the stable database must be performed before a transaction can be committed. As we pointed out in Chapter 5, a periodic checkpointing strategy may require the redoing of updates during recovery from a system crash, whereas a transaction-oriented checkpointing strategy gives rise to a simpler recovery procedure.

The use of a process-oriented architecture versus the use of a server-oriented architecture also has an impact on the sharing of buffers between concurrent users. For the SQL Server and ORACLE, buffers are shared between concurrent users and frequently updated hot spots in the database do not need to be written back until the time of a checkpoint.[5] In servers that make use of a process-oriented architecture, there is often no sharing of buffers between applications. If the same database page is buffered by two different server processes, and if it is modified by one of these server processes, it

---

[5] In fact, ORACLE also makes use of a background process to write modified pages back to the stable database asynchronously, thereby minimizing the number of pages that have to be written at checkpoint time and also ensuring free space is available in the buffer for reading in database pages demanded by applications.

becomes necessary for the other server process to invalidate its copy of the same page. Even though this adds to the synchronization overhead between server processes, it nevertheless becomes more easily adaptable to run in a multiprocessor environment.

7.7 Case Studies

In this section, we examine factors that can affect performance in each of the four SQL-based database servers discussed in this book. Our intent is to highlight features that are unique to each of these servers.

7.7.1 IBM OS/2 Extended Edition Database Manager

The IBM OS/2 Extended Edition Database Manager provides the least amount of tuning options to database designers and application developers. As a result, the IBM Extended Edition is much easier to administer as compared to the other three servers covered in this book. On the other hand, the performance of the IBM Extended Edition may not be as good under extreme workloads.

Delayed Binding Support

An access plan in the IBM Extended Edition is a database object created by either the precompiler or the binder. The act of creating the access plan is known as *binding* the application program to the database. Once created, the access plan contains the information needed by the IBM Extended Edition to access data in the most efficient way for a particular application program.

The decisions regarding which indexes to use and whether to use an index for a particular table access is determined by the IBM Extended Edition at the time the application program is bound to the database. If the physical data structures change after the program is bound, the access plan is automatically invalidated. If the application program is executed after an associated access plan has been invalidated, the IBM Extended Edition automatically rebuilds the access plan. Thus, the application program is not affected by changes resulting from the addition or removal of indexes.

The precompiler creates the information the IBM Extended Edition needs to execute the application's SQL statements against a database. The database against which the precompilation is performed must contain all the database objects that are referenced in the SQL statements in the source modules. This information is stored in an access plan, in a bind file, or both, depending on the selected precompilation option.

If the /P option (the default) is used, access plan generation (binding) is enabled. This means that an access plan is created in the database specified by the precompile command. One access plan is created for each precompiled source module. In addition to modifying the source file, the precompiler associates the application with the database with which the application will be dealing. That is, appropriate dependency information is recorded in the system relations. Unless otherwise told, the precompiler automatically binds the program to the database that contains the definition of database objects referenced in the source module, and it stores the resulting access plan in that database.

If the /B option is selected, binding is deferred. The information required to create an access plan is stored in a bind file with the .BND extension. This file contains the data required to create an access plan and can later be used with the SQLBIND command or the BIND utility function to bind the program to a desired database. One bind file is created for each precompiled source module.

If both the /P and /B options are selected, both an access plan and a bind file are created. The application is bound to a database, and a bind file will permit binding to other databases later.

The deferred binding mechanism is useful for developing generic applications. It is also useful for developing new applications against existing production databases. Thus, an application developer can use one database as a development database. Once the application is working, it can be bound to one or more production databases.

Concurrency Control Options

As we discussed in Chapter 5, the IBM Extended Edition supports three levels of isolation: repeatable read (RR), cursor stability (CS), and uncommitted read (UR). The default isolation level for Version 1.2 is cursor stability. The isolation level can be set when an access plan is bound to an application program, using the BIND command.

The IBM Extended Edition also resorts to lock escalation to reduce the number of outstanding locks in the system. When a high degree of concurrency is desired, the locklist configuration parameter should be adjusted upward to minimize the need for lock escalation.

Recovery Log File Relocation

The recovery log is used by the IBM Extended Edition to roll back uncommitted transactions and to complete committed transactions in the event of a system or application failure. By default, the log is placed in the same subdirectory as the database. It may be desirable to relocate a database log file to another disk to reduce disk head movements necessitated by the writing and logging of updates to the stable database and to the recovery log. At the same time, the database capacity can be increased since the database and log files are no longer restricted to the same disk partition. The NEWLOGPATH configuration parameter causes the relocation. The log file relocation won't be effective until all users have stopped using the database, and the database is restarted.

Database Application Remote Interface

The IBM Extended Edition's Remote Data Services allows an application to access a database on a remote database server. With Remote Data Services, an application can use the Database Application Remote Interface to allow the routine that uses the remote database to reside and execute at the location of the database rather than at the client workstation. This provides efficient access to functions that reside only on the remote database server. Additionally, it reduces communications traffic, and improves the performance of batchlike work.

To utilize the Database Application Remote Interface mechanism, the application transaction should be designed so that one client routine runs on the machine that hosts Database Requestor and a server routine runs on the workstation that hosts the IBM Extended Edition. If Database Requestor and Database Server happen to be on the same workstation, Remote Data Services bypasses the remote interface and executes the procedure locally.

The server routine must exist as an OS/2 Dynamic Link Library (DLL). The Database Requestor effectively invokes the remote DLL that includes the server routine. This DLL must reside in an OS/2 directory identified by the LIBPATH parameter in the CONFIG.SYS file.

The Database Requestor routine must issue a START USING DATABASE call before invoking the Database Application Remote Interface. The Database Requestor routine must also supply the addresses of input and output data structures. Parameters are passed to and from the server routine using a SQL descriptor area (SQLDA) structure, which is defined by Database Requestor to include variable data areas. Most fields of the SQLDA are transmitted to the server routine, which uses a reconstructed SQLDA that includes the transmitted fields. The server routine uses the reconstructed SQLDA and passes most fields of the SQLDA back to the Database Requestor routine. The server routine must pass the same number of items with the same data type and length as specified in the Database Requestor SQLDA.

The transaction may be atomic, with one call and return, or conversational, with a set of calls and returns. This configuration is determined by the value returned by the server routine. If the interaction is atomic, the server routine and all data areas are freed after information is transmitted successfully to the Database Requestor. If the interaction is conversational, the data areas are also freed after information is transmitted successfully to the Database Requestor, but the server routine is not freed. The server routine must provide an interface for the Database Requestor so it can be instructed to free itself.

7.7.2 ORACLE Server

An instance of the ORACLE is implemented with six kernel processes and one proxy process for each connected client. Each process is independently scheduled to run by the operating system. These processes share an area called the system global area (SGA) for buffer management, caching, lock management, and communications with user applications.

The six background processes supported by ORACLE are

DBWR: The Database Writer writes modified blocks of data from the SGA to the database. This process ensures that data blocks are written in the proper order (in accordance with the write ahead log protocol). It combines writes, when possible, for greater efficiency.

LGWR: The Log Writer writes log entries to disk. LGWR ensures a smooth flow of data from buffer to disk without delaying processes that are generating new redo log entries.

SMON: The System Monitor oversees the operation of the server and performs database recovery when necessitated by system or hardware errors.

PMON: The Process Monitor oversees all user processes and performs user process recovery when necessitated by system or hardware errors.

ARCH: The Archiver copies online redo log files to archival storage.

NLSN: The Network Listener "listens" on the network for connection requests to the server from client applications or other database servers. When such a connection is detected, it spawns a shadow or proxy process that performs all further communication with its client.

The shadow process reads and writes to the SGA on behalf of the user process and prevents runaway applications or unauthorized users from reading other users' data or from improperly writing to the SGA and corrupting the database.

The client applications can communicate with ORACLE using a variety of networking protocols, including Named Pipes, SPX/IPX, and NETBIOS.

Each ORACLE database consists of one or more database files and two or more redo log files. The database files contain all of the database objects: the data dictionary, the database tables, views, indexes, and rollback segments. The data dictionary includes a set of tables that the system uses as a reference guide to database objects, such as table and index definitions, user name and password information and so on. Rollback segments contain information needed to roll back or undo prematurely terminated transactions. The redo log files contain a record of updates, inserts, and deletes that need to be reapplied to the database if those changes were not written to the database before a system failure.

Multitable Clustering

An ORACLE database is divided into a number of logical storage units called tablespaces. Each tablespace consists of one or more physical database files. Tablespaces serve a number of purposes; specifically, they can be used

- To control disk space allocation for database data
- To assign specific space quotas for database users
- To provide the granularity for taking a database online and offline
- To decrease backup and recovery overhead
- To improve performance by allocating data across storage devices
- To separate user data from system, or dictionary, data
- To allocate space for different database activities (e.g., high update, read only, temporary work space)

- To group together tables with high update activities so they can be backed up more frequently

Clusters are groups of tables physically stored together because they share common columns and are often used together. Both storage cost and access time can be reduced by using multitable clustering. Tables are added to a cluster through the CLUSTER clause in the CREATE TABLE statement. A cluster may contain up to 16 tables. A cluster index provides quick access to rows within a cluster based on a cluster key. The creation of the cluster index is required before any DML operations can be performed on tables in the cluster.

Clustering forces rows from one or more tables that share the same cluster key value to be stored in the same data block. The cluster key determines how ORACLE groups the rows of the cluster. Rows with the same cluster key are stored physically close together. Each distinct cluster key value is stored only once per cluster, no matter how many tables and rows it occurs in. An optional SIZE parameter can be used to control the amount of space reserved for rows corresponding to one cluster key, and therefore the maximum number of cluster keys per data block. If size is omitted, ORACLE will store one cluster key per data block.

Array Processing

To pass SQL statement to ORACLE, the application must make a function call. These function calls incur overhead that may reduce performance, especially if the application runs in a client workstation accessing data from a server running in a different machine. ORACLE implements an array processing facility that can significantly reduce this communication overhead.

With array processing, the application can issue a SQL statement many times with a single call to ORACLE. For example, consider the following embedded SQL statement:

```
EXEC SQL
        INSERT INTO ACCOUNTS(ACC_NUM) VALUES(:acc_no);
```

If acc_no is an integer host variable, the SQL statement is passed to the server and executed once. However, if acc_no is an integer array with 100 elements, the SQL statement is passed to the server and executed 100 times, thereby causing ORACLE to insert 100 new rows into the ACCOUNTS table. In each row, the ACC_NUM column takes on the value of one of the elements of the acc_no array.

Array processing can also be used in an ORACLE precompiler program to fetch many rows with a single FETCH statement. The number of rows actually fetched can be obtained from the third element of the SQLERRD array within the SQLCA structure. When using the ORACLE Call Interface (OCI), array processing can be implemented with the following OCI calls:

OEXN( ): Executes a SQL statement multiple times. One of the arguments of this call specifies the number of times the statement is to be executed.

OFEN( ): Fetches multiple rows returned by a SQL query. One of the arguments of this call specifies the number of rows to be returned.

PL/SQL

ORACLE's PL/SQL consists of procedural language extensions to SQL (comparable to the Transact-SQL extensions in the SQL Server). PL/SQL allows application developers to mix SQL statements with procedural constructs. A unit of PL/SQL code is called a PL/SQL block. A PL/SQL block may contain data manipulation language statements like INSERT, UPDATE, DELETE, and SELECT; cursor operation statements like DECLARE, OPEN, FETCH, and CLOSE; and transaction processing statements like COMMIT, ROLLBACK, and SAVEPOINT.

In addition, a PL/SQL block may contain any of the following procedural constructs:

- Flow of control statements, including IF... THEN... ELSE, GOTO, and EXIT
- Iteration control statements such as FOR... LOOP, and WHILE... LOOP
- Assignment statements like X := Y := Z, and BONUS := CURRENT_SALARY * BONUS_MULTIPLIER
- Error handling statements such as EXCEPTION WHEN zero_divide THEN...

Application programs pass PL/SQL blocks to a PL/SQL engine. To process a PL/SQL block, the PL/SQL engine executes procedural statements and passes SQL statements to the SQL statement executor in ORACLE. The PL/SQL engine is incorporated into ORACLE RDBMS Version 6.0 with the transaction processing option, and SQL*Forms Version 3.0.

PL/SQL improves performance by reducing calls from the application to ORACLE. Reducing calls is especially helpful in networked environments where calls may incur a large overhead.

Batched Execution of SQL Statements

Two functions in the ORACLE Call Interface, OSBNDP and OTEX, can significantly enhance performance in a networked environment. OSBNDP (OCI Speed BiND by reference and Position) allows an application program to "speed bind" a set of bind variables to a cursor. It is used in conjunction with the OTEX function (OCI Transaction EXecution), which allows an application program to execute a set of cursors together in a single invocation. By executing multiple cursors in a single invocation, network traffic between the client and server is significantly reduced. Consequently, applications written using OSBNDP and OTEX should yield significant performance improvement over equivalent applications that do not make use of such constructs.

For the OS/2 environment, Dynamic Linked Libraries (DLLs) are used in conjunction with ORACLE's Pro*C preprocessor to take particular advantage of the capabilities of OS/2. This means that multiple applications can share the same libraries, reducing the size and memory required by different executables. Another advantage of the DLL format is that maintenance releases for these libraries do not require relinking of executables.

OCI speed bind by reference and position. The OSBNDP( ) function speed binds a set of bind variables to an ORACLE cursor area to ready it for the subsequent OTEX( ) call.[6] Because this call performs binding by position, all variables for the specified cursor must be bound at once in one call. At the same time, because it performs binding by reference, it only needs to be invoked once for a given ORACLE cursor area. The syntax of the OSBNDP( ) function is as follows:

```
int OSBNDP (
        cursor *cursor, unsigned int size, void *bufp[], size_t bufl[],
        int type[], short *indp[], char *buffmtp[], short buffmt1[],
        void *(*memcall)(size_t nbytes), void **memptr)
```

Table 7.1 describes the parameters included in the OSBNPP( ) statement.

---

6 OSBNDP( ) is used only with OTEX( ) and is not intended to be used with other OCI calls.

cursor	pointer to an ORACLE cursor area
size	number of elements in the arrays passed in the rest of this call (this should be the same as the number of bind variables in the SQL statement)
bufp	array of pointers to buffers for the bind values
bufl	array of lengths of buffers to bind (if a length of -1 is specified, strlen( ) of the corresponding bufp[] element is used)
type	array of SQL data types
indp	array of pointers to indicator variables (iff -1 is specified for a particular pointer, the corresponding elements in bufp[] and bufl[] are ignored; instead, NULL is bound for that variable)
buffmtp	array of pointers to format strings
buffmtl	array of lengths of format strings (if -1 is specified, strlen( ) of the corresponding buffmtp[] element is used)
memcall	client-provided memory allocator (like malloc), or NULL, or -1 if no memory allocator is used
memptr	address of a generic pointer that will be filled in by osbndp( ) (if memptr is NULL, the memcall call back function is used to allocate memory; if memptr is not NULL, it is assumed to be pointing to a valid block or memory storage enough for this call)

Table 7.1: OSBNDP parameters.

OCI transaction execute. The OTEX( ) call executes a set of cursors in a single invocation. This operation is functionally the same as executing each cursor separately but faster because it sends only one message to the ORACLE kernel.

OTEX is equivalent to a group of OEXEC( ) calls. It cannot operate on a bind variable array like OEXN( ) and will not execute PL/SQL blocks. All SQL statements are parsed in the normal way using OSQL3( ), but any bind variables must be bound using OSBNDP( ). Transactions executed across a network should show a noticeable improvement when a single OTEX( ) call is used in lieu of multiple calls to OEXEC( ). The syntax of the OTEX( ) function is

```
int OTEX (
        cursor *curarr[], unsigned int size, void *memparr[],
        void *(*memcall)(size_t bytes), void **workmem,
        unsigned int *exe)
```

Table 7.2 describes the parameters included in the OTEX( ) call.

cursarr	array to cursor data areas
size	number of cursors in the cursor array
memparr	array of pointers to client-provided memory that have been filled in by osbndp( ) (the first pointer in this array is associated with the first cursor in the cursor array, and so on)
memcall	client-provided memory allocator (like malloc), or NULL, or -1 if no memory allocator is used
workmem	address of a generic pointer (if workmem is NULL, the memcall call back function is used to allocate memory; if workmem is not NULL, it is assumed to be pointing to a valid block of memory large enough for this call)
nexe	returned value for the number of cursors executed

Table 7.2: *OTEX parameters.*

The cursors are executed in the order in which they are stored in the cursor array. If an error occurs during the OTEX( ) call, 'nexe' is loaded with the number of cursors executed (the first nexe-1 succeeded, and the next failed). The memory pointed to workmem should be allocated only the first time by setting workmem to NULL. Subsequent calls to OTEX( ) can pass in the same memory pointer as long as the number of cursors being executed is less than or equal to the number of cursors executed when the memory was allocated. The memory can then be freed when no more calls to OTEX( ) are required.

EXPLAIN PLAN

The EXPLAIN PLAN statement displays the execution plan chosen by the ORACLE optimizer for SELECT, UPDATE, INSERT, and DELETE statements. An execution plan is a series of primitive operations and an ordering of these operations that ORACLE performs to execute the statement.

Before running the EXPLAIN PLAN statement, a database table must be created to hold the output for that statement. This table can be created using a SQL script called XPLAINPL.SQL, which is included in the distribution media for ORACLE. The syntax of the EXPLAIN PLAN statement is as follows:

```
EXPLAIN PLAN
        [SET STATEMENT_ID = 'description']
        [INTO <tablename>]
        FOR <sql_statement>
```

Sequence Optimization

Business applications often use system-generated key values to uniquely identify data items. For example, new accounts are each assigned an account number typically sequenced after the last assigned account number; similarly, new tellers are assigned unique teller numbers.

Sequential numbers make it easy to identify items referenced in several tables. For example, account numbers and teller numbers are used when entering DebitCredit transactions. In a single user environment, an application adding rows with new sequence numbers can begin by selecting the maximum value from the sequence number column into a local variable, and incrementing that variable to yield a unique number. In a multiuser environment where more than one user may be adding sequence numbers simultaneously, duplicate numbers may result unless some form of concurrency control is exercised. If locking is used, one user must wait until another has committed before being allowed to proceed.

An alternative to locking might be to set up a separate table to store number sequences. The table would contain one record, storing the current value of any sequence number maintained by the system. The user could then select the new value for the new row. If the user committed immediately after obtaining the sequence number, other users could obtain another sequence number even before the row associated with the first sequence number was actually inserted.

ORACLE's sequence generator maintains sequences as system variables that are automatically incremented each time they are accessed. Duplicate values are eliminated without locks, and no transaction is required to update the sequence.

A CREATE SEQUENCE statement defines and names a sequence, so multiple sequences can be maintained concurrently. Default settings for an initial value of 0 and an increment of 1 can be overridden. The NEXTVAL attribute of a particular sequence accesses and increments the sequence value with the same syntax used for referencing a column in a table. The CURRVAL attribute just accesses the current value of a sequence. For example, if an account_number sequence has been defined, a unique account number can then be obtained as follows:

```
SELECT    account_number.NEXTVAL
FROM      DUAL
```

Dual is the dummy table ORACLE uses when a FROM clause is required but no tables are being accessed.

Concurrency Control Options

The default consistency model in ORACLE guarantees that the results of one statement are consistent. That is, each SQL statement will not see the partial results of other SQL statements. However, there are many situations where it is desirable to run multiple SQL queries against a database without interference from concurrent users, and to extend the consistency model to apply to an entire transaction. If no updates need to be performed within the transaction, it is possible to declare a read-only transaction using the following syntax:

```
SET TRANSACTION READ ONLY
```

A read-only transaction has the following characteristics:

(1) It must begin with the SET TRANSACTION statement.
(2) Only queries are allowed in a read-only transaction. Any SELECT... FOR UPDATE statement will generate an error.
(3) It can be explicitly terminated by a COMMIT or ROLLBACK statement. It is also implicitly terminated by any DDL statement.
(4) All queries within a read-only transaction are executed against the same database snapshot. In fact, the snapshot includes updates that have been performed by transactions that have completed execution as of the initiation time of the read-only transaction.

(5) No locks are held on behalf of a read-only transaction. Therefore, other users can continue to query and update data without running into concurrency conflicts with the read-only transaction.

ORACLE makes use of before images of transactions found in the rollback segments to provide a consistent view to a read-only transaction. If a read-only transaction is long running, the rollback segment may not have enough room to store the before images of transactions that commit after the read-only transaction's start. Thus, long read-only transactions may get the "Snapshot is too old" error. The situation can be remedied by increasing the size of the rollback segments or by resorting to explicit table locking.

If it is desirable to present transaction-consistent views to read-write transactions, ORACLE's default locking scheme must be altered. One option is to set the parameter SERIALIZABLE in INIT.ORA (ORACLE's initialization configuration file) to TRUE. This will ensure enforcement of the transaction serializability semantics, as stipulated by Level 2 conformance of the ANSI SQL standard. However, the concurrency penalty will be considerable. Alternatively, all SELECT statements within a given read-write transaction can tag on the FOR UPDATE option, causing write locks to be set on all table rows that are read. This option will guarantee that the read-write transaction will not see the partial results of other read-write transactions.

7.7.3 DEC Rdb/VMS

Rdb's SQL Services provides application access to Rdb/VMS and VIDA[7] databases from remote computers running a variety of operating systems, including Macintosh, MS-DOS, OS/2, ULTRIX, ULTRIX/RISC, and VMS. The client API communicates with the SQL Services server using DECnet.

The SQL Services server is implemented by one communication server and multiple execution server processes. Together, these processes accept messages from the client API applications, execute the requests against Rdb/VMS or VIDA databases, and send response messages back to the waiting API applications on the client systems. The communication server process functions as the gatekeeper and request dispatcher for the SQL Services server. The execution server

---

7 VAX to IBM Data Access.

processes take on the worker role, carrying out the requests received by the communication server. Once an execution server process finishes executing a request, it returns the results in a response message to the communication server, which dispatches it through DECnet back to the client API application.

As dispatcher, the communication server handles multiple request and response messages asynchronously, making it a multithreaded process. The dispatching technique increases request throughput and improves overall application response time. As workers, execution server processes reside in a collection of processes, called the process pool. At system startup time, the communication server creates the process pool according to definitions in a configuration file.[8] The communication server assigns a request to a execution server (of the type specified by the request) for processing. When the assigned execution server finishes with the request, it sends the results to the client application via the communication server.

Execution server processes are prestarted. When the communication server dispatches a request, the execution server process already exists and therefore does not have to be created on the fly. This arrangement eliminates the overhead of creating a process and activating an image in that process. Execution server processes are also reusable, that is, they are not terminated after use. Again, this saves process startup and image activation time.

The communication server is multithreaded, which means that it can handle multiple client requests simultaneously. Specifically, the communication server is responsible for: (1) accepting incoming client API requests, (2) assigning requests to the process pool for execution, (3) accepting the results of request execution from the process pool, and (4) returning results back to waiting client applications.

The process pool consists of one or more sets of processes, called execution server processes, that execute client API requests dispatched by the communication server. Each execution server process created at SQL Services startup is reusable by the communication server.

The SQL Services configuration file contains sets of definitions. Each definition identifies characteristics of the process pool and specifies the number of execution server sets created for the process pool, and the number of execution server processes that should populate each set.

---

[8] The configuration file can define two types of execution server processes (generic and database specific), it can also determine how many of each type to create, how long each process can be idle before being terminated, and so forth.

The communication server reads the configuration file at SQL Services system startup and creates the process pool from the definitions specified in the configuration file. A single definition creates one set of execution server processes, collectively called a subpool. The default startup process pool, created automatically by the communication server, contains one subpool of two execution server processes.

The system manager can define two classes of subpools:

Generic class execution server process (default): This is the class of execution server processes that the communication server selects by default to execute API requests. The generic class server provides client API applications with the flexibility to attach to multiple databases within a single association.

Database-specific class execution server process (optional): This class provides the same function as a generic class server, but it handles requests in a more specialized way. Modifications to applications and the server system are necessary in order to use database-specific servers. The database-specific class server can only access a single Rdb/VMS or VIDA database. This limitation is necessary because every server process in the class is preattached at system startup to a specific database through a single user account. In contrast, the execution server processes in the generic class subpool are not preattached to a database and must make a database attachment every time a client API application connects to the server system.

The communication server automatically assigns generic class execution server processes to execute API requests. The communication server uses the database-specific class of server processes instead of the default only when client applications explicitly request that class.

The structure of a Rdb database on disk varies according to options chosen by the database designer. A database can be stored in a single operating system file or in multiple files distributed across many disks. In a single-file database, all user-stored data and internal Rdb data reside in a single database root file with the default file type of .RDB. A single-file database also includes a snapshot file, which provides temporary storage for read-only data retrieval and has a default file type of .SNP. By default, both files are located on the same device and in the same directory.

A multifile database includes one or more user-defined storage area files that contain user-stored data from one or more tables or indexes. It consists of a database root file (file type .RDB), one or more storage area files (file type .RDA), and one or more snapshot files (file type .SNP). One snapshot file is created for each storage area file; these snapshot files can be placed on different devices or in different directories.

A multifile database always contains a default data storage area named RDB$SYSTEM. If no explicit storage area is specified for storing a table or sorted index, the database system stores that table or index in the RDB$SYSTEM storage area. Different data storage areas can be assigned to files on different disks to increase the number of disk drives that handle database input/output operations. When the snapshot capability is enabled for a multifile database, Rdb creates a separate snapshot area for each data storage area. When creating a storage area, the corresponding snapshot file can be specified to reside on a different disk to further spread I/O operations.

In addition, Rdb makes use of a RUJ file and an optional AIJ file for recovery purposes. A RUJ, or recovery unit journal, file is established for each user attached to the database. It contains the before images of all modified rows. The RUJ file is used by the recovery process and by user processes to roll back transactions or statements. An optional AIJ, or after image journal, file contains copies of modified rows and modified metadata of committed database transactions for a set time period. The AIJ file is used to recover the database to its most consistent state following a database restore operation.

Tables are assigned to storage areas by storage map definitions. Indexes are assigned to storage areas by STORE clauses in index definitions. A table can be divided into multiple files. This is known as horizontal partitioning.

A storage area can be specified to have either a uniform or mixed page format. A storage area defined to have a uniform page format can contain data from one or more logical areas (table rows, sorted index nodes, or hash index structures); however, each uniform format page can contain only data from one logical area. That is, only one logical area ID is allowed per page. A storage area defined to have a mixed page format can also contain data from one or more logical areas. However, each mixed format page can contain data from more than one logical area. That is, more than one logical area ID is allowed per page.

If heavy access to a single storage area causes a disk I/O bottleneck, it may be advantageous to create additional storage areas and to partition some tables across multiple storage areas. When a table is partitioned, rows are divided among storage areas according to data values in one or more columns. A given storage area will then contain only those rows whose column values fall within the range that is specified.

If a hashed index is defined on the a# column of the accounts table, the hashed index should also be partitioned to parallel the way the table is partitioned. For example,

```
CREATE STORAGE AREA accounts_sa1
FILENAME acdisk:[tp1]sa1
PAGE FORMAT IS UNIFORM;

CREATE STORAGE AREA accounts_sa2
FILENAME acdisk:[tp1]sa2
PAGE FORMAT IS UNIFORM;

CREATE STORAGE AREA accounts_sa3
FILENAME acdisk:[tp1]sa3
PAGE FORMAT IS UNIFORM;

CREATE STORAGE MAP ac_map FOR accounts
STORE USING (a#))
IN accounts_sa1 WITH LIMIT OF ('10000')
IN accounts_sa2 WITH LIMIT OF ('20000')
OTHERWISE IN accounts_sa3;

CREATE INDEX ac_hash_index
ON accounts(a#)
TYPE IS HASHED STORE USING (a#)
IN accounts_sa1 WITH LIMIT OF ('10000')
IN accounts_sa2 WITH LIMIT OF ('20000')
OTHERWISE IN accounts_sa3;
```

Indexing Options

Sorted index retrieval provides indexed sequential access to rows in a table. By contrast, hashed index retrieval provides direct retrieval of a specific row.

Batched Execution

When an application executes a prepared INSERT, DELETE, or UPDATE statement that contains parameter markers, it can control whether the API sends one row of data at a time to the server for processing or several rows at a time. Frequently, batched execution reduces the number of messages required to complete the operation.

In normal (nonbatched) execution, the API places each set of parameter marker values (an individual row) in the message buffer and sends the message to the server for execution. In batched execution, the API stores sets of parameter marker values (multiple rows) in the message buffer, but it does not send the message to the server until the application signals the end of the batched execution.

If the message buffer becomes full during batched execution, the API sends the message to the server and begins a new message in a manner that is transparent to the application. In this case, when the batched parameter marker values arrive at the server, the server stores them in a buffer until the application signals the end of the batched execution.

Concurrency Control Options

The deferred snapshot feature in Rdb is supported by the CREATE SCHEMA and ALTER SCHEMA statements by the following option:

SNAPSHOT ENABLED [IMMEDIATE | DEFERRED]

The default is SNAPSHOT IS ENABLED IMMEDIATE. When snapshots are immediate, a read-write transaction always makes copies of the rows it is about to update to the SNP file. A read-only transaction (with or without the reserving option) will always first attempt to read a row in the live RDB file (or in the appropriate RDA file in the case of a multifile database). If the row the read-only user wants is marked for update, Rdb looks at the Transaction Sequence Number (TSN) to decide if the read-only user should be sent to the SNP file.

If snapshots are deferred, then a read-write transaction needs to write to the snapshot file only if read-only transactions are attached to the database at the time the read-write transaction begins. If a user tries to start a read-only transaction while read-write transactions are active, then the read-only transaction will be forced to wait for the read-write transactions to commit or rollback before it can begin. If another read-write transaction tries to start while the read-only transaction is waiting, it will be forced to wait as well. If a read-write transaction begins while read-only transactions are active, then the read-write transaction will write before images to the snapshot file.

When snapshots are defined as immediate, read-write transactions will write before images to the snapshot file regardless of whether or not read-only transactions are active.

Access Path Display Options

Rdb makes use of a cost-based optimizer. The access plan selected by the optimizer is displayed if the *strategy flag* is turned on accordingly:

```
DEFINE RDMS$DEBUG_FLAGS "S"
```

Additionally, the *cost of access strategy flag* can be turned on to display the estimated cost and result cardinality for a query:

```
DEFINE RDMS$DEBUG_FLAGS "O"
```

These flags can also be combined as follows:

```
DEFINE RDMS$DEBUG_FLAG "SO"
```

7.7.4 Microsoft SQL Server

The Microsoft SQL Server is tightly integrated with Microsoft OS/2 LAN Manager. The SQL Server uses the LAN Manager Named Pipes Interprocess Communication (IPC) mechanism and service APIs, and is automatically identified on networks as a LAN Manager service. The SQL Server can be brought up and down remotely by LAN Manager. In addition, a flexible broadcast mechanism allows front-end applications to determine on the fly where SQL Servers are located on the network.

The SQL Server runs as a single, multithreaded OS/2 process and handles scheduling, task switching, disk caching, locking, and transaction processing within the SQL Server kernel, minimizing operating system overhead. Because of the SQL Server's client-server architecture, client applications run on separate machines, allowing the server machine to be configured optimally for the SQL Server requirements. Each SQL Server client user requires an additional 40 Kbytes of memory on the server compared to conventional systems that require as much as 512 Kbytes of server memory per user.

As a result, front-end applications that process the results of a query slowly won't slow the server down. The SQL Server doesn't have to wait for a front-end application to receive and process the returned data before working on another request. When a front-end application has finished with the contents of the return buffer, it notifies the server. Only then does the SQL Server continue to process the original query if necessary.

The major advantage of the SQL Server's multithreaded design is improved throughput—the physical number of requests that it can process per second. Throughput does not decline significantly as users are added to the system. If SQL Server processes x number of transactions per second with five users connected, it is able to process approximately 95% as many transactions per second with 60 users on the network. This also means that as users are added to the network, response time grows in a linear (rather than exponential) fashion. For example, if the response time is .5 seconds with 10 users on the network (with all users performing the same type of transaction), then the response time with 20 users on the network would be about 1 second.

In contrast, the SQL Server's architecture allows efficient use of system resources. Each user is supported through a separate execution thread inside a SQL Server process. The SQL Server can support 25 client users for each additional megabyte of memory above that needed to support the server itself.

The SQL Server's relatively low memory requirement for user applications leaves more memory available for the disk cache, which, in turn, reduces disk I/O and increases CPU efficiency. This also maximizes transaction throughput, and the SQL Server's response time, as experienced by an individual user, stays relatively constant as users are added to the network.

Stored Procedures

The stored procedures of the SQL Server are collections of SQL statements that are compiled (i.e., parsed, checked for syntax and semantics, and optimized) and stored in the server's data dictionary. Stored procedures are a key factor in the product's efficiency in transaction processing applications because they reduce network traffic and eliminate the overhead of compiling SQL transactions each time they are invoked. Stored procedures also support SQL extensions that allow branching and flow of control, such as IF... THEN... ELSE and DO... WHILE. This makes stored procedures an excellent mechanism for error checking and for enforcing data integrity within the database management system itself. In addition, stored procedures can serve as security mechanisms. A user can be given permission to execute a stored procedure without being granted access privileges on tables or views directly referenced in the stored procedure.

The SQL Server makes use of a large number of system-defined procedures that can be used as shortcuts for retrieving system table information. It also supports database administration functions that require updating of system tables.

Stored procedures are written in Transact-SQL. Transact-SQL provides special control-of-flow constructs that allow the user to control the flow of execution of SQL statements. Control-of-flow constructs can be used in single SQL statements, in batches, in stored procedures, and in triggers. Table 7.3 lists and describes the control-of-flow keywords in the SQL Server.

IF	Defines conditional execution.
ELSE	Defines alternate execution when condition is false.
BEGIN	Begins a statement block.
END	Ends a statement block.
WHILE	Repeats performance of statements as long as condition remains true.
BREAK	Exits from the end of the next outer WHILE loop.
CONTINUE	Restarts WHILE loop.
GOTO <label>	Goes to labeled position with a statement block.
RETURN	Exits unconditionally.
WAITFOR	Sets delay for statement execution.
PRINT	Prints a user-defined message or local variable on the user's screen.
RAISERROR	Prints a user-defined message or local variable on the user's screen, and sets a system flag in the global variable @@ERROR.

Table 7.3: *Microsoft SQL Server control-of-flow keywords.*

The syntax for creating a stored procedure is as follows:

```
CREATE PROCEDURE [owner.] procedure_name [;number]
[[(@parameter_name data type [= default]
 [, @parameter_name data type [= default]...] [)]]
[WITH RECOMPILE]
AS Transact_SQL_statements
```

One or more parameters can be declared in a CREATE PROCEDURE statement. Additionally, default values can be attached to declared parameters within a stored procedure. They are used when the associated parameters are omitted by the user during invocation of the stored procedure. Parameters and local variables are prefixed with a single "@". Global variables, which are system-defined predeclared variables, are distinguished from local variables by having two "@" instead of one "@" preceding their names.

Parameters passed to a procedure can take the place of only constants. The database objects (e.g., table names and column names) referenced in a stored procedure must be known at the time the procedure is created. In particular, the creation of database objects within the body of a stored procedure is limited to those objects that are explicitly named in the source of the stored procedure. In other words, the names of objects being created cannot be parameterized. Furthermore, the creation of views, defaults, rules, triggers, and other procedures within the body of a stored procedure is explicitly prohibited.

The optional semicolon and number listed after the name of a stored procedure provide for the grouping of a set of stored procedures with the same name. These groups can be dropped together using a single DROP PROCEDURE statement.

The WITH RECOMPILE option instructs the SQL Server not to save the access plan created for the stored procedure during invocation. Instead, the procedure should be recompiled on every invocation because the SQL Server uses histograms on the distribution of values within table columns in its query optimizer. Hence, the optimized plan selected for executing a stored procedure may depend on the values passed to the procedure as parameters.

The values passed to a stored procedure can be assigned to parameters implicitly by position. Alternatively, the assignment can be made explicit to take advantage of optional parameters. The syntax for invoking a stored procedure is

```
[EXECUTE] procedure_name[;number]
          [@parameter = ] value [, [@parameter = ] value]...]
```

In the TP_1 benchmark described in Chapter 8, processing a single TP_1 transaction without the SQL Server's stored procedures requires six network messages: a begin transaction, three updates, an insert, and a commit. Using stored procedures, the entire TP_1 transaction is invoked with a single EXECUTE command, requiring only a single network message, instead of six. The SQL Server also uses a shared procedure cache so that multiple users can share the same memory-resident procedure code. In addition, because stored procedures are precompiled and stored in the SQL Server, no compilation overhead is incurred when a stored procedure executes.

One notable difference between the stored procedure mechanism in the SQL Server and the PL/SQL implementation in ORACLE is that of sharing. Whereas the same stored procedure can be shared by multiple clients in the SQL Server, and one stored procedure can invoke other stored procedures, there is no provision for sharing the same PL/SQL block by more than one application. Also, a PL/SQL block cannot be named and explicitly called from another PL/SQL block using conventional procedure invocation semantics.

Query Processing Options

The SQL Server supports a number of query processing options that can be used to control the execution of stored procedures and queries. These options are enabled and disabled using the SQL SET statement.[9] They remain in force for the remainder of the user's session, unless explicitly overridden by subsequent SET statements. Table 7.4 summarizes the options that are relevant to performance monitoring and tuning in the SQL Server.

9 No special privilege is needed for executing the SET statement.

SHOWPLAN (on/off)	This option causes a description of the execution plans for subsequent queries to be displayed.
NOEXEC (on/off)	This option causes subsequent queries to be compiled but not executed. It is often used with the SHOWPLAN option to explore how the SQL Server executes different queries.
STATISTICSIO (on/off)	This option causes the number of scans, logical reads (pages accessed), physical reads (logical reads that cannot be satisfied with cached pages), and pages written for each table to be referenced in subsequent SQL statements.
STATISTICSTIME (on/off)	This option displays the time taken to parse and compile each statement, and the time taken to execute each statement to be displayed.
ROWCOUNT (number)	This option causes the SQL Server to stop processing a query after the specified number of rows has been returned. It can be turned off by setting ROWCOUNT to zero.

Table 7.4: *Microsoft SQL Server query processing options.*

7.8 Summary

As we have seen in this chapter, the performance of client-server database applications is affected by many often-tunable factors. For high-volume online transaction processing, the most critical of these factors are the server's ability to efficiently perform context-switching between multiple transactions, the available support for batching of requests and responses between the client and the server, and the server's ability to defer the synchronized writing of modified database pages until periodic checkpoints.

For ad hoc queries and decision-support applications, the provision of efficient access paths and the optimized selection of access paths are more important. Although it is important that the query optimization process be syntax independent (i.e., independent of the order in which tables and selection predicates are specified), certain nested SQL queries can prove to be too tricky for optimizers that attempt to flatten nested queries to discover efficient access paths. Such queries should simply be avoided, or else users should scrutinize the results carefully to ensure that they are correct.[10]

When there is a mix of short update transactions and long queries, the elimination of concurrency conflicts between these two categories of transactions will go a long way toward optimizing throughput and response. Systems that implement a snapshot read capability for read-only transactions provide a high degree of consistency while maximizing concurrency. Others have to trade concurrency for consistency; they resort to the use of non-two-phase locking (i.e., early release of locks) to minimize conflicts. By doing so, the repeatability of read operations within a transaction can no longer be guaranteed.

Table 7.5 lists the performance features discussed in this chapter and indicates which of the servers support these features.

Performance Features	**IBM EE**	**Oracle Server**	**DEC Rdb/VMS**	**Microsoft SQL Server**
Array Interface	N	Y	N	N
B^+-tree Index	Y	Y	Y	Y
Background Writing of Dirty Pages	N	Y	N	N
Batched Execution	N	Y	Y	Y
Clustering Index	N	Y	N	Y
Compile-time Optimization	Y	N	N	Y
Cost-based Optimization	Y	N	Y	Y
DB Application Remote Interface	Y	N	N	N

[10] Because database software vendors continually update their implementation of query optimization, we have not attempted to identify the exact deficiencies in different servers.

Performance Features	IBM EE	Oracle Server	DEC Rdb/VMS	Microsoft SQL Server
Distributing Database and Log Files	Y	Y	Y	Y
Distributing Tables and Associative Indices	N	Y	Y	Y
Explain Plan	N	Y	Y	Y
Hashed Index	N	N	Y	N
Heuristics-based Optimization	N	Y	N	N
Index Compression	N	Y	Y	N
Multitable Clustering	N	Y	N	N
Multithreaded Server	N	N	N	Y
Partitioning Table Data	N	N	Y	N
Periodic Checkpoint	Y	Y	N	Y
Runtime Optimization	Y	Y	Y	Y
Sequence Generation	N	Y	N	N
Set Checkpoint Interval	Y	Y	N	Y
Snapshot Read	N	Y	Y	N
SQL2-based Levels of Isolation	Y	N	N	N
Stored Procedures	N	N	N	Y
Transaction-oriented Checkpoint	N	N	Y	N

Table 7.5: *Comparison of performance features in four servers.*

Chapter 8
Benchmarking

Improved transaction processing performance and capacity are strong incentives for moving from client-based file-server database applications to a client-server architecture. Two benchmarks that have been widely used to measure the performance of relational database systems are the Wisconsin benchmark [Bitton et al., 1983] and the TP1 benchmark [Anon. et al., 1985]. Both use synthetically generated data and controlled workloads; however, they differ in their target application environments. Both of these benchmarks are less than perfect, and each has evolved over the years. Some of the original authors of the Wisconsin benchmark have recently developed the AS^3AP benchmark [Turbyfill et al., 1991] in an effort to address some of the deficiencies of the Wisconsin benchmark. At the same time, the popularity of the TP1 benchmark among hardware and software vendors has led to the formation of the industry consortium called the Transaction Processing Council (TPC), with a current membership of more than 30 hardware and software vendors. This council has formally developed specifications for the TPC-A and TPC-B benchmarks.

We begin this chapter with a general discussion of benchmarking, its definition, properties, and uses (Sections 8.1 and 8.2). We then examine the salient features of the Wisconsin, AS^3AP, and TPI benchmarks (Sections 8.3 through 8.5), along with their more recent derivatives, the TPC-A and TPC-B benchmarks (Section 8.6).

In Section 8.7, we highlight the published benchmark results of two implementations. Section 8.8 contains specific programs for implementing TPI transactions in each of the four servers discussed throughout this book. (For a complete treatise on benchmarking database and transaction processing systems, see Gray [1991].)

8.1 Why Benchmarks?

Benchmarking is a method of measuring the performance of a hardware or software system in a controlled environment using a standard methodology. Benchmarks are typically used by both vendors and customers for capacity planning, system design, or as a method of comparing the performance of different systems. Vendors frequently use benchmarks for marketing purposes. Occasionally, vendors also rely on benchmarks to uncover performance bottlenecks in their implementations. Customers use benchmarks to choose a system.

In general, the development of customized benchmarks require investments in programmer time, management time, and hardware and software resources. The long lead time required to develop customized benchmarks may also result in lost opportunity [Sawyer, 1991]. Thus, any attempt to develop a customized benchmark should be treated as a development project with its own goals, budget, and schedule.

Many public and proprietary database and transaction processing benchmarks exist [Inmon, 1989; Gray, 1991]. For a benchmark to be generally applicable, it must possess certain commonly cited properties [Gray, 1991; DeWitt, 1991; and Turbyfill et al., 1991]:

Relevance: The benchmark must measure the peak performance and price performance ratio of the system under test, using a realistic workload.

Simplicity: The benchmark must be simple to implement, and the performance metric must be easy to understand and interpret.

Scalability: The benchmark should be applicable to a wide spectrum of computer systems with different processing capacity, through proper scaling of the benchmark database. The longevity of a benchmark depends on its ability to adapt to the dual trends of decreasing hardware cost and increasing parallelism.

Portability: The benchmark should be specified at a high level so it can be ported to different systems and architectures.

Vendor neutrality: The benchmark must not be biased in favor of a particular implementation if it is to become a standard or *de facto* standard used by different vendors.

8.2 Performance Metrics

Whereas traditional computer performance metrics such as Whetstones, MIPs, MegaFLOPs, and GigaFLOPs focus on CPU speed, database and transaction processing benchmarks must be specific to the application domain. Ideally, they must take into consideration the following aspects of the system under test (SUT):

- Input/output architecture
- Data communications architecture
- Query optimization capabilities
- Concurrent processing capacity
- Import/export abilities
- Backup/restore abilities

The Wisconsin benchmark was first developed at the University of Wisconsin [Bitton et al., 1983]. It was originally designed to measure systems with a small database[1] (5,000 to 10,000 rows) using synthetic data for ad hoc queries and simple updates. The Wisconsin benchmark is primarily used to measure performance in a single-user environment running mostly decision-support, read-only applications. It focuses on testing the query processing and optimization aspects of a relational database system. Performance is measured in terms of the response times for various queries and updates when executed in a stand-alone (single-user) environment.

For multiuser online applications, the relevant performance factors are quite different from those measured by the Wisconsin benchmark. The key issues are transaction throughput and response times measured for a large number of users who submit their requests against large databases. Throughput is the rate at which transactions are processed through the system and is usually stated in terms of transactions per second (TPS). In high-performance systems, throughput typically reaches a maximum when there are a certain number of concurrent users, and it remains stable as more concurrent users are added. In systems that are not well suited for online transaction processing applications, throughput reaches a peak, usually at a small number of users, and then drops off precipitously as the number of users increases. The TP1 benchmark focuses on measuring the transaction throughput power, including overhead for network and presentation services in some implementations, of a system designed to support large volumes of short update transactions[2] from multiple concurrent users. Unlike the Wisconsin benchmark, average response times for TP1 transactions are not explicitly quoted, except that throughput must be measured under the constraint that a certain percentage of all transactions must have

---

1 See DeWitt [1991] for a discussion on scaling the Wisconsin benchmark for different database sizes.

2 For example, the TP1 transaction involves updating three existing records and inserting one new record.

response times below a specified limit. In addition to transaction throughput, the TP1 benchmark also introduces the notion of using ownership cost as a normalization factor for comparing systems with different acquisition and maintenance costs. This cost is taken to be the five-year capital costs of owning and maintaining vendor-supplied hardware and software in the machine room; it excludes terminal costs, communications costs, application development costs, and operations costs. The TP1 benchmark is able to condense the performance rating of a system into two simple-to-interpret numbers: transactions per second and cost per transaction per second. This attribute significantly contributes to its simplicity, scalability, portability, and vendor neutrality—many of the desirable properties of benchmarks discussed earlier.

8.3 Wisconsin Benchmark

The Wisconsin benchmark is the most frequently used single-user benchmark for relational database systems. The development of the Wisconsin benchmark was one of the first experimental attempts at evaluating performance of relational database systems. Timeliness, simplicity, and portability have contributed to the wide usage of this benchmark in industry and research environments. (The original specifications did not address the issue of scalability.) As pointed out by DeWitt [1991], a prime reason for the popularity of the Wisconsin benchmark was the benchmarking wars it triggered. The initial report describing the Wisconsin benchmark actually provided performance results for a number of commercial database products. With each new release of these products, the vendor would obtain and release a new set of benchmark numbers to claim dramatic improvements over the previous version, as well as superiority over competitor products. Had the products not been identified by name in the initial Wisconsin benchmark study, the vendors would not have had any reason to react in this way.

8.3.1 Benchmark Structure

The test database for the Wisconsin benchmark consists of three synthetic tables with identical attributes but different cardinalities. Each table has 16 attributes, 13 integer attributes, and three string attributes. The integers are two bytes and the strings are 52 bytes. Assuming no storage overhead, this results in tuple widths of 182 bytes.[3] The three tables are OneK with 1,000 rows, and two copies of TenK (TenK1 and TenK2), each with 10,000 rows. The columns and their domains are presented in Table 8.1.

Column	Data Type	Range	Remarks
unique1	int not null	0 to no. of rows	candidate key
unique2	int not null	0 to no. of rows	primary key
two	int not null	0, 1	
four	int not null	0, 1, 2, 3	
ten	int not null	0, ..., 9	
hundred	int not null	0, ..., 99	
thousand	int not null	0, ..., 999	
twothous	int not null	0, ..., 1999	
fivethous	int not null	0, ..., 4999	
tenthous	int not null	0, ..., 9999	
odd100	int not null	1, 3, 5, ..., 99	
even100	int not null	2, 4, 6, ..., 100	
stringu1	char(52) not null		candidate key
stringu2	char(52) not null		candidate key
string4	char(52) not null		four distinct values

Table 8.1: *Table columns in the Wisconsin benchmark.*

3 The original benchmarks were conducted on 16-bit machines. Many vendors have since changed their test databases to use 32-bit integers. With this change, the tuple width grows to 208 bytes [DeWitt, 1991].

The smaller table OneK has the same structure as the larger tables TenK1 and TenK2, with identical ranges and cardinalities except where the number of rows in a table precludes a unique-numbered column from having all of the integer values within the specified range. For instance, in OneK, unique1 and unique2 contain values in the range of zero to 999, whereas in TenK1 and TenK2, unique1 and unique2 values range from zero to 9,999.

This uniform structure of the test tables facilitates the construction of queries with systematic control of selectivity and output size. There are a total of 32 test queries and updates in the Wisconsin benchmark. These include

- Selections involving different selectivities
- Two-way and three-way joins
- Projections with different percentages of duplicate column values
- Simple aggregates and aggregate functions (i.e., aggregates computed over groups of values)
- Simple database modifications, including insert, delete, and update

Selections

The selection queries in the Wisconsin benchmark are designed to evaluate storage organization of the tables and indexes, the impact of selectivity factors, and the relative efficiency of outputting queries in different modes.

To isolate the cost of formatting and displaying rows to a user's terminal, the selection queries with large outputs insert their result rows into a result table. Only those selection queries with small results send their outputs to the screen. The six selections into result tables are intended to isolate the effects of communication lines and the overhead of displaying rows to the screen. The selections to the screen select one and 100 rows. They model two levels of selectivity (1% and 10%) and three storage structures (no index, primary index, and secondary index) for the selected table.

Joins

Join queries are designed to evaluate two different areas in the implementation of the database system: (1) the basic join algorithms used by the query processor and (2) the optimization of complex joins. All three join queries are based on one-to-one relationships (i.e., the joins involve primary key columns). Each is preceded by zero, one, or two selections.

The *zero-selection join query* is of the form TenK1 join TenK2'. TenK2' is formed by restricting TenK2 with a 10% selectivity predicate.

The *one-selection join query* is of the form TenK1 join TenK2, with a 10% selectivity predicate on TenK2. The latter is specified after the join predicate to test if the optimizer has the rudimentary intelligence of first applying the selection to TenK2 before performing the join with TenK1. This query is also intended for comparing against the cost of first materializing TenK2' as in the zero-selection join query, and then joining that result with TenK1.

The *two-selection join query* is of the form OneK join TenK1 join TenK2, with 10% selectivity predicates attached to each of TenK1 and TenK2.

It should be noted than the join queries fail to adequately model important types of queries that a query optimizer often must deal with. These are outer joins, sparse joins in which certain special join techniques (like the use of Bloom filters) may be fruitfully exploited, and nested subqueries that can be flattened and processed as joins and semijoins.[4]

Projections

Projection queries are designed to evaluate the strategy used by the query optimizer to eliminate duplicate rows. The results are always inserted into freshly created temporary tables. (Because the queries were originally specified in QUEL, which is the data definition and manipulation language supported by INGRES, the elimination of duplicates is implied.)

Aggregates

Aggregate queries are designed to test the algorithms used for aggregation and to determine whether an available and applicable index is effectively used for aggregate processing.

Updates

Test queries for updates are designed to measure the cost of updating a table and its associated indexes. They are also used to evaluate the overhead of concurrency control and recovery management, but not necessarily in the presence of conflicting transactions.

---

4 A semijoin is like half of a join. It makes use of the join column values in one table to select a subset of the rows in the other table with matching join column values.

Test Queries

Except where explicitly stated, results for the following test queries are always redirected to newly created tables in the database.

Q1 (no index), Q2 (clustered index), Q5 (nonclustered index): Simple select on a 10,000-row table with a 1% selectivity BETWEEN predicate.[5]

Q2 (no index), Q4 (clustered index), Q6 (nonclustered index): Simple select on a 10,000-row table with a 10% selectivity BETWEEN predicate.

Q7 (clustered index): Simple select on a 10,000-row table with a unique key, output to screen.

Q8 (clustered index): Simple select on a 10,000-row table with a 1% selectivity BETWEEN predicate; output to screen.

Q9, (no index), Q12 (clustered index), Q15 (nonclustered index): 1-Selection Join—Join two 10,000-row tables, with a 10% selectivity BETWEEN predicate on one of them.

Q10 (no index), Q13 (clustered index), Q16 (nonclustered index): 0-Selection Join—Join a 10,000-row table with a 1,000-row table. The 1,000-row table is first obtained by applying a 10% selectivity BETWEEN predicate on a 10,000-row table.

Q11 (no index), Q14 (clustered index), Q17 (nonclustered index): 2-Selection Join—Join two 10,000-row tables with a 10% selectivity BETWEEN predicate on each of them, then join the result with a 1,000-row table.

Q18: Project on a 10,000-row table with duplicate elimination to yield 100 rows.

Q19: Project on a 10,000-row table with duplicate elimination to yield 10,000 rows (because the primary and candidate keys are included).

Q20 (no index), Q23 (with index): Apply a scalar aggregate involving the minimum function on a 10,000-row table.

Q21 (no index), Q24 (with index): Apply aggregates involving the minimum function over rows from a 10,000-row table grouped by a 1% selectivity attribute.

Q22 (no index), Q25 (with index): Apply aggregates involving

---

5 That is, the same query is run under the absence or presence of different kinds of indexes.

the minimum function over rows from a 10,000-row table grouped by a 1% selectivity attribute.

Q26 (no indexes), Q29 (with indexes): Insert one row into a 10,000-row table.

Q27 (no indexes), Q30 (with indexes): Delete one uniquely identified row from a 10,000-row table.

Q28 (no indexes), Q31 (with indexes): Update one uniquely identified row in a 10,000-row table using a primary key.

Q32 (with indexes): Update one uniquely identified row in a 10,000-row table using a candidate key.

Multiple instances of each of the above queries/updates are run, and the average response time for each is computed. Each test query is run in a stand-alone mode. Thus, even though locking overhead may be incurred, no resource contention arises.

8.3.2 Critique

Perhaps the most important impact of the Wisconsin benchmark was the benchmark war it ignited by including performance results for popular commercial database systems in its original published report [Bitton et al., 1983]. In the early days of benchmarking relational database systems, the popularity of the Wisconsin benchmark—with both vendors and customers—was primarily due to its ability to measure performance in a variety of commercial relational database systems. This information allowed for quick comparisons between systems. Nowadays, the benchmark is used more often by database software vendors as a tool for tuning performance and uncovering implementation flaws, from release to release of the same product. As pointed out by Bitton and Turbyfill [1988], the workload modeled by the Wisconsin benchmark is not representative of real-world application environments because parameters chosen for the database and test queries have been deliberately limited to focus on benchmarking technology. Furthermore, a number of undesirable variables that interfere with the analysis of test results have inadvertently been introduced into the test setup (e.g., always eliminating duplicates and redirecting query results to temporary tables).

The Wisconsin benchmark fails to adequately evaluate the ability of a database system to deal with a number of important problems:

Nonstandard query specifications: Wisconsin's original queries were stated in terms of QUEL rather than SQL. QUEL does not provide control over duplicate retention and elimination. As a result, the SQL equivalents of the queries always require an explicit duplicate elimination operation, which is atypical of SQL queries. The cost of the duplicate elimination operation can distort the cost measurements.

Output redirection: Most of the benchmark queries insert their output into a newly created table rather than displaying the output on the screen. These tables do not reside on a separate disk. As a result, sequential read optimization capabilities can be affected.

Column data types and value distributions: Only two-byte integers and fixed-length character strings, all uniformly distributed, are included in the database.

Table size and structure: The test database is only five megabytes and is not properly structured for scaling.

Overly simple query set: Important query types—in particular, many types of commonly used joins (i.e., one-to-many joins, many-to-many joins, and outer joins), nested queries, and set-at-a-time updates—are not included.

Incomplete modeling of a complex application environment: Updating of multiple indexes, in simple and bulk updates, is not modeled. Validity checking on insert and update operations is not modeled. Concurrency conflicts, recovery from transaction, system, and media failures, and, in general, multiuser operations are not modeled.

Lack of a simple performance metric: Performance of a system under test is not reduced to a single number, making it more difficult to directly compare two systems.

Above all, the most serious deficiency of the Wisconsin benchmark is that it is only a single-user benchmark. The stand-alone query elapse time is the only metric considered. Measurements obtained in single-user mode can provide useful information to the system designer when they isolate the performance of access methods, query processing algorithms, or special hardware and operating system features. However, they only provide a best-case estimate for query response time in an underutilized resource environment. As such, these measurements only constitute a baseline and cannot be considered realistic approximations of what query response time would be in a real environment. Historically, this deficiency of the Wisconsin benchmark prompted the joint industry and academia effort headed by Jim Gray at Tandem Computer and the development of the DebitCredit, or TP1 OLTP, benchmark described in Anon. et al. [1985].

Several of the original authors of the Wisconsin benchmark have concluded the following retrospective evaluation:

> *The Wisconsin benchmark should be viewed as an experiment in benchmarking technology. It has been useful as one point of reference for debugging and comparing database systems. However, it cannot be depended upon as a comprehensive tool for making fair and precise comparisons between systems.*
>
> *[Bitton and Turbyfill, 1988]*

8.4 AS^{3}AP Benchmark

AS^{3}AP stands for *An ANSI SQL Standard Scalable and Portable Benchmark for Relational Database Systems*. As the name suggests, the benchmark is targeted for relational databases of a wide spectrum of sizes. Both the test database schema and the query and update workloads are expressed using constructs defined in the proposed ANSI SQL2 standard.

The AS^{3}AP benchmark is designed to measure a database's overall performance across a wide range of operations, including decision support queries, online transaction processing, and utility operations such as database loading and restoration. It addresses most, if not all, of the criticisms raised against the Wisconsin benchmark.

8.4.1 Test Database Generation

The test database consists of four tables, each with 10 columns, ranging over data types supported in the draft international standard SQL2. These include new data types such as DOUBLE, DATETIME, and VARCHAR, which are not supported in the SQL89 standard. The VARCHAR column is specified to have a maximum size of 80 and an average size of 20. Systems that do not support VARCHAR are penalized by having to allocate a fixed size for storing the VARCHAR columns. Thus, the average size of a row in the test database, when stored in a system that supports varying length character data, is 100 bytes. With fixed-length storage allocation for the VARCHAR column, this size grows to 160 bytes.

The four tables that make up the test database are

uniques: All columns in this table are unique.

hundreds: Most columns in this table have exactly 100 distinct values, and the column values are correlated. This table is intended to provide selection and projection results with exactly 100 rows.

tenpct: Most columns in this table have 10% selectivity. That is, the number of distinct values for most columns in this table is 10.

updates: This table is designed for update operations. Different distributions (e.g., uniform, normal, exponential, and zipfian) are used for different columns. Clustered, nonclustered, and hashed indexes are built on this table.

To model the maintenance of integrity constraints within the test database, the table definitions also include referential integrity specifications.

Like other scalable benchmarks, the AS^{3}AP specifications include a parameterized test database generator program that can generate tables ranging in cardinality from 10,000 rows to one billion rows (with a corresponding database size of four megabytes to 400 gigabytes).

The AS^{3}AP tests are divided into two modules: the single-user test module and the multiuser test module. The single-user test module includes utilities for loading and structuring the database, as well as queries designed to test the efficiency of access methods and the effectiveness for query optimization. The multiuser test module models different mixes of database workloads, including OLTP workloads, information retrieval workloads, and mixed workloads with a balance of short transactions, report queries, relation scans, and long transactions.

8.4.2 Scaling

As the acronym AS^{3}AP suggests, the test database is scalable to different sizes from 10^5 to 10^9 rows in each of the four tables. The logical size of the test database (i.e., the total number of bytes needed to represent the logical contents of the database, not including indexes) is defined as

(# of tuples per table) x (100 bytes per row) x 4 tables

Thus, for systems that support fixed-length records, the physical database size would be larger than the logical database size. Conversely, for systems that employ compression, the physical database size would be smaller than the logical database size.

The specifications for scaling in the AS^{3}AP benchmark also stipulate that the system under test be configured with a main memory size that is equal to or smaller than the logical database size. As in the TP1 and TPC benchmarks, the number of users to simulate in a multiuser environment also scales up with the increase in database size and is determined by the following formula:

number of users = logical database size in megabytes / 4

8.4.3 Operational Issues

The AS^{3}AP benchmark addresses operational performance issues by including measurements for initial loading of the synthesized data into the test database. The test data generator generates the test data for the four tables in ASCII format. These ASCII files must be loaded into the AS^{3}AP database, using bulk loading capabilities supported by the system under test. Since indexes are maintained on the test database, and referential integrity constraints are defined among tables, the loading times also include time for creating the specified indexes and for verifying that the defined referential integrity constraints are not violated.

To test for efficiency in sequential scanning, the integer-typed candidate key columns for the generated test tables always range between zero and the maximum number of rows, with the value '1' missing. The test queries include an unsuccessful selection involving this missing key that forces the query processor to sequentially search through the entire table. This query is aimed at testing the SUT's ability to optimize processing of queries that require sequentially scanning an entire table.

8.4.4 Single-user Tests

Single-user tests are designed to cover the following facets of database processing:

- Operational issues like bulk loading, index creation, backup, and restore
- Selections, projections, joins, and aggregates queries that process large amounts of data, including those that can take advantage of intraquery parallelism (when run on multiprocessor database machines)
- Updates that require verification of referential integrity and key uniqueness

- Parametric queries (queries that make use of host variables) that require dynamic selection of access paths at runtime

Three separate queries are used to test for the overheads associated with different output modes: the display of result rows on screen, the redirection of result rows to an ASCII file, and the insertion of the result rows into a newly created table. All other queries redirect output to a null device to eliminate the impact of output modes on the overall query processing performance.

In general, queries are arranged in an order that precludes data needed for one query from becoming memory resident as a result of the processing of a previous query.[6] On the other hand, consecutive queries that can take advantage of the same set of indexes are included to test for a system's ability to cache index pages differently from other database pages.

Update queries are designed so the database is not modified by the test suite as long as the complete suite is run in the specified order. This is achieved by interleaving special queries that save deleted rows, reinsert the deleted rows, and restore the updated rows to their original values.

8.4.5 Multiuser Tests

In the AS^{3}AP benchmark, four multiuser tests model different workload profiles:

(1) An online transaction processing workload, where each user repeatedly executes a (randomly selected) single row update against the same table. These transactions require level 3 isolation, serializability. (See Section 5.1.4 for discussion on isolation levels.)

(2) An information retrieval workload, where each user repeatedly executes a (randomly selected) single row selection against the same table. These transactions require only level 0 isolation, and dirty reads can be tolerated. (See Section 5.1.4 for discussion of isolation levels and dirty reads.)

(3) A mixed, but primarily information retrieval workload, where one user executes a cross section of 10 retrieval and update queries, and all the other users execute the same information retrieval query as in workload #2 above.

---

6 That is, consecutive queries are designed to access different portions of the test database.

(4) A mixed, but primary online transaction processing workload, where one user executes a cross section of 10 retrieval and update queries, and all the other users execute the same OLTP transaction as in workload #1 above.

As we discussed earlier, the number of concurrent users is scaled according to the logical database size. Workloads #1 and #2 are each run for a fixed period of 15 minutes. Workloads #3 and #4 are both of varying length; that is, they are run for as long as it takes to go through each of the 10 retrieval and update queries. The multiuser tests are run for throughput measurements as well as for contribution to the global performance metric (i.e., the equivalent database size metric described in the next section).[7] However, there is no provision to ensure that the system under test has reached steady state[8] before the measurements are taken. Instead, the tests are intermingled with database backup, restore, and consistency checking operations that are carefully ordered to permit the system under test to "warm up" before throughput is measured. Furthermore, the multiuser tests do not model an OLTP environment in detail; that is, terminal emulator, interjob arrival, think time, and no presentation services are not modeled at all. Instead, a number of processes are forked, each running a simple script.

8.4.6 Performance Metrics

For a particular database management system, the AS^{3}AP benchmark determines an equivalent database size. This is the maximum size of the AS^{3}AP database for which the system is able to perform the designated AS^{3}AP set of single-user and multiuser tests in under 12 hours. The equivalent database size is an absolute performance metric. It also provides a basis for comparing cost and performance of systems. The cost per megabyte of a DBMS is the total cost of the DBMS divided by the equivalent database size. The equivalent database ratio for two systems is the ratio of their equivalent database sizes. Both the cost per megabyte and the equivalent database size ratio provide global comparison metrics.

---

7 It should be noted that the throughput measurements are not directly incorporated into the global performance metric.

8 That is, when the number of transactions processed per second becomes steady.

8.5 TP1/DebitCredit Benchmark

Vendors of transaction processing systems quote transactions per second (TPS) rates for their systems. However, without a standard transaction and a standardized way to price a system supporting a desired TPS rate, it is impossible to compare the price/performance of different systems. The TP1 benchmark was originally designed to meet this requirement. It has been widely used for comparing throughput TPS and cost per TPS among transaction processing systems.

The original TP1/DebitCredit benchmark is described in a Tandem technical report (No. 85.2) and a *Datamation* article, both titled "A Measure of Transaction Processing Power" [Anon. et al. 1985].[9] TP1 models a hypothetical banking environment and defines a classic transaction processing application. The bank has one or more branches, and each branch has a number of tellers. The bank also has a number of client accounts. The test database models the cash positions of the branches, tellers, and accounts in this application environment. Each transaction is carried out by a teller at some branch, on an account that has been opened either at that branch or at some other branch. The transaction represents the work performed when a customer submits a deposit or withdrawal request on an account to a teller at some branch of the bank. It involves debiting a bank account, debiting the cash positions associated with the teller and the branch handling the transaction, inserting a history record describing the transaction, and then returning a reply to the teller's terminal.

Even though the names DebitCredit and TP1 were used interchangeably in the original Tandem report, the TP1 benchmarks implemented by various vendors depart significantly from the original DebitCredit specifications. Therefore, we will refer to the specifications in Anon. et al. [1985] as DebitCredit, and we will use the name TP1 for implementations by vendors that typically depart from the DebitCredit specifications in one way or another.

The DebitCredit benchmark database contains the following tables:

accounts: This table contains at least 100,000 accounts for every transaction per second that is achievable by the system under test (SUT). In other words, if a vendor claims 10 transactions per

---

9 The early version of this paper was distributed by Jim Gray to a number of his colleagues at Tandem and 19 other researchers and practitioners in the database world for comments and suggestions. "Anon. et al." was graciously used by Jim Gray when the paper was published to suggest that the paper was authored by the entire group [Serlin, 1991].

second, the accounts table must have at least one million records. Each account record is 100 bytes long and contains the account number, account name, branch number, and account balance. There is a unique index on account number.

branches: This table contains 10 branches for each transaction per second that is achievable by the SUT. Each branch record, representing a branch office of the bank, is 100 bytes long. It contains the branch number, branch name, and branch balance. There is a unique index on branch number.

tellers: This table contains 100 tellers for each transaction per second that is achievable by the SUT. Each teller record, representing a bank teller in a branch office, is 100 bytes long. It contains the teller number, teller name, branch number, and teller balance. There is a unique index on teller number.

history: This table contains one record for each transaction executed against the database for up to 90 days. Each history record is 50 bytes long and contains a summary of each successful transaction, including account number, branch number, teller number, the amount of deposit or withdrawal, and the time of the transaction. There is no index on this table.

Each DebitCredit transaction, as originally defined, consists of the following sequence of operations:

(1) A 100-character 3270 screen message containing a teller-generated deposit or withdrawal transaction is received from a branch via an X.25 communications line.
(2) An account record is updated to reflect the deposit or withdrawal.
(3) A branch total record is updated to reflect the deposit or withdrawal.
(4) A teller record is updated to reflect the deposit or withdrawal.
(5) A history record describing the transaction is written.
(6) A 200-byte 3270 screen message is formatted and sent to the teller terminal via an X.25 communications line.

In addition, the original DebitCredit specifications include the following finer points:

- Account keys are 10 bytes long.
- All data files must be protected by fine-granularity locking and logging (to ensure transaction serializability a decent level of concurrency).

- The log file for transaction recovery must be duplexed to tolerate single failures; data files need not be duplexed.
- Ninety-five percent of the transactions must give subsecond response times.
- Fifteen percent of the transactions are supposed to be made at branches not normally associated with the account.
- Message handling should deal with a block-mode terminal (e.g., IBM 3270) with a base screen of 20 fields. Ten of those fields are read, mapped by presentation services and then remapped and written as part of the reply. The line protocol is X.25.
- The benchmark is intended to emulate teller think-time (i.e., time for interaction between a teller and a client before a TP1 transaction can be submitted) and transaction generation distribution. Each teller submits the standard transaction every 100 seconds; it is generated as follows: (1) a branch office is selected at random; (2) a teller within the branch is selected at random; and (3) a random account is selected with an 85% probability of being from the selected branch and a 15% probability of being from another branch.

For the purpose of computing price/performance for a given system, the cost of ownership calculations include the initial purchase of all software and hardware, five years of maintenance for software and hardware, and 10 gigabytes of disk storage for 90 days of the history table.

Once the TPS and cost of ownership numbers have been identified, it is important to look at the price/performance of the solution. The TPS cost is derived by dividing the cost of ownership by the maximum sustainable TPS rated throughput. However, this measurement can be easily skewed by not following the original DebitCredit specifications faithfully and by taking advantage of loopholes not anticipated in the original specifications.

8.5.1 Common Departures in TP1 Implementations

The benchmark used by DebitCredit and described by Anon. et al. [1985] is an updated and simplified form of the Bank of America benchmark used in 1972 and 1973 to select a vendor for their online teller support system. The key environment parameters (10 million customer accounts, 10,000 tellers, 1,000 branches) were representative of the bank's requirements. In addition, with 10,000 tellers, the DBMS is faced with a load of 100 TPS.

The TP1 benchmark implemented by various hardware and software vendors is a much less vigorous and more simplified version of DebitCredit. With TP1, DBMS vendors often adjust system parameters to inflate TPS claims, using the following shortcuts:

Omission of error checks: Often, the database system does not check to make sure that the account is not overdrawn. In some implementations, the resulting balance may not even be returned to the application to permit such error checking.

Incorrect measurement of transaction response time: It is not uncommon to measure the transaction response time without including the network communications overhead. Even when such overhead is included, the use of incomparable networking environments in different implementations renders direct comparisons difficult.

Unfaithful implementation of the history table: Many vendors partition the history table into multiple tables. They then modify the transaction definition so as to cause the history records to be uniformly distributed over the multiple history tables, thereby eliminating a hot spot in the system.

Inappropriate scaling: The table sizes may not always be appropriately scaled to reflect the TPS rating of the system. Also, the number of users in the system may not reflect the transaction think-time specification that each teller submits a transaction every 100 seconds.

Nonrandom account numbers: Random number generators that come with standard language compilers are often not capable of generating random account numbers for very large tables.[10] Consequently, the account numbers generated may not be uniformly distributed over the entire database. (In fact, certain account numbers may never be referenced by the transaction generator.)

Inaccurate cost computation: Full disclosure on the computation of cost of ownership may not always be provided. The 10-gigabyte history table in the cost of ownership is sometimes omitted.

Incomplete disclosure of information: Certain key details, such as whether the log is duplexed, may not be disclosed. Sometimes,

---

[10] For example, the range may be limited to be between zero and 32,767.

the log may even be allocated in RAM disk, compromising transaction durability. Moreover, the versions of software being tested often are not fully disclosed, and the claimed TPS rating may even be based on unreleased software. In general, the benchmark code may not be provided, making independent verification of the TPS claim impossible.

Failure to reach steady state: Many database systems require periodic checkpointing to force write modified buffer pages back to the database. The TP1 benchmark may be run for such a short time that no checkpointing cost is incurred. Alternatively, the checkpointing parameters may be set artificially high to prevent checkpointing from occurring during the measurement period. In either case, the result is an inflated TPS claim.

8.5.2 Critique

In spite of its popularity, the TPI/DebitCredit benchmark has many shortcomings, as we outline here:

Not a function benchmark: The workload covers only a single type of transaction. These transactions do not fully exercise the different capabilities of an advanced database system. For example, this benchmark does not even test whether the SUT incorporates a query optimizer.

No error checking: The transaction specification does not include checking for invalid account numbers or overdrawn situations.

No insertion or deletion on the accounts, branches, and tellers tables: There is no stress testing of concurrent index manipulation operations. All index accesses are read only!

No read-only transactions: Reporting functions are assumed to be done offline. The concurrency control delays inflicted by long-running queries on the bread-and-butter short update transactions are not modeled.

Simplistic model of transaction locality: Eighty-five percent of the transactions are submitted at the home branches of the accounts.

Not originally designed to deal with client-server architecture: Message handling models dumb terminal operations and is often omitted by vendors.

The authors of the original *Datamation* article are quite aware of the limitations of the TP1 Benchmark, as shown in the conclusion of their report:

> *In closing we restate our cavalier attitude about all this: Actual performance may vary depending on driving habits, road conditions and queue lengths—use these numbers for comparison purposes only. Put more bluntly, there are lies, damn lies, and then there are performance measures.*
>
> *[Anon. et al., 1985]*

Thus, while useful as a vehicle for highlighting the strengths and weaknesses of database systems, TP1 benchmarks should not be taken as absolute measurements of database system performance.

8.6 TPC Benchmarks

The lack of precise definitions in TP1 benchmarks leaves interpretation to each vendor and increases the state of confusion among customers. More important, it has allowed vendors to make impressive, but dubious, TPS rating claims.

An industry-wide attempt to lend credibility to and to maintain a set of benchmarking standards has led to the formation of the Transaction Processing Council (TPC).[11] The prime objective of this vendor consortium is to establish OLTP-oriented benchmarks and to enable vendors to provide more accurate and reliable information on the performance of a chosen relational DBMS.

TP1 implementations generally fall into two categories, Class I and Class II, which Omri Serlin defined in the March 21, 1988 issue of the *FT SYSTEMS Newsletter*. Class I implementations are applicable to hardware vendors; they include the performance cost of terminal emulation, presentation services, and scheduling of front-end applications. Class II implementations are generally used by relational database system vendors; they do not include front-end overhead.

TPC Benchmark A is a formalized version of TP1 for Class I implementations, whereas TPC Benchmark B is the counterpart for Class II implementations. TPC Benchmark B is intended to reflect the database aspects of an OLTP environment. However, it does not

---

[11] The Transaction Processing Council was first formed in August 1988. The original members include Control Data, DEC, ICL, Pyramid, Stratus, Sybase, Tandem, and Wang. Since then, membership has grown to include over 30 transaction processing hardware and software vendors.

reflect the entire range of OLTP requirements typically characterized by terminal and network I/O. As in TP1, both TPC-A and TPC-B use a single transaction type based on the DebitCredit transaction first described by Anon. et al. [1985]. TPC Benchmark A is intended for OLTP environments. TPC Benchmark B is intended for measuring the performance of the database component in a transaction processing environment. It does not require the modeling of terminals, networking, or think time.

The metrics used for measuring performance are transactions per seconds (TPS), subject to a response time constraint, and the associated price per TPS.

Both TPC Benchmark A and TPC Benchmark B use a single, simple, update-intensive transaction to load the system being tested. This workload reflects that of an OLTP environment but does not model more complex environments where multiple types of transactions of varying complexity are run.

As in the original TP1 definition, the database contains four types of entities (tables) structured as follows:

- Rows in the accounts table are at least 100 bytes long. They include information on account_id, branch_id, and account balance.
- Rows in the branches table are at least 100 bytes long. They include information on branch_id, and branch_balance.
- Rows in the tellers table are at least 100 bytes long. They include information on teller_id, branch_id, and teller_balance.
- Rows in the history table are at least 50 bytes long. They include information on account_id, teller_id, branch_id, amount of deposit or withdrawal, and date and time of transaction.

With TPC Benchmark A, the transaction begins by reading 100 bytes from a terminal. This includes information on account_id, teller_id, branch_id, and the amount that is being deposited or withdrawn. (The branch_id refers to the branch where the teller is located.) The transaction reads the balance for the specified account, and then adjusts the balance according to the amount of deposit or withdrawal. Next, the teller balance and the branch balance are adjusted accordingly. Finally, a history record is inserted to identify the account, teller, branch, and amount involved in the transaction.

For each transaction, the teller terminal sends at least 100 user-level alphanumeric bytes, organized as at least four distinct fields that include account_id, teller_id, branch_id, and delta. As output for the transaction, the teller terminal receives at least 200 user-level alphanumeric bytes, organized as at least five distinct fields that include account_id, teller_id, branch_id, delta, and account_balance (if the transaction commits successfully).

For TPC Benchmark B, the terminal I/O and network traffic are not modeled. For each transaction, the driver presents at least four distinct fields; these are account_id, teller_id, branch_id, and amount. Each successful transaction returns to the driver the balance of the account acted upon by the transaction.

8.6.1 Clarifications from TP1/DebitCredit

The TPC specifications are intended to close many of the loopholes exploited by transaction processing hardware and software vendors for boosting their TPS claims. Unless otherwise stated, the following clarifications apply both for TPC-A and TPC-B:

Input and output parameters: The account balance must be returned at the end of the transaction. As a result, implementations that make use of the chaining or batching of SQL statements (in lieu of stored procedures), such as the OTEX mechanism in the ORACLE Server, may have to execute a separate SQL SELECT statement in order to obtain the resulting account balance.

Network environment: Whereas the DebitCredit specifications assume all terminals are connected to the system under test over a wide-area X.25 communications network, TPC-A allows the use of wide-area and local-area networks with any standard protocol. However, the TPS rating for a system under test must be qualified as tpsA-wide (for wide-area network) versus tpsA-local (for local-area network). It must be emphasized that tpsA-wide and tpsA-local ratings are not comparable.[12]

Message compression: The compression of incoming and outgoing messages in TPC-A is specifically disallowed.

ACID properties: The atomicity, consistency, isolation, and durability properties must be guaranteed for each transaction.

Scaling rules: For each nominal TPS configured, the test must use a minimum of 100,000 account records, 10 teller records, one branch record, 90*8*60*60 (=2,592,000) history records, and in

---

[12] For that matter, tpsA-local and tpsA-wide are also not comparable with tpsB ratings.

the case of TPC-A, 10 teller terminals. This compares with 100,000 account records, 100 teller records, 10 branch records, and 100 teller terminals in the original DebitCredit specifications. Because a smaller number of terminals per TPS are used in TPC-A, a somewhat higher TPS rating results.

Response time constraint: Ninety percent of all transactions started and completed during the measurement interval must have a response time of less than two seconds. This compares with 95% under one second in the DebitCredit specifications.

Physical database design rules: Horizontal partitioning of tables is allowed; however, vertical partitioning of tables is not. In other words, it is permissible to divide the history table into a number of horizontally partitioned subtables and to allow different transaction generators to use different history tables in order to minimize hot spots[13] in the database. Again, this results in a higher TPS rating.

Teller_id distribution: The transaction generation procedure must distribute transactions uniformly over all tellers.

Branch_id distribution: Since each teller is assigned to a single branch and each branch has the same number of tellers, the stipulation that transactions are uniformly distributed across tellers implies that transactions are also uniformly distributed across branches.

Home versus remote transactions distribution: The account referenced in each transaction is obtained by generating a random number x in the interval [0, 1]. If x < 0.85 or if the total number of branches is 1, a random account_id is selected over all accounts opened at the chosen branch. If x >= 0.85 and the total number of branches is greater than 1, a random account_id is selected over all accounts not opened at the chosen branch.

Delta distribution: The amount of deposit/withdrawal must be distributed uniformly between +/- 999,999.

Duration of test: Throughput measurement must begin after the system has reached "steady state" when the transaction throughput rate has stabilized. The test must run uninterrupted for at least 15 minutes but no longer than one hour.

---

[13] Hot spots are parts of the database that get frequently updated by concurrent transactions and result in concurrency conflicts. In the TPC database, the end of the history table (which is likely to be organized as a sequential file) is a hot spot because concurrent transactions will all attempt to append to it at the same time.

Checkpoint intervals: Checkpoints must be taken (at least once) during the measurement interval. This eliminates the loophole of boosting transaction throughput at the expense of lengthening the time needed to recover from system failure.

Information disclosure: A full disclosure report is required in order for results to be compliant with the TPC benchmarks. The report includes a program listing of application code and DDL statements used to define the database as well as settings for all customer-tunable parameters and options that deviate from the default setting.

Audit: An independent audit of the benchmark results is highly recommended, and the report should be made available to the public for a reasonable handling charge.

8.6.2 Differences Between TPC-A and TPC-B

Whereas TPC-A is intended to model online transaction processing environments, TPC -B focuses on measuring the performance of the database component in a transaction processing environment. TPC-B does not explicitly model the use of multiple online terminal sessions, networking, or think-time in between the submission of transactions from the same terminal. The salient differences between the two benchmarks follow:

Transaction inputs and outputs: The input for a TPC-A transaction consists of reading 100 bytes from a terminal. This input message includes the account id, branch id, teller id, and the amount of deposit or withdrawal. The output for a TPC-A transaction consists of writing 200 bytes to the terminal. This output message includes the account_id, branch_id, teller_id, and the resulting account_balance. For TPC-B, the same set of four input parameters are presented from the driver program to the system under test without being embedded in a 100-byte message. The output consists of a single account balance.

Response time definition: With TPC-A, response time is measured as the difference between the time the last byte of the output message is received at the driver (remote terminal emulator) and the time the first byte of the input message is sent from the driver. Because of the batch-oriented generation of transactions in TPC-B (no modeling of think-time), an alternate concept of residence time is defined. This time is computed as the difference between two quantities: the time just before the driver supplies the input parameters to the system under test, and the time just after the driver receives the output parameter from the system under test.

Response time reporting requirements: TPC-A requires a curve of the 90th percentile response times versus TPS be plotted at the 50%, 80%, and 100% levels of the reported TPS by varying the think-time. TPC-B defines the notion of average number of concurrently active transactions, C_R, where

$C_R = T_R * R_R$,

T_R = reported tps rate, and

R_R = average residency time for the measured transactions.

The TPS rate at two additional levels of concurrency, C_L and C_H, must also be reported graphically and must satisfy the following constraints:

$.7\ C_R <= C_L <= .8\ C_R$

$C_H >= 1.2\ C_R$

These two average concurrency levels are obtained by varying the number of transaction generators and/or the number of configured threads in a TP monitor.

8.7 Published Benchmark Results

TP1 Benchmarks have been published for both ORACLE and the SQL Server by their corresponding vendors under the OS/2 platform. In this section, we highlight the important features of the two implementations.

8.7.1 ORACLE Server

An audit of the TP1 benchmark results on the ORACLE Server was first reported by Sawyer [1989]. The implementation observed the following aspects of the original DebitCredit specifications:

- The atomicity, consistency, isolation, and durability properties of transactions were correctly implemented.
- The database records were appropriately sized.
- The number of records in the database were appropriately scaled to reflect the reported TPS rating.
- The transactions were randomly distributed over the database.

- The specified ratio of "remote" transactions to "home" transactions was accounted for in the transaction generation algorithm.
- The response time constraints on transactions were satisfied.
- The throughput measurements were taken when the system reached steady state.
- The cost for storing 90 days of history was included in the $/tps calculation.

Also noteworthy, were the following features of the implementation:

- The database was dispersed over three different disk drives to take advantage of ORACLE's flexibility for controlling the physical placement of tablespaces. (See Section 7.7.2 for a discussion of the tablespace notion in ORACLE.)
- The simulation of terminal users and think-times was not provided for. The test implementation made use of a server PC and a single client PC. The latter contained one controlling process that spawned multiple child processes. Each child process repeatedly submitted instances of the TP1 transaction without modeling think-times in between transactions. The actual number of child processes used was not reported. In fact, the actual benchmarking program was also not included in the auditor's report.
- The implementation exploited ORACLE's Transaction Execute interface, which allows for the batched execution of multiple, previously compiled SQL statements. The server executes each statement in sequence unless a SQL error is detected, in which case it stops processing statements and returns an error code to the client. Failure to update (or insert) at least one row in an update (or insert) statement is considered an error. Thus, an attempt to act on an invalid account caused the batched execution to fail.
- The ending balance of the affected account was not returned at the end of each transaction.
- The checkpointing interval was set so that no checkpoint actually took place during the period used for measuring transaction throughput.

8.7.2 Microsoft SQL Server

The published TP1 benchmark for the SQL Server used two servers, a *benchmark* server for storing the TP1 database and a *tracking* server for storing the benchmark statistics [Microsoft, 1989a, 1989b]. A special control program called *sqlqueen* coordinated the activities of multiple clients, each running the driver program called *benchw*. The latter was designed to run on both DOS and OS/2 client machines. Only a single instance of the benchw program ran on each DOS client machine because of the single tasking nature of the operating system. Using the multitasking capabilities of OS/2, up to 10 instances of benchw ran on the same OS/2 client machine to simulate multiple users of the transaction processing system.

Each instance of the benchw program started and stopped repetitive invocations of the TP1 stored procedure at the benchmark server under the direction of the sqlqueen program. At the end of the run, the benchw program sent statistics collected for the run to the tracking server. The sqlqueen program accepted controlling parameters for the benchmark, such as number of accounts, number of branches, and number of tellers in the database, identities of the benchmark and tracking servers, and duration of the run (in seconds). After the benchw clients finished running, the sqlqueen program analyzed statistics collected in the benchmark statistics database. The transaction flow logic is illustrated in Figure 8.1.

The following aspects of the implementation were also noteworthy:

- The transmission of a 100-byte input message and that of a 200-byte output message were modeled. However, no think-time in between transactions was modeled.
- A customized random number generator ensured that account numbers used in transactions were truly randomized with the total space of possible account numbers.[14]
- Both transaction logging and checkpointing were enabled. The checkpointing interval was left at the default value, which provided for full system failure recovery in five minutes.[15]
- A stored procedure was invoked to execute the transaction. The ability to include control structures in the stored procedure made it possible to check the validity of account numbers and to identify overdrawn accounts.
- Microsoft and the auditors determined that the steady state for the SQL Server TP1 benchmarks occurred approximately five

---

[14] It should be noted that random number generators found in most C language runtime libraries only generate 32,767 distinct values!

[15] The SQL Server automatically computes the appropriate checkpoint interval to ensure that recovery from system failure can be completed within five minutes.

minutes after the start of a benchmark run. Thus, the benchmarks were run for 20 minutes, and only the steady-state 15-minute readings were included in the report.

- The concurrency level used in the attained TPS rating is reported. In fact, the benchmark kit available from Microsoft[16] includes actual source programs and configuration parameters used to produce the reported numbers.

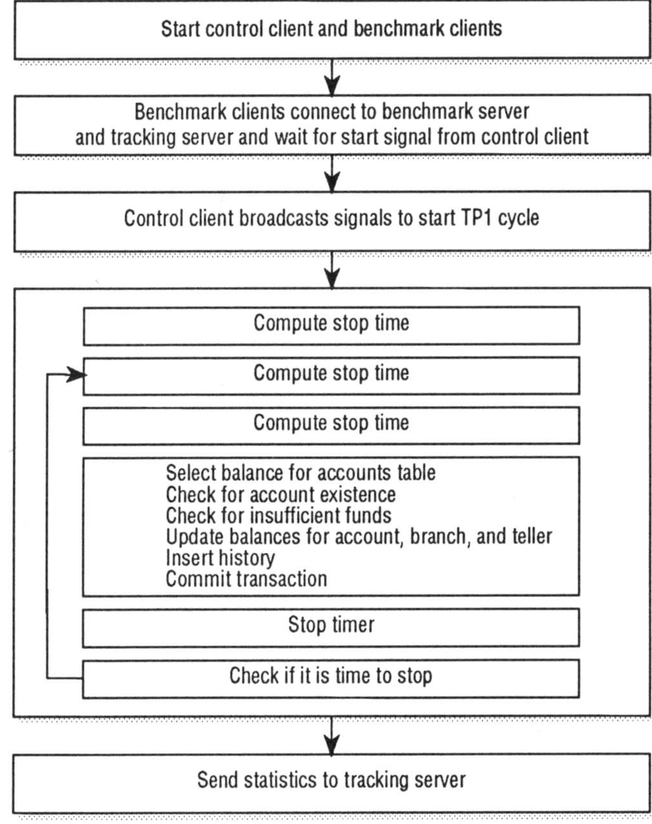

Figure 8.1: SQL Server TP1 benchmark logic.

16 The SQL Server Benchmarking kit (Microsoft part no. 098-11955) provides technical details of the benchmark configuration, benchmark results, and source and executable code for the benchmark on diskette. It can be obtained from Microsoft by calling (800) 426-9600 or by writing to Microsoft Corporation, 16011 NE 36th Way, Box 97017, Redmond, WA 98073-9717.

8.8 Sample TP1 Implementations

In this section, we provide sample programs for implementing TP1/TPC transactions on each of the servers discussed in this book. You should also refer to Chapter 9 for further discussions on application programming interfaces available to the different servers. Our emphasis is on the DML portion of the programs. As pointed out in the Microsoft SQL Server benchmark kit, most random number generators supplied with C runtime libraries are inadequate for generating random account numbers because they generate only up to 32,767 distinct numbers. See Microsoft [1989b] for a random number generator that suitably disperses transactions across the large number of accounts in the TP1/TPC environment.

In the programs, we make use of an external function get_random ( ) which, given an integral upper bound x, returns a random number that falls between 1 and x. We also make use of another external function get_delta ( ) which, given an integral upper bound y, returns a random number between -y and +y. We assume the benchmark is run for a period of time that includes a ramp-up period, a measurement period, and a ramp-down period. The external function compute_stop_time ( ) determines the time when the test should be completed. The external function not_yet_stop_time is called repeatedly to determine if the testing period has come to an end. The throughput is analyzed using a subset of the entries in the history table that correspond to transactions completed during the measurement period.

8.8.1 A TP1 Implementation on the IBM Extended Edition Database Manager

We use a static SQL implementation (SQL embedded in C) for the IBM Extended Edition Database Manager in order to take advantage of its compiled time optimization capabilities. As we shall see, this implementation is also much more compact than the ones for ORACLE, Rdb, and the SQL Server, where callable APIs (from C) are used for the client-server interface. Because IBM Extended Edition requires that all databases be cataloged at the client workstation before they can be accessed, the sqlestrd ( ) call on line 30 simply starts the desired database without explicitly connecting to the particular database server.

```
/*
** Filename: ETP1.C (TP1 using static SQL)
** Server: IBM OS/2 EE Database Manager
*/
#include <stdio.h>
#include <stdlib.h>
#include <malloc.h>
#include <sql.h>
#include <sqlda.h>
#include <sqlca.h>
#include <sqlenv.h>
extern long get_random ( );
extern long get_delta ( );
extern compute_stop_time ( );
extern not_yet_stop_time ( );
static short ERRCHK( );
EXEC SQL INCLUDE SQLCA;
EXEC SQL BEGIN DECLARE SECTION;
long  account, teller, branch, balance, delta;
char      stmt1[120], stmt2[120], stmt3[120], stmt4[120], stmt5[120],
          stmt6[120];
EXEC SQL END DECLARE SECTION;
main ( )
{
long  a = 100000;          /* number of accounts */
long  b = 1;               /* number of branches */
long  t = 10;              /* number of tellers */
long  d = 9999999;         /* maximum delta */
char  string[20];
sqlestrd ("TP1", 'S', &sqlca);
EXEC SQL DECLARE C1 CURSOR FOR
     SELECT BALANCE FROM ACCOUNT WHERE
     ACCOUNT_NUMBER = :account
```

```
        FOR UPDATE OF BALANCE;
if (ERRCHK(sqlca) < 0) return sqlca.sqlcode;
compute_stop_time ( );
for (; not_yet_stop_time ( );)
        {
        account = get_random (a);
        teller = get_random (t);
        branch = teller % b;
        delta = get_delta (d);
        EXEC SQL OPEN C1 USING :account;
        if (ERRCHK(sqlca) < 0) return sqlca.sqlcode;
        EXEC SQL FETCH C1 INTO :balance;
        if (ERRCHK(sqlca) < 0) return sqlca.sqlcode;
            balance = balance + delta;
        EXEC SQL UPDATE ACCOUNT SET BALANCE = :balance
            WHERE CURRENT OF C1;
        if (ERRCHK(sqlca) < 0) return sqlca.sqlcode;
        EXEC SQL CLOSE C1;
        if (ERRCHK(sqlca) < 0) return sqlca.sqlcode;
        EXEC SQL UPDATE TELLER SET BALANCE = BALANCE :delta
            WHERE TELLER_NUMBER = :teller;
        if (ERRCHK(sqlca) < 0) return sqlca.sqlcode;
        EXEC SQL UPDATE BRANCH SET BALANCE = BALANCE + :delta
            WHERE BRANCH_NUMBER = :branch;
        if (ERRCHK(sqlca) < 0) return sqlca.sqlcode;
        EXEC SQL INSERT INTO HISTORY
            (BRANCH, TELLER, ACCOUNT, DELTA, TIMESTAMP) VALUES
            (:branch, :teller, :account, :delta, CURRENT TIMESTAMP);
        if (ERRCHK(sqlca) < 0) return sqlca.sqlcode;
```

```
    EXEC SQL COMMIT WORK;
    if (ERRCHK(sqlca) < 0) return sqlca.sqlcode;
    }
}
short ERRCHK (struct sqlca sqlca)
{
if (sqlca.sqlcode < 0)
    {
    errrpt( );
    EXEC SQL WHENEVER SQLERROR CONTINUE;
    EXEC SQL ROLLBACK WORK;
    }
return sqlca.sqlcode;
}
errrpt( )
{
printf("%.70s (%d)\n", sqlca.sqlerrmc, -sqlca.sqlcode);
return(0);
}
```

8.8.2 A TP1 Implementation on the ORACLE Server

The following implementation makes use of the Transaction Execute mechanism in ORACLE in order to batch the SQL statements to be executed as part of the same TP1 transaction, and to minimize the communication between the front end and the database server. Because ORACLE does not support compile-time optimization, each front end must submit the same set of SQL statements that make up the TP1 transaction for compilation, before these statements can be referenced in the Transaction Execute call. While this batching mechanism in ORACLE achieves the same communication overhead optimization as the stored procedure mechanism in the SQL Server, it is much less flexible in terms of error handling. Also, the implementation here does not return the account balance that results from the execution of the transaction.

```
/*
** Filename: OTP1.C (TP1 using OTEX mechanism)
** Server: Oracle Server
*/
#include <stdio.h>
#include <stdlib.h>
extern long get_random ( );
extern long get_delta ( );
extern compute_stop_time ( );
extern not_yet_stop_time ( );
#define DEFUID "arvola/arvola@p:oracle"
#define EBL 90
/* cursor data area /*
struct csrdef
{
        char dum[64];
};
typedef struct csrdef csrdef;
/* lda is the same as a csr */
typedef struct csrdef ldadef;
main ( )
{
long        a = 100000; /* number of accounts */
long        b = 1;      /* number of branches */
long        t = 10;     /* number of tellers */
long        d = 999999; /* max delta */
long        account, branch, teller, delta;
char        string[20];
char        *uid;
char        *stmt1 = "UPDATE ACCOUNTS SET BALANCE = BALANCE + :1 "
            "WHERE ACCOUNT_NUMBER = :2";
```

```
char        *stmt2 = "UPDATE BRANCHES SET BALANCE = BALANCE + :1 "
            "WHERE BRANCH_NUMBER = :2";
char        *stmt3 = "UPDATE TELLERS SET BALANCE = BALANCE + :1 "
            "WHERE TELLER_NUMBER = :2";
char        *stmt4 = "INSERT INTO HISTORY "
            "(ACCOUNT, BRANCH, TELLER, DELTA, TIMESTAMP) "
            "VALUES (:1, :2, :3, :4, SYSDATE ( ))";
char        *stmt5 = "COMMIT";
char        errbuf[EBL];
int         err;
int         nexe;
csrdef      lda;
csrdef  *curarr[5];
void*    sbiarr[5];
void*    bufp1[2];
void*    bufp2[2];
void*    bufp3[2];
void*    bufp4[4];
long     bufl1[2];
long     bufl2[2];
long     bufl3[2];
long     bufl4[4];
short    type1[2];
short    type2[2];
short    type3[2];
short    type4[4];
char     *fmtp1[2];
char     *fmtp2[2];
char     *fmtp3[2];
char     *fmtp4[4];
```

```
short     fmtl1[2];
short     fmtl2[2];
short     fmtl3[2];
short     fmtl4[4];
short     *indp1[2];
short     *indp2[2];
short     *indp3[2];
short     *indp4[4];
void      *workmem;
int       worksize;
uid = DEFUID;
/* logon */
if (err = olon(&lda, uid, -1, NULL, -1, 0))
      {
      printf("Logon failed\n");
      exit(8);
      }
/* open cursor */
curarr[0] = (csrdef *)malloc(sizeof(csrdef));
curarr[1] = (csrdef *)malloc(sizeof(csrdef));
curarr[2] = (csrdef *)malloc(sizeof(csrdef));
curarr[3] = (csrdef *)malloc(sizeof(csrdef));
curarr[4] = (csrdef *)malloc(sizeof(csrdef));
curarr[5] = (csrdef *)malloc(sizeof(csrdef));
if (err = oopen(curarr[0], &lda, NULL, 0, -1, NULL, -1))
      {
      printf("Open cursor failed\n");
      goto badexit;
      }
if (err = oopen(curarr[1], &lda, NULL, 0, -1, NULL, -1))
      {
      printf("Open cursor failed\n");
```

```
        goto badexit;
        }
if (err = oopen(curarr[2], &lda, NULL, 0, -1, NULL, -1))
        {
        printf("Open cursor failed\n");
        goto badexit;
        }
if (err = oopen(curarr[3], &lda, NULL, 0, -1, NULL, -1))
        {
        printf("Open cursor failed\n");
        goto badexit;
        }
if (err = oopen(curarr[4], &lda, NULL, 0, -1, NULL, -1))
        {
        printf("Open cursor failed\n");
        goto badexit;
        }
if (err = oopen(curarr[5], &lda, NULL, 0, -1, NULL, -1))
        {
        printf("Open cursor failed\n");
        goto badexit;
        }
/* parse */
if (err = osql3(curarr[0], stmt1, -1))
        {
        printf("Parse failed\n");
        goto badexit;
        }
if (err = osql3(curarr[1], stmt2, -1))
        {
        printf("Parse failed\n");
        goto badexit;
```

```
    }
if (err = osql3(curarr[2], stmt3, -1))
    {
    printf("Parse failed\n");
    goto badexit;
    }
if (err = osql3(curarr[3], stmt4, -1))
    {
    printf("Parse failed\n");
    goto badexit;
    }
if (err = osql3(curarr[4], stmt5, -1))
    {
    printf("Parse failed\n");
    goto badexit;
    }
/*
** bind by reference and position
**
** 1st bind variable in SQL statement should go in the 1st element
** of the array (bufp1[0], bufl[0], etc.). Bind variable names are
** not relevant. Note that the format and format length of the
** bind variable do not matter for ORACLE integer data type
** (SQLT_INT). Format is only relevant for the packed
** decimal data type.
*/
bufp1[0] = (void*)&delta;
bufl1[0] = sizeof(delta);
type1[0] = 3;
indp1[0] = NULL;
bufp1[1] = (void*)&account;
bufl1[1] = sizeof(account);
```

```
type1[1] = 3;
indp1[1] = NULL;
bufp2[0] = (void*)&delta;
bufl2[0] = sizeof(delta);
type2[0] = 3;
indp2[0] = NULL;
bufp2[1] = (void*)&branch;
bufl2[1] = sizeof(branch);
type2[1] = 3;
indp2[1] = NULL;
bufp3[0] = (void*)&delta;
bufl3[0] = sizeof(delta);
type3[0] = 3;
indp3[0] = NULL;
bufp3[1] = (void*)&teller;
bufl3[1] = sizeof(teller);
type3[1] = 3;
indp3[1] = NULL;
bufp4[0] = (void*)&account;
bufl4[0] = sizeof(account);
type4[0] = 3;
indp4[0] = NULL;
bufp4[1] = (void*)&branch;
bufl4[1] = sizeof(branch);
type4[1] = 3;
indp4[1] = NULL;
bufp4[2] = (void*)&teller;
bufl4[2] = sizeof(teller);
type4[2] = 3;
indp4[2] = NULL;
bufp4[3] = (void*)&delta;
bufl4[3] = sizeof(delta);
```

```
type4[3] = 3;
indp4[3] = NULL;
if (err = osbndp (curarr[0], 2, bufp1, bufl1, type1, indp1,
                                fmtp1, fmtl1, malloc, &sbiarr[0]))
    {
    printf("Bind failed (array)\n");
    goto badexit;
    }
if (err = osbndp (curarr[1], 2, bufp2, bufl2, type2, indp2,
                                fmtp2, fmtl2, malloc, &sbiarr[1]))
    {
    printf("Bind failed (array)\n");
    goto badexit;
    }
if (err = osbndp (curarr[2], 2, bufp3, bufl3, type3, indp3,
                                fmtp3, fmtl3, malloc, &sbiarr[2]))
    {
    printf("Bind failed (array)\n");
    goto badexit;
    }
if (err = osbndp (curarr[3], 4, bufp4, bufl4, type4, indp4,
                                fmtp4, fmtl4, malloc, &sbiarr[3]))
    {
    printf("Bind failed (array)\n");
    goto badexit;
    }
sbiarr[4] = NULL;
/* execute */
compute_stop_time ( );
for (; not_yet_stop_time ( );)
    {
    account = get_random (a);
```

```
    teller = get_random (t);
    branch = teller % b;
    delta = get_delta (d);
    if (err = otex (curarr, 5, sbiarr, malloc,
                        &workmem, &worksize, &nexe))
        {
        printf ("Execute failed\n");
        goto badexit;
        }
    printf("Successfully completed one transaction.\n");
    free(workmem); /* free memory that was allocated by otex( ) */
    }
/* close Cursors */
if (err = oclose (curarr[0]))
    {
    printf ("Close cursor failed\n");
    goto badexit;
    }
if (err = oclose (curarr[1]))
    {
    printf ("Close cursor failed\n");
    goto badexit;
    }
if (err = oclose (curarr[2]))
    {
    printf ("Close cursor failed\n");
    goto badexit;
    }
if (err = oclose (curarr[3]))
    {
    printf ("Close cursor failed\n");
    goto badexit;
```

```
    }
if (err = oclose (curarr[4]))
    {
    printf ("Close cursor failed\n");
    goto badexit;
    }
if (err = oclose (curarr[5]))
    {
    printf ("Close cursor failed\n");
    goto badexit;
    }
/* logoff */
if (err = ologof(&lda))
    {
    printf ("Logoff failed\n");
    goto badexit;
    }
/* free memory allocated by osbndp */
free(sbiarr[0]);
free(sbiarr[1]);
free(sbiarr[2]);
free(sbiarr[3]);
free(sbiarr[4]);
/* free cursor data areas */
free(curarr[0]);
free(curarr[1]);
free(curarr[2]);
free(curarr[3]);
free(curarr[4]);
exit(0);
badexit:
    oerhms(&lda, (short)err, errbuf, EBL);
```

```
/* get error message */
errbuf[EBL-1] = '\0';
printf("Error: %s\n", errbuf);
ologof(&lda);
free(sbiarr[0]);
free(sbiarr[1]);
free(sbiarr[2]);
free(sbiarr[3]);
free(sbiarr[4]);
free(curarr[0]);
free(curarr[1]);
free(curarr[2]);
free(curarr[3]);
free(curarr[4]);
exit(8);
}
```

8.8.3 A TP1 Implementation on DEC's Rdb/VMS

Our TP1 implementation for Rdb makes use of the SQL Services interface, which is a callable API patterned after dynamic SQL. The SQL statements must be prepared (and optimized) on a per session basis, and the prepared statements are not shared by multiple clients submitting the same parameterized transaction. The code is also more verbose, compared with the other implementations in this appendix, because of the need to separately issue PREPARE and EXECUTE calls for each SQL statement.

```
/*
** Filename : RTP1.C (TP1 using SQL Services interface)
** Server : SQL Services Server / Rdb
*/
#include <stdlib.h>
#include <stdio.h>              /* standard input/output */
#include <sqlsrvda.h>           /* SQLDA structure definition */
```

```
#include <sqlsrvca.h>          /* SQLCA structure, error definition */
#include <sqlsrv.h>            /* SQL Services structure definitions */
extern long get_random( );
extern long get_delta( );
extern compute_stop_time( );
extern not_yet_stop_time( );
static create_association( );
static release_association( );
static report_error( );
main( )
{
/* Variables and structures for SQL/SERVICES API */
int     sts;                      /* return status value */
short   int execute_flag;         /* execute mode flag */
long    int  database_id = 0L;    /* database ID. Not in V1.0 */
char    *assoc_id;                /* association handle */
struct  SQLCA sqlca_str;          /* context structure */
char    long_error[120];          /* alternative error buffer */
char    *cursor_name = "C1";      /* name of cursor */
struct  SQLDA *param_sqlda1;/* parameter marker SQLDA */
struct  SQLDA *select_sqlda1; /* select list SQLDA */
struct  SQLDA *param_sqlda2;/* parameter marker SQLDA */
struct  SQLDA *select_sqlda2; /* select list SQLDA */
struct  SQLDA *param_sqlda3;/* parameter marker SQLDA */
struct  SQLDA *select_sqlda3; /* select list SQLDA */
struct  SQLDA *param_sqlda4;/* parameter marker SQLDA */
struct  SQLDA *select_sqlda4; /* select list SQLDA */
struct  SQLDA *param_sqlda5;/* parameter marker SQLDA */
struct  SQLDA *select_sqlda5; /* select list SQLDA */
struct  SQLDA *param_sqlda6;/* parameter marker SQLDA */
struct  SQLDA *select_sqlda6; /* select list SQLDA */
long int          statement_id1;
```

```
long int            statement_id2;
long int            statement_id3;
long int            statement_id4;
long int            statement_id5;
long int            statement_id6;
long a = 100000;                    /* number of accounts */
long b = 1;                         /* number of branches */
long t = 10;                        /* number of tellers */
long d = 999999;                    /* max delta */
long account, branch, teller, delta;
char string[20];
char *uid;
char *stmt0 =             "DECLARE SCHEMA FILENAME 'TP1' ";
char *stmt1 =             "SELECT BALANCE FROM ACCOUNT "
                          "WHERE ACCOUNT_NUMBER = ?";
char *stmt2 =             "UPDATE ACCOUNT SET BALANCE =
                          BALANCE + ? "
                          "WHERE ACCOUNT_NUMBER = ?";
char *stmt3 =             "UPDATE BRANCH SET BALANCE =
                          BALANCE + ? "
                          "WHERE BRANCH_NUMBER = ?";
char *stmt4 =             "UPDATE TELLER SET BALANCE =
                          BALANCE + ? "
                          "WHERE TELLER_NUMBER = ?";
char *stmt5 =             "INSERT INTO HISTORY "
          "(ACCOUNT, BRANCH, TELLER, DELTA, BALANCE, "
              "TIMESTAMP) "
          "VALUES(?, ?, ?, ?, ?, ?)";
char  *stmt6 = "COMMIT";
create_association(&assoc_id, &sqlca_str, long_error);
/* connect to the TP1 database */
sts = sqlsrv_execute_immediate(
      assoc_id,                     /* association handle */
```

```
        database_id,                /* database_id, must be zero */
        stmt0                       /* statement string */
        );
if (sts != SQL_SUCCESS)
        return report_error(assoc_id, &sqlca_str, long_error);
select_sqlda1 = NULL;
param_sqlda1 = NULL;
sts = sqlsrv_prepare(
        assoc_id,                   /* association handle */
        database_id,                /* database_id, must be zero */
        stmt1,                      /* SQL statement */
        &statement_id1,             /* prepared statement id */
        &param_sqlda1,
        &select_sqlda1);
if (sts != SQL_SUCCESS)
        return report_error(assoc_id, &sqlca_str, long_error);
sts = sqlsrv_allocate_sqlda_data(assoc_id, param_sqlda1);
if (sts != SQL_SUCCESS)
        return report_error(assoc_id, &sqlca_str, long_error);
sts = sqlsrv_allocate_sqlda_data(assoc_id, select_sqlda1);
if (sts != SQL_SUCCESS)
        return report_error(assoc_id, &sqlca_str, long_error);
select_sqlda2 = NULL;
param_sqlda2 = NULL;
sts = sqlsrv_prepare(
        assoc_id,                   /* association handle */
        database_id,                /* database_id, must be zero */
        stmt2,                      /* SQL statement */
        &statement_id2,             /* prepared statement id */
        &param_sqlda2,
        &select_sqlda2);
if (sts != SQL_SUCCESS)
```

```
    return report_error(assoc_id, &sqlca_str, long_error);
sts = sqlsrv_allocate_sqlda_data(assoc_id, param_sqlda2);
if (sts != SQL_SUCCESS)
    return report_error(assoc_id, &sqlca_str, long_error);
select_sqlda3 = NULL;
param_sqlda3 = NULL;
sts = sqlsrv_prepare(
    assoc_id,                   /* association handle */
    database_id,                /* database_id, must be zero */
    stmt3,                      /* SQL statement */
    &statement_id3,             /* prepared statement id */
    &param_sqlda3,
    &select_sqlda3);
if (sts != SQL_SUCCESS)
    return report_error(assoc_id, &sqlca_str, long_error);
sts = sqlsrv_allocate_sqlda_data(assoc_id, param_sqlda3);
if (sts != SQL_SUCCESS)
    return report_error(assoc_id, &sqlca_str, long_error);
select_sqlda4 = NULL;
param_sqlda4 = NULL;
sts = sqlsrv_prepare(
    assoc_id,                   /* association handle */
    database_id,                /* database_id, must be zero */
    stmt4,                      /* SQL statement */
    &statement_id4,             /* prepared statement id */
    &param_sqlda4,
    &select_sqlda4);
if (sts != SQL_SUCCESS)
    return report_error(assoc_id, &sqlca_str, long_error);
sts = sqlsrv_allocate_sqlda_data(assoc_id, param_sqlda4);
if (sts != SQL_SUCCESS)
    return report_error(assoc_id, &sqlca_str, long_error);
```

```
select_sqlda5 = NULL;
param_sqlda5 = NULL;
sts = sqlsrv_prepare(
        assoc_id,                   /* association handle */
        database_id,                /* database_id, must be zero */
        stmt5,                      /* SQL statement */
        &statement_id5,             /* prepared statement id */
        &param_sqlda5,
        &select_sqlda5);
if (sts != SQL_SUCCESS)
        return report_error(assoc_id, &sqlca_str, long_error);
sts = sqlsrv_allocate_sqlda_data(assoc_id, param_sqlda5);
if (sts != SQL_SUCCESS)
        return report_error(assoc_id, &sqlca_str, long_error);
select_sqlda6 = NULL;
param_sqlda6 = NULL;
sts = sqlsrv_prepare(
        assoc_id,                   /* association handle */
        database_id                 /* database_id, must be zero */
        stmt6,                      /* SQL statement */
        &statement_id6,             /* prepared statement id */
        &param_sqlda6,
        &select_sqlda6);
if (sts != SQL_SUCCESS)
        return report_error(assoc_id, &sqlca_str, long_error);
compute_stop_time( );
for(; not_yet_stop_time( );)
        {
        account = get_random(a);
         teller = get_random(t);
        branch = teller % b;
        delta = get_delta(d);
```

```
sprintf(param_sqlda1->SQLVARARY[0].SQLDATA, "%ld", account);
sts = sqlsrv_open_cursor(
      assoc_id,                /* association id */
      cursor_name,             /* handle for cursor */
      statement_id1,           /* handle for SELECT statement */
      param_sqlda1             /* parameter marker SQLDA */
      );
if (sts != SQL_SUCCESS)
return report_error(assoc_id, &sqlca_str, long_error);
sts = sqlsrv_fetch(
      assoc_id,                /* association id */
      cursor_name,             /* handle for cursor */
                               /* direction */
      0L,                      /* row number */
      select_sqlda1            /* select list SQLDA */
      );
 if (sts != SQL_SUCCESS)
return report_error(assoc_id, &sqlca_str, long_error);
sscanf(select_sqlda1->SQLVARARY[0].SQLDATA,"%ld", &balance);
sts = sqlsrv_close_cursor(assoc_id, cursor_name);
if (sts != SQL_SUCCESS)
return report_error(assoc_id, &sqlca_str, long_error);
balance += delta;
sprintf(param_sqlda2->SQLVARARY[0].SQLDATA, "%ld", delta);
sprintf(param_sqlda2->SQLVARARY[1].SQLDATA, "%ld", account);
sts = sqlsrv_execute(
      assoc_id,                     /* association handle */
      database_id,                  /* database_id, must be zero */
      statement_id2,                /* prepared statement id */
      execute_flag,                 /* execute mode */
      param_sqlda2                  /* parameter marker SQLDA */
      );
```

```
if (sts != SQL_SUCCESS)
return report_error(assoc_id, &sqlca_str, long_error);
sprintf(param_sqlda3->SQLVARARY[0].SQLDATA, "%ld", delta);
sprintf(param_sqlda3->SQLVARARY[1].SQLDATA, "%ld", branch);
sts = sqlsrv_execute(
    assoc_id,               /* association handle */
    database_id,            /* database_id, must be zero */
    statement_id3,          /* prepared statement id */
    execute_flag,           /* execute mode */
    param_sqlda3            /* parameter marker SQLDA */
    );
 if (sts != SQL_SUCCESS)
return report_error(assoc_id, &sqlca_str, long_error);
sprintf(param_sqlda4->SQLVARARY[0].SQLDATA, "%ld", delta);
sprintf(param_sqlda4->SQLVARARY[1].SQLDATA, "%ld", teller);
sts = sqlsrv_execute(
    assoc_id,               /* association handle */
    database_id,            /* database_id, must be zero */
    statement_id4,          /* prepared statement id */
    execute_flag,           /* execute mode */
    param_sqlda4            /* parameter marker SQLDA */
    );
if (sts != SQL_SUCCESS)
return report_error(assoc_id, &sqlca_str, long_error);
sprintf(param_sqlda5->SQLVARARY[0].SQLDATA, "%ld", account);
sprintf(param_sqlda5->SQLVARARY[1].SQLDATA, "%ld", branch);
sprintf(param_sqlda5->SQLVARARY[2].SQLDATA, "%ld", teller);
sprintf(param_sqlda5->SQLVARARY[3].SQLDATA, "%ld", delta);
sprintf(param_sqlda5->SQLVARARY[4].SQLDATA, "%ld", balance);
sts = sqlsrv_execute(
```

```
            assoc_id,                   /* association handle */
            database_id,                /* database_id, must be zero */
            statement_id5,              /* prepared statement id */
            execute_flag,               /* execute mode */
            param_sqlda5                /* parameter marker SQLDA */
            );
     if (sts != SQL_SUCCESS)
    return report_error(assoc_id, &sqlca_str, long_error);
    sts = sqlsrv_execute(
            assoc_id,                   /* association handle */
            database_id,                /* database_id, must be zero */
            statement_id6,              /* prepared statement id */
            execute_flag,               /* execute mode */
            param_sqlda6                /* parameter marker SQLDA */
            );
     if (sts != SQL_SUCCESS)
    return report_error(assoc_id, &sqlca_str, long_error);
    printf("Successfully executed one transaction.\n");
    }
}
create_association(assoc_id, sqlca_str, long_error)
char **assoc_id;                        /* address of association id used */
                                        /* in all SQL/SERVICES calls */
struct SQLCA *sqlca_str;                /* context structure */
char *long_error;                       /* alternative error buffer */
{
 /* Variables and structures for SQL/SERVICES API */
 struct ASSOCIATE_STR associate_str;
                                        /* Association structure */
 char *node_name;                       /* VMS node name */
 char *user_name;                       /* VMS username */
 char *password;                        /* VMS password */
```

```
static char read_buffer[512];
                                        /* protocol read buffer */
static char write_buffer[512];
                                        /* protocol write buffer */
long int read_size, write_size;
                                        /* protocol buffer sizes */
/* Other variables */
int sts;                                /* return status value */
int i;                                  /* loop counter */
/* Get the node name, username and password for the server */
/* connection. Prompt the user if not in argument vector */
node_name = "IVY";
user_name = "ARVOLA";
password = "UNREAL";
read_size = 1024;                       /* protocol buffer size value */
write_size = 1024;                      /* protocol buffer size value */
/* Set up association structure */
associate_str.CLIENT_LOG = 0;           /* disable client logging */
associate_str.SERVER_LOG = 0;           /* disable server logging */
associate_str.LOCAL_FLAG = 0;           /* this is a remote session */
associate_str.MEMORY_ROUTINE = NULL;
                                        /* use default */
associate_str.FREE_MEMORY_ROUTINE = NULL;
                                        /* use default */
associate_str.ERRBUFLEN = 512;
associate_str.ERRBUF = long_error;
                                        /* use alternative error string */
/* Connect with the server and establish an association */
sts = sqlsrv_associate(
      node_name,                        /* node name */
      user_name,                        /* user name */
      password,                         /* password */
```

```
        read_buffer,                    /* protocol read buffer */
        write_buffer,                   /* protocol write buffer */
        read_size,                      /* read buffer size */
        write_size,                     /* write buffer size */
        sqlca_str,                      /* SQLCA structure */
        &associate_str,                 /* ASSOCIATE structure */
        assoc_id                        /* Association handle */
        );
if (sts != SQL_SUCCESS)
        return report_error(*assoc_id, sqlca_str, long_error);
}                                       /* create_association */
release_association(assoc_id, sqlca_str, long_error)
char *assoc_id;                         /* association handle */
struct SQLCA *sqlca_str;                /* context structure */
char *long_error;                       /* alternative error buffer */
{
int sts;                                /* return status value */
char *stats = NULL;                     /* reserved parameter */
/*
        * release the association.
        */
sts = sqlsrv_release(assoc_id,stats);
if (sts != SQL_SUCCESS)
        return report_error(assoc_id, sqlca_str, long_error);
}                                       /* release_association */
report_error(assoc_id, sqlca_str, long_error)
char *assoc_id;                         /* association handle */
struct SQLCA *sqlca_str;                /* context structure */
char   *long_error;                     /* alternative error buffer */
{
char *stats = NULL;                     /* reserved parameter */
switch (sqlca_str->SQLCODE) {
```

```
case SQLSRV_CNDERR:
    printf("Filter runtime error.\n");
    break;
case SQLSRV_FTRSYNERR:
    printf("Syntax error in filter expression.");
    break;
case SQLSRV_INTERR:
    printf("Internal error. Examine SQLSRV.DMP and submit SPR.\n");
    break;
case SQLSRV_INVARG:
    printf("Invalid routine parameter.\n");
    break;
case SQLSRV_INVASC:
    printf("Invalid association id.\n");
    break;
case SQLSRV_INVASCSTR:
    printf("Invalid parameter in ASSOCIATE_STR.\n");
    break;
case SQLSRV_INVBUFSIZ:
    printf("Invalid read or write buffer size.\n");
    break;
case SQLSRV_INVCURNAM:
    printf("Invalid cursor name\n");
    break;
case SQLSRV_INVENVTAG:
    printf("Invalid environment tag\n");
    break;
case SQLSRV_INVENVVAR:
    printf("Invalid environment variable\n");
    break;
case SQLSRV_INVEXEFLG:
    printf("Invalid execute flag\n");
```

```
    break;
case SQLSRV_INVIDX:
    printf("Invalid sqlda_index_array\n");
    break;
case SQLSRV_INVREPCNT:
    printf("Invalid repeat count\n");
    break;
case SQLSRV_INVSQLCA:
    printf("Invalid SQLCA structure\n");
    break;
case SQLSRV_INVSQLDA:
    printf("Invalid SQLDA structure\n");
    break;
case SQLSRV_INVSTMID:
    printf("Invalid statement id\n");
    break;
case SQLSRV_MULTI_ACT:
    printf("A batched sqlsrv_execute or\n");
    printf("sqlsrv_fetch_many context is active.\n");
    break;
case SQLSRV_NETERR:
    printf("DECnet returned an error\n");
    printf("SQLERRD[0]: x%lx\n", sqlca_str->SQLERRD[0]);
    printf("SQLERRD[2]: %d.\n", sqlca_str->SQLERRD[2]);
    sqlsrv_release(assoc_id,stats);
    exit(2);
    break;
case SQLSRV_NO_MEM:
    printf("API memory allocation failed.\n");
    break;
case SQLSRV_OPNLOGFIL:
        printf("Unable to open log file\n");
```

```
    break;
case SQLSRV_PRSERR:
    printf("Fatal error in message parser\n");
    break;
case SQLSRV_SQLDA_NOTALL:
    printf("Attempt to deallocate static memory\n");
    break;
case SQLSRV_SRVERR:
    printf("The server returned an error\n");
    printf("SQLERRD[0]: x%lx\n", sqlca_str->SQLERRD[0]);
    printf("SQLERRD[2]: %d.\n", sqlca_str->SQLERRD[2]);
    sqlsrv_release(assoc_id,stats);
    exit(2);
    break;
/* SQL Errors */
case SQL_BAD_TXN_STATE:
    printf("Invalid transaction state\n");
    break;
case SQL_CURALROPE:
    printf("WARNING Cursor is already open\n");
    break;
case SQL_CURNOTOPE:
    printf("Cursor not open\n");
    break;
case SQL_DEADLOCK:
    printf("Deadlock encountered\n");
    break;
case SQL_EOS:
    printf("SELECT or cursor got to end of stream\n");
    break;
case SQL_INTEG_FAIL:
    printf("Constraint failed\n");
```

```
        break;
case SQL_LOCK_CONFLICT:
        printf("Lock conflict\n");
        break;
case SQL_NO_DUP:
        printf("Duplicate on index\n");
        break;
case SQL_NOT_VALID:
        printf("Valid-if failed\n");
        break;
case SQL_NULLNOIND:
        printf("NULL value and no indicator variable\n");
        break;
case SQL_OUTOFRAN:
        printf("Value is out of range for a host variable\n");
        break;
case SQL_RDBERR:
        printf("Rdb returned an error\n");
        break;
case SQL_ROTXN:
        printf("Read write operation in read-only transaction\n");
        break;
case SQL_SUCCESS:
        printf("Command completed successfully\n");
        break;
case SQL_UDCURNOPE:
        printf("Cursor in update or delete not open\n");
        break;
case SQL_UDCURNPOS:
        printf("Cursor in update or delete not positioned on record\n");
        break;
default:
```

```
    printf("Unknown error\n");
    printf("SQLCA.SQLCODE: %d\n", sqlca_str->SQLCODE);
    break;
} /* switch */
/* Print out error message text if present */
if (strlen(long_error) != 0)
    printf("%s\n", long_error);
return 1;
} /* report_error */
```

8.8.4 A TP1 Implementation on the Microsoft SQL Server

The following TP1 implementation for the SQL Server makes use of the stored procedure mechanism, which dramatically reduces the amount of communication between the client and the server needed to initiate and execute the transaction. The stored procedure is compiled and optimized once by the server, and the resulting access plan is saved away in the database for multiple invocations. At run time, the access plan is buffered in the stored procedure cache and shared by multiple clients. Compared with the OTEX implementation for ORACLE, it is straightforward to return the updated balance of the account referenced in a transaction.

```
/*
** Filename: SPTP1.C (TP1 using stored procedure)
** Server: SQL Server
*/
#include <stdlib.h>
#include <stdio.h>
#include <string.h>
#include <sqlfront.h>
#include <sqldb.h>
extern long get_random ( );
extern long get_delta ( );
extern compute_stop_time( );
```

```
extern not_yet_stop_time( );
int err_handler( );
int msg_handler( );
main( )
{
long account, teller, branch, balance, delta;
long  a = 100000;                      /* number of accounts */
long  b = 1;                           /* number of branches */
long  t = 10;                          /* number of tellers */
long  transid = 0;                     /* transaction id */
long  pid = 0;                         /* process id */
DBPROCESS *dbproc;                     /* connection to SQL Server */
LOGINREC *login;                       /* login information */
char  string[20], serverName[30];
int   result_code;
/* install the error-handling and message-handling routines
** (defined at the bottom of this source file)
*/
dberrhandle(err_handler);
dbmsghandle(msg_handler);
/* logon to the SQL Server named 'redwood' with user name = 'sa',
** password 'bogus', and start up database named 'bench'
*/
strcpy(serverName, "redwood");
login = dblogin( );                    /* get login record */
DBSETLUSER(login, (char *)"sa");       /* set the username */
DBSETLAPP(login, (char *)"tp1");       /* set the application name */
DBSETLPWD(login, (char *)"bogus");     /* set the password */
/* Now attempt to create and initialize a DBPROCESS structure */
if ((dbproc = dbopen(login, serverName)) == NULL)
    {
    printf("dbopen failed\n");
```

```
        return(1);                          /* exit program */
        }
dbuse(dbproc, "bench");         /* use the "bench" database */
fprintf(stdout,"Successfully logged on to SQL Server.\n");
compute_stop_time( );
for (; not_yet_stop_time( );)
        {
        account = get_random(a);
        teller = get_random(t);
        branch = teller % b;
        delta = get_delta(d);
        /* construct command to execute stored procedure at server */
        dbfcmd(dbproc, (char *)"tp1 %ld, %ld, %ld, %ld",
                        account, branch, teller, delta);
        /* send command buffer to SQL server */
        dbsqlexec(dbproc);
        /* now check the results from the SQL server */
        while ((result_code = dbresults(dbproc)) != NO_MORE_RESULTS)
            {
            if (result_code == FAIL)
                printf("tp1 failed\n");
                /* clear the pending results */
                dbcancel(dbproc);
            }
            printf("Successfully executed one transaction.\n");
        }
/* close the connection and exit */
dbexit( );
exit(STDEXIT);
}
int err_handler
                (dbproc, severity, dberr, oserr, dberrstr, oserrstr)
```

```
DBPROCESS *dbproc;
int         severity;
int         dberr;
int         oserr;
char        *dberrstr;
char        *oserrstr;
{
if ((dbproc == NULL) || (DBDEAD(dbproc)))
    return(INT_EXIT);
else
    {
    printf("DB-LIBRARY error:\n\t%Fs\n", dberrstr);
    if (oserr != DBNOERR)
        printf("Operating-system error:\n\t%Fs\n", oserrstr);
    return(INT_CANCEL);
    }
}
int msg_handler(dbproc, msgno, msgstate, severity, msgtext)
DBPROCESS *dbproc;
DBINT       msgno;
int         msgstate;
int         severity;
char        *msgtext;
{
printf
    ("SQL Server message %ld, state %d, severity %d:\n",
    msgno, msgstate, severity);
if (msgtext != (char *) 0)
    printf("\t%s\n", msgtext);
    return(DBNOSAVE);
}
create procedure tp1
```

```
    @account int, @teller int, @branch int, @delta int as
    declare @balance int
    declare @outbuff char(200)
    select outbuff =
        "1234567890123456789012345678901234567890"
      + "1234567890123456789012345678901234567890"
      + "1234567890123456789012345678901234567890"
      + "1234567890123456789012345678901234567890"
      + "1234567890123456789012345678901234567890"
    begin tran
    select @balance=balance
        from accounts
        where account#=@account
    if @balance + @delta < 0
        begin
            declare @err =
                "Account "
            + convert(varchar(8), @account)
            + " does not exist"
        raiseerror 21000 @err
        rollback transaction
        return
    end
update accounts
    set balance = balance + @delta
    where account# = @acct
update tellers
    set balance = balance + @delta
    where teller# = @teller
update branches
    set balance = balance + @delta
    where branch# = @branch
```

```
insert history values
    (@account, @teller, @branch, @balance, @delta, getdate( ))
select @outbuff
commit transaction
```

8.9 Summary

Benchmarking is a method for measuring the performance of a system in a controlled environment using a standardized methodology. Benchmarks are typically used for capacity planning, system design, or as a method of comparing the performance of different systems. For a benchmark to be generally applicable, it should possess the properties of relevance, simplicity, scalability, portability, and vendor neutrality.

In this chapter, we discussed five industry-standard database and transaction benchmarks. The Wisconsin benchmark, the most frequently used single-user benchmark for relational database systems, is well known because of the controversy it generated when first published (as the authors compared performance of several commercial relational database systems available at the time). The AS^{3}AP benchmark was developed by some of the original authors of the Wisconsin benchmark. It is designed to measure a database's overall performance across a wide range of operations, and it addresses most of the criticisms that have been raised against the Wisconsin benchmark.

The DebitCredit/TP1 benchmark is a first attempt at measuring transaction throughput in a multiuser environment, modeling both network and presentation services in a system designed to support large volumes of short update transactions. The DebitCredit/TP1 benchmark introduces the notion of ownership cost as a normalization factor for comparing systems with different acquisition, operation, and maintenance costs. Its ability to condense the performance rating of a system into two simple-to-interpret numbers—transactions per second and cost per transaction per second—contributes to its popularity among vendors of database and transaction processing systems. However, DebitCredit/TP1's lack of a formal specification leads to misuse and inflated claims by vendors.

An industry-wide attempt to establish a set of benchmarking standards has led to the formation of the Transaction Processing Council (TPC). The main objective of this vendor consortium is to establish OLTP-oriented benchmarks and to enable vendors to provide more accurate and reliable information on transaction processing information. The efforts of this council resulted in the development of TPC-A, a formalized version of DebitCredit/TP1 for hardware vendors. TPC-A includes the performance cost of terminal emulation, presentation services, and scheduling of front-end applications. TPC-B is its counterpart for relational database system vendors; it does not include the front-end overhead. Depending on how well a particular application environment matches the characteristics of one of these benchmarks, one might consider using performance numbers published by vendors for these benchmarks rather than investing in the development of a customized benchmark.

In Table 8.2, we summarize and compare the five industry-standard benchmarks discussed in this chapter.

	Wisconsin	AS^3AP	TP1	TPC-A	TPC-B
Communications Modeling	No	No	Subject to intepretation	Yes	No
Database Generation	Synthetic, uniform distribution	Synthetic, uniform distribution	Synthetic, uniform distribution	Synthetic, uniform distribution	Synthetic, uniform distribution
Industry Acceptance	Wide, RDBMS vendors	Too early to tell	Wide, hardware & RDBMS vendors	Hardware vendors, TPC consortium	RDBMS vendors, TPC consortium
Mixed Workload	Yes	Yes	No	No	No
Number of Users	Single	Single/multi	Multi	Multi	Multi
Orientation	DSS	DSS/OLTP without network	OLTP with or without network	OLTP with LAN or WAN	OLTP without network
Performance Metric	Response times of individual queries	Equivalent DB size $/megabyte	TPS $/TPS	TPS-A $/TPS-A	TPS-B $/TPS-B
Specification	Detailed	Detailed	Informal	Formal	Formal
System Size	Small	Scalable	Scalable	Scalable	Scalable
Utility Operations	No	Yes	No	No	No

Table 8.2: *Comparison of five industry-standard benchmarks.*

Chapter 9
Application Programming Interface

An application programming interface (API) is the group of system tools that allows an application to access the system. Different types of interfaces are supported in different database management systems. In this chapter, we discuss application programming interfaces for the IBM OS/2 Extended Edition Database Manager, ORACLE Server, DEC Rdb/VMS, and Microsoft SQL Server. In Section 9.1, we introduce several types of application programming interfaces: dynamic SQL, host language embedding, module language, and the callable function library interface. We proceed in Section 9.2 to discuss the SQL cursor manipulation, specifically the cursor update and delete statements. The error handling mechanism in an application program is addressed in Section 9.3, and Section 9.4 describes how to define or change the database environment of an application program. Last, in Section 9.5 we examine the application programming interfaces supported in four database management systems, and we present a summary table in Section 9.6.

9.1 Types of Interfaces

Structured Query Language can be used either interactively or in a program to access data in a database. In this section, we describe the different types of programmatic SQL interfaces: dynamic SQL, host language embedding, module language, and callable function library interface.

9.1.1 Dynamic SQL

A static SQL statement is known at the time the program is written. In contrast, a dynamic SQL statement is not known at the time the program is written but is generated during program execution.

There are three kinds of dynamic SQL statements: EXECUTE IMMEDIATE, PREPARE and EXECUTE, and PREPARE and cursor manipulation.

An *EXECUTE IMMEDIATE* statement is used for a one-time execution of a nonselect statement with no variable substitutions at execution time. The statement is prepared and executed immediately.

A *PREPARE* statement is used to create an executable SQL statement for repeated execution. If the prepared statement is a nonselect statement, an *EXECUTE* statement can be used to associate input values with the parameters in the prepared statement and to execute it.

If the prepared statement serves as a SELECT statement, the prepared statement must be associated with a cursor via a dynamic DECLARE CURSOR statement. A description of the resulting columns of a cursor specification may be obtained using the DESCRIBE statement. Furthermore, the dynamic OPEN statement is used to associate input values with parameters in the prepared statement and to open the cursor, which is positioned on a certain row. The values of the columns of that row are retrieved with a dynamic FETCH statement. The current row of the cursor can be deleted with the positioned DELETE statement. Or, the current row of the cursor can be updated with the positioned UPDATE statement. Finally, the cursor is closed with a CLOSE statement.

SQLDA

The *SQL descriptor area (SQLDA)* is used to store descriptive information associated with a dynamic SQL statement. For instance, in a DESCRIBE statement, a SQL descriptor area is used to store information about the resulting columns in a cursor specification. The information stored in the SQLDA can then be retrieved using the GET DESCRIPTOR statement. In a dynamic FETCH statement, the retrieved data of the current row can be stored in the SQL descriptor area or host variables. The data values of a SQLDA can be stored or modified using the SET DESCRIPTOR statement. In an EXECUTE or dynamic OPEN statement, a SQLDA is used to associate values with the parameter markers in the prepared statement. Prior to executing an EXECUTE or dynamic OPEN statement that uses a SQLDA, the SET DESCRIPTOR statement must be executed to provide the appropriate data.

A SQLDA consists of a *COUNT* field and zero or more item

descriptor areas. The COUNT field specifies the actual number of item descriptor areas that contain descriptions. A DESCRIBE statement sets the COUNT field of a SQLDA. If the described statement is a cursor specification, the COUNT field is set to the number of items in the select list. Otherwise, the COUNT field is set to zero.

Before executing an EXECUTE or a dynamic OPEN statement, the COUNT field must be set to the number of input values. The COUNT field is set to zero if there are no input values. Before executing a dynamic FETCH statement, the value of the COUNT field must be the same as the number of output values of the cursor specification.

Each item descriptor area in the SQLDA consists of many fields with information about the column or data value:

- **TYPE field:** Contains the data type of the value. (The code of the data type is entered.)
- **LENGTH field:** Set for a character string data type.
- **PRECISION and SCALE fields:** Set for a DECIMAL or a NUMERIC data type.
- **NULLABLE field:** Specifies whether or not the value can be null. It is set to one if the value can be null and to zero if it cannot.
- **INDICATOR field:** Contains the null indicator value associated with the data value if the NULLABLE field is set to one. If the input value is null, the indicator value must be negative one; if the data is not null, the indicator value is set to zero.
- **DATA field:** Contains the data value.
- **NAME field:** Contains the column name after the execution of a DESCRIBE statement.

Parameter Markers

A parameter marker is a placeholder for a constant anywhere in a SQL statement; it indicates that a value for the constant will be supplied later. A Parameter marker is represented by a question mark (?).

At execution time, parameter markers must be substituted with values. If the number of parameter markers are known, the parameter values can be supplied by using a list of host variables. Otherwise, the parameter values must be supplied by using a SQLDA.

In the example that follows, parameter markers are used in an INSERT statement to indicate that the values to be inserted are supplied at execution time.

```
INSERT INTO Dept VALUES (?, ?, ?);
```

X/Open SQL: ALLOCATE DESCRIPTOR

The syntax of an ALLOCATE DESCRIPTOR statement is as follows:

```
Allocate Descriptor statement ::=
        ALLOCATE DESCRIPTOR <descriptor name>
        [WITH MAX <occurrences>]
<descriptor name> ::=
        <embedded variable name> |
        <character-string-literal>
<occurrences> ::=
        <unsigned integer> |
        <embedded variable name>
```

This statement is used to allocate a SQLDA and to specify the number of item descriptor areas, which must be greater than zero. If the statement does not specify the number of occurrences, an implementor-defined number of item descriptor areas are allocated. In the example that follows, an InsertVarList SQLDA with three item descriptor areas is allocated:

```
ALLOCATE DESCRIPTOR InsertVarList
WITH MAX 3
```

X/Open SQL: DEALLOCATE DESCRIPTOR

The syntax of a DEALLOCATE DESCRIPTOR statement is

```
Deallocate Descriptor statement ::=
        DEALLOCATE DESCRIPTOR <descriptor name>
```

This statement is used to deallocate a SQL descriptor area that was previously allocated for the specified descriptor name, as shown in this example:

```
DEALLOCATE DESCRIPTOR InsertVarList
```

X/Open SQL: GET DESCRIPTOR

The syntax of a GET DESCRIPTOR statement is

```
Get Descriptor statement ::=
        GET DESCRIPTOR <descriptor name>
        <get descriptor information>
```

<get descriptor information> ::=

<embedded variable name1> = COUNT

| VALUE <get itcm number> <get item info>

[{, <get item info> } ...]

<get item info> ::=

<embedded variable name2> =

{ TYPE | LENGTH | PRECISION | SCALE |

NULLABLE | INDICATOR | DATA | NAME }

<get item number> ::=

<unsigned integer> | <embedded variable name3>

This statement is used to get information from a specified SQL descriptor area. The data type of <embedded variable name1> must be an integer. This integer is used to return the number of item descriptor areas in the specified SQLDA.

The value of <get item number> must reference an item descriptor in the SQLDA. The data type of <embedded variable name2> must match the corresponding requested information. The value of DATA is undefined if the value of INDICATOR is NULL. If the value of DATA is undefined, the value of the embedded variable associated with DATA is undefined after execution of the statement. For example, to get the number of item descriptor areas in the InsertVarList SQLDA and store the number in the NumOfItems variable, we execute the following statement:

```
GET DESCRIPTOR InsertVarList
        :NumOfItems = COUNT
```

In the next example, the GET DESCRIPTOR statement is used to get the data type and name of the second item descriptor area in the InsertVarList SQLDA:

```
GET DESCRIPTOR InsertVarList
        VALUE 2
                :type = TYPE,
                :name = NAME
```

X/Open SQL: SET DESCRIPTOR

The syntax of a SET DESCRIPTOR statement is as follows:

Set Descriptor statement ::=

    SET DESCRIPTOR <descriptor name>
    <set descriptor information>

<set descriptor information> ::=

    COUNT = {   <embedded variable name1> |
                <unsigned integer> }
| VALUE <set item number> <set item info>
    [{, <set item info> } ...]

<set item info> ::=

    {   TYPE | LENGTH | PRECISION | SCALE |
        NULLABLE | INDICATOR | DATA }
    =   <embedded variable name2>

<set item number> ::=

    <unsigned integer> | <embedded variable name3>

This statement is used to set values in the specified SQLDA. The value of <set item number> must reference an item descriptor in the SQLDA. The value of an item area is undefined if the DATA field of that item area is not set in the SET DESCRIPTOR statement. For example, to set the number of item descriptor areas in the InsertVarList SQLDA to three, we execute the SQL statement

```
SET DESCRIPTOR InsertVarList
        COUNT = 3
```

In the following example, the SET DESCRIPTOR statement is used to set the third item descriptor area of the InsertVarList SQLDA to a character data value. The variable CharDataType contains the code for a character data type.

```
SET DESCRIPTOR InsertVarList
        VALUE       3
```

```
TYPE = :CharDataType,
LENGTH = 30,
NULLABLE = 0,
DATA = "Character Data"
```

9.1.2 Host Language Embedding

An embedded SQL host program contains both programming language text and SQL text. The programming language text follows the requirements of a specific standard programming language. The SQL text consists of one or more embedded SQL statements with zero or more embedded SQL declare sections. The SQL statements are specified in the procedural part of a program and are used to specify operations on the contents of a database. The SQL declare section is specified in the data declaration part of a program. Its purpose is to enable the host program and the database system to exchange data values and information. The SQL text is prefixed with the EXEC SQL keyword and terminated with a host language specific terminator to distinguish it from the programming language text. This will be illustrated in the examples that follow.

A special SQL precompiler processes the embedded SQL host program and generates an equivalent host language program. The generated host language program is then compiled to generate an executable program.

9.1.3 Module Language

The module language is used to define a module. A module is a persistent object specified in the module language that contains a module name clause, a language clause, a module authorization clause, zero or more DECLARE CURSOR statements, and one or more procedures. A module must be associated with an application program during its execution. An application program can be associated with a single module. The establishment of an association between an application program and a module is not specified in the ANSI SQL89 standard.

Module Syntax

The syntax of a module is

```
<module> ::=
        <module name clause>
        <language clause>
        <module authorization clause>
        [<declare cursor>...]
        <procedure>...
```

Module Name Clause

The module name clause specifies a module. The module name is optional in the module name clause. However, if a module name is defined, it must be unique within the same environment. The syntax of the module name clause is

```
<module name clause> ::=
        MODULE [<module name>]
```

Language Clause

The language clause specifies the host language from which procedures in the module are invoked. If the language clause specifies a language but the program that calls a procedure in that module is not using the specified language, then the results are undefined.

The syntax of the language clause is

```
<language clause> ::=
        LANGUAGE {COBOL | FORTRAN | PASCAL | PL1}
```

Module Authorization Clause

The module authorization clause specifies the authorization identifier that is used to execute the SQL statement in the procedures. The syntax of the module authorization clause is

```
<module authorization clause> ::=
        AUTHORIZATION <authorization identifier>
```

DECLARE CURSOR Statement

A DECLARE CURSOR statement consists of a cursor name and a cursor specification clause. The cursor name should be unique within the same module. For a description of the DECLARE CURSOR statement, see Chapter 4.

Procedure

A procedure contains a procedure clause, one or more parameter declaration clauses, and a SQL statement. A procedure may be called by an implementor-defined agent. When a procedure is called, the SQL statement associated with the procedure is executed. However, if no transaction is active for that agent, then prior to the execution of the SQL statement, a transaction is initiated and associated with the current call and subsequent calls by that agent until the agent terminates that transaction.

The syntax of a procedure follows:

```
<procedure> ::=
        PROCEDURE  <procedure name>
                   <parameter declaration> ... ;
                   <SQL statement> ;
<procedure name> ::= <identifier>
```

A procedure clause is used to specify a procedure name, which must be unique within a module. The parameter declaration clause specifies a parameter name and its data type. The parameter name must be unique within a procedure. Furthermore, any parameter used in the SQL statement of the procedure must be specified in the parameter declaration of that procedure. The syntax of the parameter declaration is

```
<parameter declaration> ::=
            <parameter name> <data type>
        |   <SQLCODE parameter>
<SQLCODE parameter> ::= SQLCODE
```

The SQLCODE parameter is used to receive a return code from the execution of the SQL statement that follows the parameter declaration. Exactly one SQLCODE parameter must be specified in the parameter declaration. If the SQL statement execution succeeds but no data is retrieved, SQLCODE is set to +100. If the execution succeeds, SQLCODE is set to zero. If the execution fails, the action of the SQL statement is cancelled and SQLCODE is set to an implementor-defined negative number.

The SQL statement is a data manipulation or a transaction processing statement that is executed when the procedure is called. As previously described, after the SQL statement is executed, the

SQLCODE in the parameter declaration is set appropriately, depending on the result of the SQL statement.

9.1.4 Callable Function Library Interface

The Callable Function Library Interface consists of a set of callable function library routines that are used by the program to communicate with the database management system. The program sends SQL statements to the database management system through the callable function routines. The database management system then processes the requests and sends the retrieved query results back to the program through the callable function routines.

Callable function library interface often provides a mechanism for batched execution of SQL statements. Batched execution enhances the performance of an application by reducing the number of client/server network messages required to perform operations. For instance, in Rdb/VMS, the execute_flag parameter in the sqlsrv_execute() routine controls when the contents of the message buffer should be sent to the server for processing. For a prepared INSERT, DELETE, or UPDATE Rdb SQL statement that contains parameter markers, the execute_flag parameter specifies whether the programming interface sends single or multiple sets of parameter marker values to the server for processing. For any other prepared Rdb SQL statements, batched execution is not supported and the execute_flag should be set to indicate nonbatched execution. In the SQL Server, an application can send a series of SQL statements to the database management system using the dbcmd() routine. The SQL statements are stored in the command buffer and executed when the dbsqlexec() routine is sent.

9.2 Cursor Support

A *cursor* is a SQL object associated with a specific SELECT operation. Cursors provide a mechanism for sequentially accessing a set of selected records and processing the records one at a time. In this section, we examine the cursor update and delete statements.

9.2.1 Update Where Current Of Cursor

The syntax of an positioned UPDATE statement is

```
<update statement:positioned> ::=
        UPDATE <table name>
        SET <set clause:positioned>
                [ {, <set clause:positioned>}... ]
        WHERE CURRENT OF <cursor name>
```

This statement updates the specified columns in the current row of the cursor. The columns specified must be columns of the specified table and must be unique. Moreover, the specified table must be updatable. In the following example, a cursor is declared, opened, fetched, and then the current row is updated:

```
DECLARE  DeptCur FOR
SELECT   * FROM Dept FOR UPDATE OF DeptNo;
OPEN     DeptCur;
FETCH    DeptCur INTO :a, :b, :c, :d;
UPDATE   Dept
SET      DeptNo = 120
WHERE    CURRENT OF DeptCur;
```

9.2.2 Delete Where Current Of Cursor

The syntax of the positioned DELETE statement is

```
<delete statement:positioned> ::=
        DELETE FROM <table name>
        WHERE CURRENT OF <cursor name>
```

This statement deletes the current row of the cursor. The specified table must be updatable. For example, to delete from the Dept table the row of data that is the current row of the DeptCur cursor, we execute the following SQL statement:

```
DELETE FROM      Dept
WHERE            CURRENT OF DeptCur
```

9.3 Error Handling

When the execution of a SQL statement fails, an error is returned. The application program is responsible for handling the returned error. The error and status information are stored in the SQLCA, SQLCODE, and SQLSTATE variables. The GET DIAGNOSTICS statement is used to retrieve the status information. In addition, the WHENEVER statement can be used to specify how errors and warnings are handled in an application.

9.3.1 SQLCA

The *SQL communication area (SQLA)* is a data area containing several fields in which status information about the execution of the most recently executed SQL statement is returned. According to the X/Open Preliminary Specification (1991) Structured Query Language, the SQLCA consists of at least the following fields:

- **SQLCODE:** A signed four-byte integer field that contains a return code of the most recently executed SQL statement.
- **SQLERRD:** An array of six four-byte integers that provides additional information about the execution of the statement. The third element of the array contains a row count whose representation depends on the type of SQL statement executed. For instance, after an INSERT statement, the number of rows inserted into the table is stored; after a searched UPDATE statement, the number of rows updated in the table is stored; and after a searched DELETE statement, the number of rows deleted from the table is stored. For other statements, the value stored is implementation defined.
- **SQLWARN:** A sequence of at least eight single-character variables that denote warnings. Only the first four are specified:
  SQLWARN0: If SQLWARN0 is blank, all other SQLWARNn warning characters are also blank. If SQLWARN0 is set to W, at least one of the other warning characters has been set to W.
  SQLWARN1: If SQLWARN1 is set to W, at least one character string value was truncated when it was stored into a host variable.
  SQLWARN2: If SQLWARN2 is set to W, at least one null value was eliminated from the argument set of a function.
  SQLWARN3: If SQLWARN3 is set to W, the number of host variables specified in a SELECT or FETCH statement is different from the number of columns returned by the statement. Or, the value of COUNT specified in the SQL descriptor area referenced in the dynamic FETCH statement is less than the number of columns retrieved.

9.3.2 SQLCODE

SQLCODE specifies the integer value returned in a SQLCODE host variable for each SQL statement execution. When the SQL statement executes successfully, SQLCODE is set to zero. When the statement executes successfully but returns no data SQLCODE is set to +100. For an exception condition, SQLCODE is set to a negative value. The specific values for exception conditions are implementation defined.

9.3.3 X/Open SQL: SQLSTATE

Every executable SQL statement indicates its result status in the SQLSTATE field—a five-character-string field. SQLSTATE can contain only digits and capital letters. The first two characters of SQLSTATE indicate a class; the following three characters indicate a subclass. While class codes are unique, subclass codes are not. The meaning of a subclass code depends on its accompanied class code.

The class of SQLSTATE indicates the follow result categories:

- Class 00 means the statement executed successfully.
- Class 01 means the statement executed successfully with warning.
- Class 02 means the statement executed successfully but no rows satisfied the statement or no rows were available to fetch.
- Any class code besides 00, 01, and 02 means the statement did not execute successfully.

An application can test the entire SQLSTATE to obtain a more precise error report. SQLSTATE contains all the information SQLCODE provides. Therefore, an application should test SQLSTATE, not SQLCODE, to determine the status of a executed SQL statement.

9.3.4 WHENEVER Statement

The WHENEVER statement is used to specify how error and warning conditions are handled. Generally, the WHENEVER statement should be the first executable statement in a program to ensure that all error conditions are trapped. The syntax of the WHENEVER statement as specified in Annex B of the ANSI SQL89 standard is

<whenever statement> ::=

WHENEVER <condition> <exception action>

<condition> ::=

SQLERROR | NOT FOUND

<exception action> ::=

CONTINUE | <go to>

<go to> ::=

{ GOTO | GO TO } <goto target>

<goto target> ::=

: <host label identifier>

| <unsigned integer>

After the execution of a SQL statement in an embedded SQL host program, the value of the status variable SQLCODE is examined by the database management system. If the value of the status variable indicates "no data found" and the WHENEVER NOT FOUND statement is in effect, the exception action is triggered. If the action is a GOTO statement, then a GOTO statement of the host language is performed. If the action is a CONTINUE statement, no further action is performed.

If the status variable indicates "error" and the WHENEVER SQLERROR statement is in effect, the exception action is triggered.

9.3.5 X/Open SQL: GET DIAGNOSTICS

When a SQL statement is executed the exception information is stored in a place referred to as a *diagnostics area*. The GET DIAGNOSTICS statement is used to retrieve status information for the most recently executed SQL statement from the *diagnostics area*. The syntax of the GET DIAGNOSTICS statement follows:

<get diagnostics statement> ::=

GET DIAGNOSTICS { <statement information> |
<exception information> }

<statement information> ::=

<statement information item>

[{, <statement information item>} ...]

<statement information item> ::=

<embedded variable name 1> = { NUMBER | MORE }

<exception information> ::=

EXCEPTION <exception number> <exception info item>

[{, <exception info item> }...]

<exception number> ::=

<unsigned integer> | <embedded variable name3>

<exception info item> ::=

<embedded variable name 2> =

{ RETURNED_SQLSTATE | CLASS_ORIGIN |

SUBCLASS_ORIGIN | MESSAGE_TEXT |

MESSAGE_LENGTH | ROW_COUNT }

The various constructs of <get diagnostic statement> have the following semantics:

- The number of exceptions resulting from the execution of the most recent SQL statement is stored in the diagnostics area. It is retrieved by the NUMBER argument.
- The value of MORE is 'Y' if more exceptions were raised than were stored in the diagnostics area. Otherwise, 'N' is returned.
- The <exception number> specifies a particular exception. It must be an unsigned integer greater than zero and less than or equal to the number returned in NUMBER.
- The value of RETURNED_SQLSTATE is the value of the SQLSTATE.
- The value of CLASS_ORIGIN specifies the class portion of RETURNED_SQLSTATE. And, the value of SUBCLASS_ORIGIN specifies the subclass portion of RETURNED_SQLSTATE.
- The MESSAGE_TEXT contains the explanation of the exception. The value of MESSAGE_TEXT may be a zero-length string.
- The value of MESSAGE_LENGTH is the length of the current message returned in MESSAGE_TEXT.
- The ROW_COUNT specifies the number of rows the SQL statement processed: after an INSERT statement, ROW_COUNT is set to be the number of rows inserted into the table; after a searched UPDATE statement, ROW_COUNT equals the number of rows updated in the table; after a

searched DELETE statement, ROW_COUNT equals the number of rows deleted from the table. However, if these statements cannot obtain the number of rows modified, ROW_COUNT is set to negative one. After any other statements, the ROW_COUNT is implementation defined.

9.4 X/Open Association Management

Association management statements are used to define or change the current database environment that is accessed by the application program. The association management statements are CONNECT, SET CONNECTION, and DISCONNECT.

9.4.1 CONNECT

The syntax of the CONNECT statement is

```
<connect statement> ::=
        CONNECT TO <database environment>
        [ AS <connection name> ]
        [ USER <user identifier>
                [ WITH PASSWORD <password> ] ]
```

This statement establishes an association between the application program and a database environment. Although an application can issue multiple CONNECT statements, it is connected to only one database at a time. The database environment used in the most recently executed CONNECT statement is the active one.

9.4.2 SET CONNECTION

The syntax of the SET CONNECTION statement is

```
<set connection statement> ::=
        SET CONNECTION <connection name>
```

This statement is used to switch the association from the current connection to the specified connection. The context of the database environment is restored to its exact state at the time of the suspension. There should be no active transaction when a SET CONNECTION statement is issued; otherwise, an error is returned.

9.4.3 DISCONNECT

The syntax of the DISCONNECT statement is

<disconnect statement> ::=

DISCONNECT { < connection name> | ALL | CURRENT }

This statement terminates the association between an application program and a database environment. If a connection name is specified, then the named association is terminated. If ALL is specified, then all associations to database environments that were established in an application program are terminated. If CURRENT is specified, the currently active association is terminated and then there is no active database environment. The application must connect to a database environment using the CONNECT or the SET CONNECTION statement before executing any other SQL statements.

9.5 Case Studies

In this section, we examine the different types of application programming interfaces used in the IBM Extended Edition Database Manager, ORACLE Server, VAX Rdb/VMS, and Microsoft SQL Server.

9.5.1 IBM OS/2 Extended Edition Database Manager

In the IBM Extended Edition, the database application programs are developed using embedded SQL. In an embedded SQL program, SQL statements are embedded into the program's source code and intermixed with the programming language statements. The SQL statements consist of an embedded SQL declaration section and a set of embedded SQL statements.

Embedded SQL Declaration Section

Variables referenced in a SQL statement must be declared before the variables are referenced. To declare those variables, an embedded SQL declaration section is used. An embedded SQL declaration section may be coded in the application program whenever variable declarations can appear, in accordance with the rules of the host language.

The BEGIN DECLARE SECTION statement marks the beginning of a host variable declaration section, and the END

DECLARE SECTION statement marks the end. Both statements must be paired and cannot be nested. Only host variable declarations can be included within the declare section.

Embedded SQL Statements

Each embedded SQL statement is prefixed by the keywords EXEC SQL to distinguish it from the host language. In addition, each embedded SQL statement is terminated by a semicolon.

Embedded SQL statements include all SQL commands and the flow control commands that integrate the standard SQL commands within a procedural programming language.

The following list includes all valid SQL commands in the IBM Extended Edition:

ALTER TABLE	
CLOSE	
COMMENT ON	
COMMIT	
CREATE INDEX	
CREATE TABLE	
CREATE VIEW	
DECLARE CURSOR	(embedded SQL only)
DELETE	
DELETE CURRENT OF	(embedded SQL only)
DESCRIBE	(embedded SQL only)
DROP	
EXECUTE	(embedded SQL only)
EXECUTE IMMEDIATE	(embedded SQL only)
FETCH	(embedded SQL only)
GRANT	
INCLUDE	(embedded SQL only)
INSERT	
LOCK TABLE	
OPEN	
PREPARE	(embedded SQL only)

REVOKE

ROLLBACK

SELECT INTO (embedded SQL only)

UPDATE

UPDATE CURRENT OF (embedded SQL only)

WHENEVER (embedded SQL only)

As indicated, some SQL commands can only be embedded in an application program. We focus here on these specific embedded SQL statements.

DECLARE CURSOR. The syntax of the DECLARE CURSOR command in the IBM Extended Edition is

<declare cursor> ::=

DECLARE <cursor name> CURSOR [WITH HOLD]

FOR { <select statement> | <statement name> }

This statement defines a cursor by giving it a name and by associating it with a particular SELECT statement. The cursor is not allocated until it is opened. The WITH HOLD option is a cursor attribute that maintains resources across multiple units of recovery. The WITH HOLD option is specific to the IBM Extended Edition and is not supported in the ANSI SQL89 standard.

DELETE CURRENT OF. The syntax of the embedded DELETE CURRENT OF command in IBM Extended Edition is

<delete current of cursor> ::=

DELETE FROM { <table name> | <view name> }

WHERE CURRENT OF <cursor name>

This statement deletes the current row of the cursor. The table specified must be the same specified in the FROM clause of the cursor definition.

DESCRIBE. The syntax of the embedded DESCRIBE command in the IBM Extended Edition is

<describe> ::=

DESCRIBE <statement name> INTO <descriptor name>

The DESCRIBE statement is used to obtain information about a prepared statement. The statement name specifies the name of a prepared statement, and the descriptor name specifies a SQLDA.

Information about the specified prepared statement is assigned to the SQLDA when the DESCRIBE statement is executed. The DESCRIBE statement is not supported in the ANSI SQL89 standard.

EXECUTE. The syntax of the embedded EXECUTE command in the IBM Extended Edition is:

```
<execute> ::=
        EXECUTE <statement name>
        [ { USING DESCRIPTOR <descriptor name> }
        | { USING <host variable list> } ]
```

This statement executes the prepared SQL statement specified in the <statement name>. The optional USING clause is used to provide a list of host variables whose values are substituted for the parameter markers in the prepared statement. The list of host variables can be specified in the USING clause or provided by the SQLDA specified in the USING DESCRIPTOR clause. The ANSI SQL89 standard does not support the EXECUTE statement.

EXECUTE IMMEDIATE. The syntax of the embedded EXECUTE IMMEDIATE command in the IBM Extended Edition is

```
<execute immediate> ::=
        EXECUTE IMMEDIATE <host variable>
```

This statement prepares an executable form of a SQL statement specified in the host variable. It then executes the prepared statement and destroys the executable form. The statement specified in the host variable must be a valid SQL statement other than a BEGIN DECLARE SECTION, CLOSE, DECLARE, DESCRIBE, END DECLARE SECTION, EXECUTE, EXECUTE IMMEDIATE, FETCH, INCLUDE, OPEN, PREPARE, SELECT, or WHENEVER statement.

The statement string must not begin with EXEC SQL and must not end with a statement terminator. Moreover, the statement must not include parameter markers or references to host variables. The EXECUTE IMMEDIATE statement is not supported in the ANSI SQL89 standard.

FETCH. The syntax of the embedded FETCH command in the IBM Extended Edition is

```
<fetch> ::=
        FETCH <cursor name>
        { INTO <host variable list>
```

| USING DESCRIPTOR <descriptor name> }

This statement positions a cursor on the next row of its result table and assigns the values of that row to the host variables or the SQLDA. The USING DESCRIPTOR clause is not supported in the ANSI SQL89 standard.

INCLUDE. The syntax of the embedded INCLUDE command in the IBM Extended Edition is

<include> ::=

INCLUDE { SQLCA | SQLDA }

This statement inserts declaration of SQLCA or SQLDA into a source program. It is not an executable statement and is not supported in the ANSI SQL89 standard.

OPEN. The syntax of the embedded OPEN command in the IBM Extended Edition is

<open> ::=

OPEN <cursor name>

[{ USING DESCRIPTOR <descriptor name> }

| { USING <host variable list> }]

This statement opens a cursor so it can be used to fetch rows from its result table. The optional USING clause is not supported in the ANSI SQL89 standard.

PREPARE. The syntax of the embedded PREPARE statement in the IBM Extended Edition is

<prepare> ::=

PREPARE <statement name>

[INTO <descriptor name>]

FROM <host variable>

This statement creates an executable SQL statement, called a prepared statement, from a character string form of the statement. The prepared statement can then be executed repeatedly.

If the INTO <descriptor name> clause is specified and the PREPARE statement is successfully executed, information about the prepared statement is stored in the SQLDA specified by the <descriptor name>. The ANSI SQL89 standard does not support the PREPARE statement.

SELECT INTO. The syntax of the embedded SELECT INTO command in the IBM Extended Edition is

<select into> ::=

<select clause> INTO <host variable list>

<table expression>

This statement produces a result table consisting of at most one row, and it assigns the values in that row to the specified host variables. If the result table is empty, the SQLCODE is set to +100 and no values are assigned to the host variables.

UPDATE CURRENT OF. The syntax of the embedded UPDATE CURRENT OF command in the IBM Extended Edition is

<update current of cursor> ::=

UPDATE { <table name> | <view name> }

SET <column name> = { <expression> | NULL }

[{, <column name> = { <expression> | NULL } } ...]

WHERE CURRENT OF <cursor name>

This statement updates the current row of the cursor. The table specified must be the same specified in the FROM clause of the cursor definition. Moreover, the specified cursor must be updatable.

WHENEVER. The syntax of the embedded WHENEVER command in the IBM Extended Edition is

<whenever> ::=

WHENEVER { NOT FOUND | SQLERROR | SQLWARNING }

{ CONTINUE | { { GOTO | GO TO} <host label> } }

This statement specifies the action to be taken when a given exception condition occurs. The SQLWARNING option is not supported in the ANSI SQL89 standard.

With Hold Option on a Cursor

In the IBM Extended Edition, the WITH HOLD option on a cursor is used to maintain resources across multiple units of recovery.

The syntax of the WITH HOLD option is

<declare cursor> ::=

DECLARE <cursor name> CURSOR [WITH HOLD]

FOR { <select statement> | <statement name> }

Depending on whether the units of recovery are committed or rolled back, the effect of the WITH HOLD option on a cursor differs. For units of recovery ending with COMMIT, the opened cursors defined by the WITH HOLD option remain open. The cursor is positioned before the next logical row of the result table. In addition, all prepared statements that reference open cursors defined by WITH HOLD are retained, and all locks are released, except table locks for open cursors defined by the WITH HOLD option. After a COMMIT request, cursor manipulations such as FETCH and CLOSE are valid. The UPDATE and DELETE CURRENT OF CURSOR on rows that are fetched within the same unit of recovery on cursors defined WITH HOLD are also valid after COMMIT.

For units of recovery ending with ROLLBACK, all open cursors are closed, all prepared statements are dropped, and all locks acquired during the unit of recovery are released.

Example Program

```
/* This program executes a SELECT statement using a cursor.
** The purpose is to demonstrate the usage of embedded
** SQL in IBM Extended Edition.
*/
#include <stdio.h>
#include <stdlib.h>
#include <malloc.h>
#include <sql.h>
#include <sqlda.h>
#include <sqlca.h>
#include <sqlenv.h>
/* Defines and declares SQLCA structure. */
EXEC SQL INCLUDE SQLCA;
/* Defines SQLDA structure. */
EXEC SQL INCLUDE SQLDA;
/* Declare the program variables used in the SQL statements. */
EXEC SQL BEGIN DECLARE SECTION;
    char stmt[120];
    int account;
EXEC SQL END DECLARE SECTION;
```

```
main (argc, argv)
   int        argc;
   char   *argv[];
{
     /* Start database TP1. */
     sqlestrd ("TP1", 'S', &sqlca);
     if (sqlca.sqlcode != 0)
     {
               printf("Error in Start Database: sqlcode = %ld.\n",
                    sqlca.sqlcode);
     }
     /* Store the SELECT statement into the stmt variable. */
     strcpy (stmt, "SELECT * FROM ACCOUNT ");
     strcat (stmt, "WHERE ACCOUNT_NUMBER = ?");
     /* Set up checking for error condition. */
     EXEC SQL WHENEVER SQLERROR GOTO error;
     /* Compile and prepare the SELECT statement.
     ** The prepared statement is called S1.
     */
     EXEC SQL PREPARE S1 FROM :stmt;
     printf ("Successfully compiled stmt.\n");
     /* Set up the SQLDA for the SELECT statement. */
     EXEC SQL DESCRIBE S1 into :sqlda;
     /* Declare a cursor using the S1 statement. */
     EXEC SQL DECLARE C1 CURSOR FOR S1;
     printf ("Successfully declared cursor.\n");
     /* Assign a value to the account host variable. */
     account = 100;
     /* The parameter marker in the SELECT statement is
     ** replaced by the value of the account variable when
     ** the cursor is opened.
     */
```

```
53.     EXEC SQL OPEN C1 USING :account;
54.     /* Fetch a row in cursor C1, the data are stored in the
55.     ** sqlda descriptor.
56.     */
57.     EXEC SQL FETCH C1 USING DESCRIPTOR :sqlda;
58.     /* Close the C1 cursor. */
59.     EXEC SQL CLOSE C1;
60.     /* Stop using the TP1 database. */
61.     sqlestpd(&sqlca);
62.     if (sqlca.sqlcode != 0)
63.     {
64.             printf("Error in Start Database: sqlcode = %ld.\n",
65.                     sqlca.sqlcode);
66.     }
67.     return(0);
68. error:
69.     EXEC SQL ROLLBACK WORK;
70.     return( sqlca.sqlcode);
71. }
```

This program begins with include files. The files sqlca.h and sqlda.h define the SQLCA and SQLDA structures used in the application. The sqlenv.h file provides the definition of the START USING DATABASE (sqlestrd) and STOP USING DATABASE (sqlestpd).

The INCLUDE SQLCA statement in line 13 defines and declares the SQLCA structure. The SQLCA is used by the database manager to store the results of executing a SQL statement. The INCLUDE SQLDA statement in line 15 defines the SQLDA structure.

The BEGIN DECLARE SECTION and END DECLARE SECTION statements in lines 17 through 20 enclose the declaration of host variables. Host variables are used to pass data into the database manager or to hold data retrieved from the database manager. In this example, the stmt and account host variables are used to pass data into the database manager.

The main routine starts with the sqlestrd routine call in line 26. This call connects the program to the database. The program requests shared access to the database TP1.

The WHENEVER statement in line 36 specifies that when a SQL error occurs, the program should transfer control to the error label in line 68. The error label instructs the database manager to rollback the uncommitted work and exit the program.

The PREPARE statement in line 40 prepares the SQL statement stored in the stmt variable. The prepared statement is called S1. The DESCRIBE statement in line 43 obtains information about the output data in the prepared S1 statement. The information is stored in the SQLDA structure.

In line 45, the DECLARE cursor statement declares the C1 cursor using the prepared statement S1. The OPEN cursor statement in line 53 opens the C1 cursor by first substituting the parameter marker in the S1 statement with the value in the account host variable; it then executes the S1 statement. The cursor is fetched with the results stored in the SQLDA by the FETCH statement in line 57. And, the CLOSE cursor statement in line 59 closes the C1 cursor.

Finally, for normal program exit, the sqlestpd routine is called in line 61 to close the connection between the program and the TP1 database.

9.5.2 ORACLE Server

The application programming interfaces supported in the ORACLE Server are ORACLE Call Interfaces library routines and embedded SQL. An application developed using the ORACLE Call Interfaces does not require any preprocessing of the source program because the ORACLE Call Interfaces routines are C routines. On the other hand, an application developed using embedded SQL must be preprocessed by a language precompiler. Then the precompiler-generated program needs to be compiled to create an executable.

ORACLE Call Interfaces

The ORACLE Call Interfaces (OCIs) are library subroutines that allow high-level language applications in C, COBOL, or FORTRAN to access and manipulate data in an ORACLE database. The OCIs support all SQL query, data manipulation, data definition, and data control facilities that are available in interactive ORACLE SQL. They include routines that handle client-server connection, parameter binding, SQL statement processing, error message, and transaction control. In the following pages, we describe each OCI routine.

Connection routines. Connection routines create and terminate a client-server connection. Table 9.1 describes three connection routine calls.

Call	Description
OLOGOF	Disconnects a program from ORACLE and frees all ORACLE resources owned by the program. A commit on all outstanding transactions is automatically issued on a successful OLOGOF call. However, if the OLOGOF call fails, all outstanding transactions are rolled back.
OLON	Establishes communication between ORACLE and a user program. A program can log on to ORACLE multiple times, but only one OLON call and user name can be active at one time.
ORLON	Establishes concurrent communications between ORACLE and a user program through SQL*NET. Communication takes place through the logon data area (LDA) and the host data area (HDA) defined within the user program. The ORLON call connects the LDA to ORACLE.

Table 9.1: Connection routines in ORACLE Call Interfaces.

Binding routines. Before the statement is executed, the parameter markers and output select list must be bound. Binding routines are used to bind variables to substitution variables or output data. Specific binding routine calls are described in Table 9.2.

SQL statement routines. SQL statement routines prepare and execute SQL statements. Table 9.3 describes specific SQL statement routine calls.

Result table routines. Result table routines contain routines for fetching data from the server. Table 9.4 describes the specific result table routine calls.

Error message routines. The error message routines are used to return the error from the ORACLE Server to the user program. Table 9.5 describes two specific error message routine calls.

Call	Description
OBNDRN and OBNDRV	Associates the address of a program variable with a specified SQL substitution variable. OBNDRN specifies SQL substitution variables numerically. OBNDRV specifies SQL substitution variables symbolically by name. One of these calls must be issued for each program variable after the OSQL3 and before the OEXEC call.
ODEFIN	Defines an output buffer for a specified field in a select list of a SQL query. It is usually called after a call to ODSC. ODEFIN must be called once for each field in the select list. The output buffers defined by ODEFIN are the buffers that will be used by OFETCH.
ODSC	Used for SQL queries. This call allows programs to dynamically determine the number and data types of fields returned from a query. ODSC references each field in the select list as if each were numbered consecutively from left to right, beginning with one.

Table 9.2: *Binding routines in ORACLE Call Interfaces.*

Call	Description
OEXEC	Executes the SQL statement associated with the specified cursor. The OEXEC call must be preceded by a successful OSQL3 call.
OEXN	Similar to the OEXEC call, but it allows the user to take advantage of the ORACLE array interface by supporting operations using an array of bind variables.
OSQL3	Associates a SQL statement with a cursor and passes the statement to ORACLE for parsing. The parsed representation of the SQL statement is then stored in the ORACLE context area associated with the cursor data area. Subsequent calls reference the SQL statement by cursor name.

Table 9.3: *SQL statement routines in ORACLE Call Interfaces.*

Call	Description
OCLOSE	Disconnects the association of a cursor from the ORACLE context area. The OCLOSE call frees all resources obtained by the OOPEN, OSQL3, and OEXEC calls using the cursor.
OFEN	Similar to the OFETCH call except that it allows the user to take advantage of the ORACLE array interface by supporting fetching of multiple rows into an array of variables with a single call.
OFETCH	Returns rows of a query result to the user program, one row at a time. Each OFETCH call returns the next row from the set of rows that satisfy a query. After each OFETCH call, the rows processed count in the cursor data area is incremented.
ONAME	Retrieves the names of select list fields of a SQL query. The maximum length of a field name is 240 bytes.
OOPEN	Ties the cursor data area in the user program to a context area in the ORACLE user process.

Table 9.4 Result table routines in ORACLE Call Interfaces.

Call	Description
OERHMS	Returns ORACLE error message text. OERHMS allows the user to retrieve an arbitrarily long error message.
OERMSG	Also returns ORACLE error message text. However, OERMSG truncates the error message to 70 characters.

Table 9.5: Error message routines in ORACLE Call Interfaces.

Transaction control routines. Transaction control routines are used to set the automatic commit options and to commit or rollback a transaction. Specific transaction control routine calls are described in Table 9.6.

Call	Description
OBREAK	Asynchronously aborts any currently executing OCI function associated with the specified logon data area (LDA). OBREAK is the only ORACLE call allowed when other ORACLE functions are in progress.
OCAN	Informs ORACLE that the operation in progress for the specified cursor is complete. Any resources associated with the specified cursor are freed, but the association of the cursor with an ORACLE context area is still maintained.
OCOF	Disables automatic commit of every SQL data manipulation statement.
OCOM	Commits the current transaction.
OCON	Enables autocommit. By default, autocommit is disabled at the start of an OCI program.
OOPT	Sets the rollback or wait options. This call is not supported in ORACLE RDBMS Version 6.0 or later.
OROL	Rolls back the current transaction.

Table 9.6: *Transaction control routines in ORACLE Call Interfaces.*

Example Program

The following is an example program using OCI calls.

```
/* This program executes a SELECT statement to get the
** department name of a particular department number using
** the ORACLE Call Interfaces.
*/
#include <stdio.h>
#include <stdlib.h>
/* User ID and password */
```

```
#define DEFUID          "scott/tiger@p:oracle"
#define EBL             90  /* Length of the error buffer. */
/* Definition of the cursor data area */
struct csrdef
{
        short  csrrc;                           /* return code */
        short  csrft;                           /* function type */
        unsigned long           csrrpc;         /* rows processed count */
        short  csrpeo;                          /* parse error offset */
        unsigned char           csrfc;          /* function code */
        unsigned char           csrfil;         /* filler */
        unsigned short          csrarc;         /* reserved, private*/
        unsigned char           csrwrn;         /* warning flags */
        unsigned char           csrflg;         /* error flags */
        unsigned int            csrcn;          /* cursor number */
        struct  {
            struct  {
                unsigned long tidtrba;          /* rba of first block of
                                                ** table.
                                                   */
                unsigned short tidpid;          /* partition id of table */
        unsigned char  tidtbl;  /* table id of table */
            } ridtid;
            unsigned long ridbrba;              /* rba of datablock */
            unsigned short ridsqn;              /* sequence number of row in
                                                   ** block.
                                                   */
        } csrrid;
        unsigned int            csrose;         /* os dependent error code */
        unsigned char           csrchk;         /* check byte */
        unsigned char           crsfill[26];    /* private, reserved fill *
};
```

```
typedef struct csrdef CSRDEF;
main (argc, argv)
        int     argc;
        char    *argv[];
{
        char    *uid;
        char    *stmt = "SELECT DName FROM Dept WHERE
                DeptNo = :1";
        char    errbuf[EBL];
        int     err;
        short deptNameL;     /* length of the department name */
        char    *deptName; /* Pointer to the department name string */
        CSRDEF lda;          /* The logon data area */
        CSRDEF selCur;       /* The cursor data area */

#define         LDA         &lda
#define         SELCUR      &selCur
        uid = DEFUID;
        /* Logon to ORACLE using the DEFUID string */
        if ( err = olon(LDA, uid, -1, (char *)-1, -1, 0) )
        {
            printf("Logon failed\n");
            exit(1);
    }
        /* Associates the SELCUR cursor to a context area in the
        ** ORACLE user process.
        */
        if (err=oopen(SELCUR, LDA,(char *)-1, -1, -1,(char *)-1, -1))
        {
            printf("Open cursor failed\n");
            goto errexit;
        }
```

```
/* Parse the SQL statement in the stmt string and associates
** the statement with the SELCUR cursor.
*/
 if ( err = osql3(SELCUR, stmt, -1) )
 {
     printf("Parse failed\n");
     goto errexit;
 }
/* Describe the column in the select list of "stmt" to
** determine the maximum length of the department name.
*/
if (err = odsc(SELCUR, 1, &deptNameL,(short *)-1,(short *)-1,
     (short *)-1,(char *)-1,(short *) -1,(short *)-1 ) )
 {
     printf("Describe failed\n");
     goto errexit;
 }
/* allocate the string for the department name, 1 is added for
** the terminating null character.
*/
deptName = malloc (deptNameL + 1);
/* Defines deptName as an output buffer for the first item in
** the select list of the SELCUR cursor.
*/
if ( err = odefin(SELCUR,1,deptName,deptNameL+1,CHRSTR,-1,
(short *)-1,(char *)-1,-1,-1,(short *)-1,(short *)-1)
 {
     printf("Define failed\n");
     goto errexit;
 }
/* Bind the substitution variable in the SELECT statement. */
if ( err = obndrn(SELCUR, 1, &deptNo, sizeof(deptNo), INT,
```

```
            -1, (short *) -1, (char *)-1, -1, -1) )
    {
        printf("Bind failed.\n");
        goto errexit;
    }
    /* Get the department number. */
    printf("Enter the department number : ");
    scanf("%i", &deptNo);
    /* Execute the statement in the SELCUR. */
    if ( err = oexec(SELCUR) )
    {
        printf("Execute failed\n");
        goto errexit;
    }
    /* Fetch the SELCUR cursor. */
    if ( err = ofetch(SELCUR) )
    {
        printf("Execute failed\n");
        goto errexit;
    }
    printf(" The department name for department number %d is %s",
            deptNo, dName);
    /* Close Cursors */
    if ( err = oclose(SELCUR) )
    {
        printf("Close cursor failed.\n");
        goto errexit;
    }
    /* Logoff */
    if ( err = ologof(LDA) )
    {
    printf("Logoff failed.\n");
```

```
133.            goto errexit;
134.        }
135.        /* free memory allocated for the department name */
136.        free(dName);
137.        exit(0);
138.    errexit:
139.        /* get error message */
140.        oerhms( LDA, (short)err, errbuf, EBL );
141.        errbuf[EBL-1] = '\0';
142.        printf("Error: %s\n", errbuf);
143.        /* Close Cursors */
144.        if ( err = oclose(SELCUR) )
145.        {
146.            printf("Close cursor failed\n");
147.        }
148.        if ( err = ologof(LDA) )
149.        {
150.            printf("Logoff failed\n");
151.        }
152.        exit(1);
153. }      /* main */
```

In this program, the cursor data area is defined in lines 11 through 39. A cursor is a 64-byte data area that contains status information about an active SQL operation. A cursor is associated with an ORACLE context area by issuing an OOPEN call. Furthermore, a cursor is associated with a SQL statement by issuing an OSQL3 call. Every subsequent OCI call then references that SQL statement by passing a cursor as a parameter.

The OLON call in line 57 is used to establish communication between ORACLE and the user program via the logon data area (LDA). After establishing a connection, the OOPEN call in line 65 ties the cursor data area to a context area in the ORACLE user process. ORACLE uses context areas to execute SQL statements and to store processing information.

The OSQL3 call in line 73 associates a SQL statement with the SELCUR cursor and passes the SQL statement to ORACLE for parsing. The parsed representation of the SQL statement is stored in the ORACLE context area associated with the cursor data area. In line 81, the ODSC call is used to return the maximum size of a field returned as the result of a query in the SELCUR.

The ODEFIN call in line 93 defines an output buffer, deptName, for the dName field in the select list of the stmt string. The output buffer defined by ODEFIN is the buffer that will be used by OFETCH.

In Line 100, the OBNDRN call associates the address of the program variable deptNo with the :1 substitution variable in the stmt string. The OEXEC call in line 110 uses the value of deptNo to substitute for the :1 variable when executing the SQL statement.

The OFETCH call in line 116 returns rows of a query result, one at a time. Each column of the query is stored in a buffer identified by a previous ODEFIN call. In our example program, the column returned from the query is stored in the deptName variable.

The OCLOSE call in line 124 disconnects a cursor from its associated ORACLE context area. It also frees all resources obtained by the OOPEN, OSQL3, and OEXEC calls using the specified cursor.

The OLOGOF call in line 130 disconnects the program from ORACLE and frees all ORACLE resources owned by the program. A commit is automatically issued on a successful OLOGOF call, and all currently opened cursors are closed. Finally, if an error occurs, the OERHMS call in line 140 returns an arbitrarily long ORACLE error message text.

Embedded SQL

As we mentioned earlier, embedded SQL refers to the use of SQL statements embedded within a procedural programming language. It is a collection of all SQL commands and the flow control commands that integrate the SQL commands within a procedural programming language. Each embedded SQL statement is prefixed by the keywords EXEC SQL to distinguish it from the host language.

The ORACLE SQL commands that can be used only in an embedded SQL program are

CLOSE CURSOR

COMMIT

CONNECT

DECLARE CURSOR

DECLARE DATABASE

DECLARE STATEMENT

DELETE

DESCRIBE

EXECUTE

EXECUTE IMMEDIATE

FETCH

INSERT

OPEN

PREPARE

ROLLBACK

SAVEPOINT

SELECT

UPDATE

WHENEVER

CLOSE CURSOR. The syntax of the embedded CLOSE CURSOR statement in the ORACLE Server follows. This statement releases resources associated with an opened cursor.

```
<CLOSE cursor> ::=
        CLOSE <cursor name>
```

COMMIT. The syntax of the embedded COMMIT statement in the ORACLE Server is

```
<Commit> ::=
        [AT <dbname>] COMMIT [WORK] [RELEASE]
```

This statement makes permanent any changes made in the current transaction. The optional dbname clause specifies the database where the COMMIT should be executed. The RELEASE option is used to release resources and to disconnect from the database. The optional AT clause and the RELEASE keyword are not supported in the ANSI SQL89 standard. Moreover, the WORK keyword is a required keyword in the ANSI SQL89 standard.

CONNECT. The syntax of the embedded CONNECT statement in the ORACLE Server is

```
<connect> ::=
        CONNECT :<user_password> [AT <dbname>]
        [USING :<dbstring>]
```

This statement connects users to the specified ORACLE RDBMS. The CONNECT statement is not supported in the ANSI SQL89 standard.

DECLARE CURSOR. The syntax of the embedded DECLARE CURSOR statement in the ORACLE Server is

```
<declare cursor> ::=
        [AT <dbname>] DECLARE <cursor> CURSOR
                FOR { <select statement> | <statement name> }
```

This statement defines a cursor by giving it a name and by associating it with a particular SELECT statement. The SELECT statement can also be specified by providing the name of a prepared SELECT statement. The cursor is not allocated until it is opened. The optional AT clause and the <statement name> are not supported in the ANSI SQL89 standard.

DECLARE DATABASE. The syntax of the embedded DECLARE DATABASE statement in the ORACLE Server is

```
<declare database> ::=
        DECLARE <dbname> DATABASE
```

This statement declares the name of a remote database that is referenced in subsequent SQL statements specified by the AT clause. The DECLARE DATABASE statement is not supported in the ANSI SQL89 standard.

DECLARE STATEMENT. The syntax of the embedded DECLARE STATEMENT statement in the ORACLE Server is

```
<declare statement> ::=
        DECLARE <statement name> STATEMENT
```

This statement assigns a SQL variable name to a SQL statement. The declared statement can be referenced in the PREPARE, EXECUTE, or EXECUTE IMMEDIATE statements. The ANSI SQL89 standard does not support the DECLARE STATEMENT statement.

DELETE. The syntax of the embedded DELETE statement in the ORACLE Server is

```
<delete:positioned> ::=
        [AT <dbname>] [FOR :<host_integer>]
        DELETE [FROM] <table> [ <alias> ]
        [WHERE { <condition> | CURRENT OF <cursor> } ]
```

This statement removes rows from a table or view. The FOR clause specifies a limit on the number of iterations of the DELETE statement when arrays are used in the WHERE clause. The optional AT and FOR clauses are not supported in the ANSI SQL89 standard.

DESCRIBE. The syntax of the embedded DESCRIBE statement in the ORACLE Server is

```
<describe> ::=
        DESCRIBE BIND VARIABLES FOR
                <statement name> INTO <descriptor name>
```

This statement allocates and initializes a descriptor to hold host variable descriptions from a previously prepared SQL statement. The DESCRIBE statement is not supported in the ANSI SQL89 standard.

EXECUTE. The syntax of the embedded EXECUTE statement in the ORACLE Server is

```
<execute> ::=
        [AT <dbname>] [FOR :<host_integer>]
                EXECUTE <statement_name>
                [USING <values_list>]
```

This statement executes a nonselect statement that has been previously prepared. Input host variables are passed to the statement via the USING clause. The EXECUTE statement is not supported in the ANSI SQL89 standard.

EXECUTE IMMEDIATE. The syntax of the embedded EXECUTE IMMEDIATE statement in the ORACLE Server is

```
<EXECUTE IMMEDIATE> ::=
        [AT <dbname>] EXECUTE IMMEDIATE
                { :<host_string> | <string_literal> }
```

This statement prepares and executes a SQL statement containing no host variables. The EXECUTE IMMEDIATE statement is not supported in the ANSI SQL89 standard.

FETCH. The syntax of the embedded FETCH statement in the ORACLE Server is

```
<FETCH> ::=
        [FOR :<host_integer>] FETCH <cursor_name>
        { INTO <host_variable_list> | USING <descriptor> }
```

The FETCH statement positions the cursor on the next row to be retrieved and assigns the values of the current row to the referenced host variables. The FOR clause specifies that the statement is to be executed as many times as the value of host_integer or the sizes of the relevant arrays, whichever is less. The optional FOR clause and the FETCH USING statement are not supported in the ANSI SQL89 standard.

INSERT. The syntax of the embedded INSERT statement in the ORACLE Server is

```
<insert> ::=
        [AT <dbname> ] [FOR :<host_integer> ]
                INSERT INTO [<user>.] <table>
                        [ ( <column> { , <column>} ...) ]
                VALUES ( { <values_element> [ { , <value_element> } ...]
                                |     <query> } )
```

This statement is used to add rows to a table. The optional AT and FOR clauses are not supported in the ANSI SQL89 standard.

OPEN. The syntax of the embedded OPEN statement in the ORACLE Server is

```
<open> :=
        OPEN <cursor_name>
                [ USING { <host_variable_list> | <descriptor name> } ]
```

This statement allocates a cursor structure for the previously declared cursor. The statement then evaluates the query referenced in the cursor declaration and substitutes the host variable names supplied in the USING clause into the WHERE clause of the query. The optional USING clause is not supported in the ANSI SQL89 standard.

PREPARE. The syntax of the embedded PREPARE statement in the ORACLE Server is

```
<prepare> ::=
        PREPARE <statement_name>
                FROM { :<host_variable> | <string_literal> }
```

This statement parses the SQL statement and gives it a statement name. The SQL statement specified in the host variable or the literal string is not preceded by the EXEC SQL clause. The ANSI SQL89 standard does not support the PREPARE statement .

ROLLBACK. The syntax of the embedded ROLLBACK statement in the ORACLE Server is

<rollback> ::=

[AT <dbname>] ROLLBACK [WORK] [RELEASE]

[TO [SAVEPOINT] <savepoint>]

This statement aborts the current transaction, discards all changes in the current transaction, and releases all locks. The RELEASE option is used to release resources and to disconnect from the database. The TO SAVEPOINT clause is used to rollback a partial transaction to a previously declared <savepoint>. The optional RELEASE keyword, and the AT and TO clauses are not supported in the ANSI SQL89 standard. Moreover, WORK is a required keyword in the ANSI SQL89 standard.

SAVEPOINT. The syntax of the embedded SAVEPOINT statement in ORACLE is

<savepoint statement> ::=

SAVEPOINT <savepoint>

This statement specifies a point in a transaction to allow rollback of a partial transaction to that point. The SAVEPOINT statement is not supported in the ANSI SQL89 standard.

SELECT. The syntax of the embedded SELECT statement in the ORACLE Server is

<select (embedded) > ::=

[AT <dbname>] [FOR :<host_integer>]

SELECT <select_list>

INTO :<host_variable> [{, :<host_variable> }...]

FROM <table_list>

[WHERE <condition>]

[CONNECT BY <condition> [START WITH <condition>]]

[GROUP BY <expr> [{, <expr>} ...]

[HAVING <condition>]]

[{ UNION | INTERSECT | MINUS } SELECT ...]

[ORDER BY { <expr> | <position> } [ASC | DESC]

[{ ,{ <expr> | <position> } [ASC | DESC]}...]]

[FOR UPDATE OF <column> [{ , <column> } ...]

[NOWAIT]]

This statement retrieves rows from the specified table. The returned values are assigned to the output host variables. The optional AT and FOR clauses are not supported in the ANSI SQL89 standard. For a description of the syntactic differences between an ORACLE SELECT statement and the ANSI SQL89 standard SELECT statement, see Section 4.2.

UPDATE. The syntax of the embedded UPDATE statement in the ORACLE Server is

```
<update> ::=
        [AT <dbname>] [FOR :<host_integer> ]
                UPDATE <table>
                SET <column> [ {, <column>}...] =
                { ( <value> [ {, <value>} ...] | <query> }
                [ WHERE { <condition> |
                        CURRENT OF <cursor name> } ]
OR
        [AT <dbname>] [FOR :<host_integer> ]
                UPDATE <table>
                SET <column1> = { (value) | <query> }
                [{, <column1> = { (value)|<query> } } ...]
                [ WHERE { <condition> |
                CURRENT OF <cursor name> } ]
```

This statement modifies the data in a specified table. The optional AT and FOR clauses are not supported in the ANSI SQL89 standard.

WHENEVER. The syntax of the embedded WHENEVER statement in the ORACLE Server is

```
<whenever> ::=
        WHENEVER
                { NOT FOUND | SQLERROR | SQLWARNING }
                { CONTINUE | GOTO <label_name> | STOP }
```

This statement specifies how error and warning conditions are handled. Neither the SQLWARNING nor the STOP construct is supported in the ANSI SQL89 standard.

Example Program

```
/* This program executes a SELECT statement using a cursor.
** The purpose is to demonstrate the usage of embedded
** SQL in ORACLE.
*/
#include <stdio.h>
#define USERNAME "SCOTT"
#define PASSWORD "TIGER"
/* Include the SQL communication area. */
EXEC SQL INCLUDE sqlca;
/* Include the SQL descriptor area. */
EXEC SQL INCLUDE sqlda;
/* Declare the program variables used in the SQL statements. */
EXEC SQL BEGIN DECLARE SECTION;
char *userName = USERNAME:
char *password = PASSWORD;
char stmt[120];
int account;
EXEC SQL END DECLARE SECTION;
/* Declare the select descriptor. */
SQLDA *selectDA;
/* External declaration of the sqlald() function. */
extern SQLDA *sqlald();
main (argc, argv)
        int  argc;
        char     *argv[];
{
        /* Set up checking for error condition. */
        EXEC SQL WHENEVER SQLERROR GOTO ErrExit;
        /* Connect to the ORACLE TP1 database. */
        EXEC SQL CONNECT :userName IDENTIFIED BY :password;
            AT TP1 USING p:oracle;
```

```
/* Store the SELECT statement into the stmt variable. */
strcpy (stmt, "SELECT * FROM ACCOUNT ");
strcat (stmt, "WHERE ACCOUNT_NUMBER = ?");
/* Compile and prepare the SELECT statement.
** The prepared statement is called S1.
*/
EXEC SQL PREPARE S1 FROM :stmt;
printf ("Successfully compiled stmt.\n");
/* Allocate storage space for the select descriptor.
** Set the maximum number of select list columns to 40.
** Set the maximum length of column name and indicator name
** to 30.
*/
selectDA = sqlald(40, 30, 30);
/* Initialize count of array elements. */
select->N = 40;
/* Set up the SQLDA for the SELECT statement. */
EXEC SQL DESCRIBE SELECT LIST FOR S1 into :selectDA;
/* Declare a cursor using the S1 statement. */
EXEC SQL DECLARE C1 CURSOR FOR S1;
printf ("Successfully declared cursor.\n");
/* Assign a value to the account host variable. */
account = 100;
/* The parameter marker in the SELECT statement is
** replaced by the value of the account variable when
** the cursor is opened.
*/
EXEC SQL OPEN C1 USING :account;
/* Fetch a row in cursor C1, the data are stored in the
** sqlda descriptor.
*/
EXEC SQL FETCH C1 USING DESCRIPTOR :selectDA;
```

```
64.         /* Close the C1 cursor. */
65.         EXEC SQL CLOSE C1;
66.         exit(0);
67. ErrExit:
68.         EXEC SQL ROLLBACK RELEASE;
69.         exit(1);
70. }
```

This example begins with the include file for the standard Input/Output routines. The INCLUDE SQLCA statement in line 9 defines and declares the SQLCA structure, which is used by the database manager to store the results of executing a SQL statement. The INCLUDE SQLDA statement in line 11 defines the SQLDA structure.

The BEGIN DECLARE SECTION and END DECLARE SECTION statements in lines 13 through 18 enclose the declaration of host variables, which are used to pass data into the database manager or to hold data retrieved from the database manager. In this example, the userName, password, stmt, and account host variables are used to pass data into the database manager.

The WHENEVER statement in line 28 specifies that when a SQL error occurs, the program should transfer control to the ErrExit label. The ErrExit label in line 67 instructs the database manager to rollback the uncommitted work and exit the program.

The CONNECT statement in line 30 connects the user to the TP1 ORACLE database. The PREPARE statement in line 38 prepares the SQL statement stored in the stmt variable. The prepared statement is called S1.

In line 45, the SQLDA for the prepared statement is allocated by the sqlald() routine. The allocated SQLDA is called selectDA and contains 40 elements. Each element can contain a 30-character column name and a 30-character indicator name.

The DESCRIBE statement in line 49 obtains information about the output data in the prepared S1 statement. The information is stored in the selectDA SQLDA structure.

The DECLARE cursor statement in line 51 declares the C1 cursor using the prepared statement S1. The OPEN cursor statement in line 59 first opens the C1 cursor by substituting the parameter marker in the S1 statement with the value in the account host variable, then executes the S1 statement. The cursor is fetched with the results stored in the SQLDA by the FETCH statement in line 63. Finally, the CLOSE cursor statement in line 65 closes the C1 cursor.

If an error occurs in any of the SQL operations, program control will go to the ErrExit in line 67 and will execute the ROLLBACK command in line 68 to rollback the uncommitted SQL operations.

ROWID

Every row in the ORACLE Server database is associated with a pseudocolumn that corresponds to the address of that row. That address is represented by the keyword ROWID and can be retrieved with a SQL query. The ROWID returned from a query is a hexadecimal string that contains three pieces of information necessary to locate a row. The ROWID specifies a particular row of a particular block in a particular database file in which the row actually resides.

ROWID is a unique identifier for a row in a given table. It provides the fastest means of accessing a particular row. However, because a row's ROWID changes as the row changes position within a table, ROWID cannot be used as a table's primary key.

Although ROWID can be used in the SELECT and WHERE clause of a query, it is not stored in the database and is not updatable. In the example that follows, the ROWID and the department number are retrieved:

```
SELECT    ROWID, DeptNo
FROM      Dept
```

The results are

ROWID	DeptNo
00000008.0000.0002	10
00000008.0003.0002	20
00000008.0007.0002	30
00000008.000A.0002	40
00000008.000D.0002	99

Data Type Coercion

Different data types may be referenced in a comparison. The ORACLE Server uses data conversion to resolve differences. To perform the data type conversion, ORACLE can convert the constant to the column's defined data type; it can convert the column's value to the data type of the constant, or it can convert one column's data type to another column's data type.

Data conversion is context dependent. Hence, rather than rely on implied or automatic conversion, the user should specify explicit conversions using SQL functions. The data type conversion functions are TO_CHAR, TO_NUMBER, and TO_DATE. The following example is used to demonstrate the usage of the TO_CHAR, TO_NUMBER, and TO_DATE functions in a SELECT statement:

```
SELECT   TO_CHAR(120+3) CHAR123,
         TO_NUMBER("456") NUMBER456,
         TO_DATE('January 01, 1991', 'Month dd, YYYY')
         DATEVALUE
FROM     Dept
WHERE    DeptNo = 10
```

The result is

CHAR123	NUMBER456	DATEVALUE
123	456	January 01, 1991

Protected-Mode Development Utility

The protected-mode development kit (PDK) is included with Pro*C for MS-DOS workstations. Pro*C is a C precompiler for the ORACLE embedded SQL programs in C. Pro*C converts a C program with embedded SQL statement into a C program that can access and manipulate data in an ORACLE database. The PDK includes a conversion utility called EXE2PXE, which allows a programmer to prepare properly linked programs for use in protected mode.

In order to develop MS-DOS protected-mode applications, after installing Pro*C for MS-DOS Workstations, all Microsoft C libraries must be updated.

To update the Microsoft C libraries, it is neessary to have the large model libraries LLIBC.LIB, LIBH.LIB, and LLIBFA.LIB. The Microsoft libraries are usually found in the directory C:\MSC\LIB. Once the libraries are found, the following steps must be completed:

(1) Go to the directory where the library enhancements are located. For Microsoft C, these updates are located in the directory C:\ORACLE5\PRO\PROT\MSCP.

(2) Install the library enhancements by running the INSTMSC utility and typing

```
C> INSTMSC C:\MSC\LIB
```

The install utility INSTMSC creates a library called LLIBCAP.LIB, which is a version of the Microsoft C runtime library that allows the user to link programs for protected mode. LLIBCAP.LIB is placed in the \MSCP subdirectory when INSTMSC is finished. The original Microsoft C libraries are not modified.

(3) Perform the conversion, by typing EXE2PXE <filename> at the MS-DOS operating system prompt.
The EXE2PXE utility converts .EXE files to their protected-mode equivalents (.PXE) only if the .EXE files are linked using the runtime library LLIBCAP.LIB created by INSTMSC.BAT.
The utility returns the file with the .PXE extension. In order to run this program, the user should create a command file that loads and executes the .PXE executable.

(4) Create the command file by copying PLOADR.COM to the name of the .PXE file in the MS-DOS operating system prompt:

```
C> COPY PLOADR.COM <filename>.COM
```

9.5.3 DEC Rdb/VMS

In Rdb VMS, the database application programs are developed using the library routines in the SQL/Services or the module language.

SQL/Services

SQL/Services is a client-server component of the Rdb/VMS that allows application programs running on various types of computers to access DIGITAL Standard Relational Interface (DSRI) compliant databases on other computers. The client requests a set of services from the server through a common interface. The server responds by processing client requests, calling the server function to execute requests, and sending results back through the common interface.

The SQL/Services Application Programming Interface is a set of callable routines that the client uses to access SQL/Services functions. The SQL/Services routines include association routines, SQL statement routines, result table routines, utilities routines, and data/metadata routines.

Association routines. Association routines create and terminate client-server associations and control the association environment. Specific association routines are included in Table 9.7.

Routine	Function
sqlsrv_associate	Creates a client-server association.
sqlsrv_release	Terminates a client-server association in an orderly fashion. Sends a message to the server requesting termination of the association, disconnects the network link, and releases all client resources related to the association.
sqlsrv_abort	Terminates a client-server association immediately.
sqlsrv_set_environment	Sets new values for environment variables on the server. Environment variables are used to control date, time, numeric output formats, and string-matching modes.
sqlsrv_get_environment	Gets the current setting of environment variables.
sqlsrv_set_server_class	Identifies the class of execution server processes assigned by the communication server to execute a client request once an association is established.

Table 9.7: Association routines in Rdb SQL/Services.

SQL statement routines. SQL statement routines prepare and execute SQL statements and release prepared SQL statement resources. These routines map directly to the dynamic SQL interface. Table 9.8 describes specific SQL statement routines.

Routine	Function
sqlsrv_prepare	Prepares a dynamic SQL statement.
sqlsrv_execute	Executes a prepared SQL statement.
sqlsrv_execute_immediate	Prepares and executes a SQL statement.
sqlsrv_release_statement	Releases client and server statement resources associated with a prepared statement.

Table 9.8: SQL Statement routines in Rdb SQL/Services.

Result table routines. Result table routines contain routines for fetching data from the server. Table 9.9 describes specific result table routines.

Routine	Function
sqlsrv_open_cursor	Opens a cursor by associating a cursor name with a prepared statement identifier. Also allocates the cursor data structure.
sqlsrv_set_filter	Associates a Boolean expression with a cursor to filter out unwanted rows from the result table before results are sent to the client.
sqlsrv_fetch	Retrieves one row of data from an opened cursor.
sqlsrv_fetch_many	Requests that multiple rows of data be fetched and transmitted to the client in one message.
sqlsrv_close_cursor	Closes an open cursor.

Table 9.9: *Result table routines in Rdb SQL/Services.*

Utilities routines. The utilities routines are used to allocate and deallocate memory for the SQLDA data buffer and indicator variable fields. Specific utilities routines are described in Table 9.10.

Routine	Function
sqlsrv_allocate_sqlda_data	Allocates memory for the SQLDA data buffer and indicator variable fields.
sqlsrv_free_sqlda_data	Deallocates memory for the SQLDA data buffer and indicator variable fields.

Table 9.10: *Utilities routines in Rdb SQL/Services.*

Data/metadata routines. The data/metadata routines provide access to data and metadata stored in the SQLCA and SQLDA structures. Specific data/metadata routines are described in Table 9.11.

Routine	Function
sqlsrv_sqlca_error	Returns from the SQLCA structure the error codes for the last statement executed.
sqlsrv_sqlca_error_text	Returns from the SQLCA structure the error text for the last statement executed.
sqlsrv_sqlca_num_batch_rows	Returns from the SQLCA structure the number of rows processed in a batch operation.
sqlsrv_sqlca_count	Returns from the SQLCA structure the number of rows processed by a statement.
sqlsrv_sqlda_sqld	Returns the number of active columns in the SQLDA.
sqlsrv_sqlda_column_name	Returns from the SQLDA the column name for a particular column and stores it into the variable passed in the call.
sqlsrv_sqlda_column_type	Returns from the SQLDA information about the data type of a particular column.
sqlsrv_sqlda_bind_data	Binds the storage allocated in the program to the SQLDA.
sqlsrv_sqlda_unbind_data	Releases all variables bound with the sqlsrv_sqlda_bind_data routine.
sqlsrv_sqlda_map_data	Returns from the SQLDA the type, length, null value, and address of data for a column.
sqlsrv_sqlda_unmap_data	Frees any unwanted resources used by the sqlsrv_sqlda_map_data routines.

Routine	Function
sqlsrv_sqlda_get_data	Copies data from the SQLDA to a program.
sqlsrv_sqlda_set_data	Copies column information into the SQLDA.

Table 9.11: Data/metadata routines in Rdb SQL/Services.

Example Program

An example program using the Rdb SQL/Services follows:

```
#include <stdlib.h>
#include <stdio.h>              /* Standard input/output. */
#include <sqlsrvda.h>           /* SQLDA structure definition. */
#include <sqlsrvca.h>           /* SQLCA structure, error definition.  */
#include <sqlsrv.h>             /* SQL Services structure definitions. */
static create_association();
static report_error();
main (argc, argv)
int   argc;
char     *argv[];
{
    /* Variables and structures for SQL/SERVICES API */
    int  return_code;                 /* return status value. */
    short int execute_flag;           /* Execute mode flag. */
    long int database_id = 0L;        /* Database ID. */
    char *assoc_id;                   /* association handle. */
    struct SQLCA sqlca_struc;         /* Context structure. */
    char *cursor_name = "C1";         /* Name of cursor. */
    struct SQLDA *param_sqlda;        /* Parameter marker SQLDA */
    struct SQLDA *select_sqlda;       /* Select list SQLDA */
    long int statement_id;            /* statement id */
```

```
char *stmt0 = "DECLARE SCHEMA FILENAME 'TP1'";
char *stmt1 =
     "SELECT * FROM ACCOUNT WHERE
     ACCOUNT_NUMBER = ?";
/* Set up an association with the server. */
     create_association (&assoc_id, &sqlca_struc);
     /* connect to the TP1 database */
     return_code = sqlsrv_execute_immediate(
                         assoc_id,          /* association handle.*/
                         database_id,       /* database_id, must be zero. */
                         stmt0              /* statement string. */
                         );
     if ( return_code != SQL_SUCCESS)
          return report_error(&sqlca_struc);
     select_sqlda = NULL;
     param_sqlda = NULL;
     /* Prepare the stmt1 statement. */
     return_code = sqlsrv_prepare(
               assoc_id,               /* association handle. */
               database_id,            /* database_id, must be zero. */
               stmt1,                  /* SQL SELECT statement. */
               &statement_id,          /* Prepared statement id. */
               &param_sqlda,
               &select_sqlda);
     if (return_code != SQL_SUCCESS)
          return report_error(&sqlca_struc);
     /* Allocates data for the parameter marker sqlda. */
     return_code = sqlsrv_allocate_sqlda_data(assoc_id,
                                                  param_sqlda);
     if (return_code != SQL_SUCCESS)
          return report_error(&sqlca_struc);
     /* Allocates data for the select item list sqlda. */
```

```
return_code = sqlsrv_allocate_sqlda_data(assoc_id,
                                         select_sqlda);
if (return_code != SQL_SUCCESS)
    return report_error(&sqlca_str);
printf ("Successfully compiled stmt1.\n");
/* Get the value for the parameter marker. */
get_params(param_sqlda);
/* Open cursor for the prepared statement_id SELECT
** statement.
*/
return_code = sqlsrv_open_cursor(
        assoc_id,       /* association id */
        cursor_name,    /* handle for cursor */
        statement_id,   /* handle for SELECT statement */
        param_sqlda1    /* parameter marker SQLDA */
        );
if (return_code != SQL_SUCCESS)
    return report_error(&sqlca_struc);
/* Fetch the opened cursor_name cursor. */
return_code = sqlsrv_fetch(
        assoc_id,       /* association id */
        cursor_name,    /* handle for cursor */
        0,              /* direction (reserved) */
        0L,             /* row number (reserved) */
        select_sqlda    /* select list SQLDA */
        );
if (return_code != SQL_SUCCESS)
    return report_error(&sqlca_struc);
/* Close the cursor_name cursor. */
return_code = sqlsrv_close_cursor(assoc_id, cursor_name);
if (return_code != SQL_SUCCESS)
    return report_error(&sqlca_str);
```

```
        /* Release the association with the server. */
        return_code = sqlsrv_release(assoc_id, NULL);
        if (return_code != SQL_SUCCESS)
            return report_error(&sqlca_struc);
}   /* main */
create_association(assoc_id,sqlca_str)
char            **assoc_id; /* address of association id used
                            ** in all SQL/SERVICES calls. */
struct SQLCA    *sqlca_str;  /* context structure */
{
    /* Variables and structures for SQL/SERVICES API */
    struct ASSOCIATE_STR associate_str;/* Association structure. */
    char        *node_name;         /* VMS node name. */
    char        *user_name;         /* VMS username. */
    char        *password;          /* VMS password. */
    static char read_buffer[512];    /* Protocol read buffer.*/
    static char write_buffer[512];  /* Protocol write buffer. */
    long int    read_size, write_size;/* Protocol buffer sizes. */
    int         return_code;        /* return status value. */
        /* Set the node name, username and password values for
        ** the server connection.
        */
        node_name = "NODENAME";
        user_name = "USER";
        password = "PASSWORD";
        read_size = 512;   /* protocol read buffer size value */
        write_size = 512;  /* protocol write buffer size value */
        /* Set up association structure */
        /* disable client logging.*/
        associate_str.CLIENT_LOG=0;
        /* disable server logging. */
        associate_str.SERVER_LOG=0;
```

```
        /* this is a remote session. */
        associate_str.LOCAL_FLAG = 0;
        /* use default alloc routine.   */
        associate_str.MEMORY_ROUTINE = NULL;
        /* use default free routine.  */
        associate_str.FREE_MEMORY_ROUTINE = NULL;
        associate_str.ERRBUFLEN = 512;
        /* use default error buffer. */
        associate_str.ERRBUF = NULL;
        /* Connect with the server and establish an association.
        */
        return_code = sqlsrv_associate(
                        node_name,      /* node name. */
                        user_name,      /* user name. */
                        password,       /* password. */
                        read_buffer,    /* protocol read buffer.        */
                        write_buffer,   /* protocol write buffer.   */
                        read_size,      /* read buffer size. */
                        write_size,     /* write buffer size. */
                        sqlca_struc,    /* SQLCA structure. */
                        &associate_str, /* ASSOCIATE structure. */
                        assoc_id        /* Association handle. */
                        );
        if (return_code != SQL_SUCCESS)
            return report_error(sqlca_struc);
}       /* create_association */
get_params(param_sqlda)
struct SQLDA    *param_sqlda;   /* Parameter marker SQLDA. */
{
        int   i;                /* loop counter */
        int   len;              /* temporary */
        char s[80],*p;    /* temporary */
```

```
        for (i = 0; i < param_sqlda->SQLD; i++) {
            /* SQLD contains the number of parameter markers */
            switch(param_sqlda->SQLVARARY[i].SQLTYPE) {
                /* branch on the data type of the parameter */
                case SQLSRV_ASCII_STRING:
                        /* null-terminated strings */
            case SQLSRV_GENERALIZED_NUMBER:
              do {
                        printf("Enter value for:   ");
                        printf("%s\n", param_sqlda
                        >SQLVARARY[i].SQLNAME);
                        printf("Maximum length is: ");
                        printf("%d\n", param_sqlda
                        >SQLVARARY[i].SQLLEN);
                        printf("DATA> ");
                        gets(param_sqlda
                        >SQLVARARY[i].SQLDATA);
                        len = strlen(param_sqlda
                        >SQLVARARY[i].SQLDATA);
                        if (len == 0)
                            printf("Value required. Please reenter.");
                        } while (len == 0);
                  break;
                case SQLSRV_VARCHAR: /* counted string */
              do {
                        printf("Enter value for:   ");
                        printf("%s\n", param_sqlda
                        >SQLVARARY[i].SQLNAME);
                        printf("Maximum length is: ");
                        printf("%d\n", param_sqlda
                        >SQLVARARY[i].SQLLEN);
                        printf("DATA> ");
                        gets(s);
```

```
                /* Get the length and write it into the
                ** first word of the buffer. Set a
                ** pointer to the next byte and copy
                ** in the ASCII data. */
                len = strlen(s);
                p = param_sqlda
                >SQLVARARY[i].SQLDATA;
                *(short int *)p = len;
                p += sizeof(short int);
                strncpy(p,s,len);
                if (len == 0)
                printf("Value required.  Please reenter.");
            } while (len == 0);
            break;
        case SQLSRV_GENERALIZED_DATE:
        /* null-terminated string */
            do {
                printf("Enter value for:   ");
                printf("%s\n", param_sqlda
                >SQLVARARY[i].SQLNAME);
                printf("Maximum length is: ");
                printf("%d\n", param_sqlda
                >SQLVARARY[i].SQLLEN);
                printf("Format is: ccyymmddhhmissff\n");
                printf("DATA> ");
                gets(param_sqlda
                >SQLVARARY[i].SQLDATA);
                len = strlen(param_sqlda
                >SQLVARARY[i].SQLDATA);
                if (len == 0)
                    printf("Value required.  Please reenter.");
                } while (len == 0);
                break;
```

```
204.                    default:
205.                            printf("Invalid data type: %d\n",
206.                                param_sqlda
                                    >SQLVARARY[i].SQLTYPE);
207.                            gets(s); /* dispose of value */
208.                            break;
209.                    } /* switch */
210.            } /* for */
211.            return(SQL_SUCCESS);
212. } /* get_params */
213. report_error(sqlca_str)
214. struct SQLCA    *sqlca_str;                 /* context structure */
215. {
216.            /* Print out error code */
217.            printf("The returned error  code is: %d\n",
218.                    sqlca_str->SQLCODE);
219.            return 1;
220. } /* report_error */
```

In this example program, the create_association routine in line 26 sets up the association structure and creates an association between the application and the communication server by calling the *sqlsrv_associate* routine in line 128. After setting up an association, the *sqlsrv_execute_immediate* routine in line 28, with the DECLARE SCHEMA statement as a parameter, connects the application to the TP1 database.

The *sqlsrv_prepare* routine in line 38 prepares the SELECT statement specified in the variable stmt1. If the execution of the *sqlsrv_prepare* routine is successful, the *sqlsrv_allocate_sqlda_data* routine in lines 48 and 53 are executed to dynamically allocate data and indicator variables for the parameter markers and the select list items.

In line 59, the get_params routine gets the values for the parameter markers in stmt1 and stores the values in the parameter marker descriptor area. The *sqlsrv_open_cursor* routine in line 63 opens a cursor for the prepared SELECT statement identified by the variable statement_id, using the information in the parameter marker descriptor area. After opening the cursor, the data are retrieved using the *sqlsrv_fetch* routine in line 72.

The cursor is closed by the *sqlsrv_close_cursor* routine in line 82. Finally, the *sqlsrv_release* routine in line 86 releases the association and deallocates the resources associated with the association.

In the following section, we discuss the Rdb SQL/Services routines used in this example program.

Rdb SQL/Services Routines

***sqlsrv_associate* routine.** The sqlsrv_associate routine creates a link between an application and the communication server, using the node name and the optional user name and password parameters. It also creates an association handle used in subsequent routine calls and binds specific variables to the association:

```
extern int sqlsrv_associate(
        char                    *node_name,
        char                    *user_name,
        char                    *password,
        char                    *read_buffer,
        char                    *write_buffer,
        long int                read_buffer_size,
        long int                write_buffer_size,
        struct SQLCA            *sqlca_str,
        struct ASSOCIATE_STR    *associate_str,
        ASSOCIATE_ID            *associate_id);
```

A description of the parameters in the sqlsrv_associate routine follows:

node_name	Specifies the node name of the VAX system on which the server resides.
user_name	Specifies the user name of the account within which the execution server process session runs.
password	Specifies the password of the account within which the execution server process session runs.
read_buffer	Specifies the buffer used by the API to receive messages from the communication server.
write_buffer	Specifies the buffer used by the API to build messages to send to the communication server.

read_buffer_size	Specifies the size in bytes of the API buffer that receives messages.
write_buffer_size	Specifies the size in bytes of the API buffer that sends messages.
sqlca_str	Specifies the SQLCA structure.
associate_str	Specifies an ASSOCIATE_STR structure, which is used to define optional association characteristics.
associate_id	Contains the address of the newly allocated associate_id returned by the sqlsrv_associate routine.

sqlsrv_execute_immediate routine. The sqlsrv_execute_immediate routine prepares and executes the SQL statement stored in the sql_statement parameter:

```
extern int sqlsrv_execute_immediate(
        ASSOCIATE_ID    associate_id,
        long int        database_id,
        char            *sql_statement);
```

The parameters in the sqlsrv_execute_immediate routine are

associate_id	Specifies the active association.
database_id	The database_id parameter must be set to zero. Database is referenced within the SQL statement syntax.
sql_statement	Specifies the SQL statement to be prepared and executed.

***sqlsrv_prepare* routine.** The sqlsrv_prepare routine prepares a SELECT statement:

```
extern int sqlsrv_prepare(
        ASSOCIATE_ID    associate_id,
        long int        database_id,
        char            *sql_statement,
        long int        *statement_id,
        SQLDA_ID        *param_marker_sqlda,
        SQLDA_ID        *select_list_sqlda);
```

The parameters in the sqlsrv_prepare are

associate_id	Specifies the active association.
database_id	The database_id parameter must be set to zero.

	Database is referenced within the SQL statement syntax.
sql_statement	Specifies the SQL statement to be prepared and executed.
statement_id	Contains the identifier of the prepared statement returned by the sqlsrv_prepare routine.
param_marker_sqlda	Specifies the SQLDA structure used for parameter markers.
select_list_sqlda	Specifies the SQLDA structure used for select list items.

***sqlsrv_allocate_sqlda_data* routine.** The sqlsrv_allocate_sqlda_data routine dynamically allocates data and indicator variable:

```
extern int sqlsrv_allocate_sqlda_data(
        ASSOCIATE_ID    associate_id,
        SQLDA_ID        sqlda_str);
```

The parameters in this routine are

associate_id	Specifies the active association.
sqlda_str	sqlda_str is a SQLDA structure containing a SQLVAR array. The API writes the address of the newly allocated SQLDATA and SQLIND fields into this array.

***sqlsrv_open_cursor* routine.** The sqlsrv_open_cursor routine opens a cursor for the prepared SELECT statement identified by the statement_id parameter:

```
extern int sqlsrv_open_cursor(
        ASSOCIATE_ID    associate_id,
        char            *cursor_name,
        long int        *statement_id,
        SQLDA_ID        param_marker_sqlda);
```

The parameters in this routine are described as follows:

associate_id	Specifies the active association.
cursor_name	The cursor_name parameter contains the result table identifier. All cursor operations must use the cursor_name to identify the cursor.
statement_id	Contains the identifier of the prepared statement returned by the sqlsrv_prepare routine.
param_marker_sqlda	Specifies a SQLDA structure defining the parameter marker values for the prepared SELECT statement.

sqlsrv_fetch routine. The sqlsrv_fetch routine fetches a row of data into the specified select_list_sqlda parameter:

```
extern int sqlsrv_fetch(
        ASSOCIATE_ID    associate_id,
        char            *cursor_name,
        short int       direction,
        long int        row_number,
        SQLDA_ID        select_list_sqlda);
```

The parameters in the sqlsrv_fetch routine are described as follows:

associate_id	Specifies the active association.
cursor_name	The cursor_name parameter contains the result table identifier. All cursor operations must use the cursor_name to identify the cursor.
direction	Reserved. Must be set to zero.
row_number	Reserved. Must be set to zero.
select_list_sqlda	Specifies a SQLDA structure in which to store the row.

***sqlsrv_close_cursor* routine.** The sqlsrv_close_cursor routine closes the specified cursor:

```
extern int sqlsrv_close_cursor(
        ASSOCIATE_ID    associate_id,
        char            *cursor_name);
```

The parameters in this routine are:

associate_id	Specifies the active association.
cursor_name	The cursor_name parameter contains the result table identifier. All cursor operations must use the cursor_name to identify the cursor.

***sqlsrv_release* routine.** The sqlsrv_release routine commits active transactions on the server and terminates the association. In addition, this routine disconnects the network link and releases the client association resources:

```
extern int sqlsrv_release(
        ASSOCIATE_ID    associate_id,
        char            *stat);
```

The parameters in the sqlsrv_release routine are:

associate_id	Specifies the active association.
stat	Must be a null pointer and should be set to zero.

Database Keys

Database keys are internal pointers to specific rows of a table in a database. In a SQL query, the keyword DBKEY is used to refer to the database key of a table row.

A database key provides fast access to a table row because retrieval through a database key is direct and bypasses any indexed or sequential searches. Moreover, because the access is direct, the database system locks only the row retrieved or updated and thus reduces locking of data.

The scope of a database key refers to the duration in which the database system guarantees that a particular row's database key will point to that row only and will not be reused even if the row is deleted. In the CREATE SCHEMA, DECLARE SCHEMA, and IMPORT statements, the user can specify the database key scope to be for the duration of a transaction or for the duration of an attachment to the database.

With the database key scope specified in the CREATE or DECLARE SCHEMA statements, database keys are guaranteed to be unique. Therefore, singleton SELECT statements based on database keys will always return at most one row. The returned row is always the same, unless the row was deleted.

DBKEY can be used as a value expression only in the context of a select list item or a basic predicate that equates DBKEY to another value expression. For example, to select the DBKEY of the Dept table, we execute the following SQL statement:

```
EXEC SQL SELECT DBKEY FROM Dept;
```

And, to update the EName of the Emp table using the DBKEY in the equality comparison, we execute the SQL statement

```
EXEC SQL UPDATE Emp
        SET EName = "EXAMPLE"
        WHERE DBKEY = :dbkey_var;
```

The RETURNING DBKEY clause in an INSERT statement directs SQL to return the database key for the inserted row into a host variable, as shown in the following example:

```
EXEC SQL INSERT INTO Emp(EName)
        VALUES ("USER")
        RETURNING DBKEY INTO :dbkey_var;
```

There are several restrictions that apply to a DBKEY:

(1) SQL never converts database keys to another data type. The host parameters that receive database key values should be declared as a fixed-length character strings.

(2) Database keys vary in length. Database keys are eight bytes long for base tables and (8*number of tables named in a view) bytes long for views. The host parameter should be declared long enough to hold the longest anticipated database key. If the host parameter is too short to hold a database key, SQL returns an error.

(3) Rows in result tables created by specifying functions, the GROUP BY clause, or the HAVING clause in a select expression do not have database keys associated with them.

Module Language

The SQL module language provides special keywords and syntax that allow procedures containing SQL statements to be called from any host language, including languages that are not supported by the SQL precompiler.

The SQL module language also provides a calling mechanism for host language programs to execute SQL statements contained in a separate SQL module file. The SQL module file contains module language elements that specify a single SQL module. Futhermore, a SQL module includes one or more procedures, each of which consists of parameter declarations and a SQL statement.

The host language program uses procedure calls to specify a particular SQL module procedure and supplies actual parameters to that SQL module procedure. A call to a procedure in a SQL module causes the SQL statement in the procedure to be executed.

Using SQL module language instead of precompiled SQL is advantageous for several reasons. First, module language allows SQL module procedures to be called from any host language, whereas the SQL precompiler supports only specific languages. Second, with the SQL module language, all SQL statements are contained in a separate SQL module file; therefore, the source program does not contain two languages in the same file. And third, by calling SQL modules, programs can work around the restrictions of the SQL precompiler.

Rdb SQL Module Language Syntax

The syntax of the Rdb SQL module language is as follows:

```
<module language> ::=
    MODULE [ <module name> ] LANGUAGE <language name>
    AUTHORIZATION <auth id>
    [ <declare statement list> ]
    <procedure list>
<declare statement list> ::=
    <declare statement> [ {, <declare statement>}...]
<procedure list> ::=
    <procedure> [ {, <procedure> } ... ]
<procedure> ::=
    PROCEDURE <procedure name>
    <param declaration list> ;
    <sql statement> ;
<param declaration list> ::=
        <param declaration> [ {, <param declaration> }...]
<param declaration> ::=
        { <parameter item> | SQLCA | SQLCODE |
          [<parameter>] SQLDA
        }
<parameter item> ::=
        <parameter>
        { <data type> | <domain name> | <record type> }
        [ BY DESCRIPTOR  [CHECK] ]
<record type> ::=
        RECORD
        { <item list> | FROM <path name> |
          INDICATOR ARRAY OF <array length>
                <exact numeric type>
        }
        END RECORD
<item list> ::=
        <item> [ {, <item>} ... ]
```

```
<item> ::=
            <item name> { <data type> | <record type> }
<exact numeric type> ::=
            { SMALLINT | INTEGER | QUADWORD | TINYINT }
                    [ <n> ]
            | { DECIMAL | NUMERIC }
                    [ ( <n> [ , <n> ] ) ]
<language name> ::=
            { ADA | BASIC | C | COBOL | FORTRAN | PASCAL |
            PL1 | GENERAL
            }
```

The components of this statement are described here.

MODULE [<module name>]. The <module name> is an optional name for the module. It can be any valid VMS name. If no module name is specified, the default is SQL_MODULE. The module name must be unique among the modules that are linked together to form an executable program.

LANGUAGE <language name>. The <language name> specifies the name of the host language in which the program that calls the procedures is written. GENERAL is used to represent languages that do not have the corresponding language name keywords. The host language determines the kinds of data types that the SQL module processor considers valid in the formal parameter declarations of the module. The host language also identifies the default mechanism for passing parameters to and from a host language source file.

AUTHORIZATION <auth id>. This statement specifies the authorization identifier for the default schema.

[<declare statement list>]. The declare statement can be any of the following: DECLARE SCHEMA, DECLARE CURSOR, DECLARE TRANSACTION, DECLARE TABLE, or DECLARE STATEMENT.

The <declare statement> clause is optional. All DECLARE statements must be positioned together after the language clause of the module. All DECLARE statements except DECLARE TRANSACTION can be repeated. No punctuation is required to separate DECLARE statements or to separate the declare statement section from the procedure section.

PROCEDURE <procedure name>. The procedure name is used in the host language calls to specify a particular procedure. A procedure name can be any valid VMS name.

<param declaration>. The parameter declaration section defines one or more parameters. Parameters in a SQL module procedure allow values to pass between a database, the SQL statement in a procedure, and variables in a host language program. All procedures must have a parameter to pass the value of SQLCODE from the database to the host language program.

Table 9.12 describes the elements of a parameter declaration.

Item	Description
<parameter>	The name for a formal parameter.
<data type>, <domain name>	Specifies the data type of the formal parameter. The ata type specified must be equivalent to the data type of the host variable declaration for the actual parameter. A user can specify a SQL data type by using <data type> or <domain name>. A user can also pass records and indicator arrays to SQL module language procedures and retrieve data dictionary record declarations using the <record type> clause.
<record type>	Specifies the beginning and end of the record in a module language parameter declaration. A record definition cannot contain a SQLDA, a SQLCODE, or a SQLCA. A record definiton does contain the following: *<item name>:* Specifies the name of an item in a record. Item name cannot be duplicated at the same level in the same record declaration. *FROM <path name>:* Specifies the data dictionary path name of a data dictionary record definition. *INDICATOR ARRAY OF*: Specifies a one-dimensional array of elements with a specified data type. An indicator array provides indicator parameters for fields in the host structure. The indicator array must have at least as many elements as the record defintion has.
BY DESCRIPTOR	Specifies that the formal parameter will be passed to the calling program module by descriptor.

Item	Description
CHECK	Specifies that SQL compares at run time the data type, length, and scale of the descriptor for an actual parameter to what was declared for the procedure parameter in the SQL module. If there is a mismatch, SQL returns an error.
SQLCODE	A formal parameter that SQL uses to indicate the execution status of the SQL statement in the procedure. The SQLCODE formal parameter does not require a data type declaration; it defaults to INTEGER data type. The SQLCODE parameter must be passed by reference.
SQLCA, SQLDA	A formal parameter for the SQLCA or SQLDA. The calling program module must declare a record that corresponds to the structure of the SQLCA or SQLDA, and must specify that record declaration as the calling parameter for the SQLCA or SQLDA formal parameter.

Table 9.12: Elements of a parameter declaration.

<sql statement>. The <sql statement> section refers to an executable SQL statement. The SQL statement must use names specified in the formal parameters of the procedure wherever it refers to parameters. The SQL statement must also end with a semicolon.

Example Program

The SQL module file here is referenced in the C program immediately following.

```
MODULE employees
        LANGUAGE C
        AUTHORIZATION Peterson
DECLARE SCHEMA PATHNAME 'CONFIDENTIAL'
DECLARE names cursor FOR
        SELECT EmpNo FROM Emp
        WHERE EmpName LIKE matchString
```

```
PROCEDURE SetTrans
        SQLCODE;
SET TRANSACTION READ ONLY;
PROCEDURE OpenCursor
        SQLCODE,
        matchString CHAR(14);
Open names;
PROCEDURE FetchInto
        SQLCODE,
        name CHAR(14);
Fetch names INTO name;
PROCEDURE CloseCursor
        SQLCODE;
CLOSE names;
Procedure RollbackTrans
        SQLCODE;
ROLLBACK;
```

The following example of a C program calls procedures in the above SQL module file.

```
/*
** This C program calls procedures in a SQL module to list
** employees name that matches a LIKE predicate.
*/
/* Declarations of entry points in the SQL module.
*/
extern void SetTrans(int *sqlcode);
extern void OpenCursor(int *sqlcode, char *matchString);
extern void FetchInto(int *sqlcode, char *name);
extern void CloseCursor(int *sqlcode);
extern void RollbackTrans(int *sqlcode);
main()
{
```

```
14. int sqlcode = 0;
15. char empName[15];
16. char likeString[15] = "S____";
17.         /* Start a read only transaction. */
18.         SetTrans( &sqlcode);
19.         /* Open the cursor and supply the string to be matched. */
20.         OpenCursor(&sqlcode, likeString);
21.         printf("Matching Employees:\n");
22.         do  /* Fetches the selected result to empName. */
23.         {
24.             FetchInto( &sqlcode, empName);
25.             if (sqlcode == 0)
26.                 printf("%s\n", empName);
27.         } while (sqlcode == 0);
28.         /* if sqlcode is not 100(No More Record), display an error. */
29.         if (sqlcode  != 100)
30.             printf(" SQL error code = %d\n", sqlcode);
31.         /* Close the opened cursor. */
32.         CloseCursor( &sqlcode);
33.         RollbackTrans( &sqlcode);   /* finish transaction. */
34. }   /* main */
```

In this example, lines 7 through 11 contain the external declaration of the procedures in the SQL module. The SetTrans() procedure call in line 18 executes the SetTrans SQL procedure which, in turn, executes the "SET TRANSACTION READ ONLY" statement in line 10 of the SQL module file and returns the status code in the sqlcode parameter.

The OpenCursor() procedure call in line 20 passes sqlcode and likeString as parameters and opens a cursor. The likeString parameter corresponds to the matchString formal parameter in the OpenCursor() procedure declaration in line 13 of the SQL module file. The matchString parameter is used as a variable in the DECLARE CURSOR statement in the SQL module.

The FetchInto() procedure call in line 24 passes sqlcode and empName as parameters. The value of the current row is stored in the name formal parameter of the FetchInto() procedure. The empName parameter corresponds to the name formal parameter in the FetchInto() procedure declaration in line 18 of the SQL module file. Thus, the value of empName is updated by the FetchInto() procedure call.

The CloseCursor() procedure call in line 32 closes the names cursor by executing the CLOSE names statement in line 21 of the SQL module file. And, the RollbackTrans() procedure call in line 33 rolls back the current transaction.

9.5.4 Microsoft SQL Server

The application programming interface provided by the Microsoft SQL Server is the DB-LIBRARY functions. Through DB-LIBRARY, values in program variables can be sent to the database, and data from the database can be placed in program variables for manipulation by an application.

DB-LIBRARY

DB-LIBRARY is a set of C functions and macros that allow user applications to interact with the SQL Server. DB-LIBRARY includes functions that

- initialize the connection between an application and the SQL Server
- send TRANSACT-SQL statements to the SQL Server
- process the results of a SQL statement
- handle error conditions and warning messages
- perform data type conversion
- provide information about the interaction with the SQL Server
- process browse mode
- handle text and image data types
- process control flow

The DB-LIBRARY approach is different from the "embedded SQL" type of language interface. In the embedded SQL interface, the source program must be preprocessed by a language precompiler. In the DB-LIBRARY interface, no preprocessing of the source program is required since the DB-LIBRARY functions are C functions.

Programming with DB-LIBRARY typically involves a few basic steps:

(1) Logging on to the SQL Server.
(2) Placing TRANSACT-SQL statements into a buffer and sending them to the SQL Server.
(3) Processing the results returned from the SQL Server, one

statement at a time, row by row. The results can be stored in program variables and used by the application.

(4) Handling DB-LIBRARY errors and SQL Server messages.

(5) Closing the connection with the SQL Server.

DB-LIBRARY functions communicate with the SQL Server through the DBPROCESS structure, which serves as the connection between the application and the SQL Server. An application may have more than one DBPROCESS, and each DBPROCESS is completely independent of any other DBPROCESSes.

The DBPROCESS structure consists of (1) a pointer to a command buffer that contains TRANSACT-SQLstatements for transmission to the SQL Server, (2) a pointer to result rows returned from SQL Server, and (3) information on various aspects of SQL Server interaction. Most DB-LIBRARY functions require a DBPROCESS as the first parameter, and many of the DB-LIBRARY functions extract information from the DBPROCESS. Applications access and manipulate components of the DBPROCESS structure only through DB-LIBRARY functions, not directly.

The LOGINREC structure is the login record that contains information the dbopen function uses to log on to the SQL Server.

Example Program

The following example program shows the basic framework of many DB-LIBRARY applications. The program opens a connection to Microsoft's SQL Server, sends two TRANSACT-SQL SELECT statement to the SQL Server, and processes the resulting rows.

```
/* This program connects to the SQL Server and executes two SQL
** statements. The results are retrieved and displayed.
*/
#include <sqlfront.h>
#include <sqldb.h>
/* Forward declarations of the error handler and message handler
*/
int err_handler();
int msg_handler();
main()
{
/* The connection with SQL Server. */
```

```
DBPROCESS *dbproc;
/* The login information. */
LOGINREC *login;
DBCHAR   number[40];
     /*
     ** Install user-supplied error and message
     ** handling routines.
     */
     dberrhandler(err_handler);
     dbmsghandler(msg_handler);
     /* Get a LOGINREC. */
     login = dblogin();
     /* Set up the login user name and password.
     ** Also specifies the application name as example.
     */
     DBSETLUSER(login, "user");
     DBSETLPWD(login, "password");
     DBSETLAPP(login, "example");
     /* Get a DBPROCESS structure for communication
     ** with SQL Server.
     */
     dbproc = dbopen(login, "sql_server");
     /* Retrieve some columns from the "authors" table
     ** in the "pubs" database.
     */
     /* Activate the "pubs" database. */
     dbuse(dbproc, "pubs");
     /* Put the TRANSACT-SQL statement into the command
     ** buffer.
     */
     dbcmd(dbproc, "SELECT DeptNo From Dept");
     /* The following SQL statement is send to the DB-LIBRARY
```

```
    ** by calling dbcmd() twice. A space is need at the end of
    ** the first statement to prevent the running together of the
    ** words Emp and WHERE when the second dbcmd()
    ** concatenates the two statements.
    */
    dbcmd(dbproc, "SELECT EmpNo FROM Emp ");
    dbcmd(dbproc, "WHERE EName = 'Smith'");
    /* Send the command to SQL Server for execution.*/
    dbsqlexec(dbproc);
    /* Process the results of each TRANSACT-SQL
    ** statement.
    */
    while ((return_code = dbresults(dbproc)) !=
            NO_MORE_RESULTS)
    {
        if (return_code == SUCCEED)
        {
            /* Bind results to program variables. */
            dbbind(dbproc, 1, STRINGBIND, (DBINT)0,
                number);
            /* Retrieve and print the result. */
            while (dbnextrow(dbproc) !=
                            NO_MORE_ROWS)
                {
                        printf("The number is : %s\n", number);
                } /* while (dbnextrow ...) */
            } /* if (return_code ... ) */
        } /* while (return_code ...) */
        /* Close the connection to SQL Server. */
        dbexit();
} /* main */
/* The err_handler() routine handles the DB-LIBRARY error
```

```
** messages.
*/
int err_handler(
        DBPROCESS   *dbproc,
        int         severity,
        int         dberr,
        int         oserr,
        char        *dberrstr,
        char        *oserrstr)
{
        /* if the dbproc is DEAD or NULL, return the EXIT code. */
        if ( (dbproc == NULL) || (DBDEAD(dbproc)))
            return(INT_EXIT);
        else
        {
            /* Display the error message and cancel the error. */
            printf("DB-LIBRARY error:\n\t%s\n", dberrstr);
            if (oserr != DBNOERR)
                printf("Operating-system error:\n\t%s\n",
                        oserrstr);
                return(INT_CANCEL);
        }
}   /* err_handler */
/* The msg_handler() routine handles the DB-LIBRARY warning
** messages.
*/
int msg_handler(
        DBPROCESS   *dbproc,
        DBINT       msgno,
        int         msgstate,
        int         severity,
        char        *msgtext)
```

```
109. {
110.     printf("SQL Server message %ld, state %d,",
111.             msgno, msgstate);
112.     printf(" severity %d:\n\t%s\n", severity, msgtext);
113.     return(0);
114. }   /* msg_handler */
```

This example illustrates the commonly used functions in most DB-LIBRARY applications. Two header files, *sqlfront.h* and *sqldb.h,* are required in all source files that use DB-LIBRARY functions. The sqlfront.h file defines symbolic constants such as the function return values and exit values. It also includes typedefs for data types. The sqlfront.h file must appear first in the file. The sqldb.h file contains additional definitions and typedefs, most of which are used only by the DB-LIBRARY functions. In lines 4 and 5, the sqlfront.h and sqldb.h files are included.

The *dberrhandler* routine in line 21 supplies a user function to handle DB-LIBRARY errors. When a DB-LIBRARY error occurs, DB-LIBRARY immediately calls this user-supplied error handler, which completely determines the response of DB-LIBRARY to any error that occurs. It tells DB-LIBRARY whether to abort the program, return an error code, or keep trying, in the case of a timeout error.

Value	Action
INT_EXIT	Prints an error message and aborts the program.
INT_CANCEL	Requests the DB-LIBRARY function that caused the error to return FAIL.
INT_CONTINUE	Continues to wait for one additional timeout period. At the end of that period, calls the error handler again. For nontimeout errors, this value is considered an error and is treated as INT_EXIT.

Table 9.13: *Possible values returned from the error handler routine.*

The user-supplied error handler must return one of the values listed in Table 9.13 in order to direct DB-LIBRARY to perform particular actions. If the user does not supply an error handler, DB-LIBRARY returns FAIL from the DB-LIBRARY function that caused the error and continues executing the program.

The *dbmsghandler* routine in line 22 supplies a user function to handle the SQL Server messages. When DB-LIBRARY receives a SQL Server warning or informational message, it immediately calls this message handler. The message handling function should not call any DB-LIBRARY functions because calls to DB-LIBRARY functions can generate messages, which could result in infinite recursion. Thus, the message handler must return a value of zero to DB-LIBRARY.

The *dblogin* routine in line 24 allocates a LOGINREC structure for use in the dbopen routine. The *DBSETLUSER* routine in line 28 sets the user name field of the LOGINREC structure; the *DBSETLPWD* routine in line 29 sets the password field of the LOGINREC structure; and the *DBSETLAPP* routine in line 30 sets the application name field of the LOGINREC structure. After setting the various components of the LOGINREC structure, the *dbopen* routine in line 34 uses the information in the LOGINREC structure to communicate with the network and then logs in to the SQL Server. The dbopen routine also allocates and initializes a DBPROCESS structure.

The *dbuse* routine in line 39 activates the "pubs" database. The *dbcmd* routine in lines 43, 50, and 51 stores the specified SELECT statements to the command buffer of the DBPROCESS structure. These stored SQL statements are executed by the *dbsqlexec* routine in line 53.

The *dbresults* routine in line 57 sets up the next statement in the command batch for processing. The dbresult routine is called until there are no more results to be processed. The *dbbind* routine in line 63 binds a result column to a program variable. The *dbnextrow* routine in line 66 gets the next row of the retrieved data from the DBPROCESS. The dbnextrow routine is called until there are no more rows.

Finally, the *dbexit* routine in line 74 closes and frees all DBPROCESS structures created in the application.

In the following section, we discuss the DB-LIBRARY routines used in the example program.

DB-LIBRARY Functions

dblogin. The syntax of the dblogin function is

```
LOGINREC    *dblogin()
```

This function allocates a LOGINREC structure for use in the dbopen routine. All components in the LOGINREC are initially set to NULL. Various other functions supply components of the LOGINREC. For instance, the DBSETLUSER and DBSETLPWD functions set the user name and password that DB-LIBRARY used when logging in, and the DBSETLAPP sets the name of the application.

dbopen. The syntax of the dbopen function is as follows:

```
DBPROCESS *dbopen(    LOGINREC     *login,
                      char         *servername)
```

This function allocates and initializes a DBPROCESS structure. It also sets up communication with the network, logs in to the SQL Server, and initializes any default options.

In the function, the login parameter is a pointer to a LOGINREC structure. The servername parameter specifies the SQL Server that the user wants to connect to. If this is a null string, a local SQL Server is used.

If everything is correct, a DBPROCESS pointer is returned. Otherwise, NULL is returned if a DBPROCESS structure could not be allocated or initialized, or if the user failed to login to the SQL Server.

dbuse. The syntax of the dbuse function is:

```
RETCODE dbuse(        DBPROCESS    *dbproc,
                      char         *dbname )
```

This function executes a TRANSACT-SQL USE statement for the specified database for a particular DBPROCESS. Specifically, it sets up the statement and calls the *dbsqlexec* and *dbresults* functions.

The dbuse function uses the dbproc provided by the caller and its command buffer. Any existing statements in the buffer are lost, and the command buffer is cleared by the dbuse function when it is finished.

The dbproc parameter specifies the DBPROCESS structure, and the dbname parameter specifies the database name to be switched to. The dbuse function returns SUCCEED or FAIL, depending on the result of executing the USE statement on the specified database.

dbcmd. The syntax of the dbcmd function is

```
RETCODE     dbcmd(    DBPROCESS    *dbproc,
                      char         *cmdstring )
```

This function adds text to the command buffer in the DBPROCESS structure. Specifically, it adds to the existing command buffer but does not delete or overwrite the current contents except after the buffer has been sent to the SQL Server by executing the dbsqlexec or dbsqlsend routine.

In the function, the dbproc parameter specifies the DBPROCESS structure that is the handle for a particular workstation/SQL Server process. Additionally, the cmdstring parameter specifies a null-terminated character string that is copied into the command buffer. The dbcmd function returns SUCCEED or FAIL.

The user can call dbcmd repeatedly. Sequential calls of dbcmd are concatenated together. It is the application's responsibility to ensure that any necessary blanks appear between the end of one line and the beginning of the next.

After a call to the dbsqlexec or dbsqlsend function, the first call to either the dbcmd or dbfcmd function automatically clears the command buffer before the new text is entered. However, if the database option DBNOAUTOFREE is set, the command buffer is cleared only by an explicit call to the *dbfreebuf* function.

The *dbfcmd* function is similar to the dbcmd function except that dbfcmd takes additional parameters and interprets the cmdstring as a format string that is passed to sprintf along with any additional parameters.

dbsqlexec. The syntax of the dbsqlexec function is

```
RETCODE      dbsqlexec( DBPROCESS    *dbproc )
```

This function sends SQL statements stored in the command buffer of the DBPROCESS to theSQL Server. Once dbsqlexec has returned SUCCEED, *dbresults* must be called to process the results.

This function also returns SUCCEED or FAIL. The most command reason for failing is a TRANSACT-SQL syntax error or the SQL Server permission violation. Other reasons include incorrect column or table names. The dbsqlexec function also fails if previous results were not processed or if no statement was specified.

If a series of commands is sent to the SQL Server and if one or more of the commands contains a syntax error, the SQL Server processes none of the commands, and dbsqlexec returns FAIL.

dbresults. The syntax of the dbresults function is

```
RETCODE      dbresults( DBPROCESS *dbproc )
```

This function sets up the next statement in the command batch for processing. It is called after the dbsqlexec or dbsqlok function returns SUCCEED. The dbresults function must be called for each statement in the command batch, regardless of whether the statement returns a row. If the application code does not know how many statements are in the batch, dbresults can be called until it returns NO_MORE_RESULTS, which indicates that there are no more results to be processed. The dbresults function also returns SUCCEED or FAIL.

dbbind. The syntax of the dbbind function is

```
RETCODE dbbind(
        DBPROCESS     *dbproc,
        int           column,
        int           vartype,
        DBINT         varlen,
        BYTE          *varaddr )
```

This function binds result columns to program variables. Data comes back from the SQL Server one row at a time. Dbbind directs DB-LIBRARY to copy the data for a regular column into a program variable. When each new row containing regular data is read using the dbnextrow or dbgetrow function, the data from the designated column in that row is copied into the program variable with the address specified in the varaddr parameter. A separate dbbind call must be executed for each regular column that is to be copied. A result column can be bound to only one program variable. The calls to dbbind must be made after a call to dbresults and before the first call to dbnextrow.

In the function, the dbproc parameter specifies the DBPROCESS structure that is the handle for a particular workstation/SQL Server process. The column parameter specifies the column number of the row data that is to be copied to a program variable. The first column is number one.

The vartype parameter describes the data type for binding. It corresponds to the data type of the program variable that receives the copy of the data from the DBPROCESS. The varlen parameter specifies the length of the program variable in bytes. For fixed-length vartypes, such as MONEYBIND, this length is ignored. For character, text, binary, and image types, varlen must describe the total length of the available destination buffer space. The varaddr parameter specifies the address of the program variable to which the data is copied. Calling dbbind with a NULL varaddr parameter breaks a previously set binding. The dbbind function returns SUCCEED or FAIL.

dbnextrow. The syntax of the dbnextrow function is

```
STATUS    dbnextrow( DBPROCESS    *dbproc )
```

This function makes available the next data row through the dbproc. Normally, each row is processed in turn by repeatedly calling dbnextrow. If row buffering is disabled, the user must continue calling dbnextrow until it returns NO_MORE_ROWS.

The dbnextrow function returns one of the following five values:

REG_ROW: Returned if a regular row is read.

The computeid of the row: Returned if a compute row is read.

NO_MORE_ROWS: Returned if there are no more rows to be read or if the statement did not return any rows.

BUF_FULL: Returned if buffering is turned on and reading the next row would cause the buffer to be exceeded.

FAIL: Returned if the function was unsuccessful.

dbexit. The syntax of the dbexit function is

```
void dbexit(void)
```

This function closes and frees all DBPROCESS structures created as a result of an application program. No value is returned by dbexit.

Browse Mode Support

The SQL Server allows users to browse through database rows and to update their values one row at a time. This process involves several steps because each row must be transferred from the database into program variables before it can be browsed and updated. Since a row being browsed is not the actual row residing in the database, the program must be able to ensure that changes to variable values can be used reliably to update the original database row. In a multiuser situation, the program must ensure that updates made to the database by one user do not incorrectly overwrite updates recently made by another user. A timestamp column in the database tables provides the information necessary to regulate this type of multiuser updating.

To browse and update a table, the user must complete the following steps:

(1) Select result rows containing columns derived from one or more database tables.

(2) If appropriate, change values in the columns of the result rows, not the actual database rows, one row at a time.
(3) Update the original database tables, one row at a time, using the new values in the result rows.

In the SQL Server, these steps are implemented in a program as follows:

(1) Execute a SELECT statement to generate the resulting table. The SELECT statement must include the FOR BROWSE clause.
(2) Copy the result column values into program variables, one row at a time, and change the values if appropriate.
(3) Execute an UPDATE statement that updates the database row corresponding to the current result row. The WHERE clause of the UPDATE statement must reference the timestamp column to handle multiuser updates. Such a WHERE clause can be obtained via the dbqual function.

In order to use browse mode, several criteria must be met. First, the SELECT statement must end with the keywords FOR BROWSE. In addition, the tables to be browsed and updated must have a unique index and a timestamp column. The third criteria requires that a valid correspondence be established between the result column and the database column to be updated. And, last, the browse mode usually requires two DBPROCESS structures—one for selecting the data and another for performing updates based on the selected data.

Table 9.14 describes the browse mode functions.

Function	Description
dbcolbrowse	Indicates whether the source of a result column can be updated via browse mode.
dbcolsource	Returns a pointer to the name of the database column from which the specified result column was derived.
dbfreequal	Frees memory allocated by the dbqual function.
dbqual	Returns a pointer to the WHERE clause that specified the timestamp condition and the unique index values of the current row.
dbtabbrowse	Indicates whether a particular table can be updated in browse mode.

Function	Description
dbtabcount	Returns the number of tables involved in the current SELECT statement.
dbtabname	Returns the name of a table based on its number.
dbtabsource	Returns the name and number of a table from which a particular result column was derived.
dbtsnewlen	Returns the length of a new value in the timestamp column after a browse mode udpate.
dbtsnewval	Returns the new value of the timestamp column after a browse mode update.
dbtsput	Puts the new value of the timestamp column into the given table's current row in the DBPROCESS.
dbwritetext	Sends a text or image value to the SQL Server.

Table 9.14: The browse mode functions in DB-LIBRARY.

Example Program

The following example program shows how some browse mode functions are used:

```
/**********************NOTE ***********************
** The Emp table must has a timestamp and an unique index
** in order to be browsable.
*/
#include <sqlfront.h>
#include <sqldb.h>
/* Forward declarations of the error handler and
** message handler.
*/
int err_handler();
int msg_handler();
```

```
main()
{
/* The connections with SQL Server. */
/* DBPROCESS used for SELECT with FOR BROWSE
** clause.
*/
DBPROCESS *dbproc;
/* DBPROCESS used for update. */
DBPROCESS *updproc;
/* The login information. */
LOGINREC *login;
DBCHAR   name[40];
/* The qualptr is used to point to the WHERE
** clause appropriate for updating dbproc's
** current data row.
*/
char              *qualptr;
/*
** Install user-supplied error and message
** handling routines.
*/
          dberrhandler(err_handler);
          dbmsghandler(msg_handler);
          /* Get a LOGINREC. */
          login = dblogin();
          DBSETLUSER(login, "user");
          DBSETLPWD(login, "password");
          DBSETLAPP(login, "example");
          /* Get a DBPROCESS structure for communication
          ** with SQL Server.
          ** dbproc is used for the execution of the SELECT statement.
          ** updproc is used for the update operation.
```

```
*/
dbproc = dbopen(login, "sql_server");
updproc = dbopen(login, "sql_server");
/* Activate the "property" database. */
dbuse(dbproc, "property");
/* Put the TRANSACT-SQL statement into the command
** buffer.
** The FOR BROWSE clause is specified in the
** SELECT statement.
*/
dbcmd(dbproc,
        "SELECT EName FROM Emp FOR BROWSE");
/* Send the command to SQL Server for execution.*/
dbsqlexec(dbproc);
/* Process the results of each TRANSACT-SQL
** statement.
*/
while ((return_code =  dbresults(dbproc)) !=
          NO_MORE_RESULTS)
{
        if (return_code == SUCCEED)
        {
                /* Retrieve and print the result. */
                while (dbnextrow(dbproc) !=
                NO_MORE_ROWS)
                {
                    /* Retrieve the name value.*/
                    name = *((DBCHAR *) (dbdata(dbproc, 1)));
                    /* Update the record with the retrieved
                    ** name equals Smith.
                    */
                    if (strcmp(name, "Smith")  == 0)
```

```
                              {
                                  /* The dbqual() routine returns a
                                  ** WHERE clause suitable for use in
                                  ** updating the current row of the
                                  ** dbproc.
                                  */
                                  qualptr = dbqual(dbproc, 1, "");
                                  /* Update the name field to contain
                                  ** "Testing" using the updproc.
                                  */
                                  dbcmd(updbproc,
                                  "UPDATE Emp SET EName=");
                                  dbfcmd(updproc, "%s ", "Testing");
                                  /* Specified the qualifying WHERE
                                  ** clause obtained from the dbqual
                                  ** function.
                                  */
                                  dbcmd(updproc, qualptr);
                                  dbsqlexec(updproc);
                                  dbresults(updproc);
                                  /* Deallocate the memory allocated
                                  ** by the dbqual() function.
                                  */
                                  dbfreequal(qualptr);
                              }   /* if (strcmp(....) )*/
                          }   /* while (dbnextrow().... ) */
                  }       /* if (return_code ...)  */
          }       /* while (return_code ... ) */
          /* Close the connection to SQL Server. */
          dbexit();
}         /* main */
```

In this example, two DBPROCESSes are allocated in lines 45 and 46. The dbproc is used to select data from the Emp table. In order to use browse mode, the FOR BROWSE clause is specified in the SELECT statement of the dbproc in line 55.

In lines 85 to 94, the updproc is used to update the current data row of the dbproc. The *dbqual* function in line 81 is used to provide a pointer to a WHERE clause suitable for use in updating the current row of the dbproc. The *dbfreequal* function in line 98 is used to deallocate the memory allocated by the dbqual function.

9.6 Summary

In this chapter, we examined the different types of application programming interfaces supported in the IBM OS/2 Extended Edition Database Manager, the ORACLE Server RDBMS, DEC's Rdb/VMS, and the Microsoft SQL Server. We summarize the application programming interfaces supported in each system in Table 9.15.

Application Programming Interface	ANSI SQL89	IBM EE	ORACLE Server	DEC Rdb/VMS	Microsoft SQL Server
Dynamic SQL	No	Yes	Yes	Yes	No
Embedded SQL	Yes	Yes	Yes	Yes	No
Direct Call Interface	No	No	Yes	Yes	Yes
Module Language Support	Yes	No	No	Yes	No
Fetch Multiple Rows	No	No	Yes	No	No
SQL Cursors	Yes	Yes	Yes	Yes	No

Table 9.15: Summary of the application programming interfaces.

Chapter 10
Distributed Database Systems

The proliferation of powerful workstations interconnected by local area networks, along with the increasing interconnections from workstations to mainframes, has led to a tremendous potential for sharing data among heterogeneous hardware and software systems. In fact, the emergence of distributed databases has been touted as one of the most significant new developments in the commercial database world since relational databases. Though there is considerable confusion and hype in the marketplace over the definition of a distributed database, the reality is that a distributed database system potentially can provide a wide spectrum of capabilities. And though many years of research have gone into the development of technical solutions for distributed database problems, the first commercial distributed database systems have emerged only recently with a very rudimentary set of capabilities. No vender has yet announced, let alone delivered, a full-function distributed database implementation.

We open this chapter in Sections 10.1 and 10.2 with a brief discussion on the rationale behind the distributed database and a look at two approaches for developing a distributed database. Then, in Section 10.3 we examine some of the desirable capabilities of a distributed database system. This is followed in Section 10.4 by a look at Date's rules for distributed databases.

In Sections 10.5 and 10.6, we go on to identify the more important technical problems that must be addressed in the implementation of a distributed database, and we examine the level of distributed capabilities found in four popular SQL-based database servers. As always, we conclude the chapter with a summary.

For our discussions in this chapter, we make use of the following working definition of a distributed database:

A distributed database system is a collection of data which is distributed across many computers possibly at different sites. The computers are connected by a communication network. The system must support local applications at each computer as well as global applications in which more than one computer is involved.

[Ceri and Pelagatti, 1984]

10.1 Why Distributed Databases?

The earliest distributed database research emphasized the locality of reference, increased processing capacity, scalability of operations, and improved data availability afforded by a distributed database in a homogeneous environment; however, most commercial applications are not quite ready to take advantage of many of the esoteric capabilities addressed by the early prototypes—systems that required development of a distributed database from scratch. The desire for site autonomy and the high cost of migrating existing applications to a truly distributed database (one that presents a single-system image to all applications) have deterred database software vendors from developing systems that require the relinquishing of control over local data and/or the rewriting of existing applications.

In recent years, the demand for distributed database capabilities has been fueled mostly by the decentralization of business functions to address customer needs and by the mergers and acquisitions that run so rampant in the corporate world. As a result, there is a strong requirement among enterprises for the ability to cross-correlate data stored in different existing heterogeneous databases. At the same time, advances in hardware, software, and networking technologies have made decentralization reliable and cost effective and the development of heterogeneous distributed database capabilities more feasible.

10.2 Approaches for Developing a Distributed Database

There are at least two distinct approaches for developing a distributed database: (1) a *bottom-up* approach of integrating existing databases running on heterogeneous systems into a virtual distributed database for global applications, while at the same time preserving existing applications that run against individual single-site databases; and (2) a *top-down* approach of decomposing a logically centralized database schema (against which all applications run) into fragments and allocating those fragments to sites of a distributed system [Ceri et al., 1987].

10.2.1 Bottom-up Integration

The bottom-up integration approach is particularly suitable for enterprises with a decentralized organization and computation structure. The proliferation of departmental and personal databases in these enterprises is likely to have created "islands of information" in a heterogeneous hardware and software environment. Under such a scenario, a heterogeneous distributed database can provide a virtual, integrated view of the existing databases. Because enterprises have invested tremendous amounts in their existing DBMS environments, it is important that the development of a heterogeneous distributed database preserves existing single-site applications as well as the autonomy of departments owning the existing databases.

10.2.2 Top-down Distribution

The top-down distribution approach is more suitable for a homogeneous environment where uniformity can be exploited to provide improved performance and reliability. The approach is particularly appropriate for distributed databases that are developed from scratch (such as when a new database is designed for use in a distributed environment). Alternatively, when a single-site database has grown to exceed the operating limits of its existing host database system, it becomes desirable to reconfigure the existing single-site database into a distributed database that spans multiple homogeneous sites. Under this approach both fragmentation transparency and replication transparency are more readily supported. In addition, global data integrity constraints can be automatically enforced by the distributed database system, since all applications will be operating against the same global database schema.

Within the top-down design approach, the global conceptual schema of a distributed database is first defined. Integrity constraints can be specified on objects in this global schema without regard to how they would eventually be allocated to sites in the distributed database system. Next, data objects in the global schema are optionally divided into fragments. Subsequently, each object or object fragment is allocated to a site, or optionally is replicated at multiple sites. Finally, physical database design (such as choosing the set of indexes to be maintained) is performed on each allocated object or object fragment.

The most important reason for using the top-down approach to design a distributed database is to maximize the data independence afforded to applications. With all applications working against the same global database schema, it becomes possible to dynamically alter the allocation of data to sites in the distributed system. This optimizes the prevailing access pattern without incurring the high cost of application conversion. Of course, to fully exploit this flexibility, the database designer needs tools to monitor access patterns as well as to evaluate the merits of different data allocation strategies.

10.3 Spectrum of Distributed Capabilities

As discussed by Sheth and Larson [1990] and Ozsu and Valduriez [1991], the characteristics of a distributed database systems can be measured along three dimensions: autonomy, distribution transparency, and heterogeneity.

10.3.1 Autonomy

Autonomy refers to the distribution of control. It represents the degree to which sites within the distributed database system may operate independently. When a distributed database is built on top of existing databases, an important measure of autonomy is whether single-site applications can continue to run.

One extreme in the autonomy dimension is *tight coupling* among sites, which presents the illusion of a single integrated database to users and applications. Each site in the distributed database system has complete knowledge of the state of the system and can control the processing of user requests that span data at multiple sites.

An intermediate alternative is *semiautonomy*, where sites in the distributed database system voluntarily decide to participate in the federation and make their data sharable. Typically, each local system requires some modifications to become aware of other sites in the federation.

Another extreme is *total isolation.* Each site in the distributed database system is a stand-alone server and is unaware of the other sites. In this case, the distributed database system must be completely layered on top of the local systems, and its capabilities to coordinate and optimize activities that span multiple sites may be severely limited.

10.3.2 Distribution Transparency

Distribution transparency refers to the extent to which the distribution of data to sites (including the fragmentation and replication of logical data objects and their allocation) is shielded from users and applications. It represents the degree of freedom a database designer may have in distributing data to trade off

- storage cost
- retrieval and update efficiency and
- overheads for maintaining intersite constraints like fragment integrity and replica consistency

In general, the following data distribution strategies are possible (as identified in IBM [1989e]):

Basic distribution tables: The unit of distribution is at the level of individual tables. Each table can be stored at a site where it is most frequently accessed.

Extracted tables: This is an inexpensive form of replication. The user extracts a table using an arbitrary query on tables in the distributed database and stores the result at one site. Once extracted, there is no longer any linkage between the source tables and the target table. In most cases, the extracted table is treated as read only, representing a single snapshot of the source tables at a certain point in time.

Snapshot tables: A snapshot table is similar to an extract table except that linkage is maintained between the source tables and the snapshot table. Periodically, the snapshot table is refreshed by reprocessing the distributed query associated with the snapshot table definition. In some cases, the snapshot table may also be refreshed using a differential file mechanism, which keeps track of and transmits just those changes made to the source tables since the last refresh operation.

Replicated tables: For this distribution strategy, multiple copies of the same logical table are stored in different sites of the distributed database system. The usual objectives for replication are retrieval efficiency and reliability. When multiple copies are kept up-to-date, queries can be processed against any one of them. Updates, on the other hand, need to be applied to all the copies synchronously.

Fragmented tables: A fragmented table is divided into several usually nonoverlapping portions. The objective is to store portions of a logical table at different locations that maximize locality of reference. Two basic strategies for fragmentation are possible: *horizontal fragmentation*, which refers to the division of the original table into subsets of rows, and *vertical fragmentation,* which refers to the division of the original table into subsets of columns.

The characteristics of rows that belong to a particular horizontal fragment are usually specified using a simple qualification predicate. Only rows that satisfy the associated predicate are found in a given horizontal fragment. Two kinds of horizontal fragmentation can further be distinguished. *Primary fragmentation* refers to the division of a table into fragments using several predicates that involve only attributes in the table. *Derived fragmentation* refers to the fragmentation of a table T_2 based on the fragmentation scheme applied to another related table T_1. For example, suppose T_2 contains a foreign key column that references or matches a primary key column in T_1. T_1 is decomposed into two horizontal fragments F_{11} and F_{12}. Then T_2 can be divided into two corresponding horizontal fragments F_{21} and F_{22}, such that F_{21} contains rows with foreign keys that match primary keys of rows contained in F_{11}, and F_{22} contains rows with foreign keys that match primary keys of rows contained in F_{12}. In this case, if there is a need to join T_1 and T_2 based on the primary key/foreign key referential relationship, we can infer that both F_{11} joined with F_{22} and F_{12} joined with F_{21} will be empty. Thus, we can compute the join between T_1 and T_2 as the union of two joins between corresponding fragments: F_{11} with F_{21}, and F_{12} with F_{22}.

To provide better control on redundancy, horizontal fragments are typically kept disjoint (i.e., their associated qualification predicates cannot be simultaneously satisfiable by any row in the table). Vertical fragmentation, on the other hand, requires the replication of one or more key columns in each fragment. In general, fragments should be designed so it is possible to reconstruct the original table, by taking either the union of fragments or the join of fragments. In addition to horizontal and vertical fragmentation, *mixed fragmentation* can also be used by alternating horizontal and vertical fragmentation (i.e., applying horizontal fragmentation to vertical fragments and vertical fragmentation to horizontal fragments).

It should be noted that the above notions of distribution are stated from the viewpoint of top-down distributed database design. When a distributed view is constructed over autonomous existing databases, these notions must be adapted slightly. Instead of distributing a logical table into fragments, the database designer must treat existing tables as fragments of a global logical table. Whereas disjointness of horizontal fragments is relatively easy to enforce in a top-down designed distributed database, disjointness of horizontal fragments in a bottom-up integrated distributed database may not always be assumed, unless the fragment definition predicate is attached as an integrity constraint on fragments that may reside at database systems supplied by different vendors.

Just as relational databases are expected to provide a high degree of data independence by hiding the physical representation from end users and applications, distributed databases ideally should hide different aspects of data distribution from end users and applications. This gives rise to the notions of location transparency, fragmentation transparency, and replication transparency. Supporting these notions pervasively impacts metadata management, concurrency control, reliability management, and query optimization in the distributed database system, as we discuss in Section 10.4.

10.3.3 Heterogeneity

Heterogeneity in distributed systems may occur in various forms, ranging from hardware platforms, operating systems, networking protocols, and local database systems. Different hardware and operating systems may use different data representations (e.g., different representations for floating point numbers, different byte ordering for integers, and different encoding for characters). Additionally, different communication protocols may require the use of gateways, which are difficult to implement because of the heterogeneity involved. And finally, different database systems may use different data models, thereby posing schema translation and query translation problems.

Many database software vendors have targeted cross-platform compatibility as a major selling point. As a result, they have ported their systems to run in heterogeneous hardware and system software environments, thereby providing the simplest form of heterogeneous distributed database access. A bigger challenge, however, comes from heterogeneities due to differences in the local database systems. An enterprise may have a decentralized organizational structure, and different organizations within the enterprise may have different functional requirements and hence different database systems. At the same time, database systems acquired over a period of time may be based on different technologies. Because some of the early heterogeneous database system prototypes were concerned with integrating systems that supported hierarchical, network, and relational database systems, they were bogged down dealing with differences such as database structures, built-in integrity constraints, and query languages. But with the popularity of the relational data model and the standardization of SQL, integrating heterogeneous SQL-based servers into a distributed system is a much more tractable problem. However, even when local database systems are all SQL based, semantic heterogeneity problems (such as differences in naming conventions, differences in scale, missing data, and conflicting data) must be solved. At the same time, without any standardization in transaction management primitives and techniques (e.g., concurrency control, commit, and recovery protocols), heterogeneity at the system level poses major obstacles to achieving distributed transactions across heterogeneous local systems.

10.4 Technical Problems

Though vendors of SQL-based database servers have started to incorporate distributed database capabilities into their products, many technical problems must be addressed to provide a full-function distributed database solution. In this section, we discuss the major technical problems in developing a full-function distributed database system and some of the solutions proposed in the related literature.

10.4.1 Directory Management

Directory management refers to the management of schema and other forms of metadata in the distributed database system. To process a query or a transaction against data stored at multiple sites, metadata describing the underlying data must be available at the site where the query or transaction is submitted. In general, metadata can be stored centrally, distributively, or in a fully replicated manner. Each of these approaches has different tradeoffs.

For example, storing the metadata centrally at some master site minimizes updating costs but at the expense of retrieval efficiency and availability. At the same time, it would not be consistent with the goal of maximizing site autonomy. Should the master site fail, other sites would not be able to continue query and transaction processing.

Alternatively, storing the metadata distributively implies that a distributed query against the metadata may have to be posed before any user query can be processed. This storage option maximizes autonomy of the individual sites but at the expense of retrieval efficiency.

The other option—storing the metadata in a fully replicated way—makes the data readily available for query and transaction processing. However, this method introduces the complexity of maintaining mutual consistency among copies of the replicated metadata. There is also the potential for loss in site autonomy; a site may not be able to modify its metadata in the event of failures at other sites.

A comprise between storing metadata distributively and storing fully replicated metadata is to store metadata together with the data being described, and to cache metadata at sites where queries are submitted. Of course, when metadata is cached, it becomes necessary to verify the freshness of metadata used in the processing of a given query.

Schema Caching

In practice, a more optimized approach to storing metadata is to augment the distributed storage approach with caching of metadata from remote sites. That is, each site stores metadata describing data under its own control. In addition, each site keeps a cache of metadata retrieved from other sites. Before processing a distributed query, a site examines its cache to determine if metadata concerning remote tables referenced in the query is available locally. If so, no retrieval will need to be performed against remote metadata.

Schema caching leads to the additional technical problem of how to ensure that the cached metadata is up-to-date. Two approaches are available: either the owner of the metadata can actively invalidate other sites' caches whenever the owner makes a schema change, or a version numbering scheme can be used to validate the cached metadata used in processing a distributed query. For example, when a subquery is sent to a remote site for processing, the originating site specifies a version number of the cached metadata used to formulate the subquery. If the remote site undergoes schema changes after the time the metadata was cached by the query's originating site (i.e., the schema version number is incremented), then the subquery will be rejected by the remote site. In this case, the query's originating site must refresh its own metadata cache and restart processing for the failed query.

Dependency Tracking

In a production environment where queries and transactions are of a repetitive nature, it is advantageous to select an optimized plan for a given query or transaction at compile time instead of at execution time. That is, it should be possible to store the optimized execution plan and reuse it for many different executions. However, this notion introduces a dependency from the stored execution plan to the underlying metadata. That is, if the metadata changes, the stored execution plan must be invalidated and regenerated. This dependency problem exists even for centralized database systems that support compile time optimization. It is exacerbated in a distributed environment because of the distributed nature of the metadata.

One way to simplify dependency tracking is to sacrifice site autonomy. For example, when one site caches (imports) metadata from another site, the exporting site can register that export. Thus, when the exporting site needs to change a schema, it can ensure that all importing sites are notified before the change is made. (Thus, the schema change will fail if any importing sites are not operational at the time.) At the importing sites, access plans can be generated based on the imported schema information, and dependencies of those access plans can be recorded locally. Since the imported schema information is guaranteed to be up-to-date, optimized subplans can be sent to a remote site for execution without revalidation. This is because prior to a schema change at the export site, all the import sites are requested to invalidate any access plans that are dependent on the imported schema information.

10.4.2 Distributed Concurrency Control

Concurrency control is necessary to ensure that multiple users do not interfere with each other. The problem is more complicated in a distributed environment than a centralized environment. There is also one major difference: whereas intratransaction concurrency is not particularly important in a centralized system running under a single processor, it is critical in a distributed environment if the presence of multiple processors is exploited for processing the same transaction.

Deadlock Avoidance or Detection

Locking is widely accepted as the method of choice for synchronizing concurrent users. When transactions span multiple database servers, and when each server acquires locks on behalf of a distributed transaction in an incremental fashion, it is possible to run into distributed deadlocks that may not be detected by individual servers using local locking information.

Whereas some centralized database systems perform continuous deadlock detection, deadlock avoidance or periodic deadlock detection is more appropriate in a distributed environment because of the communication overhead for maintaining the locking information used to achieve continuous deadlock detection.

In general, deadlock avoidance is simpler to implement than deadlock detection, but it has the disadvantage of unnecessarily rolling back transactions. It is most suitable for an environment that includes heterogeneous servers. Periodic deadlock detection requires the collection of 'waits-for' information from multiple sites to determine if there are cycles in the global 'waits-for' graph. Some decentralized algorithms for detecting deadlocks do not require that all 'waits-for' information be gathered at one central site. However, such algorithms usually assume a simplified transaction execution model in which each transaction is active at one site at a time, thus implying that there is no intratransaction concurrency. Unless these decentralized algorithms are generalized inexpensively to deal with a more general transaction execution model, their practicality is limited.

Distributed Deadlock Avoidance

A conservative scheme for using locking in a distributed environment is to disallow deadlocks from occurring. Suppose a unique priority can be assigned to each transaction in the distributed database system. It is then possible to selectively grant locks to transactions in such a way that deadlocks can never occur. For example, the *wait-die* and *wound-wait* strategies [Rosenkrantz et al., 1978] are used to determine the appropriate actions to take when a transaction T_i requests a lock that is currently held by T_j:

wait-die: If priority(T_i) > priority(T_j) then Ti waits, else T_i dies.

wound-wait: If priority(T_i) > priority(T_j) then wound T_j, else T_i waits.

The terms *wait, die,* and *wound* are interpreted from Ti's point of view. Wait refers to T_i queuing after T_j to wait for the lock. Die refers to T_i committing suicide and restarting. Wound refers to an attempt by T_i to preempt T_j by requesting the distributed transaction manager to abort T_j. However, T_i must still wait for T_j to release the lock before it can proceed, and the request to abort T_j may not always succeed. It is possible that T_j might have already committed by the time the request to abort arrived at the distributed transaction manager. Even so, the contested lock will be released by T_j, and T_i will be able to acquire the desired lock and proceed.

One way to assign priorities to transactions is to make use of their relative ages or timestamps: the older the transaction, the smaller the timestamp and the higher the priority. In this case, a distinct timestamp must be generated for each transaction at the time the transaction starts. The simplest strategy to guarantee that the timestamps generated by different sites in a distributed database system are unique is to treat each timestamp as a concatenation of two numbers: (1) the local clock at the transaction's home (originating) site forming the high-order bits and (2) the home site's unique site number forming the low-order bits.

Decentralized Deadlock Detection

Path pushing is a decentralized deadlock detection technique first pioneered in IBM's R* prototype. It detects global deadlocks without centrally collecting all the waits-for information from all sites in the distributed database system. Periodically, each site analyzes its local waits-for graph (WFG) for cycles and lists all paths in the WFG. For each path in the form T_i -> ... -> T_j, it sends the path information to every site where Tj might be blocked because of a lock wait.[1] As originally designed, a transaction in R* is active at one site at a time, making it easy to determine exactly what site should receive information concerning a particular path in the WFG. Suppose T_3 is initially executing at site 1. When T_3 needs to access some data from site 2, it does a remote procedure call (RPC) to site 2, and its activities at site 1 are suspended until the RPC returns. In other words, the path pushing algorithm sends the information about a particular path only when the transaction at the end of the path has initiated an RPC to another site. Since only one RPC can be sent on

---

1 If the subtransactions of a transaction are actively acquiring locks at different sites simultaneously, it may be difficult to determine the sites where Tj might be active and hence the set of sites that should receive the path information.

behalf of a transaction from one site at a time, information about a particular path needs to be pushed only to one other site.

When a site receives a WFG path from another site, it augments its own WFG with the received information. If the augmented WFG contains a cycle, it selects a victim transaction and attempts to abort that transaction. If it finds a newer or longer path that was not previously present in the local WFG and that satisfies the criterion for being pushed, it forwards this information to appropriate sites.

Consider the following WFGs at sites 1, 2, and 3:

WFG^1: T_1 -> T_2 -> T_3, and T_3 has made a RPC to site 2

WFG^2: T_3 -> T_4, and T_4 has made a RPC to site 3

WFG^3: T_4 -> T_2

When site 1 sends its path information to node 2, the augmented WFG at site 2 becomes

WFG^2: T_1 -> T_2 -> T_3 -> T_4

Since site 2's WFG has changed, it sends its path information to site 3, whose WFG now becomes

WFG^3: T_1 -> T_2 -> T_3 -> T_4 -> T_2

WFG^3 now contains the cycle involving T_2, T_3, and T_4.

Replica Update Synchronization

If the distributed database system supports replication transparency, then it is necessary to synchronize updates to replicated data. If the system also supports the notion of a primary copy of each replicated data object, it is possible to funnel write locks through the primary copy and to propagate such locks to the other replication sites. On the other hand, if the purpose of replication is to provide high availability, then it is appropriate to treat all copies as equals. In this case, a write-write conflict between two transactions can easily turn into a deadlock situation. For example, transaction T_1 locks copy C^1 and then attempts to lock copy C^2. Meanwhile, transaction T_2 attempts to lock the two copies in reverse order. Since each is requesting a lock held by the other, T_{16} and T_2 are deadlocked. To minimize the cost for propagating updates to replicated copies, it is often desirable to batch together the acquisition of update locks at replication sites at the end of a transaction. The potential danger here is that the probability of deadlocks will increase.

10.4.3 Distributed Transaction Management

A distributed transaction is a sequence of operations involving data from multiple sites that must be carried out as one atomic unit. For instance, consider a transfer of funds between two accounts belonging to different subsidiaries of a bank holding company. Suppose each subsidiary maintains it own account database. First, the application debits $10,000 from the source account in the first subsidiary, then it credits $10,000 to the target account in the second subsidiary. Because the transaction involves two databases, this transaction may have to be committed sequentially at the two databases. That is, the debit is committed at the first database, and then the credit is committed at the second database. However, if the network connection fails after the application debits the source account but before the target account can be credited, then the owner of the first account has effectively lost the funds being transferred. Thus, to ensure transaction atomicity, either both databases must commit the transaction or both must abort it.

The challenge of distributed transaction management is to make sure that each transaction is executed in an atomic fashion, and that updates performed by one transaction are seen by another transaction in their entirety, or not all. If data replication is supported transparently, then mutual consistency among the replicas and continued accessibility in the presence of site failures must also be addressed.

Two-phase Commit

The problem of atomic commitment is to ensure that all participants of a distributed transaction either commit or abort. The fundamental requirements for achieving atomic commitment are as follows:

(1) Each participant must arrive at the same commit or abort decision.
(2) Each participant has veto power; unanimous consensus is required for a commit decision.
(3) Each participant must not reverse its decision once a unanimous decision is reached.

The conventional approach to achieving atomic commitment is to use a two-phase commit protocol. This protocol involves the use of a *transaction coordinator* (which can be served by one of the transaction's participants) to collect the necessary status information from all participants of a distributed transaction. During the first phase, the coordinator requests each participant to prepare to commit the transaction. The coordinator then waits for votes from the participants. If all votes are positive, then the coordinator instructs all participants to commit; otherwise, the coordinator instructs those participants that have voted yes to abort. (Those that have voted no can go ahead and abort their local portion of the distributed transaction without waiting for the final decision from the coordinator.) In general, prior to casting a yes vote, a participant is free to unilaterally abort the transaction. However, once a participant sends a yes vote to the coordinator, the participant must wait for the final commit or abort decision from the coordinator and then terminate the transaction accordingly.

When the user issues the COMMIT WORK statement in SQL, the first phase of the two-phase commit process begins. The coordinator then sends *PREPARE* messages to the participants in parallel. Each participant that is willing to commit the transaction force writes a *prepare* log record before returning a *YES VOTE* to the coordinator. The participant is now said to be in the *prepared* state. If a participant is not willing to commit the transaction, it force writes an *abort* record and returns a *NO VOTE* to the coordinator. Since each participant is allowed to veto the commitment of a transaction, a participant that votes no can go ahead and abort the transaction, release its locks, and forget about the transaction. The coordinator forgets about the transaction after receiving acknowledgments from all the participants.

After the coordinator has received votes from all participants, the second phase of the two-phase commit protocol begins. If all votes are positive, the coordinator force writes a *commit* log record, moves to the *committing* state, and sends *COMMIT* messages to the participants. Each participant, on receiving the *COMMIT* message, force writes a *commit* log record, sends an acknowledgment to the coordinator, completes commit activities for the transaction (such as releasing locks), and forgets about the transaction. If at least one vote is negative, the coordinator force writes an *abort* log record and sends *ABORT* messages only to those participants that have voted positively. Each participant, on receiving the *ABORT* message, force writes an *abort* log record, sends an acknowledgment to the coordinator, completes abortion of the transaction, and forgets about the transaction.

The purpose of requiring participants to acknowledge both *COMMIT* and *ABORT* messages is to make sure that they are aware of the final outcome of the transaction, before the coordinator forgets about the transaction. By force writing *commit* and *abort* log records, a participant never has to ask the coordinator about the outcome of the transaction during recovery processing.

Decentralized Termination

A simple two-phase commit algorithm presents one problem: if the coordinator fails after it has collected all the positive votes but before it sends the commit decision, then all the other participants must remain blocked (that is, they will be unable to release locks on resources held by the transaction) until the coordinator recovers. To get around this problem, a decentralized termination protocol can be used to minimize the amount of blocking in the event of coordinator failure. In such an instance, the participants can communicate with each other and determine whether any one of them has already committed or aborted the transaction. If so, all other participants that are prepared can follow suit and adopt the same decision. Of course, such a strategy would require that each participant knows the identities of all other participants. Therefore, when the coordinator sends the *PREPARE* messages to the participants, it is possible to piggyback on those messages information about the identities of the participants, so no extra messages should be incurred during normal operations.

Three-phase Commit

The three-phase commit protocol is designed to allow sites that remain operational to safely terminate a distributed transaction in the presence of coordinator site failure. During the second phase, the participants do not directly commit the transaction. Instead, they only enter into a *prepared-to-commit* state. By doing so, it becomes possible to elect a new coordinator should the existing coordinator fail. The new coordinator can then determine to commit or abort the transaction without worrying about the possibility of contradicting the decision of the original coordinator. When the original coordinator recovers it simply defers to the decision reached by participating sites that have remained operational, rather than resuming its previous coordinator role.

When the user issues the *COMMIT WORK* statement in SQL, the first phase of the three-phase commit process begins. The coordinator then sends *PREPARE* messages to the participants in parallel. Each participant that is willing to commit the transaction force writes a *prepare* log record before returning a *YES VOTE* to the coordinator. The participant is now said to enter the *prepared* state. If a participant is not willing to commit the transaction, it force writes an *abort* record and returns a *NO VOTE* to the coordinator. Since each participant is allowed to veto the commitment of a transaction, a participant that votes no can go ahead and abort the transaction, release its locks, and forget about the transaction.

When the coordinator receives all *YES VOTEs*, it sends *PRECOMMIT* messages to the participants. The coordinator only sends *COMMIT* messages to the participants when it has received acknowledgments (*ACK* messages) to the *PRECOMMIT* messages.

The termination protocol for three-phase commit is based on the following principle: If at least one participant that remains operational has not entered the precommit state, then the transaction can be safely be aborted; if at least one participant that remains operational has entered the precommit state, then the transaction can be safely committed.

Because the above two conditions are not mutually exclusive, there are situations where it is safe to either commit or abort the transaction. A termination protocol that always commits a transaction when it is safe to either commit or abort is said to be *progressive*. However, the simplest strategy to terminate a three-phase commit is to make use of a centralized, nonprogressive protocol. The first step involves electing a new coordinator. The coordinator then proceeds accordingly:

(1) If the new coordinator is in the precommit state, it sends *PRECOMMIT* messages to all the other participants that are operational. It then waits for acknowledgments before sending *COMMIT* messages to the operational participants.
(2) If the new coordinator is already in the commit state, it sends *COMMIT* messages to the operational participants.
(3) Otherwise, it sends *ABORT* messages to the operational participants.

If the new coordinator has not already entered the precommit state, the protocol can be made progressive by requiring the new coordinator to inquire about the recorded status of the transactions for all operational participants. Thus, if any of the operational participants are in the precommit state, the transaction can be committed.

While the three-phase commit protocol eliminates blocking situations that arise due to site failures, it is liable to terminate a transaction in a nonatomic fashion if network partitioning occurs. That is, if the network is partitioned because of communication failures, there is the danger that one group of participants of a distributed transaction may decide to commit the transaction while another group may decide to abort the transaction. This shortcoming is not found in the two-phase commit protocol. Later in this chapter, we describe how the three-phase commit protocol can be adapted into a quorum-based commit protocol that is resilient to network partitions.

Replica Recovery

Since a major objective for replicating data is to improve availability, it is imperative that retrievals and updates continue in the presence of failures at one or more replication sites. Thus, replicas stored at failed sites can become out-of-date. Therefore, when a site recovers from a previous failure, it must bring its replicas up-to-date before using them to process new transactions. It is important that such recovery be performed in a differential fashion to minimize the amount of data transfer required. That is, the recovering site should obtain updates it missed during its failure from other replication sites and re-apply them, instead of obtaining a complete copy of each replicated object from another site. Furthermore, it is desirable to have recovery of replicated data at a recovering site take place incrementally. For example, when a replicated table is updated, it should be usable for processing new transactions. It should not be necessary to wait for the recovery of all tables that have replicas at the recovering site before any of those tables can be used to process new transactions.

Network Partition Complications

The problems associated with achieving non blocking atomic commitment and replicated update control are complicated by the potential partitioning of the communication network. A *network partition* occurs when sufficient failures among links in the network result in groups of sites being isolated from each other. Under such a scenario, when site A cannot communicate with site B, it cannot assume that the latter is not operational. Instead, site A must make the worst case assumption that site B is operating within another partition of the network. To achieve atomic commitment, a coordinator must now ensure that no other coordinators in other partitions of the network may come to different decisions about terminating a transaction. In such a case, the notions of *commit* and *abort quorums* should be introduced, requiring the coordinator to obtain the appropriate quorum before terminating a transaction. To guard against updates to a replicated data object in different partitions of the network, it is also necessary to introduce the notions of *read* and *write quorums*. In other words, some minimal number of copies of a replicated data object must be present within a partition before that object can be read or written.

Quorum-based Commit

The three-phase commit protocol described earlier can be made resilient against network partitions through the introduction of *commit* and *abort quorums*:

- Each site i involved in the transaction is assigned a positive and integral number of votes V_i.[2]
- Let V be the sum of the votes of all sites involved in the transaction.
- A commit quorum of V_c votes must be collected before the transaction is committed.
- An abort quorum of V_a votes must be collected before the transaction is aborted.
- V_a and V_c must be chosen such that $V_a + V_c$ is greater than V.

The quorum-based three-phase commit protocol works as follows:

- After sending *PRECOMMIT* messages in the second phase, the coordinator tries to collect V_c positive votes before sending *COMMIT* messages to the participants.
- If one or more negative votes are received instead, the coordinator sends *PREABORT* messages to the participants and waits for their acknowledgments before sending *ABORT* messages.

In this protocol, termination and restart operations are slightly more complicated, compared to the nonblocking three-phase commit protocol. Restarting sites must participate in the formation of quorums. Furthermore, sites that have participated in building a commit quorum cannot subsequently change their direction and participate in building an abort quorum. Therefore, after a new coordinator has been elected and has solicited state information from the participants, a centralized termination protocol for the quorum-based three-phase commit functions as follows:

(1) If at least one site has committed, the coordinator sends *COMMIT* messages to the other participants.

(2) If at least one site has aborted, the coordinator sends *ABORT* messages to the other participants.

(3) If the number of votes from sites in the precommit state is greater than or equal to V_c, the coordinator sends *COMMIT* messages to the other participants.

(4) If the number of votes from sites in the preabort state is greater than or equal to V_a, the coordinator sends *ABORT* messages to the other participants.

---

2 This number can be different for each site.

(5) If the number of votes from sites in the precommit state, plus the votes from sites that are in the prepared state is greater than or equal to V_c, the coordinator sends *PRECOMMIT* messages to those sites that are in the prepared state, and waits for condition #3 above to occur.

(6) If the number of votes from sites in the preabort state, plus the votes from sites that are in the initial or prepared state, is greater than or equal to V_a, the coordinator sends *PREABORT* messages to those sites that are in the initial or prepared state, and waits for condition #4 above to occur.

(7) Otherwise, the coordinator continues to wait to hear from recovering sites.

Replica Control in a Partition Prone Network

The problem of maintaining consistency of a replicated distributed database is magnified if network partitioning occurs as a result of communication failures. During a network partitioning situation, the network is split into two or more partitions of operational sites. Sites within each partition can communicate with each other but not with sites in other partitions. From the point of view of sites in any single partition, the situation is indistinguishable from the simultaneous failure of all sites in other partitions. Thus, if network partitioning is a possibility, then sites cannot trust their own perception of the states of other sites; any site that is incommunicado may actually be operational in another partition on the network. Therefore, special care must be taken so that participants in a transaction terminate their subtransactions consistently, and that replicated copies of data are not updated in multiple partitions in an inconsistent way.

The fundamental problem of managing replicated data is that partitioning is symmetric: when site A cannot communicate with site B and considers site B unavailable, site B may, in turn, assume that site A has become unavailable. Therefore, partition-resilient replica control protocols typically exploit some asymmetry to distinguish partitions holding accessible logical data objects from partitions holding inaccessible objects:

Site majority protocol: Within this protocol, all data objects are accessible only in the partition that contains a majority number of sites in the network. This implies that sites in minority partitions cannot perform any update access to their stored data. Notice that in the presence of a potential network partition, the availability of a logical data object is unaffected by its replication factor. While straightforward to implement, this protocol does not guarantee high data availability.

Copy majority protocol: In this protocol, a particular data object is accessible only in a partition that contains a majority number of copies of that object. This allows the database designer to fine tune the availability of the data objects.

Weighted majority protocol: This protocol is similar to the copy majority protocol, except that copies of data objects at different sites are assigned different weights. Majority is then interpreted as a weighted sum that exceeds the weighted sum of all copies in other partitions. Thus, strategically placed copies can be given higher importance by being assigned heavier weights.

Quorum-based protocol: With this option, each copy of a logical data object is assigned a number of votes. Associated with the logical data object is the number of votes required for a read operation to succeed (*read quorum*) and for a write operation to succeed (*write quorum*). A data object is accessible only if a quorum is established when physical operations are applied to copies. In other words, even a read operation must ensure that a majority number of copies are accessible.

Virtual partition protocol: This protocol is an optimized version of the quorum-based protocol, which maximizes the efficiency of read operations. It makes use of the notion of a virtual partition that consists of a collection of sites that can cooperate in transaction processing. By requiring that sites join a virtual partition in a controlled way, a data object is made read accessible or write accessible if the number of votes held by copies in the virtual partition exceeds the read (or write) threshold for that object at the time the virtual partition is established. The quorum-based protocol, on the other hand, requires that votes be counted whenever a logical operation is translated into physical access.

10.4.4 Distributed Database Administration

In this section, we address the problems related to the administration of a distributed database. These problems include providing a naming scheme that will make tables from multiple sites visible to an application, granting appropriate privileges to remote users, and archiving distributed data to guard against catastrophic failures.

Distributed Object Naming

To reference data objects at multiple sites, each data object must be uniquely named. One way to guarantee that all generated names are unique is to use a name server. However, this reduces site autonomy: should the name server fail, no other sites will be able to add or drop database objects. Alternatively, the name space can be partitioned so that each site can generate unique names without conflict. One simple strategy to achieve name space partitioning is to qualify all database and user names with a site name. For example, IBM's R* makes use of systemwide names that are made up of four components:

<owner's home site name>

<owner name>

<table name> @

<birth site>

Authorization Control

At one extreme, authorization control can be decentralized. Each user can be assigned a login ID at each local database. Permissions are granted by local database administrators and enforced by local database management systems. Intermediately, authorization control can utilize systemwide user IDs but with permissions granted and enforced at the local databases. At the other extreme, authorization control can be completely centralized. For instance, each user is given a systemwide login ID; permissions are granted on a systemwide basis by a systemwide database administrator over an integrated view of the distributed database; and enforcement is carried out by a systemwide global query processor.

Each server in the distributed system has a set of users known to it. If server A only knows about local users, other remote users requiring access to data stored at A must provide a login ID that is known to A. In other words, a user may have to use different login IDs in order to access data at different sites. On the other hand, if user names are qualified by site names, and if the authorization subsystem can deal with privileges granted to remote users, then a user can use a single login ID to access data from multiple sites.

One potential advantage of centralized authorization control is that a user can be given access to certain distributed aggregated views while being denied access to the underlying raw data. For example, consider two tables Employees (emp#, salary) and

Works_for (emp#, dept#) that are located at different sites. It may be desirable to grant select privilege to certain employees on a distributed view Avg_dept_sal (dept#, avg_sal), which was obtained by joining the Employees and Works_for tables, rather than granting the employees select privilege to the underlying tables.

Archival Checkpoints

An archival checkpoint is essentially a consistent snapshot of a distributed database. To provide recovery from committed, but erroneous, transactions, the distributed database must be restored to some previous consistent state, and transactions that have committed beyond that point must be rolled forward. Additionally, recovering from media failure where both the database and the recovery log are lost requires the use of a global consistent snapshot. In this case, the only way to regain consistency is to globally restore the database back to some previous consistent state. The probability of such catastrophic failures can be reduced if the log and the database are stored on different disk drives, and if the log is locally replicated. In other words, if erroneous transactions are logically undone by running compensating transactions, and if logs are duplicated or triplicated, then the global checkpointing problem may be finessed.

10.4.5 Distributed Query Optimization

The major difference between query optimization in a distributed environment and query optimization in a centralized environment is that the distributed environment adds the cost of intersite communication. Furthermore, dimensions for optimization are added to the distributed environment when additional levels of transparencies are introduced.

Join Sequencing

The complexity of join sequencing is compounded in a distributed environment by communication costs. Also, depending on the particular networking environment, it may make sense to minimize response time instead of minimizing the total weighted sum of CPU, I/O, and communication costs. (For example, for a lightly loaded distributed database system, it may be desirable to trade total weighted cost for improved response time, by taking advantage of the idled processors for more parallel processing.)

Binding Operation to Site

Whenever a high-level operation involves data from more than one site, it is possible to perform the operation at different sites. For example, to join a table from site 1 with a table at site 2, it is possible to choose site 1, site 2, or even some other site 3 as the execution site.

In general, the choice of execution site will affect the transmission costs incurred for shipping the operands to that site, as well as the costs for processing subsequent operations. Cost is affected because the result of the operation will be located at the execution site, and that result may be needed for a subsequent operation performed at yet another site.

There are a number of important methods for joining a pair of tables R and S, which reside at sites 1 and 2, respectively. (Each method has a symmetrical counterpart in which the roles of R and S are exchanged. Let's assume R is the outer table and S is the inner table in the following discussion.)

Ship one operand: Ship S to site 1 and perform the join based on "local optimization." This method has variants according to the method used for the local join.

Semijoin (R, S): Project S on the join attribute to obtain S', then ship S' to site 1. At site 1, join S' with R, and transmit the result R' to site 2. Finally, join R' with S at site 2.

Distributed nested loop: For each row of R, send a request to site 2 for the matching rows from S. This method allows for the use of available indexes on S at site 2.

Distributed merge scan: Sort the outer table R. For each distinct join column value of R, request from site 2 the matching rows from S.

Ship both operands: Ship both tables to a third site and perform the join at that site (in anticipation that the result will be needed at the third site either for subsequent operations or as the final output for the query).

In evaluating the cost of each alternative, the corresponding local processing costs and message costs must be summed.

Central Versus Distributed Query Compilation

A query against distributed data can be compiled either at a central site (at the site where the query is submitted), or compiled distributively at those sites that contain data referenced in the query.

Compiling at a central site generally implies that authorization control will be checked at that site and that this central site will send optimized subplans to the execution sites. One consequence of this approach is that if the query submission site is subverted by unauthorized users, security in the entire distributed system may be compromised. The alternative to centralized compilation and authorization checking is to have only the query submission site select a high-level execution plan, and to instruct each of the execution sites to optimize its individual piece of the distributed query. Under this scheme, authorization control can be checked at the individual sites. The basic tradeoff is efficiency versus site autonomy. If maximum efficiency is to be achieved, then centralized compilation may be preferred. On the other hand, if sites cannot trust each other blindly, or if heterogeneous components at different sites are involved, then distributed query compilation is essential.

The one other advantage of using distributed query compilation is that upgrading database system software is much easier at each site without global synchronization. Compiled execution plans generated at one site will not have to be executed at another site.

Fragment Access Optimization

The problem of fragment access optimization arises when the distributed system provides fragmentation transparency. For example, consider a table R fragmented into R_1 and R2 at different sites, and a table S fragmented into S_1 and S_2 at some other disjoint set of sites. Now consider a join between R and S. It is possible to reconstruct R and S from their fragments before doing the join. Alternatively, the join can be performed distributively. That is, it can be computed as the union of four fragment-level joins: R_1 join S_1, R_1 join S_2, R_2 join S_1, and R_2 join S_2. In general, the join operation can be distributed over the union operation—totally, partially (reconstruction of just the left operand or just the right operand), or not at all. Because the costs associated with different distribution strategies vary, and because no single strategy dominates all others under all circumstances, fragment access optimization requires the estimation of costs for different strategies, and the selection of the cheapest one.

It is also possible that the fragment definition for R is derived from the fragment definition of S. Consequently, it may be inferred that R_1 joined with S_2, and R_2 joined with S_1 will both be empty. In other words, the join can be computed as the union of R_1 joined with S_1, and R_2 joined with S_2.

Replica Access Optimization

When the distributed database system supports replication transparency, another dimension in query optimization becomes relevant. Essentially, when a replicated table is referenced in a query, the database system has the freedom of using any of the copies for processing the query. Using different copies can lead to very different data transmission costs. When a fragmented table R is to be joined with a replicated table S, the number of possibilities is further compounded: it may be desirable to use more than one copy of S simply because different copies of S may be co-located with different fragments of R.

Optimization in a Multidatabase System Environment

Query optimization in a multidatabase system environment is complicated by the autonomy and heterogeneity requirements. Sheth and Larson [1990] identify three feasible query optimization design approaches for such an environment:

Simplest strategy: Each remote table referenced in a distributed query results in a single table query to the corresponding site retrieving the minimal subset of rows and columns needed for processing the query. The results of all the subqueries are assembled at the query's originating site for final processing. This strategy essentially treats each remote site as an access method that can support simple selection and projection operations on individual tables.

Slightly optimized strategy: The global query is decomposed into a set of maximal subqueries, one for each site that contains one or more tables referenced in the query. This optimization requires minimal intelligence in the distributed query optimizer to identify the maximal subqueries that can be processed at each site; it relies on the individual site to optimize the subquery sent to it.

More optimized strategy: Rather than always sending the results of the subqueries to the query's home or coordinator site, they may be sent to participant sites. This allows operations to be performed in such a way that communications costs are minimized.

10.4.6 Distributed Integrity Maintenance

Increasingly, semantic integrity constraints associated with a database are centrally enforced by the database system, rather than being implemented by front-end applications. This guarantees that there are no trap doors to violating the database's integrity. To support distribution transparency, a truly distributed database system must be prepared to enforce integrity constraints that span data residing at multiple sites.

Fragment Integrity

To achieve locality of reference, it is often desirable to divide a top-down designed database into fragments and to assign those fragments to different sites. A table can be divided into horizontal or vertical fragments. Each horizontal fragment can be defined in terms of a fragment qualification predicate. (Vertical fragments are simply projections that include the primary key.) When an update is conducted against a fragmented table and the fields used in the fragmentation predicates are updated, rows should be migrated from one fragment to another. If the database system provides fragmentation transparency, then the migration of rows from one fragment to another should also be automated. An inexpensive and pragmatic alternative may be to disallow updates on fields used in fragmentation qualification predicates. This puts the burden on applications that want to perform such operations to decompose them into deletions from the source fragments, followed by insertions into the target fragments.

Distributed Integrity Constraints

When a distributed database is designed top-down, the logical schema is defined first. Subsequently, tables may be fragmented, replicated, and allocated to different sites. If referential integrity constraints or uniqueness constraints exist in the logical schema, and if the data involved in a particular constraint is allocated to different sites, then an enforcement scheme for such global integrity constraints must be devised.

10.5 Truly Distributed Capabilities (Date's Rules)

Various industry experts have defined rules or yardsticks for assessing the level of capabilities provided by a distributed database system, just like Codd has defined the rules for measuring the faithfulness of a relational implementation [Codd, 1985]. One such rule set has been put together by C.J. Date of the Codd and Date Consulting Group [Date, 1987]. The fundamental principle behind Date's Rules for Distributed

Databases is that a distributed database system should look exactly like a nondistributed system to the end-user or application programmer. Subsidiary to this principle are 12 rules, which can be divided into three groups based on our previous discussions on the three dimensions of distributed database capabilities.

The first three rules are related to the autonomy dimension discussed in Section 10.3:

Rule 1. Local autonomy: Local data should be locally owned and managed. Security, integrity, and storage representation must be locally controlled. There are, however, exceptions to this rule. For example, integrity constraints may have to span multiple sites. Also, whenever a site participates in a distributed transaction and agrees to precommit the transaction, it must temporarily relinquish its control over local data involved in the transaction, and it must await a decision from the transaction coordinator regarding the final (commit or abort) fate of the transaction. In other words, local autonomy and other rules in Date's 12 subsidiary rules may have conflicting requirements, and it may not be possible to satisfy all of these rules in any single distributed database implementation.

Rule 2. No reliance on a central site for any particular service: This rule guards against any site becoming a performance/reliability bottleneck. The implication of this rule is that schema management, query processing, concurrency control, and recovery management must all be conducted in a decentralized fashion.

Rule 3. Continuous operation: There should not be any planned shutdowns. Thus, the adding or removing of sites to the distributed database system, creating or dropping tables, and upgrading the *DBMS* release at one site should cause little or no interruption to the operation of the entire distributed database system.

The next five rules are related to the notion of distribution transparency, which was also discussed in Section 10.3:

Rule 4. Location independence: Users need not know where data is physically stored. As a result, application logic can be simplified and data migration to achieve locality of reference can be made transparent.

Rule 5. Fragmentation independence: It should be possible to divide a logical table into fragments for storage at different sites in order to improve locality of reference. Users do not need to be aware of the fragmentation in their formulation of queries and updates. The distributed database system will avoid accessing irrelevant fragments while processing a retrieval or update request. As mentioned earlier, this rule may conflict with the objective of local autonomy (Rule 1).

Rule 6. Replication independence: It should be possible to store copies of a table at different sites to improve locality of reference and continued availability in the event of site failures. Again, users should not be aware of the replication. Instead, the distributed database system should optimize the selection of copies for retrievals and propagate updates to all the available copies. Copies that become outdated as a result of site failures must be rolled forward automatically before being used in subsequent query and transaction processing. Again, this rule conflicts with the objective of local autonomy (Rule 1). Under a network partitioning scenario, a site may, in some cases, not be able to access even its local copies of replicated data objects unless it is willing to jeopardize global consistency and transaction serializability in the distributed database.

Rule 7. Distributed query processing: Where appropriate, query processing should be carried out in a distributed fashion. For example, it should not be necessary to move all relevant data to the query initiation site to process operations that reference data from multiple sites.

Rule 8. Distributed transaction management: A transaction is a unit of work, a unit of concurrency, and a unit of recovery. Just like a transaction in a centralized database system, a distributed transaction that updates tables from multiple sites must be atomic, serializable, and durable. If sites fail in the course of distributed transaction processing, recovery (timely, consistent termination) of the subtransactions at participating sites must be automated. As discussed earlier, this rule may conflict with the objective of local autonomy (Rule 1) because of the potential for a participant to become blocked during a multiphase commit protocol due to the untimely failure of the coordinator(s).

The final four of Date's 12 rules are related to the heterogeneity dimension discussed in Section 10.3:

Rule 9. Hardware independence: The same distributed database system software should run on different hardware systems and should participate as equal partners in the distributed system.

Rule 10. Operating system independence: The same distributed database system software should run on different operating systems. Sites running on different operating systems must be able to participate in the same distributed database system.

Rule 11. Network independence: It should be possible to interconnect sites of the distributed database systems on local area networks and wide areas networks, using different networking protocols such as SNA, DECNet, TCP/IP, and OSI.

Rule 12. DBMS independence: It should be possible for local database systems supplied by different vendors to participate in the same distributed database system.

As Date points out, there is no such thing as an "ultimate" distributed database system. Different users will attach different degrees of importance to different objectives. While it is useful to identify the many objectives of developing a distributed database system, we must bear in mind that some of these objectives (rules) may conflict with others. For example, local autonomy (Rule 1) is not necessarily compatible with distributed transaction management (Rule 8), fragmentation independence (Rule 5), and replication independence (Rule 6). Distributed transaction management requires sites to participate in atomic commitment protocols like two-phase or three-phase commit. Once a site has acknowledged a request to prepare to commit a distributed transaction, it must relinquish control over the ultimate fate of the transaction to the transaction's coordinator. Likewise, the needs to keep table fragments consistent with their definitions and replicated data in synchronization may imply that when a site is involved in a network partition, it may not be allowed to read or update a local replica, lest transaction serializability be lost.

10.6 Case Studies

In this section, we examine the rudimentary distributed database capabilities implemented in each of the popular SQL-based servers covered in this book.[3] Our emphasis is on capabilities available on the OS/2 platform. In some cases, related products provided by the

---

3 In the case of IBM OS/2 Extended Edition Database Manager, which does not currently implement any distributed database capabilities, we turn to IBM's widely described R* prototype for our case study. The R* prototype is expected to significantly influence future distributed database implementations, both inside and outside IBM.

same vendors may have more advanced capabilities under other operating system platforms. We will only briefly touch on some of these more advanced capabilities.

10.6.1 IBM OS/2 Extended Edition Database Manager

The Extended Edition Database Manager supports neither transactions that span multiple databases at different nodes nor queries that span multiple databases. However, as early as 1988, IBM announced extensions to the Common Programming Interface (CPI) under its System Application Architecture (SAA). These extensions support heterogeneous distributed database access against four IBM relational database products running on different operating system platforms, including the OS/2 Extended Edition Database Manager, DB2, SQL/DS, and SQL/400.

IBM's Distributed Database Strategy

Though IBM has developed the most complete distributed database system prototype under the R* project, it has been slow to deliver any commercial distributed database capabilities. In an IBM-sponsored supplement to the September 1989 issue of *DBMS* magazine, IBM espoused the following milestones toward developing fully distributed database support [IBM, 1989e]:

Remote request: A request is essentially a SQL statement. With remote requests, a user can read and update data at a remote site. To issue a remote request, a user first connects to a remote database site and then issues a single SQL request. The remote site executes the request, returns the results and then implicitly commits the transaction.

Remote unit of work: A group of requests can be executed as an atomic unit (transaction) at a remote site. An application can read or update data at multiple sites, with the restriction that each transaction must reference only tables from one site.

Distributed unit of work: Each request can be executed against a single site, and the requests within a distributed unit of work (transaction) collectively can execute on multiple sites. The requests can be committed or recovered as a unit.

Distributed request: Requests involving multiple tables at multiple sites are possible. In addition, several such requests can be grouped as a transaction.

In other words, support for queries and updates against multiple tables at multiple sites in the same SQL statement will not be available until the final phase of IBM's distributed database development. Put yet another way, the more complex issues like location transparency, fragmentation transparency, and replication transparency also won't be addressed until the final phase.

Currently, the notion of a distributed unit of work is not uniformly supported against IBM's relational database systems. It is only supported against DB2 sites but not against SQL/DS sites or against the database managers of OS/400 and OS/2 Extended Edition. Furthermore, a distributed unit of work against multiple DB2 sites is restricted to update tables from only a single site.

Though IBM has yet to ship any real distributed database product, given the development history of the DB2, SQL/DS, and OS/2 Extended Edition Database Manager, and given the influence of the original System R prototype on these products, it is natural to assume that the distributed capabilities prototyped in R* (the distributed version of System R) will find their way into future IBM database product releases. The following sections highlight some of the approaches adopted in the R* prototype.

R* Objectives

R* is a homogeneous distributed database system. All sites in the system execute the same database management software on the same operating system platform, and they communicate using the same networking protocol. The architecture of the R* implementation has been influenced heavily by the following design objectives:

Distribution transparency: Queries posed in SQL should not be sensitive to the location of the referenced tables. It should be possible to migrate tables from one site to another. System administration activities must be possible both locally and remotely.

Site autonomy: The database is distributed over hardware controlled by different administrative organizations. Therefore, the design of the distributed database system must consider the legitimate need of each site to control its own data. That is, each site must be able to access its own data when the network is not available. Each site also must have authorization control over its local data. When multisite queries are bound to local data, it must be possible to invalidate that binding locally without obtaining the consent of remote sites that may be unavailable at the time.

Object Naming

The site autonomy objective dictates that the object name space within the distributed database system be partitioned by site. Specifically, each table within the distributed database must be uniquely identifiable. Each site must be able to create unique names for tables without consulting other sites. Furthermore, the distribution transparency objective requires support for migrating tables from one site to another (to improve access efficiency) without affecting existing applications. R*'s naming convention to satisfy these requirements is to make use of four-part systemwide names (SWN) for objects such as tables and views. Each SWN includes the creator's user ID, the creator's home site, the object name, and the object's birth site. The first two components together identify a user in the distributed system. The first three components collectively provide unique identification for each object, among objects born within the same site. Since each site has a unique site name, each is free to give birth to new objects with unique SWNs without having to consult other sites. The SWN for an object never changes, even when it is migrated from one site to another. Consequently, applications can refer to objects by their SWNs without any sacrifice in location independence. R* also supports the definition of synonyms for SWNs so that SWNs are not required to be exposed to users and application programs.

Database Introduction

To meet R*'s objective of site autonomy, two sites must be explicitly introduced to each other before they can cooperate in distributed query and transaction processing. This is accomplished with a new INTRODUCE DATABASE statement:

```
INTRODUCE DATABASE  <database1>
TO                  <database2>
AT                  <network address for database 2>
IDENTIFIED BY       <database1_password>
                    <database2_password>
```

This statement can be executed asynchronously by the DBA at each site for each remote site with which the DBA desires to enter into a bilateral data sharing agreement. A user at <database1> can access database objects at <database2> (and vice versa) only when the DBAs of both sites have indicated their willingness to share data with each other.

Catalog Management

Because of the desire for site autonomy, each site only maintains catalog information on objects to which it has given birth and on objects for which it is providing storage. By requiring each site to keep track of the current storage location of each object, information should be available from the birth site if the object has not been migrated to another site. Otherwise, the birth site should have up-to-date information regarding the current location of the object. Thus, the catalog information request can be redirected to that site. In other words, two remote sites at most might have to be consulted (i.e., one level of indirection) to obtain catalog information for an object identified by its SWN.

To minimize the catalog retrieval overhead in processing distributed queries, each R* site caches and timestamps catalog information retrieved from remote sites to avoid repeated remote access. When an execution plan is sent to a remote site, the recipient site uses timestamp information associated with the cached catalog entries used to generate the execution plan; this verifies that those entries are still valid. Otherwise, the execution plan is rejected, and the query's home site must refresh its cache of catalog information before reprocessing the query.

Site-to-Site Authorization

When two sites communicate, it is important to verify that the other party is really the intended site. R* makes use of a password mechanism for site-to-site verification upon initial communication between two sites. When a user accesses data from multiple sites, passwords are verified only once. Each site trusts the user ID provided by the other site; it only ensures that the identified user is authorized to access the data referenced by SQL statements.

Transaction Management

R* supports the bracketing of multiple SQL statements accessing distributed tables into transactions with the atomicity, consistency, isolation, and durability properties. Each transaction is assigned a global transaction ID at the site where the transaction is initiated. Concurrency control is provided using two-phase locking, with locks held until the transaction is committed or aborted. Distributed deadlock detection is achieved using the path pushing algorithm discussed in Section 10.4.2.

R* uses two variations of the standard two-phase commit

protocol to achieve atomic commitment of distributed transactions. These variations are aimed at minimizing the number of intersite messages, the number of times that log entries have to be force written to stable storage, and the accelerated release of locks at sites that have participated only in read-only subtransactions.

Presumed Abort

In the presumed abort optimization of the two-phase commit protocol, when the recovery manager at the coordinator site of a distributed transaction finds no information about a transaction when inquired, it presumes that the transaction has been aborted. The consistent use of this deduction by the recovery manager facilitates the design of a two-phase commit algorithm in which the coordinator can forget about an aborted transaction earlier. In fact, when the coordinator receives a negative vote and makes the decision to abort the transaction, it simply broadcasts the abort message to all participants, writes an *abort* record in the log without necessarily forcing it, and forgets about the transaction. Similarly, when a participant receives an *ABORT* message, it is not required to acknowledge it.

Another feature of the presumed abort protocol relates to the possibility of discovering that the subtransactions performed by some participants in the distributed transaction are read only. When a participant has not performed any database update, it does not need to write log records and can release its locks and forget about the transaction immediately, after sending its vote to indicate that it is read only. In fact, the participant does not even need to know whether the transaction will eventually commit or abort.[4]

If all the participants are read only, then the coordinator does not need to enter the second phase of the commit. It just force writes a commit record, releases its locks, and forgets about the transaction. When some of the participants are read only and others have performed updates, those that have performed updates are the only participants that have to enter the prepared state.

Presumed Commit

Like the presumed abort protocol, the presumed commit protocol deduces that when no information is available to the recovery manager at the coordinator's site, the transaction is to be committed.

---

4 Since it is read only, the final outcome of the transaction is not going to affect the local data at all.

The duality of protocols leads to an approach in which aborts have to be acknowledged while commits do not. Before the coordinator sends *PREPARE TO COMMIT* messages to participants, it force writes a *collecting* record to the log to keep track of the identities of the participants. When the coordinator receives votes from the participants, it decides to commit or abort the transaction. If it decides to commit the transaction, it force writes a *commit* record, broadcasts a commit message to the participants, and forgets about the transaction. In this case, participants are not required to acknowledge the *COMMIT* message. On the other hand, if the decision is to *abort* the transaction, the coordinator force writes an abort record in the log and sends *ABORT* messages to the participants. Participants must acknowledge receipt of this message, and the coordinator must not forget about the transaction until all participants have acknowledged receipt of the *ABORT* message. As in the case of presumed abort, read-only participants can send a *VOTE READ-ONLY* message and not participate in the second phase of the protocol.

Query Processing/Optimization

Consistent with its objective for site autonomy, R* employs a distributed query compilation strategy. Each distributed query is processed by a *master* site and a number of *apprentice* sites. The master site is responsible for performing high-level query optimization and for generating a global execution plan that specifies (1) what subqueries should be executed at each site and (2) how intermediate results should be sent from one site to another.

Since the unit of distribution in R* is an individual table, each table is stored entirely at one site. A distributed query is any SQL statement that references tables at sites other than the query submission site. The query submission site functions as the master site. It coordinates the optimization of all SQL statements embedded within an application program. The optimizer at the master site is responsible for making all intersite decisions, such as the order in which intersite joins are to be performed, the site where each intersite join is to be performed, and the strategy for shipping a table from one site to another (ship whole vs. fetch match).

Intrasite processing strategies (e.g., the order in which tables within the same site involved in the query are to be joined, the method for performing each local join operation, and the access path to be used for each local table) are suggested by the master site to apprentice sites. However, final access path decisions on tables stored within an apprentice site, as well as the generation of local access plans, are delegated to the apprentice sites. (This gives rise to the possibility of local sites tuning their physical database design without necessarily invalidating entire global execution plans.) The master site sends the global execution plan, along with the original textual SQL statement, to each of the apprentice sites involved in processing the distributed query.

The master site is responsible for authenticating the user submitting a distributed query, and the apprentice site verifies that the execution plan is coming from the indicated site. The apprentice site trusts that the master site has already completed the user authentication and will not attempt to authenticate the user once more. Intersite authentication and communication of the authorized user ID is done only once; subsequent intersite requests on behalf of the same user can be processed without re-authenticating the requesting site and without retransmitting the user ID.

Each apprentice site deduces its role in processing the received SQL statement from the global execution plan and generates a local execution plan for its portion of the query. This local plan is saved and bound to local objects at the site. Thus, certain local schema changes can take place without affecting the global execution plan. Affected local plans can be regenerated locally. Because local plans are saved, subsequent query executions can be initiated using a small message identifying the query plan.

The global plan distributed by the master site includes

- A modified version of the original query with all synonyms for tables and views substituted by their systemwide names.
- Version numbers of catalog entries for the tables, views, and columns referenced in the query and used by the master site for global query optimization.
- A high-level representation of the master execution plan that is devoid of internal representations.

Dependency Tracking

The access module at each site depends on the continued existence and validity of database objects stored at that site. Such dependency information is explicitly cataloged at each site in two kinds of catalogs. The *usage catalog* has one entry for each table, view, or index used in the local access module for a distributed query. The *authorization catalog* for each object type (such as table, view, or index) has one entry for each object referenced by that access module. When an object is dropped or migrated, the authorization catalog is searched, and affected access modules are invalidated. When an access module is invalidated, its entries in the usage catalog are used to identify other authorization catalog entries that should be removed. The next time an application program attempts to execute an invalidated access module, it is automatically recompiled.

Optimizer Validation

Experiments on validating performance of the R* optimizer have been reported [Lohman and Mackert, 1986; Mackert and Lohman, 1986]. Some interesting results were obtained, including the following:

Fetch match versus ship whole: Shipping the entire inner table to the join site and storing it there dominates the fetch-match strategy, which incurs prohibitive message costs for each outer row even in high-speed networks. This result can easily be generalized to the situation of nested SQL subqueries involving tables from different sites. It would be preferrable to materialize selected subsets of tables at the same site, create indexes on join columns in the materialized tables, and perform tuple substitution locally rather than distributively.

Semijoins: Consider the joining of tables R at site 1 and S at site 2 based on columns R.a and S.b. Let's suppose the join result is to be assembled at site 1. Rather than shipping table S in its entirety to site 1, it is possible to minimize the data transmission cost by identifying exactly what subset of rows in S can participate in the join. This is achieved by projecting R onto its joining column R.a, eliminating duplicates from this projection,[5] and sending the result to site 2. This set of distinct R.a column values can be used at site 2 to determine what rows of table S can participate in the join operation. Essentially, any row in S with a value for S.b that matches any value in R.a will participate in the join and therefore should be sent to site 1. The act of reducing S to a subset of rows that can join with R is referred to as a semijoin reduction of S by R. If the join result is to be assembled at a site 3, then the projection of S semijoin reduced by R on the column b can be sent to site 1 to perform a semijoin

---

5 This can be done particularly efficiently if R is indexed on Column a. The leaf pages in the B-tree index can be scanned to obtain all the distinct index key values, avoiding the need to scan the entire table, projecting on the join column, and eliminating duplicates from the result.

reduction on R. The result can subsequently be transferred to site 3 where the final join operation can be carried out.

Bloom joins: Hashing is an efficient technique for grouping together matching values. Bloom joins use Bloom filters as a hashed semijoin to filter out rows that do not have matching counterparts in the other table being joined. As in semijoins, Bloom joins are intended to reduce the size of tables that have to be transferred. The Bloom filter is a large vector of bits that are initially all set to zero. The Bloom filter on S is computed by scanning rows in S, hashing the join column value of each row to a particular bit in the bit vector, and turning on that bit with the vector. The bit tables used in Bloom joins are typically much smaller than the join column values transmitted in semijoins. Whereas a semijoin requires executing an extra join to reduce the inner table, Bloom joins only need an additional scan in no particular order.

10.6.2 ORACLE Server

Version 6.0 of the ORACLE Server supports distributed query but not distributed update. (A two-phase commit capability has been announced for Version 7.0.) ORACLE supports gateways to DB2 and SQL/DS, and these foreign databases can participate as part of an ORACLE Server distributed database. However, these gateways are not available on the OS/2 platform. Multiple instances of ORACLE for OS/2, however, can be part of a distributed database.

ORACLE's definition of a distributed database is a set of networked databases stored on multiple computers but that appear as a single logical database to users. Each database is controlled by its own local database management system. That is, each local database is autonomous and is administered separately and independently from the other databases.

Using SQL*Net, ORACLE's communication software, the ORACLE Server can communicate on a wide range of local and wide area networks. When ORACLE databases on different computers communicate with one another, one database acts as a client and the other as a server. With ORACLE distributed databases, users can access multiple database servers simultaneously and transparently. For example, database tables from multiple servers can be joined into a single view. DBAs can set up applications to take advantage of location transparency: the location of the data does not have to be specified by the application designer or user. If specific tables are not located in the default ORACLE Server, that server uses SQL*Net to access the appropriate remote database tables. In processing distributed queries, the ORACLE Server employs a completely distributed data dictionary and does not attempt to cache remote dictionary entries during the processing of multiple queries that originate from the same site.

Database Links

In the ORACLE Server, the SQL command CREATE DATABASE LINK creates a path from a user's primary database server to another database server. The information required to create a database link is the same as that required to access a server. The user must have access to an account (user name and password combination) on the destination server. A single user connection is called a *private database link.* Multiple database users may connect using a common user name; this is called a *public database link.* Only DBAs may create public database links. The syntax for creating a database link is as follows:

```
CREATE [PUBLIC] DATABASE LINK <linkname>
CONNECT TO <username> IDENTIFIED BY <password>
USING <connect_string>
```

Table 10.1 describes each of the parameters included in this statement.

Parameter	Definition
PUBLIC	Keyword that represents all users except those who have a private database link with the same name.
<linkname>	Name of the database link.
<username>	Valid user name on the database server.
<password>	Password corresponding to the user name.
<connect_string>	Character string for specifying the server and SQL*Net driver.

Table 10.1: *Parameters for database link creation.*

If the DBA creates a public database link without a user name or password, the user's user name and password are assumed. If a user does not have an account on the remote server, access is denied. A user can grant access to his/her tables and views to all users with the keyword PUBLIC.

As the number of databases on a network increases, it becomes beneficial to organize and simplify data access across the distributed database system. This streamlining can be achieved by the use of two options: *synonyms* and *views listing database links and synonyms.*

To establish location transparency, one must create synonyms for tables or views located on the servers in the distributed database management system. A *synonym* is a name for a specific remote table or view that includes a database link. The syntax for creating a synonym is

```
CREATE SYNONYM <name> FOR
<tablename>@<connecting_string>
```

After defining a synonym, the data can be accessed as follows:

```
SELECT * FROM <name>
```

To ensure location transparency from all locations in the network, "chains" of synonyms can be established. By chaining synonyms of tables and views across many servers, users can issue SQL statements without knowing where the tables or views reside. Nesting synonyms in this way allows users to access data from a given server by going indirectly through any number of servers.

Concurrency Control

Because ORACLE queries are executed using the multiversion consistency read mechanism, deadlocks are not possible for queries that span multiple databases. Also, because no update transactions can span multiple databases, there is no special need to synchronize retrievals at multiple databases to ensure that multidatabase updates are atomic with respect to distributed queries.

10.6.3 DEC Rdb/VMS

Version 4.0 of VAX Rdb/VMS allows an application to use more than one database or attachment to a database in the same transaction. However, SQL statements are restricted to referring to tables from a single database only. Thus, distributed queries that span tables from multiple databases can be implemented only at the application level, but updates on tables across multiple databases can be performed in the context of a distributed transaction. Because DEC supports a variety of other database management products like VAX DBMS, and VIDA, Rdb uses a VMS utility called DEC distributed transaction manager (DECdtm) to achieve atomic commitment of multidatabase transactions. In fact, DECdtm allows a distributed transaction to span multiple DEC database products.

Distributed Deadlock Avoidance

When deadlocks occur on the same node or cluster, the VMS distributed lock manager detects and resolves the deadlock. For deadlocks that span multiple systems, a timeout mechanism is provided:

The logical name RDM$BIND_LOCK_TIMEOUT_INTERVAL can be set at the operating system level to control the amount of a time a transaction waits for locks.

The SET TRANSACTION statement also accepts a WAIT <interval> option to specify the lock timeout interval. If specified, it overrides whatever default was previously established, for the transaction on hand.

The DECLARE TRANSACTION statement also accepts a WAIT <interval> option. In this case, the same timeout is applied to all subsequent transactions executed within the same application.

Two-phase Commit

DECdtm's implementation of the two-phase commit protocol involves the following participants:

Resource managers: Each resource manager is an attachment to the database product that supports the two-phase commit protocol. Possible resource managers include Rdb/VMS, VAX DBMS, and VIDA.

Transactions managers: Each transaction manager coordinates the activities of resource managers located on the same node. The transaction manager keeps track of all local resource managers involved in a particular distributed transaction. The DECdtm utility at each node plays the role of the transaction manager at that node.

Coordinator: The transaction manager at the node where the application is initiated plays the role of coordinator in the two-phase commit protocol. The coordinator generates a transaction identifier when a distributed transaction starts. The coordinator also keeps track of all local resource managers and remote transactions involved in a particular distributed transaction.

DECdtm provides the following system services to applications:

SYS$START_TRANS: This call starts a distributed transaction. For transactions that span only Rdb and VIDA databases, the application can make this call implicitly or explicitly. For transactions that involve Rdb as well as VAX DBMS, this call must be invoked explicitly.

SYS$END_TRANS: This call commits a distributed transaction if all the participants vote yes, or it rolls back the transaction if any of the participants votes no.

SYS$ABORT_TRANS: This call rolls back a distributed transaction.

Starting a Distributed Transaction

The procedure for starting a distributed transaction is as follows:

(1) The application invokes the local DECdtm (the distributed transaction's coordinator) for the SYS$START_TRANS service.
(2) The coordinator generates a unique identifier for the transaction and returns it to the application.
(3) The application instructs local and remote resource managers to join the distributed transaction, specifying the transaction identifier.
(4) Each resource manager notifies its local transaction manager that it is joining the distributed transaction identified by the given transaction identifier.
(5) Each remote transaction manager informs the coordinator of its involvement in the distributed transaction.

Referencing Tables From Multiple Databases

When an application is compiled without the logical name SQL$DISABLE_CONTEXT set to true, all transactions that attach to multiple databases are treated as distributed transactions.

Multiple databases can be attached simultaneously using the DECLARE SCHEMA statement, along with the use of a database alias. This alias can subsequently be used to qualify table names referenced in SQL statements. If an application calls SYS$START_TRANS service explicitly, then the transaction can only be committed or aborted by calling SYS$ABORT_TRANS and SYS$END_TRANS explicitly. If the transaction is implicitly started, then the COMMIT and ROLLBACK statements should be used.

If the SYS$START_TRANS service is used explicitly, the returned transaction identifier must be put into a context structure. This context structure must be explicitly referenced in a SQL statement to cause that statement to be executed as part of the specified transaction. Consider the following example:

```
EXEC SQL USING CONTEXT :<context_variable>

<embedded SQL statement>
```

Committing a Distributed Transaction

To commit a transaction, the following steps are completed:

(1) The application invokes the coordinator DECdtm for the SYS$END_TRANS service.

(2) The coordinator, upon receiving the SYS$END_TRANS call, instructs all local resource managers and remote transaction managers to enter the prepare phase of the transaction.

(3) The remote transaction managers instruct their local resource managers to enter the prepare phase of the transaction.

(4) When the resource managers receive instructions to prepare to commit, they write sufficient information to stable storage that will permit them to commit or roll back the transaction at a later time when a consensus of the transaction's outcome can be reached. Essentially, each resource manager writes all changes to the database and writes a prepare record to the recovery unit journal (RUJ) file. In the case of a process or image failure, the prepare record indicates to the database recovery (DBR) process that the database is involved in part of a distributed transaction; therefore, the DBR process should consult with the transaction manager to decide whether to commit or rollback the changes. Furthermore, all changes made during the transaction are logged in the after image journal (AIJ) file and written to the database file. A prepare record is also written to the AIJ file.

(5) When the information is written to stable storage, the resource manager is considered prepared. The resource manager then returns a yes vote to the transaction manager.

(6) The transaction manager evaluates the votes from the resource managers on its node. If all the votes on a remote

node are positive, the remote transaction manager returns a yes vote to the coordinator. If any of the votes are negative, the remote transaction manager returns a no vote.

(7) The coordinator evaluates the votes it receives from local resource managers and remote transaction managers. If all votes are positive, the coordinator writes a commit record to the log. The transaction now enters the commit phase. At this point, the commitment of the distributed transaction at all of the involved resource managers is assured. No matter what happens, the transaction will eventually commit the changes to the affected databases. If any of the votes are negative, the coordinator instructs the resource managers to roll back the transaction.

(8) The coordinator instructs the local resource managers and the remote transaction managers to complete the commit processing. The coordinator then returns control to the application so that the transaction manager can start another transaction if desired. Asynchronously, the coordinator waits for acknowledgments from local resource managers and remote transaction managers. If the application tries to start a new transaction at a database that has not finished the previous commit processing, the transaction will be forced to wait.

(9) Each remote transaction manager forwards the commit instruction to its local resource managers. Then, each resource manager writes a commit record to its log and truncates the RUJ file before returning an acknowledgment to its local transaction manager. Each remote transaction manager collects acknowledgments from the local resource managers before sending acknowledgments to the coordinator.

Because the remote transaction managers and resource managers must acknowledge commit and abort instructions from the coordinator, DECdtm supports neither the presumed commit nor the presumed abort optimization.

Termination Protocol

DECdtm does not make use of any decentralized termination protocol. Therefore, if the coordinator fails after collecting votes from the participating resource managers but before it has a chance to disseminate the commit decision, the resource managers are required to wait for the recovery of the coordinator.

If a resource manager fails before voting to commit or abort, the entire transaction must be aborted as follows:

(1) When a transaction manager notices the failure of a local resource manager, it immediately informs the coordinator that it will not be able to commit its portion of the distributed transaction.
(2) The coordinator then instructs each local resource manager and remote transaction manager to rollback the transaction.
(3) Each resource manger uses its RUJ file to rollback the transaction's changes. An abort record is also written into the AIJ file.

If the resource manager fails after it has sent a positive vote, the following events take place:

(1) A database recovery (DBR) process is created on recovery. The DBR process examines the RUJ file and finds a prepare record.
(2) The DBR process asks the local transaction manager for the outcome of the transaction. The remote transaction manager in turn asks the coordinator if necessary.
(3) The coordinator tells the transaction manager to either commit or abort the transaction; this information is propagated back to the resource manager.
(4) The DBR either commits or aborts the transaction, as directed by the local transaction manager.
(5) If the coordinator is not reachable, the DBR process does not allow databases with unresolved transactions to be accessed. If there is a communication failure between a remote transaction manager and the coordinator, Rdb provides an escape mechanism that allows use of manual intervention to force commitment or abortion of an unresolved transaction. However, if the two-phase commit process is circumvented, it must be performed consistently at all the resource managers, or serializability will be compromised.

10.6.4 Microsoft SQL Server

The SQL Server supports updates across multiple servers but does not support distributed queries or distributed deadlock detection. The UNIX version of the SQL Server also supports remote procedure calls. Thus, an application may invoke a stored procedure at one server which, in turn, invokes other servers using the remote procedure call mechanism. Server-to-server remote procedure calls can be used to enforce integrity constraints and business rules on distributed data.

The SQL Server also opens its architecture as widely as possible to allow other databases to be integrated into its client-server architecture. Sybase's Open Server mechanism provides a consistent method of receiving SQL requests or remote procedure calls from an application based on Sybase's Open Client (DB Library) interface. At run time, an application program issues a database RPC to the distributed database system, which may consist of any combination of SQL Servers and Open Servers. If the data is stored in a non-Sybase source, the Open Server provides the necessary data type and network connection to allow the Open Client to process the resultant data.

The Open Server consists of two logical components: a server network interface and event-driven utilities. The server network interface manages the network connection and accepts requests from client programs running Open Client or database RPC from another SQL Server. Event-driven utilities in the Server Library provide the logic to ensure that client requests are passed to the appropriate user-developed handler and are completed properly. The utilities also ensure that the returned data is formatted correctly for the client program.

Two-phase Commit Support Library

The two-phase commit service allows an application to coordinate updates among multiple SQL Servers. However, unlike the two-phase commit implementation in Rdb, more burden is put on the application to orchestrate the two-phase commit activities.

One SQL Server is designated as the Commit Server. It functions as a record keeper to help the application determine whether to commit or abort transactions. The responsibility for coordinating a distributed transaction rests primarily with the application. The SQL Servers where retrievals and updates are performed are referred to as the participants (participating SQL Servers) of the transaction. The Commit Server can be chosen from among the participating SQL Servers. Alternatively, a different SQL Server can be chosen to play the role of Commit Server.

A distributed transaction that involves multiple SQL Servers is performed by submitting Transact-SQL statements to the participating SQL Servers via DB-Library functions and macros. An application opens a session with each server, issues the retrieval and update commands, and then prepares to commit the transaction. Through DB-Library, the application issues the following statements to each participating server:

(1) A begin transaction statement, with information identifying the application name, the transaction name, and the name of the server that is to serve as the commit server.
(2) The Transact-SQL retrieval and update statements.
(3) A prepare transaction statement to indicate the end of the transaction and that the application is prepared to commit.

After the application has issued all the updates to the participating SQL Servers, the two-phase commit process begins. In the first phase, the application requests that each participating SQL Server prepares to commit and waits for response from each of them. If all the participating SQL Servers respond positively to the prepare request, the application issues the commit transaction statement to the participating SQL Servers. The application then tells the Commit Server that the transaction is complete.

The Commit Server plays a passive role in coordinating the distributed transaction. It functions purely as a record keeper and returns the last known status of a given distributed transaction when inquired.

If all SQL Servers participating in a distributed transaction are prepared to commit, the application notifies the Commit Server to mark the transaction as committed. Once this happens, commitment of the transaction is assured, even in the presence of subsequent failures.

If the application or any of the participating SQL Servers fails before the prepare transaction statement, the transaction is rolled back. If a SQL Server or the application program fails after the prepare but before the commit, the participants communicate with the Commit Server to determine if the transaction should be committed or rolled back.

As in the Rdb two-phase commit implementation, the SQL Server does not use a decentralized termination protocol. Therefore, should the application and the commit server both fail at an inopportune time, other participants will not be able to terminate their subtransactions and will be forced to wait.

The role of the application program is to deliver the Transact-SQL statements to the participating SQL Servers in appropriate order, using the proper DB-Library functions and macros. The role of the Commit Server is to provide a single place where the commit/rollback status is maintained. The participating SQL Server communicates with the Commit Server only if a failure occurs during the two-phase commit protocol.

The application communicates with the Commit Server through a separate SQL Server DBPROCESS, which is separate from those used for processing retrievals and updates in the transaction. The SQL Server that functions as the Commit Server can also be one of the servers participating in the transaction.

If any SQL Server must terminate a distributed transaction after it has acknowledged the prepare request from the application, either because communication with the application has been dropped or because the Server has previously crashed and is now recovering, it initiates a Probe Process to determine the last known status of the transaction.

The SQL Server's two-phase commit service library includes the following calls:

open_commit: Opens a connection with the Commit Server. It takes the login ID of the user initiating the session (DBPROCESS) and returns a pointer to a DBPROCESS structure for use in subsequent commit service calls.

start_xact: Records the beginning of a distributed transaction and stores initial information about the transaction (DBPROCESS ID, application name, transaction name, and the number of sites/DBPROCESSes participating). It returns a commID that uniquely identifies the transaction among those for which the Commit Server is providing commit service.

build_xact_string: Builds a name string for use by each SQL Server participating in the transaction (to be used in the begin transaction and prepare transaction statements). This string encodes the application's name, the transaction's name, the SQL Server that is functioning as the Commit Server, and the commID.

commit_xact: Informs the Commit Server that the transaction is to be committed.

abort_xact: Informs the Commit Server that the transaction is to be aborted.

remove_xact: Informs the Commit Server to decrement the count of SQL Servers still participating in the transaction.

close_commit: Terminates the session with the Commit Server.

scan_xact: Prints the status of a single transaction if a commID is specified; otherwise all commit service records are printed.

stat_xact: Returns the status of a distributed transaction.

Potential Problems

Presently, there appears to be a number of glitches in the SQL Server's two-phase commit implementation. First, the Commit Server may not always be able to garbage collect information about a distributed transaction. If the application fails after receiving an acknowledgment for a commit transaction statement, but before it has a chance to inform the Commit Server to decrement the count of SQL Servers still participating in the transaction (using the remove_xact call), then the Commit Server may not be able to forget about the transaction. This is because the Commit Server is never informed of the identities of the SQL Servers participating in the transaction; it only knows the number of participating SQL Servers that may be interested in the outcome of the transaction.

In addition, the maximum number of SQL Servers that will be participating in a transaction must be specified prior to start of the transaction (in the start_xact call). There is no way to dynamically add more participants to a distributed transaction.

Another drawback is that the burden of coordinating commitment of the distributed transaction falls primarily on the application. In fact, the service provided by the Commit Server is quite minimal. And last, the SQL Server does not make use of any global transaction identification scheme for lock management. Therefore, if multiple subtransactions are performed on the same database (using different DB processes), these subtransactions cannot share locks.

10.7 Summary

There is considerable confusion in the commercial database world over the definition of a distributed database. Though many years of research have gone into the development of technical solutions for distributed database problems, the first commercial distributed database systems have emerged only recently with a very rudimentary set of capabilities.

Chris Date, in his "Twelve Rules for Distributed Databases," has identified the most often quoted yardsticks for assessing the level of capabilities provided by a distributed database system. The fundamental principle behind Date's rules is that a distributed database system should look exactly like a nondistributed system to the end-user or application programmer. In this chapter, we further divided these rules into three groups, along the three dimensions of autonomy, distribution transparency, and heterogeneity. Autonomy refers to the distribution of control. It represents the degree to which sites within the distributed database system may operate independently. Distribution transparency refers to the extent to which the distribution of data to sites is shielded from users and applications. And, heterogeneity refers to differences in the form of hardware platforms, operating systems, networking protocols, and local database systems. As Date points out, there is no such thing as an "ultimate" distributed database system: different users will attach different degrees of importance to different objectives. Many of the Date's 12 rules (objectives) are in fact conflicting and therefore not satisfiable simultaneously.

We also surveyed in this chapter many of the technical problems that must be solved in order to implement different aspects of distribution transparency. As summarized in Table 10.2, solutions to many of these problems remain to be implemented in commercial database systems.

Distributed Database Features	IBM R*	ORACLE Server	DEC Rdb/VMS	Microsoft SQL Server
Application Coordinated 2PC	N	N	N	Y
Archival Checkpointing	N	N	N	N
Automatic 2PC	Y	N	Y	N
Basic Distribution Tables	Y	Y	Y	Y
Caching of Catalog Entries	Y	Y	N	N
Centralized Catalogs	N	N	N	N
Centralized Deadlock Detection	N	N	N	N
Centralized Query Compilation	N	N	N	N
Decentralized Deadlock Detection	Y	N	N	N

Distributed Database Features	IBM R*	ORACLE Server	DEC Rdb/VMS	Microsoft SQL Server
Decentralized Termination	N	N	N	N
Dependency Tracking	Y	N	N	N
Distributed Catalogs	Y	Y	Y	Y
Distributed Integrity Constraints	N	N	N	N
Distributed Object Naming	Y	Y	Y	Y
Distributed Query Compilation	Y	Y	N	N
Distribution Transparency	Y	Y	N	N
Extracted Tables	Y	Y	N	N
Foreign Database Introduction	Y	Y	N	N
Fragment Access Optimization	N	N	N	N
Fragment Integrity	N	N	N	N
Fragmented Tables	N	N	N	N
Heterogeneity	N	Y	Y	N
Join Sequence Optimization	Y	N	N	N
Name Server	N	N	N	N

Distributed Database Features	IBM R*	ORACLE Server	DEC Rdb/VMS	Microsoft SQL Server
Name Space Partitioning	Y	Y	Y	Y
Presumed Abort	Y	N	N	N
Presumed Commit	Y	N	N	N
Quorum-based Commit	N	N	N	N
Replica Access Optimization	N	N	N	N
Replica Recovery	N	N	N	N
Replica Update Synchronization	N	N	N	N
Replicated Tables	N	N	N	N
Resiliency Against Network Partitions	Y	Y	Y	Y
Site Autonomy	Y	Y	Y	Y
Site Binding Optimization	Y	N	N	N
Snapshot Tables	Y	N	N	N
Three-phase Commit	N	N	N	N

Table 10.2: *Comparison of distributed database features.*

Chapter 11

SQL Extensions for Next Generation Applications

The distributed database directions extend and enrich the client-server architecture. They support peer-to-peer distributed computing in which different nodes can act both as clients and servers. In addition to the distributed database directions, a number of "intelligent database" directions are becoming increasingly prominent as SQL extensions. In this chapter, we discuss these directions, indicating how some can be integrated into actual products.

We begin in Section 11.1 with an overview of the evolution of intelligent databases. Then, in Section 11.2, we discuss some of the SQL2 and SQL3 extensions that incorporate richer relational semantic constructs in SQL. In Section 11.3, we examine how many systems, including ORACLE and Sybase, have extended SQL with general-purpose programming control structures, such as WHILE loops, IF-THEN-ELSE statements, and so on.

Our focus shifts in Section 11.4 to intelligent database extensions. Here, we discuss how SQL can be extended with each of the object-oriented concepts of abstract data typing, inheritance, and object identity. In fact, some of the proposed SQL2 and SQL3 standard extensions incorporate aspects of object orientation. We also describe how inferencing rules can be integrated in SQL and how deduction can be used to extract knowledge from existing databases. Finally, we discuss how, in addition to the support of BLOBs, SQL implementations can provide a richer semantics of multimedia data types, such as TEXT, IMAGE, and VOICE.

11.1 The Evolution of Intelligent Databases

The evolution of the database is illustrated in Figure 11.1. The forerunners of database management systems were "generalized" file routines. In the 1950s and 1960s, *data definition* products were developed by large companies. This laid the foundation for *network* database management systems. The underlying data model of these databases presented users with a network view of their databases. This network view consisted of record types and one-to-many relationships among the record types. The network model allowed a record type to be involved in more than one relationship. A less general model was a tree-structured hierarchical relationship among record types, which was the basis of the *hierarchical data model.* The hierarchical data model allowed a record type to be involved in *only one* relationship as a parent and also *only one* relationship as a child.

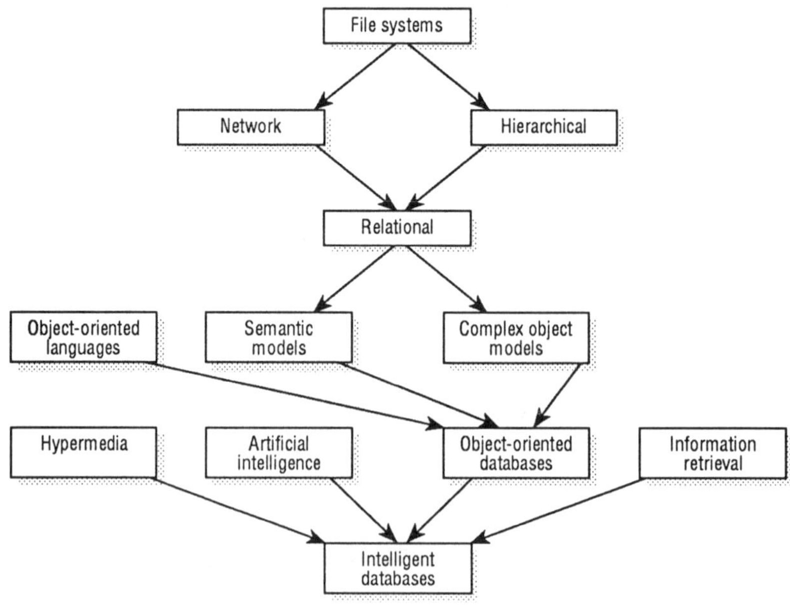

Figure 11.1: *Evolution of database data models.*

Both the hierarchical and network data models were primarily *navigational*. Furthermore, the owner-member relationship (for the network model) or parent-child relationship (for the hierarchical model) were explicitly stored in the database records. In order to provide more flexibility in organizing large databases and alleviate some of the problems of the earlier models, Ted Codd introduced the *relational data model* in the early 1970s. Relational database management systems became increasingly popular in the 1980s and their use and popularity is steadily increasing in the 1990s. The relational model is simple and elegant. The underlying theory is based on the mathematically well founded and well understood concepts of relational algebra and first-order predicate calculus.

Commercial relational systems and the propagation of relational databases stem from the success of the System/R [Astrahan et al., 1976] and INGRES [Stonebraker et al., 1976] relational database implementation efforts. System/R was an ambitious research project which paved the way for a number of commercial implementations from IBM, including DB2, SQL/DS, and the OS/2 Extended Edition Database Manager, which is discussed extensively in this book.

In the late 1980s, almost all the commercial database management systems were either based on the hierarchical, network, or relational model. Still, there were several alternative database modeling proposals. One of the earliest of these was the *semantic data model*. Semantic data models used the *node* and *link* representation schema of semantic networks. Each node is an *entity type*. Similar to types in programming languages, an entity type represents a set of objects (entities), all having the same attributes. An attribute is a function that can apply to an entity in the entity type. The name of an entity type also identifies the *extension* (set of all instances) of the entity type. Entity types are analogous to classes, entities are analogous to instances, and attributes are analogous to instance variables.

Semantic data models are primarily used as design tools for underlying relational or network databases. The forerunner of the semantic model was the famous entity-relationship model introduced by Chen [1976]. The semantic data modeling approach was not the only one that tried to add more semantics to the more traditional data models. There were a number of data models that attempted to *incrementally* extend the relational data model, to allow more flexibility while maintaining a solid theoretical foundation.

The object space in the relational model consists of a collection of flat tables. Each table is a set of rows (or tuples). The column values in each row (attributes of tuples) can only be instances of base atomic types such as integers, floats, or character strings. The flat-table representation is known as the *first normal form. Complex object* models attempted to relax the first normal form restrictions, while maintaining the strong theoretical foundation of the relational model. With a nested and more general complex object model, more general object spaces can be constructed using *set* and *tuple* object constructors. The "column" values could thus be tuples, sets of base values, or sets of tuples (i.e., relations). If the model supports object identity, the sets and tuples could be referentially shared. Hence, users can construct arbitrary graph-structured object spaces and avoid the "unnatural" foreign key joins of the relational model.

The complex object models and the semantic data models laid a strong foundation for the development of a number of object-oriented databases, both in research and in industry. Concepts such as complex objects, object identity, inheritance, and set- and tuple-valued attributes propagated into these powerful object-oriented database systems. Each object-oriented database was influenced by one or more of the complex and semantic data modeling alternatives.

A different, but equally significant, development in the evolution of the database was the incorporation of inferencing and logic-based models in the early and mid 1980s. Through the launching of a number of fifth-generation projects (such as ICOT in Japan, and MCC in the U.S.), PROLOG became increasingly popular. PROLOG provided an implementation logic programming. PROLOG programs consisted of collections of declarative rules. The interpretation of these rules utilized *unification* and SLD resolution. PROLOG implementations were primarily in-RAM systems with little or no access capabilities to bulk extensional databases.

There were several attempts to integrate PROLOG and SQL. For example, PROSQL [Chang and Walker, 1986] was one such attempt, which incorporated SQL statements in the premises of PROLOG rules. A more recent attempt was *Intelligent SQL* [Khoshafian, 1991a].

Other models, such as the Calculus of Complex Objects [Bancilhon and Khoshafian, 1986, 1989], the Logic-Data-Language (LDL) [Tsur and Zaniolo, 1986], and the NAIL!, project from Stanford [Ullman, 1988] attempted to provide complete conceptual models that incorporated deduction in a declarative, rule-based database system. Unlike the PROLOG (which has backward chaining, left-to-right, top-down, goal-directed execution semantics), these models provided a more consistent and general logic-based semantics. More specifically, in the CCO, LDL, and NAIL! models, the order of the rules and the order of the predicates that appear in the premises of the rules do not influence the behavior or the operational semantics of the logic programs. This enhances the expressibility and generality of the logic-based database management systems. The generality and the ability to have consistent semantics of logically equivalent programs paved the way for a number of query optimization techniques, especially in the area of recursive queries [Bancilhon and Ramakrishnan, 1986].

Thus, the next evolutionary step after object-oriented and inferencing/logic-based databases was the *intelligent database*. The intelligent database integrates inferencing *and* object orientation. Object orientation models the real-world persistent object spaces directly, whereas inferencing is important both as a declarative style of programming and as a base technology to perform inductive reasoning about databases. Object orientation augmented with inferencing provides a powerful model to support complex applications in the 1990s. Intelligent databases also incorporate direct support of multimedia data types, such as text, images, and voice. The intelligent database user-interface provides a high-level hypermedia programming environment to the user. Moreover, intelligent database tools allow users to discover intricate relationships in their persistent object spaces automatically.

11.2 SQL2 and SQL3 Directions

As we mentioned earlier, the database language SQL was adopted by ANSI in 1986. In 1989, an extension that incorporated integrity constraints was accepted by ANSI; throughout this book we refer to the standard with the integrity constraints as *ANSI SQL89*.

In the section that follows, we give a brief overview of the incremental extensions introduced by SQL2. The SQL2 extensions are primarily incremental enrichments of the features of the SQL standard. Then, in Section 11.2.2, we give a more detailed description of the enhancements introduced by SQL3. The SQL3 extensions attempt to integrate richer "intelligent" database constructs in SQL (object-oriented and deductive capabilities).

11.2.1 SQL2

After the accepted version of the ANSI SQL, the standardization effort concentrated on an upward compatible enhancement referred to as SQL2. The SQL2 standard is in an almost *near completion* status, and is expected to be adopted sometime in 1992. Several of its features are described here.

Richer type system: In addition to the character string and numeric data types of the SQL standard, SQL2 supports BIT, DATE, TIME, TIMESTAMP, and INTERVAL. As we discussed earlier, several of these data types are currently supported by the SQL database management systems surveyed in this book.

Internationalization and better support of character strings: SQL2 supports collating sequences, which provide the rules for comparing the character in different character sets. In addition, SQL2 supports a number of character string operations such as concatenation, extraction of substrings, conversion to and from lowercase/uppercase, and so on.

Domains: SQL2 allows the user to create and name domains (specific ranges of values) using the built-in data types or other domains. This provides a restricted form of specialization through restriction [Khoshafian and Abnous, 1990].

Different environment and parameter setting: SQL2 incorporates the notion of a session. Within a session, a user can execute a number of transactions. SQL2 provides a rich collection of settings for different parameters in a session. A user initiates a session through a *connect/disconnect* statement to different SQL environments. A user can specify whether an integrity constraint is to be enforced just before a transaction commits (deferred mode) or immediately. In addition, a user can specify the access mode of a transaction (e.g., *read only* or *read/write*) and can change authorization IDs, time zones, and the like.

Levels of isolation: SQL2 supports different levels of isolation, which can be explicitly set through the <set transaction statement>. There are four levels of isolation: 0, 1, 2, and 3. Isolation level 3 guarantees serializability; whereas the other weaker levels can result in transactions reading each other's intermediate result (i.e., nonserializable execution).

Richer relational semantics: SQL2 also introduces a number of constructs that better capture the underlying relational conceptual model of the language. For instance, it enriches the referential integrity constraint through cascaded deletes. (As we saw in Chapter 3, the IBM OS/2 Extended Edition Database Manager supports cascaded deletes.) Another important and interesting extension that provides richer relational semantics is the direct support of natural, inner, and outer joins. As we discussed in Chapter 4, joins provide a more direct representation of relational operations. Although SELECTs could achieve the same functionality, the direct support of joins provides a cleaner and clearer expression of the same operations.

Although SQL2 provides many additional extensions to the SQL89 standard, the features we have outlined here summarize the main advantages of SQL2 over the SQL89 standard.

11.2.2 SQL3

Though substantial, the SQL2 extensions are primarily *incremental* extensions. Concurrent with the SQL2 standardization effort, there is an effort to define a SQL3 standard, which will encompass a number of intelligent database features. In fact, many proposed features that are deemed "advanced" are incorporated into SQL3. It will be quite some time before SQL3 is accepted as a standard—one estimate is 1995! Therefore, some of the concepts in SQL3 are much less stable than those of SQL2.

The remainder of this chapter will be devoted to the envisioned features of the intelligent database extensions of SQL. Although it is hard to analyze a moving target such as the future SQL3 standard, it is now clear that a number of prominent and important intelligent database extensions will be integrated into SQL3. The intelligent database features that could be integrated into SQL are discussed in detail in Section 11.4. Now, we present a brief survey of some of the intelligent database concepts that are likely to be included in SQL3. These include object-oriented extensions, integrity constraint extensions, recursion support, roles as a security mechanism, and savepoints.

Object-oriented Extensions

Two object-oriented extensions are included in the SQL3 proposals: user-defined abstract data typing and inheritance.

User-defined abstract data typing. Most SQL systems come with a built-in collection of base types: INTEGERS, FLOATing point numbers, CHARACTER strings, DATE, TIMESTAMP, and so on.

To be more flexible and to satisfy user needs for extensibility, a trend has developed to enrich these abstract data types and to support additional types. A more realistic approach is to allow the users to develop *their own abstract data type* in some host language (such as C). Subsequently, tables could be defined with column values that are of the user-defined abstract data types. The operations and methods of the abstract data types could be used in SQL statements. Note that user-defined abstract data typing can be thought of as a generalization of DOMAINs, which are supported in SQL2 and further enhanced in SQL3.

Inheritance. Inheritance hierarchies can be defined for domains or abstract data types, and for tables. The abstract data type inheritance is similar to inheritance of classes in object-oriented systems. Classes do not have extensions. Table definitions, on the other hand, define both structure and extension. SQL3 includes a proposal for table inheritance. Inheritance for tables has a set-inclusion semantics, which is discussed in Section 11.4.

Other equally useful object-oriented extensions that could be incorporated in SQL include *tuples* (structured-valued attributes), *arbitrary set-valued attributes*, and *object identity*. These also are all discussed in detail in Section 11.4

Integrity Constraint Extensions

The SQL3 proposal extends the integrity constraint enhancements of SQL2 and introduces the notion of *triggers*. A trigger is a SQL subprogram that gets activated when a specific database operation is performed. We discussed triggers in Chapters 2 and 4 and described how several of the popular SQL servers discussed in this book support triggers.

As in many existing commercial SQL database management systems, triggers in SQL3 can be associated with database INSERT, DELETE, or UPDATE statements. When a trigger is associated with one of these operations for a table, the action in the trigger gets executed.

Recursion

SQL is not Turing complete. One implication of this is that some interesting computations cannot be performed using vanilla SQL (e.g., ANSI SQL89). For instance, the *transitive closure* of a relation cannot be evaluated using the SQL standard (or SQL2 for that matter). Figure 11.2 illustrates a binary relation and its transitive closure. The figure depicts a graphical representation of the relation. The transitive closure evaluates all the *paths* between the nodes; the paths which are evaluated *transitively* are illustrated through dashed lines.

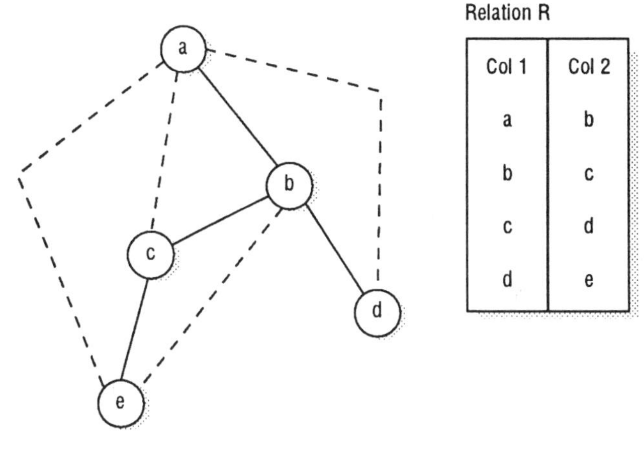

Figure 11.2: *Binary relation and its transitive closure.*

There is a SQL3 proposal to evaluate the *RECURSIVE UNION* of a relation. This could be used to evaluate the transitive closure. A simplified syntax for the RECURSIVE UNION is

<initial expression>

RECURSIVE UNION

<result column list>

<iteration expression>

In evaluating the transitive closure of R as R U R^2 U R^3 ..., the <initial expression> is R and the <iteration expression> evaluates the R^n:

```
SELECT     P, C
FROM                 R
RECURSIVE UNION      TCR(A, C)
SELECT               TCR.A, R.C
FROM                 R
WHERE                TCR.C=R.P
```

Security

The SQL3 proposal includes an extension of the GRANT/REVOKE mechanism of SQL. It introduces the concept of a *role* in an attempt to satisfy several deficiencies in the existing SQL security mechanism. In most SQL systems, privileges are granted and revoked to and from users on a table-by-table basis. Realistically users play *roles* when running applications: administrative roles, secretarial roles, manager roles, developer roles, and so on. In most cases, each time an application is run, it is run by a user playing a certain role. Of course, the same user might have different roles. Existing security mechanisms do not incorporate the notion of a role. This means it is much more laborious and error prone to GRANT/REVOKE privileges on individual objects. In addition, it is much more difficult to switch users, as all the privileges of a user U1 need to be granted to a user U2 if U2 is replacing U1. Furthermore, with existing security mechanisms, users playing different roles will have privileges on objects that they should not have in a particular role. For instance, if the same person is both a manager and a payroll administrator, then as a manager that person should not be allowed to access personnel financial records. The current privilege mechanism cannot handle this notion of grouping and granting collections of privileges on objects.

Thus, role is a collection of authorized actions on persistent database objects. Unlike GRANT/REVOKE privileges, which must be assigned on individual tables and objects, the role mechanism allows users to be granted privileges on *all* the objects in an application. This extra level of roles solves both problems of the existing GRANT/REVOKE privilege mechanism.

Savepoints

The ROLLBACK statement in the SQL standard roles back any changes made to a database by the current transaction. SQL3 extends this notion with the notion of *savepoints*, which allows *partial* rollback of a transaction (up to a specific savepoint).

Thus, users can create savepoints through a SAVEPOINT <savepoint name> statement, and rollback to a specific savepoint through a ROLLBACK TO SAVEPOINT <savepoint name> statement.

Savepoints are nested within one another. For example, consider the following:

```
SAVEPOINT S1
INSERT INTO T1 ...
SAVEPOINT S2
INSERT INTO T2
SAVEPOINT S3
INSERT INTO T3
    ...
```

If we execute

```
ROLLBACK TO S1
```

then both savepoints S2 and S3 will be destroyed (and, of course, the inserts onto T2 and T3). If we execute

```
ROLLBACK TO S2
```

then savepoint S3 will be destroyed (and also, the insert into T3).

Savepoints are very useful since they allow a transaction to rollback up to the point where an exception was raised (vs. the entire transaction, which is the case with the existing ROLLBACK mechanism of the SQL standard). Thus, with the savepoint mechanism much larger and consistent transactions and programs can be constructed, and "loss of work" can be minimized.

11.3 Control Structures in SQL

SQL is a declarative database language that is (at least) as powerful as relational calculus. However, as mentioned earlier, SQL is not Turing complete. For instance, as we discussed earlier, it is not possible to evaluate the transitive closure of a relation using SQL. In fact, to perform more complex computations, SQL statements are often *embedded* in a host programming language, such as C or Ada. Besides the inconvenience of preprocessing the embedded SQL, this conventional approach results in an *impedance mismatch* between the host language and the embedded SQL. Conventional languages such C or Ada are procedural. Database query languages such as SQL are higher level and more declarative. Therefore, applications involving both languages mix (*mismatch*) these different programming paradigms. Furthermore, the data types in the different languages (SQL and C, for instance) are not the same and have to mapped onto one another.

To alleviate the problems of the dual language/dual environment scenario, a number of dialects of SQL have introduced *control structures* to the language. Of course, these languages cannot be used for full-blown system development. Nevertheless, they *do* alleviate some of the needs for control structure or lack of computational power of the SQL standard.

Extending SQL *only* with procedural constructs has a serious drawback. The problem is that the *declarative* language SQL is extended with *procedural* constructs. SQL is a relational language and the relational model has a clean underlying mathematical model/semantics underneath. Providing only a procedural extension is really a step in the wrong direction. What is really needed is a declarative reasoning extension.This would allow the specification of more powerful complex queries (such as the transitive closure) and problems, while maintaining a solid mathematical foundation. The proposed SQL3 extension with recursion, discussed earlier, is a step in the right direction. In Section 11.4 we discuss more general and advanced strategies for supporting declarative rules on SQL databases.

The following are examples of SQL extensions that introduce control structures to the language:

Oracle's Procedural Language (PL) SQL has several control structures, seamlessly integrated with SQL. These control structures include

IF-THEN-ELSE statements:

```
IF <cond> THEN <statements>
[ELSEIF <cond>
THEN <statements> ...
ELSE <statements>]
END IF
```

WHILE loops:

```
WHILE <cond>
LOOP
<statements>
END LOOP
```

FOR loops:

FOR <var> IN <range>

LOOP

<statements>

END LOOP

And other constructs, such as

LOOP...ENDLOOP,

GOTO statements,

RAISE to raise exceptions, and so on.

Similar to Oracle's PL/SQL, the TRANSACT-SQL of the Microsoft SQL Server also incorporates control structures. More specifically, TRANSACT-SQL includes

IF...ELSE statements:

IF <cond>

<statements>

[ELSE <statements>]

WHILE Loops:

WHILE <cond> <statements>

BEGIN ... END Blocks:

BEGIN <statements> END

And other constructs, such as

GOTO statements,

BREAK/CONTINUE,

RETURN,

PRINT,

RAISERROR, and so on.

These procedural control flow extensions usually include *variables*. For example, variables are used to control the execution of the FOR loop in PL/SQL. Similarly, TRANSACT-SQL uses *local* variables of the form @<variable name>. These variables are declared using a DECLARE statement and assigned values through SELECT statements. The use or "scope" of a variable is within the enclosing procedure (hence the name *local*).

11.4 Intelligent Databases

All the incremental and more radical extensions of SQL are elements of the next generation databases, namely, *intelligent databases.* As we stated earlier, intelligent databases integrate

- Object orientation
- Deductive rules (artificial intelligence)
- Information retrieval capabilities
- Multimedia data types and hypermedia object spaces

Figure 11.3 illustrates the technologies integrated into intelligent databases. Most of these features will be presented in the context of a SQL prototype called *Intelligent SQL.* Some of the elements of Intelligent SQL were presented in the object-oriented data base (OODB) task group in May of 1990 [Khoshafian, 1991a]. More detailed inheritance and generalization properties of Intelligent SQL are presented by Chan et al. [1991]; features and architecture of intelligent database engines supporting intelligent SQL are presented by Khoshafian et al. [1990]. In addition, Khoshafian and Thieme [1991] present deductive reasoning extensions to SQL systems.

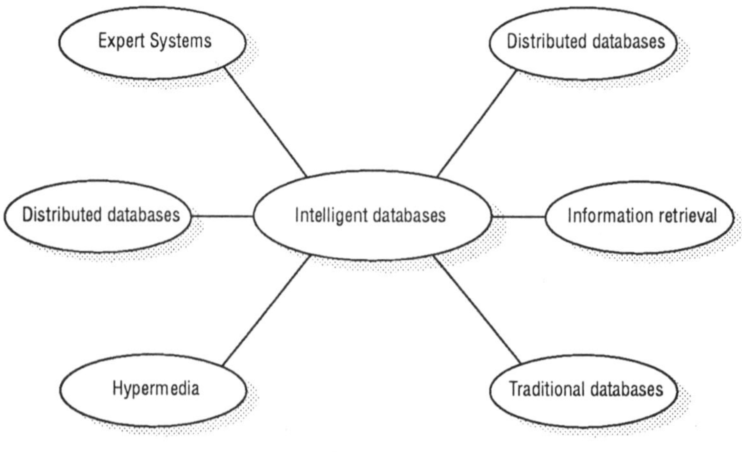

Figure 11.3: *The technologies integrated into intelligent databases.*

Intelligent SQL is neither the first nor the only database language that incorporates object-oriented or other intelligent database constructs into a relational language. In fact, we mentioned previously that a number of object-oriented features such as user-defined abstract data typing and inheritance, are being integrated into the next generation SQL3 standard. Other examples include PROSQL [Chang and Walker, 1986], which interfaced PROLOG with SQL/DS, and the POSTGRES [Stonebraker and Rowe, 1986; Stonebraker et al., 1990] experimental database management system, which extended a relational system with abstract data types, constructed types (similar to *tuple* types in Intelligent SQL), and a rule system. Even some object-oriented databases have used object-oriented extensions of SQL as their query language. For example, Iris [Fishman et al., 1987] from Hewlett-Packard supports an extension of SQL called Object SQL, which allows querying of an object-oriented database using SQL-like syntax. In addition, the Ontos object-oriented database management system supports a dialect of SQL (Ontos SQL), which incorporates object-oriented features [Ontologic, 1991].

11.4.1 The Intelligent Database Architecture

As we stated earlier, intelligent databases represent the merging of a number of distinct paths of technological development. Until recently, these technologies were treated in isolation, with each technology being only *weakly linked* to others. For instance, expert systems have relied on little more than file-transfer protocols to gather data from databases. Due to the phenomenal growth in each field, the connections to the other fields did not have time to form. Now that these technologies have reached a stage of maturity, it is possible to define an overall unifying structure for viewing all these fields. Intelligent databases provide a common approach to the access and use of information for analysis and decision making.

The top-level architecture of the intelligent database consists of three levels: high-level tools, a high-level user interface, and an intelligent database engine, which supports a deductive object-oriented data model.

As Figure 11.4 illustrates, this is a staircase-layered architecture. Users and developers may independently access different layers at different times. The details and functionality of each level is described by Parsaye et al. [1989]. Here we provide a brief overview.

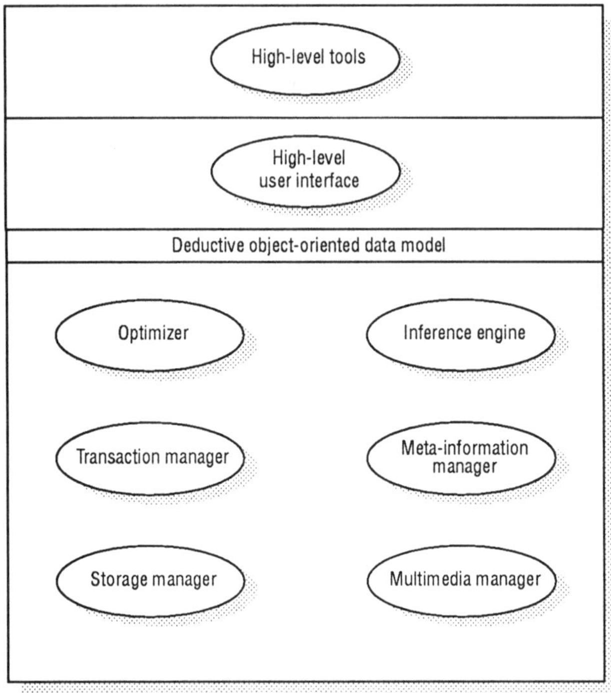

Figure 11.4: *The architecture of intelligent databases.*

The first of these levels is that of high-level *tools*. These tools provide the user with a number of facilities: intelligent search capabilities, data quality and integrity control, and automated discovery. These high-level tools represent an external library of powerful tools. Most of these tools may be broadly classified as information management techniques, similar to spreadsheets and graphic representation tools. They look and work much as their stand-alone equivalents, but they are modified so as to be compatible with the intelligent database model. They are object-oriented, and their basic structure mirrors the object representation methods of the intelligent database model.

The second level is the *high-level user interface*. This is the level that users interact with directly. In other words, it is this level that creates the model of the task and the database environment that users interact with. It has to deal as much with how the user wants to think about databases and information management as with how the database *engine* actually operates. Associated with this level are a set of representation tools that enhance the functionality of the intelligent database.

The user interface is presented in two aspects. First, there is a core model that is presented to the user. This core model consists of the object-oriented representation of information, along with a set of integrated tools for creating new object types, browsing among objects, searching, and asking questions. In addition, there is a set of high-level tools, which enhance the functionality of the intelligent database system for certain classes of user.

The base level of the system is the *intelligent database engine* and its data model. This model allows for a deductive object-oriented representation of information, which can be expressed and operated on in a variety of ways. The engine includes backward- and forward-chaining inference procedures, as well as optimizing compilers, drivers for the external media devices, and version handlers.

The intelligent database engine, with its deductive object-oriented data model, is the underlying repository for integrated applications and products using the high-level tools and the high-level user interfaces. The engine is the *core* and the most important component of future systems. The intelligent database engine provides the functionality and the performance for supporting integrated applications. In addition, access to other databases, distributed inferencing, and database management systems can be achieved through the intelligent database engine.

Intelligent database engines consist of two components: the deductive object-oriented data model and the intelligent database engine.

The deductive object-oriented data model. This model provides the interface to the layers above. DOOD is the basic core intelligent database language. Applications intending to use the intelligent database engine submit programs written in DOOD. As its name suggests, DOOD incorporates object-oriented modeling capabilities.

The intelligent database engine. The engine compiles, optimizes, and executes DOOD programs. Figure 11.4 depicts some of the components of the architecture: the optimizer, the inference engine, the meta-information manager, the transaction manager, the multimedia data manager, and the storage manager.

In a client-server architecture, the high-level tools and the high-level user interface will execute in client nodes. Most of the components of the intelligent database engine will execute on server nodes. Like most SQL-based client-server systems, in order to access the server, an application programming interface on the client side will allow the user-interface layers (or "language" layers) to interact with the server. This interaction is illustrated in Figure 11.5. Note that the inference engine, the storage manager, the transaction manager, and so on are all under server control. This provides a natural and clean partitioning of functionality where the access and control of the concurrently shared databases are left to the server and the (often compute-intensive) display and visual analysis are performed in the client nodes.

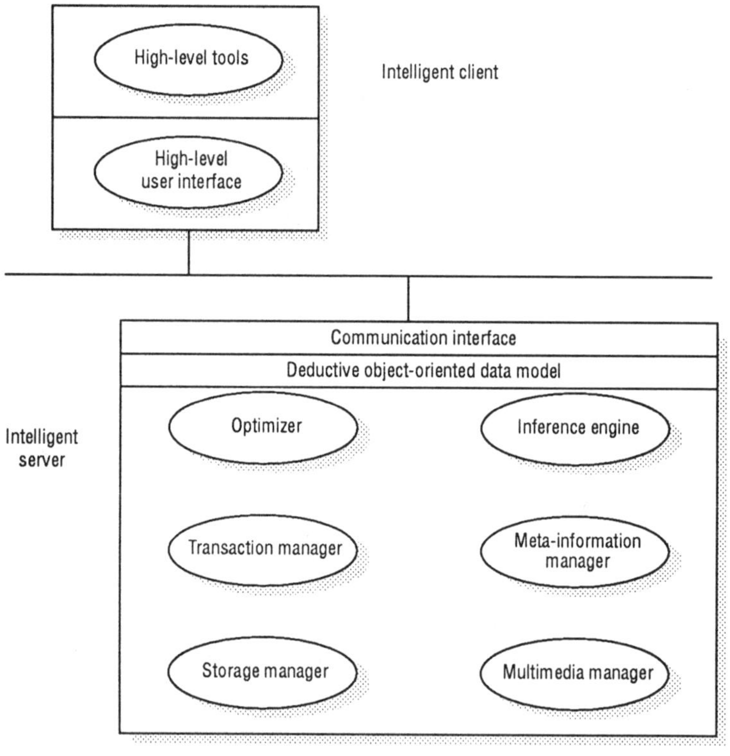

Figure 11.5: Intelligent databases in client-server architectures.

11.4.2 The Deductive Object-oriented Data Model

The intelligent database strategy is to capture and represent the deductive, object-oriented, and multimedia capabilities of intelligent databases. One option is to create an entirely new language with these capabilities. Another alternative is to extend an existing database language with these features. Recently emerging intelligent and object-oriented database products have chosen one or the other approach. Some have introduced new languages, whereas others have extended the most popular relational language standard, namely SQL. In fact, as we discussed earlier, a number of the proposals in the next generation SQL3 standard do incorporate inferencing and object-oriented extensions. Both approaches—extending SQL or providing a "higher level" interface language on top of a SQL system—have merits. As the focus of this book concerns developing SQL applications, we believe there are several advantages to extending SQL. One distinct advantage is that SQL is the most popular relational language, endorsed by most of the prominent vendors of relational database management systems. Furthermore, SQL is a declarative language, with a clean underlying relational model. In addition, SQL has the advantage of being the only relational language that is standardized. And finally, it is the interface database language of the most popular relational database servers.

However, it should also be mentioned that similar to the visual and graphical interfaces to SQL engines, it is possible to have *intelligent programming interfaces* to SQL databases. These programming interfaces can be more general and higher level than SQL. An extreme example is the natural language interface. Less ambitious interfaces include declarative languages supporting intentional and extensional databases, such as the Bancilhon-Khoshafian Calculus of Complex Objects [Bancilhon and Khoshafian, 1989] or LDL [Tsur and Zaniolo, 1986].

Here, we present the integrated intelligent database capabilities in DOOD primarily as an extension of SQL called *Intelligent SQL*. Intelligent SQL combines three main categories of extensions to SQL:

Deductive rules: These allow inferencing or proving goals from within database queries.

Object-oriented features: The purpose of these features is to model the real world as closely as possible using abstract data typing, inheritance, and object-identity.

Multimedia data types: Such data types allow more direct access to multimedia objects through the database data manipulation language.

Deductive Rules and SQL

The integration of expert systems (rule-based systems) and databases is becoming increasingly important to a larger class of users and applications. Expert systems have proliferated diverse applications such as medicine, mathematics, business applications, and configurations of complex systems. Additional application areas include office automation, surveillance systems, manufacturing, oil refinery, and battlefield management. However, although most of these applications use large data (knowledge) bases, the integration of rule-based systems and database management systems remains "loosely" coupled.

There are two commonly used "loose" coupling strategies for AI-DBMS interconnection. In the first strategy, the Inference Engine submits queries (e.g., in SQL) to the database engine as illustrated in Figure 11.6a. Besides the lack of integration of the two languages (the rule-based language and SQL), the performance penalty of this scheme is severe. Furthermore, it is very difficult to perform inferences and prove goals under a consistent transaction model of computation, since typically only the database management system is under transaction control. Thus, the same goal in the same expert system shell session could generate different proofs because of modifications in the underlying databases. In addition to the query and data "traffic," in many cases, the inference engine replicates the functionality of the database engine in its search, optimization, and storage strategies.

Alternatively, a rule-based system (expert system shell) could read data files generated by databases (e.g., dBASE .dbf file) and then process the data locally, as illustrated in Figure 11.6b. There are numerous problems with this approach. For one thing, the integrity and concurrency control of the database files could easily be violated (since accesses and updates are performed through a foreign application without going through the database management system). Moreover, the rule-based system must understand and manipulate different file formats generated by different database management systems. Sometimes the internal structures of these file formats are proprietary. The previous technique did not have this problem since the AI front end communicates with the DBMS through the SQL standard, which is supported by most vendors of database management systems.

The intelligent database approach is to have a "tight" coupling of the engines; this is illustrated in Figure 11.6c.

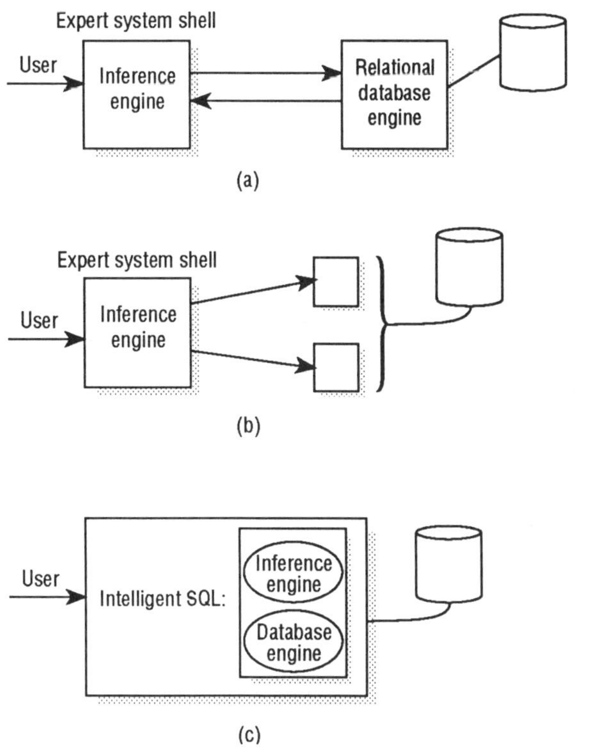

Figure 11.6: Integrating databases and expert systems.

Besides the inferencing and deductive capabilities of rule-based systems, through rules it is possible to perform some very interesting computations which could not be implemented through SQL. We saw earlier how the SQL3 dialect was extended with the recursive union operation to support the evaluation of the transitive closure of a relation.

Inferencing rules, either as an extension of SQL or a higher level interface on top of SQL-based databases, support powerful *declarative* constructs to perform complex computations on tables. As we mentioned, in order to make SQL more computational complete, some systems have extended SQL with *only* procedural constructs. SQL is a relational language and the relational model has a clean underlying mathematical model (embodied in relational algebra) Providing *only* procedural extensions to the language to support more complex problems is a step in the wrong direction [Khoshafian and Thieme, 1991].

The integration of rules with SQL in systems like Intelligent SQL will allow the user to have:

SQL SELECT statements in the premise of if-then rules, and

Logical predicates in the WHERE clauses of SQL statements

To understand the use of rules with SQL, let's consider the following schema:

```
CREATE TABLE Employee(
        Name            CHAR(20),
        Age             INTEGER,
        Address         CHAR(40),
        Rank            CHAR(1),
        Salary          INTEGER)

CREATE TABLE Manages(
        ManagerName     INTEGER,
        EmployeeName    INTEGER
        Duration        INTEGER)
```

We define three rules to find all direct and indirect subordinates of a manager. First, we have the SubordinateOf predicate, which is defined through two rules:

Employee SubordinateOf Manager

IF

Employee ReportsTo Manager

and the second rule:

Employee SubordinateOf Manager

IF

Employee ReportsTo ImmediateManager

AND

ImmediateManager SubordinateOf Manager

The ReportsTo predicate is defined through a rule involving a SQL statement

```
        Employee ReportsTo Manager
    IF
        SELECT EmployeeName AS Employee, ManagerName AS Manager
    FROM Manages
```

With these rules, we can ask the intelligent database management system to tell us who are the subordinates of John:

```
    ?X SubordinateOf John
```

where ?X will bind X to the names of John's subordinates. Similarly, we can determine who are the supervisors of Mary:

```
    Mary SubordinateOf ?S
```

where ?S will bind S to the names of the supervisors of Mary.

To find the names and addresses, names of supervisors under 30, and the names and ranks of all employees who report to them we have:

```
        SELECT    S.Name, S.Address, E.Name, E.Rank
        FROM      Employees S, Employees E
        WHERE     E.Name SubordinateOf S.Name
        AND       S.Age <= 30
```

The Object-oriented Constructs in Intelligent SQL

The three main concepts of object orientation are encapsulation, inheritance, and object identity [Khoshafian and Abnous, 1990]. All three concepts can be integrated in Intelligent SQL.

Abstract Data Types

We noted previously that the next generation SQL3 standard incorporates user-defined abstract data typing. For abstract data typing, methods and operations can be associated with: user-defined data types, such as a stack; tuple types, such as an address; and tables, such as employees and departments.

The user-defined abstract data typing concept is, in fact, an extension of another useful concept being supported by several commercial databases, namely, *user-defined functions.* SQL systems typically come with a built-in collection of aggregate functions: AVERAGE, MAX, MIN, COUNT, SUM, and so on. Many systems allow the users to define their own functions (and to invoke these functions in SQL statements), using either a fourth-generation language (such as dBASE), a general-purpose programming language (such as C), or a procedural extension of SQL (such as TRANSACT-SQL).

As we mentioned earlier, there is a SQL3 proposal for user-defined abstract data typing. Without getting bogged-down in a particular syntax, here we show a simple generic stack type example, which can be used in Intelligent SQL tables. The generic Stack class has Push and Pop methods. The type parameter will allow us to create stacks of different types of objects.

```
CREATE CLASS Stack[T] (
INSTANCE VARIABLES (
        ARRAY StArr[M] of T,
        Top INTEGER);
METHODS (
Push
Stack X T -> Stack
(St Stack, Value Integer
St.Top = St.Top + 1
St.StArr[St.Top] = Value
RETURN St);

Pop
Stack -> T
(St Stack
St.Top = St.Top - 1
    RETURN StArr[St.Top + 1]); ))
```

Once the data type stack is defined, it can be used in Intelligent SQL tables:

```
CREATE TABLE Account(
    AccountNumber    INTEGER,
    Location         CHAR(20)
    Payables         Stack[DOLLAR])
```

and Intelligent SQL queries:

```
    SELECT    AccountNumber, Pop(Payables)
    FROM      Account
    WHERE     Location = "New York"
```

Inheritance

Inheritance is a very powerful object-oriented concept that can be used to organize the structure and instances of persistent tables. Inheritance achieves software reusability and software extensibility. Through inheritance, we can build new software modules or object spaces (e.g., tables) on top of existing hierarchies. This avoids redesigning and recoding everything from scratch. New types, classes, and structures can *inherit* both the behavior (operations, methods, etc.) and the representation (columns, attributes, etc.) from existing types. Inheriting behavior enables *code sharing* (and hence, reusability) among software modules. Inheriting representation enables *structure sharing* among data objects. The combination of these two types of inheritance provides a most powerful modeling and software development strategy.

The SQL3 standard supports inheritance through a *IS-A* construct. Here, we use SPECIALIZES instead of IS-A. In fact, it is also possible to start from existing tables, discover commonalities, and GENERALIZE to supertables. Specialization and generalization in Intelligent SQL are discussed in Khoshafian et al. [1991].

Here is a simple example of table inheritance involving persons, employees, and students:

```
CREATE TABLE Persons(
    Name        CHAR(20),
    Age                  INTEGER,
    Address     CHAR(40))

CREATE TABLE Employees
    SPECIALIZES Persons(
    Salary      FLOAT,
    Rank        INTEGER)

CREATE TABLE Students
    SPECIALIZES Persons(
    GPA         FLOAT,
    Major       CHAR 10)

CREATE TABLE StudentEmployees
```

SPECIALIZES Employees, Students

To retrieve the age and address of all employees who earn more than $50,000, we have

```
SELECT    Age, Address
FROM      Employees
WHERE     Salary > 50k
```

In other words, the Employees table inherits the columns Name, Age, Address from Persons.

Similarly, to obtain the name, GPA, and salary of all student-employees who are over 30 years old we have

```
SELECT    Name, Salary, GPA
FROM      StudentEmployees
WHERE     Age > 30
```

Since the definition of a table incorporates both the definition of a *structure and extension* (the set of all rows of the table), table inheritance in Intelligent SQL has a *set inclusion* semantics. This means that if a table T2 is a subtable of table T1, then the elements (rows) of T2 are also elements of T1. This is illustrated in Figure 11.7.

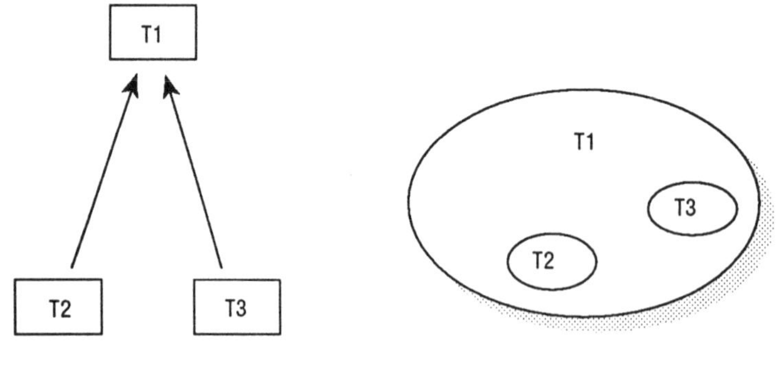

Figure 11.7: *Table inheritance in Intelligent SQL with set inclusion semantics.*

One important implication of the set inclusion semantics is that when we execute a query such as

```
SELECT    Name
FROM      Persons
WHERE     Age < 20
```

we will retrieve the names of all student-employees who are less than 30 years old, "plain" students (nonemployees) who are less than 30 years old, "plain" employees (nonstudents) who are less than 30 years old, and "plain" people (neither students nor employees) who are less than 30 years old.

Another implication of set inclusion semantics is that on any deletion or modification of a set of tuples in a supertable, the corresponding tuples are deleted or modified in all subtables. For instance, the statement

```
DELETE FROM    Persons
WHERE          Age >= 30
```

will delete all student-employees, "plain" students, "plain" employees, and other persons who are over 30.

Tuple-valued Attributes

In this section, we illustrate how tuple types are incorporated in Intelligent SQL. With tuples, users will be able to construct complex persistent object spaces and retrieve complex structures *without* joins.

One serious problem with normalization (especially first normal form) is that naturally occurring structures cannot be represented directly. Consider the example of a person's address. An address consists of a street number, street name, city, state, and zip code. This cannot be thought of as set of atomic values; each piece has a different meaning. Still, there are several ways to store an address in the relational model. Minimally, we can store the address as a long string of characters, but the structure of address is lost. The user then has to worry about the different fields and attributes within the long field. Qualification on different fields of address becomes either difficult or impossible.

Another possibility is to capture the different fields of address in the *name* of the attribute (e.g., different fields for AddressNumber, AddressName, AddressCity, AddressState, and AddressZipCode). This option loses the logical *aggregation* of the address fields. The table definition looks strange and the association of the different fields to the same logical object must be done by the user.

A third alternative is to store addresses in a separate table and perform joins to retrieve the different fields of address. Although this option avoids some of the pitfalls of the other two alternatives, it incurs the extra overhead of *joins* to retrieve the fields of a persons address. Moreover, the table of addresses is not an interesting *grouping*, since, in most cases, users retrieve addresses through a person's record.

Thus, the most natural representation for an address is to allow *tuple-valued attributes*. With this alternative, the address will be a tuple and exist as a single logical entity, instead of being spread across multiple fields or tables. Yet, the user will be able to access and update each field separately.

Intelligent SQL supports tuple types as in

```
CREATE TUPLE ADDRESS(
Str #           INTEGER,
StName          CHAR(20),
City            CHAR(20),
Zip             INTEGER,
State           CHAR(20))
```

—which represents an Address tuple. From this, we can create the Persons table, which uses the Address tuple type

```
CREATE TABLE Persons(
Name            CHAR(20),
Dob             DATE,
HomeAddr        ADDRESS)
```

An extended "dot" notation is used to retrieve different values of the tuple-valued attributes. For example, to retrieve the state where Jim lives, we have

```
SELECT  HomeAddr.State
FROM    Persons
WHERE   Name="Jim"
```

Similarly, we can retrieve the name and date of birth of all persons living in Concord:

```
SELECT  Name, Dob
FROM    Persons
WHERE   HomeAddr.City = "Concord"
```

Object Identity

The tuple support discussed thus far does not allow tuples to be *referentially shared* [Khoshafian and Valduriez, 1990]. For instance, we cannot have two people reference the *same* address: the addresses need to be either replicated or stored separately in another relation. As we discussed in the previous section, both of these options have problems and do not provide a direct modeling and representation of the real worlds.

Since it is natural to *share* tuple values (e.g., addresses) and objects in general, Intelligent SQL also supports *object identity* for tuples. Object identity organizes the objects or instances of an application in arbitrary graph-structured object spaces. Identity is the property of an object that distinguishes the object from all other objects in the application [Khoshafian and Copeland, 1986; Khoshafian and Abnous, 1990]. In programming languages, identity is realized through memory addresses. In relational SQL-based databases, identity is realized through primary keys. User-specified names are used in both languages and databases to give unique names to objects. Each of these schemes compromises identity.

In a complete object-oriented system, each object will be given an identity that will be permanently associated with the object, immaterial of the object's *structural* or *state* transitions. The identity of an object is also independent of the *location* or address of the object. With object identity users can *referentially share objects.* Object identity provides the most natural modeling primitive to have the same object be a subobject of multiple parent objects. Object identity in Intelligent SQL will practically remove the need for having referential integrity constraints.

Object identity can also be associated with atomic-valued attributes (i.e., base types). This makes a great deal of sense for fields that store multimedia data types. For example, if an image is shared in current database engines, it must be normalized in a separate table and subsequently joined with the referencing table. With object identities, all the rows accessing the long field can have direct references to the object.

To indicate objects with identity, we use the REF or OBJECT construct. Consider the example of employees and departments, where departments can share the picture of the building in which they are located:

```
CREATE TABLE Departments(
        CompanyName       CHAR(20)
        DeptName          CHAR(20),
        Budget            FLOAT,
        BldAddr           OBJECT ADDRESS,
        BldPicture        OBJECT IMAGE)
```

Here, the building address is an object with an identity. Many departments can have the *same* address: the company's address. If the company moves and all its departments are relocated, all we need to do is modify the values of the street number, street name, city, state, and zip of the company address. Since the departments are referencing the same object they will acquire these values automatically. The same is true of the building picture.

With object identity, we can also reference rows of tables as tuple objects. For instance, we can have the Dept attribute and Manager attribute in an Employee table reference the corresponding table entry directly:

```
CREATE TABLE Employees
    SPECIALIZES Persons(
                        Salary          FLOAT,
                        Dept            REF ROW Departments,
                        Manager         REF ROW Employees)
```

To retrieve the salary, the manager's name, and the picture of the department building of employee Joe's department we have

```
SELECT Salary, Manager.Name, Dept.Building.Picture
FROM Employees
WHERE Name = "Joe"
```

Multimedia Data Types

Multimedia data types (text, images, voice, video) are becoming increasingly popular. Some relational systems support multimedia data types that can be arbitrarily large. For instance, Microsoft's SQL Server supports TEXT and IMAGE fields with up to 2 gigabytes in each row! Of course, long fields can be stored in operating system files. Storing them in the database allows the multimedia data to be shared concurrently by many users, under transaction control. In most relational database systems that support long fields (alternatively called BLOB, LONG VARCHAR, IMAGE, TEXT, etc.), the functionality is primarily that of storing and accessing the fields, without much consideration of *data typing* (structure + operations).

Intelligent SQL provides special operators and predicates to query and retrieve multimedia objects. It extends the BLOB or long data field object support of some existing relational database management systems with more *intelligent* multimedia types. The "intelligence" in the multimedia type support is exhibited either through *content searches* of multimedia objects, or through the association of attributes and different operations with multimedia object structures.

Text Data

Text documents constitute the most popular medium of storage in the office environment. However, in the typical office automation environment, full-text management and record management are completely independent. Users must interact with two independent and unrelated products to perform table searches and searches for long text fields within table rows. In the typical office environment, Information Management and Database Management are decoupled.

Intelligent databases integrate information and record-database management. There have been a number of proposals to integrate full-text querying capabilities into SQL. The most notable of these is the SFQL proposal [AIA/ATA, 1990].

Here, we describe a simple Intelligent SQL approach that allows users to create, update, and retrieve text fields based on full-text Boolean expressions. The Intelligent SQL approach is similar to SFQL in many aspects, the most important of which is the provision of complex Boolean searches. The Boolean expressions can appear in SQL WHERE clauses, in conjunction with the usual search expressions

If T is a text-valued field then an expression of the form:

```
["Term1" AND "Term2" ... AND "Termn"] IN T
```

can appear as a SQL predicate. This expression is a predicate which is true if and only if all of the terms Term1, ..., Termn are in T. Of course, other kinds of Boolean expressions involving OR and NOT are also allowed.

The following query retrieves the author and publisher of all books published before 1986 covering either "object orientation" and "databases" or "semantic data models."

```
SELECT    Author, Publisher
FROM      Books
WHERE     ["Object Orientation" AND "Databases" OR
          "Semantic data models"] IN BookText
AND                 Year <= 1986
```

The schema of Books is

```
CREATE TABLE Books(
    Author          CHAR(20),
    Publisher       CHAR(20),
    BookText        TEXT,
    Year            INTEGER)
```

Another important aspect of text retrieval is the RANK or RELEVANCE of the returned text. For instance, if we are searching for the occurrence of a particular term and that term occurs, say, 10 times in one record and 100 in another, clearly the second record is more "relevant." Frequency of count is often used as a measure of relevance [Salton, 1983, 1989]. If we want the same query to also return the rank or relevance, we have

```
SELECT    Author, Publisher, RANK(BookText)
FROM      Books
WHERE     ["Object Orientation" AND "Databases" OR
          "Semantic data models"] IN BookText
AND       Year <= 1986
```

Image Data

Image data can correspond to graphs, charts, moving video images, two-dimensional bit-maps, or groups of shapes. Images can be generated by scanners, or imported from external .PCX, TIFF, or other image files. Images can also be used to represent spatial or geographic data.

Images can be represented and stored in vector format as groups of shapes at specific positions and with specific sizes, shades, and colors. In general, the memory requirements using vector format are less than the bit-mapped storage of the same image. However, vector format is not as general as bit-maps.

Since each of these formats has relative advantages and functionalities, Intelligent SQL supports both raster and a number of vector images such as points, rectangles and polygons. The database engine will support grid files and other types of accelerators to enhance the retrieval and update of image data types.

Supporting tuple-valued attributes as in the object-oriented extensions of SQL will help us cluster the media-specific information with the multimedia field.

For spatial (vector image) data types, Intelligent SQL has built-in data types such as RECTANGLE and POINT. Each of these data types is a tuple type, which can further be specialized by the user. More specifically, RECTANGLE is given by

```
CREATE TUPLE RECTANGLE(
        LOW-LEFT    XY-POINT,
        UP-RIGHT    XY-POINT,
```

```
        SCALE          FLOAT,
        ORIGIN         POINT,
        PICTURE        OBJECT IMAGE)
```

Here, LOW-LEFT and UP-RIGHT indicate the lower-left and upper-right corners of a rectangle; the scale and origin provide the necessary information to place the rectangle on the IMAGE. The (optional) IMAGE field stores either the image contained in the rectangle or the image of the environment in which the rectangle is contained (e.g., the rectangle contains a map and the IMAGE is the map of Madison, Wisconsin).

Similarly POINT is a built-in data types given by

```
    CREATE TUPLE POINT(
        POINT          XY-POINT
        SCALE          FLOAT,
        ORIGIN         FLOAT
        PICTURE        OBJECT IMAGE)
```

where SCALE, ORIGIN, and IMAGE are as before, and XY-POINT is a tuple giving the X and Y coordinates of a point:

```
    CREATE TUPLE XY-POINT(
        X-COORD        FLOAT,
        Y-COORD        FLOAT)
```

Following the Pictorial SQL (PSQL) proposal [Roussopoulos et al., 1988], associated with the "spatial" data types RECTANGLE and POINT, Intelligent SQL has a number of built-in operations such as COVERED-BY, OVERLAPS, CLOSEST, PERIMETER, and AREA. As an example, to retrieve the city name, state, and population of all cities a unit distance from the point [4,9], with a population greater than 1 million we have

```
    SELECT    City, State, Population
    FROM      Cities
    WHERE     Location COVERED-BY {4 +/- 1, 9 +/- 1}
    AND       Population > 1,000,000
```

Here, the schema of Cities is

```
CREATE TABLE Cities(
    City          CHAR(20),
    State         CHAR(20),
    Location      POINT)
```

Intelligent SQL can also perform a juxtaposition query of dissimilar information stored in multiple spatial objects. For example, if REC1 and REC2 are rectangles we can specify predicates in SQL WHERE clauses such as

```
REC1 OVERLAPS REC2
REC1 BORDERS REC2
REC1 COVERED-BY REC2
```

11.5 Summary

In this chapter, we discussed SQL extensions for the next generation applications and client-server architectures. In addition to the distributed database functionalities discussed in Chapter 10, a number of "intelligent" database features are in development; these will be integrated into the next generation of database servers.

Specifically, we described a number of SQL2 and SQL3 directions being proposed for future SQL standards. We also discussed the deductive (AI/database integration), object-oriented, and multimedia extensions in the context of a prototype dialect of SQL called Intelligent SQL. These deductive capabilities allow SQL statements to appear in the premises of rules, and rule predicates appear in SQL search conditions. Moreover, we saw how the object-oriented constructs of Intelligent SQL, such as abstract data typing and inheritance, are also part of the SQL3 proposal and are incorporated in several existing commercial database management systems. Finally, we illustrated how TEXT, IMAGE, VOICE, and spatial multimedia types could be incorporated in SQL.

Chapter 12
Summary

It is interesting to reflect on the major forces that have made client-server computing a reality. The introduction of the PC in the early 1980s helped redefine the computing architecture and user applications. These "toys" of the early 1980s have become legitimate solutions in less than a decade as the processing power and storage capacity of PCs increased. Powerful PCs and workstations are now used more and more as "downsizing" application platforms, which, until a few years ago, were the exclusive domain of minicomputers and mainframe computers.

The 1980s also saw the success of the local area network (LAN). While the LAN started out modestly as a way to share expensive printers and disks, it is now used as the basis of connectivity, sharing vital business data, electronic mail, and decision support. As more PCs and workstations are linked, they form a powerful, but cost effective, environment to satisfy computing requirements in a very flexible way.

The advent of more affordable hardware and storage has brought about a new phenomenon—the proliferation of online data. Distributed access to this data is a natural requirement in a LAN environment, and it has created new opportunities for database management systems. These systems have reached a level of maturity whereby they can take advantage of this opportunity. The invention and refinement of the relational model, the understanding of the division between the front end and the database engine, the breakthroughs in concurrency control, recovery, and optimization in the 1970s and 1980s are all proven concepts. Thus, it is not surprising to find that some of these database management systems took the next natural evolutionary step: they became the database servers in the increasingly lucrative market of the client-server environment.

During the 1980s, we also witnessed the adoption of the graphical user interface environment for implementing applications. With this came the pressure and challenge to create user friendly applications in which details such as data access, communications, and security are "given" and considered not very interesting to the user. The availability of database servers that could take care of these matters enabled application implementers to concentrate on the user-centric problems. This division of labor is the very essence of cooperative client-server environment.

Finally, we have seen, in the past few years, very active effort to standardize languages, protocols, data types, error messages, and the like. All of these make it more feasible for the user to have portable applications accessing data from multiple data sources.

Client-server computing offers many other advantages over traditional approaches. First, resource allocation is scalable in the sense that servers can be added to the network to handle more data and requests. Also, because the interface is formalized, a server can be replaced by a more powerful machine without affecting the overall architecture of the applications.

Since most of the complex tasks of database processing have been offloaded to the database servers, inexpensive PCs can serve as effective platforms for applications accessing server data. This cost saving factor forms a powerful incentive for Management Information Systems to downsize traditional applications from minicomputer and mainframes.

Client-server architecture also helps return ownership of data back to the MIS. Since all data processing is performed by central database management systems, important aspects of data such as integrity, security, backup procedure, and transaction processing can be properly monitored. This could be the setting of a win-win situation for users and the MIS—the users are happy because they are obtaining professional support as members of the MIS environment, and the MIS staff are happy because they can integrate all these (once considered) "lost" PCs into their structure.

12.1 Foundation of Client-Server Computing

The foundation of the client-server concepts discussed in this book is the relational database model. This model allows us to represent data as a set of tables, where each table is simply a collection of rows and each row is a collection of values. This simple model has many major advantages over other forms of data models (such as network and hierarchical). Relational query languages are much more declarative than the navigational languages of the earlier models. Furthermore, the underlying theory of the relational model is based on the mathematically well understood concepts of relational algebra and first-order predicate calculus.

The term *relational data model* is sometimes used loosely by vendors. As we discussed, Codd's Twelve Rules for Relational Database Management can be a helpful tool in evaluating database products. In fact, the ANSI committee on SQL has expanded its initial standard to address many of the issues mentioned in these rules. The foundation of the rules is based on the requirement that a DBMS should not have to resort to nonrelational facilities to achieve any of its data manipulation capabilities, such as data definition, data manipulation, integrity, querying, and so on. For example, if SQL is the relational facility, then using it alone should provide you with all the power to manage data. This rule is important for client-server computing because it enforces a clean interface to a database system.

In general, relational database servers that "play by the rules" offer the following advantages: (1) a complete high-level query language insulates the user and application programs from the physical and logical structures of the underlying data management capability; (2) the same language is used for both data and metadata, hence the interface between the client and server is simplified; (3) integrity constraints are centrally enforced and shared by all clients; and (4) ease of distribution of data is achieved because the users do not need to know where the data is physically stored.

The relational model provides the foundation and theoretical framework to model data. The details, such as the kinds of data types and integrity constraints, are left to the implementers of the model. Standards, such as the ANSI SQL89, attempt to give some guidelines to the data definition portion of the model. The data types in SQL89, for instance, cover only very basic types such as character, integer, float, real, and decimal. Many vendors provide additional data types such as date, time, timestamp, binary, and long uninterpreted bit strings. As multimedia and object-oriented technologies mature, an increasing number of data types will be introduced by the vendors. Thus, standardization of data types is certain to be one of the most active areas of concern among standards bodies.

Integrity constraints allow database designers to express additional semantics on the data and enforce "rules of conduct" on data usage. Currently, only a small number of constraints are available to express various well formed conditions such as existence condition (NOT NULL), uniqueness property within a table (unique and primary key), and intertable constraints (foreign key). The trend is for vendors to provide more declarative integrity constraints to database designers that are directly enforceable by the servers. There are several significant advantages to having more semantics attached to the data and directly understood and enforced by the database engines. First, the application logic is simplified because much of the data correctness-checking will be performed by the server. Second, since the constraints are associated with the data, they can be shared by all applications of the database, and even more importantly, these constraints can be centrally managed by the database administrator.

The data definition constructs found in current servers are the most diverse facilities as compared to other types of constructs. Facilities such as database and schema creation, domains for table columnsdefinition, triggers, and the various options for referential integrity constraints and authorization constraints, differ considerably from vendor to vendor. Standardization of these constructs is currently underway; however, it will take some time for all vendors to conform to the terminology and definition of the constructs.

Manipulating data in the relational model, as illustrated through SQL, is nonprocedural in the sense that users specify only "what" data they need and not "how" the data should be retrieved. The separation of the logical property of the data from the physical implementation of the data is referred to as data independence. Data independence allows the database designer to tune and modify the physical storage structures of the database without having to rewrite the portion of the applications using the database. As a result, applications are more maintainable and tunable.

The data manipulation constructs found in most servers conform to standards such as the ANSI SQL89 much more closely than their data definition counterparts. Nevertheless, significant differences among server vendors can be found in built-in scalar functions (e.g., date, math functions), set operators (e.g., intersect and difference), special predicates (e.g., set membership), and special arithmetic operators (e.g., bitwise And, Or, and Not). Even the universal SELECT statement has many variations in the details of outer join, cursors, nested statements, and predicates such as ALL and EXIST. The proposed standards SQL2 and SQL3 contain many of these constructs; but until they are better defined, significant differences will be seen in commercial products. Applications that require accessing data from multiple servers in different platforms need to stay with the subset of SQL that all servers support. The tradeoff is that they will not be able to take advantage of specific features found in many servers.

12.2 Server Technologies

In Chapters 5 through 8, we discussed the technologies that a database server needs to deal with. Specifically, we covered transaction processing, database administration, performance enhancement, and benchmarking.

The intuitive meaning of a transaction is that either the entire sequence of operations of the transaction or nothing at all is applied to the database. Transaction processing includes two highly interrelated components—concurrency control and recovery management. Together, they guarantee the atomicity, consistency, isolation, and durability properties of transactions.

Concurrent control is used by database systems to synchronize the operations of concurrent transactions and to ensure correct operations by guarding against mutual interference. The objective is to allow concurrent transactions performing interleaving operations on shared database objects as if they are executed serially against the database. This concept is called serializability. Most commercial database systems use locking as the main mechanism for concurrency control. Several major, proven locking concepts were discussed in this book. The first is the so-called multigranularity locking, where different sizes of lockable database units, or granules, such as database, table, page, row, and field are used to synchronize potentially conflicting operations to the database. In general, the coarser the lock granule, the lower the bookkeeping overhead but the lower the degree of concurrency. Multigranularity locking also covers the concept of intention locks. Here, the idea is to improve on concurrency by declaring a transaction's intention on the kind of operations it will perform on a database object; in this way, others transactions with compatible intentions on the same object are allowed to hold compatible locks.

A powerful, yet simple, discipline to ensure serializability based on locking is the concept of two-phased locking. The protocol is that no locks can be released before a transaction has acquired all the locks needed for processing, and no new locks can be acquired once any of the locks have been released by the transaction. Two-phased locking can be simply implemented by releasing locks only at the end of the transaction.

Recovery management allows a transaction to roll back changes in the case of concurrent conflict and also to redo changes in the case of system recovery. Both the before and after images of the updated database object need to be recorded in logs to allow rollback and recovery to occur. Again, a powerful, but simple, protocol called the write-ahead log (WAL) is used by most commercial database systems to support recovery from transaction, system, and media failures. With the write ahead log protocol, the before images of the database object are recorded in the recovery log before the database object is updated in place. Furthermore, before a transaction is committed, its after images are recorded in the recovery log.

Most commercial database systems employ these basic concepts in concurrency control and recovery. However, there are significant differences in the details of their implementation. For example, some systems offer more granule types than others, while others exploit the before images of the log to provide multiversion concurrency control so that read-only transactions are never blocked. Most high-performance systems employ sophisticated checkpointing techniques to avoid force writing dirty pages after every transaction. And, some systems use data snapshots to offload some of the congestion of the database. There is a movement in transaction processing toward a new generation of techniques that (1) combine traditional locking concepts with optimistic concurrency control, (2) employ optical disks as recovery logs to simplify recovery management, and (3) offer more options of concurrent operations at the expense of serializability for practical purposes.

As we discussed earlier in this book, the factors affecting the performance of a server's operations are diverse. For decision-support applications with many ad hoc queries to the server, the ability of the server to provide efficient access paths and optimized selection of access paths is crucial. Most current commercial servers support B-tree indexing as the primary access method; access path selection is achieved through a combination of ad hoc and dynamic programming techniques based on statistics gathered on the data distribution. SQL provides additional challenges to the query optimizers, especially in the area of nested queries. Most current systems either fall short in their search for an optimal way of processing nested queries or they attempt to "flatten" the queries and discover the optimal access paths as a whole. Flattening nested queries can be very difficult. In fact, in many instances, servers that perform nested query transformation are very slow and sometimes they produce incorrect results.

For high-volume transaction processing, the performance of a server is affected primarily by three factors: (1) the architecture of the server, where it is crucial to provide efficient context-switching between concurrent transactions; (2) the interaction protocol between the server and the client, where it is important to provide batched requests and responses to minimize traffic on the network; and (3) the transaction manager, where appropriate lock modes and efficient checkpointing are needed to batch update pages to minimize traffic on the disk.

In systems that support both short update transactions and long queries, a number of techniques exist to boost performance by eliminating concurrency conflict. Multiversion and snapshot of database objects are the most popular of these. Another source of performance boost involves trading consistency for concurrency. For example, during a potentially long browse session, it may be desirable to release some of the record locks in order to minimize conflicts, thereby violating the two-phased locking protocol and compromising serializability.

Formally measuring performance of a system is the difficult and sometimes controversial area of benchmarking. For many years, because of the lack of a generally applicable benchmark with formal definition, performance was based on subjective evaluation and claims by vendors. For a benchmark to be generally applicable, it has to possess the properties of relevance, simplicity, scalability, portability, and vendor neutrality. In addition to these general guidelines, a benchmark designer needs to model a diverse number of areas spanning communications, database generation, number of concurrent users, data operation types, and system size. Currently, the Wisconsin benchmark is the most frequently used single-user benchmark for small relational database systems. The AS^3AP benchmark is an attempt by the original authors of the Wisconsin benchmark to offer a wider range of operations. The DebitCredit/TP1 benchmark is the first popular benchmark embraced by commercial database vendors designed to measure a large volume of short transactions in a multiuser environment; its model includes network and presentation services. However, TP1's lack of formal definition leads to abuse and exaggerated claims by some vendors. The formation of the Transaction Processing Council (TPC) and the subsequent creation of the TPC-A and TPC-B benchmarks represent the effort put forward by the relational vendors consortium to establish a formal OLTP benchmark that provides more accurate and reliable information on transaction processing. This selfpolicing effort is very encouraging and will be more widely accepted as client-server computing matures.

12.3 Application Programming Interfaces

Application programming interfaces (APIs) are used to send client requests to database servers. The major types of application program interfaces include dynamic SQL, embedded SQL, direct call interface, and module language support. Many vendors support more than one API type. Very often, it is a tradeoff between ease of use versus efficiency. For example, using dynamic or embedded SQL in a host environment is more programmable and readable than using direct call interface with the predefined parameters. However, the latter very often provides significant performance advantages. The effort by standards groups like Remote Database Access (RDA) and the SQL Access Group (SAG) to standardize on data access API to increase the interoperability and portability of applications is gaining momentum.

12.4 Twelve Rules for Client Applications

In this book we did not cover PC database application development tools and products such as forms, report generators, and GUI development environments. However, we do provide (in the Appendix) 12 rules which ensure portability, performance, autonomy, and completeness of client-server applications. They provide guidelines to client application designers in realizing the basic benefits of client-server computing; namely, the division of labor with as little duplication of effort as possible and the full exploitation of each other's strengths in order to achieve the best possible application. We believe these rules should also be used as evaluation guidelines for client applications. The portability rules ensure that there is a way to port the same applications across different servers running in different platforms without excessive modification of the application. The performance rules guard against client applications abusing the privilege as a client to a server for ease of implementation; they also guard against compromising the performance and power of the underlying server. The autonomy rules enforce the clean separation between a client and a server so both sides can continue to evolve independently in the areas in which they are good. And, the completeness rules provide guidelines to measure the richness of solution that a client application provides to the users in the areas of end-user tools, host environment, and server connections.

12.5 Future Evolution of Client-Server Computing

There are two major trends in the area of client-server computing: distributed databases and intelligent database extensions of SQL.

The term *distributed database* is very often misused and abused by vendors. Loosely speaking, current client-server solutions can be considered part of the distributed database solution because they provide for the separation of data and applications. However, if one were to use the formal definition of the term, it would appear that the first commercial distributed database systems have emerged with a very primitive set of capabilities—even though many years of research have gone into the identification of distributed database problems and some of their solutions. The 12 rules developed by Chris Date help to clearly define the intention and basic capabilities of distributed databases. The major concept of these rules is that a distributed database system should behave exactly like a nondistributed system to the end user and the application developer. Three principles can be derived from this concept. The first is the principle of autonomy, which states that all sites within a distributed database system should be able to operate independently. The second is the principle of distributed transparency; this states that the distribution of data to sites within a distributed database system should be shielded from users and applications. And, the third is the principle of heterogeneity, which requires that users and applications be shielded from the hardware platforms, operating systems, and networking protocols of the sites.

Clearly, a large number of technical problems must be solved before all of Date's rules can be satisfied. Aside from the distributed version of technical problems facing a nondistributed database, such as distributed catalog manager, query optimization, integrity constraints, concurrency control, recovery, and deadlock detection, there are many other problems peculiar to distributed database systems. These include heterogeneous two-phased commit, fragmentation, global naming scheme, and caching of foreign objects.

Distributed databases are difficult to realize all at once. However, they are a very natural evolutionary goal for current client-server applications. In fact, if the current trend continues, slowly but surely, servers will absorb more and more distributed database features into their products.

There are several additional paths of evolution that the next generation of client-server computing may adopt. We have combined these extensions under the term *intelligent databases*. We have also presented possibilities of intelligent databases through a prototype dialect of SQL called Intelligent SQL. Intelligent database extensions currently focus on several areas: (1) capturing more semantics in the relational model, (2) adding control structures in SQL to allow it to express larger units of application logic, (3) absorbing some of the object-oriented features found in most object-oriented database systems into the SQL language, (4) integrating inference rules into SQL to achieve more expressive power such as recursion, and finally (5) adding more multimedia data types and their access methods into SQL and the database engine. Each of these areas is very promising and exciting, and we believe that all of these sets of features will be found in future database systems. In fact, many of these features are addressed in SQL2 and SQL3, and several vendors have begun adding some rudimentary version of a small set of these features in their products. While most of these activities will occur on the server's side, client applications will reap the benefits of a "smarter" server, a richer language to express data manipulation logic, and more native support of many of the multimedia data types. At the same time, they will be completely shielded from having to know how the data is distributed and how the integrity constraints are enforced. All of these point to an increased opportunity for the user of client applications to produce more exciting, efficient products.

Client-server database computing is clearly here to stay. While there will always be obstacles to overcome, such as the natural resistance of moving to the new environment, the initial cost of downsizing, and the lack of widely accepted standards, the technologies are quickly maturing to the point where the benefits will simply be too overwhelming to ignore. The future is certain to be very exciting in terms of technology in the distributed database arena and in terms of SQL extensions, but more important, the future will present a solution framework to the complex, heterogeneous world of information.

Appendix

Guidelines for Client Application Software

As database-server technology grows in popularity, the impetus shifts increasingly on developers to create applications that access server data and take advantage of the many new features and capabilities that database servers provide. The move toward providing server access to new and existing client PC or workstation applications and the trend toward more graphical user interfaces are probably the two most important driving forces in application development today.

In this appendix, we examine the client application software that provides database-server access and we describe the features and attributes that you should look at when evaluating database application software.

Client Application Software

In contrast to terminal-based applications running on large platform computers, applications running on PC and workstation computers originally maintained all their own data and performed all their own data processing. After a proliferation of different data formats and the accumulation of large and unwieldy files storing data on different file servers, we now see a trend toward standardization of data access and a new role for more centralized data processing.

As database servers take on the task of centralizing data storage and data processing functions, applications can focus more on managing local tasks and providing better interaction with the user. For example, PCs and workstations can perform more processing-intensive operations such as those required to support mouse, pen, and other point-and-click operations in graphical user interface and event-driven programming systems like Windows 3.0 or Presentation Manager.

The delegation of services performed by both database servers and client PC and workstation computers follows a natural division of labor, taking into consideration the relative strength of each resource. Since the database server automatically handles many of the more difficult and complex data processing tasks, such as concurrency control (locking) and transaction processing, the application's responsibility in such matters is simply to issue requests for data and to handle returning data. As a result, database applications are smaller, more portable (since standard SQL data access commands are used), and easier to develop and maintain. Figure A.1 illustrates the new roles of both client and server.

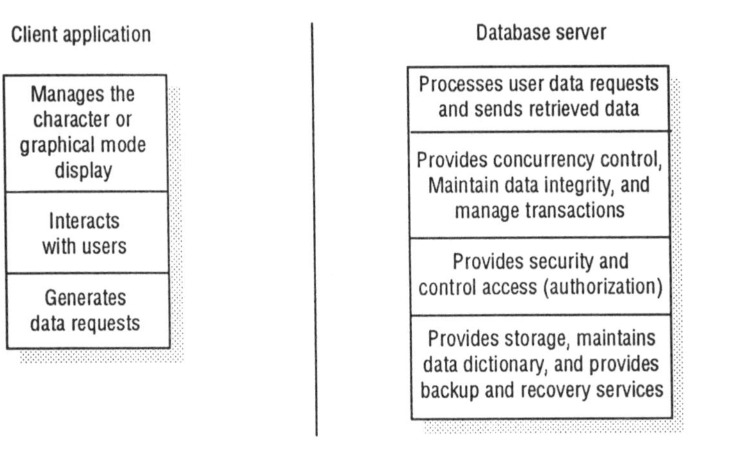

Figure A.1: *Client application and database-server software operations.*

Variety of Database Application Types

Several different types of client application software products that can be used to access database-server data are available today. End-user "decision support" software packages that provide functions such as query, report generation and database administration are one type. These packages come "out-of-the-box" ready to access one or more database servers. The Lotus 1-2-3 spreadsheet from Lotus, the database desktop publishing dbPUBLISHER product from Digital Composition Systems, the R&R for SQL Reportwriter from Concentric Data Systems, and Q&E from Pioneer Software are examples of this type of product.

A second type of client application product is composed of PC database application programs that, in addition to providing end-user tools, offer development tools that allow creation of custom database applications that access server data. An example is the dBASE IV Server Edition, which provides a complete set of tools for designing objects such as forms, queries, menus, and reports. It also provides a high-level application programming language (4GL) into which you can embed SQL statements that access server data. Additional examples of this type of product include DataEase from DataEase International, Paradox SQL Link from Borland, Omnis from Blythe Software, and Advanced Revelation from Revelation Technologies.

There are other types of programs that should also be considered for database application development. These include computer-aided software engineering (CASE) packages and tools such as AD/Cycle from IBM, ADW/Workstation from KnowledgeWare, and ORACLE CASE Tools from Oracle. In addition, other "object" or specific window environment-oriented products such as SQLWindows from Gupta, Object1 from mdbs, and Objectview from Matesys are considerations.

Server Access in Heterogeneous Environments

The simplest server access arrangement is a single type of application that accesses a single vendor database server (or multiple servers all of the same type); however, this is not often very practical. It is more likely that users in different groups will require different software packages, which may or may not all access the same sources of data. Thus, it is important that applications be able to access many different or "heterogeneous" sources of data (possibly involving one or more database servers provided by different vendors). Similarly, applications must peaceably coexist with other different or heterogeneous clients who may all be on the same network, concurrently accessing and operating with the same data. Figure A.2 shows how different application software products might be used to access the same server data.

As we see in the next section, a number of specific criteria allow for a diverse mix of both client applications and data resources, while assuring their peaceful coexistence.

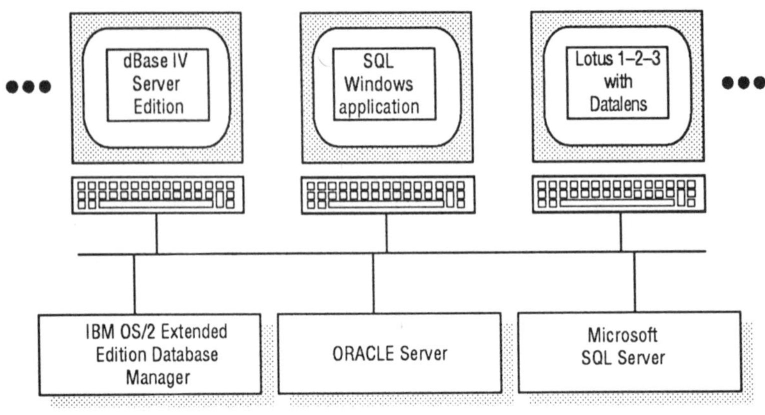

Figure A.2: The heterogeneous client- and database-server environment.

Criteria for Evaluating Client Software

Although we've talked in this book about the advantages of database servers and the benefits that client-server computing provide, there still is no guarantee that you will benefit from these advantages when you set up various software packages on different PCs. Your particular system or the applications you run to access server data may impose specific limits on the database server or may otherwise limit its capability or performance.

To provide an analogy, you might have an automobile engine capable of going very fast or pulling a lot of weight, but if your vehicle has balding tires, you're not going to do either. Thus, it's important when evaluating various end-user and application development products first to make sure they meet all the basic functional requirements for the type of operations your application is to perform. Then, you need to check the way in which applications access different database servers to make certain that they do not create artificial restrictions on server operations, impose a large overhead on configuration or server performance, or otherwise "paint you into a corner."

Here, we describe various criteria by which you can evaluate software when choosing applications that access server data for your own use. The following list summarizes 12 basic attributes (as they pertain to a client application accessing server data) that a "good" client will provide. We go into some detail and provide examples on how each attribute may affect your database server's operation.

Rule 1. Preservation of server autonomy: Let the server do what it does best. Don't abuse the privilege enjoyed as a client application accessing server data.

Rule 2. Preservation of client autonomy: Client software should behave and operate the same when connected to a database server as when it operates on local or stand-alone data.

Rule 3. Server-independent applications: Client software should be portable and should run the same when accessing data across different database servers operating on a variety of different hardware, operating system, and network platforms.

Rule 4. Accessibility of server-specific features: Applications should provide a way to access the specific features and constructs of particular database servers. In some cases, implementing these features may reduce server-independent operations (rule 3); however, users and particularly developers should be able to access specific server features when necessary to achieve the best possible performance.

Rule 5. "Live" data access support: Client software should operate on "live" server data! Also, an application should provide up-to-date information on server schema data. Downloading and uploading server data (a practice carried out by some client software packages) reduces the database server to a glorified file server.

Rule 6. Minimal workstation impact for adding server access: Accessing server data should minimally impact the requirement for workstation hardware, memory, and disk space. Client software should not require additional memory or disk space for processing or downloading server data, or additional space for replicating database server schema and catalog data.

Rule 7. Completeness of connectivity options: How complete a connectivity solution does a particular software package provide? This question should be answered both in terms of the number and types of database servers accessed as well as the manner in which these connections can be made.

Rule 8. Local prototyping opportunity: In particular, application development software should provide the capability to prototype and test an application using local data and resources—without requiring a major investment up front in the database server and network hardware and software needed to implement the final installed client application.

Rule 9. Completeness of end-user tools: For software used primarily by end users, look for as complete a set of end-user tools as possible. This will allow users to fully access the capabilities of a particular server without much assistance or without requiring custom application programming.

Rule 10. Completeness of application development environment: To simplify the process of application creation, client software used to develop applications should have as complete a set of development tools as possible. For example, the software might include tools for designing the user interface as well as the display, entry forms, and reports used within an application.

Rule 11. An open system host language environment: While it is important that a software package provide robust and fully functional end-user tools "out-of-the-box," users should also be allowed to change the way in which a particular product works. No matter how complete a "hard-wired" product's tool set is, it cannot generally meet the needs of all users or accommodate different levels of user expertise or experience. Without an accessible host language interface underlying the tools a particular product provides, users are stuck with the functionality that the original software designers put into the box.

Rule 12. Adherence to standards: All major database servers are approaching standardization in the use of SQL dialect and in the protocols used for server access. It is crucial for client software to adhere to these standards and to evolve with them to protect the investment made in applications. Conforming to existing standards also improves the interoperability among various client application/database server combinations.

Rule 1: Preservation of Server Autonomy

The first rule that client software should observe is the preservation of server autonomy. Stated more simply, client software should operate in such a way as not to violate common rules of behavior or "etiquette" established for accessing server data. Adherence to this rule allows the server to do what it does best and helps to maintain the independent operation of each individual database server as well as the independent operation of client applications with respect to each other.

For example, since one of a database server's primary responsibilities in the client-server equation is to optimize data sharing and concurrency, clients should not routinely lock up large amounts of data. Moreover, client software should not allow users to bypass security and authorization checks. This is particularly important in environments where a number of different client software packages are all accessing the same server.

This first rule also requires that client software not let "dirty" data (that which has not been committed as part of a transaction) be entered into database-server tables. Similarly, the failure of particular clients should not impact the availability of the server (or server data) to other clients. As an example, some systems implement transaction logging at the client PC or workstation. Thus, if an application running on the client crashes, there will be no way to kill a transaction because the rollback information is stored on the "dead" client workstation's machine.

Observation of this rule by client applications allows peaceful coexistence among client applications and independence of database-server operations from client operations, thereby providing optimization opportunity to the server. On the other hand, violation of this rule results in compromises of data integrity, and performance degradation in server operations.

Rule 2: Preservation of Client Autonomy

Similar to client applications respecting the autonomy of a server, application software should maintain the autonomy of the client (from the server). The goal and technical challenge of adhering to this second rule is that client software should behave and operate the same when connected to a database server as when it operates on locally maintained or stand-alone data. This means that the presence of an active server connection should not adversely affect client software or applications, restrict or slow their operation, affect the "look and feel" of an application, or otherwise intrude excessively in the affairs of a client application user.

As an example of adherence to this rule, if the database server crashes, a client should be able to continue operating as an independent workstation. Similarly, since there are times when a database server may not be available (e.g., when using a notebook computer to store data that will later be uploaded to the server), client software should support access and storage of both local and server data.

Client software should also try to handle the location of data as transparently as possible and should insulate the user from the details to access data on a particular server. Client software should support native server datatypes and perform any required datatype mapping as transparently as possible. In addition, the type of scalar functions and expression capability provided for operations with each of the various datatypes supported by a particular database server should also be evaluated.

When accessing data from multiple servers, client applications should work the same and access data in the same way, regardless of the particular server from which data is accessed. (For example, client software may map the error messages returned by individual database servers to common consistently phrased messages used within the application.) Where client software may also allow simultaneous or distributed access of data from one or more database servers from the same or different vendors, the same goal of providing "transparent" and "seamless" data access also generally applies.

Observation of this second rule by client applications will allow (1) minimal additional training for client application users, (2) smoother integration of more data sources without major impact on users, and (3) better protection of user investments in applications because of the transparency of connectivity.

An example of a client software that violates the client autonomy rule is Paradox SQL Link in which only a subset of its functionality is available for server data. The View and Edit commands, for instance, work only with native Paradox data. Another example of software violating rule 2 can be found in the dBASE IV Server Edition. In this product, none of Control Center tools work on server data. Rule 2 is only observed at the dBASE/SQL level when the same language constructs can be used for both local and server data.

Rule 3: Server-independent Applications

This third rule specifies that client applications, particularly application development software, should be portable and should run the same when accessing data across different database servers operating on a variety of different hardware, operating system, and network platforms. This rule implies the existence of a query language mapping layer in the client software to access remote database servers.

As supplemented by rule 7, (Completeness of Connectivity Options), and application's adherence to rule 3 is critical to organizations that need to support many different types of servers from a number of different vendors, and that want to write uniform interfaces that talk to each one. Depending on the variety of different platforms you need to support, you should evaluate the number of different server connections and the variety of connectivity options that are available.

Apple Computer's Data Access Language (DAL) and Borland's dBASE IV Server Edition are examples of software in which a designer may write a single application that operates transparently even when accessing database servers having different SQL dialects.

It is also important to keep in mind that there may be a tradeoff in the desire to support server-specific features (rule 4) and the desire to have applications operate the same across different servers. Each of the two products mentioned above provide a common SQL dialect that may be used to develop server-independent applications. In this case, the completeness of the "baseline" functionality of the standard SQL dialect provided by client software may determine how easy it is to take advantage of server-specific features without requiring application developers to learn and implement the specific SQL dialect of each supported server.

Observation of this rule ensures the user's investment in applications because the same application can run regardless of what server contains the data source.

Paradox requires the user to embed server-specific SQL commands in PAL, their programming language, thus all applications are server dependent. This deficiency can be remedied by using QBE to express the required data access and embedding the QBE definition in the application.

Rule 4: Accessibility of Server-specific Features

The key goal specified by rule 4 is that client software, particularly software packages allowing application development, should enable users to take advantage of and tap into the specific features of a particular database server. While incorporating features and capabilities specific (and unique) to an individual server may reduce the portability of applications and may require some custom application design, it is nonetheless important to allow developers to do so.

It might be especially important, for example, to allow developers access to specific features and contructs provided by a server in situations where performance is an issue and the application must run as efficiently as possible on a particular platform. This rule might also be significant in cases where a particular server provides certain features not yet available in other servers (e.g., support of BLOB and long text fields), or where a server follows unique and different file-naming or object-creation conventions.

Client software (both end user and application development) should be able to directly access most if not all server features. For example, a client application should be able to access all server structures such as tables, views, indexes, and catalogs. Also, end-user tools such as queries, entry forms, and reports should all be able to operate against and update server data, and they should be able to integrate whatever server features and capabilities (such as security, access, and data integrity control) are available using a particular database server. Observation of this rule allows client developers to fully exploit the total power of the server.

Some specific examples of adherence to rule 4 are allowing an application running against the IBM Extended Edition Database Manager to access its referential integrity features—or—using the SQL Server to take advantage of triggers and special stored and system procedures.

Software products that violate this rule include Oracle's SQL*FORM and SQL*Report Writer. Oracle's Server Long Text fields cannot be accessed. Another example is Paradox's SQL Link in which the BLOB fields from the SQL Server are automatically truncated. Perhaps the most serious violation of rule 4 is the one-cursor only limitation imposed by Paradox, which severely restricts the power of the server.

Rule 5: "Live" Data Access Support

Client software needs to operate on "live" server data! Users should not have to resort or be forced into looking at snapshots of old data. We can't really emphasize this rule enough. Any translation, downloading and uploading of data, or other operation involving "snapshot" data reduces the effectiveness of your application and will probably annoy the end user a great deal. That's because, invariably, there will be times when a user performs some operation on a set of data, only to have the operation fail because the data is no longer available or it has been changed. (See also the important discussions regarding read consistency and multiversioning in Chapter 5.)

You should be particularly concerned with a number of areas when evaluating client software for operation with live data: the generation of queries and reports, "browsable" data tables and views, and the creation and modification of database objects. In addition to actual server table data, applications should also provide up-to-date information on server schema data, which specifies server catalog or data dictionary information, the names of database objects, and so on. In general, an application should provide up-to-date information on server schema data without slowing down client operations, replicating data, or requiring extra disk space storage on the client's machine.

Observation of rule 5 provides timely, accurate data, without expensive overhead of storage at the client level. Violation of this rule could make client-server computing an impractical solution because the very purpose of having an architecture in which the server deals with the data and the client deals with the front end is abused.

Paradox SQL Link requires all server data to be locally stored in order to manipulate this data. For small applications with a small amount of data required from the server, the space and time penalty may be acceptable. However, in most sizable applications, this lack of live data support makes such an approach totally useless.

Rule 6: Minimal Impact on Workstations

Just as adding server access should not significantly change the operation of an existing application, it also should not significantly impact the client PC or workstation requirements for hardware, memory, and disk space. The client software might have considerable workstation requirements of additional memory or disk space for temporarily processing or downloading server data.

When adding server access to an existing application, however, it is reasonable to require additional space to load network and connectivity software or to add connectivity library functions to an existing package. Client software may also provide memory management support and configuration options to minimize the impact that adding server access imposes on workstation memory and disk space requirements. For example, in the DOS arena, many applications are now bundled with a memory manager program and they may also provide some other capability for disk caching. Some products may also use real and extended mode switching (for PCs using 286- and 386-based processors) to allow access to network connectivity packages and protocols available in different LAN environments.

Rule 7: Completeness of Connectivity Options

The availability of connectivity options may dictate, to a large extent, the choice of both database-server and client-application software. Your selection may be based on both the number and types of database servers that may be interconnected or accessed as well as the manner in which these connections can be made.

As with database software, when evaluating client software, you should look carefully at all the connectivity options a particular package supports, determine the ones you need, and then read the fine print to make sure the client software supports all the various options for accessing data from particular servers. One key factor that might dictate your selection is where data in your business or organization is currently stored. Other influences might be the type of PCs and workstations you need to connect and the type of LAN hardware and software you have already installed. Some of more common servers on the market include the Microsoft SQL Server, the IBM OS/2 Extended Edition, the ORACLE Server, Informix, DB2, and Gupta.

Other influences specific to client applications are the ability to connect to one or more different servers (possibly using different networking protocols to access servers on different operating system platforms), and the ability to connect to more than one database server at a time (from the same or different vendors). Similarly, you may want to look at whether an application is available on all the different operating systems you need, such as DOS, OS/2, or UNIX, and whether the application uses various graphical user interfaces, such as Windows 3.0, Presentation Manager, or X-Windows, on those platforms.

Observation of rule 7 allows the flexibility of writing applications accessing data from many server types. This is a crucial requirement for corporate MISs where a heterogeneous environment is the norm rather than the exception.

Oracle tools such as SQL*FORM and SQL*Report Writer can access many platforms where ORACLE Server runs. Paradox SQL Link allows access to Microsoft's SQL Server, ORACLE, and the IBM OS/2 Extended Edition. Advanced Relevation and DataEase/SQL allow two-phased commit among different servers.

Rule 8: Local Prototyping Opportunity

This rule applies primarily to client application development software. Optimally, this type of software should provide the capability to prototype and to test an application using local data and resources without requiring a major investment in database-server and network hardware and software. After a prototype is built and a majority of the development effort is complete, you can install the client application and be assured that it will run with very few changes.

This rule implies that you need a complete local development environment, including a local SQL database engine and a 3GL or 4GL language environment that can be used to prototype a complete application. In particular, this capability might be desirable for first-time users or developers; however, it might also be beneficial in situations where quick feedback from end users is required. This type of environment can also serve as an educational forum for first-time users of relational databases, SQL, and database application design and programming tools in general.

Adherence to rule 8 allows a cheaper and quicker way to develop applications and provides an opportunity for developers to experiment and educate themselves before a big commitment has to be made as to which server to purchase. The dBASE IV Server Edition is an example of client application satisfying this rule because the local SQL environment is available to the developer. All other products that employ a simple "pass-through" mechanism without their own local SQL engine fail to satisfy this rule.

Rule 9: Completeness of End-user Tools

For software that is to be used primarily by novice and end users, you should consider applications that provide as complete a tool set as possible. End users should be able to perform a broad range of simple database tasks without assistance. Additionally, they should be able to perform many sophisticated, nontrivial operations without requiring the design of a custom application program, which may further burden an overloaded application development or MIS staff.

End-user tools include items such as query and reporting tools, display and entry form designers, database design and administration tools, and automatic application program generation. In many cases, end users can interactively query the database and can design all their own display, browse, and entry forms as well as create reports on the data they want to retrieve from one or more database servers.

Observation of rule 9 permits a flexible way for end users to interact with server data. Most front-end applications currently available have extensive end-user tools to deal with server data. One exception is the dBASE IV Server Edition in which direct interaction with server data is limited because the Control Center tools are not enabled for server data.

Rule 10: Complete Application Development Environment

Rule 10 applies mostly to client software used by application developers or members of MIS and IS staff responsible for creating business and enterprise applications. To simplify the process of application creation, client software used to develop applications should have as complete a set of development tools as possible. These tools typically include those used for designing elements of the user interface, that is, elements such as the display, entry forms, and reports used within an application.

Development tools might also include debugging tools to test applications, and an application generator to automatically generate executable programs. (The client software may be based on 4GL, CASE, or object-oriented design models to simplify the creation of sophisticated applications.) In addition, the client software might provide additional database administration tools to help set up database objects, migrate data to the server, and set up security for access to the data.

The tools available to developers should allow integration of server-specific and generic database server capabilities into custom database applications. Thus, client software should incorporate as complete an implementation of SQL as possible, tightly integrated into whatever host application development language or environment the product provides. The tools should also allow control or interaction with database servers to define operations such as transaction processing (spanning both local and server data updates), concurrency and other related issues such as deadlock detection and prevention, and data validation on server data.

Gupta's SQL Windows, the dBASE IV Server Edition, and Oracle Tools all have extensive development environment. Advanced Revelation and DataEase/SQL contain limited debugging facilities for application developers.

Rule 11: Open System Host Language Environment

While it is important that a software package provide robust and fully functional end-user tools, users need to be able to customize the operation of software to meet their individual preferences and requirements. No matter how complete and robust a product is, it generally cannot meet the needs of all users or accommodate all levels of user expertise or experience; thus, users should be allowed to change it. More specifically, in regard to application development products, by making a host language interface accessible to users, users can customize the functionality that the original software designers put into the product.

On the application development side, client software should incorporate as complete as possible implementation of SQL. Also, the SQL implementation for databaser servers should be tightly integrated into whatever host application development language or environment the product provides. By building tools on top of a native host language that is also made available to developers, you allow users to extend the functionality of software, or customize it to match their own requirements or preferences. As a result, you can extend the life of software and protect a potentially large investment in existing applications.

Adherence to rule 11 allows application customizability. Many front-end applications do not provide a host language environment, and thereby fail to satisfy this rule. Most major client software products such as dBASE, Paradox, and Oracle Tools use their proprietary languages or standard 3GLs such as C as their host environment.

Rule 12: Adherence to Existing Standards

All major database servers are approaching standardization in the the use of SQL dialect and the protocols used for server access. It is crucial for client software to adhere to these standards and to evolve with them to protect the investment made in applications. Conforming to existing standards also improves the interoperability among various client application/database server combinations.

Change is one of the constants in the PC hardware and software industry. Developers must work constantly to stay ahead of their competition by designing or redesigning existing software packages to adapt to new trends in the marketplace and to run on new hardware and software platforms.

While users want new features, they also have other concerns when considering to adopt new software, especially when a large number of users are involved, when major investments or changes in systems are at stake, or when training are required. In particular, software that adheres closely to existing standards for graphical user interfaces (such as Windows and Presentation Manager) and standards for SQL and remote access of server data can go a long way in eliminating the risks involved in adopting new programs.

Conforming to existing standards, particularly regarding the use of SQL, can also improve portability of applications and reduce application development costs when designing applications that access multiple database servers. Following existing graphical interface standards can simplify the design of new programs and can reduce the cost of training new users as applications operate in the same way and use similar navigation techniques.

Current standards for SQL have been detailed by the American National Standards Institute (ANSI), the International Standards Organization (ISO), and most recently, IBM's SAA standard for multiplatform SQL portability. Standards for graphical interfaces and "presentation" have developed through products such as the Apple Desktop Interface, Windows 3.0, and Presentation Manager. On UNIX computer and Next platforms, similar graphical user interface standards have developed from products such as X-Windows and Motif. For more details on graphical user interfaces see Khoshafian and Abnous [1990].

Networking and Remote Database Access (RDA) standards have been developed using the Open Systems Interconnect (OSI) model prepared by the ISO group and the Institute for Electronic and Electrical Engineers (IEEE). In addition, the SQL Access Group (SAG), a consortium of hardware and software vendors, has developed a standard for interoperability and portability of SQL-based applications.

Bibliography

Abrial, J. 1974. Data Semantics. In *Data Base Management,* eds. J.W. Klimbie and K.L. Koffeman. North-Holland.

AIA/ATA. 1990. *SFQL: Structured Full-Text Query Language, AIA/ATA Subcommittee 89-9C Specification* December 1989; revised February 1990.

ANSI. 1986. *Database Language—SQL.* American National Standards Institute, Incorporated.

ANSI. 1989. *Database Language—SQL with Integrity Enhancement.* American National Standards Institute, Incorporated.

Anon. et al. 1985. A Measure of Transaction Processing Power. *Datamation* 31(7).

Armstrong, W.W. 1974. Dependency Structures of Data Base Relationships. *Proceedings of the 1974 IFIP Congress.* North-Holland.

Astrahan, M. et al. 1976. System R: A Relational Approach to Data Management. *ACM Transactions on Database Systems* 1(2).

Bancilhon, F. et al. 1983. VERSO: A Relational Back-end Data Base Machine. *Proceedings of the 2nd International Workshop on Database Machines.*

Bancilhon, F., T. Briggs, S. Khoshafian et al. 1987. FAD—A Simple and Powerful Database Language. *VLDB Conference Proceedings.*

Bancilhon, F. and S. Khoshafian. 1986. A Calculus for Complex Objects. *ACM PODS Conference Proceedings.*

Bancilhon, F. and S. Khoshafian. 1989. A Calculus for Complex Objects. *Journal of Computer and System Sciences* 38(2).

Bancilhon, F. and R. Ramakrishnan. 1986. An Amateur's Introduction to Recursive Query-processing Strategies. *ACM SIGMOD Conference Proceedings.*

Barter, R. 1989. *CASE*METHOD™ Entity Relationship Modeling.* Addison-Wesley.

Bayer, R., E. Elhardt, H. Heller et al. 1980. Parallelism and Recovery in Database Systems. *ACM Transactions on Database Systems* 5(2).

Beeri, C., R. Fagin, and J.H. Howard. 1977. A Complete Axiomatization for Functional and Multivalued Dependencies. *ACM SIGMOD International Conference on Management of Data.*

Bernstein, P.A., V. Hadzilacos, and N. Goodman. 1987. *Concurrency Control and Recovery in Database Systems.* Addison-Wesley.

Bernstein, P.A. and N. Goodman. 1981. Concurrency Control in Distributed Database Systems. *ACM Computing Survey* 13(2).

Bitton, D., D.J. DeWitt, and C. Turbyfill. 1983. Benchmarking Database Systems: A Systematic Approach. *Proceedings of the 1983 Very Large Database Conference.*

Bitton, D. and C. Turbyfill. 1988. A Retrospective on the Wisconsin Benchmark. In *Readings in Database Systems*, ed. M. Stonebraker. Morgan Kaufmann.

Ceri, S., B. Pernici, and G. Wiederhold. 1987. Distributed Database Design Methodologies. *IEEE Proceedings Special Issue on Distributed Database Systems* 75(5).

Ceri, S. and G. Pelagatti. 1984. *Distributed Databases: Principles and Systems.* McGraw-Hill.

Chan, A., S. Khoshafian, R. Abnous et al. 1991. Intelligent Object-oriented Features in Distributed Databases. *IEEE COMPCON Conference Proceedings.*

Chang, C.L. and A. Walker. 1986. PROSQL: A Prolog Programming Interface with SQL/DS. In *Expert Database Systems, Proceedings of the First International Workshop*, ed. L. Kerschberg. Benjamin-Cummings.

Chen, P.P. 1976. The Entity-Relationship Model—Toward a Unified View of Data. *ACM Transactions on Database Systems* 1(1).

Codd, E.F. 1970. A Relational Model for Large Shared Data Banks. *Communications of the ACM* 13(6).

Codd, E.F. 1979. Extending the Database Relational Model to Capture More Meaning. *ACM Transactions on Database Systems* 4(4).

Codd, E.F. 1985. Is Your DBMS Really Relational? *Computer World* October 14, 1985.

Conte, P. 1989. SAA Distributed Database: In Search of Consistency. *Database Programming & Design* 2(8).

Daniels, D., P. Selinger, L. Haas et al. 1982. An Introduction to Distributed Query Compilation in R*. In *Distributed Data Bases*, ed. H.J. Schneider. North-Holland.

Date, C.J. 1987. Twelve Rules for a Distributed Database. *Computer World* June 8, 1987.

DEC. 1990a. *VAX Rdb/VMS Guide to Database Maintenance and Performance, Part 1*. Digital Equipment Corporation.

DEC. 1990b. *VAX Rdb/VMS Guide to Using SQL/Services*. Digital Equipment Corporation.

DEC. 1990c. *VAX Rdb/VMS Installation Guide*. Digital Equipment Corporation.

DEC. 1990d. *VAX Rdb/VMS SQL Reference Guide, Part 1*. Digital Equipment Corporation.

DeWitt, D.J. 1991. The Wisconsin Benchmark: Past, Present, and Future. In *The Benchmark Handbook for Database and Transaction Processing Systems*, ed. J. Gray. Morgan Kaufmann.

Edelstein, H. 1990. Distributed Databases. *DBMS* September 1990.

Everest, G.C. 1986. *Database Management: Objectives, System Functions, and Administration*. McGraw-Hill.

Finkelstein, R. and C. White. 1989. Auditor's Report. Ashton-Tate/Microsoft SQL Server TP1 Benchmark, May–June 1989; Performance Computing and Colin White Consulting, August 1989.

Fishman, D. et al. 1987. Iris: An Object Oriented Database Management System. *ACM Transactions on Database Systems* 5(1).

Garcia-Molina, H. and R.K. Abbott. 1987. Reliable Distributed Database Management. *IEEE Proceedings Special Issue on Distributed Database Systems* 75(5).

Gold-Bernstein, B. 1990. Does Client-Server Equal Distributed Database? *Database Programming & Design* 3(9).

Goldring, R. 1990. Application Design for Distributed DB2. *Database Programming & Design* 3(9).

Gray, J., ed. 1991. *The Benchmark Handbook for Database and Transaction Processing Systems.* Morgan Kaufmann.

Gray, J., P. McJones, M. Blasgen et al. 1981. The Recovery Manager of the System R Database Manager. *ACM Computing Survey* 13(2).

Groff, J.R. and P.N. Weinberg. 1990a. Transaction Processing. *DBMS* December 1990.

Groff, J. and P. Weinberg. 1990b. *Using SQL.* Osborne/McGraw-Hill.

Hall, P., J. Owlett, and S. Todd. 1976. Relations and Entities. In *Modeling in Data Base Management Systems*, ed. G.M. Nijssen. North-Holland.

Hammer, M. and D. McLeod. 1981. Database Description With SDM: A Semantic Database Model. *ACM Transactions on Database Systems* 6(3).

Harder, T. and A. Reuter. 1983. Principles of Transaction-oriented Database Recovery. *ACM Computing Surveys* 15(4).

IBM. 1988. *System Application Architecture: Common Programming Interface Database Reference.* International Business Machine Corporation.

IBM. 1989a. *IBM Operating System/2 Extended Edition Version 1.2 Database Manager Structured Query Language (SQL) Reference.* International Business Machines Corporation.

IBM. 1989b. *IBM Operating System/2 Extended Edition Version 1.2 Database Manager Administrator's Guide.* International Business Machines Corporation.

IBM. 1989c. *IBM Operating System/2 Extended Edition Version 1.2 Database Manager Programming Guide and Reference*, Vol. 1: Guide. International Business Machines Corporation.

IBM. 1989d. *IBM Operating System/2 Extended Edition Version 1.2 Database Manager Programming Guide and Reference*, Vol. 2: Reference. International Business Machines Corporation.

IBM. 1989e. Inside IBM's Database Strategy. *DBMS* IBM-sponsored Supplement. 2(9).

Inmon, W.H. 1989. Benchmarking the Benchmarks. *Database Programming & Design* 2(8).

Khoshafian, S. 1989. A Persistent Complex Object Database Language. *Data and Knowledge Engineering* 3, 1988–1989.

Khoshafian, S. 1990. Insight Into Object-oriented Databases. *Information and Software Technology* 32(4).

Khoshafian, S. 1991a. Intelligent SQL. *Computer Standards and Interfaces* 13(1–3).

Khoshafian, S. 1991b. Modeling With Object-oriented Databases. *AI Expert* October 1991.

Khoshafian, S. and R. Abnous. 1990. *Object Orientation*. John Wiley.

Khoshafian, S., R. Blumer, and R. Abnous. 1991. Inheritance and Generalization in Intelligent SQL, ANSI OODBTG Standardization Workshop, *Computer Standards and Interfaces* 13(1–3).

Khoshafian, S. and T. Briggs. 1988. Schema Design and Mapping Strategies for Persistent Object Models. *Information and Software Technology* December 1988.

Khoshafian, S. and G. Copeland. 1986. Object Identity. *OOPSLA Conference Proceedings*.

Khoshafian, S., K. Parsaye, and H. Wong. 1990. Intelligent Database Engines. *Database Programming & Design* 3(7).

Khoshafian, S. and L. Thieme. 1991. Declarative Reasoning Extensions to Commercial SQL Database Management Systems. *IEEE COMPCON Conference Proceedings*.

Khoshafian, S. and P. Valduriez. 1990. Persistence, Sharing, and Object Orientation: a Database Perspective. In *Advances in Database Programming Languages*, eds. F. Bancilhon and P. Buneman, Addison-Wesley.

Kim, W. 1982. On Optimizing an SQL-like Nested Query. *ACM Transactions on Database Systems* 7(3).

Kulkarni, K. and M. Atkinson. 1986. EFDM: Extended Functional Data Model. *The Computer Journal* 29(1).

Kung, H.T. and J.T. Robinson. 1981. On Optimistic Methods for Concurrency Control. *ACM Transactions on Database Systems* 6(2).

Kuper, G. and M. Vardi. 1984. A New Approach to Database Logic. *ACM PODS Conference Proceedings*.

Landers, T. and R. Rosenberg. 1982. An Overview of Multibase. In *Distributed Data Bases*, ed. H.J. Schneider. North-Holland.

Lindsay, B.G. 1987. A Retrospective of R*. *IEEE Proceedings Special Issue on Distributed Database Systems* 75(5).

Lindsay, B.G., L.M. Haas, C. Mohan et al. 1984. Computation and Communication in R*: A Distributed Database Manager. *ACM Transactions on Computer Systems* 2(1).

Litwin, W., L. Mark, and N. Roussopoulos. 1990. Interoperability of Multiple Autonomous Databases. *ACM Computing Surveys* 22(3).

Lohman, G., D. Daniels, L. Haas et al. 1984. Optimization of Nested Queries in a Distributed Relational Database. *VLDB Conference Proceedings.*

Lohman, G. and L.F. Mackert. 1986. R* Optimizer Validation and Performance Evaluation for Local Queries. *ACM SIGMOD Conference Proceedings.*

Lohman, G., C. Mohan, L. Haas et al. 1985. Query Processing in R*. In *Query Processing in Database Systems*, eds. W. Kim, D. Batory, and D. Reiner. Springer-Verlag.

Mackert, L.F. and G. Lohman. 1986. R* Optimizer Validation and Performance Evaluation for Distributed Queries. *VLDB Conference Proceedings.*

Maier, D. 1983. *The Theory of Relational Databases.* Computer Science Press.

Martyn, T. and T. Hartley. 1990. Semantics and Logical Errors Using SQL. *Database Programming & Design* 3(6).

McGoveran, D. 1990. Evaluating Optimizers. *Database Programming & Design* 3(1).

McGoveran, D. and C. White. 1990. Clarifying Client-Server. *DBMS* 3(12).

Microsoft. 1989a. *SQL Server On-line Transaction Performance.* Microsoft Corporation.

Microsoft. 1989b. *SQL Server Benchmarking Kit.* Microsoft Corporation.

Microsoft. 1990a. *Microsoft SQL Server Installation Guide.* Microsoft Corporation.

Microsoft. 1990b. *Microsoft SQL Server Language Reference.* Microsoft Corporation.

Microsoft. 1990c. *Microsoft SQL Server Programmer's Reference.* Microsoft Corporation.

Microsoft. 1990d. *Microsoft SQL Server System Administrator's Guide.* Microsoft Corporation.

Mohan, C. and B. Lindsay. 1983. Efficient Commit Protocols for the Tree of Processes Model of Distributed Transactions. *ACM Proceedings of the 2nd SIGACT/SIGOPS Symposium on Principles of Distributed Computing.*

Mylopoulos, J., P. Bernstein, and H. Wong. 1980. A Language Facility for Designing Database-Intensive Applications. *ACM Transactions on Database Systems* 5(2).

NSTL. 1990. SQL Servers: Performance Optimization and Data Integrity. *Software Digest Buyer's Alert* 7(6).

Obermarck, R. 1982. Distributed Deadlock Detection Algorithm. *ACM Transactions on Database Systems* 7(2).

Ontologic. 1991. *ONTOS Object Database Documentation Set.* Ontologic, Incorporated.

Oracle. 1989a. *Advanced Performance Tuning Guide: ORACLE Server for OS/2.* Oracle Corporation.

Oracle. 1989b. *Database Administrator's Guide: ORACLE Server for OS/2.* Oracle Corporation.

Oracle. 1989c. *Programmer's Guide to the ORACLE Call Interfaces (OCIs).* Oracle Corporation.

Oracle. 1989d. *Server Manager User's Guide: ORACLE Server for OS/2.* Oracle Corporation.

Oracle. 1989e. *Setting Up the Server: ORACLE Server for OS/2.* Oracle Corporation.

Oracle. 1989f. *SQL Language Reference: ORACLE Server for OS/2.* Oracle Corporation.

Oracle. 1989g. *Utilities User's Guide: ORACLE Server for OS/2.* Oracle Corporation.

Ozsu, T. and P. Valduriez. 1991. *Principles of Distributed Database Systems*. Prentice Hall.

Parsaye, K., M. Chignell, S. Khoshafian et al. 1989. *Intelligent Databases*. Wiley.

Reiner, D., M. Brodie, G. Brown et al. 1985. The Database Design and Evaluation Workbench (DDEW) Project at CCA. *Database Engineering* 7(4).

Rosenkrantz, D.J., R.E. Stearns, and P.M. Lewis II. 1978. System Level Concurrency Control for Distributed Database Systems. *ACM Transactions on Database Systems* 3(2).

Roussopoulos, N., C. Faloustos, and T. Sellis. 1988. An Efficient Pictorial Database System for PSQL. *IEEE Transactions on Software Engineering* SE-14(5).

SAG. 1990. *SQL Access Group Technical Specification, X/Open DMWG/SQL Access Base Document*

Salton, G. 1989. *Automatic Text Processing*. Addison-Wesley.

Salton, G. and M.J. McGill. 1983. *An Introduction to Modern Information Retrieval*. McGraw-Hill.

Sawyer, T. 1989. *Auditor's Report of ORACLE Server TP1 Benchmark Results*. Codd and Date, Incorporated.

Sawyer, T. 1991. Doing Your Own Benchmark. In *The Benchmark Handbook for Database and Transaction Processing Systems*, ed. J. Gray. Morgan Kaufmann.

Schek, H. and M. Scholl. 1986. The Relational Model With Relational Valued Attributes. *Informational Systems* 11(2).

Selinger, P.G. and M. Adiba. 1980. Access Path Selection in Distributed Database Management Systems. *Proceedings of the International Conference on Data Bases*, eds. S.M. Deen and P. Hammersly. University of Aberdeen.

Selinger, P.G., M.M. Astrahan, D.D. Chamberlin et al. 1979. Access Path Selection in a Relational Database Management System. *ACM SIGMOD Conference Proceedings*.

Serlin, O. 1991. The History of DebitCredit and the TPC. In *The Benchmark Handbook for Database and Transaction Processing Systems*, ed. J. Gray. Morgan Kaufmann.

Sheth, A.P. and J.A. Larson. 1990. Federated Database Systems for Managing Distributed, Heterogeneous, and Autonomous Databases. *ACM Computing Surveys* 22(3).

Skeen, D. 1982. A Quorum-based Commit Protocol. *Proceedings of the 6th Berkeley Workshop on Distributed Data Management and Computer Networks.*

Stonebraker, M. et al. 1976. The Design and Implementation of INGRES. *ACM Transactions on Database Systems* 1(3).

Stonebraker, M. and L.A. Rowe. 1986. The Design of POSTGRES. *ACM SIGMD Record* 15(2).

Stonebraker, M., L.A. Rowe, and M. Hirohama. 1990. The Implementation of POSTGRES. *IEE Transactions on Knowledge and Data Engineering* 2(1).

Sweet, F. 1989. Optimistic Concurrency Management. *Database Programming & Design* 2(11).

Templeton, M., D. Brill, A. Hwang et al. 1983. An Overview of the Mermaid System—A Frontend to Heterogeneous Databases. *Proceedings of EASCON.*

Teorey, T.J. 1990. *Database Modeling and Design: The Entity-Relationship Approach.* Morgan Kaufmann.

Thomas, G., G.R. Thompson, C.W. Chung et al. 1990. Heterogeneous Distributed Database Systems for Production Use. *ACM Computing Surveys* 22(3).

Tillman, G.D. 1990. The Trouble With Two-Phase Commit. *Database Programming & Design* 3(9).

Transaction Processing Council. 1989. TPC Benchmark™ A Standard Specification. For further information contact TPC Administrator, c/o Shanley Public Relations, 777 North First Street, Suite 600, San Jose, CA 95112-6311. Phone: (408) 295-8894, Fax: (408) 295-2613. Also In Gray, J. ed. 1991. *The Benchmark Handbook for Database and Transaction Processing Systems.* Morgan Kaufmann.

Transaction Processing Council. 1990. TPC Benchmark™ B Standard Specification. Ibid.

Tsur, S. and C. Zaniolo. 1986. LDL: A Logic-based Data Language. *VLDB Conference Proceedings.*

Turbyfill, C., C. Orji, and D. Bitton. 1991. AS^3AP An ANSI SQL Standard Scalable and Portable Benchmark for Relational Database. In *The Benchmark Handbook for Database and Transaction Processing Systems*, ed. J. Gray. Morgan Kaufmann.

Ullman, J. 1988. *Principles of Database and Knowledge-Base Systems.* Computer Science Press.

Wiorkowski, G. and D. Kull. 1989. Optimizers: The Invisible Hand of the DBMS. *Database Programming & Design* 1(9).

Wong, H. 1983. Design and Verification of Information Systems. Ph.D. Thesis, University of Toronto.

X/Open SQL. 1991. *X/Open Snapshot SQL Remote Database Access.* X/Open Company.

Yu, C.T. and C.C. Chang. 1984. Distributed Query Processing. *ACM Computing Surveys* 16(4).

Zaniolo, C. 1983. The Database Language GEM. *ACM SIGMOD Conference Proceedings.*

Index